MW01222443

Law and Multinationals: *An Introduction to Law and Political Economy*

John J. Bonsignore

University of Massachusetts, Amherst

PRENTICE HALL, Englewood Cliffs, New Jersey 07632

Library of Congress Cataloging-in-Publication Data

Bonsignore, John J.
Law and multinationals: an introduction to law and political economy/John J. Bonsignore.
p. cm.
Includes index.
1. International business enterprises–Law and legislation.
2. International business enterprises–Government policy.
3. International business enterpises–Law and legislation–United States.
4. International business enterprises– Government policy–United States. I. Title.
K1322.B67 1994
341.7′53–dc 20 94-10768
CIP

Production Editors: Alan Dalgleish, Anne Graydon, and Lisa Kinne
Acquisitions Editor: Donald Hull
Manufacturing Buyer: Herb Klein
Copy Editor: Pat Johnson
Cover Designer: Maureen Eide

A Paramount Communications Company
Englewood Cliffs, New Jersey 07632

Printed in the United States of America

10 9 8 7 6 5 4 3 2 1

ISBN 0-13-524414-5

Prentice Hall International (UK) Limited, *London*
Prentice Hall of Australia Pty. Limited, *Sydney*
Prentice Hall Canada Inc., *Toronto*
Prentice Hall Hispanoamericana, S.A., *Mexico*
Prentice Hall of India Private Limited, *New Delhi*
Prentice Hall of Japan, Inc., *Tokyo*
Simon & Schuster Asia Pte. Ltd., *Singapore*
Editora Prentice Hall do Brasil, Ltda., *Rio de Janeiro*

Our laws are not generally known; they are kept secret by the small group of nobles who rule us . . . [I]t is extremely painful to be ruled by laws that one does not know.

F. Kafka, The Problem of Our Laws.

Above all, the people must never be sentimental.

B. Traven, Government

An American Worker about 1955.

Contents

Preface

Books on multinationals seem to be out of date before they reach print. This drives everyone interested in multinational study to periodicals and instantaneous retrieval systems rather than books, and writers find themselves more like stockbrokers hanging over the latest quotations in a rapidly moving market than scholars mulling over what will stay significant for the foreseeable future. Yet gravitation toward the current and episodic has a counterpressure in the desire to make some long-term sense out of what is going on minute by minute. And despite the speed of current developments in international enterprise and its consequences, there are some very old themes equally in evidence—for example, winners and losers in the economic order.

For a text to be adequate, age-old relationships must accompany the utterly new—for example, the demise of the state-run capitalism in the Soviet block. It is just as unwise to reject everything written before the current year as it is to be confident that old forms of enterprise and their consequences have remained unchanged.

Waves come crashing over multinational study continually. Now it is the pulping of the Amazon; then it is the reunification of Germany or the opening of what has been "communist" Vietnam to foreign investment and private property holding. If no topic is fully safe to consider permanent, the fear that whatever might be discussed is indefensible produces utter paralysis, leading nowhere. One must try, therefore, to come to an understanding of the multinational phenomenon, knowing better; that is, knowing that whatever is said cannot be good enough or permanent enough.

Even though it is hard to tell which thematic wave to ride and which to pass up, I have gone forward. A compromise has been struck, with the first seven chapters offering what I see to be an orientation that might offer some degree of permanence: definition of the subject, and the legal preconditions for the multinational phenomenon found in the United States experience.

The later themes and materials are chancier, but blend the perennial with the transient, so that even if surfaces change, some issues and methods for the study might have lasting value. Land, labor, and capital have been around for a while, and the international contest for the control of land, labor, and capital will also be around for a while, even if some particulars of the contest change.

It should be admitted frankly that I often started out on a theme, and then browsed as I would through books in a library. This led to this; that led to that. The Caterpillar strike threw me back to older themes in labor law and history, and forward to the internationalization of labor. A worker in the United States, *whether blue collar or white collar*, must keep glancing over the shoulder to see just where production will take place next, and whether a pink slip will declare that what may have been thought to be a lifetime job will be over within weeks. A chance reading about Nike and athletic shoes in *Harper's* magazine carried me to the annual reports of Nike, and to the general consideration of enterprise processing zones where Nikes and other products are assembled. Then it was on to the *maquiladora zones* of Mexico and the North American Free Trade Treaty (NAFTA), which could make everywhere in Mexico an export processing zone, and everyone from the Arctic reaches of Canada to Guatemala *casual labor*, fitting or not fitting into the multinational imagination.

Just when the topic seemed spent and without a conclusion, I was invited, probably because I was put on the wrong mailing list, to a four–day meeting of international business heavyweights in Washington for the low, low sum of $1500—if I took advantage of early registration discounts! With the price of attendance three-fourths of the *annual* per capita income of Mexico, and about three times the *annual wages* of a Nike shoe assembler in Indonesia, I was instantly forced to merge in my thinking the conference assumptions about world leaders, with export processing zones, and world followers. (I did not attend.) And so went other sections of the book.

I never knew exactly where topics would lead or how long the coverage of a topic would have to be. In fact, if I had known, I might not have been foolhardy enough to begin. At the point when one is ready to give up—like hope at the bottom of Pandora's box—there comes a realization that in multinational study all paths lead to comparable places. Once the panic over the size and dynamism of the field subsides, any number of itineraries may be imagined that will produce a decent understanding. For example, one can randomly pick a country, a commodity or service, or a multinational company, and before long the makings of a primer on law and political economy begin to emerge.

The field does have complexities, and every professional must both cope with complexities and make them part of their stock in trade. Three educational approaches may be taken, given the abundant technicalities of international commerce and the law–government systems that surround them: (1) A little knowledge is a dangerous thing; no teaching is better than potentially misleading teaching. (2) Students unschooled in international business must be offered material that has been purged of technical coverage lest they become "lost." (3) Some technical materials must appear even though they make the head hurt, but technical materials must always be considered with an eye on results and systemic consequences.

Consistent with the usual authorly practice of saving the preferred for last, I have chosen the third way. Technical materials are used to show how lawyers practice, to see how companies structure their businesses, and to assess the problems in bringing corporations within the regulatory powers of law–government systems, and not out of a compulsion to "cover everything." In taking this approach, I hope that students will appreciate the beauty of the human hand; it can grasp and let go. Technical detail can be held, and then let go, freeing the mind to see how technical details fit larger wholes.

Throughout the writing of this book, I was accompanied by the spirit of my father, whose picture appears opposite this preface. He and my mother, both now deceased, made great sacrifices, not only to see me through my education but also to impart to me the abiding belief that learning, and hard work at learning, are valuable.

As I was working, I sometimes had mental discussions with my father, in which he said:

> Your mother and I did what we could to give you the education that we did not have. What have you found out? Tell us about big business, family member to family member, without the false fronts and posturing that might take place in classrooms, among academics, or other strangers. We want as straight a story as you can tell about contemporary business and international business law. We want to know where people like us stand in these systems. Are these systems likely to help us, and protect us, or should we run for our lives?

In keeping with this self-assumed familial responsibility, there is more straight talk and less academic posturing in this text than you might expect. I tried to conscientiously combine factual coverage with theoretical discussion, but I did not mince words once I knew what words I would use if I were talking with my parents. There is, therefore, a viewpoint throbbing away throughout this text. This should come as no surprise, since all authors need moral sentiments that are strong enough to carry them through the seemingly endless task of writing a book.

You need a viewpoint, too—*your own* viewpoint, based on your own reflections, and open to the new information that will inevitably bombard you in the years ahead. What book do *you* plan to write about multinationals? Imagine a future conversation with me where I say:

> I did what I could to start you out on the subject of multinationals . . . what have *you* found out? Give me the straight story, as you would tell it . . .

If this book drives you toward a continual evaluative mood, and pushes you toward a lifetime awareness of a phenomenon that will inevitably touch your life and the lives of those you care about most, then the book will have accomplished its purposes.

There are some people to whom I would like to give thanks, without burdening them with responsibility. To my four sisters, Florence, Mary, Aurelia and Anita, and my brother, Joseph. To my seven children: John, Joan, Ruth, Carol, Patricia, Alice, and Fenna. To my partner, Marie, and her daughter Risha. To my friends Tom Martens, Steve Davis, and Randy Boivin.

In academic life, I have both accomplices and friends: Nancy Hauserman at the University of Iowa, who thought enough of me to tell me when something I had written was not good enough; Art Wolfe of Michigan State University and William Elliott of Saginaw Valley University, whom I can call in the middle of the night if I must; and Harry T. Allan of the University of Massachusetts, who is my mentor and longtime friend.

Special thanks go to Don Hull, Anne Graydon, and Pat Johnson of Prentice Hall, who encouraged the project and did all that they could to improve the manuscript.

PART 1
Law and Political Economy

CHAPTER 1

Alternatives Forgone

This is a study of multinationals, the law affecting them, and the intimate connections between legal orders and the political economies in which they are found. As such it is not simply a law book, an economics book, or a book on politics, all subjects that can be studied separately. Life does not come with labels—this transaction is legal, that political, that economic—nor can bits of life be neatly segregated. Yet it is on such an assumption that most scholarly disciplines are premised. Kenneth Boulding spoke of the acquisition of knowledge in a discipline as the *orderly* loss of information, meaning that some aspects of a question must deliberately be neglected if we are to make any sense of anything. Some of the doors of our perception need to be closed, some sentiments that would intrude upon systematic thinking repressed.

There is, of course, a casualty in the accumulation of knowledge while losing information. What we do as a matter of necessary convenience—looking at a piece instead of the whole—might mean that we have picked the wrong piece to consider and, in doing so, have lost what we should have kept firmly in mind. Similarly, by setting boundaries we have excluded a consideration of relationships between one branch of learning and another.

Tight boundaries might work to a limited extent in the natural sciences, but they have no place in any subject remotely connected to social study. Rigorous closure will inevitably obscure the very purposes that are said to be at the center of legal, economic, and political inquiry: how justice is best achieved, what makes for an equitable distribution of limited material resources, or the maximization of human potential through the most appropriate handling of power. The more restricted the field of inquiry, the less that can be said of any consequence (but the more precisely it can be said).

Take the "simple" transaction of buying a house and the lot on which it stands for some cash down and a mortgage. What sign or label should the transaction carry? It is a legal event with an agreement, deed, and mortgage. It is an economic event with the allocation of land to the buyer and the allocation of cash to a seller. It is a political event with the new owner getting a valuable right to exclude the state, police, and unwanted others from the premises ("It's ours, get out," sometimes works!). The purchase starts a social round of neighborhood and connections with people who were once strangers; thoughts about social futures probably contributed significantly to the decision to purchase in the first place. On the less sentimental front, it starts a relationship of up to thirty years with a bank.

The purchase is also a cultural episode, home ownership being an integral part of the American dream of prosperity, success, and minimum social standing. It is also a psychic event, the phrase "our home" resonating through the mind, carrying powerful symbols.

If the purchase of a house and lot can raise a rich network of subjects, what of the prolific effects of the activities of multinational corporations like Exxon, which has approximately $90 billion of assets worldwide in petroleum, natural gas, chemicals, coal, and other minerals? How many lives are touched by Exxon here and abroad and in what ways?

For simplicity's sake only three of the many possible threads of inquiry are taken up with respect to multinationals like Exxon. Lopping off other angles of vision may be costly, as any artist, anthropologist, or historian could quickly reckon on seeing what has been included and what has been excluded in this text. And yet, even taking up just three—the legal, the economic, and the political—will be regarded by some as too ambitious. They know that to try to say too much may result in saying nothing in sufficient depth. But making the account limited and manageable defeats any chance of an overall perspective on multinationals, which seems to be the more pressing need as the multinational phenomenon intrudes more and more into our consciousness.

The closing down of alternative visions need not be so devastatingly quick, and this first chapter allows for some coverage of methods and themes that will ultimately have to be put to one side. The first chapter may be considered a gentle wave goodbye to perfectly legitimate ways to study the relationships among people who differ. It contains three excerpts: a parable from the writer Franz Kafka entitled "The Refusal"; a second from a journalist, Susan Faludi, who writes about Hawaii and the relationship of the current generation of native Hawaiians to non-Hawaiians on the Islands; and a third from an anthropologist-novelist, B. Traven, on the world views of preindustrial Mexico. Like the phrase "our home" these powerful stories will continue to resonate in our minds, even as we leave them behind.

"The Refusal," by Franz Kafka (1883–1924), is at once a very old story and a truly modern story. The characters are ordinary people moving about in a small town with a folksiness that we can easily recognize. Yet they encounter problems that are too modern to be relegated to ancient fantasy. If the parable is as strong a teaching device as some claim it to be, this one of Kafka's may tell all we ever need to know about the relationship of many people to system.

THE REFUSAL*

Our little town does not lie on the frontier, nowhere near; it is so far from the frontier, in fact, that perhaps no one from our town has ever been there; desolate highlands have to be crossed as well as wide fertile plains. To imagine even part of the road makes one tired, and more than part one just cannot imagine. There are also big towns on the road, each far larger than ours. Ten little towns like ours laid side by side, and ten more forced down from above, still would not produce one of these enormous, overcrowded towns. If one does not get lost on the way one is bound to lose oneself in these towns, and to avoid them is impossible on account of their size.

But what is even further from our town than the frontier, if such distances can be compared at all—it's like saying that a man of three hundred years is older than one of two hundred—what is even further than the frontier is the capital. Whereas we do get news of the frontier wars now and again, of the capital we learn next to nothing—we civilians that is, for of course the government officials have very good connections with the capital; they can get news from there in as little as three months, so they claim at least.

Now it is remarkable and I am continually being surprised at the way we in our town humbly submit to all orders issued in the capital. For centuries no political change has been brought about by the citizens themselves. In the capital great rulers have superseded each other—indeed, even dynasties have been deposed or annihilated, and new ones have started; in the past century even the capital itself was destroyed, a new one was founded far away from it, later on this too was destroyed and the old one rebuilt, yet none of this had any influence on our little town. Our officials have always remained at their posts; the highest officials came from the capital, the less high from other towns, and the lowest from among ourselves—that is how it has always been and it has suited us. The highest official is the chief tax-collector, he has the rank of colonel, and is known as such. The present one is an old man; I've known him for years, because he was already a colonel when I was a child. At first he rose very fast in his career, but then he seems to have advanced no further; actually, for our little town his rank is good enough, a higher rank would be out of place. When I try to recall him I see him sitting on the veranda of his house in the Market Square, leaning back, pipe in mouth. Above him from the roof flutters the imperial flag; on the sides of the veranda, which is so big that minor military maneuvers are sometimes held there, washing hangs out to dry. His grandchildren, in beautiful silk clothes, play around him; they are not allowed down in the Market Square, the children there are considered unworthy of them, but the grandchildren are attracted by the Square, so they thrust their heads between the posts of the banister and when the children below begin to quarrel they join the quarrel from above.

This colonel, then, commands the town. I don't think he has ever produced a document entitling him to this position; very likely he does not possess such a thing. Maybe he really is chief tax-collector. But is that all? Does that entitle him to rule over all the other departments in the administration as well? True, his office is very important for the government, but for the citizens it is hardly the most important. One is almost under the impression that the people here say: "Now that you've taken all we pos-

*Franz Kafka, *Parables and Paradoxes* (New York: Schocken, 1974), pp. 161-175.

sess, please take us as well." In reality, of course, it was not he who seized the power, nor is he a tyrant. It has just come about over the years that the chief tax-collector is automatically the top official, and the colonel accepts the tradition just as we do.

Yet while he lives among us without laying too much stress on his official position, he is something quite different from the ordinary citizen. When a delegation comes to him with a request, he stands there like the wall of the world. Behind him is nothingness, one imagines hearing voices whispering in the background, but this is probably a delusion; after all, he represents the end of all things, at least for us. At these receptions he really was worth seeing. Once as a child I was present when a delegation of citizens arrived to ask him for a government subsidy because the poorest quarter of the town had been burned to the ground. My father the blacksmith, a man well respected in the community, was a member of the delegation and had taken me along. There's nothing exceptional about this, everyone rushes to spectacles of this kind, one can hardly distinguish the actual delegation from the crowd. Since these receptions usually take place on the veranda, there are even people who climb up by ladder from the Market Square and take part in the goings-on from over the banister. On this occasion about a quarter of the veranda had been reserved for the colonel, the crowd filling the rest of it. A few soldiers kept watch, some of them standing round him in a semicircle. Actually a single soldier would have been quite enough, such is our fear of them. I don't know exactly where these soldiers come from, in any case from a long way off, they all look very much alike, they wouldn't even need a uniform. They are small, not strong but agile people, the most striking thing about them is the prominence of their teeth which almost overcrowd their mouths, and a certain restless twitching of their small narrow eyes. This makes them the terror of the children, but also their delight, for again and again the children long to be frightened by these teeth, these eyes, so as to be able to run away in horror. Even grownups probably never quite lose this childish terror, at least it continues to have an effect. There are, of course, other factors contributing to it. The soldiers speak a dialect utterly incomprehensible to us, and they can hardly get used to ours—all of which produces a certain shut-off, unapproachable quality corresponding, as it happens, to their character, for they are silent, serious, and rigid. They don't actually do anything evil, and yet they are almost unbearable in an evil sense. A soldier, for example, enters a shop, buys some trifling object, and stays there leaning against the counter; he listens to the conversations, probably does not understand them, and yet gives the impression of understanding; he himself does not say a word, just stares blankly at the speaker, then back at the listeners, all the while keeping his hand on the hilt of the long knife in his belt. This is revolting, one loses the desire to talk, the customers start leaving the shop, and only when it is quite empty does the soldier also leave. Thus wherever the soldiers appear, our lively people grow silent. That's what happened this time, too. As on all solemn occasions the colonel stood upright, holding in front of him two poles of bamboo in his outstretched hands. This is an ancient custom implying more or less that he supports the law, and the law supports him. Now everyone knows, of course, what to expect up on the veranda, and yet each time people take fright all over again. On this occasion, too, the man chosen to speak could not begin; he was already standing opposite the colonel when his courage failed him and, muttering a few excuses, he pushed his way back into the crowd. No other suitable person willing to speak could be found, albeit several unsuitable ones offered themselves; a great commotion ensued and messengers were sent in search of various citizens who were well-known speakers. During all this time the colonel stood there motionless, only his chest moving visibly up and down to his breathing. Not that he breathed with difficulty, it was just that he breathed so conspicuously, much as frogs breathe—except that with them it is normal, while here it was exceptional. I squeezed myself through the grownups and watched him through a gap between two soldiers, until one of them kicked me away with his knee. Meanwhile the man originally chosen to speak had regained his composure and, firmly held up by two fellow citizens, was delivering his address. It was touching to see him smile throughout this solemn speech describing a grievous misfortune—a most humble smile which strove in vain to elicit some slight reaction on the colonel's face. Finally he formulated the request—I think he was only asking for a year's tax exemption, but possibly also for timber from the imperial forests at a reduced price. Then he bowed low, remaining in this position for some time, as did everyone else except the colonel, the soldiers, and a number of officials in the background. To the child it seemed ridiculous that the people on the ladders should climb down a few rungs so as not to be seen during the significant pause and now and again peer inquisitively over the floor of the veranda. After this had lasted quite a while an official, a little man, stepped up to the colonel and tried to reach the latter's height by standing on his toes. The colonel, still motionless save for his deep breathing, whispered something in his ear, whereupon the little man clapped his hands and everyone rose. "The petition has been refused," he announced. "You may go." An undeniable sense of relief passed through the crowd, everyone surged out, hardly a soul paying any special attention to the colonel, who, as it were, had turned once more into a human being like the rest of us. I still caught one last glimpse of him as he wearily let go of the poles, which fell to the ground, then sank into an armchair produced by some officials, and promptly put his pipe in his mouth.

This whole occurrence is not isolated, it's in the general run of things. Indeed, it does happen now and again that minor petitions are granted, but then it invariably looks as though the colonel had done it as a powerful private person on his own responsibility, and it had to be kept all but a secret from the government—not explicitly of course, but that is what it feels like. No doubt in our little town the colonel's eyes, so far as we know, are also the eyes of the government, and yet there is a difference which it is impossible to comprehend completely.

In all important matters, however, the citizens can always count on a refusal. And now the strange fact is that without this refusal one simply cannot get along, yet at the same time these official occasions designed to receive the refusal are by no means a formality. Time after time one goes there full of expectation and in all seriousness and then one returns, if not exactly strengthened or happy, nevertheless not disappointed or tired. About these things I do not have to ask the opinion of anyone else, I feel them in myself, as everyone does; nor do I have any great desire to find out how these things are connected.

As a matter of fact there is, so far as my observations go, a certain age group that is not content—these are the young people roughly between seventeen and twenty. Quite young fellows, in fact, who are utterly incapable of foreseeing the consequences of even the least significant, far less a revolutionary, idea. And it is among just them that discontent creeps in.

For discussion

1a. With a writer as careful as Kafka, it is safe to assume that no detail in the story is accidental or carelessly placed. What impels him to select certain images—small towns, frontiers, generic uniforms, a pipe, ladders, silk clothes, verandas, blacksmith, colonel-tax collector, bamboo sticks, and so on—and what mood is he trying to evoke in the reader through the use of these images and the contexts in which they are found?

With what character or characters does he want us to identify? When we reach the end of the story, in what emotional place are we supposed to be?

What events or episodes in the story stand out?

b. Does his story seem true to life, or is it implausible and irrelevant to contemporary readers?

2. Kafka has a negative effect on readers, as written comments on Kafka by students reveal:

"Kafka talks in circles."

"I haven't got the vaguest idea of what he is getting at. If he wants to say something about law, about economic relationships, or politics why doesn't he come right out and say it?"

"I read this thing four times (the first time that I have ever done this in college!) and just threw it down in frustration. I wrote something but I was just bs'ing because I was lost."

"These people got exactly what they deserved and wanted. I know I am supposed to write two pages but it all comes down to this—tough luck townspeople!"

What irritates us most about the story? (What irritates us most could tell us the most.)

3. Try to translate Kafka's parable into a straight prose essay entitled, "Law, Economics, and Politics." Kafka, for all the difficulty there is in pinning him down, does seem to have some ideas on these subjects.

4. What is Kafka's politics? It seems that he does not like the order that prevails, but in what direction would he have us move to change things? What should the 17–20-year-olds do next?

5. In some student writings it is said that the townspeople are ignorant and need to become educated. Just what is it that they need to know? If you were their teacher, what course of study would you design for them so that in the future they would not experience refusals like the one they got in the story?

For all of the inflation of Kafka as a consummate social scientist who tells us all we would ever need to know about the place of moderns in systems, most readers would demand more evidence before endorsing his prophecies unqualifiedly.

We turn next to the writing by a journalist on present-day Hawaii. We already know something about Hawaii from television—a gigantic wave curling majestically toward shore, rugged Hawaiian natives furiously paddling a huge outrigger canoe, lush jungles leading to volcanic peaks, a thin stream emptying into a small, clear, pure pool where young lovers surface and laugh softly. Beyond that, for those who have never flown United, there is a pleasant haze.

BROKEN PROMISE: HOW EVERYONE GOT HAWAIIANS' HOMELANDS EXCEPT THE HAWAIIANS

By Susan C. Faludi

Staff Reporter of *The Wall Street Journal*[*]

HONOLULU—"You just hang on, Mr. Afong," U.S. Sen. Daniel Inouye said at a public hearing in 1989 to 91-year-old Henry Afong, a frail native Hawaiian who had been on a waiting list since 1952 for land promised his people under a federal law. "You just hang on." Mr. Afong's daughter, Annie Stevens, remembers the senator's advice with some bitterness: Six months later, her father, an aspiring rancher from the Big Island, was dead.

Politicians have been telling native Hawaiians to hang on for 70 years, ever since Congress passed the Hawaiian Homes Commission Act in 1921, setting aside nearly 200,000 acres in scattered tracts across the islands. Congress hoped to save the dying Hawaiian people by returning a small portion of land taken from them in what even a U.S. president had called the unlawful federal seizure of Hawaii in 1893.

The federal act requires the state to lease modest residential, farm and pastoral homestead lots for $1 a year to any Hawaiian with at least 50% native ancestry. It instructs the state to provide the infrastructure of utilities, roads and water. And it promises to provide native Hawaiians with home and farm loans to get started.

Firing Ranges and Car Lots

But many decades later, more than 60% of the land has been rented at bargain-basement prices to non-natives—many of them belonging to the richest and most powerful families in the islands—or swapped or simply given away to other government agencies. The area where Mr. Afong hoped to raise a few head of cattle, for example, has been leased for many years by Parker Ranch, the nation's second-largest private ranching business. The ranching corporation pays the state $3.33 an acre each year to use the property, locking up 27,000 acres of homelands.

"It's not like we are paying nothing," says Robert L. Hind III, Parker Ranch's livestock manager. And he says Parker Ranch has helped out the native Hawaiians—for instance, by leasing them cows to get started.

BROKEN PROMISE: HAWAIIANS WAIT IN VAIN FOR THEIR LAND

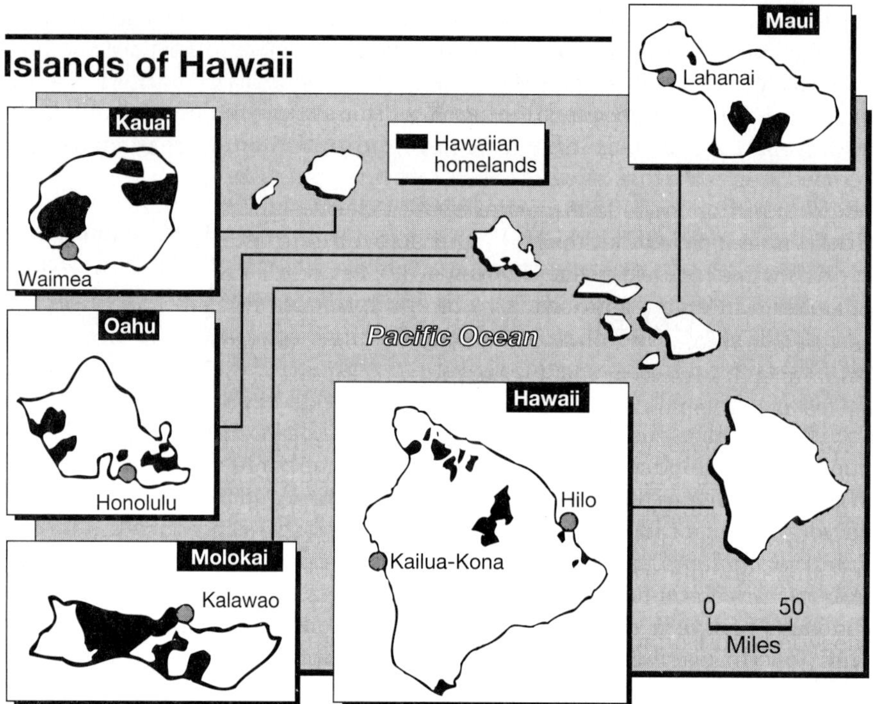

Other land has gone to multinational corporations for quarrying and mining operations, to the U.S. military for the Pacific naval headquarters, to state agencies for waste-water treatment plants and airports and cemeteries, to mayors and legislators for their own private companies and personal estates, to prominent businessmen for auto dealerships and shopping strips and tourist attractions, and to shrewd investors who have turned around and subleased the property for as much as eight times their rent.

A Vast Waiting List

Native Hawaiians, who are the poorest and most ill-housed population in the state, hold just 17.5% of the acreage. In the law's entire history, only 3,700 of the tens of thousands of families who have been eligible have actually been allowed to settle on the homelands. While about 5,500 families have been awarded land, the state bars more than a third of them from moving onto their land because it lacks basic infrastructure—which the state itself is supposed to build.

Others do have homes, built under government programs by subcontractors, but many of the structures are falling apart or deemed substandard by state inspectors. Meanwhile, native Hawaiians who have applied for homelands languish on a ballooning waiting list, now 21,000 names and decades long.

State officials maintain they are at least compensating the native Hawaiians in other ways, albeit belatedly: The state agreed last year to make up for the seizure of more than a million acres of native lands 100 years ago by paying a cash settlement to a state agency that aids native Hawaiians. They say they are making some progress in awarding homelands, but that implementing the law has been frustrated by a lack of funds, which are needed to provide loans to the homesteaders as well as for roads and utilities. So, they say, they must lease land to non-natives to generate revenue for the Department of Hawaiian Home Lands, which administers the act.

The department's director, Hoaliku Drake, says she believes applicants for homelands are "mostly high middle class. A lot of them own land already." She adds, "People should be disciplined enough to wait." As for the substandard houses, she says, ""Well, they're probably just getting a little old."

A number of outside audits conducted on behalf of various state and federal agencies have found the homelands department plagued by bureaucratic incompetence and underfunding. A 1983 joint federal-state task force, a Hawaiian governor, a state attorney general and several courts have concluded that the state government has consistently violated the 1921 act.

Little has been done about the violations, however, in part because the act itself authorizes only the federal government, not native Hawaiians, to sue the state for breaking the homelands law. And the federal government has never taken legal action.

At the U.S. Interior Department, the homelands' administrative agency on the federal level, officials say they feel no obligation to enforce "that darn law," as Timothy Glidden, the Interior Department's sole designated officer for the homelands act, refers to it. "I have a whole page full of other responsibilities," says Mr. Glidden. "I spend very little time on it."

Hawaii has a strong economy and huge cash reserves: State government boasted a $456.3 million surplus in fiscal 1991. But many of the 50,000 native Hawaiians currently eligible under the 1921 act haven't participated in the boom. According to a 1990 state-sponsored study of the 200,000 people who are any part native Hawaiian, more than 2,000 of them live in cardboard boxes, rusted cars or on the beaches—and 40% of the homeless Hawaiians have been on the waiting list for a homestead for more than seven years. As the state's housing crisis mounts, the number of native Hawaiians on the waiting list has ballooned, more than doubling in the past six years even though officials have at times purged the list of inactive names.

Until recently, the state allocated very little money for the homelands department—it has had the smallest staff and budget of any state agency—and the federal government allocated no funds at all. But at the same time, when financing is available, the agency has been slow to take advantage of it. Indeed, the federal government has allocated $1.2 million for the department every year since 1988—and the department has spent none of it. At one point, a local circuit court judge actually ordered the department to request funds from the state Legislature.

In addition, in the past two decades the homelands department allowed millions of dollars of state capital-improvement-project bond funds to lapse unspent, state records show. It has also left $24 million in cash untouched in various banks. "Because of delays, we haven't been ready to use that money," says the agency's deputy director, John Rowe.

Moreover, he says the costs of many construction projects were higher than expected, and rather than seek more

HANDS OFF THE WATERMELON KING

MOLOKAI, Hawaii—An Indiana businessman named Larry Jefts is the watermelon king of Hawaii, thanks to some fancy dancing around the federal homelands law.

Under the 1921 act, native Hawaiians aren't allowed to sublease their plots. But without sufficient loans, infrastructure or water to farm or build on their land, many have illegally rented the property to big corporations or non-native entrepreneurs. Mr. Jefts became the state's largest watermelon producer by buying up the right to farm from Hawaiians. The few holdouts here eventually couldn't compete with him, filing for bankruptcy.

The homelands department is aware of Mr. Jefts's practices, but has adopted a hands-off attitude. "The department has not really come out and told him to lay off," says George Helm, the agency's district manager in Molokai. "The way we handle it is, it's okay as long as it's a verbal agreement and not a lease."

"The topic . . . is something I cannot talk about," Mr. Jefts says of his dozen "crop-sharing agreements" with the Molokai farmers. "It takes you down a road you don't want to go." He adds, "There are no written agreements anywhere, so there is nothing to talk about."

financing from the government, the department just decided to let the bonds lapse. "If (the bids) were above (the cost of the project); we chose not to go through with it, because we'd have to go back and get more funds," he explains.

Yet the department has spent plenty of money to help develop homelands leased by non-natives, a list of whom has read over the years like a Who's Who of state politics and business. They have included J. Atherton Richards (the late former trustee of the powerful Bishop Estate charity, who had a 9,370-acre ranch on homelands). Diamond Head developer and Aloha Air founder Ruddy F. Tongg (who had a 1,126-acre ranch) and state legislator Harvey Tajiri (who operates his campaign headquarters and auto body shop on homelands and who, in the early 1980s, made a substantial profit off the land by subletting it for six times the amount he was paying the Department of Hawaiian Home Lands).

"I'm a businessman," Mr. Tajiri says, and people who object to his making a profit off the homelands "don't understand business." Mr. Tajiri says his position played no role in getting the land. "Being in a public office actually works to my disadvantage," he says, "because a lot of things get misinterpreted to mean that I have favorable treatment. So I have to watch my step even more."

Mr. Tongg's son Ronald, who most recently ran Tongg Ranch, says, "I don't have any qualms" about having rented native Hawaiian land since 1966 for less than $6 an acre per year. "My thing doesn't have anything to do with their thing," he says of the native Hawaiians. "To be perfectly frank, if they haven't gotten their land or it's been mismanaged or whatever, that's their problem. I don't mean to be so cold and uninterested, but when you get right down to it, that's the bottom line." Mr. Tongg says that after his 25-year lease expired a few months ago, he decided not to renew because the department wanted to raise the rent "four to five times," an increase that Mr. Tongg deemed "incredible."

The homelands agency recently allotted $1.4 million to ease traffic and put up street lights around Prince Kuhio Shopping Center, a sprawling mall in Hilo built on homelands leased by non-natives. The department also put in a road there because "we thought it would be a good addendum to the shopping center," says Mr. Rowe, the agency's deputy director. And it has spent millions of dollars installing infrastructure in two industrial parks that serve only non-native lessees. Mr. Rowe says that expenditure was acceptable because it "was designated economic development."

On Kawaihae, on the northern coast of the Big Island, nearly 200 native Hawaiians have been awarded homeland lots, but they have been waiting since 1986 for basic capital improvements, such as running water and electricity, to make their land livable. The homelands department received a $990,000 appropriation to install the infrastructure in 1979, before the land was even awarded, but delayed so long the appropriation lapsed unspent.

Mr. Rowe says the funds were allowed to lapse because when the department considered using the money, the amount it wanted to spend exceeded the state's annual cap on the agency's expenditures.

Squatting on Their Own Land

Mr. Rowe says Kawaihae is still in the "design stages." The department forbids homesteaders to move onto their own land before the infrastructure is in place, and often evicts those who try. Joanie Dela Cruz and her sister Josephine each got awarded half-acre lots at Kawaihae after years on the waiting list, but they weren't permitted to settle on them. Between them, they have three jobs—Josephine works all day cleaning rooms at a nearby resort hotel and half the night delivering newspapers. But she still can't afford the high Hawaii rents.

So first, the sisters and their four children squatted on a nearby beach for two years, until the police threw them off. "The Hawaiian has no home but the beach," says Joanie Dela Cruz. Frustrated, they quietly moved onto Josephine's boulder-strewn plot with their four children, erecting a plywood shack and bathing in a nearby public restroom.

Last year, the department sent Josephine Dela Cruz a letter warning her she might be evicted. After an extended battle, she thwarted the move by securing a county building permit.

Many of the more than 1,000 native Hawaiians who have received homes from the department find the problems don't end after they claim occupancy. On the east coast of Kauai, "Auntie" Rachel Rapozo lives in a development of more than 60 homes built under a department contract in the 1970s. She and her husband moved here after spending 30 years on the waiting list. First, she recounts, the sewage backed up—again and again and again. Then the floor started sinking. Then the roof began caving in and had to be replaced. Now the second roof is collapsing. The electrical wiring is hazardous and hardly works. "I have only two lights here," she says, as she moves in the dim house, stepping around the pots that collect water from the many roof leaks. "Try staying in darkness for 10 years."

While Mrs. Drake, the department director, says the only problem is that the homes in the development are getting old, her public relations director, Hardy Spoehr, who is sitting by her side as she speaks, interrupts to say: "There were a lot of problems actually with those homes." He adds: "We're building the roofs for the third time. . . . There have been sewage problems that have resulted from freak, well, not freak but—ah, not an understanding of the topography under those homes."

Illegal Occupants

Most of the non-native lessees obtained their land rights illegally, because the 1921 act reserved the land for natives. Leasing to non-natives was supposedly allowed under a 1965 state law that empowered the department to rent to non-natives, but that didn't make it legal because the federal statute can be amended only by Congress. It wasn't until 1986 that Congress approved the practice as part of blanket approval of a raft of amendments that the state had made without congressional authorization since Hawaii's statehood.

By that time, former state legislator and Maui Mayor Elmer Cravalho, who sponsored the 1965 bill, had already been enjoying his 15,000-acre homelands plantation for 19 years. After the bill passed, he was one of the first non-natives to sign up, at $1.60 an acre a year. He now pays $2.50 an acre. "Where is the conflict of interest?" he asks in response to a question. He says his support for leasing to non-natives "contributed greatly to the financial capability" of the homelands program.

Sometimes the department has simply given property away to non-natives for a game reserve, military depot or the like. In 1984, Gov. George Ariyoshi ordered the department to rescind nearly 30 of these illegal deals, covering about 30,000 acres. The state attorney general, meantime, decreed the U.S. Navy's occupation of 1,400 acres of prime homelands near Honolulu to be a "fundamental breach of trust."

But the department, in most cases, rescinded the agreements only on paper. It has not evicted the offending land users, which include state and federal agencies. The Department of Hawaiian Home Lands made one attempt to evict, mounting a court challenge to the U.S. Navy's occupancy of Oahu homelands. But the judge found that the department had waited too long to sue.

Forty Years on the List

Even when the department charges non-natives for leases, the rates are often bargains. At least 15 non-natives in recent years have subleased their homelands to others at a substantial profit, state records show. The department once considered appropriating some of the profits, but abandoned the plan when the lessees threatened legal action. One of them, George Madden, a wealthy developer, calls the agency's efforts "obnoxious." By leasing homelands, he says, "I am contributing to those 20,000 people (on the waiting list) drawing nearer to realization of their homes."

Actually, only a tiny handful are getting anywhere on the list. At the beginning of 1990, the homelands department announced it would build 448 new houses during the year. It built 16. Last fiscal year, the department gave out only 30 loans to the thousands of applicants. "We aren't ready with the loans because there have been some delays in putting in infrastructure," explains Mr. Rowe.

Sonny Kaniho's family has been on the waiting list for nearly 40 years; he is one of 139 so-called "Aged Hawaiians" who applied for lots in 1952 but never got them. His father, also on the list, died waiting. His grandparents, ironically, were evicted from their land when the state laid claim to 108,000 acres on the Big Island under the 1921 act.

When Mr. Kaniho retired in the 1970s, after 24 years in the U.S. Navy, he went to Honolulu to inquire about the 1952 list. Department officials told him the list "never existed," he says. At the state archives, he found it without much trouble—published in a 1952 newspaper. Mr. Kaniho was No. 14. It took years

'WE ARE STILL AT THE BOTTOM OF THE BARREL'

As mistreated as they were, some other native Americans received far more compensation for the seizure of their lands. In 1971, native Alaskans, for instance, received $1 billion and 40 million acres of land from the federal government. "The Indians have come a long way, but we Hawaiians are still at the bottom of the barrel," says Healani Doane, 81, who fruitlessly applied for homestead land in 1929.

"Hawaiians are the only indigenous group in this country who have gotten no formal recognition of their sovereign rights," says Alan Murakami, litigation director of the Native Hawaiian Legal. Corp. "And ironically, Hawaiians are the ones with the most compelling case for federal recognition." Unlike other native American groups, the Hawaiian Kingdom had several formal international treaties with other nations, plus consulates and a network of diplomats.

Many native Hawaiians attribute their 70 years of frustration to the flaws in the 1921 homelands act itself, to homelands department mismanagement, to machine politics and to their own political impotence.

They bemoan their fate in private, but they also have one of the smallest turnouts on Election Day.

Recently, a native Hawaiian "sovereignty movement" has sprung up, complete with a shadow government. But the natives' numbers are dwindling. Between native Hawaiians' terrible health statistics and the state's 46% interracial marriage rate, the native Hawaiian population has nearly been obliterated. There were a million native Hawaiians at the time of Captain Cook's landing in 1778; now there are only 11,000 full-blooded Hawaiians—and only 50,000 people have the 50% or more Hawaiian blood required to claim a homelands lot.

and a court battle to force the department to reinstate the list, which it finally did in 1984. Still, the Aged Hawaiians waited for their land.

Above the Frost Line

In the meantime, politically influential native Hawaiians, including homeland department officials, were moved ahead of the claims of the Aged Hawaiians, receiving large parcels. In 1965, Albert Akana, the agency's project manager on the Big Island, was jumped past more than 100 people on the 1952 list to get a 300-acre ranch. "Yeah, I was lower down on the list," says Mr. Akana, who says the department picked him to serve as a "role-model" rancher to other Hawaiians. His ranching effort fizzled, however, and he used the land to build and sell boats.

Mr. Kaniho, on the other hand, was repeatedly arrested and served jail terms for trespassing on homeland pastures in protest of the Aged Hawaiians' treatment. Finally, last fall, just before the statewide election, the homelands department announced it would award some land to the Aged Hawaiians. Then it revealed that the size of the lots would be reduced. Homestead pasture lots, as opposed to residential lots, are supposed to be 300 acres because it takes at least that much acreage to sustain livestock on the arid land. But the lots now were cut to as small as 10 acres. And Mr. Rowe says it probably will take "years" before there will be any water, utilities or roads. "The land is pretty much useless," says Mr. Kaniho, now 69 years old. His lot is above the frost line.

Battles Over Water

Native Hawaiians who have farmed and ranched the homelands find they often are crowded out by the big non-native corporations that lease neighboring homelands. On Kauai, Hawaiian homesteaders have less than 900 acres, while the Kekaha Sugar Co., a subsidiary of giant Amfac Inc., leases about

A PEEK INSIDE THE 'X' FILE

HONOLULU—Veteran staff members of the Department of Hawaiian Home Lands say the agency has been a hotbed of patronage and favoritism for many years.

Ray Ah Nee, a department manager for more than 30 years, recalls that one former director, Abraham Piianaia, required staffers to consult a secret file marked "X" before awarding any land. That file, Mr. Ah Nee says, contained a list of politically connected people who were to get land before Hawaiians on the official waiting list.

"I was so dumbfounded when I saw it," says Mr. Ah Nee. But when he told a judge about it, during a court case in which a native Hawaiian woman unsuccessfully complained that the department exercised favoritism in its handling of the waiting list, "the judge got mad at me for talking about it."

Mr. Piianaia acknowledges that he kept such an "X" folder. In fact, he says he kept several. But, he says: "that doesn't at all imply that there was an attempt to give those guys a jump over other people." He says the "X" files were only meant as a way "to keep track of who called in to say, 'Oh, I'm a friend of so and so.' 'I'm Senator so and so and I'm calling for so and so.' There's nothing wrong with that."

Asked if any of the people in the "X" file did get a jump, Mr. Piianaia says: "Hardly any."

15,000 acres of homelands at $3.79 an acre. Kekaha Sugar also has exclusive rights to all the available water from the nearby Waimea River and the entire network of irrigation ditches.

With little water, only two native Hawaiians still try to ranch their land. One of them is Joe Manini, whose grandparents were driven off their ancestral land on Kauai at gunpoint in the 1890s. He received permission in writing from the Hawaiian Homes Commission, which supervises the department, to tap into Kekaha's irrigation ditch. But in 1989, when he installed his pipe, the company got an injunction. The court ruled that the sugar company had a valid prior claim on the water, and that Mr. Manini's use of the water would cause the company "lost income" and "irreparable harm."

The department didn't back him up. Mr. Rowe says that while Mr. Manini did have the department's permission to tap into the ditch, "at the same time we were in the process of negotiating with Kekaha" and the department didn't want to jeopardize the negotiations. What became of these talks? "I don't know," Mr. Rowe says. "I think we are still negotiating."

Mr. Manini, however, says the department is "only a blockade to Hawaiians getting on the land." His herd is down to four skinny cows. He supports his children and diabetic wife with two jobs. Nights he pumps cesspools. Days he works as a tractor operator for the Robinson Sugar Co.

Gov. John Waihee, the first part-Hawaiian governor, whose own father died while on the waiting list, has taken some steps to increase state funding of the homelands department. He also promoted passage of a bill that allows native Hawaiians to sue over violations of the 1921 act in some circumstances. "Only in the past few years has the program begun to turn around despite the odds," he says. His policies have "begun to pay off," he says.

But the right-to-sue bill bars suits over violations that occurred before 1988. And if native Hawaiians win any damages, the bill requires them to give the money to the Office of Hawaiian Affairs—a controversy-plagued agency that many native Hawaiians don't trust. During the first three years of Gov. Waihee's first term—through 1989, the latest year for

...AND THE HIGHEST SUICIDE RATE, TOO

About 200,000 of Hawaii's one million-plus residents are any part Hawaiian. By most measures, they are the most impoverished group in the state.

Their downward slide began as soon as Captain Cook arrived. First, Western disease came close to wiping them out; next, the influence of missionaries nearly obliterated cultural traditions and social structure; and, finally, white planters lay claim to virtually all prime land and natural resources. Over the years, native Hawaiians have been relegated to the lowest rung of the islands' social and economic ladder.

The consequences of the overthrow of the kingdom of Hawaii by the United States are not confined to historical wrong or compensable claims for lost ancestral land rights and interests, wrote three members of the Native Hawaiians Study Commission in their report to the federal government in 1983. "Dispossession and defeat also have psychological, social and cultural consequences."

A 1990 state study found that about 1% of native Hawaiians are homeless. They represent about 30% of the state's homeless population, far higher than their percentage of the general population.

Native Hawaiians also have the worst housing in the state. According to U.S. Census data, they live in the most crowded conditions and are the most likely of any ethnic group in Hawaii except Filipinos to have partial to no plumbing in their homes.

According to state figures, 15% of native Hawaiians are below the poverty line, compared with 8% of the total population. Native Hawaiians also have twice the unemployment rate of the state's general population and represent 30% of its recipients of Aid to Families With Dependent Children. About 15% of native Hawaiians receive AFDC assistance versus 6% of the total population.

Native Hawaiians have the lowest life expectancy of any ethnic group in the state, the highest death rates from heart disease, cancer, diabetes, hypertension and strokes and the highest infant mortality rate. They have the lowest education levels in the state and the highest suicide rate.

which statistics are available—the awarding of home lots slowed even more, while the amount of acreage leased or licensed to non-natives climbed by another 8,319 acres, department records show. Gov. Waihee says the awarding of home lots slowed because his administration had made installing infrastructure on the homelands a "major priority."

Fed up, about 19 families on the waiting list took to squatting a few years ago on a homeland beach on Kauai called Anahola, a Hawaiian word meaning "time set aside." It is a beach the county wants to turn into a park for tourists. The families planted a community garden, tapped the county electric lines and built a big A-frame in the sand. "My father waited all his life for his land," says Michael Grace, the Anahola squatters' unofficial leader. "That's not going to happen to me."

But in July, a few days after eclipse-gawking tourists had left the islands, state police and the National Guard arrested the squatters for trespassing and bulldozed the A-frame.

Mrs. Drake, the homelands department director, says the squatters weren't playing fair. "They should wait their turn," she says. "They should follow the list." But one squatter, Daniel Manaku, has no faith in this system.

"It's a hit list, that's what it is to me," he says. "They put you on a list and they let you die."

THE PRINCE'S PLAN IS CO-OPTED

In 1893, a group of businessmen, backed by U.S. Marines, toppled the popular Hawaiian queen and took over the islands, including 1.5 million acres that were supposed to go to native Hawaiian commoners according to a decree by the Hawaiian king in 1848. President Grover Cleveland commissioned an investigation and concluded that the takeover was "a lawless occupation."

President Cleveland was ignored by Congress, however, and the businessmen began selling chunks of the 1.5 million acres to fellow merchants and planters. When the Hawaiian islands were later annexed to the United States, the islands' government acknowledged that this acreage belonged to native Hawaiians, and ceded it to the United States with the stipulation that it be held in trust for native Hawaiians. The federal government then lopped off about 20 percent of the land for its own use, mostly for military bases.

Nearly 30 years after the businessmen's coup, it looked as if native Hawaiians would at least get to rent a small sliver of the 1.5 million acres. The Hawaiian Homes Commission Act began as a well-meaning effort by Prince Jonah Kuhio, the part-Hawaiian territorial delegate to Congress, who saw urban slums, venereal disease and cholera rapidly killing off the Hawaiians and hoped that returning Hawaiians to the land could save them. "The Hawaiian race is passing," he mourned in 1920. "And if conditions continue to exist as they do today, this splendid race of people, my race, will pass from the face of the earth."

But no sooner did Prince Kuhio float his plan in Congress than it was co-opted by sugar and pineapple planters, who saw it as a way to secure their own uncertain futures. Their leases on 26,000 prime acres were about to expire and a general homesteading law threatened to transfer their lucrative holdings to other hands.

So the planters struck a deal with the territory's politicians. Get rid of general homesteading, allow planters to keep their lands, and in exchange they would agree to allot less than 200,000 acres of "fourth-class" lands to native Hawaiians for homesteading. They made sure that the homelands department's first directorate was sympathetic—its executive secretary was George Cooke of Castle & Cooke, one of the Big Five planter powers.

The ceded lands of the native Hawaiian commoners, meantime, were still being held in trust by the federal government. With statehood in 1959, the U.S. required that this land and the revenues it generated be used for "the betterment" of native Hawaiians, but that never happened.

Finally, in 1978, a state constitutional convention instructed the state government to compensate native Hawaiians for the ceded lands' lost revenues. More years passed without action. In 1990, the state government settled the matter by agreeing to pay a state agency $100 million plus $8.5 million a year, to be used to aid native Hawaiians. However, the state agency charged with this task, the Office of Hawaiian Affairs, is plagued by poor budget controls, mismanagement and cronyism, according to two outside audits in 1986 and 1990.

The Office of Hawaiian Affairs, while conceding that many of the auditors' findings are "reasonable and acceptable," blames its problems on uncertain funding and "complex and sometimes ambiguous relationships with other agencies of state government."

For discussion

1. Kafka's townspeople and the Hawaiians in Susan Faludi's story both get refusals. Compare the two stories for similar and dissimilar features.
2. About Kafka, it was asked whether a straight essay on law, economics, and politics could be teased out of his story. Here it would seem that there is much more tangible material with which to do it. If this capsule on Hawaii were all that we had to go on, what would we conclude about the interconnections among law, economics, and politics?

3a. What is the state of the law of the United States and Hawaii regarding the rights of natives to homelands? Is all law adverse to them, or are there some desirable features from their standpoint? If law has a mixed character rather than being either totally favorable or totally unfavorable, what effects might law have on the native Hawaiians? Should the Hawaiians renounce law as a means of redress, or try to use its favorable elements?

b. If a group of native Hawaiians were to consult you as their lawyer, what would you advise?

4. What should 17–20-year-old Hawaiians do either by themselves or in conjunction with their older kin?
5. The story refers to multinationals. How do multinationals affect native Hawaiian land claims?

Writer B. Traven can be called an anthropologist-novelist since his knowledge of Indian life in Mexico was so intimate that if one visits Southern Mexico today, almost one hundred years after the period in that his writing was set, one can still find some of the characteristics that he described in his stories.

His main themes are the relationships between Indians and Ladinos, who controlled all of the important institutions of the country, and the efforts of the Indians to maintain their culture in the face of very difficult odds. In the following, an Indian is not pitted against a Ladino, but a more distant outsider, E. L. Winthrop of New York.

ASSEMBLY LINE

B. Traven[*]

Mr. E. L. Winthrop of New York was on vacation in the Republic of Mexico. It wasn't long before he realized that this strange and really wild country had not yet been fully and satisfactorily explored by Rotarians and Lions, who are forever conscious of their glorious mission on earth. Therefore, he considered it his duty as a good American citizen to do his part in correcting this oversight.

*"Assembly Line" from *The Night Visitor and Other Stories* by B. Traven. Copyright © 1966 by B. Traven. Reprinted by permission of Hill and Wang, a division of Farrar, Straus and Giroux, Inc.

In search for opportunities to indulge in his new avocation, he left the beaten track and ventured into regions not especially mentioned, and hence not recommended, by travel agents to foreign tourists. So it happened that one day he found himself in a little, quaint Indian village somewhere in the State of Oaxaca.

Walking along the dusty main street of this pueblecito, which knew nothing of pavements, drainage, plumbing, or of any means of artificial light save candles or pine splinters, he met with an Indian squatting on the earthen-floor front porch of a palm hut, a so-called jacalito.

The Indian was busy making little baskets from bast and from all kinds of fibers gathered by him in the immense tropical bush which surrounded the village on all sides. The material used had not only been well prepared for its purpose but was also richly colored with dyes that the basket-maker himself extracted from various native plants, barks, roots and from certain insects by a process known only to him and the members of his family.

His principal business, however, was not producing baskets. He was a peasant who lived on what the small property he possessed—less than fifteen acres of not too fertile soil—would yield, after much sweat and labor and after constantly worrying over the most wanted and best suited distribution of rain, sunshine, and wind and the changing balance of birds and insects beneficial or harmful to his crops. Baskets he made when there was nothing else for him to do in the fields, because he was unable to dawdle. After all, the sale of his baskets, though to a rather limited degree only, added to the small income he received from his little farm.

In spite of being by profession just a plain peasant, it was clearly seen from the small baskets he made that at heart he was an artist, a true and accomplished artist. Each basket looked as if covered all over with the most beautiful sometimes fantastic ornaments, flowers, butterflies, birds, squirrels, antelope, tigers, and a score of other animals of the wilds. Yet, the most amazing thing was that these decorations, all of them symphonies of color, were not painted on the baskets but were instead actually part of the baskets themselves. Bast and fibers dyed in dozens of different colors were so cleverly—one must actually say intrinsically—interwoven that those attractive designs appeared on the inner part of the basket as well as on the outside. Not by painting but by weaving were those highly artistic effects achieved. This performance he accomplished without ever looking at any sketch or pattern. While working on a basket these designs came to light as if by magic, and as long as a basket was not entirely finished one could not perceive what in this case or that the decoration would be like.

People in the market town who bought these baskets would use them for sewing baskets or to decorate tables with or window sills, or to hold little things to keep them from lying around. Women put their jewelry in them or flowers or little dolls. There were in fact a hundred and two ways they might serve certain purposes in a household or in a lady's own room.

Whenever the Indian had finished about twenty of the baskets he took them to town on market day. Sometimes he would already be on his way shortly after midnight because he owned only a burro to ride on, and if the burro had gone astray the day before, as happened frequently, he would have to walk the whole way to town and back again.

At the market he had to pay twenty centavos in taxes to sell his wares. Each basket cost him between twenty and thirty hours of constant work, not counting the time spent gathering bast and fibers, preparing them, making dyes and coloring the bast. All this meant extra time and work. The price he asked for each basket was fifty centavos, the equivalent of about four cents. It seldom happened, however, that a buyer paid outright the full fifty centavos asked—or four reales as the Indian called that money. The prospective buyer started bargaining, telling the Indian that he ought to be ashamed to ask such a sinful price. "Why, the whole dirty thing is nothing but ordinary petate straw which you find in heaps wherever you may look for it; the jungle is packed full of it," the buyer would argue. "Such a little basket, what's it good for anyhow? If I paid you, you thief, ten centavitos for it you should be grateful and kiss my hand. Well, it's your lucky day, I'll be generous this time. I'll pay you twenty, yet not one green centavo more. Take it or run along."

So he sold finally for twenty-five centavos, but then the buyer would say, "Now, what do you think of that? I've got only twenty centavos change on me. What can we do about that? If you can change me a twenty-peso bill, all right, you shall have your twenty-five fierros." Of course, the Indian could not change a twenty-peso bill and so the basket went for twenty centavos.

He had little if any knowledge of the outside world or he would have known that what happened to him was happening every hour of every day to every artist all over the world. That knowledge would perhaps have made him very proud, because he would have realized that he belonged to the little army which is the salt of the earth and which keeps culture, urbanity and beauty for their own sake from passing away.

Often it was not possible for him to sell all the baskets he had brought to market, for people here as elsewhere in the world preferred things made by the millions and each so much like the other that you were unable, even with the help of a magnifying glass, to tell which was which and where was the difference between two of the same kind.

Yet he, this craftsman, had in his life made several hundreds of those exquisite baskets, but so far no two of them had he ever turned out alike in design. Each was an individual piece of art and as different from the other as was a Murillo from a Velásquez.

Naturally he did not want to take those baskets which he could not sell at the market place home with him again if he could help it. In such a case he went peddling his products from door to door where he was treated partly as a beggar and partly as a vagrant apparently looking for an opportunity to steal, and he frequently had to swallow all sorts of insults and nasty remarks.

Then, after a long run, perhaps a woman would finally stop him, take one of the baskets and offer him ten centavos, which price through talks and talks would perhaps go up to fifteen or even to twenty. Nevertheless, in many instances he would actually get no more than just ten centavos, and the buyer, usually a woman, would grasp that little marvel and right before his eyes throw it carelessly upon the nearest table as if to say, "Well, I take that piece of nonsense only for charity's sake. I know my money is wasted. But then, after all, I'm a Christian and I can't see a poor Indian die of hunger since he has come such a long way from his village." This would remind her of something better and she would hold him and say, "Where are you at home anyway, Indito? What's your pueblo? So, from Huehuetonoc? Now, listen here, Indito, can't you bring me next Saturday two or three turkeys from Huehuetonoc? But they must be heavy and fat and very, very cheap or I won't even touch them. If I wish to pay the regular price I don't need you to bring them. Understand? Hop along, now, Indito."

The Indian squatted on the earthen floor in the portico of his hut, attended to his work and showed no special interest in the curiosity of Mr. Winthrop watching him. He acted almost as if he ignored the presence of the American altogether.

"How much that little basket, friend?" Mr. Winthrop asked when he felt that he at least had to say something as not to appear idiotic.

Fifty centavitos, patroncito, my good little lordy, four reales," the Indian answered politely.

"All right, sold," Mr. Winthrop blurted out in a tone and with a wide gesture as if he had bought a whole railroad. And examining his buy he added, "I know already who I'll give that pretty little thing to. She'll kiss me for it, sure. Wonder what she'll use it for?"

He had expected to hear a price of three or even four pesos. The moment he realized that he had judged the value six times too high, he saw right away what great business possibilities this miserable Indian village might offer to a dynamic promoter like himself. Without further delay he started exploring those possibilities. "Suppose, my good friend, I buy ten of these little baskets of yours which, as I might as well admit right here and now, have practically no real use whatsoever. Well, as I was saying, if I buy ten, how much would you then charge me apiece?"

The Indian hesitated for a few seconds, as if making calculations. Finally he said, "If you buy ten I can let you have them for forty-five centavos each, señorito gentleman."

"All right, amigo. And now, let's suppose I buy from you straight away one hundred of these absolutely useless baskets, how much will they cost me each?"

The Indian, never fully looking up to the American standing before him, and hardly taking his eyes off his work, said politely and without the slightest trace of enthusiasm in his voice, "In such a case I might not be quite unwilling to sell each for forty centavitos."

Mr. Winthrop bought sixteen baskets, which was all the Indian had in stock.

After three weeks' stay in the Republic, Mr. Winthrop was convinced that he knew this country perfectly, that he had seen everything and knew all about the inhabitants, their character and their way of life, and that there was nothing left for him to explore. So he returned to good old Nooyorg and felt happy to be once more in a civilized country, as he expressed it to himself.

One day going out for lunch he passed a confectioner's and, looking at the display in the window, he suddenly remembered the little baskets he had bought in that faraway Indian village.

He hurried home and took all the baskets he still had left to one of the best-known candymakers in the city.

"I can offer you here," Mr. Winthrop said to the confectioner, "one of the most artistic and at the same time the most original of boxes, if you wish to call them that. These little baskets would be just right for the most expensive chocolates meant for elegant and high-priced gifts. Just have a good look at them, sir, and let me listen."

The confectioner examined the baskets and found them extraordinarily well suited for a certain line in his business. Never before had there been anything like them for originality, prettiness and good taste. He, however, avoided most carefully showing any sign of enthusiasm, for which there would be time enough once he knew the price and whether he could get a whole load exclusively.

He shrugged his shoulders and said, "Well, I don't know. If you asked me I'd say it isn't quite what I'm after. However, we might give it a try. It depends, of course, on the price. In our business the package mustn't cost more than what's in it."

"Do I hear an offer?" Mr. Winthrop asked.

"Why don't you tell me in round figures how much you want for them? I'm not good in guessing."

"Well, I'll tell you, Mr. Kemple: since I'm the smart guy who discovered these baskets and since I'm the only Jack who knows where to lay his hands on more, I'm selling to the highest bidder, on an exclusive basis, of course. I'm positive you can see it my way, Mr. Kemple."

"Quite so, and may the best man win," the confectioner said. "I'll talk the matter over with my partners. See me tomorrow same time, please, and I'll let you know how far we might be willing to go."

Next day when both gentlemen met again Mr. Kemple said: "Now, to be frank with you, I know art on seeing it, no getting around that. And these baskets are little works of art, they surely are. However, we are no art dealers, you realize that of course. We've no other use for these pretty little things except as fancy packing for our French pralines made by us. We can't pay for them what we might pay considering them pieces of art. After all to us they're only wrappings. Fine wrappings, perhaps, but nevertheless wrappings. You'll see it our way I hope. Mr.—oh yes, Mr. Winthrop. So, here is our offer, take it or leave it: a dollar and a quarter apiece and not one cent more."

Mr. Winthrop made a gesture as if he had been struck over the head.

The confectioner, misunderstanding this involuntary gesture of Mr. Winthrop, added quickly, "All right, all right, no reason to get excited, no reason at all. Perhaps we can do a trifle better. Let's say one-fifty."

"Make it one-seventy-five," Mr. Winthrop snapped, swallowing his breath while wiping his forehead.

"Sold. One-seventy-five apiece free at port of New York. We pay the customs and you pay the shipping. Right?"

"Sold," Mr. Winthrop said also and the deal was closed.

"There is, of course, one condition," the confectioner explained just when Mr. Winthrop was to leave. "One or two hundred won't do for us. It wouldn't pay the trouble and the advertising. I won't consider less than ten thousand, or one thousand dozens if that sounds better in your ears. And they must come in no less than twelve different patterns well assorted. How about that?"

"I can make it sixty different patterns or designs."

"So much the better. And you're sure you can deliver ten thousand let's say early October?"

"Absolutely," Mr. Winthrop avowed and signed the contract.

Practically all the way back to Mexico, Mr. Winthrop had a notebook in his left hand and a pencil in his right and he was writing figures, long rows of them, to find out exactly how much richer he would be when this business had been put through.

"Now, let's sum up the whole goddamn thing," he muttered to himself. "Damn it, where is that cursed pencil again? I had it right between my fingers. Ah, there it is. Ten thousand he ordered. Well, well, there we got a clean-cut profit of fifteen thousand four hundred and forty genuine dollars. Sweet smackers. Fifteen grand right into papa's pocket. Come to think of it, that Republic isn't so backward after all."

"Buenas tardes, mi amigo, how are you?" he greeted the Indian whom he found squatting in the porch of his jacalito as if he had never moved from his place since Mr. Winthrop had left for New York.

The Indian rose, took off his hat, bowed politely and said in his soft voice, "Be welcome, patroncito. Thank you, I feel fine, thank you. Muy buenas tardes. This house and all I have is at your kind disposal." He bowed once more, moved his right hand in a gesture of greeting and sat down again. But he excused himself for doing so by saying, "Perdóneme, patroncito, I have to take advantage of the daylight, soon it will be night."

"I've got big business for you, my friend," Mr. Winthrop began.

"Good to hear that, señor."

Mr. Winthrop said to himself, "Now, he'll jump up and go wild when he learns what I've got for him." And aloud he said: "Do you think you can make me one thousand of these little baskets?"

"Why not, patroncito? If I can make sixteen, I can make one thousand also."

"That's right, my good man. Can you also make five thousand?"

"Of course, señor. I can make five thousand if I can make one thousand."

"Good. Now, if I should ask you to make me ten thousand, what would you say? And what would be the price of each? You can make ten thousand, can't you?"

"Of course, I can, señor. I can make as many as you wish. You see, I am an expert in this sort of work. No one else in the whole state can make them the way I do."

"That's what I thought and that's exactly why I came to you."

"Thank you for the honor, patroncito."

"Suppose I order you to make me ten thousand of these baskets, how much time do you think you would need to deliver them?"

The Indian, without interrupting his work, cocked his head to one side and then to the other as if he were counting the days or weeks it would cost him to make all these baskets.

After a few minutes he said in a slow voice, "It will take a good long time to make so many baskets, patroncito. You see, the bast and the fibers must be very dry before they can be used properly. Then all during the time they are slowly drying, they must be worked and handled in a very special way so that while drying they won't lose their softness and their flexibility and their natural brilliance. Even when dry they must look fresh. They must never lose their natural properties or they will look just as lifeless and dull as straw. Then while they are drying up I got to get the plants and roots and barks and insects from which I brew the dyes. That takes much time also, believe me. The plants must be gathered when the moon is just right or they won't give the right color. The insects I pick from the plants must also be gathered at the right time and under the right conditions or else they produce no rich colors and are just like dust. But, of course, jefecito, I can make as many of these canastitas as you wish, even as many as three dozens if you want them. Only give me time."

"Three dozens? Three dozens?" Mr. Winthrop yelled, and threw up both arms in desperation. "Three dozens!" he repeated as if he had to say it many times in his own voice so as to understand the real meaning of it, because for a while he thought that he was dreaming. He had expected the Indian to go crazy on hearing that he was to sell ten thousand of his baskets without having to peddle them from door to door and be treated like a dog with a skin disease.

So the American took up the question of price again, by which he hoped to activate the Indian's ambition. "You told me that if I take one hundred baskets you will let me have them for forty centavos apiece. Is that right, my friend?"

"Quite right, jefecito."

"Now," Mr. Winthrop took a deep breath, "now, then, if I ask you to make me one thousand, that is, ten times one hundred baskets, how much will they cost me, each basket?"

That figure was too high for the Indian to grasp. He became slightly confused and for the first time since Mr. Winthrop had arrived he interrupted his work and tried to think it out. Several times he shook his head and looked vaguely around as if for help. Finally he said, "Excuse me, jefecito, little chief, that is by far too much for me to count. Tomorrow, if you will do me the honor, come and see me again and I think I shall have my answer ready for you, patroncito."

When on the next morning Mr. Winthrop came to the hut he found the Indian as usual squatting on the floor under the overhanging palm roof working at his baskets.

"Have you got the price for ten thousand?" he asked the Indian the very moment he saw him, without taking the trouble to say "Good Morning!"

"Si, patroncito, I have the price ready. You may believe me when I say it has cost me much labor and worry to find out the exact price, because, you see, I do not wish to cheat you out of your honest money."

"Skip that, amigo. Come out with the salad. What's the price?" Mr. Winthrop asked nervously.

"The price is well calculated now without any mistake on my side. If I got to make one thousand canastitas each will be three pesos. If I must make five thousand, each will cost nine pesos. And if I have to make ten thousand, in such a case I can't make them for less than fifteen pesos each." Immediately he returned to his work as if he were afraid of losing too much time with such idle talk.

Mr. Winthrop thought that perhaps it was his faulty knowledge of this foreign language that had played a trick on him.

"Did I hear you say fifteen pesos each if I eventually would buy ten thousand?"

"That's exactly and without any mistake what I've said, patroncito," the Indian answered in his soft courteous voice.

"But now, see here, my good man, you can't do this to me. I'm your friend and I want to help you get on your feet."

"Yes, patroncito. I know this and I don't doubt any of your words."

"Now, let's be patient and talk this over quietly as man to man. Didn't you tell me that if I would buy one hundred you would sell each for forty centavos?"

"Si, jefecito, that's what I said. If you buy one hundred you can have them for forty centavos apiece, provided that I have one hundred, which I don't."

"Yes, yes, I see that." Mr. Winthrop felt as if he would go insane any minute now. "Yes, so you said. Only what I can't comprehend is why you cannot sell at the same price if you make me ten thousand. I certainly don't wish to chisel on the price. I am not that kind. Only, well, let's see now, if you can sell for forty centavos at all, be it for twenty or fifty or a hundred. I can't quite get the idea why the price has to jump that high if I buy more than a hundred."

"Bueno, patroncito, what is there so difficult to understand? It's all very simple. One thousand canastitas cost me a hundred times more work than a dozen. Ten thousand cost me so much time and labor that I could never finish them, not even in a hundred years. For a thousand canastitas I need more bast than for a hundred, and I need more little red beetles and more plants and roots and bark for the dyes. It isn't that you just can walk into the bush and pick all the things you need at your heart's desire. One root with the true violet blue may cost me four or five days until I can find one in the jungle. And have you thought how much time it costs and how much hard work to prepare the bast and fibers? What is more, if I must make so many baskets, who then will look after my corn and my beans and my goats and chase for me occasionally a rabbit for meat on Sunday? If I have no corn, then I have no tortillas to eat, and if I grow no beans, where do I get my frijoles from?"

"But since you'll get so much money from me for your baskets you can buy all the corn and beans in the world and more than you need."

"That's what you think, señorito, little lordy. But you see, it is only the corn I grow myself that I am sure of. Of the corn which others may or may not grow, I cannot be sure to feast upon."

"Haven't you got some relatives here in this village who might help you to make baskets for me?" Mr. Winthrop asked hopefully.

"Practically the whole village is related to me somehow or other. Fact is, I got lots of close relatives in this here place."

"Why then can't they cultivate your fields and look after your goats while you make baskets for me? Not only this, they might gather for you the fibers and the colors in the bush and lend you a hand here and there in preparing the material you need for the baskets."

"They might, patroncito, yes, they might. Possible. But then you see who would take care of their fields and cattle if they work for me? And if they help me with the baskets it turns out the same. No one would any longer work his fields properly. In such a case corn and beans would get up so high in price that none of us could buy any and we all would starve to death. Besides, as the price of everything would rise and rise higher still how could I make baskets at forty centavos apiece? A pinch of salt or one green chili would set me back more than I'd collect for one single basket. Now you'll understand, highly estimated caballero and jefecito, why I can't make the baskets any cheaper than fifteen pesos each if I got to make that many."

Mr. Winthrop was hard-boiled, no wonder considering the city he came from. He refused to give up the more than fifteen thousand dollars which at that moment seemed to slip through his fingers like nothing. Being really desperate now, he talked and bargained with the Indian for almost two full hours, trying to make him understand how rich he, the Indian, would become if he would take this greatest opportunity of his life.

The Indian never ceased working on his baskets while he explained his points of view.

"You know, my good man," Mr. Winthrop said, "such a wonderful chance might never again knock on your door, do you realize that? Let me explain to you in ice-cold figures what fortune you might miss if you leave me flat on this deal."

He tore out leaf after leaf from his notebook, covered each with figures and still more figures, and while doing so told the peasant he would be the richest man in the whole district.

The Indian without answering watched with a genuine expression of awe as Mr. Winthrop wrote down these long figures, executing complicated multiplications and divisions and subtractions so rapidly that it seemed to him the greatest miracle he had ever seen.

The American, noting this growing interest in the Indian, misjudged the real significance of it. "There you are, my friend," he said. "That's exactly how rich you're going to be. You'll have a bankroll of exactly four thousand pesos. And to show you that I'm a real friend of yours, I'll throw in a bonus. I'll make it a round five thousand pesos, and all in silver."

The Indian, however, had not for one moment thought of four thousand pesos. Such an amount of money had no meaning to him. He had been interested solely in Mr. Winthrop's ability to write figures so rapidly.

"So, what do you say now? Is it a deal or is it? Say yes and you'll get your advance this very minute."

"As I have explained before, patroncito, the price is fifteen pesos each."

"But, my good man," Mr. Winthrop shouted at the poor Indian in utter despair, "where have you been all this time? On the moon or where? You are still at the same price as before."

"Yes, I know that, jefecito, my little chief," the Indian answered, entirely unconcerned. "It must be the same price because I cannot make any other one. Besides, señor, there's still another thing which perhaps you don't know. You see, my good lordy and caballero, I've to make these canastitas my own way and with my song in them and with bits of my soul woven into them. If I were to make them in great numbers there would no longer be my soul in each, or my songs. Each would look like the other with no difference whatever and such a thing would slowly eat up my heart. Each has to be another song which I hear in the morning when the sun rises and when the birds begin to chirp and the butterflies come and sit down on my baskets so that I may see a new beauty, because, you see, the butterflies like my baskets and the pretty colors on them, that's why they come and sit down, and I can make my canastitas after them. And now, señor jefecito, if you will kindly excuse me, I have wasted much time already, although it was a pleasure and a great honor to hear the talk of such a distinguished caballero like you. But I'm afraid I've to attend to my work now, for day after tomorrow is market day in town and I got to take my baskets there. Thank you, señor, for your visit. Adiós."

And in this way it happened that American garbage cans escaped the fate of being turned into receptacles for empty, torn, and crumpled little multicolored canastitas into which an Indian of Mexico had woven dreams of his soul, throbs of his heart: his unsung poems.

For discussion

1. In this third story of refusal, the Indian stands his ground and succeeds, at least in the sense that it was his will that prevailed rather than Winthrop's. How can his success be explained against the backdrop of the prior two stories of "little guy" failure?
2. If the Indian were a guest lecturer in a modern economics class—for example, one entitled the Economics of Resource Allocation—would his appraisal of his situation be consistent with sound economic theory, or would he be laughed out of the class as a fool?
3. Winthrop may have gone home baffled because the Indian did not grab at the chance to break out of the cycle of dirt farming and customer abuse. The Indian was rejecting modernity, specialization, development, and the highest and best uses of his time and efforts. Was Winthrop right?
4. What if Winthrop had come home impressed by the lessons of the Indian, and had resolved that in the future he would insist upon an integral connection among all the things that he did in his own life? He announces to his friends, "Either things have meaning or they shouldn't be done. Yes sir. I learned that from an Indian in Mexico. He treated me like I was his kid brother, and I deserved it!"

   Do his friends reply, "So we are to become Indians?—Come on"?

   Imagine the lines of discussion that would ensue as Winthrop tries to transform his new aspirations into a life plan. (What seems to make this imaginative exercise not so far-fetched is that the hundreds of students who have read Traven's story are rooting for the Indian to stand his ground, and stick to his style of life; they find his position compelling and attractive. Thus, while a life like Winthrop's is far and away the more likely career prospect for them, students feel drawn toward the Indian and not Winthrop.)

CONCLUSION

The strength of literary geniuses like Kafka is that they refuse to perform a reductionist assault on the richness of life. The complex is not mindlessly simplified; the paradoxical is left paradoxical and not tortured into a false place. Yet their creations rise above, or more accurately stay well below, a debilitating vagueness that would discourage our efforts to come to terms with them. On the contrary, Kafka's stories, if a touch mysterious, are engaging, graphic, and memorable, driving us inward toward choice rather than outward toward the accumulation of mere information.

The journalist, when avoiding the occupational disease of writing the quick and dirty story based on instant sources, can perform an equally valuable function. Albert Camus, a writer of fiction and a journalist, spoke in his notebooks about the kind of mental alertness that he hoped he could maintain. He spoke of a visitor to a strange city who arrives at night; night precludes putting the new place into preconceived order. When morning arrives, the vagueness and frailty of definition disappears and by the end of the first day what had been strange, imposing, or frightening has been trivialized and rendered totally familiar. According to Camus, the conscious person needs to maintain the stance of the visitor to an unfamiliar city at night.

Most journalists are daytime travellers, and their work can safely be dispatched to the recycling box. There are exceptions, such as the work done by Susan Faludi in the Hawaiian story. She has dug beneath the surface and revealed unpleasant facts. They might have been facts that she would have preferred not to find, and she could have prevented herself from finding them if she had chosen the right "sources." Perhaps she let the story tell itself. In any case, her story proves the worth of journalism in understanding contemporary problems in law and political economy.

All of the foregoing material presents the perspectives of people out of power, status, wealth, and privilege—people whose stories are generally not told, let alone given consequential weight. One must wonder why it takes the writer of fiction or the occasional journalist to bring the common person to our attention.

CHAPTER 2

Business and Legal Models

For Franz Kafka and just plain peasants from all periods and places, the daily round has never been broken into component parts. Homelife and worklife, family and community, and living and learning have never been so sharply demarcated as they are for most moderns. Perhaps it is the absence of clocks in some places that best typifies the differences across cultures. The clock breaks time into regular intervals to be assigned to well-defined tasks, with time to be saved or spent like currency.

Disciplines as studied in school share the fragmentation and specialization of the rest of modern life. If students find a certain charm in reading about the integrated life of the Indian peasant of B. Traven's story, they would also feel a certain impatience if storytelling were to comprise a major focus of their education. The peasant listens to dreams, but for moderns dreams represent weakness or a suspicious departure from pragmatic purposes. To the extent that students are trying to learn a living, excessive dreaminess would be considered a waste of time.

Academics share the student aversion for the ethereal and get down to the serious business of their specialized visions very soon after their studies begin. For the business person it is the bottom line or whatever else, besides profit, will contribute to the survival of the business organization. The lawyer gets down to cases or focuses on techniques to get a client's work done, even if a preoccupation with technique to the exclusion of purposes can lead in the longer term to personal and systemic disaster. Political scientists, with a methodological tool box borrowed from the hard sciences, may struggle for respectability by perfecting the *form* of their inquiry even when perfect form can trivialize the results. For the more venturesome political theorists, beliefs can get in the way. Too much questioning of system legitimacy—by raising the awesome reach of economic power and its corrupting effects—could make disbelievers not only of their students but of themselves as well.

Economists, with a similar and even deeper penchant for natural science methods, often reduce life to economic rationality and apply mathematical formulas where any self-respecting peasant would cringe at the mindless simplicity being injected into life in the name of rigor. Where life is bigger than the model, some economists pare life down to fit the models rather than enlarging the models. This is especially so where power intrudes upon economic analysis at every turn, and yet is considered "outside" the analysis, and ruled irrelevant.

A student who is not inclined toward the specialization that permeates modern education might try to undo disciplinary specialization by taking a smorgasbord of courses across a number of departments of the university. After such a campus-wide sampling, would the student be less afflicted by the mental deformity that results when students study exclusively in one department or discipline? Not necessarily. While it is of course true that a student exposed to more angles of vision would be better off than one with single vision, the total returns from studying successive specialties might be substantially less than one might hope to be the case. A series of specialized subjects need not provide an assessment of the whole; the parts may be simply parts, either too small or too inconsequential to contribute to the piecing together of a meaningful whole, and specialists will most probably leave whatever integration is to be done for the students to do on their own.

What are the dominant patterns of analysis that characterize the discrete subjects of business, political science, economics, and law, and how would an explicit integration of these otherwise separate areas of the study of multinational business offer better prospects than a students' hopscotching across departments to get a general picture of the multinational corporation?

There seem to be two promising beginnings toward answering this largely unanswerable question. First, the focal questions of a discipline and the preferred ways that practitioners in the calling have for answering them can be outlined. The table of contents of introductory texts or the course descriptions and syllabi for courses disclose favored methods and subject matter. Unfortunately, what is routinely *excluded* from consideration may be far harder to pinpoint, and what is left out may be more critical than what is left in! It is the exclusions from regular coverage that are especially important in a field like multinationals, which presents many novel elements.

A second approach follows from the first. Some people are renegades from the disciplinary orthodoxies in which they were trained. Their rebellion might have been in part inspired by a discomfort over the questions customarily asked in their disciplines and the questions their disciplines have ruthlessly excluded. This partial dissatisfaction—it is usually partial rather than complete—with their home disciplines may have been produced by a burning question to which the discipline offered no satisfactory answers, or worse, never pursued.

A business person may wonder whether all parties to an international business deal are really benefitting from it, or whether what is good for General Motors really is good for the United States or the other countries where General Motors operates. A lawyer, despite having been repeatedly told in law school that justice, like truth, can never be satisfactorily explained, may still thirst for justice, and may feel discomfort at merely implementing a corporate client's will with the necessary paperwork. A political scientist may ask about the real forces behind voting, legislation, or policy making—just where does power fit into political analysis, and is there too much power in some people and too little, or none, left over for others? An economist might ask about the effects of economic power on law or politics—if money talks in a society, what language does it speak, to whom, through what intermediaries, and with what effects on the allocation of goods and services? Big questions like the foregoing usually take people beyond the boundary of their disciplines.

I. THE FOCAL CONCERNS OF BUSINESS, MODELS OF INTERNATIONAL BUSINESS, AND CONTEMPORARY TRANSFORMATIONS OF THEM

What contemporary businesses are concerned about can be determined in part by the kind of schooling they promote. For domestic businesses of all types, there are a number of areas of study that have been perennially valued as contributing directly and indirectly to the profitability or longevity of firms. Finance, accounting, marketing, and management comprise the principal foci for business in theory and practice. Surrounding these "functional" areas, which appeared in business school curricula many years ago, there are newer areas of study such as computer systems and quantitative methods, which are considered germane in all of the functional areas. As glosses on functional and related study, one might also survey business law or business ethics, law an early arrival in business education, ethics traceable to post-Watergate concerns that professionals without a grounding in ethics could become social menaces.

Strictly speaking, law and ethics could be considered epiphenomenal, a fancy way of saying that they are not essential to being a successful participant in business. One would not utterly fail in the operational aspects of a business were the subjects of law and ethics excluded from the curriculum. In fact, these subjects might even cause excessive squeamishness that could impair business effectiveness. Some of the resistances to law and ethics in business schools stem from the aversion to controversial issues surrounding product safety, whistle-blowing, discriminatory hiring practices, or workplace and environmental hazards, to say nothing about capital flight from the United States to countries overseas, sharp tax practices by businesses, or the uses and abuses of the corporate form of business organization.

The central question as one moves from domestic business to international business is whether the core business curriculum as augmented by such subjects as law or ethics remains adequate *by simple extension* of existing courses, or whether a deeper revision of business study must be done to bring business education up to the speed of world enterprise. Said differently, is international business simply *additive*—more of the same—or does the internationalization of enterprise require a top-to-bottom *qualitative shift* in the focal concerns of business and business education?

Some models for thinking about international enterprise suggest that multinationals will call for revolutionary rather than evolutionary changes in business education. Just as students of management had to import more and more from psychology and sociology to make any meaningful statement on the administration of organizations, so too the parameters of business study will have to be transcended to comprehend the multinational phenomenon.

But this time the direction of transcendence will be toward *political economy*, the general name given for the interplay between economic and political forces, or the interplay between state power and property–production systems. Law, as a dimension of the political, may be the place where artifacts from political–economic struggles pile up, and the study of law and the multinational corporation may offer one of the best vehicles in schools of business and elsewhere for rendering the usually invisible, visible.

It is now commonplace knowledge that business can no longer be considered a narrow subset of economics—*applied economics*, as it used to be called—and political-power questions can no longer be limited to the organizational infighting within a particular firm. Businesses will be dragged unwillingly, but more probably willingly, into more and more "nonmarket" arenas, "outside" the businesses, sometimes with lawyer–lobbyists at their sides.

For the more circumspect students of enterprise this development may not seem especially novel. Businesses have always had to be mindful of the contexts—cultural, social, political, and economic—in which they have operated. And they have not been passive with respect to those environments. Instead, they have cultivated environments helpful to enterprise through advertising and public relations.

Nevertheless, there may be inhibitions about making political economy an explicit dimension of business study. For years business people have publicly stated their aversion to politics and have said that they prefer a political context that leaves them alone to succeed or fail in the marketplace—"getting government off the backs of business." To recognize that no business can even begin to operate in the international context without running into politics at every level, both at home and abroad, does not take penetrating vision; a random issue of the *Wall Street Journal* makes the point uncontestably.

The reluctance to open up the business curriculum to the full study of the interconnection between business and political–legal contexts may have a different source. The introduction of the politics of international enterprise can spread to dangerous wonderment about the relationship between business and domestic politics. Are the same forces that are *at the surface* of international business just a little *below the surface* of domestic businesses? If so, once the intimate connection between business and politics at the international level becomes familiar, business at all levels can never be studied apolitically again. Such a fear can conservatize business curricula and create an impulse to stick closer to economically oriented study.

Some Contemporary Models for International Business

Contemporary models being developed for international business suggest lines of stability and change. The first, called for convenience the *typical model*, depicts some of the factors in decisions to multinationalize activities of an enterprise through the establishment of foreign subsidiaries. The model is typical in that its primary focus is economic, using simple extensions of techniques developed in business studies for the appraisal of any business opportunity or new product line. The typical model is supplemented by a schematic of an integrated manufacturing network that represents a multinational with worldwide options for production.

The second set of models extends the allocation models to include political dimensions; all multinationals routinely include political considerations in the calculus of location decisions, although not necessarily overtly. Two political models are presented; the first is a *passive* or *naive political model* in which a business takes a political system as given, and either rejects location within it, or enters and adapts to political restraints; this model adds to the purely economic-business model in a limited way.

The second political model—*active political*—includes the more likely situation, where a firm engages in political activity to create more favorable conditions in which to operate. Political activity ranges from out-and-out bribery, which comes to the minds of students first because it is so understandable, to the more subtle forms of political activity, such as lobbying, the formation of industry associations, or long-term public educational programs designed to make the political world more amenable to enterprise needs.

Location Decisions

Most multinationals are among the largest organizations in the world, each with a number of systems, subsystems, and affiliations located virtually everywhere. The organizations for production, marketing, finance, accounting, and management all have centers and subcenters, but not every functional area of the business necessarily overlaps with another in the same place. Production units may be kept close to raw materials, labor, or ultimate market destinations; marketing may occur with different intensities everywhere; finance may be situated in New York, London, or other money centers; accounting and data systems are usually located at headquarters or large regional subheadquarters; management may be centralized or decentralized, depending on the type of decision. Organizational and logistical complexities multiply in the large organization, increasing the costs of coordinating and executing multinational decisions in multiple locations. Nevertheless, judging from the growth in size and range of multinational corporations in the period since World War II, their managements must have seen net advantages accruing to the firms from worldwide networks.

The following model (Chart 1) depicts, in simplified form, location decisions of a multinational:[1]

Each multinational continually assesses its current locations and where it might relocate or discontinue activities to maximize *allocation efficiencies*,

[1]See generally, Yves Doz, *Strategic Management in Multinational Companies*. (New York, Pergamon, 1986), pp. 2–5. See also J. Dunning, "The Eclectic Paradigm of International Production, *Journal of International Business Studies* (Spring, 1988), pp. 1–25.

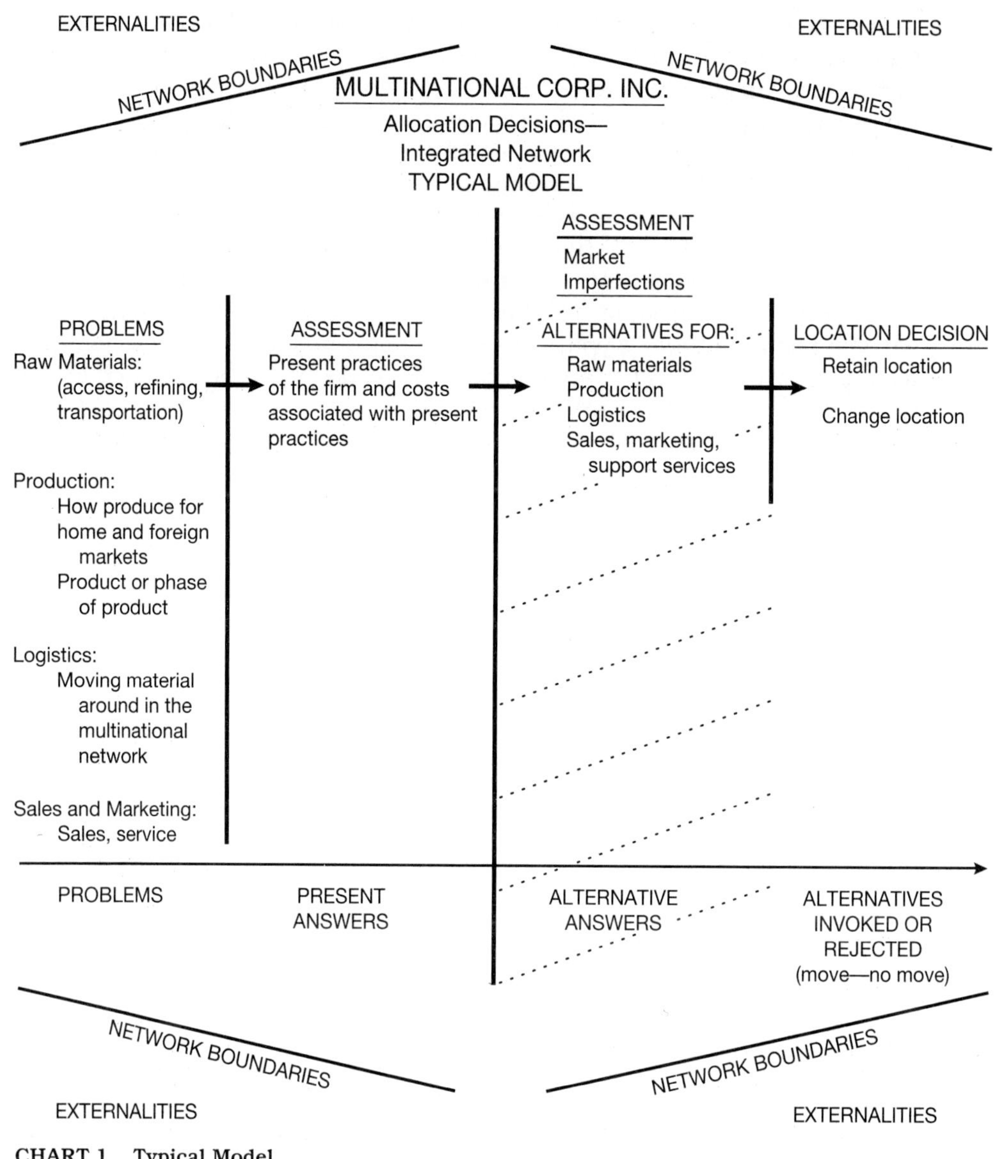

CHART 1 Typical Model

that is, doing the right things in the right places at minimum costs, maximum revenues, and hence greatest net returns. Decisions include all inputs to the enterprise, including land, labor, and capital, and the locations of inputs, end uses, and all logistical points in between. The import–export question also entails the assessment of costs and revenues.

It must be remembered that the integrated multinational can import and export to and from *itself*, since it controls both ends of all transactions. Should the United States market be supplied by domestic production or by overseas production? Should foreign markets be supplied from United States-based production or from foreign country-based production? Or will it be best from the firm's standpoint to use both production systems for different products or phases of production?

Where there are *phases* of production, intermediate products may be made for incorporation into ultimate products at later stages—for example, automobile transmissions made in Eastern Europe, assembled into cars in France, and then shipped for sale in the United States market; or electronic components assembled in the Far East for further assembly in the United States or nearby Mexico. Location decisions are made for each phase of production, using the criteria outlined above—costs, revenues, and net return.

Market imperfections, the name given to different prices in different markets, are close to the center of location strategies. Market imperfections are not as difficult to grasp as the name implies. For example, in 1983, chateaubriand steak for two with a bottle of wine and three-waiter service cost $16 at a classy hotel in Guadalajara, Mexico. Other things being equal—which they are not—every New Yorker would have preferred to eat out in Guadalajara at those prices instead of paying $100 for the same meal in New York. Even though one cannot always take advantage of differences in prices and value for money in different places, multinational corporations pay close attention to market imperfections. When market imperfections appear, such as differentials in wage rates and fringe benefits, multinationals might be able to tap them; when they dry up, as they have partially done for textile production and assembly work in Hong Kong, the multinational can restart the assessment process and consider alternative locations for the work.

The model in Chart 2 amplifies the typical model, showing a simplified version of the manufacturing network of an integrated multinational.[2]

Many aspects of the decisions involving location of firm activities can be totally analytical in the old sense of the word, using economic analysis or conventional business techniques for assessing the costs and benefits of a decision. The underlying goal of the calculus would be what produces the most for the least.

Externalities is the name given to costs or benefits "outside" the firm. Multinational managers use externalities to maximize profitability. For example, compensation for workers' injuries can be *internalized* as a cost of doing business or can be external to the firm and not a cost. The firm would incur no cost or less cost if the law of the place where a firm does manufacturing does not require an employer to pay compensation for worker injuries (or where the rate of compensation is comparatively low, or where the state itself maintains a system for taking care of injured workers without full assessment of the costs against the firm).

[2]Doz, *op. cit.*, p. 8.

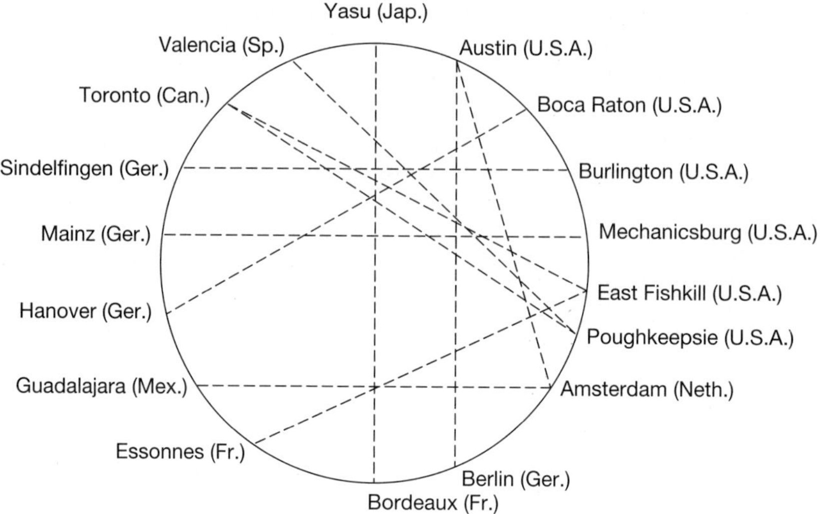

CHART 2 Amplified Typical Model

Another common example of externalities concerns pollution and whether the polluter must pay for pollution and take steps to eliminate pollution. If so, pollution costs figure into the profit and loss of the firm, or are "internalized." If, as has been true for most of U.S. industrial history, firms do not have to fully account for environmental damage, the costs of pollution need not be accounted for by the polluting firm. In an integrated multinational network like that depicted in the foregoing chart, there will be many more options for controlling costs, and externalizing costs, than would be true of an exclusively domestic company. As an economic matter, then, a multinational will choose to locate in places with minimum liability for worker injuries and where environmental costs would not be charged to the enterprise.

Externalities can be of other types. A school system is a benefit to a firm since, if workers need to read, it is less costly to a firm when a publicly funded school teaches them. Similarly, New York is a favorite place for financial firms to locate because of the tremendous amount of free information and low-cost communications that a financial firm can use when it locates there.

The foregoing diagram of a multinational network reveals a second critical feature. Allocative efficiencies are judged for the system *as a whole*, without regard to the benefits or detriments incurred by the *constituent units* of the integrated system. This judgment raises an immediate political problem since while the multinationals can move, people in the particular locations in the integrated network may not be able to move. It is not accidental that organized labor in the United States is upset by the free trade agreement between the United States and Mexico, where the average daily wage rates may be under $10 per day and fringe benefits inconsequential. Shifts of production to Mexico might benefit the multinational *as a whole*, but not necessarily the workers in all of the *affected units* of production. (This point does not reach the question of the across-the-board reduction of labor power when virtually all companies have numerous production sites for the same product or production phase, and can raise or lower production at particular locations. It also does not reach the sometimes disastrous impact on communities where production is discontinued or significantly reduced.)

International Business and Politics

This discussion of the gains and losses from allocation decisions and integrated production systems takes us closer to politics and the potential interference or noninterference by political forces with the discretion of multinational managers in shaping corporate strategies. Multinational corporations can, of course, avoid political limitations altogether by refusing to locate corporate activities in hostile political environments, or in places where compliance costs eat up economic advantages. No doubt this has been the case with Cuba since the 1956 Revolution, when multinational properties were nationalized. Until the Soviet Union gets a convertible currency and agrees to recognize private property and wider managerial discretion for outsiders, it too will remain an uncongenial place for multinational location.

Where the costs of bringing multinational behavior into compliance with state constraints are sufficiently low, location will occur. The *passive political model* in Chart 3 shows some of the possibilities.[3]

At point A, the multinational prerogatives are total and political limits are nonexistent; this could approximate the case in a "banana republic," where there are few if any consequential limits imposed upon foreign companies. At B, the multinationals would have no prerogatives, and political power over them is plenary. This could be the case of Cuba after the Cuban Revolution, and to a lesser extent is presently the case with members of the old Soviet Union. Points C and D represent different degrees of state tolerance or resistance to multinational discretion, points where regimes are neither totally pliable nor totally intransigent with respect to multinational preferences. At C and D, some allocative efficiencies might have to be sacrificed by the multinational, but the sacrifices might not offset all efficiencies.

There are a number of unrealistic elements in the passive political model that make it naive:

1. It would be rare for a multinational to be passive and not interventionist with respect to state policy. The banana republic may itself be an *end result* of a long history of interventionist strategizing designed to minimize state restrictions, and not a political context that was in its present configuration when the first multinational arrived.
2. The model might carry the implicit assumption that a multinational would prefer a totally noninterventionist state over all other possible

[3]The chart here is based on the discusssion in Doz, *op. cit.*, Chapters 1 and 2.

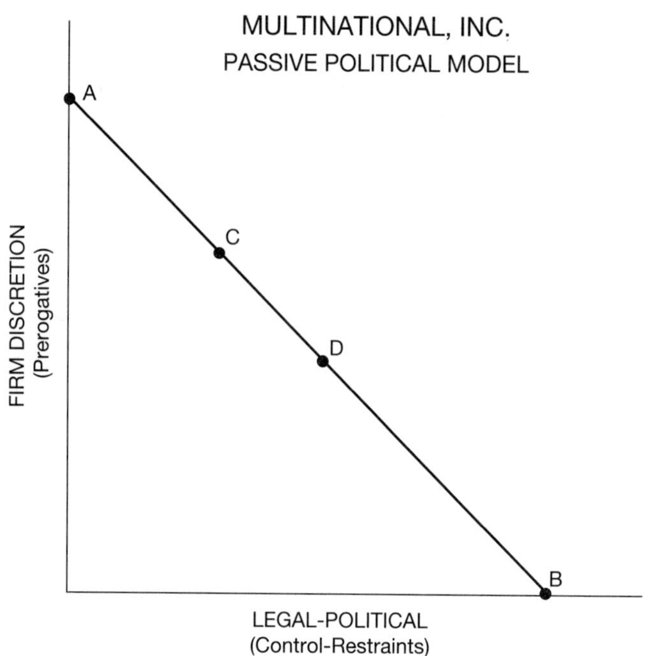

CHART 3 Passive Poltitcal Model

relationships with the state. While a multinational would clearly favor inaction by a state to hostile interference, the multinational would find even more desirable a state that "intervenes" *positively* by granting state subsidies—for example, interest-free loans, government-furnished land and plant, tax holidays, infrastructural support (roads, bridges, systems for water and sewage disposal), exclusive marketing or production licenses, state purchasing contracts, worker training, and the like.

By ironic twist, costs usually internalized to a business can be externalized when the company gets the state involved in the right way. This beneficial realm of state action will not be noticed when the focus remains exclusively on the negative impacts of a state.

3. The model understates the extent to which multinationals over time become enmeshed with affairs of state, and obliterate the line between public and private activity. The end point has been reached when multinational definitions of rationality become equivalent to state definitions of reality. Compare: "What's good for General Motors is good for the United States."

A more complex model becomes necessary to identify the more common condition of the politically active multinational; see Chart 4.[4]

[4]This is a simplified version of what J. Boddewyn discusses in "Political Aspects of MNE Theory," *Journal of International Business Studies* (Fall, 1988), pp. 341–359.

CHART 4 Active Political Model

MULTINATIONAL, INC.

Political Actors	Means	End or Goals
Internalized as staff (employed) External to the firm (bought) *Examples* Political risk assessors Consultants "Door openers" "5% people" Lawyers, lobbyists Publicists	*Examples* Bribery Business coalitions Lobbying Legal structuring of relationships Lawsuits	1. Avoiding negative sanctions (narrowing the gap between private desire and public purpose) 2. Gaining access to state largesse and subsidies 3. Increasing costs of rivals (local or international) 4. Rendering public policy equivalent to private policy (see 2. above) 5. Infiltrating general consciousness itself with business values

Chart 4 is an abbreviated version of one developed by Jean Boddewyn to supplement the usual models for allocation decisions. He saw his task to identify the political behavior of multinationals and incorporate political dimensions in the models of multinational behavior, which usually exclude political costs and benefits.

Boddewyn has two main analytical strategies: the identification of *political actors* used by international enterprises, and the full range of *political means* that the enterprises employ to achieve favorable outcomes. The actors include political risk assessors, legal and other "advisers," "door-openers," five percent people (those who are paid a percentage of the gains achieved), and public relations specialists. The means include both legal and illegal ones: bribery, local "advisers," industry associations and coalitions, lawyers and other professional servicers, lobbyists, and public relations.[5] Some of the methods are focused and designed to achieve immediate results, while others are diffuse and long term, like the promotion of a "good business climate." (The phrase "business climate" obscures more than it reveals. *Climate* cannot be changed; it either rains or it doesn't. "Business climate," on the other hand, is open to influence and adjustment. It happens every day in every capitol of the world, in Washington, D.C., in state capitols, and in every other situs of government on earth.)

The multinational can either make these political providers a part of the company, internalizing them as staff, or can engage their services in what Boddewyn terms the "political market," where desired political services are bought and sold like any other commodity or service. We may be reluctant to think of a "political market" as equivalent to any other market, given the ethical implications of buying private advantage and otherwise "privatizing" public resources, but once our initial shock is over, the presence of a

[5]Ibid., pp. 343, 348–357.

market of this type reveals what has become routine multinational corporate behavior. Facing activities like these squarely rather making believe they never occur can be the start of serious thinking about a critical and usually hidden aspect of international business.

What is it that a multinational wants to accomplish through its political activity? Clearly, the company wants to avoid negative sanctions that would make it more expensive to do business, and to narrow the gap between the company's interest, and the state's definition of the public interest. Second, the company would like to have as big a piece of state largesse as it can get. Third, it might want to increase the costs to business rivals or reduce access by rivals to a desired area. Last, and over the longer run, the international company might desire to establish *hegemonic* influence, a condition in which its desires and state action become fully congruent, without constant heroics and expense to accomplish the perfect fit.[6]

The models discussed here have been simplified to illustrate a process and show one type of extension of business thinking about multinationals. A fuller account of the political strategizing of multinationals would also include all activities in the country where the multinational is headquartered—both the cultivation of a domestic law and state policy so that it does not interfere with allocation decisions (as well as the domestic law and policy that facilitates allocation decisions). There is no practical reason why a multinational would limit political activity to other countries, and they don't.

The foreign policy of the home country can affect the law and policy of countries where multinationals locate and operate. Where nationalization of company property occurs, multinationals will lobby the governments where they are headquartered for protection. The Bay of Pigs invasion of Cuba would probably have restored property expropriated from multinationals after the revolution led by Castro. The Chilean government of Salvador Allende was overthrown with CIA assistance after it expropriated the property of multinational corporations.

The foregoing were times of political crisis. Foreign policy concerns multinationals day to day as well; with substantial oil coming from the Middle East, would an oil company be casual about foreign policy in the Middle East? Could the temptation to help shape the foreign policy of the United States in the Middle East be resisted?

These multiple levels of politics—in other countries, in the country where the multinational is headquartered, and across countries through diplomacy and interstate relations—show how much of a gap now exists between school visions and the commonplace political strategizing of international companies. Where the economic–business modeling for decision-making ends, political process models begin, since politics can impose additional costs on multinationals or generate benefits for the companies.

[6]Ibid., pp. 352–359.

II. LAW STUDY, FOCAL CONCERNS OF LAW, CONTEMPORARY LAW IN THEORY AND PRACTICE

As a second part of this chapter, we consider the field of law as studied and practiced. The field of multinational corporations has slowly insinuated its way into the professional imagination and training, but there has to be an inventory of just how much change will be required in the legal profession if it is to adequately encompass the multinational phenomenon. Law practitioners in the large elite firms of major cities have already moved well beyond their legal training to serve their international business clients. However, law schools have lagged behind practice.

Undergraduate Law Study—Problems and Prospects

Unlike the study of business, law is studied primarily at the graduate level, with undergraduates taking only a course or two as part of their university studies. The assessment of law and multinationals should begin with the expectations of undergraduates as they encounter a course on law and multinationals. What are they? Will they be met?

There are two distinct impediments to the public understanding of law in theory or practice. Perceptions of law have been so thoroughly shaped by television and other popularizations of legal subjects that these images—however misleading they may turn out to be upon closer study—take on a life of their own with important personal, educational, and political consequences.

"L. A. Law" can swell law school applications, despite a simultaneous drop in solid career prospects for new lawyers. The program may create dreams based on the lives of lawyers *on the program*, even at a time when fewer of the dreams can be fulfilled in real life. In an earlier era, Perry Mason as portrayed by Raymond Burr had more to do with popular understandings about lawyers and legal process than volumes written by legal scholars. Perry defended criminal cases to a jury, winning every one of them. At the same time the program was avidly watched, most real-life lawyers never practiced criminal law, never went to court, and never tried a case to a jury. By most counts, over 90 percent of criminal cases ended without any trial, by jury or otherwise, through negotiated pleas of guilty.

"People's Court," a favorite because it lets viewers play judge during Judge Wapner's recess, reinforces notions that there is a court for everyone and law offers quick redress for whatever wrongs the average person might experience. "Divorce Court" provides family law themes with the same effects. Few viewers stop to consider that the results reached in small claims courts or divorce courts are utterly without transcending impact; that is, they have no abiding consequences in law at all, despite their seriousness for the people involved.

One could say that these programs about life in the fast lane of Los Angeles law practice, about murder trials brought to a sudden, eye-opening conclusion, or about the backyard and household disputes of America, do no serious harm, and, on the contrary, provide some learning about law as well as an interesting diversion. It must be remembered that for tens of millions these programs are the only connection to legal education available.

There is reason to pause. With no regular coverage of bloodless subjects like commercial banking (which could cost the American taxpayer hundreds of billions of dollars if significant numbers of commercial banks go the way of the savings and loan institutions of the 1980's) television viewers get only a small and largely inadequate legal education. Issues that will profoundly affect their lives are missing because they have little entertainment value.

The presentation of law through the media presents a grand obstacle to the type of law study envisioned in this text. If undergraduates are asked what interests them in law or why they might be attracted to law study, their responses will mirror what has already excited them about law from television and newspapers. They are interested in criminal law, family law, and the law governing automobile accidents. Beyond these first-mentioned interests they might want to know more about the law applicable to personal finance—buying a house, making a will, or getting satisfaction from a retailer at the local shopping mall. These areas call for adding law dimensions to preexisting factual information, and do not exact the heavy start-up costs that subjects like banking or international business would require.

If most students know from nightly news broadcasts or the local papers that the solvency of the commercial banking system has become more precarious, beyond this awareness there is an unpleasant haze as to just why it is banks could be in trouble, and what, if anything, needs to be changed to get them out of trouble. Trying to get a solid answer to questions like these makes the head hurt and could send the student reeling back to Judge Wapner and "People's Court" reruns. When there is too great a distance between knowing how to use an ATM card and understanding the strengths and weaknesses of the commercial banking system, students might want to give up before they start.

Like banking, the subject of multinationals taps no down-home familiarity. Students will know from the daily papers that the United States no longer has the entire world economy at its disposal and discretion, and that literally all career aspirations in the United States will succeed or fall based on the decisions of the largest business aggregations ever assembled in human history. But beyond these impressions there may be the same unpleasant haze that surrounds banking.

Ten years ago students never got that far. They would ask, "What's international business got to do with me?" Now the interconnectedness of the world has become common knowledge, but the learning required to catch up with international developments may look too formidable, and there might be a temptation to leave the field to "experts."

The task of this text is to make the subject of multinationals as engaging and *familiar* as "L.A. Law," "Perry Mason," "People's Court," "Divorce Court," or whatever television shows replace them as the primary vehicles for bridging the lay world and the law world. We have already learned from the case of the native Hawaiians that ignorance of large-scale, economic-political forces will never be blissful; on the contrary, it can kill. The experience of the native Hawaiians should serve as a warning that ordinary people can never casually delegate vital aspects of their welfare to others; that there may be no help like self-help; that no interpretation of political-legal-economic reality is better than one's own interpretation. If there is no assured trip to the promised land for people who think for themselves, at least there is less likelihood that they will become instant suckers to the first con artists who come along.

It might be consoling for undergraduates to learn that many experts from law and elsewhere are equally bewildered by the multinational corporate phenomenon. There is now a frantic effort underway in law schools to discard nationally based legal education, and develop a professional curriculum more consonant with internationally based enterprises. This reworking of curricula may be compared with what was discussed earlier with respect to business training; some of the older learning in law will continue to be relevant, but the multinational phenomenon will inevitably cause a top-to-bottom shift in legal education.

One only has to realize that, by moving out of a country, an international company can often leave an unwanted legal system behind. Law, developed over a long time and elaborately articulated for domestic application, can be sloughed off by businesses with the speed of electronic transmission. This one fact has to fill domestically oriented teachers with fear; they face annihilation, not novelty. If across time the capital sin of a lawyer is to be naive about practical affairs, the older law school curriculum cannot be lovingly preserved without creating a sinful breach between law school and professional work, between the older law world and the world of contemporary business–politics that has overwhelmed it.

Law School

Many of the stereotypes about what goes on in law school are true: the law school begins and ends with case study; there are no preliminary overviews, no interim summaries of what the cases already studied might stand for, and no clinching wrap-ups at the close of courses, the close of each year of study, or at the end of law school. Law schools make only two promises to students, both of which they keep: (1) students will learn to think like lawyers; and (2) they will become case-hardened; that is, after reading hundreds of cases they will be roughly familiar with many areas of law and will generally know what problems a legal system handles and the way it handles them.

Robert Hutchins, a famous educator originally trained in law, said that law school taught him how to work hard but didn't give him much of a sense of the purposes of the work. Charles Reich dubbed lawyers "professional knife-throwers," because they had a better sense of targets and tactics than they did of purposes. Rather than being ashamed of an instrumental orientation, lawyers are often proud of their sticktoitiveness, their preoccupation with getting results, and their dismissing from consideration issues that have no ready answers. They consider themselves practical, and in many, *but not all*, senses of the word, they are.

When beginning law students get down to cases, they do not always stop on the word "down" and see it as a narrowing of focus, but that is just what happens. Instead of bemoaning their giving up breadth of perspective for the specialized depth that comes with studying case after case after case, they more probably feel that their education has at last begun after years of undergraduate meandering. The cases are real. They have an outcome. A judge has pronounced a rule that may be committed to memory and applied to comparable cases. Teachers encourage fancy verbal footwork in and around cases, and everyone is very busy trying to get to the bottom of things, or so it seems.[7]

There are some implicit understandings just below the surface of case study. First, every story has two sides, and legal materials are sufficiently open-textured that each side in a controversy can make an equally plausible argument with authoritative support. Given the argumentative impasse to which every well-trained advocate can bring a case, the decisions about which side has merit can never be resolved by mere lawyers, and must be delegated to judges. The sooner students jettison their evaluative moods and get down to the business of framing arguments and positions—in short, become "objective"—the sooner the student has begun to think like a lawyer.[8]

As arresting as the beginning student finds the case method to be, distinctly diminishing returns set in when an engaging vehicle is taken to extremes, and what might appear to be "limitations" of an excellent teaching-learning device become out-and-out disastrous when a field like multinationals becomes the subject of study.

The focus in law school is *United States* federal and state *judge-made* law. Other sources of law, for example, legislatures, federal or state, or the countless regulations and rulings made by administrative agencies of all types at the state and federal levels of government are relatively neglected. The multinational corporation operates within and sometimes beyond many regimes of law, and a knowledge of the national and state legal system derived from cases cannot be stretched for an easy application to multinational corporate activity.

In addition, the cases are *appellate* cases; only a tiny sliver of commercial disputes makes it as far as an appeal, after noncourt resolutions of troubles have failed, and after another court has already worked on the problem. Excluded are out-of-court negotiations, settlements, arbitrations, and other alternative dispute mechanisms, as well as most trials from which no appeal has been taken. The appellate case dominates the legal imagination at the

[7]Legal thinking and its limits are discussed in J. Bonsignore, "Law as a Hard Science," II *American Legal Studies Forum* (1977) 47.

[8]John Noonan, *Persons and Masks of the Law* (New York: Farrar, Straus, 1976) Chapter 1.

very time in history when appellate litigation reaches less and less significant commercial activity.

While the multinational corporation can be found in appellate litigation—some cases are included in this text—there are other settings both inside and outside the United States where multinational law and policy are shaped with far greater frequency. Lawyers *in practice* will appear in a variety of settings having learned *after graduation* what "representation" of a multinational requires. These free-wheeling practitioners might look back at their law school training as quaint, or, as Hutchins did, a curriculum that taught them to work long hours tenaciously, and practice disciplined self-denial, but one that was otherwise quite irrelevant to the performance of much of their work.

In focusing on selected *formal* settings of rule making and policy formation, the law school neglects *informal* ones. One of the most critical aspects of a formal legal system is the delegation of power to other institutions. In the plantation South when slavery was practiced, the state promised to stay out of master–slave relationships, thereby delegating to the master, his overseer, and other appointees full control of the plantation: rulemaking, determining when rules were broken, and what penalties—from beatings to losses of privileges—ought to be imposed.

In contemporary times there have been comparable delegations of power to certain institutions, for example, staying out of day-to-day university governance, or not intruding upon family affairs except in well-defined situations like child abuse or other domestic violence.

One of the most important delegations by the legal order to an institution "outside" formal law has been the delegation of power to businesses—local, national, and multinational. By and large, the state does not interfere with the way businesses are run, and yet it is "under" these *non–state regimes of law–government* that most people spend half their waking hours. One would think that, since businesses are the places where most rule making occurs, where most rules are interpreted, and where most administration of punishments and rewards is made, these nonstate legal settings would be systematically studied by "lawyers." These informal places make up in volume and direct effects what they lack in notoriety. Instead, the study of law stops with the fact of delegation of power, and it is only when the rare disputes spill over from a realm of delegated power—"reach the courts"—that the legal system takes any interest in them at all.

Among businesses, by far the most consequential delegation of political-legal power has been made to the multinational corporation, and even though more and more welfare turns on how these giant nonstate regimes behave, most of their activities fall outside the bounds of legal consciousness and control. If domestic enterprise is underregulated, international business is even less so, a point that will not be lost in later chapters.

The last main deficiency in contemporary professional legal education must be expressed elliptically: law study concerns law study. Beyond the ellipse lies the idea that law is studied as an isolated phenomenon rather than as one linked to politics and economics. The price of depth in learning the language and practices of legal formalism is the loss of wide enough vision to see the effects of law on other aspects of life and the effects of life on workings of law. The better the legal professional, at least as the law school would define professional, the more mentally deformed is the graduating lawyer—a cruel way, but a realistic way, to put the gain–loss attendant to traditional legal training.

Well, so what? Most of the people who read this text will not necessarily become lawyers or need to concern themselves with the current contours of the legal imagination. The short answer is that everyone needs to know the limits of legal vision in order to know the kind of work lawyers are likely to do, and to assess the adequacy of law as a mechanism for controlling unwanted multinational corporate behavior in the United States and elsewhere. In addition, to effectively link law study with political economy, the lack of range of legal inquiry and vision must be charted.

Models of Law

Each profession develops models that both explain the principal activities of the calling and let practitioners think better of themselves rather than worse. All critics or renegades discredit prevailing models and in doing so raise unpleasant theories or facts that the profession would like to disregard. If lawyers are characterized as a bunch of shysters, ambulance chasers, or sharks, they wince. If law is seen as a power play—"It's not what is just, but who you know that counts" or "money talks"—the legitimacy of the legal order as well as the careers of lawyers have been called into question. If these common negative appraisals are valid, lawyers, whatever their personal integrity, will be stuck in a system where many believe honesty will continually be sacrificed to power and expediency.

Contrast the foregoing with more sympathetic images of lawyers and the legal orders in which they practice. The lawyer may be seen as a friend to those who have no friends, or a helper to those who would otherwise be powerless in the face of formidable opponents. Almost as often as lawyers have been vilified as near-crooks, they have been raised to the level of folk heroes, and by ironic twist some who freely engage in lawyer-baiting might in the next breath announce their plans to go to law school (perhaps in self-defense).

The version of the legal order that most appeals to lawyers is based on the work of Roscoe Pound, a lawyer, teacher, and judge whose long legal career had an enormous influence on generations of teachers and practitioners.[9] Pound began by asking where conflict originates, and he attributed conflict to scarcity. "[W]e all want the earth" he declared, "and compete over just how much can be possessed to the exclusion of others." Legal systems arise in response to scarcity, as a means of minimizing the friction and waste that

[9]David Wigdor, *Roscoe Pound* (West: Greenwood, 1974).

inevitably accompany competing claims to material returns and life space. People who do law work are "social engineers" whose task is "making the goods of existence, the means of satisfying the demands of men living together in a politically organized society, if they cannot satisfy all the claims that men make upon them, at least go around as far as possible."[10] Pound thus made lawyers part of the solution to scarcity and not part of the problem.

Pound then asked how a legal system makes the best allocation, given competitive rivalries. Legal systems "balance competing interests," determining which interest to advance and secure by reference to rules of law and the overall goals that every legal system endorses: controlling interpersonal aggression, assuring that promises will be kept, securing property, and discouraging intentional or careless behavior that injures other people. These goals Pound designated *jural postulates*; like the axioms of geometry, they are the starting assumptions and goals in all legal orders.

In addition to keeping track of rules and how a given outcome will square with the jural postulates, a legal system must accommodate to the social-economic context in which it is found, so that there will not be a gross breach between what the legal order decrees and working beliefs and practices extrinsic to law. If a society is centered around the automobile and industrial production, horses and agriculture will have to be given lesser weight by courts.[11]

Pound thus provided a theory of the sources of conflict—scarcity; a theory of justice—"minimizing waste" or a "balancing of conflicting interests"; the functions of legal systems—adjudicating rival claims; the principal referents for evaluating claims—rules, postulates, and "the times"; and a theory of change—rejected claims, reasserted over time, can be reevaluated and recognized. (See Chart 5.)[12]

As noted, the model of Pound appeals to legal professionals because as "social engineers" they do constructive, benevolent work on problems that are not of their own making. So conceived, lawyers and judges rise above the conflicts with which they help society come to terms. Their work may be unpleasant, since conflict and trouble do not warm the heart, but is nevertheless necessary, lest a society come totally apart through unresolved rivalries.

Pound's understanding may be labeled the Neutral Arbiter Model of Law and many critics have disputed the explanatory power of his model by challenging the neutrality of law and his assumption that law has exclusively benevolent effects.

Laura Nader, a legal anthropologist, observed that legal systems, rather than being purely neutral and benevolent, have a variety of purposes and consequences, some nice and some not so nice: (1) therapy to participants, (2) education and reinforcement of social values, (3) restoring harmonious relations,

[10]Roscoe Pound, *Social Control Through Law* (New Haven: Yale, 1942), 111.

[11]Ibid., pp. 113–115.

[12]For Pound's model and additional discussion of Pound's conception of legal systems and the evaluations of claims, see John Bonsignore et al., *Before the Law* (Boston: Houghton Mifflin, 1989), pp. 63–82.

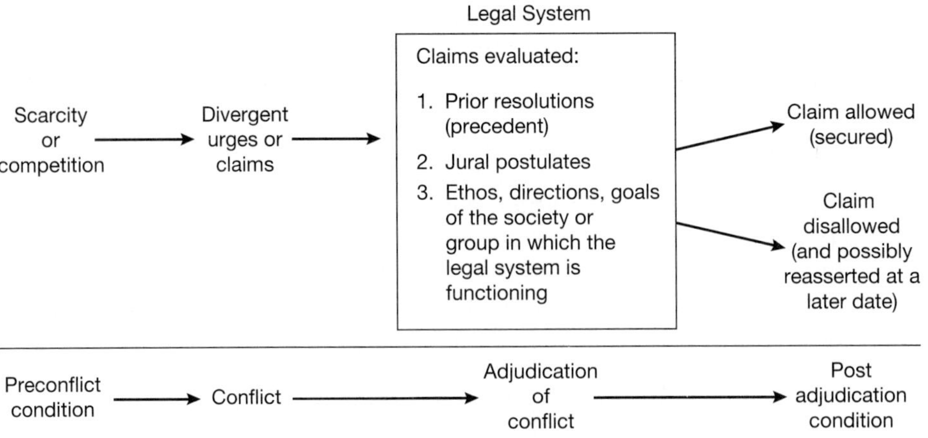

CHART 5 Pound's Model of Conflict and the Role of Legal Systems

(4) ruining one's enemies, (5) raising revenue, (6) gaining economically over another, (7) preventing the formation of factions, and (8) development of factions. Pound's notion of law as "resolving" conflict or minimizing friction and waste looks simple-minded against the plenary list drawn by Nader.[13] In sorting out the legal strategizing and effects of law in the field of multinationals, Nader's more circumspect approach should be kept firmly in mind.

Mark Gallanter, in a provocative essay on the nature of contested cases, took a different tack with equally telling effects of Pound's notion of how claims are adjudicated. He contended that it is a mistake to look first to rules of law as a guide to the outcomes of lawsuits. The *parties* and their *access to resources*, including but not limited to legal representation, have more to do with outcomes than rules of law. *Repeat Players*, the name he gives to resourceful participants who regularly use law, have a much better chance to prevail than those who are only occasional participants (*One-Shotters*). The repeat players, with the help of lawyers on retainer, shape their legal affairs to maximize their chances over time of favorable legal outcomes. They are less concerned with short-term, quick-hitting returns from legal systems than they are for long-term results.

Under his theory, the persistent practices of repeat players as a group over a long period of time make their participation in legal systems more highly successful than it would be for the average person. Over time, the system will not be neutral but biased toward the powerful.[14]

Bringing Pound's theory back into the discussion, we can see that the parties in his model are presumed to be on equal footing, with no claimant

[13]L. Nader, "The Anthropological Study of Law," 67 *American Anthropologist* (1965), pp. 20-21.

[14]M. Galanter, "Why the Haves Come Out Ahead," *Law and Society Review* (1974), pp. 95ff.

coming to the legal system possessing any special advantages of the type that Gallanter attributes to repeat players. Nor does Pound acknowledge the buildup of advantage over time that the repeat players as a group achieve. One only has to imagine oneself in a legal contest against a multinational corporation to sense the systemic advantages that Gallanter identifies and Pound neglects.

In the antitrust suits against IBM, which lasted for more than a decade, IBM and its lawyers wore out not only rival computer companies, who were not trifling in size or impoverished of legal resources, but also the Antitrust Division of the U.S. Department of Justice. All opponents gave up in total defeat. The case epitomizes the strategic advantages that accrue to the well-financed, well-represented litigant in a system that professes neutrality.[15]

Pound's model also fails to acknowledge political factors in the legal system. Judges in his legal order use legitimate criteria for decision making, and their political predilections play no part. There are also no *systemic* political predispositions and according to Pound legal contestants stand equal before the law regardless of their income, power, status, or wealth.

Currently in American law schools there is a critical legal studies movement that focuses on the political-power dimensions of law.[16] Teachers identified with the movement argue that the system can claim no legitimacy, given the endemic biases in law toward powerful groups. They contend that most legal discussions obscure the role of political forces, and at times justify outcomes that are not all that far from naked, illegitimate power. While the multinational corporation has not been a main interest of this renegade professional group, their abiding thesis of systemic illegitimacy can be tested through multinational study.

Lawyers

The American lawyer can best be characterized by the kind of work done and for whom. The life of Thomas Jefferson presents the early American lawyer as a Renaissance man who moved without loss of stride across disparate fields—farming, science, law, engineering, architecture, and government at all levels, local to international. He did everything from drafting the Declaration of Independence to designing buildings and inventing household gadgets. Jefferson's law training consisted of working with an established lawyer for five years, an extension of the apprentice system of the craft production extant at that time in American history.[17]

Lawyers trained in this way became "solos" and the sometimes heard expression, "I'll just hang out my shingle" refers to the individual lawyer who would hang out a small sign announcing his availability for the general prac-

[15]James Stewart, *The Partners* (New York: Simon & Schuster, 1983) R. De Lamarter, *Big Blue: IBM's Use and Abuse of Power* (New York: Dodd, Mead, 1986).

[16]See, for example, David Kairys, *The Politics of Law* (New York: Pantheon, 1982).

[17]Adrienne Koch et al. (eds.), *The Life and Selected Writings of Thomas Jefferson* (New York: Random, 1944).

tice of law. The lawyer did both "office work" and trial work. The sole-practitioner model, lawyer as rugged individualist trying cases for all comers, was the dominant model of law work until well into the twentieth century, and still attracts writers for television and the movies. Even though the lawyers on "L. A. Law" are in a medium-sized firm, they still have intimate contacts with individual clients, and go to court rather than work on straight office assignments. Since the L. A. lawyers confer with their colleagues continually, the model of lawyering to be synthesized from program might be called the Gregarious Trial Advocate Model.

Anyone with a little experience about the transformation of law practice from solos to firms knows that "L. A. Law" significantly distorts the realities of modern practice. In life, firm lawyers frequently work on fairly drab assignments, far from the din of courtroom battles, in quiet offices all alone, with their time divided into six-minute bits to efficiently match lawyer input with client billings. Work has become specialized by field of law, such as taxes or commercial real estate, or by parties represented, such as insurance companies or personal injury plaintiffs. Firm practice, as firms grow in size to the over-200-lawyer level in the largest cities, probably warrants the designation of Lawyer as Monkish Specialist or Lawyer as Billable Hours.[18]

The disenchantment of many younger, highly skilled lawyers may be traceable to the gross breach between dreams of law practice, some based on television, and the actual experience. Law teachers, who on occasion are considered soft-headed for not being in the thick of law practice, may also be simultaneously envied by lawyers who are mired in highly technical, dispirited work.

None of the above models of lawyering reach the work done on behalf of multinationals, even though aspects of all of the foregoing "stages" of lawyering can be found somewhere in the legal profession. The multinational lawyer can best be described as a thinker in a legal-business-political environment. The lawyer has become more free-floating not only around courts but also around legislatures and administrative agencies, and the more amorphous "political circles," bringing multinational lawyers closer to their colonial counterparts for the ambiguity of their daily rounds than to the traditional Wall Street lawyer who was pretty much "practicing law."

This newer lawyering can be designated Lawyer as Lobbyist or Lawyer as High-Level Go-Between, or Lawyer as Just Like George Ball. George Ball, whose ideas on multinationals will be detailed later, started his career in a large Chicago firm. He might have been a twelve- or fifteen-minute-bite-man, doing the work that has typified corporate law practice since the turn of the century. He then went to Washington, D. C., where he eventually became Undersecretary of State during the Johnson administration. After that, he went to Wall Street as an investment banker with Lehman Brothers.[19]

[18]For a description of the Cravath model of large law firm recruitment, organization, and promotion, see Stewart, *op. cit.*, pp. 367–375.

[19]George Ball, *The Past Has Another Pattern—Memoirs* (New York: Norton, 1982) pp. 20, 21.

Ball summed up his career as a succession of "cross fertilizations," moving in and out of law practice, and between government and business. He found these mixed roles "enormously useful to (him) and to (his) clients."[20] He had become a lawyer-problem solver with an international orientation, using conventional legal approaches among other possible approaches. At the levels where he functioned, there are no clear lines separating law, politics, and business. This is why he must be considered a thinker in a legal-political environment rather than a straight corporate lawyer. Modern commercial life had demolished the parameters of law, or to put it biologically, the membranes once separating law, politics, and business had become fully permeable.

James Stewart, who at one time was an associate at an elite New York law firm, gave a rare glimpse in his book, *The Partners*, of what goes on at the highest level of corporate law practice. If the world of the largest firms will seem unfamiliar to readers, it is because very few people know what goes on inside them. This remote, but highly important, corner of the law world is described in Stewart's introduction. There follows his account of the role of lawyers in high-level international negotiations for the release of 52 American hostages held in Iran in 1979.[21]

PROFILE OF THE ELITE LAW FIRM

On December 12, 1980, lawyers from law firms representing America's richest and most powerful banks gathered secretly in the 32nd-floor conference room at the midtown offices of Shearman & Sterling in New York City's Citicorp skyscraper. For most of the lawyers attending, the circumstances were unique but the cast of characters familiar: the same senior partners from the same law firms they had been working with or against in major financial transactions for years. The meeting's host, John Hoffman, the Shearman & Sterling partner representing Citicorp, greeted his colleagues like old friends: Bruce Nichols, from Davis Polk & Wardwell representing Morgan Guaranty Trust; Frank Logan, from Milbank, Tweed, Hadley & McCloy representing the Chase Manhattan Bank; Richard Simmons from Cravath, Swaine & Moore representing Chemical Bank; and others, together representing the country's twelve largest banks.

Then Hoffman dropped a bombshell on the assembled bank lawyers: acting on behalf of his client, Citibank, he was secretly negotiating with the revolutionary government of Iran for the release of the American hostages. These negotiations were being conducted not by the State Department, not by the President, not by the Pentagon, but by John Hoffman—a partner in a New York law firm that most Americans had never heard of and, throughout the hostage ordeal, never would hear of. In his hands, and the collected hands of the partners from the elite law firms gathered together that day, would ultimately rest the fate of American lives, power, prestige and money.

[20]He is interviewed in the documentary, "Controlling Interest," California Newsreel (1978). His essay on multinationals is in Chapter 5.

[21]Stewart, *op. cit.*, 13–17. Copyright © 1983 by James Stewart. Reprinted by permission of Simon &Schuster, Inc. and ICM.

If Alexis de Tocqueville were describing American lawyers today as an "aristocracy," as he did more than 150 years ago, he would mean the kind of partners from the kind of law firms meeting at Shearman & Sterling that day. There are about 500,000 lawyers practicing in the United States today; among them are personal injury, criminal, divorce and real estate lawyers, practicing in towns and cities, alone and in small groups as partners. Only a tiny fraction of that number—roughly 3,000—practice in the elite blue chip corporate firms which occupy the pinnacle of the profession. [The number of elite lawyers, their salaries, and the size of the firms where they work were lower when Stewart wrote, but the substance of his description of this type of law practice has not changed. —Ed.]. From their plush offices high in skyscrapers in the nation's financial centers, these lawyers survey the rest of the profession with at least a touch of arrogance and disdain.

Binding together these lawyers and law firms and distinguishing them from all others is their representation of America's major banks, financial institutions and corporations, the country's greatest concentrations of economic power. Only such clients can afford the elite corporate law firms and the kind of law practice for which the firms pride themselves—one in which no stone is left unturned, no matter how seemingly insignificant, and with virtually no regard for time or money. Indeed, if pressed, this is the explanation most often offered by top corporate lawyers to justify their representation of wealthy clients: it permits them to perfect the craft of lawyering to an extent that poor clients cannot possibly afford. It is what makes them, in their own eyes, the best. The representation of such clients is concentrated in the hands of the partners in the elite corporate firms to an extraordinary degree. At nearly all of the largest, most important and most complicated financial transactions and conflicts which take place, partners from the same small group of elite law firms are present. It is no coincidence that such events are among the country's most significant economic, social and political events as well.

These law firms dominate the legal affairs of their principal clients, even though large banks and corporations always have lawyers within their corporate staffs, known as "in-house" counsel. The firms have developed the capacity to handle a very wide range of the kinds of specialized legal problems which arise in corporate and financial transactions, as well as the manpower to handle very large and complex problems. As a result, the elite corporate firms are themselves large and diversified. None is smaller than 150 lawyers; the largest, Shearman & Sterling, is almost 350 lawyers. Most have at least 200, with a support staff at least as large.

At all such firms, lawyers are divided into partners, the more senior and experienced lawyers who share the profits and risks of the firm and make the management decisions; and associates, younger lawyers who are employed by the firm at an annual salary and may ultimately be tapped for partnership. Most of the legal problems handled by this kind of firm are so large that they require a number of lawyers, which gives rise to what is known as "pyramid" staffing—a single partner or small group of partners who preside over a larger pool of associates. Within the firms, as a whole, there are always more associates than partners. More than any other factor, it is the capacity of the firms to staff matters in such a fashion—and to bill clients for associates' work at rates that far exceed associate salaries—which produces the firms' immense profitability. Their partners earn incomes that rival and often exceed those of the top executives in their client corporations—upwards of $350,000.

There is an aura about the elite corporate law firms that is not quite duplicated anywhere else. It makes itself felt in the tastefully conservative, even faintly shabby, office decor; in the oil portraits of the long-dead founding partners; in the prestige addresses; in the polite but cool formality displayed by the lawyers in the firm, who invariably wear dark suits and dignified ties. The firms project an image of unshakable prosperity and security, of tradition and excellence, of permanence. It is the image of the old-line WASP financial establishment, one that is carefully burnished and maintained.

It is a world for which lawyers are well prepared at the country's most prestigious law schools. At nearly all of the elite corporate firms, many of the partners have been educated at Harvard Law School, itself a bastion of the kind of values reflected in the blue chip firms. Harvard Law graduates have dominated the upper reaches of the legal profession to a far greater degree than any other school or college, and their similar professional training has in turn influenced other lawyers at their firms. As Robert Swaine, a partner in Cravath, Swaine & Moore, wrote unapologetically in 1948, "The firm has taken most of its associates from the law schools of Harvard, Columbia and Yale, although . . . there was a conscious effort to take at least one man a year from other law schools of high repute such as Pennsylvania, Cornell, Virginia, Michigan and Chicago." To that list today would be added Stanford, California (Berkeley) and probably New York University. Despite occasional gestures of hiring an associate from a "lesser" local law school, graduation from one of the top ten law schools is almost a prerequisite for employment at one of the elite firms.

The similar educational background helps explain the homogeneity of the lawyers in the firms despite the absence of any overt discrimination in hiring and promotion. To interview at the prestigious law schools, all firms today sign statements that they do not discriminate on the basis of race, creed, ethnic origin, sex and, in many cases, sexual preference. Historically, there was discrimination, especially against Jews. (Virtually no blacks or women applied.) If there is discrimination today, it is extremely subtle, even unconscious, reflecting a generalized preference for people who will "fit in" and work well with clients. All of these firms now have lawyers who are Jewish, black, female; vestiges of discrimination are, ironically, most apparent in the degree to which some such lawyers have aped their WASP counterparts. There is little, if any, affirmative action at any of the most prestigious firms.

The elite corporate firms are also old; their traditions have been handed down from one generation of lawyers to another, and they have deep roots in the business and financial communities they serve. Most were founded before the turn of the century, with established clients who took advantage of the boom in the American economy which ensued. No firm founded since the Second World War has managed to enter these elite ranks; some old established firms have, however, slipped out of them.

Of these traditions, one of the most deeply rooted is secrecy. As Alexander

Forger, a partner at Milbank, Tweed, Hadley & McCloy, explains: "Our clients tell us that one of our great attributes is an ability to cope with problems in a low-profile way. We *never* seek public attention. Discretion is essential. Clients never even have to ask for confidentiality. We assume that our clients don't even want it known that they are consulting counsel."

The elite corporate firms have never needed publicity to attract clients; indeed, their reputation for secrecy is more valuable in that regard. Such a policy has also had the effect of almost entirely shielding such firms from public scrutiny, since knowledge of how and what they do has been largely confined to their partners and, to a much lesser degree, their clients. . . .

IRAN[22]

It was April 25, 1980. The United States military attempt to rescue the American hostages in Teheran had ended in humilitating failure. The fifty-two hostages were dispersed from the American Embassy into secret locations, and the likelihood of their release seemed more remote than ever. In the wake of the raid, all contacts between the United States government and the revolutionary regime in Iran abruptly ceased.

Most Americans reacted to the failed attempt with feelings of frustration and anguish, but it was particularly worrisome for John Hoffman, a partner at the New York law firm of Shearman & Sterling. Lately, it seemed, nearly everything that happened to the fifty-two American captives in Teheran had a direct bearing on the interests of his own most important client, Citibank, the nation's second-largest bank. Citibank was caught squarely between the United States government and the Iranians. The bank had millions of dollars in outstanding loans to Iranian entities; the Iranians, in turn, had additional millions in Citibank deposits, which had been frozen by President Jimmy Carter shortly after the hostages were seized the previous November.

[22]Ibid., 19–52.

The main leverage the United States still seemed to have with the Ayatollah and his revolutionary government was the frozen assets in American banks like Citibank. It had become obvious to Hoffman that without a satisfactory settlement of the hostage situation, the Iranian assets would remain frozen, the Citibank loans to Iran would not be repaid, and there was nothing he or the bank could do about it. Now that settlement looked hopeless.

On the Tuesday morning after the raid, Hoffman dutifully called 29-year-old associate Margaret Wiener into his office for their weekly strategy conference on the Iranian situation, though it was hard to know now what strategy could possibly do any good. Citibank had been sued by the Iranians in Paris soon after the freeze. Hoffman was overseeing the litigation. Wiener and he began to discuss the impact of the raid on the already tortuous progress of that case. Shortly after they began, the phone rang. . . .

. . .Wiener heard the excited voice of Peter Mailander, a German lawyer in Stuttgart who often worked with Shearman & Sterling on Citibank matters. . . Mailander told the Shearman & Sterling lawyers that he had been contacted by lawyers representing revolutionary Iran, and they wanted him to get in touch with Hoffman to "explore an economic solution to the worldwide litigation problems." Hoffman was electrified by the news. For months he had been casting lures in every direction he could think of, desperately hoping that he would make some kind of contact with the Iranians themselves. . . .

Mailander explained that he had been contacted by Herbert Wagendorf and Peter Heineman, two German lawyers who were representing the government of Iran and Bank Markazi, Iran's central bank. Wagendorf and Heineman claimed that they had been instructed by Iranian President Abolhassan Bani-Sadr; Nasir-O-Sadat Salami, Iran's Minister of Finance and a board member of Germany's Krupp industry, in which the Iranian government was a principal stockholder; and Behzad Nabavi, the head of Bank Markazi. The Iranians had asked their German lawyers to begin settlement negotiations with Citibank on the following conditions: Iran would not put forward any more money as collateral, and the existence of their negotiations must be kept absolutely secret. They emphasized that any leak would produce emphatic denials from the Iranian officials and the negotiations would be terminated.

Hoffman's voice was calm when he told Mailander that he would consider the proposal, but when he hung up and turned to Wiener, elation sparkled in his face. He reiterated the need for secrecy, then raced to Shearman & Sterling's library, where the two lawyers fed the names of Bani-Sadr, Nabavi and Salami into the firm's computerized information banks. What they discovered reinforced the plausibility of the German approach. . . . Of course, it wasn't clear that the Ayatollah himself knew anything about the approach or would support it, and it was hard to know the status of any of the various factions struggling for power within Iran. . . .

Hoffman immediately called Hans Angermueller, Citibank's senior executive vice president and a former partner at Shearman & Sterling, who in turn pulled Walter Wriston, Citibank's chairman, out of a board meeting. The bank executives gave Hoffman their authority to pursue the Iranian approach. Hoffman then notified one other senior partner at his firm, Robert Clare, Jr., the head of the firm's banking department, and notified and obtained approval from officials at the State Department, Treasury Department and the White House, all of whom were then stalemated in their own efforts.

Ten days later, Hoffman stood in Kronberg, West Germany, looking up at the mock-medieval battlements of the Schloss Hotel, a castle built by Kaiser Wilhelm II for his mother. Inside this fantastic and unlikely setting were the German lawyers who were representing Iran. And on Hoffman's shoulders rested the fate of the $8 billion in frozen Iranian assets and, as later events would demonstrate, the fate of the fifty-two Americans held captive in Iran.

There is no better bedrock for a major corporate law firm than a great and powerful bank as a client; it is, in fact, practically a prerequisite for inclusion among the most elite law firms in the country. Obviously, the larger the bank, and the more comprehensive a law firm's grasp on its outside legal work, the better. Two law firms so dominate the outside work of major banks that they would belong in the first rank of law firms for that reason alone: Shearman & Sterling, which represents Citibank, and Davis Polk & Wardwell, which represents Morgan Guaranty Trust.

The importance of a major bank client to a large corporate law firm is based on the sheer volume and regularity of its legal needs. The major American banks today represent some of the greatest concentrations of wealth in the world. Because of the power which stems from such economic resources, they are also among the most heavily regulated institutions in the country, subjected to an unending stream of statutes and regulations. . . . While banks like Citibank and Morgan Guaranty may be officially based in New York, they do business all over the world. . . . A bank can make hardly any decisions that do not have legal implications. Citibank, the country's second-largest after Bank of America, has an in-house legal staff of ten; Shearman & Sterling has almost 350 lawyers, more than half of whom work on Citibank matters at one time or another, their work ranging from reviews of mundane loan agreements to restructuring the Polish national debt.

Representing a major bank like Citibank or Morgan Guaranty also guarantees a major law firm vital exposure in the sophisticated financial markets which generate other legal business as well. In addition to its principal work for Citibank, Shearman & Sterling has added thirty other foreign and domestic banks as clients, including the Bank of Montreal in Canada and the Japanese Fuji Bank. Its extensive international banking work in such areas as Eurodollar financings and transactions has brought it into contact with many foreign governments and foreign corporations; such clients today include the Saudi Arabian Royal Commission; De Beers Consolidated Mines, the South African mining and manufacturing concern; Sonatrach, the North African oil company; the government of Abu Dhabi; and many others. The international scope of the firm's work is reflected in its far-flung network of branch offices located in San Francisco, Paris, London, Abu Dhabi and Hong Kong; overall, about 60 percent of the firm's work is international. . . .

For these principal reasons, bank work . . . is done at something of a discount. Usually, the banks pay the firms a large annual retainer, and hours are charged against the retainer at a rate discounted slightly from the law firms' usual formula hourly rate. This does not mean that bank work is not highly profitable. In many cases, it is the custom for someone else to pay the bank's legal fees. . . at the firm's full rates. Much bank work also lends itself nicely to the pyramid staffing pattern. A single partner, for example, can easily oversee a large number of associates who review loan agreements. And the discount encourages bank executives, as one partner put it, "to just pick up the phone any time they feel like it and talk to us without worrying about our hourly rates." Picking up the phone, of course, triggers the clock for the time which will eventually be deducted from the retainer, . . . Though law firm partners do not like to emphasize this aspect, one obvious reason for the discount is to discourage the major banks from keeping most of their legal work in-house. . . .

Citibank and its predecessors have been Shearman & Sterling's most important client since 1891. . . .

On November 13, 1979, . . . President Carter had frozen all Iranian deposits in American banks in retaliation for the seizure of the United States Embassy in Teheran and the taking of American citizens as hostages. That step immediately sent outside counsel for the banks scurrying to bank conference rooms across the country. Citibank naturally turned to Shearman & Sterling, which already had some experience with freezes and asset seizures. . . . Russia in 1917, China in 1950, Cuba in 1963 and Vietnam in 1975.

Within the White House there had been a great deal of reluctance to impose the freeze in the first place. In strategy meetings in Washington, presided over in large part by presidential counsel Lloyd Cutler, previously a partner in the Washington firm of Wilmer, Cutler & Pickering, and a former associate at Cravath, Swaine & Moore, there was concern that the freeze would "trigger the Great Depression of 1979," according to Cutler. Not only did the government of Iran and its various entities have billions of dollars on deposit in American banks, but worldwide faith in the integrity of the American banking system might have been jeopardized, leading any foreign depositors who feared political reprisal to withdraw their assets precipitously.

It was just such a threat, however, which finally led Carter to impose the freeze. At 4:00 A.M. on the morning of November 13, eight days after the seizure of the hostages, the Iranians impetuously announced that they were withdrawing all of their assets from United States banks. "That resolved all doubts," Cutler recalls, and by the time the Iranians tried to collect, the presidential order implementing the freeze had been executed and the Iranians were turned away by the banks.

One of the banks to take the lead in refusing to release the Iranian assets was Morgan Guaranty, which acted on the advice of two of its lawyers at Davis Polk & Wardwell, Bruce Nichols and Bartlett McGuire. Morgan Guaranty, though it is only the fifth-largest U.S. bank in assets, wields an influence disproportionate to its size. It was founded by financier John Pierpont Morgan, as the private banking firm of J. P. Morgan & Co.; and the nature of its clientele—it had traditionally serviced only the wealthiest individuals and corporations—and the secrecy which has surrounded its operations have made it one of the world's most influential and powerful banks.. . .

. . . Davis Polk in some ways itself resembles the kind of clients attracted to Morgan Guaranty. Historically, it has epitomized the "white shoe" law firm, and it still has many . . . partners listed in the Social Register. . . .

Though Morgan Guaranty and Morgan Stanley remain mainstays of Davis Polk's practice, the firm has diversified from that base to an even greater extent than has Shearman & Sterling. Among its major corporate clients are International Telephone & Telegraph, International Paper, Johns-Manville, LTV Corporation, McDermott, Inc., and R. J. Reynolds. . . . In addition to Morgan Stanley, it represents Merrill, Lynch . . . and Smith Barney . . . in investment circles.

When executives at Morgan Guaranty learned of the asset freeze, they first called Bruce Nichols, the Davis Polk corporate partner who acts as a liaison with the bank and oversees most of its work within the firm. Nichols is something of a legend within Davis Polk. Though he eschews company politics and membership on firm committees, his position at the head of the bank work makes him one of the firm's most powerful partners. Like Hoffman, he graduated from Princeton and from Harvard Law School, and his reputation for legal brilliance within the firm is matched only by his reputation for eccentricity. He is a confirmed bachelor who dresses fastidiously but conservatively and, on the rare occasions he is not working at the firm, cultivates an expensive taste in food, wine and opera. To most associates he seems aloof and distant, preoccupied with weighty legal questions. Many associates are afraid to work for him, intimidated by his brilliance and the great deference he is shown by other partners in the firm. . . .

To assist him with the Iran matter, Nichols tapped Bartlett McGuire. . . .

. . . [T]he Davis Polk partners had two major questions on their minds: What did the freeze mean in practical terms? And how could Morgan Guaranty protect its own interests? Morgan had what McGuire describes as a "substantial exposure," about $80 million in loans outstanding. Like most of the major American banks, Morgan also held deposits of Iranian entities in its branches in London, Paris and Frankfurt. . . .

As for the freeze itself, Nichols and McGuire advised the bankers to issue instructions stopping payment to all its domestic and foreign branches. That decision itself took some deliberation . . . The freeze itself raised some serious legal questions. Foremost among them was the status of Iranian deposits in Morgan's foreign branches. There was no question that the President had the constitutional authority to freeze the assets located in the United States, but most of Iran's deposits were in the foreign branches. Did the President have the power to freeze assets located on foreign soil? No one was sure. . . . As for the bank's own $65 million in claims, it decided to launch a search for Iranian assets located in countries where litigation by Morgan could secure a judgment against them. The Davis Polk lawyers sent instructions to lawyers in England, France and Germany, including a lawyer in Frankfurt, Bodo Schlosshan, an old friend and a former associate at Davis Polk.

On April 17, another presidential directive appeared, as well as regulations implementing the freeze. These orders enabled the banks not only to freeze the Iranian assets in foreign branches but also to set off their own claims against Iran against the Iranian deposits. . . . Cutler now concedes that he and the President knew their authority in this regard was questionable. "If nothing else, we knew we could snarl the Iranian assets for years in the ensuing litigation." . . .

As Morgan Guaranty, Citibank and the other American banks proceeded with the set-offs, Davis Polk's man in Germany, Schlosshan, located a rich cache for any claimant against the government of Iran—the Krupp industrial complex in Essen. Before the Iranian revolution, the Shah's government had made a major investment in the German steel and heavy equipment manufacturer, and much to the delight of the Davis Polk lawyers, that investment was held in the name of the government of Iran. The revolutionary government had become the successor owner, and Salami, the Finance Minister, was a member of Krupp's board of directors.

On Monday morning, April 28, . . . Schlosshan was on the courthouse steps armed with the papers necessary to attach Iran's interest in Krupp on behalf of Morgan Guaranty. An attachment, in a sense, is a temporary seizure of property by the court. The court does not actually award the property to the party obtaining the attachment, but it puts the property within the control of the court. . . . Thus, in this case, the German court would hold Iran's interest in Krupp. . . .

The attachment was granted. . . . The government of Iran was notified that one of its prized foreign assets had been tied up by an American bank, acting independently of the United States government. Citibank quickly followed Morgan Guaranty's lead. . . . Iran had its German lawyers, Wagendorf and Heineman, file a motion in the German court to set aside the attachment. It was clear, however, . . . that an ultimate resolution . . . could take years to determine. And Iranian lawyers were already getting a sour taste for Western litigation. . . .

Furthermore, after the American banks set off their claims against the Iranian deposits in foreign branches, Iran had instituted litigation in Paris to declare such set-offs illegal and to reclaim the foreign deposits, raising many of the questions about presidential authority. . . . It had become obvious to the American bank lawyers . . . that the French were going to be content to juggle that judicial hot potato as long as necessary to avoid any politically embarrassing outcome.

It was this complicated web of litigation, which had effectively tied Iran's hands in world financial markets, to which the German lawyers evidently referred when they told Hoffman they wanted to negotiate a solution to the "worldwide litigation problems."

At about the same time that they called Citibank's lawyers, Wagendorf and Heineman, the German lawyers for Iran, also approached Davis Polk. . . .

Nichols, McGuire and Donaldson Pillsbury, another Davis Polk partner met to consider the Iranian approach through the German lawyer. . . . The Davis Polk lawyers declined an invitation to travel to Germany to meet with Wagendorf and Heineman.

. . . After the initial flurry of excitement about the asset freeze, life returned to routine at Davis Polk.

Not so at Shearman & Sterling, where Hoffman felt instinctively that something would break. . . .

Hoffman does little to alter the image of the banking lawyer as the drab, colorless counterpart to his cautious and meticulous banking clients. Shearman & Sterling's midtown offices (the firm also has expansive quarters at 53 Wall Street) are bright and modern, but Hoffman's own corner office is conservatively furnished in somber colors and antique furniture reproductions, decorated with family photos. Hoffman looks younger than his 48 years, despite his gray hair, and dresses in regulation pinstripes. He is all that a bank lawyer is expected to be—thorough, meticulous and cautious—but as one associate puts it, "he has a vision." He loves to tackle the broad complexities of a new project. . . .'

As the head of Shearman & Sterling's twenty-seven-lawyer midtown litigation group, he has plenty of opportunity for such intellectual activity. He and his group work almost exclusively on litigation matters for Citibank, but most of it is threatened or prospective litigation, and Hoffman's goal is to head it off before it actually gets to court. Hoffman is the kind of litigator, in fact, who almost never appears in a courtroom. As a result, his principal litigation skill is negotiation, and it is as a hard-nosed negotiator that he has earned his reputation within the firm. . . .

More than any other bank lawyer, Hoffman was also in a position to circulate the results of his thinking. Besides his close friendship with Angermuller, the former Shearman & Sterling partner at Citibank, he had close personal and professional ties to lawyers serving in the Carter administration. Robert Carswell, Deputy Secretary of the Treasury with primary responsibility for the asset freeze, was also a former partner at Shearman & Sterling and had worked closely with Hoffman. Robert Mundheim, general counsel for the Treasury, had been an associate at Shearman & Sterling before becoming a law professor at the University of Pennsylvania. Lloyd Cutler, whose firm in Washington, Wilmer, Cutler & Pickering, often handles matters in the capital for Citibank, is a friend of Hoffman's.

"I was in contact with the government people on a daily basis," Hoffman recalls. "They wanted to know about the pending litigation . . ., a matter of great concern to the government because the legality of the freeze in foreign branches was the issue. If we'd lost, the U.S. financial leverage was gone." Hoffman met in Washington periodically with Carswell and Mundheim, keeping them abreast of developments. Hoffman also began sending out his own signals to the Iranians. . . .

When Hoffman reached Carswell in Washington over the weekend to tell him about the call, Carswell was interested but hardly as excited as Hoffman. . . . "We had agreed we'd see the bank lawyers whenever they wanted," Carswell recalls, "and they'd march down. We had endless contacts with every conceivable bank lawyer. What really happened for six months was a lot of probing that came to nothing." . . . "The U.S. government wasn't talking to Iran then," Carswell says. "The raid had killed every approach we had under way. Sure, I told Hoffman to go ahead and talk. But I didn't have any great expectations."

Although Carswell won't talk about it, Hoffman was not the only bank lawyer who contacted him that week claiming to have had feelers from revolutionary Iran, but Carswell was not so willing to bestow the support to others that he had given Hoffman. Bank of America had also been contacted by Iran's German lawyers and given much the same message as Hoffman. . . .

Bank of America is the country's largest bank, and it was also exposed to the greatest risks in the Iranian situation—$2.5 billion in deposits. Unlike the other major banks involved, however, it did not turn most of the legal work over to its outside counsel. . . . The lawyer in charge was Thorne Corse, the bank's senior in-house counsel for international matters.

. . . "A. P. Giannini, the bank's founder, was not enamored of lawyers. He hired Samuel Stewart away from Cravath, Swaine & Moore to become the bank's inside general counsel. . . ." Today, Bank of America has 140 lawyers on its staff, and spreads its outside work among a number of law firms.

. . . According to Corse, Carswell told him that "no negotiations will be permitted as long as the hostages are still being held." In retrospect, Corse isn't sure why Hoffman got the go-ahead and he didn't, especially since Bank of America had more at stake. "It may have been that Citibank was approached slightly before we were," Corse says. "On the other hand, there was speculation that Hoffman was tapped because he and Carswell and Hans Angermueller (the Citibank executive vice president) were all former partners at Shearman & Sterling. . . .

Hoffman . . . went to work immediately, flying to Washington for a briefing. . . . Carswell reminded Hoffman that, given the government freeze, any settlement would be subject to the approval of the United States government, and asked him to keep the government informed. He also made clear what had become an implicit condition of Hoffman's daydreams: There would be no United States government approval of any financial settlement that did not include the release of the United States hostages. When Hoffman returned to New York, he cabled the German lawyers to state the conditions for negotiations. He accepted the Iranian demand for secrecy, and added another condition to those stated by Carswell: Citibank would not enter into an agreement which did not contain an across-the-board settlement for all the United States banks that were holding frozen Iranian assets. One day later, the Iranians accepted his conditions.

Hoffman's diplomatic efforts were shrouded in the most careful security precautions ever taken at Shearman & Sterling. Hoffman always traveled alone and rarely used the telephone to discuss his progress. He used fictitious names to make hotel reservations. Within the government, only Carswell, Mundheim, Owens, Christopher, Cutler, Treasury Secretary William Miller, Secretary of State Cyrus Vance and President Carter were informed; at Shearman & Sterling, Hoffman told only senior banking partner Robert Clare, Jr., Wiener, and his secretary. Unknown to these participants, he also began discussions with one other lawyer: Frank Logan, a partner at New York's Milbank, Tweed, Hadley & McCloy, which represents Chase Manhattan Bank, the financial citadel of the Shah. . . .

. . . Chase Manhattan . . . had no independent contacts with representatives of Iran after the revolution. The mere mention of the Chase Manhattan Bank or its chairman, David Rockefeller, was enough to make a revolutionary Iranian see red. Rockefeller, after Carter, was probably the American most hanged in effigy by Iranian militants. It was risky for Hoffman to talk to Logan. . . .

That risk was minimized in the person of Francis Logan. Modest, almost self-effacing, he is the kind of lawyer for whom secrecy is instinctive. He considers even the name of his client to be confidential information, and for 25 years has never spoken to a reporter. Associates at Milbank are intimidated by his rectitude, his taciturnity and above all by his encyclopedic knowledge of banking law and procedure. . . .

"I couldn't get involved in any conflicts of interest," Logan recalls thinking. "I didn't want to get involved in anything which might embarrass my client. It was also clear to me that this was a matter of great importance, and we would have to bear in mind the public interest. I hope history's verdict will be that we served the public interest without sacrificing our duty to our clients, and our duties as officers of the court." Those reservations aside, Logan began to help Hoffman. . . . When Hoffman reached Germany for the first meeting with the lawyers representing Iran, he was armed with what was called Plan C—a complex arrangement for a simultaneous financial settlement and release of the hostages, the joint product of their efforts. (Plans A and B had been discarded. . . .)

. . . Only five lawyers were present: the two German lawyers representing Iran; Citibank's two German lawyers, Mailander and Klaus Gerstenmaier; and Hoffman, with Gerstenmaier's wife acting as translator. The group focused on a few of the mechanical problems, but Hoffman was more interested in establishing a rapport with the lawyers for Iran. The meeting made little substantive progress—Hoffman never brought out Plan C. . . . "I was ready to lay some plans on the table, but I wanted some clear signals from their Iranian principals to continue. I wanted evidence of real authority." Hoffman considered asking for some kind of written grant of authority but decided against it. . . .

The summer of 1980 was a period of confusion within Iran. The hostages had been dispersed from the American Embassy in Teheran, the United States had renounced further attempts to retrieve them by force, and there were no negotiations between the American and Iranian governments. In Iran, the struggle for power between the clerics . . . and the so-called moderates . . . continued. . . .

During that summer, Hoffman, the German lawyers and Roger Brown, an English solicitor who . . . had been called into the negotiations by the lawyers for Iran, continued to hammer out details of Plan C in a series of meetings in Paris, London, Bermuda and even Hoffman's own home in suburban Chappaqua, New York.

Though it eventually required voluminous paperwork . . . the basic principles of Plan C were relatively simple. Plan C envisioned that Iran would pay off all of its syndicated loans with its assets that had been frozen in the foreign branches of the American banks. Iran's frozen domestic assets—those already located in the United States—would be held pending resolution of the unliquidated claims [Claims are "liquidated" where not in dispute, "unliquidated" when there may be dispute about amounts—ed.] against Iran. Since Iran had more in foreign branch deposits than the liquidated claims against it, the excess—about $1.8 billion—would be unfrozen and deposited in the Iranian central bank, Bank Markazi. Plan C had obvious appeal for Citibank, and Hoffman assumed that it would be equally appealing to the other American banks, which, except for Chase Manhattan, didn't even know the negotiations were proceeding. The American banks' syndicated loans, which represented the vast amount of debt owed by Iran to American banks, would be paid off in full.

The Iranian lawyers never made a counterproposal. Over and over, Hoffman and the German lawyers repeated the details of Plan C, . . . In September, Ayatollah Khomeini announced formal conditions for the release of the hostages, which Hoffman viewed as a positive step toward settlement. The Iranian lawyers continued to shuttle back and forth between Teheran and the meetings with the bank lawyers, but there were communications problems after the outbreak of the Iraq-Iran war in November.. . . [B]y late November 1980, a final Plan C was ready. Iran's German lawyers took it to Teheran, and Hoffman flew to Dusseldorf in anticipation of a favorable response.

He was bitterly disappointed. Shortly after his overnight flight from New York, Iran's German lawyers called with the message that Plan C—Hoffman's cherished product of six months' effort—was unconditionally rejected. They offered no comment or explanation.

. . . The three lawyers felt that the plan's failure must have stemmed from opposition by the clerics as a result of the Iraqi war. The war had placed enormous strain on Iran's crippled financial reserves; and, they reasoned, Plan C called for paying off the loans too quickly, further depleting Iran's financial strength. But no solution to that problem seemed evident, and their spirits sagged. . . .

At seven the next morning, the lawyers reconvened, and Hoffman felt new determination. Overnight he had had a new idea—what was to become Plan D. . . . "There didn't seem any alternative," he says. "It was obvious that there would be no hostage release without a financial settlement." The essence of Plan D was an attempt to accommodate what the lawyers assumed was Iran's reluctance to pay back all of its syndicated loans to the American banks at once out of its frozen assets. Plan D called for Iran to pay only the current overdue interest on its syndicated loans. The banks would then continue the loans with repayment guarantees from the government of Iran and the central bank of Iran, and Iran's assets would be unfrozen.

If Iran was prepared to accept the existence of further financial ties to American banks, Plan D was obviously a much more favorable proposition. But for that very reason, Hoffman no longer felt that he could act alone for banks other than his own client, Citibank. . . .

On December 12, lawyers for the country's twelve most powerful banks gathered in Shearman & Sterling's 32nd-floor conference room. Later dubbed "the gang of twelve," or simply "the twelve," the lawyers represented an extraordinary concentration of banking expertise. Nichols and Pillsbury were there from Davis Polk on behalf of Morgan Guaranty, as was Milbank's Logan for Chase Manhattan. Richard Simmons, a partner at Cravath, Swaine & Moore, attended for Chemical Bank; Thomas Cashel, from New York's Simpson Thacher & Bartlett, represented Manufacturers Hanover Trust. Hamilton Potter, Jr., from New York's Sullivan & Cromwell, appeared on behalf of both European American Bank and Marine Midland. Bank of America was represented by Thorne Corse. Rounding out the twelve were Bankers Trust (represented by White & Case in New York), Irving Trust (represented by Winthrop, Stimson, Putnam & Roberts in New York), First National Bank of Chicago (represented by Debevoise & Plimpton in New York) and Continental Illinois (represented by Mayer, Brown & Platt in Chicago).

The meeting followed two days of furious phone calls by Hoffman: first to Carswell and Mundheim in Treasury, to Warren Christopher in the State Department, and then to the chairmen and principal lawyers for each of the syndicate banks. To each, he outlined briefly the nature of his undertaking and stressed the need for secrecy. Even so, the lawyers weren't prepared for the scope of Hoffman's efforts when he explained them in detail at the meeting. Pillsbury, in particular, says he was "amazed" that the contact he had earlier discounted "proved to be a more direct pipeline than anything the United States government had."

Corse was a little piqued, annoyed with Carswell for letting Hoffman proceed even though Bank of America had the largest stake in the outcome. But he had to admit he was impressed with Hoffman's efforts, and he too was amazed by the tight secrecy which had been maintained.

. . . Hoffman began to outline his concept for Plan D and passed out copies of a draft. With surprising speed, but with bank lawyers' typical appetite for mechanical detail, the group of lawyers absorbed the concept and turned to a discussion of some of the practical details of working out a Plan D financial settlement which would coincide with a release of the hostages.

Those practical problems proved to be simple in concept but enormously complicated in the execution. Where were Iran's frozen assets? How much was there? What kind of transfer would be necessary, and how could it be executed? What kind of authority and what kind of documents could initiate the payments? It was obvious, for example, that simply identifying Iran's assets would be an enormously difficult task. Although the twelve banks had acted as agents for the syndicated loans, more than 300 banks had actually participated in those transactions, some domestic and some foreign. The Treasury Department had been trying for months to locate the Iranian assets located in literally hundreds of American financial institutions and their foreign branches and subsidiaries. . . .

"There was an immediate appreciation of the hard technical problems," Logan recalls. "But the meeting was businesslike, low key. Everyone immediately pitched in." There were no strangers in the group; many of the lawyers had known one another for twenty-five years or more and had attended the same law schools (most had gone to Harvard and Columbia). Lawyers involved repeatedly echo Logan, who says, "One of the most important factors was the fact that we knew each other well. We trusted one another. We had confidence in everyone's legal skills and judgment." . . .

At the end of the meeting on December 12, the lawyers divided into working specialty groups. Hoffman assumed a general oversight role. Logan became the head of a "drafting" group, with responsibility for preparation of all the documents which would eventually be necessary to transfer the assets. Cashel, the Simpson, Thacher partner, agreed to head the "figures" committee, in charge of assembling data on the location and extent of the Iranian assets. To help him, the banks retained the accounting firm of Peat, Marwick, Mitchell & Co. . . .

Shortly after the December 12 meeting, the Citibank negotiations with the German lawyers representing Iran, known in Washington as the "bank channel," and the United States government's own negotiations, which had resumed through Algerian intermediaries, began to coalesce. Carswell at Treasury was still reluctant to rely too heavily on the bank channel—he didn't know who was on the Iranian end of it, and he was pressing Warren Christopher in Algiers to have the Algerians take up financial negotiations with the Iranians—but he recognized that whatever the source of a financial settlement, the banks would have to be involved, and the same backup work would eventually be necessary. The government didn't have the manpower, so he directed the Federal Reserve Board of New York to work with the lawyers representing the twelve. . . .

Then, on December 21st, "the whole thing blew up," Carswell recalls. That day, the Iranians publicly announced the terms of the financial settlement they had in mind—payments by the United States which totaled an astounding $24 billion. . . .

Hoffman and the bank lawyers were equally surprised. The outrageous financial demands appeared to have the support of Behzad Nabavi, the Bank Markazi head and Bani-Sadr ally who they assumed was among those Iranians on the other end of their negotiating channel. While they knew that the German lawyers also had contacts within the clergy, they had always presumed that the Bank Markazi faction would predominate in a financial settlement. . . . Even more surprisingly, negotiations through the bank channel continued as though the demands hadn't been made.

The importance of the bank channel finally became clear to Carswell and the Carter administration shortly before New Year's Day. The Algerians had returned to Teheran on December 26, and during discussions in the next three days the Iranians told the Algerians that negotiations intended to reach a financial settlement were already taking place with the American banks. Since the Algerians had made no headway in that area, they suggested merging the United States and bank negotiations into the bank channel. On January 3, 1981, Carswell flew to New York to brief Hoffman; and on January 8, Shearman & Sterling became the official site of the financial negotiations. Hoffman cancelled his twenty-fifth wedding anniversary trip to the Seychelles Islands scheduled for that week.

Beginning January 8, lawyers for the twelve began intensive round-the-clock negotiating and drafting. Computer runs were being performed at least twice a day to update the financial data. Daily meetings were held with the team of lawyers representing Iran: Roger Brown and Nigel McEwen from Coward Chance in London; the two German lawyers; and Leonard Boudin, the well-known American antiwar lawyer who was retained by Bank Markazi. Hoffman and several lawyers moved into the Waldorf-Astoria Hotel, but few were actually finding any time to sleep there. Clean clothes were at a premium, and Shearman & Sterling secretaries kept running out to buy shirts at a nearby Bancroft clothing store.

By Saturday night, January 10, most of the details had been hammered out. That night, in a series of twenty-minute sessions with Iran's lawyers in a Shearman & Sterling conference room dubbed the "dentist's chair," a lawyer for each of the banks separately negotiated the rate of interest each bank would pay Iran on the frozen assets it had held. Late that night, the deal was complete.

Sunday morning, the lawyers waited. An eerie calm prevailed in the Shearman & Sterling offices; the typewriters, the telexes, the computers were quiet. Hoffman put in a few calls to Boudin and to the Iranian lawyers; they were unavailable. Around 2:30 that afternoon, the lawyers for Iran arrived with an Iranian national—Iran's delegate to the International Monetary Fund and the only "real" Iranian the lawyers would ever meet—and asked to speak with Hoffman. . . .

Hoffman suddenly had haunting memories of the baffling rejection of Plan C months before. The Iranian banker did not look like someone about to conclude the $8 billion deal which had been painstakingly finished the night before. The Iranian's first statement confirmed Hoffman's premonition. He rejected outright any notion that Bank Markazi or the Islamic Republic of Iran would guarantee repayment of the loans which were being deferred.

The American lawyers were stunned. Guarantees of repayment—a Koranic guarantee from the Islamic Republic and a full guarantee from Bank Markazi—had been a cornerstone of Plan D, and it had never been questioned by any of the negotiators for Iran. It had been made clear at the outset that the American banks wouldn't *consider* deferring Iran's repayment of the outstanding loans without a guarantee of eventual repayment.

Unfazed, the Iranian proceeded to demand the American lawyers' "last written offer." Hoffman, slightly confused, said that Plan D *was* their last written offer. This seemed to make no impression; the Iranian simply kept parroting his demand for their "last written offer," almost like a record stuck in a single groove. . . . Finally, Hoffman cut him short. "I can tell you that nothing further will develop," he said. "This meeting is closed and we probably will not be speaking to you again." . . .

"It was the low point," Hoffman recalls, "and I wanted them to know it. They had overplayed their hand." Hoffman had emphasized all along that if no agreement was reached by Inauguration Day, the slate would be wiped clean. . . . Now there were only nine days left. . . .

But thirty minutes later, the English solicitor Brown and the German lawyers for Iran were back at Shearman & Sterling, minus their Iranian client. "Let's talk," Brown told Hoffman. The lawyers for Iran told the Americans that the Iranian banker was in tears by the time he got off the elevator after the meeting, unable to understand what had gone wrong. He had simply adopted an Iranian merchant's style of negotiating. By the time the lawyers for Iran left this time, Plan D was alive again.

Hoffman called Carswell after the meeting to brief him on their progress; and for the first time, Carswell sounded a little desperate. He exhorted the bank lawyers to "cut a deal they could live with" and then "sell it to the Iranians." The people in Washington, too, had now realized that time was running out.

In the meantime, intensive work proceeded on the mechanics of the fund transfer. Carswell called Mundheim (who had retired from the Carter administration to resume teaching . . .) and asked him to travel to Europe to arrange for a depository bank that would act as an intermediary. . . . American banks would transfer by telex all the Iranian funds held in foreign branches to the Federal Reserve Bank of New York, which would in turn transfer those assets, in gold if necessary, to an intermediate depository bank. When the Iranian authorities received word that the assets were in the hands of the intermediary bank, according to the plan, the hostages would be released, and the intermediary bank would forward the assets to any bank Iran designated, presumably Bank Markazi. . . .By Thursday morning, the mechanisms were in place in London and New York to execute the modified Plan D.

That day, Hoffman had just returned to his office after lunch when Cutler and Carswell got on the phone from Washington to report a major breakthrough in Algeria. The Algerian negotiators had just presented Christopher with a new financial proposal, a proposal which, much to their amazement, looked something like Hoffman's old Plan C. . . .

. . . Iran proposed paying off all the syndicated loans out of its deposits in the foreign branches of United States banks. These it valued at $3.7 billion. As for the unliquidated claims, which it valued at $5.1 billion, it proposed creation of an escrow fund out of which payments would be made once the merits of the claims were determined. The balance of the frozen assets would be returned to Iran, and the hostages would be released.

. . . Though Hoffman didn't know it at the time, the earlier Plan C had not been rejected by the clerics, as Hoffman had assumed, but by the Bani-Sadr faction, which was then in decline and apparently believed it needed a spectacular financial coup to re-establish its power and legitimacy. . . . This time, the clerics embraced Plan C as a solution which solved the hostage crisis and left it with no lingering financial obligations to the American banks.

. . . There seemed only one area of difference: the interest owed on the frozen assets. The Iranian proposal asked $800 million; the banks' plan, worked out in the "dentist's chair" negotiations over Plan D, called for payments of only $670 million. After the frustrations Hoffman had already endured, those differences seemed minor. It looked as though action might be at hand. He, Cutler and Carswell scheduled a meeting at the State Department for 11:00 A.M. the next day. It was time for the lawyers for the twelve to act.

Secretary of State Edmund Muskie opened the meeting, which convened that morning in the State Department's elaborate briefing room. Cutler did most of the initial presentation, stressing that the deal promised to be almost incredibly favorable for the United States banks—full, accelerated repayment of the outstanding syndicated loans. He stressed the fate of the hostages, emphasizing tacitly that public opinion might easily blame the banks for their fate. Nonetheless, the proposal posed some problems for the bank lawyers. . . . The first of these was the priority to be given the syndicated loans. Such an arrangement favored the banks with large syndicated loans—like Chase Manhattan and Morgan Guaranty—at the expense of those banks whose unliquidated claims against Iran were more substantial, such as Bank of America and Bankers Trust. . . .

Interest rates posed a greater problem. Iran had asked for $800 million in interest on the frozen assets held by the banks, and while no one knew for sure where that figure had come from, it looked like it might be the highest interest rate negotiated by the lawyers for Iran in the individual sessions in New York applied to all the banks. This was approximately a 17 percent annual rate spread over a 14-month period, and some of the American banks—especially Bank of America and Bankers Trust—didn't want to pay such a high rate, because they had larger interest-bearing deposits. Tension mounted. . . .

After lunch, Nichols took Cutler aside. "Why don't you, Muskie, Carswell and the government people stay out of the meeting?" Nichols asked Cutler. "Give us an hour to have a little dogfight." Cutler followed his advice, and when they returned, an agreement had been reached. The $130 million difference would be paid by the banks into an escrow account on a pro rata basis based on the size of interest-bearing Iranian deposits, and the interest question would later be submitted to international arbitration.

. . . [A]midst the euphoria of the agreement was a nagging anxiety on the part of some of the lawyers present. The debate over the interest rates was the first crack in the united front that had been maintained by the bank lawyers—a reminder that the public interest was not necessarily foremost, and that the client's was. Even the fate of the fifty-two hostages had not obscured that fact at the meeting.

Back in London, Mundheim was on his way to dinner at the American ambassador's residence. . . . When Mundheim arrived at the ambassador's, he learned that the deputy governor of the Bank of England was on the guest list, and asked Ambassador Kingman Brewster, Jr. to arrange a secret meeting between them during the course of the evening. When the somewhat bewildered English banker was brought into the ambassador's study, Mundheim explained the turn in the negotiations and the implications for the Bank of England: instead of merely being a conduit for the funds, the bank would be required to act as a stakeholder—to keep much of the frozen assets on deposit in an escrow account. . . . Would the Bank of England—and Britain itself—be willing to become involved in the crisis for such a long period of time?

Mundheim left the dinner at about 1:00 A.M. . . . At his hotel, Carswell called him from Washington with the news that the Algerians had insisted that the Bank of Algeria act as the final conduit. . . . Could he, the deputy governor, and some of the bank lawyers in London be in Algiers the next morning?

Mundheim spent the night on the telephone and, with the active help of ambassador Brewster, secured the consent of the Bank of England. At 10:00 A.M. the next day, Warren Christopher's State Department plane landed at a private airstrip outside London. Waiting to board were Mundheim, the Bank of England's deputy governor and head cashier, Logan and Corse. . . .

On the plane, Logan and Mundheim began working out the mechanics of the new deal on scraps of paper, stuffing important notes into their pockets. At about 1:00 P.M., the plane touched down in Algiers and taxied to a remote corner of the airport where the lawyers were hustled into armored police cars. . . .

The next five days Logan remembers only as a blur. As soon as they arrived, Warren Christopher, the Deputy Secretary of State, briefed the lawyers on the plan which had been proposed by the Iranians the day before. . . .

Shortly after, the lawyers and Mundheim were introduced to the Algerian negotiators, who politely shook their hands and then told Mundheim that they wanted the bank lawyers out. For some reason, they didn't trust anyone who was not a U.S. government official. . . .

It made their drafting efforts considerably more difficult. Corse and Logan were responsible for the actual preparation of most of the documents and for collecting the financial data from their colleagues in New York. But they were implementing political agreements which were constantly changing. . . . "We'd get it on paper," Corse recalls with some irritation, "and then we'd get word that 'it didn't mesh' with the political agreement. We'd ask why—and get no answer. They saw all of our work, but we couldn't see theirs, even though their negotiations were going on right upstairs in the embassy."

According to Logan, . . . "We just kept going. You had to. Desperation and elation alternated. . . . It was a continuous mental and physical effort, with little to eat and even less sleep. . . .

Following the breakthrough on January 16, an excited Hoffman flew back to New York to supervise the last hurried attempts to complete the inventory of Iranian assets and to arrange the financial transfer out of the Federal Reserve Bank of New York. Lawyers for the twelve resumed round-the-clock drafting at the offices of Shearman & Sterling. But the heightened time pressure, the lack of sleep, and the prospect of a final resolution to the agonizing crisis all contributed to a tinderbox atmosphere. It nearly exploded on January 17.

That Saturday, lawyers for the twelve regrouped for a final review of the transfer mechanism and asset data. . . . But during the discussion of the transfer procedures, a problem resurfaced which had pervaded all of the negotiations, that of attachment.

The plan which had been worked out for the mechanical transfer of the assets was designed to alleviate the mistrust between the Iranians and the U.S. government. According to the plan, a single payment order for the $5.3 billion in Iranian assets on deposit in the foreign branches of U.S. banks would be sent by Bank Markazi to the London office of Coward Chance, Citibank's English solicitors. Copies would immediately be sent to the twelve banks, which would in turn instruct the Federal Reserve Bank in New York to debit their accounts for the respective amounts. Once the Federal Reserve Bank of New York had done so, it would credit the Bank of England.

The Bank of England in turn would credit the Central Bank of Algiers, a step which, together with the transfer of some gold and securities, it certified to the Algerian government. When copies of the Bank of England's certification reached the U.S., Iranian and Algerian governments, the Iranians were required to release the hostages. As soon as they cleared Iranian air space, the Algerian government would instruct the Bank of England to release $3.7 billion back to the New York Federal Reserve Bank, which would in turn pay off Iran's loans from the U.S. banks. The Bank of England would hold an escrow account for the disputed unliquidated claims, and the residue would be transferred to Bank Markazi.

Though all of these transfers would take place electronically in a matter of hours, the assets would, in a physical sense, be moving from Europe, to the United States, to England, to Algeria, and finally to Iran. During the fleeting period when those assets touched down in the United States, they could be subject to an attachment order issued by any U.S. federal court—just as Citibank and Morgan Guaranty had attached Iranian assets that were physically present in West Germany—and there were hundreds of American companies with big claims against Iran, greedy for the chance to tie up Iranian funds which might eventually be awarded to them by a court decree.

The lawyers for the twelve had recognized this problem from the beginning, but the likelihood of an attachment—and the resulting halt in the flow of assets which would undoubtedly destroy the entire hostage release arrangement—was considered remote. No one knew that billions of dollars in Iranian assets would be briefly exposed to attachment as they touched down in the United States, and they wouldn't know where or when. That is, except for the obvious—the lawyers for the twelve knew the plan, and knew exactly when and where the assets could be seized.

One lawyer at that meeting on Saturday evening recalls that Bank of America's lawyer Timothy Atkeson from Steptoe & Johnson seemed particularly subdued, even uneasy. Suddenly Atkeson plunged into the discussion, talking vaguely about the fact that he and his law firm also represented some major industrial clients with outstanding contract claims against Iran. Such clients were precisely the kind who would, under ordinary circumstances, be interested in the possibility of attachment. As this realization dawned, silence fell over the assembled lawyers, then Hoffman, his voice grave, ordered Atkeson out of the room. Had he dallied, another lawyer says, he would have been forced out the door.

"We had to get him out," Hoffman recalls, even though he and Atkeson were close friends and Steptoe & Johnson often handled Washington, D.C., matters for Shearman & Sterling. "We had no margin for error. These stakes were very, very high."

Atkeson had to be stopped, and urgently. He was a live wire that could ignite the entire hostage deal with a simple piece of paper in any federal court. The bank lawyers knew they had a legal handle for action against Steptoe & Johnson in the event it tried an attachment: if the law firm tried to stop the assets on behalf of one or more of its other clients, it would be jeopardizing the chance for its bank client, Bank of America, to recover its outstanding syndicated loans. . . .

They, in turn, notified Cutler, Civiletti and Muskie. The attachment problem was one that had been anticipated—and feared—at the highest levels of government. . . . Muskie had sternly warned at the previous day's meeting that "the full resources of the U.S. government would be deployed against anyone who attempted to block the transfer."

Now that threat was made more specific. Word was passed to Atkeson and the other lawyers that both Air Force I and Air Force II were standing by, ready to fly a squad of Justice Department lawyers anywhere in the country if Steptoe or any other firm tried to interfere. Justice Department lawyers were already on location, armed with the necessary papers, in Washington, New York and Boston, the most likely sites for an attachment attempt. . . .

In the unlikely event that an attempt by Steptoe actually succeeded, the government was prepared to obtain review by the U.S. Supreme Court in less than four hours. The Supreme Court had immediately been alerted to the potential problem and justices were standing by. . . .

By Sunday evening, all was ready for the asset transfer. The computers in New York, which take four hours to warm up, were turned on. Twelve phone lines from the banks were open to Hoffman in Washington and to the Shearman & Sterling conference room, as well as lines connecting Washington, New York, London and Algiers. Because the Iranians didn't want a plane leaving the Teheran airport at night during the Iraqi war, the target time was set for dawn on Monday, Teheran time. The lawyers waited for the single telex order to London from the Iranians, the signal to set the asset transfer in motion. By now, all the basic agreements had been signed by the bankers and government representatives, including President Carter's own order unfreezing the Iranian assets. Carter went on national television to announce the imminent release of the hostages.

The morning dawned in Teheran, but nothing happened. Where was the telex? Hoffman called Algiers; there had been no information. He called the lawyers in Germany representing the Iranians; they had heard nothing. Then the snag appeared. Through the Algerians, Hoffman learned of an eleven-page appendix to the escrow agreement which had been drafted by Logan and Corse in Algiers and attached to the final papers. Basically, the attachment contained technical instructions related to the escrow account which would be maintained by the Bank of England, and the language had already been approved by the government negotiators in Iran. Someone, however, had needlessly inserted Bank Markazi as a signatory to the escrow agreement—and Nabavi seized this as a last opportunity to upset the deal. . . . Once they learned the problem, Logan, Corse and Hoffman solved it in thirty seconds by simply dropping the language. . . . But in all the confusion, and because of bad connections, an entire day was lost. It was now 10:30 P.M. on Inauguration eve. . . .

For Hoffman, the waiting had become an agony. Nightfall was approaching in Teheran, after which there would be no hostage release. Hoffman would have felt better if, as he had advocated all along, there had been a standard formal closing in London, with all the lawyers and representatives involved. Then he could simply have sat down with the Iranians, and if there were any last-minute problems they could have been dealt with on the spot. But the principals acting on behalf of Iran—whoever they were—had refused to budge from Teheran. . . .

At midnight, Hoffman set up an open line to the Coward Chance conference room in London. Someone stayed on the phone at all times, in touch with a lawyer who watched the telex machine for the red warning light indicating that a transmission was in progress; but nothing happened. Then, at 2:40 A.M., Hoffman shouted to his colleagues in Washington, "The light's on!" and everyone jumped to his feet and gathered around the phone. Hoffman told London that he wanted transmission read instantly as it came over the wire, but there was nothing. In London, the light blinked out. Frantic inquiries soon revealed that the machine had been triggered by a wrong number a sleepy and unsuspecting caller had haphazardly dialed.

But shortly after, the light blinked on again, and this time a transmission began. "Read the test number," Hoffman shouted, and the lawyers waited breathlessly as they listened for the series of numbers. As they were read over the phone, Hoffman couldn't believe what he was hearing. The code number was wrong. As he later described it, "It was like being handed a forged check."

. . . But as the telex transmission continued, it soon became apparent that practically nothing had been accurately recorded and transmitted by the Iranians. . . .

As soon as the wrong test code appeared, Hoffman got on the phone to the lawyers in London, who were able to reach the Iranian transmitters by telephone. The Iranians claimed the erroneous code had resulted from simple typing errors, and they agreed to transmit a corrected test code, which finally appeared on the London telex at about 3:00 A.M. But as for the garbled names and figures, the Iranians refused to make any corrections. Instead, the lawyers received a final threatening message over the telex: "Responsibility for the fate of the 52 American hostages rests entirely with you."

Ordinarily, no bank lawyer would authorize the transfer of $8 billion on the strength of such documents. Even simple typographical errors have derailed closings and caused associates to be disciplined. But these were not ordinary circumstances, and as patriotic duty and the fate of the hostages swept aside reservations about client obligations and prudent behavior, the usually calm and cautious lawyers became militant. . . . Finally, at 6:44 A.M., January 20, the money completed its global circulation and flowed into the Bank of England. . . . [N]o attachment attempts had been made. . . .

Six hours later, the plane carrying the American hostages took off from the Teheran airport. The $3.7 billion in assets were electronically credited to the accounts of the twelve American banks whose lawyers, in a sense, had just bought the hostages' release.

Comments and Questions

1. This substantial excerpt of Stewart captures some of the complexities that accompany the practice of law–politics by members of elite law firms. The following may help uncover some elements in the banking freeze–hostage negotiations that are worth keeping in mind:
   a. It was earlier contended that lawyers for multinationals behave more like thinkers in a business-legal-political environment than strictly legal thinkers. Does John Hoffman meet this description?
   b. Stewart states that the banks are "subjected to an unending stream of statutes from foreign, federal, state, and local governing bodies." Do you get the feeling from reading about these negotiations that the banks were being controlled by the government, or do you get the idea that the negotiations were being shaped by the banks and their lawyers?
   c. There seem to have been many informal connections between John Hoffman and members of the Carter Administration. Would you have expected these relationships, or were you surprised by them?
   d. In speaking about the lawyers for Morgan Guaranty Trust Company, Stewart said that they had two main questions: What did the freeze mean in practical terms? and How could Morgan Guaranty protect its own interests?
   Logan, the lawyer for Chase Manhattan, says: "I hope history's verdict will be that we served the public interest without sacrificing our duty to our clients, and our duties as officers of the court." The story had a happy ending—the banks got their money, Iran got some funds for its war effort against Iraq, and the American hostages were returned home. Had the story unfolded differently, could there have been conflicts between the lawyers' duties to their clients and their duties to country and the hostages? What implications might potential conflicts have on the delegation of diplomatic functions to private lawyers?
   e. Early in the episode there was a debate as to the applicability of U. S. banking law and presidential orders on foreign deposits and foreign branches of United States banks. Would the banks have any reluctance to endorse a *wholesale* application of American banking laws worldwide?
   f. The lawyers for the banks in question seem to have long-standing personal ties to each other which facilitated their working out a collective resolution of the negotiations with Iran despite some

tensions. Looking beyond the Iran episode, what do you see to be the effects of the numerous informal connections among the lawyers for the banks?

g. Based on the Iran case report, what are the interconnections among law, politics, and banking? Does one dimension predominate over another? Is there any priority of importance that can be attached to each?

CONCLUSION

Albert Camus, in his bone-chilling book entitled *The Plague,* wrote about the reluctant recognition of the plague by a doctor:

> When leaving his surgery on the morning of April 16 Dr. Bernard Rieux felt something soft under his foot. It was a dead rat lying in the middle of his landing. On the spur of the moment he kicked it to one side, and without giving it further thought, continued on his way downstairs. Only when he stepped forth into the street did it occur to him that a dead rat had no business to be on his landing.[23]

A dead rat—the antithesis of sanitation and health—violates everything Doctor Rieux stands for. Rather than diving into the medical implications of a dead rat and a possible plague, he kicks the problem to one side, at least for a moment. In the end his seeing the rat will not let him carry on business as usual, but it is only after a pause that he allows the prospect of a plague sweeping across the city, and a full quarantine of every citizen, to reach his consciousness.

Contemporary professionals, facing a world changing about their feet, might be inclined to behave like Dr. Rieux. They would rather not. Rather not what? Business teachers and business people generally do not want to acknowledge that the world of enterprise has been so intermingled with the state and politics that the old words "government regulation of business," "independent businessman," as well as the old dichotomy "public sector/private sector" have been drained of meaning.

Law teachers and lawyers prefer to see themselves as helpers and facilitators of all people regardless of their class, status, wealth, or power and not moral derelicts from their duty to advance justice through the promotion of democratic values and economic equality.

The net result across business and law may be a collective kicking of rats off landings, and a merger of disciplines may be the only way to offset the ability of people in each field to deal exclusively with what they prefer, and reject the rest. After merger, no one field can dump unwanted issues and findings beyond the boundaries of the field.

[23](1947), p. 9.

The rat is power—greater power than has ever been assembled in human history for good or for evil. Power raises unpleasant facts that must either be acknowledged and squarely faced or purged in the interest of academic tranquility and a carefree professional life.

If power questions are purged, scholarship will become a mere propagandistic distraction, and postgraduate life no more than a pursuit of power, money, and wealth, with a few winners of large prizes, and many losers who may or may not casually accept their ill fortune and powerlessness.

In the next two chapters we will see that business people and lawyers are not alone in their desire to avoid the hardest questions. Political scientists and economists have developed techniques for excluding what is especially troubling. And yet some questions must be answered if we are to achieve any understanding of multinationals and their effects.

CHAPTER 3

Politics

The central questions in politics are the allocation of power and the nature of the state. International business requires the enlargement of the scope of politics to include the international, or interstate systems, in addition to national state systems. The following discussion refers to national politics, but in the next section on political economy, other levels of political activity will be added to the coverage.

What students learn in high school social studies, political scientists would call the *pluralist* state.[1] According to the pluralist tradition, power resides in individual persons who authorize others to be their representatives and advance their interests as state action is formulated and implemented. That power resides in the people has been assumed since the Declaration of Independence, when the right to revolt against Great Britain was deemed to be inherent in the people. Abraham Lincoln at Gettysburg restated the principle of popular sovereignty when he defined the national challenge to be the preservation of government *of, by,* and *for* the people.

Students also commit to memory at an early age the United States' being a government with *separation of powers*; the executive, legislative, and judicial branches are independent and autonomous, and the power of each branch can be "checked" by the other, potentially rival, branches. This structure of countervailing powers is said to insulate against excesses should one branch usurp power and act in derogation of the general interest or will.

In the foregoing structure of government, abiding legitimacy depends upon the faithful execution of the will of the people and those in public office not only winning but also keeping popular support. The ability to form coalitions and interest groups to vote people out of office as well as put them in affirms the contingent status of incumbents, and despite the fact that most contemporaries would wince in disbelief if their elected representatives were described as their "public servants," as a matter of organizing principle this is what they are said to be.

The system as designed minimizes the persistence of injustice, since those who are discontented can mobilize and join with others and "throw the bums out." That this prospect may be bleaker than some would like to admit is suggested by the current support for term limitation, according to which even if voters cannot get incumbents out, their terms would expire after a fixed time in office.

[1]For the central concepts of the pluralist state, see Robert Dahl, *A Preface to Democratic Theory* (Chicago, U. of Chicago Press, 1956).

Once in office, successful candidates are expected to continue to advance the interests of their constituents. With a country as large and geographically diverse as the United States, there will inevitably be differences of political opinion, but all interests can or will find a voice in the political process. State action results from the balancing and mediating of many voices, such that any action undertaken by the state will reflect a consensus or the most workable compromise among competing interests.

This process of balancing among competing political interests parallels the textbook version of the judicial process, which also is said to entail "a delicate balancing of conflicting interests." The state, like the good judge, is expected to rise above rival interests and become the voice of the people as a whole.

Thus, if the pluralist conception of politics holds true in experience, no group will expect to have its own way politically, but no group will be unduly disgruntled either, since presumably no other group has unqualifiedly prevailed. The expectation that people govern, that power will be shared and not monopolized, and that the state will not be captured by any dominant interest group leads pluralists to claim that the system of government in the United States is the most legitimate in all of history.

In both academic circles and in random barrooms around the country, substantial doubts have arisen about the operation of this textbook version of government. Academics question the assumption that the majority, or significant subsets of society, materially affect government policy and law. In barrooms, while patriotism remains high and no revolution seems imminent, many nevertheless wonder about the future chances of the "average person" or "ordinary workers."

Some deep-seated split exists between love of country and love of government. Even though the Iraq War received almost unqualified endorsement, the government, and especially the Congress, continually receives low approval ratings as the custodian of the general welfare. The fatalistic statement, "What do you expect from the politicians?" says that people routinely expect that the government will not protect "the public," but instead will be self-serving, or likely to act in the interests of some, and not all.

The most persistent criticism of the pluralist theory of power allocation and the fairness of state action has come from marxists. They argue that the so-called separation of powers is largely illusory; that the "branches" of government move in the same direction and not in opposition, and therefore assert no consequential checks and balances on one another.

Critics on the left also contend that all parts of the government derive their values from the same source—economic elites and their spokespeople, who circulate into and out of government posts. Rival groups do not necessarily mobilize and exert their influence on government, and, on the contrary, those who are well-situated economically wind up with a persistent advantage in mobilizing and setting public agendas, regardless of what party wins an election.

Barroom theoreticians sometimes take the same position as leftists, even though they will deny their affinity to marxist notions as soon as the label that best fits their politics is attached to their viewpoints. "Them that has gets," "Money talks," "You can't fight city hall," "They feather their own nests" capture popular disenchantment, the growing belief in entrenched privilege, and the increasing disbelief in responsive government. However, the barroom critics of government are just that—critics; there is no fleshing out of the critique with evidence or a political agenda, and no countervailing action is envisioned.

To press the marxist critique further, legal, political, and economic forces are said to contribute simultaneously to the *proletarianization* of the middle class as the general standard of living falls, and reinforcement of the position of those who are powerful in the economy. Institutions ranging from law to politics to education to religion support the transfer of wealth from one group to another, a practice that could not succeed without active cooperation across the entire institutional spectrum of capitalist culture.

Given the chronic disadvantages and the persistent failure to reverse the prevailing pattern of privilege, one might ask what sustains loyalty. For the last 100 years, marxists have predicted an imminent revolution led by the disadvantaged once they *fully* realize that established political channels are thoroughly dominated by those who have everything to lose by change. Marxists contend that when peaceful prospects *utterly* dry up and are seen as exercises in futility, interclass hostilities will intensify to the point of violent revolution. Loyalty still persists because conditions have not reached dire levels, but according to marxist prophecies those levels will be reached—someday.

John Gaventa in his book *Power and Powerlessness*[2] argues that both the pluralists and the marxists are wrong, but they are wrong for different reasons. Oddly enough, they share an optimism about the elimination of persistent injustices over time that, according to Gaventa, the historical evidence does not support. The pluralists are wrong in predicting that a discontented electorate can and will become politically active, form interest groups and force a desired response from the state; the marxists are wrong in believing that injustices across classes will *inevitably* produce irreconcilable class rivalries and rebellion. Both liberals and marxists envision shifts in power, and not a stable power system in which silence and injustice can coexist for a surprisingly long time. It is on this odd combination of silence and injustice that Gaventa focuses.

Based on a study of a region of Appalachia spanning an almost 100-year period, Gaventa divides power into three dimensions, which are cumulative and complementary. He begins with an economically based power system that later becomes overlaid with a political dimension. Finally power is *hegemonic*, meaning that ideas about power, and who should and who should not have it, are buried deep in each person's psyche. The power–powerless relationship is complete and most stable when the powerless accept their fate, or even argue on behalf of those who are in power.

[2](Urbana: U. of Illinois Press, 1980).

In the first phase, in the late nineteenth century, a London-based company consolidated mining properties in Southern Appalachia that were once held as farms and woodlands by mountain people. In the second phase, local elites—lawyers, politicians, and petty business people were "recruited" and given a partial stake in the success of coal mining and related ventures; their share was a cut above that of the general work force, but involved no ownership in the main venture. When it was discovered that not everyone would benefit from the business boom, these mid-range local allies were helpful in preventing challenges from the mountaineer–miners, who by this time had become impoverished, and had lost their escape route back to subsistence farming; they no longer had any land.

The third phase involved hegemonic power, power relationships that had been fully internalized *by the powerless*. Images like progress, prosperity, and modernity were the property of the elite, leaving the "hillbillies" with old-fashioned, traditional values—individualism within kinship relationships. Instead of being virtues, these latter qualities were declared to be the causes of their poverty. The mountaineers were caught between other people's values from which they were foreclosed, and values that were theirs, but publicly regarded worthless and not translatable into material sustenance.

Once power relationships were fully internalized, overt force through the courts and the police did not have to be used to control dissent, and local spokespeople for the company did not have to continually fight off criticism of the injustices that continued to pile up. When the mountaineer–miners no longer believed in any chance of successful opposition and had virtually abandoned their sense of entitlement, the entrenchment of power-powerlessness was complete. In the eyes of the losers, the powerful had won—eternally and *almost deservedly*.[3]

Gaventa's theory of power entails a base in economics, the installation of barriers around that base, and finally power-supporting imagery. Ideology and mythology help implant the inevitability of the power system in the minds of people most likely to be hurt by the power system. In the end the powerless might be inclined to give up. According to Gaventa, nothing fails like persistent failure and nothing succeeds like persistent success; over a very long period economic returns and power relationships never did "even out."

Gaventa's thesis seems even more dismal than that of the strident marxists, who at least lighten their grim prophecies of violent class conflict with more hope for the future. But then we can recall our surprise that the townspeople in Kafka's *Refusal* welcomed the adverse decision of the colonel as the one outcome on which they could always depend; they were neither politically assertive nor physically aggressive, despite the denial of a perfectly reasonable request. Gaventa's theory of hegemonic power explains the

[3]Ibid., pp.13–72. For a comparable point on British society, see G. Orwell, "Such, Such Were the Joys," in Volume IV, *Collected Essays, Journals and Letters 1945–1950* (New York: Harcourt Brace, 1968), p. 330.

POWER, COAL VALLEY[4]

1st Dimension	2nd Dimension	3rd Dimension
Control of material resources—land, transportation, and related businesses	Control of institutions—lawyers, politicians, education, religion	Control of images—"progress," "prosperity," "hillbilly"; ideology—"Hard work rewards all," and myths—"Everyone gains, unless personally deficient"
Coercion—law, court orders, sheriff	Barriers against effective protest	Internalized restraints—surrender without fight, or even being conscious of surrender
Protest	Protest deflected or put in harmless channels	Silence
Visible power	Secondary actors visible, primary power holders not visible	Hegemonic power—generally invisible

[4]Gaventa, op. cit., pp.3–83.

response of Kafka's townspeople; they no longer expect change, or claim anything for themselves except ritualistically, and are politically paralyzed by a profound sense of their own worthlessness.

Unlike Kafka and Gaventa, pluralists might predict resistance by the townspeople, and marxists violence at the perennial oppression by The Colonel and his army. Nothing happens. A perverse equilibrium set in and the townspeople help adjust the noose around their own necks. The abiding popular sentiment is fear, not rebellion. Kafka the writer and Gaventa the political scientist concur, making Kafka's story even more troubling than it was when we first read it.

THE STATE AND THE ECONOMY

Ralph Miliband in his *The State and Capitalist Society*[5] reaches a comparable conclusion to Gaventa, focusing on the anatomy of the modern state rather than a detailed theory of power. He divides the state into constituent parts:

1. *The executive*. These are the highest officials and their appointees—for example, the Clinton Administration and White House appointees to head governmental agencies. These come and go with the election returns and the successes and failures of political parties.
2. *The bureaucracy*. Unlike the above, who are transients, the bureaucracy continues across administrations. They are there upon the

[5](New York: Basic, 1969).

arrival of newly elected officials and their appointees and are there when they leave.

3. *The legislature.* In the United States, the U.S. Senate and the House of Representatives.
4. *The judiciary.* The United States Supreme Court and the federal court system.
5. *Agencies of force.* The military, the CIA, and other agencies.
6. *The mini-states.* In the United States the 50 states and the territories, each with its own elected officials and their appointees, bureaucracies, legislatures, judicial systems, and agencies of force.[6]

So far, this summary of Miliband does no more than remind us that the state is bigger than the elected officials and their appointees, and repeats what might be read in any primer on the American political system.

Miliband takes the analysis further. Not all of the constituent elements of the state need be of the same political orientation. Political differences across the chambers of the state may be seen most vividly in countries where the army is preeminent, and the executive, legislative, and judicial branches, with other values, hold inconsequential power and sometimes different values.

When Corazon Aquino "took over" in the Philippines after the long regime of the dictator Ferdinand Marcos, she had no control over the bureaucratic carryovers, the army, or the judiciary from the Marcos years. These differently inclined chambers of the Philippine state not so subtly toned down all of the reforms she had promised in her campaign against Marcos, but especially those in the area of the organization of the economy and land reform.

In the early Reagan years, some parts of the federal bureaucracy, most notably the Environmental Protection Agency and the Civil Rights Commission, but other agencies as well, differed with the president over how zealously to enforce the laws these agencies were charged by Congress to uphold. The lawyers at the EPA threatened to quit if Reagan and his appointees discouraged effective enforcement of environmental laws and regulations that antedated Reagan's election. The lawyers wound up quitting. This episode of presidential–bureaucratic conflict offers an example of checks and balances within a state working, at least up to the time when the lawyers quit.

The two cases suggest that the political persuasions of a state cannot necessarily be lumped together in one whole; investigators must inventory each subpart of a state and not simply focus on a few highly visible participants in state action.

According to Miliband, it is far more common for there to be political congruence across the subsets of the state than for there to be significant differences. He endorses the marxian position that the ruling ideas (the ideas premising state action) will most often be the ideas of the ruling elite, who

[6]Ibid., pp. 49–55.

derive their power from the economic order. Moreover, he contends that class-based state power is reinforced by media and educational institutions, neither of which, for all the politicians' complaints about hostile media or radical academics, take positions grossly disparate from those taken by the powerful.[7]

This consensus across the subsets of the state and in all media and educational settings does not have to be complete. In fact, power may be more stable where discontentment has some voice. The cross-institutional consensus needs to provide only a political center of gravity, an edge in institutional life. Trivial controversies—those which do not threaten power or wealth—can orbit unthreateningly around this central organizing tendency based on economic power.[8]

Power and the Circulation of Elites

Just how do the ideas of economic elites become the ruling ideas? The institutional meanderings of the lawyers who negotiated the Iran hostages release, introduced in Chapter 2, suggest that elites who circulate into and out of critical state positions do not encounter grossly different values when they move back and forth between private practice and government assignments. Miliband believes that common class background or education eliminates the potential for policy disagreements.

Scarcely anyone of working-class origins makes it to either private or public circles of power.[9] Talented people from the middle class who are recruited to state positions identify with those with higher class and status rather than remembering their middle class origins or identifying downward with the working class.[10] Political parties in all major capitalist countries do not inject dramatically different policies despite their carrying names like the Labor party or Liberal party or even Socialist party. On the contrary, Miliband finds that some of the "left" parties may impose more austerity upon the classes that elected them than "center" or "rightist" parties do.[11] In the end participants, regardless of class background or political party, pose no threat to the status quo.

Miliband, once readers can get around the antipathy he arouses for his overt marxism, raises important tests of the pluralist understanding of government in a capitalist society. He calls for a closer consideration of all the subparts of the state to see just how each connects to enterprise and economic power bases. Eisenhower, a good Republican and former military man,

[7]Ibid., pp. 119–145.

[8]Ibid., pp. 179–181.

[9]C. W. Mills, in *The Power Elite* (New York: Oxford, 1956) made the overall argument on cross-institutional consensus among elites.

[10]Miliband, op. cit., pp. 39–43; 60–67. The precarious social place of the middle class and its concomitant conservative politics is best explained in G. Orwell, *The Road to Wigan Pier* (New York: Harcourt Brace, 1958).

[11]Miliband, op. cit., pp. 102-106.

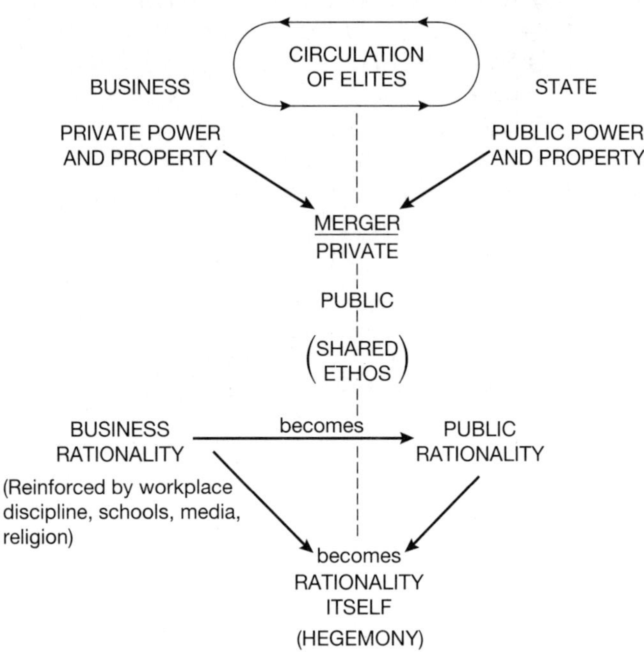

FIGURE 3-1 The Miliband Model

warned of a military–industrial complex, presumably out of fear that the autonomy of the state as a whole might be compromised by an overemphasis on military procurement and the kind of economy that goes with it.

That would be one type of state capture from among other possibilities. It could be that a circumspect inventory reveals that the system of checks and balances is alive and well, and that the general interest commonly prevails over limited interests, such as wealth and the power that usually goes with it. But then again an inventory could yield disappointing results.

If we look back to the profile of the contemporary multinational corporate lawyer in the preceding chapter, Miliband's thesis might produce a startling observation: the multinational lawyer as a thinker in a business-legal-political environment *tries to fulfill the marxist prophecy that the state enacts the will of economic elites*. The superlawyer tries to make the ideas of their multinational clients the ruling ideas.

Using Miliband to reconsider the style and scope of legal education, we would underscore the obsolescence of the conventional curriculum. Contemporary lawyers must know not only how to practice law (the ins and outs of the judicial system) but also how to practice "the state" in the United States and everywhere else a business might locate. Law work has moved far beyond the old realms of strictly legal advice or "going to court" to any facet of the state whose action might impinge on the welfare of the multinational. Those lawyers who are opposed to multinationals will need to know their opposition thoroughly, and be able to follow their business-oriented opponents to wherever critical state policies are in conflict.

If we look back still further to the discussion of business activism on the political front, Miliband's thesis has application. He provides a checklist of the places, institutions, and political actors where businesses and their spokespeople will be likely to seek advantages. Where state activity will affect a business is where the business and its advocates will converge—the White House, the halls of Congress, administrative agencies, and so on. Opponents who chafe at multinational domination of the affairs of state will also have an unpredictable itinerary, and will need to take their resistance beyond courts to wherever problems take them.

CASE STUDIES IN POLITICS

The story of the native Hawaiians and the account of the bank lawyers negotiating in the Iran hostage case suggest that journalists may offer a more accessible starting place for the discovery of the interconnection between business and politics than conventional theoretical works. A steady immersion in narratives about particular companies, countries, or even commodities like coal, oil, or wheat can become the basis for working out one's own thoughts on what forces, political or economic, pull in what directions with what consequences. *The Wall Street Journal*, *The Investors Daily*, the *London Financial Times,* and *The Economist* offer steady reporting of "case histories" in business and politics that can be dissected by the perceptive reader and then integrated into a more comprehensive understanding that can guide insights as to where things are going and for what reasons.

The strength of journalistic accounts is the journalist's penchant for details—who is doing what, where, and for what declared purposes. Readers can rather painlessly gather information about the business world, which at this point in history intersects with the world of politics at every turn. It might be surprising how little distance needs to be traveled in one's reading before becoming highly sensitized to this point. If one expects political dimensions to be hidden, the opposite often turns out to be the case.

Besides the political slant of the creators of these publications, the weakness of journalistic accounts is their atheoretical stance. Readers can get lost in the details of a story or be distracted by personalities and not see structural elements with transcending implications. Like law students who read case after case without necessarily making interconnections among the cases, readers of journalistic accounts may get details without coherence. Good theory tells what to look for in a story, whereas a good story cries out for a theory. Perhaps the way out of this tension is the right sequence of study, testing theory against narrative accounts, and once the study is further along, establishing a regular rhythm in study between stories and theory that maximizes the return from both.

We follow that plan here and distill from two book-length accounts (Ron Chernow, *The House of Morgan*[12] and Peter Collier et al., *The Rockefellers*[13])

[12](New York: Simon & Schuster, 1990).

[13](New York: Signet, 1976).

the relationship between prominent business families and politics. Like other journalistic accounts, these long stories raise the risk of losing readers in details and personalities, and neglecting structural threads. But they provide relatively easy access to the relationship between businesses and the acquisition and preservation of power by critical actors.

Dynastic Wealth—The Rockefellers and the Morgans

Two families stand out among all others in the business history of the United States—the Rockefellers in oil and derivative investments, and the Morgan family in finance, railroading, steel and other corporations. The following joke summarizes the central place of Morgan and Rockefeller in American business history:

> Who made the world, Charles?
> A. God made the world in 4004 B.C., but it was reorganized in 1901 by James J. Hill, J. Pierpont Morgan, and John D. Rockefeller.[14]

Even though these private economic power bases were at times antagonistic to one another, they nevertheless shared a similar evolution, which bears on our theme.

In the first phase there was a consolidation of economic position. Rockefeller began in Cleveland as a grain trader in the civil war years, moved into oil with the opening of the Pennsylvania oil fields, and consolidated control over oil refining until in 1880 his companies controlled over 95 percent of all of the refining capacity of the United States.[15] At one point profits were rolling in at such an astounding rate that John D. Rockefeller could not spend them, invest them, or give them away with the ease that people who have never had substantial money might expect would be the case.[16] Rockefeller confessed to being in this unusual kind of trouble, and hired a specialist to help him systematically get rid of his money (some of it).[17]

The Morgan company began before Rockefeller's Standard Oil with banking partnerships in London, Paris, and New York. At the end of the nineteenth century the center of gravity of the company moved slowly toward the United States. The banks went international relatively early, in part because finance followed trade, which was international long before industrial companies internationalized their operations.[18] In their peak years, the Morgan interests claimed to be involved with the financial affairs of virtually all the leading corporations in America.[19] A congressional committee investigating corporations in 1912 corroborated the intimate connections between corporations and financial institutions, which then meant the Morgans and a handful of interlocked New York banks:

[14]Chernow, op. cit., p. 78.

[15]Horowitz, op. cit., p. 29.

[16]Ibid., pp. 49–53.

[17]Ibid., p. 51.

[18]Chernow, op. cit., pp. 3–16; 23–28.

[19]Ibid., pp. 153, 156.

> . . . directorships in 112 corporations, and spanning the worlds of finance, railroads, transportation, and public utilities. In this era of relationship banking, board seats often meant a monopoly on a company's business. During the previous decade the House of Morgan had floated almost $2 billion in securities—an astronomical sum for the time.[20]

Both the Rockefellers and Morgans are known for entrepreneurial inventiveness. John D. Rockefeller realized that oil could be controlled only *after it was produced*, when transported, refined, and distributed, and not at the well head, where furious competition among wildcat drillers prevailed. He and his partners worked with railroads on a rebate–drawback system (they arranged rebates on their own shipments and drawbacks on the oil shipments of their competitors) that gave them a competitive advantage over other refiners, and finally drove rival companies into consolidating their operations into what would ultimately become Standard Oil.[21]

Since no national company could be easily coordinated under the then prevailing corporate law, a Rockefeller lawyer, Samuel Dodd, invented the business trust; the shareholders of constituent companies put their stock into the trust and the trustee issued shares in the trust. The trust managers could then operate the entrusted companies as a single national enterprise—Standard Oil—which virtually monopolized oil refining.[22]

The company was eventually dissolved after an antitrust case in 1911 but continued to operate *de facto* even after the dissolution because Standard was broken up by distributing the stock of the participating corporations *pro rata* to the holders of shares in Standard Oil holding company.[23]

The trust device was also used by J. Pierpont Morgan in finance, to arrange and rearrange corporate America. The principal purpose of trusts was the elimination of competition among rival businesses, and though it is true that competition cannot be excluded forever, transient monopolies and oligopolies can be indispensable in generating wealth. In John D. Rockefeller's case the wealth has extended to four more generations of his family.

A change in New Jersey law eliminated the need for trusts by allowing *holding companies* which could own other companies. Standard Oil of New Jersey was organized in 1899 to do according to New Jersey law what had been done roundabout through the trust device. It was the New Jersey holding company that was dissolved after the antitrust case in 1911. The holding company gave even greater potential to the corporation, which was already a superhuman legal creation, existing in perpetuity, aggregating unprecedented capital everywhere, for any lawful purpose. No multinational corporation could exist without the holding company privileges first granted under New Jersey corporate law.[24]

[20]Ibid., p. 152.

[21]Horowitz, op. cit., pp. 28, 33–34.

[22]Ibid., p. 29.

[23]Ibid., pp. 58, 68, 160–61.

[24]For details of the evolution of corporate law to accommodate new business organization, see Chapter 5.

Rockefeller found competition ruinous and wasteful, a position that Morgan shared. When railroads because of overcapacity and duplication of services were engaging in "destructive" competition, Morgan as financier acted as a neutral arbiter of their differences, earned fees for refinancing the corporations, and sometimes wound up in control through the use of the voting trust. (Stockholders would put their voting power in a trust for a period of years, thereby transferring political control to the trustee while continuing to earn income on the shares entrusted.)[25]

At the time Pierpont Morgan became active in railroad finance, railroads were as atomistic as the producers and refiners of oil had been in the early days of Rockefeller. When Morgan and others were done there were fewer, more powerful railroads more likely to pay their indebtedness when it came due.

Morgan's real coup came with the formation of the United States Steel Corporation, which linked rival producers and integrated all aspects of steelmaking. United States Steel was the first billion dollar corporation in the United States and provided a pattern of *vertical* integration—ore to finished products—and *horizontal* integration—joining those who might otherwise be purchasers or sellers in the same markets. United States Steel accomplished on a domestic scale what integrated international companies would attempt on a world scale in post-World War II years.[26]

Intensifying public criticism of the Rockefellers and the Morgans was at first shrugged off by them; they could retreat into the private enclaves of their businesses and residential hideaways. Vanderbilt, a railroad man, had said, "The public be damned,"[27] an extreme maxim that might have been privately seconded by the Rockefellers and Morgans. More likely, the latter men would have explained their business practices less negatively; they were trying to eliminate inefficiencies and waste in enterprises, and were therefore acting in the public interest, and not exclusively for themselves. Since the long run would be their vindication, they saw no need to justify their behavior.[28]

John D., largely through silence, was able to skate through some early public hearings on the railroad rebate system and a conspiracy among railroad men and oil men to maximize profits of both at the expense of oil producers and non-Rockefeller-affiliated refiners. His son, John Jr., was not so fortunate with the congressional hearings held in 1915 surrounding the Ludlow, Colorado coal strike in which corporate and state forces were pitted against miners.

After a number of deaths, martial law had been declared in Colorado, and the confrontation collapsed only after a bitter struggle. The public, at least for the moment, was aligned with the miners against the Rockefellers, and John Jr. and his advisers saw a need to be more active in cultivating the right public images and state policies with respect to corporations and labor.[29]

[25]Chernow, op. cit., pp. 38, 68–69, 152–153, 189.

[26]Ibid., pp. 81–86.

[27]Quoted in Chernow, op. cit., p. 42.

[28]Chernow, op. cit., pp. 67–68; Horowitz, op. cit., pp. 23–25.

[29]Horowitz, pp. 106–129.

Pierpont Morgan had already had his shock with the Pujo congressional hearings in 1912. As outlined above, the hearings revealed the intimate connection between industrial enterprises of all types and their bankers. Many in the Morgan group thought that the hearing, though nominally won by Pierpont, was his physical undoing—he died shortly after the hearings were concluded. More important, the Morgan partners realized that the state could impose serious limits on corporate power through antitrust laws and bank regulation in response to populist pressures, and public animosity could not simply be shrugged off as inconsequential to business success.[30] The Morgans and the Rockefellers reluctantly came to realize the need to resist the states' imposing unwanted controls upon their prerogatives.

The foregoing states only one-half of the long relationship among the Rockefellers, the house of Morgan, and the state. Alongside the impulse to resist the intrusion upon corporate discretion, there was a simultaneous recognition that the state could be highly useful as well as a threat. People to this day are thrown off by the public statements that businesses want government off their backs and to go it alone.

A more careful study of the relationship of enterprises to the state would reveal that enterprises want the right kind of state intervention rather than no intervention at all. This was the case when the Rockefellers and others desiring to consolidate corporations for national management benefited from the New Jersey law authorizing holding companies.

Some of the details of the relationship between the House of Morgan and the state can be taken first. As financiers some of their most profitable transactions came from acting as investment bankers in floating government debts and seeing that they were later paid. Their business in public finance developed before many countries had refined systems for raising money for public works and warfare.[31] (This practice of private placement of public indebtedness continues to this day, as we will later see through the study of the third world debt crisis in Chapter 11.) The financing of public indebtedness created a mutually beneficial relationship between banking and the state that moderated antagonisms between them.

The stand of the Morgan interests regarding the creation of the Interstate Commerce Commission in 1887 helps destroy any myth about enterprises having an across-the-board resistance to government intervention. The Morgans saw that the Commission could reduce the chaos in free enterprise railroading. Private efforts to smooth out competition had failed, and the right kind of government intervention was needed to enhance railroad profitability.[32]

The Morgan position on the creation of the ICC shows that his company had priorities regarding the relationship between enterprises and regulation, and not blanket opposition: government planning was superior to competition, and private planning was superior to either. The ICC reforms were favored after private possibilities had been exhausted.

[30]Chernow, op. cit., pp. 155–161.

[31]Ibid., pp. 205–229.

[32]Ibid., p. 56.

In the days before the Federal Reserve system in the United States, private bankers were expected to come forth and inject stability in times of financial panics like the one that occurred in 1907. The later creation of the Federal Reserve both limited private banking discretion *and* freed private bankers from the burdensome duty of being lenders of last resort to save other financial institutions in times of crisis. Moreover, bankers could influence the policies and direction of the Federal Reserve, and experience a net advantage while being "regulated." (The first director of the Federal Reserve bank of New York was a Morgan man, and the Federal Reserve and the United States Treasury continue to this day to draw key personnel from money center banks.)[33]

It was during the First World War and thereafter that relationships between the state and banking became more intimate. When U.S. government loans to Great Britain would violate the declared neutrality of the United States, the Morgan Company advanced "credits" needed to finance the Allied war effort. The Morgan company opened a procurement office for Great Britain in the United States and bought billions of dollars worth of munitions and supplies. On the transaction Morgans made a one percent commission, but astute observers saw the profits coming from the interest that Morgans had in suppliers as well as from the commissions. These transactions led to postwar charges of House of Morgan profiteering.[34]

Because the House of Morgan operated in Great Britain, France, and the United States, questions were continually raised about the national loyalties of the firm. For whom were the Morgan interests working? Were they, because of their long connections to Great Britain and France, more loyal to those countries than to the United States, or were they more loyal to the United States, since most of their financial power was centered in New York?

But if Americans wondered whether the Morgans were captives of the British, many in Britain wondered whether the Morgans could be entrusted with war procurement, especially when Morgan-controlled companies in the United States were among the suppliers. It could also have been that the Morgans were loyal to neither, or to both. Were the Morgans *citizens* of anywhere, or were they making straight business decisions without patriotic sentimentality? The debate over the loyalties of multinational companies to particular countries continues to this day.[35]

Up to the Great Depression, when unwanted limitations were placed on banking, a much more cooperative relationship between the state and the House of Morgan developed, with Morgan partners taking posts with the government and freely circulating with diplomats in shaping foreign policy in Italy, China, Mexico, and other countries. Finance and diplomacy never being far apart, there came to be such an amalgamation of private and public purpose that the two were often indistinguishable in this period.[36]

[33]Ibid., pp. 181, 182.

[34]Ibid., pp. 186–192.

[35]Ibid., pp. 191–203.

[36]Ibid., pp. 230–244, 336–345.

Depression legislation separated investment banking from commercial banking, and the House of Morgan was divided in two halves, J. P. Morgan Company, a commercial bank, and Morgan Stanley Company, an investment banking company that took over from the predecessor company the placement of stocks, bonds, and other securities. (As in the case of the breakup of the Standard trust, the formal severing of connections did not end informal relationships, including representation by the same law firm.)[37]

A 1980 Senate study of interlocking corporate directorates disclosed that the J. P. Morgan Company still had over 600 interconnections via boards of directors with leading industrial corporations and other financial institutions of the United States. There were bigger banks, and J. P. Morgan was no longer exclusively dominant in American corporate finance, but it was still there and still big.[38]

The Rockefellers arrived at a more cordial relationship with the state by a different route. Like Morgan, John D. Sr. favored keeping still and letting populist-inspired storms swirl on by his enterprises. When populism reached the legislatures, it was handled matter-of-factly, like any other business expense. The following letters to a United States Senator from John D. Archbold of Standard suggest the directness in handling political matters:

> Feb. 16, 1900
>
> My Dear Senator:
>
> Here is another very objectionable bill. It is so outrageous as to be ridiculous, but it needs looking after and I hope there will be no difficulty in killing it . . .
>
> Very sincerely yours,
>
> John D. Archbold

> April 17, 1900
>
> My Dear Senator:
>
> I enclose you a certificate of deposit to your favor for $15,000 . . . I need scarcely again express our great gratification over the favorable outcome of affairs. . .
>
> Very sincerely yours,
>
> John D. Archbold[39]

Another commentator said that Standard Oil had done everything with the legislature of the State of Pennsylvania except refine it![40] Students

[37]Ibid., pp. 384–388.

[38]The interlocking of banking with industrial corporations is discussed in Chapter 6.

[39]Horowitz, op. cit., p. 56.

[40]Ibid., p. 29.

expect that if there is a connection between enterprise and the state, it will take the form of direct bribes. In the early days of buccaneer capitalism there was more candor about buying political influence. It was explained in part as a necessary evil to head off unwanted and unnecessary regulation.

John D.'s son Junior and his experiences in 1913 in the Ludlow, Colorado coal strike at the Rockefeller-controlled Colorado Fuel and Iron Company changed the above pattern, although the older practice of campaign contribution–legislative influence continues to the present day. Over 40 people had been killed at Ludlow, and Junior realized that the Rockefeller interests could be jeopardized if they remained silent or worked strictly behind the scenes to head off negative state action.

A proactive rather than a reactive stance—getting out in front of problems and "getting believed in" by the general public—was worked out for Junior by Ivy Lee, one of the first public relations specialists, and MacKenzie King, an early practitioner in the new field of "industrial relations." Lee and King combined to create the right "climate of opinion" and a recommended course of action not antagonistic to Rockefeller interests. With their help, Junior went from being a "murderer" of innocent women and children to a benevolent pioneer in the field of labor relations.

At a national conference convened by President Wilson on labor at which labor, business, and the public were to be represented, Junior appeared as spokesperson *for the public*; like the textbook version of the ideal state, Junior had risen above the labor–business conflict to assume the role of a public-spirited citizen. That is how far his image had been reconfigured in the few short years after Ludlow.

A Rockefeller Plan for labor, also know as the American Plan, was advanced that stressed cooperation between workers and their employers in the form of "company unions." The union would function as a labor-management council and not as a contentious organization made up exclusively of workers. The Rockefeller Plan was so subtle that Junior was criticized by fellow business people as being pro-union. In fact, he had simply concluded that if unions were inevitable, they might as well have a design that impinged least on managerial prerogatives. (Company unions were outlawed under later labor law as inadequately representative of worker interests.)

Lee and King were part of a growing staff of professional managers of Rockefeller family interests in business and philanthropy. The Office, as it was called, was staffed by advisers of all types: lawyers, financiers, publicists, and directors of philanthropies, including the large Rockefeller foundations. In the end, The Office was not simply guiding the Rockefellers in their personal business; it was charting the future of the United States.[41]

Over many years, fields of interest normally associated with government and the public sector were systematically pursued either through The Office or through the Rockefeller-endowed foundations. Health, medicine, education, religion, conservation, atomic energy, military policy, foreign poli-

[41]Ibid., pp. 115–143.

cy, social science research, industrial relations research, population policy, Third World development priorities, and many others were the subjects of debate and strategizing in Rockefeller think tanks. The Office was never referred to as the Office of Hegemony, but without exaggeration such a title could be attached to its functions.[42]

The advantage of an office is that it is an office. A group is regularly and steadily working on projects that, if done sporadically, will fizzle out for lack of nurturing. It goes without saying that the Rockefellers and other powerful aggregations did not have things completely their own way throughout the course of American history; the family has cyclically been in and out of public favor. But the presence of an office with an agenda improved the odds, and like the house advantage of 0 and 00 on a roulette table, gave the Rockefeller interests a long-run advantage.

The family office became the training ground for a number of Junior's sons, of whom John III, Nelson, and David have special significance for students of multinationals. John III took an interest in the Far East and population. It was his belief that the problems in many parts of the world were traceable to population growth that had outstripped the carrying capacities of the economies where the people lived.

A growing number of experts funded by the Population Council and the foundations contended that United States foreign policy ought to be premised on population controls in developing countries, since population posed "one of the greatest obstacles to economic and social progress and the maintenance of political stability in many of the less developed areas".[43]

The focus on population was a distinctively safe approach to world economic problems. Poverty and its accompanying miseries were traceable to there being too many people in the world, and the multinationals through the more efficient organization of production could help alleviate them. Alternative theories—that outside interferences were making the lives of indigenous people more austere than they otherwise would be, or that the multinationals were exacerbating the maldistribution of local wealth and income—were effectively displaced not only as foci for United States foreign policy but also in the way most people thought about such problems as world hunger. Multinationals, by integrating "less developed countries" (also called "underdeveloped" countries) into a world economy were seen as the solution to a problem that was not of their own making.

Nelson Rockefeller, Junior's second son, took a special interest in Latin America, and especially Venezuela, after visiting companies affiliated with Standard as part of his early training. By this time, the Jersey Standard had integrated operations back to oil production and controlled a substantial share of Venezuelan crude. Mexico, which nationalized its oil fields at the end of the 1930s, had set a dangerous precedent for a developing country to follow, and threatened private ownership of oil everywhere. Nelson took it upon himself to try to shape a different outcome in Venezuela.

[42]Ibid., pp. 49–55, 138–143, 246–248, 275–276, 297–301.

[43]Ibid., pp. 285–288.

His answer was VBEC (Venezuela Basic Economy Corporation), an offshoot of IBEC (International Basic Economy Corporation), corporations originally designed to blend public and private investment and to insure that Venezuela would not simply be a place where valuable commodities were extracted with nothing left for Venezuelans. The purposes of VBEC changed over time from improved food distribution, services, and promoting nonoil businesses to a straight profit-making enterprise that posed no threat to ordinary capitalistic ventures. VBEC and IBEC were prototypes for multinational business organizations, especially in agribusiness.[44]

Nelson also took an appointment in the government of Franklin Delano Roosevelt as Coordinator of Inter-American Affairs. In Washington, Nelson, now *with a federal budget*, created a Mini-Office within the national government and helped shape the Latin American policy of the United States.[45] When World War II was over, he served as an unofficial delegate at the formation of the United Nations in San Francisco, and advocated the admission of countries like Argentina whose own fascism and wartime affiliation with European fascists jeopardized its admission to the UN. If Argentina was fascist, it was not communist, suggesting a distinction that would be critical in determining friendly and unfriendly countries for a long time to come.[46]

In addition, Nelson was a four-time governor of the state of New York, an unsuccessful republican candidate for President, and finally Vice President under Gerald Ford, after Richard Nixon resigned under threat of impeachment. A more intimate connection between the Rockefellers and politics at all levels cannot be imagined.

The career of David, Junior's youngest son, also intersected with politics. He was active on both the near front—New York City politics and city planning—and the distant front—world politics—through Chase Manhattan Bank, where he served as Chairman of the Board. The Chase, created out of a number of merged banks, was an outgrowth of Standard Oil revenues and at one time was the largest bank in the United States.

Chase became heavily involved in international finance, where, as noted above in the discussion of the House of Morgan, the line between business and government often disappears. Development strategies often turn on the availability of finance, and Chase thus became intimately involved in policies for economic development not only in Latin America but also in other parts of the world. David was also a principal in the Council on Foreign Relations, an influential group formed by the Rockefellers for the study of the foreign policy of the United States.[47]

In addition to the brothers themselves, there was a steady stream of Rockefeller professionals moving between New York and Washington to serve in official and unofficial capacities in both Democratic and Republican admin-

[44]Ibid., pp. 261–262, 411–412, 540–541.

[45]Ibid., pp. 211–213, 226–232.

[46]Ibid., pp. 234–241.

[47]Ibid., pp. 311–313, 402-431.

istrations. The term *eastern establishment* may have been inspired in part by these professional commuters between business and government. Many people who had been affiliated with the Rockefellers served in influential positions: John Foster Dulles, Secretary of State for Eisenhower; Dean Rusk, Secretary of State to Kennedy and Johnson; Henry Kissinger, Secretary of State and foreign policy adviser in the Nixon and Ford administrations; Zbigniew Brzezinski, Foreign Policy Adviser to President Jimmy Carter.

A number of positions can be taken on this "circulation of elites":

1. There is no fundamental conflict between private purpose and public purpose, so it makes no difference that appointees to government posts were once affiliated with powerful private groups and are likely to return to them after their time of appointment has elapsed.
2. There may be a fundamental conflict between private purpose and public purpose, but the appointees can be counted on to resolve conflicts in favor of the public interest rather than the private interest.
3. There will be fundamental conflicts between private purpose and public purpose, and the appointees will resolve them in favor of the private purpose in derogation of the public purpose.

The Iran hostage case presented in the previous section can be put under (1); the bankers were paid and the hostages were released. But one can easily imagine the hostage case becoming a situation envisioned in (2) or (3) above, and that is what would worry people about lawyers for the money center banks (including Chase, where the deposed Shah of Iran had his money) taking on diplomatic roles. A comparable question arises whenever a prominent person from the private sector takes a public appointment.

If the need is for expertise, it appears logical that experts from the "private sector" be recruited for appointments. The claim can always be made that upon the assumption of public service, appointees shed their prior mental orientations and put the public interest first. Nevertheless, skeptics not only doubt that this can be done, but also expect a compromising of the public interest where it conflicts with the private interest.[48]

Might not Nelson and others from the Rockefeller organizations who took governmental posts have acted simply out of a desire to render public service, like making a no-strings-attached gift to a church or school, or funding useful research through endowed foundations? Yes and no. The Rockefellers clearly viewed their public service as being in the interests of the country rather than self-serving. But it is not hard to find substantial overlap between positions that might be helpful to the Rockefellers as business people and the public positions they advocated.

Two general points will have to suffice concerning an issue that would require lengthy biographies to definitively prove. A main debate after World War II concerned the postwar organization of the economy of the United

[48]An early warning on the subordination of public interests to private interests is Robert Fellmuth, *The Interstate Commerce Omission* (New York: Grossman, 1970).

States and the world. Was it to be capitalistic or socialistic? At the bottom of this debate lay two grand themes. First, power—is power to be privately held and exercised with minimal state surveillance, or publicly held with extensive public decision making? The capitalist answer entails private power holding with state surveillance limited to cases of manifest abuses.

Second, property—what can be property, how is property to be held, in what quantities, and by whom? The capitalist answer is that anything can be privately held property (including buried treasure, like oil), in unlimited amounts (subject only to monopoly laws), and forever (using the corporate form of ownership). The socialist approaches to property, which limit any or all of the above, would have been anathema to the Rockefellers, the enterprises from which they derived their wealth, and to all other families and enterprises similarly situated. Their preferred direction for state policy comes tumbling out of these indispensable needs; the state must not challenge private power and private property. With high stakes like these, Rockefeller involvement in matters of state was necessary, rather than a public-spirited hobby.

A second general point concerns the preferred economic systems in other countries. Nationalization or other schemes of public control of oil or other critical resources jeopardize the ability of multinationals to own and develop them, to privately determine the rate of use or conservation, and to choose the disposition of output and the recipients of the proceeds therefrom. Accordingly, "development" must follow the same lines as domestic policy regarding the allocation of power and the holding of private property, if the existing stakeholders of power and wealth holders are to persist.

From this perspective, the formation of VBEC and other policies advocated by the Rockefellers in Venezuela were perfectly predictable measures designed to deflect nationalistic pressures for the control of oil.

CONCLUSION

At this point we have almost become buried in these illustrative examples of the relationship of business to power and the state. The theory of John Gaventa would have had us look for an economic base and then the construction of political insulation around that economic base to prevent interferences with it. The movement of both Morgan and the Rockefellers toward more involvement in politics instead of retreating to their economic strongholds supports his contentions; their strongholds could not have been kept strongholds without extending perimeters to include politics.

Gaventa would also predict that the holders of power would cultivate certain images and encourage habits of thought conducive to the persistence of power rather than its overthrow. The "philanthropic work," "public service," foundation-funded research, establishing colleges and universities, and working with churches can be characterized in several ways: first as charitable and public-spirited, second as self-serving and private, and third as mixed—not necessarily devoid of kindness, but also designed to head off unfavorable images of the Rockefellers as mere money grubbers who don't deserve their privileges.

There is also some confirmation of the thesis of Ralph Miliband in these accounts of dynastic wealth. A complete list of the circulation of elites between the Morgan and Rockefeller interests and the state would be long. What these elites did—serve private interests, public interests, or both—has taken authors full-length works to answer. On what chambers of the state they brought their influence to bear has also required exhaustive historical proof. Nevertheless, it can safely be said that the efforts to shape public affairs was certainly made, even if it was not always completely successful.

As the stakes got higher and especially when business and finance became international, the political activities of the business families and their commercial networks became more intense, the reverse of the expectation that once money is made the focus can shift to philanthropy or unrewarded public service.

CHAPTER 4

Political Economy

A German philosopher at one time wondered whether philosophy would one day devour itself.[1] Philosophy had become so focused on semantics and logic chopping that it had totally abandoned the original purposes for which philosophy had been studied—discovery of what might be a good life to lead, and what kinds of society are worth trying to cultivate. Just as philosophy had reached a dead end by cutting itself off from the world and inquiry that mattered, so too, until the current period, *pure* or *positive* economics had become thoroughly dominated by truncated inquiry and overrefined models and was losing any utility in helping us find our way in the modern world.

How are *equitable* systems of production and distribution to be organized and maintained? Can markets, private property, and historical divisions of labor be relied upon to make scarce resources go around as far as possible? The avoidance of qualitative judgments that questions of this type require meant that economics ran the greater risk of devouring itself. The costs of avoiding value-laden questions and using highly refined, but often irrelevant economic models could become too high.

THE BOUNDARIES OF ECONOMICS

The separation of economics from values can be found in Joseph Schumpeter's *The Theory of Economic Development.*[2] After acknowledging that "social process" is an indivisible whole, he states the areas of inclusion and exclusion for economics:

> . . . [E]conomic facts result of economic conduct. And the latter may be defined as conduct directed towards the acquisition of goods... [S]ince we are concerned only with that economic conduct which is directed towards the acquisition of goods through exchange or production, we shall restrict the concept to these types of acquisition *while we shall leave that wider compass to the concepts of economic motive* and *economic force*, because we need both of them *outside* the narrower field within which we shall speak of economic conduct. [emphasis added][3]

Schumpeter's definition of economic facts leads to a modest claim for the discipline of economics. The economist will not deal with everything touching

[1]E. Cahn, "Law in the Consumer Perspective," 112 *University of Pennsylvania Law Review* (1963).

[2](New York: Oxford, 1961).

[3]Ibid., p. 3.

on economic activity, for example, what impels people to behave in economic ways, or where economic forces lead. Economists *as economists* need not consider all *sources* of economic facts nor all of the *effects* of economic activity.

To push Schumpeter's definition of the field further, how does an economist know when to stop studying or trying to explain things, and when to start delegating problems to people outside economics? As soon as the economist finds that a *causal* role is noneconomic, he says:

> If I could say . . . that . . . ground rent is founded on the differences in the qualities of land, the economic explanation would be completed. If I can trace particular price movements to political regulations of commerce, then I have done what I can as an economic theorist, because political regulations of commerce do not aim immediately at the acquisition of goods through exchange or production and hence do not fall within our concept of purely economic facts.[4]

For Schumpeter and many economists, economics as a science ends where qualitative choices and the political process begin. Rather than being imperialistic and following promising leads across the disciplinary boundary, many economists simply stop and mind more limited business. This enables them to say that their discipline is *value free*. (One of the curious aspects of Schumpeter's own career was his failure to follow his own prescriptions regarding the appropriate domain for economists; his most serious works endorsed monopoly profits as a source of innovation in an economy, and he preferred capitalism over socialism.)[5]

A more contemporary example of economic orthodoxy comes from the World Bank and its chief economist, Lawrence Summers, on toxic wastes and whether to put them in less developed countries (LDCs). The following is excerpted from a 1991 memorandum (leaked to the press).[6]

MEMORANDUM, *Lawrence Summers*

December 12, 1991

Just between you and me, shouldn't the World Bank be encouraging more migration of the dirty industries to the LDCs? I can think of three reasons:

(1) The measurement of the costs of health-impairing pollution depends on the forgone earnings from increased morbidity and mortality. From this point of view a given amount of health-impairing pollution should be done in the country with the lowest cost, which will be the country with the lowest wages. I think the economic logic behind dumping a load of toxic waste in the lowest-wage country is impeccable and we should face up to that.

(2) The costs of pollution are likely

[4]Ibid., p. 5.

[5]See R. Lekachman's preface to J. Schumpeter, *Can Capitalism Survive?* (New York: Harper, 1978).

[6]A copy of the Summers memorandum is on file with the author.

to be non-linear as the initial increments of pollution probably have very low cost. I've always thought that under-populated countries in Africa are vastly under-polluted; their air quality is probably vastly inefficiently low [sic] compared to Los Angeles or Mexico City. Only the lamentable facts that so much pollution is generated by nontradable industries (transport, electrical generation) and that the unit transport costs of solid waste are so high prevent world-welfare-enhancing trade in air pollution and waste.

(3) The demand for a clean environment for aesthetic and health reasons is likely to have very high income-elasticity. The concern over an agent that causes a one-in-a-million change in the odds of prostate cancer is obviously going to be much higher in a country where people survive to get prostrate cancer than in a country where under-5 mortality is 200 per thousand. Also, much of the concern over industrial atmospheric discharge is about visibility-impairing particulates. These discharges may have very little direct health impact. Clearly trade in goods that embody aesthetic pollution concerns could be welfare-enhancing. While production is mobile the consumption of pretty air is a non-tradable.

Comments and Questions

1. Before going further, examine carefully the statements made by Summers and indicate what a fair reading of them would be.
2. The Summers memorandum was taken very seriously by environmentalists and by spokespeople in other countries. The Brazilian minister for environmental affairs found the memorandum to be "an insult to thinking people all over the world."[7]
3. There are a number of economic or near-economic terms and phrases in the memorandum that warrant decoding and reflection:
   a. . . . the *costs* of health-impairing pollution depends on the *forgone earnings* from increased morbidity and mortality . . .
   b. The *costs* of pollution are likely to be *non-linear* . . .
   c. *under-populated* countries in Africa are vastly *under-polluted.*
   d. *unit transport costs* of solid waste prevent *world-welfare enhancing trade in air pollution and waste.*
   e. The demand [for a clean environment] is likely to have *high income-elasticity.*
   f. the concern over an agent that causes a one-in-a-million *change in the odds* of prostate cancer is obviously much higher in a country where people survive to get prostate cancer . . .
   g. Clearly trade in goods that embody aesthetic pollution concerns could be *welfare enhancing.*

[7]*LA Times,* March 1, 1992, p. M5.

REPLY OF LAWRENCE SUMMER[8]

After the publication of portions of the memorandum in a number of prominent magazines and newspapers, Summers came forth with an explanation. He said that the story had "quoted selectively" from a memorandum that had been circulated for discussion within the World Bank. He added that, "it is not my view, the world bank's view, or that of any sane person that pollution should be encouraged anywhere, or that dumping of untreated toxic wastes near the homes of poor people is morally or economically defensible.

According to Summers, the purpose of the memorandum had been "to sharpen the debate on important issues by taking as narrow-minded an economic perspective as possible" and "to clarify what had been rather vague internal discussion." He also said that he "deeply regreted the misunderstandings my memo caused."

Despite these disclaimers, environmental groups and spokespeople in other countries continued to be bothered by what in its best light was insensitive and in poor taste as a joke, and in its worst light, was an accurate reflection of the World Bank's problematic environmental record.

The World Bank said that the Summers memorandum was "merely trying to provoke debate," which it certainly did. Readers can draw their own conclusions about the disingenuousness of the Bank's reaction and Summers's own reaction to the unauthorized publication of his memorandum. What seems more critical is the implicit affirmation that economics is or can be "value free" and that economists can simultaneously defend taking a "narrow-minded" approach that produces "inescapable logic" while in the next document disavowing where that approach and logic lead. If what Summers himself says about sanity is true, then by his own admission economic method and logic can lead to insane conclusions for which he must take responsibility.

Self-imposed limitations on the proper domain of economics have been the complement of self-imposed limitations placed by pluralist political scientists on their work. Economists excluded "value questions," such as the way power and privilege influence economic decisions, at the same time that pluralist political scientists when studying power neglected the economic determinants of power. The result, by design, accident, or expedience, has been a critical gap between the two disciplines. Neither group, if disciplinary orthodoxies are followed, need systematically consider what all *political economists* take to be the central question of political economy—the way power systems and production-distribution systems are interconnected.

[8]Summers reply, *The Economist* (Feb. 15, 1992), p. 6.

POLITICAL ECONOMY

Political economists, with a history longer than the pure economics defined by Schumpeter or perhaps Summers, acknowledge that the boundaries between economics and politics cannot be strictly drawn without rendering both economics and politics meaningless, and worse, an obstruction to understanding. For a time, the consideration of political economy, which had a very promising start with works like Adam Smith's *Theory of Moral Sentiments* and *The Wealth of Nations* or Marx's *Capital* and J. M. Keynes's *General Theory of Employment, Interest, and Money,* fell into disuse and discredit. Because political economy was considered to be so mathematically imprecise, and it was not until the surfacing of "radical economics" in the 1960s that the field of political economy was dusted off for renewed scholarly attention.

Multinational enterprise and its prolific consequences was one topic that kept slipping out from under conventional economic explanations, and played a large part in the resuscitation of political economy. The late Stephen Hymer, one of the prominent radical economists, came to the limits of his training and needed to move further:

> Both in my study of Ghana and my study of foreign direct investment, the disproportion between the questions I was asking and the tools I had to deal with them grew daily. But I was a reformist and tried to incorporate what I was learning about society and politics into the analytical framework of economics. I held too fast to what I had learned in school.[9]

Two ideas stand out in Hymer's commentary: first, there was a "disproportion" between problems and the available answers; and second, he was a reluctant radical, that is, he preferred to stay within his training but simply could not. Rather than cut the world down to disciplinary size, he resolved to go where the problems took him, beyond the boundaries of straight economics.

After moving well beyond his training, Hymer asked:

> What will be the effect . . . of the tendency of the system to produce poverty as well as wealth, underdevelopment as well as development? . . . A regime of North Atlantic Multinational Corporations would tend to produce a hierarchical division of labor between geographical regions corresponding to the vertical division of labor within the firm. It would tend to centralize high level decision-making occupations in a few key cities in advanced countries, surrounded by a number of regional subcapitals, and confine the rest of the world to lower levels of activity and income . . . Income, status, authority, and consumption patterns would radiate out from these centers along a declining curve and the existing pattern of inequality and dependency would be perpetuated. The pattern would be complex, just as the structure of the corporation is complex, but the basic relationship between different countries would be of superior to subordinate, head office and branch plant.[10]

[9]R. Cohen, et al., "Making of a Radical Economist" in Stephen Hymer, *The Multinational Corporation: A Radical Approach* (New York: Cambridge, 1979), p. 277.

[10]S. Hymer, "The Multinational Corporation and the Law of Uneven Development," in *Economics and World Order* (New York: Macmillan, 1972), p. 114.

Is the foregoing commentary what one would expect from an economist? The average person might say yes, since all of Hymer's prophecies look so close to production and distribution systems that they would seem to be pertinent subjects for economists to explore. If the approach of Hymer were to be used on the question of toxic wastes and what should be done with them, would the analysis of Hymer match the analysis of Summers and the World Bank? Probably not. Hymer would no doubt demand more circumspection. The result might be a map of toxicity that parallels his description of the flow of economic benefits from multinational networks, with the unwanted toxic wastes going to the underdeveloped countries: products out, toxicity in; those who get most would suffer least, and those who get the least would suffer the most.

Many economists would dismiss Hymer's commentary, and the extension of his approach to the problems of toxic wastes, as nothing more than a series of polemical statements of political preference that cannot be systematically studied, quantified, or resolved. His selection of the "wrong" domains of study pushed Hymer beyond the community of economists, as MIT's initial decision not to publish his controversial Ph.D. dissertation attests.[11] By contrast, Summers obeys disciplinary rules and thereby stays officially sane, and free to draw insane conclusions that can be disavowed, when challenged.

Martin Staniland in his useful book, *What is Political Economy*?[12] expands on the doubts raised by economists like Hymer about the adequacy of the discipline, and gives three critiques of straight economics that inspired the revival of the abandoned field of political economy:

1. *Explanatory critique*. Without a consideration of power or other "noneconomic" factors, economists cannot explain economic behavior. If psychology and values produce economic preferences, then economists are not free to assume them away and choose their own starting points for analysis.
2. *Political critique*. Economists practicing "pure" economics are power blind, to the point where even the subject of monopolies found in all the basic texts does not usually take them to a consideration of power. Monopolies are considered simply to be the opposite of pure competition, and are not studied for what they might disclose about the impact of power in so-called free markets.
3. *Moral critique*. It was a combination of the political critique and the moral critique that activated radical economists in the 1960s. A "self-contained professional discourse" obscured values implicit in the dis-

[11]Charles Kindleberger wrote the foreword to the posthumous publication by MIT of his thesis, *The International Operation of National Firms; A Study of Foreign Direct Investment* (Cambridge: MIT, 1976).

[12](New Haven: Yale, 1985).

course while simultaneously declaring illegitimate value judgments and policy preferences. Lawrence Summers in his pollution memorandum at the World Bank seems to both reject a value-laden analysis while writing a memorandum filled with value implications. Radical economists demand a better fit between economics and the world, between economist as economist and economist as person, and less breach between technique and principle.[13]

International Political Economy

Once back on the academic agenda, what have been the focal concerns in political economy, especially those relevant to the study of multinationals? Just how are systems of political power related to systems of production–distribution?

As one might expect, the theoreticians from the marxist side endorsed *economic determinism* along the lines of Stephen Hymer and Ralph Miliband, whose thesis was discussed in the last chapter. Wealth was translated into power. Economic position comes first and politics follows; the ruling ideas are the ideas of the economic elites.

Others found cases of *political determinism*, political power translated into economic advantage. Scholars studying cases from postcolonial Africa found a scramble for political control of the newly constituted states, which in turn could be translated into economic power and privilege.[14]

Still others contended that whether power controls production–distribution systems or those systems shape political systems need not be answered, because the two are mutually reinforcing; there is an *ongoing* and *reciprocal interaction* between wealth and power, one rarely occurring without the other. The accounts of dynastic wealth in the last chapter support the third thesis, at least for all periods subsequent to the one when the economic base was first established.

Theories of cause and effect or a reciprocal relationship between power and wealth have special consequence in the study of multinationals. Must a particular nation-state bring its policies into congruence with economic facts of life, or can a particular nation state resist economic forces when they are inconsistent with local needs as the nation-state would define them?[15] These questions were once asked only about "developing countries" and not about fully industrialized countries.

People of the United States are now asking whether United States politics, its economy, and, in the end, American freedom and a high standard of living will be conditioned by the place of the United States in the world economy. Will the same rules apply in the United States as have frequently

[13]Ibid., pp. 18–23.

[14]Christopher Clapham, *Third World Politics* (Madison: U of Wisconsin Press, 1985), pp. 39–44.

[15]For a valuable introduction to the tensions between host country welfare and international capital, see H. Schwartz, *In the Dominions of Debt* (1989), pp. 1–30.

applied elsewhere?[16] Economic determinists would say that as the world economy goes, so must go the politics of particular countries, including the politics of United States. Political determinists might conclude that the ultimate source of economic behavior, including markets, is political, rendering the decisions about nation-state welfare not exclusively determined by external economic forces. Interactionists might argue that the question cannot be answered cleanly, although many do seem to believe that over the long term economic forces restrict the political options open to a country.

Apologists for multinationals usually argue that companies face substantial limits on their discretion from the political systems in which they operate.[17] Critics of multinational power argue that multinationals can bring even recalcitrant nation-states into compliance with their objectives through an array of strategies—playing one political system off against another,[18] for example, two weak nation-states both vying for multinational investment; threatening to withdraw investment from a strong nation-state unless political conditions are kept favorable; using political influence in powerful nation-states like the United States to gain political leverage over a weaker nation state; "covertly" subverting an uncooperative political regime,[19] or simply coopting reluctant political regimes wherever they occur,[20] along the lines suggested in the earlier discussion of the political dimensions of business activity.

These divergent contentions about the interplay between economic and political forces revitalizes the study of history: Who has determined what? Under what conditions? Have nation-states been autonomous with respect to large enterprises and other nation-states, or have they been nonautonomous and subservient? Before turning to the contemporary debate over the viability of nations and the fate of national sovereignty, a brief survey of some of the principal theories of international political economy suggests the range of debate.

International Political Economy—Background

Ideas about international political economy are complicated by the multiple levels of politics that are potentially pertinent to the study. In the United States there are local governments at the town, city, and county level, there are the 50 state governments, there is the national government, and there is at least some international government as established by treaties or other recognized networks, such as those engendered by the United Nations.

[16]Richard Barnet, *The Lean Years* (New York: Simon & Schuster, 1980), and B. Bluestone, et al., *The Deindustrialization of America* (New York: Basic, 1982).

[17]Exxon Corporation, "Multinational Enterprises," Undated company publication. See also Doz, *op. cit.*

[18]Richard Barnet et al., *Global Reach* (New York: Simon & Schuster, 1974), pp. 254–302.

[19]Noam Chomsky, *Necessary Illusions* (Boston: South End, 1989); Donald Herman et al., *Manufacturing Consent* (New York: Pantheon, 1988).

[20]Nora Hamilton, *The Limits of State Autonomy* (Princeton: Princeton U. Press, 1982).

Additional governmental interconnections are pertinent when a company "arrives" in a "host country"—treaties between home and host country, the host country national system, and the local governmental system of the host country.[21]

The multiplicity of political "levels" that may be involved when businesses internationalize leads to the claim by multinationals that they are "highly regulated" or even "overregulated." Critics of multinationals debate the efficacy of this or that level of government in imposing consequential control over multinationals, and some argue that the more systems that might apply, the fewer there are that *actually do* apply; too many cooks spoiling the regulatory broth, or more likely, many cooks with ineffective utensils, standing around, cooking nothing. The most extreme of these positions is that the multinationals operate lawlessly, that is, without serious political-legal restraints on their behavior or discretion wherever they operate.

Since, as noted in Chapter 2, the focus on prohibitions imposed by government misses the cooperation with enterprises by governments, the extreme view should be rephrased; multinationals are *outside* for purposes of prohibition but *inside* for the purposes of subsidy, a condition where the cooks are usually not cooking, but when they are, they are cooking on special order for the international companies and their local political and business affiliates.[22]

There are also multiple levels of economy, and multiple levels and types of markets, sometimes coterminous with national boundaries and geographic demarcations, but sometimes not. As we will later see in the case of grain, the market is a world market, rendering national or regional markets subordinate to world market conditions. At the other extreme, there are *mini-reciprocity systems* where production and trade are strictly local; these are without significance beyond the locality.[23] (This is where the basket maker of B. Traven's story in Chapter 1 would fit in.) If there is a trend, the trend is toward more and more integration of the local into the world; there are likely to be fewer and fewer mini-reciprocity systems as time goes on. But this said, the world market is scarcely monolithic or made of homogeneous subsets. To specialists in tin, the markets outside tin may be "foreign" with different participants up and down the stages of production and uses of tin.

People in the United States are now being continually reminded that the United States is no longer simply a national economy and that the world economy must be taken into account in all economic and political calculations. Some theorists, such as Immanuel Wallerstein, whose "world-economy" thesis we will consider later, contend that there is only one economy—the world economy—which renders all other "economies" subservient and dependent,

[21]For a case involving the relationship of national law to treaties, see the case of *Sumitomo Shoji America, Inc.* v. *Avagliano* in Chapter 10.

[22]For an example of multinational control of a national law–government system (Honduras), see Chapter 8. Also see Daniel Schirmer, et al. eds., *The Philippines Reader*, (Boston: South End, 1987), pp. 225–272.

[23]Immanuel Wallerstein, *The Politics of the World Economy* (Cambridge: Cambridge U Press, 1984), pp. 147–151, 163–165.

and all political systems eventually become subservient to world economic imperatives.[24]

The increasing importance of the world economy is probably what excites the interest in multinational study among university students, since multinationals are the dominant players in transnational economic activity; students sense that careers and the multinational corporation will intersect. And if what Wallerstein says is true, multinationals will be major forces in politics everywhere.

"Regional economies" are also coming into prominence—the European Economic Community, ASEAN among countries of the Far East; ANDEAN among South American countries, and the free trade agreement just made covering the United States, Canada, and Mexico (NAFTA). Other regional economies—Comintern, which commercially joined the old Soviet Bloc—no longer exist. Whether these regional economic arrangements are movements within a world economy to promote more effective involvement in it, or steps backward from the rigors of a world economy is debatable.

In the case of the disintegration of Comintern, it appears that countries that were once part of Comintern are being integrated, at least for the moment, into the world economy, with heavier multinational corporate involvement. In the case of the trade treaty involving the United States, Mexico, and Canada, one wonders whether a North American regional economy is motivated by defense against the European Common Market and Japan—the creation of an island of strength as the position of the United States worsens in the world economy.

Selected Theories of International Political Economy

These complexities acknowledged, what have international political economists said about relationships among peoples and countries of the world, and what are their prophecies about the future? Extreme positions can taken first, since they show parameters of thought. They are extreme according to their belief or nonbelief in the need for political control of economic affairs. The differences in their prophecies come down to whether they believe that everyone everywhere will live happily ever after if economic forces are allowed to run their course without political interference (liberal theory), or whether they believe that depoliticized economic organization will be disastrous to everyone, everywhere (marxist theory).

As one would expect, there are theories in between the above, some calling for greater protection of "national interests" without necessarily adopting socialism, limiting by national law what free-wheeling international entrepreneurs might desire to do (neo-mercantilist theory). Others look beyond the nation-state systems toward "international regimes" that would create the right institutional balance between business-economics and law-politics (regime theory). If the economy is a world economy, then the regime theorists foresee a parallel law–government system developing alongside econom-

[24]Ibid., pp. 47–57, 80–85.

ic activity to cure the organizational mismatch between an international economy and nationally based rules and institutions. Still other theorists argue that regime theorists have run way ahead of international realities; more careful case studies must be compiled before jumping to the conclusion that "world law" now exists.

The theories at the extremes—the liberal theory ("liberal" used here in the sense of minimizing political constraints on economic decisions and letting businesses run their course) and the world-systems theory (world socialism to confront worldwide exploitative economic activity) share some common assumptions, even though their adherents wind up in very different places. They are both economic determinists, meaning that they both believe that all political systems have economic forces as their causal element.[25]

In the case of liberal theorists, political intervention will inevitably fail because it flies in the face of economic rationality and the efficient allocation of resources, which can be left only to private parties. World theorists argue that as economies go, so must eventually go politics at all levels, but instead of producing a better and efficient economy with widespread and egalitarian participation, the world theorists predict a world economy dominated by fewer and fewer people with benefits and burdens highly stratified depending on class; benefits moving to the "core" industrialized countries and detriments piling up in "peripheral," underdeveloped countries.[26]

The liberals predict more stability—world peace through economically connected countries, whereas the world-system theorists expect more and more conflict and "anti-systemic" behavior,[27] as inequalities in power and wealth build to the breaking point. World socialism is the end point for world systems theorists, but it is not clear when or how anti-systemic action will bring it about and where the world socialism will originate.

Theorists of the foregoing persuasions also have very little confidence in the nation-state, but their lack of confidence has different bases. The liberals believe that the nation-state imposes irrationality, which impedes the beneficial workings of economic decisions. Since they predict that in the long-run benefits and detriments will even out through market forces, and long-run equilibria will be established across all sectors of the world economy, the best policy is one where nation-states get out of the way.[28]

The world-system theorists also believe that the nation-state systems are ineffective, but they regard them as ineffective for different reasons. Even where a nation-state attempts to act in good faith to protect local interests in face of undesirable market results, its actions will inevitably fail in the face of an economy whose scope exceeds the enforcement capabilities of any nation-state.

[25]Staniland, op. cit., pp. 105, 106, 140–145.

[26]Wallerstein, op. cit., pp. 80–85; F. Cardoso, et al., *Dependency and Development in Latin America* (Berkeley, U of California Press, 1979).

[27]Ibid., pp. 127, 130–145.

[28]The liberal theory, also called *classical trade theory*, can be found in most elementary economics texts.

In addition to the idea that any nation-state is "mismatched" or "overmatched" when acting in good faith against world actors, the world-economy theorists add ideas about cooptation—the alignment of companies with powerful people of a nation-state who might otherwise take positions antagonistic to business. The likelihood that nation-states can act or will act effectively in a world economic system appears remote. Hence world theorists contend that anti-systemic action (that is, action taken against both the multinational and the nation-state) is the most likely long-run probability.[29]

Neo-mercantilist and *regime* theories fall somewhere in between the liberal and world-theorist schemes.[30] Both are politically driven theories, rejecting at least partially the economic imperatives implicit in the liberal and world-system theories. The neo-mercantilists (named for the seventeenth- and eighteenth-century nation-state trade policy) do not give up on the nation-state as a source of economic and trade policies to protect national interests.[31] They argue that national limits are neither obstructionist as the liberal theorists might contend, nor doomed to being ineffective or coopted as the world-theorists might contend.

The neo-mercantilists do have the practical argument that the nation-state offers the only effective counter to unwanted international business practice if market forces do not work. If the long-run equilibria and promised lands exist only in the dreams of liberal economists, and a world socialist millennia is 100 years away, the nation-state, for all its deficiencies, may be, for the moment, it.

Regime theorists argue that even though the regulatory effectiveness of nation-state systems is declining, the international scene is not so lawless or free of political constraints as some of the foregoing theories might imply. But first, what are "regimes?"

> ... sets of implicit or explicit principles, norms, rules, and decision-making procedures around which actors' expectations converge in a given area of international relations. Principles are beliefs of fact, causation and rectitude. Norms are standards of behavior defined in terms of rights and obligations. Rules are specific prescriptions and proscriptions for action. Decision-making procedures are prevailing practices for making and implementing collective choice.[32]

International regimes, so defined, seem like legal systems of a vague type. If they do exist, then the nation-state might be more expendable as the source of regulation than the neo-mercantilists think, since the control of international business activity, where necessary, can devolve to higher and more effective international "regimes." Some regime theorists say that regimes exist and are growing, citing the cases of the GATT system of trade

[29]Wallerstein, op. cit., pp. 135–145.

[30]Ibid., pp. 52–57, 77–96.

[31]Staniland, op. cit., pp. 105–110.

[32]Stephen Krasner, ed., *International Regimes* (1983), p. 2.

negotiations or the international finance "structure" that has arisen around international credit and the Third World debt crisis.[33]

Other theorists dismiss regime theory as largely wishful thinking and illusory. Professor Susan Strange[34] argues that it might be more productive of understanding of international developments to bypass the "international institutions" which preoccupy the regime theorists and follow the actual deals cut among the powerful players in international business:

> In matters of investment for future production . . . the most notable achievements . . . have . . . come through piecemeal bargaining. Most of the key bargains have been struck between governments . . . and large manufacturing and processing enterprises, some state-owned, some private, some syndicates of both. Since these arrangements will radically affect future relations of production in the world economy and the relative economic prospects of states and their governments, they cannot be ignored with impunity.[35]

Strange wants to avoid the grand theorizing that might be implicit in liberal theories, world-systems theories, "regime theories," and to a lesser extent neo-mercantilist theories. Like a lawyer, she seems to want to get down to cases before creating theory and drawing conclusions about best explanations. Her goal in constructing "bargaining maps" and assessing the net outcomes of bargaining would be to answer fundamental questions:

> . . . who gets what . . .
> What is the net result and for whom, in terms of order and stability, wealth and efficiency, justice and freedom, and in terms of all the opposite qualities—insecurity and risk, poverty and waste, inequity and constraint?[36]

Unlike what some regime theorist seem inclined to do, Strange does not gloss over the fact that there may be distinct losers in international regimes. World-systems theorists, discussed earlier, may have jumped to the right conclusion, but it is simply too early to tell without more case studies and evidence.

As we look across all of these selected theories, what can be said? Some call for no political action, some for extensive political action, even revolution where necessary. Some call for nationally based action, others for the firming up of existing international "regimes" or the creation of better ones. Still others call for gathering more information on international economic and political affairs before drawing unwarranted conclusions.

From the perspective of the multinational corporation, some theories of international political economy are more threatening to their legitimacy than others. The world-economy theory posits that the international capitalist order is the most brutal of all history and must be abandoned or overthrown;

[33]Ibid., J. Finlayson et al., "The Gatt and the Regulation of Trade Barriers," pp. 273–314; B. Cohen, "Balance of Payments Financing," pp. 315–336.

[34]Ibid., S. Strange, "Cave Hic Dragones!," pp. 337–354.

[35]Ibid., pp. 352, 353.

[36]Ibid., p. 354.

the neo-mercantilist theories rationalize "protectionist" measures taken in a nation's self-defense against what multinationals might prefer to do. Regime theories condone toleration of contemporary economic developments if appropriate international regimes are developed to alleviate tensions. Liberal theories are premised on leaving whatever corrective actions are needed to market forces rather than political forces; left alone, multinationals can do harm for only limited time.

From the standpoint of the "average person" from "anywhere," some theories are more frightening, some more consoling. The world-economy theorists find far more losers than winners in the international economic system, regardless of where people live. The liberal finds some "short-term losers" but many "long-term winners," if economies can be kept apolitical. Neo-mercantilists, in concluding that the nation-state can still assert meaningful controls on multinationals, offer some hope that national systems can check multinational corporate abuses. International regime theorists may be finding "systems" that are, on closer observation, either too ethereal to be effective, or too remote to be of much help locally.

For discussion

1. How would the foregoing theories be put in a chart form to show the principal differences and similarities among them? These charts can be constructed in small groups and then brought back to the class for discussion.
2. Which of the theoretical explanations had most appeal to your small group? To the class as a whole?
3. Buy a single issue of the *Wall Street Journal* and read as much of it as time permits. Which theory or theories of political economy seem to be most useful in understanding the news stories and features of the paper? (*Note:* Theories will rarely be referred to explicitly, and the material in the newspaper must be integrated with the theory by you.) Which theories or aspects of theories seem most helpful? Which less so?
4. Pick a sample of speech reprinted in *Vital Speeches* made by a government official or the CEO of a multinational corporation. What seems to be the theory of political economy underpinning the speech? (*Note*: As was the case with the *Wall Street Journal*, there will not necessarily be explicit references to theory by the speechmaker; this can make the exercise of digging out the theory implicit in the speech especially instructive.)

Compare notes on the preceding exercises in class. How helpful are the theories in explaining the overall directions in international political economy being reported or talked about? Do other theoretical explanations discovered through the exercise offer better insights?

5. Read an article selected at random from the monthly periodical *Multinational Monitor*. (This magazine is highly critical of multinationals.) What is the theory of political economy in the sample article? What action is called for? What is the level of action (local, national, or international) that would be required to address the criticism being made?

Nations and Nationalism in a World Economy

We are living in an odd time. The historical positions of the political left and right on the worth of sovereign nation-states and the desirability of promoting nationalism have been reversed and jumbled, and on some issues, by ironic twist, have become identical.

Parties on the left, whether of anarchical or marxist persuasion, have always preferred an internationalist position, considering the nation-state parochial and the wrong level for establishing cooperative relationships. People are citizens of the world and not a particular nation. Marx in his *Manifesto* encouraged *working men [sic] of all countries* "to unite." The International Workers of the World (IWW), an anarchically oriented union prominent around the turn of the century in the United States, carried in its name the preference for international labor organization.

The antipathy of leftists to nationalism had a number of elements, including a distrust of patriotism, the perennial control of national politics by those who were oppressing the constituencies to whom they wanted to appeal—workers, immigrants, and on some occasions women and blacks; and the nation's being primarily an engine of warfare to secure propertied interests rather than a means for peaceful cooperation and universal welfare.

Both anarchists and marxists attended the First International held over a period of years between 1864 and 1876, but they divided very early over the appropriate place of the state. Was the state to be taken over and reconfigured to secure economic and political equality for all, or was the state so *inherently* flawed that any state, regardless of who controlled it, would eventually become an order of oppression and not of liberty? The anarchists rejected the state outright. The marxists, however, wanted to take the state over and use it to institutionalize revolutionary principles. Despite marxist consolations to the anarchists that the state would "wither away" once economic injustices had been purged, the anarchists bolted and became opposed to marxism thereafter.[37]

Distrust of the state and nationalism was reinforced by the experiences with European fascism of the 1930s and World War II, which brought a number of nations to barbaric extremes.[38] It took a system to kill more than 6,000,000 people in cold blood, and that system was a nationalistically driven state. Intense nationalism and feelings of racial-ethnic supremacy furnished

[37]G. Woodcock, ed., *Anarchism* (1962), pp. 26, 27; *The Anarchist Reader* (Atlantic Highlands: Harvester, 1977), pp. 72, 73.

[38]Barbara Ward, *Nationalism and Ideology* (New York: Norton), (1966), pp. 11–15.

the motivation, but the state provided the method-apparatus. Understandably, after such experiences few would casually endorse powerful states, nationalism, and the patriotism that went with them, although to win the war against fascism, the Allies imitated the very behavior—state propaganda, spy networks, huge munitions expenditures, and militarism—to which they said they were unalterably opposed.[39]

In the post-World War II years, the left modified its international stance and encouraged "wars of national liberation" to end colonialism. If the most appropriate level of political activism continued to be the world, that objective would have to be postponed until the elimination of the vestiges of imperialism. Nationalism, a good organizing principle for the short term, could yield to a better organizing principle later.

At present, the left is divided as to whether to continue a nationalistic focus.[40] The national level appeals since it often represents the only place for effective political action, but nationalism may in the end be ineffective in confronting inequities traceable to an economy and business organizations that operate worldwide. Despite virtually everyone's believing that marxists and anarchists are the same, the anarchists still reject the marxist confidence in the state, but they agree that large aggregations of capital and power have destructive, class-stratified effects. In the end the anarchists want to eliminate the excess power that has accompanied both nations and the international extensions of nations.[41]

The political right in the United States has been more overtly nationalistic for a long time. The support for American imperialism in Latin America, the annexation of the Philippines as a colony around the turn of the century, and later, the support of laws limiting immigration and imposing protective tariffs are early indicators of a nationalistic stance on empire, citizenship, and economy.

Now the right is justifiably confused. If it follows current political policies, it is being asked to reject the isolationism that it might prefer, accept "foreign aid," and be willing to integrate the U.S. economy into a world economy that may not include them and the people they care about most. The economic life they need to save may be their own, and in their off hours they sound as unconvinced about the prospects of international businesses leading them to a promised land as people on the left have always been.

Further, there has been a reversal of the historic positions of the Republicans and some Democrats on free trade and protectionism. Earlier in history, tariffs on imports were supported by Republicans and opposed by Democrats; "protectionism," now a dirty word, was at one time endorsed by Republicans and not Democrats. At present, some Democrats and organized labor seem to be more inclined toward protectionism than they have ever been—especially if a less pejorative word can be substituted for it.

[39]G. Orwell, *Collected Essays*, Vol. I (New York: Harcourt Brace, 1968), pp. 376, 405.

[40]Wallerstein, op. cit., pp. 122–131.

[41]Richard Falk, *The End of World Order* (New York: Holmes & Meier, 1983), pp. 277–298.

White-collar workers seem less distant politically from organized labor than used to be the case, perhaps because of unprecedented layoffs and forced retirements in the recession-depression of the early 1990s. At one time white-collar workers seemed to believe that what the corporation said was largely right, and followed the "politics" of the corporation routinely. Now they may be becoming more disillusioned about the worth of unstinting loyalty to the corporation and its preferred political stances.[42] Capital flight to other countries has become a flight from all workers regardless of the color of their collars. "Restructuring" restructures everyone, not merely those on the low end of the status hierarchy. "Rightsizing" or "downsizing" can leave them out.

Thus even though corporations still encourage team play, too many white-collar workers are being cut from the team for them to take their companies as seriously as they once may have done. The prospect of white-collar workers' becoming more highly critical of multinationals and asserting this position politically where they vote—nationally and locally—appears greater than it has ever been.

High-level executives, who at one time might have favored tariff protection or other limits on free trade, now embrace free trade (except when they are in particular industries, such as steel and autos, that want protective tariffs).

One-third of imports to the United States are *intra*company transfers—goods moving from one controlled subsidiary to another; therefore, the "foreign competition" is not always foreign. In after-dinner speeches, the CEOs of major corporations often claim that they and their corporations are "world citizens," not tied to parochial ideas like nation-states, national economies, or particular geographic locations.[43] If common folk on the political right heard these speeches, their usual endorsement of private property and other business values might be shaken.

Perhaps it is small business values or older corporate values and not multinational corporate values that the mainstream right embraces.[44] Meanwhile, if multinational executives are not packing their bags to attend a marxist or anarchist International, their cosmopolitan speeches on the obsolescence of the nation-state and the need for world citizenship sometimes makes it sound as if they are!

There are reasons why many groups, including multinationals—if it comes right down to it—are unwilling to declare the nation-state irrelevant. For the marxists, state power is the object of takeover, for liberals, a unit of world government needed for at least limited purposes; for the conservatives,

[42]W. Whyte's *The Organization Man* (Garden City: Doubleday, 1956) would read like a bad joke to contemporary executives. Executives of the 1950s expected to work for life for a company, believing that if one were loyal to the company, the company would be loyal in return.

[43]See, for example P. Townley, "Going Global in the '90's", LVI *Vital Speeches* July 15, 1990, pp. 589–593.

[44]This could be the appeal of Ross Perot, who, despite owing his own success to the formation of a large computer service company, nevertheless extols older business values.

a citadel for the preservation of nativist values; and for multinationals, an indispensable source of political, financial, and legal support. Multinationals would not be able to last more than a few years without the support of the nation-states where they operate or have their headquarters. For the critical present, the nation-state is secure, if sometimes for dubious purposes.

This absence of alternatives keeps both the political left and the political right engaged, even though the left might want to be more international under the different circumstances, and the right less so. The right is still attached to the flag, patriotism, and notions of America First, which run counter to jettisoning a national base and becoming world citizens. However, the right is also presently allied to the Republican party, which could be dragging some people toward a world economy and trade policies that they would not like very much if they studied them more carefully.

Second, when it comes to law, with few exceptions, the nation-state is the only place where effective law can be made and enforced. Therefore, for want of viable alternatives, the near-term abandonment of the nation-state looks improbable. But the place of the state in contemporary thinking and action will continue to be extremely hard to follow, as the preceding discussion of the currents and cross currents of contemporary theories intimates.

Writing by political economists reflects the current debate about the future of the nation-state. Liberal political economists are inclined to regard nation-states as unnecessary impediments to allocative efficiencies, which would occur more cleanly were there no nation-states with whom businesses had to contend. Marxists are divided, some endorsing the old stand that the nation-state causes more harm than it is worth and simply postpones the inevitable need for international organization, while others say that if taken over, the nation-state offers at least some place to stand against international corporate power.

Neo-mercantilists see the nation-state as a useful source of protection of "national interests." "International regime" theorists contend that the international field is not really so lawless after all, and that "international regimes" can supplement or replace national legal systems as necessary to provide dispute resolution mechanisms.

Reading the *Wall Street Journal* for a single week with an eye on the nationalism debate will reveal bewildering currents and cross currents on the issue, sometimes marked by the same people taking different positions as they travel in different circles. The debate, when it moves beyond the abstractions of position–counter position, affects the policy of the United States on multinationals; how is not always easy to determine.

Case Studies in Political Economy

A. Grain Dan Morgan, the author of *Merchants of Grain*,[45] was an accidental political economist. As a writer for a newspaper, he was given an assignment that on the surface looked straightforward enough—do a story about an

[45](New York: Penguin, 1979).

unprecedented grain deal between the United States and the Soviet Union. While such a trade might appear utterly unremarkable today, at the time many Americans were incensed at the prospect that the United States would be feeding its archenemy in the cold war.

Expecting to write this story like any other, Morgan was in for a surprise:

> I suddenly experienced every reporter's nightmare; I found myself in the middle of a big story, and had no source. *The Washington Post* had assigned me to a brief stint in Moscow and I arrived at about the time when rumors began circulating in the United States that some companies had sold the Russians $1 billion worth of grain. How to confirm the story? What were these companies? Where were they? We had no idea. As usual the Russians were not talking. And the American government was not much help either. The U.S. Embassy seemed as ignorant as the foreign correspondents . . . Only one thing was clear: the grain companies were no paper-shuffling middlemen, jotting down orders with stubby pencils. The Russian government, second most powerful in the world, was negotiating with them, and the most powerful government apparently did not know what they were up to. The companies had authority, aura, mystery . . .[46]

Fortunately for us, Morgan could not write the quick and dirty story. Instead he went off to the library to see what "background" information he could find. It was skimpy:

> I soon found mysel]f fashioning my own historical narrative out of the bits and pieces that were available. This was an interesting lesson in its own right. Multinational scholarship of the kind required for inquiry into a subject like the grain trade is still in its infancy. The focus of historical research still seems to be on individual countries and their rulers, rather than on the world and its resources . . . That is why "unlicensed historians" like myself—free as we are from academic conventions—have made the perilous crossing into the historians' territory for better or for worse.[47]

His first findings alarm most people who read the book. Five companies, all privately held by seven families, controlled virtually all the grain trade of the world. (There are now six, since the merger of a Japanese trading company with a relatively small United States trader.) The companies were in all aspects of the trade: buying and selling in cash markets and on the commodities futures markets, as well as storing, transporting, and processing grain. (All except farming! Ironically, farmers throughout the world have come and gone with the changes of weather and prices, prosperity and debt foreclosures, while the families of traders have stayed in place for over one hundred years.)

The traders move within and beyond governments. Cargill and Continental, the companies with greatest presence in the United States, are highly interested in agricultural policies and trade policies.[48] Shifts in subsi-

[46]Ibid., pp. 14, 15.

[47]Ibid., p. 15.

[48]Ibid., pp. 188–200.

dies to farmers change prices, and subsidies for the promotion of grain exports produce more profits for the grain companies, as does the storage of grain owned by the government under agricultural support programs. The United States government under P.L. 480 has provided financing for many international grain purchases by other countries.[49]

At the same time they deal with grain grown in the United States, the traders also deal with the grains of other countries—Canada, Australia, India, and even the Soviet Union when it has surplus instead of shortage. Their orientation therefore moves quickly beyond the strictly domestic; orders to buy can be filled from alternative sources of supply, and multiple commodities can move across several countries for cash or barter. As global companies, they often do not simply move from one system of legal-political control to another, but as often transcend legal-political control altogether. The companies cite their willingness to deal with customers of all political ideologies as a social contribution, but particular countries attempting to manage agricultural systems and maximize the welfare of their own citizens may not appreciate the cosmopolitan stance of the companies, and want to assert more control over them than they are capable of doing.[50] Not many languages besides money, buyers, sellers, and logistics are spoken in the grain trade.

The movement in and out of territorially bound systems can be neatly illustrated by the following example. In it, grain moves two ways, first through the transportation network from point A to point B, and a second way—on paper—by a not-so-direct route:

> Once Cargill has its Panama and Geneva subsidiaries in place, it [can] play as freely as any other multinationals. When Cargill sells a cargo of corn to a Dutch animal-feed manufacturer the grain is shipped down the Mississippi River, put aboard a vessel at Baton Rouge, and sent to Rotterdam. On paper, however, as tracked by the Internal Revenue Service, its route is more elaborate. Cargill will first sell the corn to Tradax International in Panama, which will "hire" Tradax/Geneva as its agent; Tradax/Geneva then might arrange the sale to a Dutch miller through its subsidiary Tradax/Holland; any profits will be booked to Tradax/Panama, a tax haven company, and Tradax/ Geneva would earn only a "management fee" for brokering the deal between Tradax/Panama and Tradax/Holland.[51]

Such invocation-rejection of nations and their legal systems for tax purposes have been made more difficult by tax law changes since the time Morgan published his book, but the multinational corporations usually stay more than one step ahead of the IRS tax hounds and with the rewards from tax avoidance so high, tax strategizing is no doubt going on as you read this book.

Morgan makes a number of points about political economy. First, world

[49]Ibid., pp. 336–350.

[50]See Ibid., pp. 298–304, for a confrontation between Continental Grain and the country of Zaire in which Continental prevailed.

[51]Ibid., p. 272.

economic systems are not congruent with political-legal systems that are national, making fictitious transactions like the previous one "practical." Second, the grain trading companies are legally active and not passive, that is they create the right legal results and do not sit around waiting to obey whatever law may affect them. Third, in the eyes of the prime movers in grain, actual farming is strictly for suckers—the money is in grain trading and logistics, and not in actual production. Fourth, grain trading is non ideological; it deals with buyers and sellers wherever there is effective demand, that is, demand backed by acceptable money.

The most troubling conclusion about the grain trade that Morgan offers is that the trade runs on money and not to meet human need. In many cases feeding hungry people cannot be squared with the grain trade unless, through government subsidies like those available under P.L. 480, grain purchases are financed.[52]

Morgan could not have predicted that a simple assignment would have led to meanderings across the grain trade and beyond:

> [G]rain is a subject that takes a student down a thousand paths—back into history, forward into the future of an already overcrowded planet, and always across borders, borders of ideology, nationality, and geography. Through wheat, for example, I saw the close connection between two enormous events,the settling of North American prairies and the Industrial Revolution, with its insatiable need for bread. Instantly, the Nineteenth Century seemed less remote ... Study grain long enough and the world shrinks ... I was left with no doubt that the companies at the center of the grain distribution system are not only wealthy but important and very powerful.[53]

By a twist of fate, Dan Morgan became what was earlier said to be a characteristic of the multinational lawyer—a thinker in a multifaceted environment, going where answers to problems might be found, and breaking out new terrain when the accessible ones proved inadequate to the task. His dogged determination to get to the bottom of things is a quality worth emulating, and his book may be the best first book on multinationals for the newcomer to the field to read.

For discussion

> How can Morgan's method be transferred to other settings, and commodities or services?

B. Supertankers and the Ocean Transport of Oil Instead of nosing around musty grain elevators as Dan Morgan did, Noel Mostert, author of *Supership*,[54] climbed aboard a supertanker at Rotterdam bound for the Middle East and a load of crude oil. The *Ardshiel*, on which he sailed, was a

[52]Ibid., pp. 443–468.

[53]Ibid., pp. 21, 22.

[54](New York: Knopf, 1974).

VLCC—very large crude carrier—ten times larger than the older style 20,000-ton tankers. One quarter of a mile long and taking over three miles and twenty minutes to stop when underway, these superships revolutionized ocean shipping of oil and permanently changed the relationship of humankind to nature and the ecology of oceans.

Mostert wrote his book before the *Exxon Valdez* ran aground off Alaska, but he fully anticipated that such an accident would happen, since accidents of even greater magnitude had already happened. (The *Torrey Canyon*, which broke in half off the coast of Great Britain and France in 1967, lost 3.6 times the amount of oil as *Exxon Valdez*. *Exxon Valdez* at 10.1 million gallons does not even make it to the top ten list of "spills," some of which occurred after Mostert wrote.)

Early in his discussion, Mostert makes an odd claim: "They are the biggest ships that have ever been, their dimensions being one of the technological audacities of the century. Most of all, however, they qualify because no other ships have ever been so universally important, *none more political*" [emphasis added].[55]

A political ship. Is Mostert personifying the supership casually, or does he really mean that the ship is political? He is dead serious. The ships, at the edge of and sometimes beyond maritime engineering knowledge, are injecting unprecedented risks of unseaworthiness, collisions, and explosions that change the relationships between shippers of oil and the ecosystems that may be affected by their actions. The use of huge oil carriers raises many political questions that are largely unanswered to this day.

The ships themselves are of multinational "citizenship" typically built in Japan, owned and financed in the United States or other industrialized countries; insured in London; repaired in Europe or the Far East; sailed under the flag of Liberia, Panama, or other non-maritime country offering a "flag of convenience"; and crewed by nationals from just about anywhere, based on expense. The *Torrey Canyon* case ensnared investigators in a legal thicket that quickly became political:

> [T]he task of trying to pin down a flag of convenience ship within any accessible frame of legal jurisdiction is well-nigh impossible. The *Torrey Canyon* was owned by the Barracuda Tanker Corporation, a financial offshoot of the Union Oil Company of California, which leased the ship and had in turn subleased the ship to British Petroleum Trading Limited, which was a subsidiary of British Petroleum Company. The ship, built in the United States, and rebuilt in Japan, was registered in Liberia, insured in London, and crewed by Italians.[56]

Mostert concludes:

> For an international lawyer any suit involving such a vessel must, one assumes, be the sort of stuff of which dreams of eternal litigation are made.[57]

[55]Ibid., p. 15.

[56]Ibid., p. 60.

[57]Ibid., p. 60.

Given this legal labyrinth, it might have been understandable why instead of fussing over niceties, the British and French governments simply grabbed a sister ship to the *Torrey* when it came into a port amenable to legal procedures, and held the ship until they could negotiate a settlement of $7.5 million with the insurers.

The *Ardshiel*, on which Mostert sailed, was owned by the P & O Lines, a British company going back to the days of the British Empire. Its crew reflected ancient class stratifications of England and also mirrored the contemporary division of labor between First World and Third World. In England, as one moves out of London and northward, one drops in class, and the ship's hierarchy replicated this pattern. The captain and chief officers were from London and southern England. Navigation officers were from the northern and western counties, and the engineers were "Geordies" from the northern coal country near Scotland. The captain was a brusque taskmaster, looking back to the good old days of real discipline and proper respect. The engineers practiced a working class egalitarianism reminiscent of miners, and humanized on-board life to the extent possible on a ship as overwhelming as a supertanker. The rest of the crew were from places in the old empire: Hong Kong (4), India (10), and Pakistan (20). Even the placement and size of cabins, and the deck levels where they were located, reflected these divisions of class and status—heads and brain work above; hands and manual work below.[58]

The demand for supertankers was an outgrowth of Middle East tensions and the closing of the Suez Canal that rendered it economical for ships to circumnavigate Africa. They provided the biggest boat for the buck, and despite known risks, could at the time they were introduced sail relatively free from regulation. (Some law was later enacted in the United States covering routine and accidental spilling of oil.)

The supership exemplifies the allocation efficiencies discussed in Chapter 2 on business modeling. Instead of determining where to locate business activities for the least cost and the greatest revenues, the decision to use supertankers turned on the best relationship between the size of ship, its costs, and the cost per ton of crude shipped. The supertankers won out over smaller ships. It took no more crew to sail larger ships than smaller ones; the necessary power plant did not go up in perfect proportion with the size of the ship; and one ship rather than multiple ships carrying equivalent cargoes saved port charges, pilotage, and general administration. In 1967 superships met the critical criterion: it cost $3.29 per ton for a round trip to Europe via the Suez Canal using 80,000-ton ships, and $2.40 per ton using 200,000-ton tankers rounding Africa.[59]

Ecological costs do and do not enter into calculations. The risk of loss and damages can be calculated and "priced out" like any other contingency. (Compare the costing out of toxicity in the World Bank memorandum considered earlier in this chapter.) But as every grade school child is now taught,

[58]Ibid., pp. 85–108.

[59]Ibid., p. 73.

mere money can never be commensurate with the long-term and cumulative destruction of the environment. To use another contemporary example, Exxon will pay $1 to 2 billion in fines and damages for the *Exxon Valdez* grounding, but everyone concedes that environmental impacts are not amenable to pure monetization.

Most of Mostert's account deals with the not so felicitous relationship between economic expediency and environmental safety. The ships were of dubious structural soundness and underpowered for the various waters they had to navigate. On a single trip a supertanker like the *Ardshiel* might move from tropical heat to Southern Hemispheric winter, from wide open ocean to tight navigation in and around Europe; these varying conditions raise numerous design problems.

Some maritime terms like *load lines* can baffle the amateur, but a closer study of their application can reveal the trade-offs made between costs and safety. Where a ship sails in winter or through especially rough seas, loads must be adjusted accordingly (the load line or "marks" show the maximum level to which a ship may be loaded). An overloaded tanker in winter storms could be unseaworthy, but a lighter tanker means less payload and more cost per ton of oil shipped. Ships traveling around the Cape of Good Hope (once called the Cape of Storms) face some of the most difficult water and weather conditions in the world. To shippers it might seem senseless to adhere to more stringent load lines when only this relatively small stretch of the Middle East run might require them. They would therefore resist the imposition of international standards to that end.[60]

In general, safety standards lag behind business practices. Mostert outlines the steps then necessary to implement international standards:

> From the start, IMCO's [the IMCO—Intergovernmental Maritime Consultative Organization] concern was safety at sea, but in recent years by far its biggest concern has become pollution at sea and the framing of laws to prevent it . . . The way it does this, or anything that needs to be framed as international, is to call an international diplomatic conference. Invitations are sent out according to UN protocol lists . . . Not everyone of course attends, and any sea law we have is by and large the work of those who do . . . The majority of delegates who . . . may not know too much about maritime affairs are inclined to defer to the advice of the IMCO's technical committees and to those among them who have shipping knowledge. The latter would always be the delegates of the principal maritime powers.
>
> The complications deepen when one considers how many of the IMCO's international laws come into force. At the end of its sessions, the diplomatic conference adopts a so-called convention . . . This then has to be ratified by domestic legislation in the parliaments of IMCO members. A convention becomes international law when two-thirds of the IMCO's membership has deposited these articles of ratification. This usually takes years and years.[61]

[60]Ibid., pp. 195–197.

[61]Ibid., p. 197.

We see the same organizational mismatch in the maritime field as we saw with respect to the grain trade, where companies can move into and out of legal jurisdictions. Shipping firms and other principals in oil transporting can race ahead of constraints with the speed of agreements among companies, while regulatory bodies must deal with multiple levels of political organization, international to national. Delay and cumbersomeness are only the beginning. The influence of the companies on the content of the regulations via the representatives to international organizations, and later in "home" countries during the ratification process, is a separate, consequential matter. Moreover, whatever law is passed is not self-executing.

Mostert's concerns over the construction and operation of the giant tankers took him back to his boyhood memories of the waters off South Africa:

> I have always felt that if you set me blindfolded upon all manner of shores I would know at once by the smell and by its very air upon my skin which was the South Atlantic: one was very close to it in a small boat, to the seal,... penguins, and walrus that broke surface to calmly regard one, and to the exhilaration of that icy kelpy water exhaling into hot sunshine, such a cool impact, even in the most intense heat, like the clout upon one's nostrils of freshly cut watermelon.[62]

A few sentences later he dampens his own reveries: "More oil has been spilled, dumped, and slopped into the waters around the Cape than in any other single area of the world."[63]

The ships described by Mostert are more than political ships—they are political-economic ships, because they cause an intersection of politics and economics at every point. Looking back over the previous chapters, we can see that the supership starts with business choices about allocation of resources—the most ship for the least cost. Next business choices are facilitated by the superlawyers, who work out the intricacies of cross-national transactions covering everything from construction, to registration, to chartering and operation.[64] They become subjects for political economy by their environmental impacts alone, even though environmental impacts do not exhaust the issues they raise.

Like Morgan, Mostert suggests a method, a relatively easy if painful one, for improving one's understanding of modern enterprise and its consequences. If readers climb up on his back as he climbs aboard the *Ardshiel*, they will be carried to places from which they cannot quite return.

CONCLUSION

Thomas Kuhn in his famous *Structure of Scientific Revolutions* asked what it meant to be a scientist. The question that got him started concerned people

[62]Ibid., p. 185.

[63]Ibid., p. 185.

[64]See Chapters 9 and 10 for additional coverage of the legal complexities traceable to flags of convenience.

who thought themselves to be scientists but whose work was later discredited by knowledge that proved their "science" fanciful and wrong. He came to the conclusion that being a scientist did not depend upon one's finding the truth for now and evermore. Kuhn's central observation is that being a scientist has a different basis than the ultimate validity of one's work.

His answer concerned paradigms which he defined to be an accepted and shared world view, and accepted methods within that world view. Early scientists believed that the earth was the center of the universe and conducted experiments consistent with that "understanding." In an important sense, the fact that Copernicus later rendered these understandings obsolete did not matter. The earth-centered scientists were *talking to one another* in ways that they could all understand. Eventually, experiments rendered their world view untenable and it took a Copernicus to straighten everyone out, create a new world view, and provide ample room for new "scientists" to test the sun-centered theory he developed.

Kuhn established the idea that scientists are part of a community practicing an agreed reality, in good faith, and with no intention of upsetting their community or its understanding with revolutionary breakthroughs. Copernicus annihilated older astronomy, and it is quite understandable that many did not welcome him with open arms: if he was right, their life work was obsolete, their community destroyed, and they faced a forced choice of adapting, or leaving the field.

All disciplines are constructed along the lines identified by Kuhn. The newcomer to business, law, political science, or economics learns what the field or discipline expects, and eventually takes a place in the community of agreed values and approaches. Implicit is the promise not to rock the disciplinary boat, to threaten the community and its understanding, or to render one's fellow practitioners obsolete. These are professions of joint faith, analogous to accepting the credos and orthodoxies of a religion. If the disciplinary orthodoxies no longer fit the world, the first impulse will be to cut the world down to size rather than face unpleasant facts or reconsider the worth of the orthodoxies.

These were the dilemmas that Stephen Hymer faced. No doubt, he was trying to mind disciplinary business, get a doctoral dissertation written and be on his way, but the problems he confronted kept slipping outside the world view and research regimes that his training had provided. The fact that MIT did not follow the customary practice of publishing his thesis (they published it after his death) attests to the threat that boundary breaking presents to a discipline. It also suggests that to play with disciplines will not be received with good graces; in embarking on new ventures, the rebel states a willingness to leave the community, and to kill the community in the process. If Hymer were right, they were all wrong, and their learned writing irrelevant—not a pleasant prospect, even for those who, for the record, are committed to creative scholarship.

In a field of study like multinationals, disciplinary boundaries can be outstripped in five minutes. When one starts from a discipline and then considers the world, serious censorship of fact must be undertaken if the discipline in its given form is to survive. When one starts with problems, as Dan Morgan did with grain and Noel Mostert did with supertankers, the usefulness of specialized vision falls away.

Over these first chapters the task has been to bring ourselves to the edge of several disciplines and demonstrate the frailty of relying on any one of them to adequately enlighten us on the subject of multinationals. Fortunately, as students we are not like old scientists wedded to any one understanding, although we may share the impulse of seasoned disciplinarians to avoid novelty wherever possible because we do not know where it will take us. Like them we may want to cut the world down to size. Or we may go where the problems take us—a far more interesting, if troubling, journey.

PART 2
Legal Antecedents of Multinationals

CHAPTER 5

The Evolution of the Modern Corporation—from Corner Store to Cosmocorp

The multinational corporation both builds on and transcends the corporate form of business organization as it evolved under the law of the United States. Starting from the present time and then dropping back into the history of corporate law can be instructive, since organizational forms have undergone such momentous changes over the last 100 years. Today multinational corporations hold vast amounts of property, including other corporations and affiliated subsidiaries, everywhere in the world, in perpetuity. For example, Mobil Corporation, which in 1992 had assets of $40.5 billion, revenues of $63.5 billion, and earnings of $0.86 billion, operates all over the world.[1] It is not only vertically integrated to include all aspects of oil from the wellhead to final markets, but it is also a conglomerate company involved in oil, natural gas, coal, chemicals, plastics, and land development.

Mobil, while among the largest multinationals, is in no way exceptional in the use of the corporate form of business organization. One good place to begin learning about the unprecedented size and scope of modern business can be the annual reports of Mobil or other comparable multinationals from which information like the foregoing may be readily obtained. Caterpillar, Inc. is an easier multinational to profile than an international oil company, but it still provides plenty to think about.

I. PROFILE OF A MULTINATIONAL CORPORATION—CATERPILLAR INC.

A. Overview[2] Caterpillar Inc., with worldwide revenues of $10.1 billion in 1991, has its headquarters in Peoria, Illinois. Holt Brothers, a predecessor company, became involved in the 1880s with agricultural equipment, developing a horse-drawn combine with chain links that meant fewer breakdowns

[1] Mobil Corporation, 1992 Annual Report

[2] Based on W. Ross, "Caterpillar," in *International Directory of Company Histories* (Chicago: St. James, 1991), Vol III, pp. 450–453.

on the larger and larger tracts of land being cultivated. The Holts moved next to power sources, and substituted the steam engine for the horse on tractors and other equipment for plowing and grain harvesting.

In 1910, Peoria became the center for manufacturing and after a year the Holt Company had 625 employees. The company exported tractors to Canada and Mexico in this period and became specialists in vehicles capable of moving over forbidding terrain. World War I, with its trench warfare and shell-cratered battlefields, made the "tank" an indispensable weapon of warfare and over 10,000 Holt vehicles were used by the Allies in Europe.

Caterpillar Tractor Company was formed in 1925 with domestic production, sales, and outlets, and dealerships in Australia, Europe, and Africa. With sales in 1929 of $52 million, Caterpillar next became important as an exporter of tractors and combines to the Soviet Union for use on the vast collective farms. By 1931 diesel engines had come into common use and Caterpillar equipment was used not only in farming but also on the public works projects of the Depression era.

World War II spurred demand for tank engines and for all types of construction equipment. Sales in 1945 had reached $230 million and employment 18,300. After the war there was heavy demand for equipment to rebuild Europe, and Caterpillar established its first overseas production subsidiary, Caterpillar Tractor Ltd., in Great Britain. In 1954 Caterpillar opened subsidiaries in Brazil and by 1956 had established subsidiaries in Australia and Scotland. By this time Caterpillar had also broadened its production base in the United States with new factories in Iowa, Pennsylvania, and Wisconsin and distribution centers in Illinois and Colorado.

Presently the corporation has at least 75 subsidiaries owned in whole or in part in the United States and around the world. These legally separate entities are engaged in finance, production, and distribution. Like many other multinationals, Caterpillar also has joint ventures with a number of companies as well as countless contractual connections with other companies for the supply of components and services.

The history of the relationship of Caterpillar to the United Auto Workers, the principal union dealing with the company, has been very stormy for three decades. In 1961 12,600 workers at Peoria walked off the job. In 1964 there was another strike. After the 1961 strike Caterpillar announced a joint venture with Mitsubishi for the production of equipment in Japan, and after the second strike Caterpillar opened a production subsidiary in Belgium. In 1966 and 1979 there were more confrontations with the UAW, with a long strike and extensive negotiations. Owing to layoffs, a wage freeze, and benefit cuts, there was a seven-month-long strike in 1982.

After what had been described in the late 1980s as a new spirit of cooperation between labor and management to cut costs and improve quality, the older confrontational politics recurred in 1991, when there was another long strike.

Across the company's history, the center of product development and production has remained in the United States, but Caterpillar has also become a worldwide company with substantial production and distribution outside the United States. Whether this internationalization was simply to serve markets more efficiently and competitively, an act of self-defense against union labor, or a systematic plan to break the union by multiple sourcing of components and products, or some combination of these, has been a long-standing debate that has intensified in recent years.

B. Multinational Aspects of the Company The annual report for 1989 states the company's world orientation:

> The 1980's will be remembered by many as the decade of "globalization" as companies in diverse industries expanded their presence in the international marketplace.
>
> Caterpillar's global presence is one of its primary competitive strengths. Long before globalization became a trend, Caterpillar was serving customers around the world . . .
>
> We began manufacturing outside the United States in Great Britain in the 1950's. Now, four decades later we build products in more than 30 facilities in North and South America, Europe, Asia, and Australia. We also have contract manufacturing and licensing agreements in 14 countries. Parts are distributed from 22 facilities located in ten countries. Our supplier network spans the globe . . .[3]

Students of multinationals are especially interested in details on particular themes: where the company has facilities for production and distribution, where sales occur, where profits are earned, and the levels of employment in the United States and abroad: To what extent is Caterpillar an "American" company? These can be taken up in succession, using information from the company's annual reports, and reports made by the company to the Securities Exchange Commission.[4]

A small conclusion can precede the details that lead up to it. Caterpillar is still a major producer of equipment in the United States and is one of the country's leading exporters, with one percent of the country's total exports, and one-half of the exports of manufactured products. It has more sales overseas than it does domestically.

One might want to jump to the conclusion that Caterpillar also makes more profits overseas. However, costs, revenues, and profits for an integrated multinational company can be slippery figures, owing to the intracompany assignment of costs, and the discretionary allocation of revenues across subsidiary companies in the Caterpillar network.

The work force worldwide is getting smaller, and the work force in the United States is far smaller than it was as recently as 1979. The shrinkage is attributable to plant closings and the substitution of capital for labor both

[3]Caterpillar Inc., 1989 Annual Report, p. 6.

[4]These reports include the company's annual reports, 10K reports, and proxy statements, all of which are submitted to the Securities Exchange Commission. The following analysis is based on these public reports.

in the United States and elsewhere in the world. The overall shift in the company to a world company since the 1950s, increasing automation, and more extensive use of "outsourcing" for company production inputs can explain the increasingly bitter conflicts in labor negotiations.

C. Facilities Buried within the data on expenditures for land, buildings, machinery, and equipment are some trends. Using the company's data, we see that the company spent a total of $6.7 billion from 1981 to the end of 1991, $5.08 billion in the United States and $1.59 billion outside the United States. In the five years from 1987 through 1991 the company spent $4.18 billion, of which $3.05 billion was spent within the United States and $1.35 billion outside. For the five-year period, 27 percent of expenditures were outside the United States; for the whole period, 23 percent were outside. In 1981, 15 percent of the net property values of the company were outside the United States. In 1991, 27.6 percent of the net property values were outside the United States. The decade was marked by a number of plant closings within the United States and the announcements of more. Most plant closings took place in the United States, but some closings and consolidations occurred abroad as well—for example, in the United Kingdom, Canada, and Brazil.

CATERPILLAR, INC. EXPENDITURES ON FACILITIES[5] (IN MILLIONS)

Year	U.S.	Outside U.S.	Total	%Outside
1981	729	107	836	13
1982	454	80	534	7
1983	265	59	324	18
1984	162	72	234	30
1985	180	49	229	21
1986	238	93	331	28
1987	337	156	493	32
1988	584	209	793	26
1989	814	275	1089	25
1990	708	331	1039	32
1991	610	164	774	21
Totals	5081	1595	6676	24
1987–1991	3053	1135	4188	27

The overall number of production facilities has remained about the same, but the composition of them has changed. In 1981 the company had 21 plants in the United States; three in the United Kingdom; two each in Brazil, France, and Canada; and one each in Belgium and Australia. In 1991 the production array included 19 plants in the United States, three in France, two in Brazil, and one each in Australia, Belgium, Canada, Indonesia, Mexico, and the United Kingdom. (The foregoing does not include joint ventures.)

[5]SEC Reports.

D. Sales Sales of Caterpillar machines and engines are worldwide. Sales outside the United States, with the exception of the mid-1980s, have been greater than sales in the United States, by growing percentages, as the following chart of sales from 1979 through 1991 shows.

CATERPILLAR, INC. SALES (IN BILLIONS)[6]

Year	U.S.	Outside U.S.	Total	% of Total Outside
1979	3.51	4.1	7.6	54
1980	3.7	4.8	8.59	56
1981	3.97	5.18	9.15	57
1982	2.80	3.67	6.46	57
1983	2.93	2.49	5.42	46
1984	3.82	2.76	6.58	42
1985	3.77	2.96	6.73	44
1986	3.98	3.34	7.32	46
1987	4.29	3.89	8.29	47
1988	5.07	5.18	10.43	50
1989	5.13	5.75	11.13	52
1990	5.15	6.28	11.43	55
1991	4.4	5.78	9.83	59
Totals	52.52	56.18	108.97	51
1987–1991	24.04	26.88	51.11	53

Sales differ by foreign market, although Caterpillar has presence in all significant markets. The 1991 annual report shows where foreign sales (in billions) take place:

Europe	1.78
Asia/Pacific	1.41
Africa/Middle East	1.14
Latin America	0.873
Canada	0.658

Closely related to the level and place of sales is the source of the product that meets the sales. Again taking the company's figures (the figures can be distorted by what constitutes "the product" in an integrated world production system), of the total foreign 1991 sales of 5.7 billion, 3.5 billion were from U.S.-produced product and 2.2 from non-U.S. manufactured product. (The annual report does not show the source of the product for U.S. sales, that is, whether it was exclusively domestic product or from imported product.)

E. Profits Just where Caterpillar makes its profits will have to be skipped, for the most part, even though the question screams out for an answer as we pore over the data on production and sales. A small paragraph buried in the fine print of the company's 1992 Proxy Statement tells why it is so difficult to state the sources of profit in an integrated world company:

[6]SEC Reports.

> The product of subsidiary company's manufacturing operations located outside the United States, in most instances, consists of components manufactured and purchased locally which are assembled with components purchased from related companies. As a result, the profits of these companies do not bear any definite relationship to their assets, and individual subsidiaries' results cannot be viewed in isolation. Prices between Caterpillar companies are established at levels deemed equivalent to those which would prevail between unrelated parties.[7]

What does this mean? It is saying that when it comes to profitability in an integrated company, something meaningful can be said about the whole company, but much less can be said about subsidiary parts. Intracompany transfers—the movement of product within the company—is done at *assigned* prices, which raise or lower costs and revenues, and hence the "profits" allocable to a subsidiary unit.

A down-home illustration may clarify why it is so difficult to establish the levels of profit for subsidiaries of Caterpillar or other multinationals with integrated world operations. Assume that a person decides to run a sophisticated backyard vegetable garden using five wholly owned and managed subsidiaries: one, a seed and fertilizer supplier; the second, a soil preparation company; the third, a planting firm; the fourth, a harvesting enterprise; and a fifth business to manage consumption or sales. What "costs" or "revenues" are to be allocated to each subsidiary? You answer, "It makes no difference to the gardener—owning all gardening companies means that everything is going into and out of the same pocket." True. Taken as a whole—the gardening project—inputs and outputs can be compared. About the subparts of the process, *much less* can be said regarding the relative worth of contributions, and the assignment of values to them will be at least a tad arbitrary.

So too, with the integrated international company. There are some bases for determining the contributions and returns properly allocable to a subsidiary, but they can be quite fragile on closer scrutiny. What is the worth of a triple-bent-left-hand widget that will ultimately be assembled into a bulldozer at another subsidiary? The material quoted from the proxy statement addresses this difficulty and warns about the arbitrariness in determining the profits of subsidiaries of an integrated company. Not irrelevant to the cost/revenue problem is tax planning.

F. Employment What have been the overall levels of employment by Caterpillar, how have employment levels been changing over time, and where are people employed? The chart on page 133, drawn from annual reports, answers some of the questions.

Since 1979 overall employment has been reduced by 35,764 jobs, or 40 percent. Employment has fallen by 30,575 jobs or 44 percent in the United States and by 5189 jobs or 25 percent outside the United States. Of the roughly 15,000 people employed outside the United States in 1991, 8690 were in Europe and 4845 in Latin America. The jobs that may have been "exported" by Caterpillar were not primarily to the Third World and cheap labor. (The

[7]Ibid., p. 43.

CATERPILLAR, INC. YEAR-END EMPLOYMENT[8]

Year	U.S.	Outside U.S.	Total	% Outside
1979	69,244	20,156	89,400	22.5
1980	68,500*	19,000*	87,500*	21.7
1981	67,748	18,174	85,922	21.1
1982	46,247	15,059	61,306	24.5
1983	43,666	14,431	58,097	24.8
1984	46,341	15,283	61,624	24.8
1985	37,753	15,907	53,616	29.6
1986	35,895	17,836	53,731	33.1
1987	36,938	17,525	54,463	32.2
1988	41,370	19,188	60,558	31.6
1989	41,979	18,430	60,409	30.5
1990	40,895	17,553	58,488	30
1991	38,669	14,967	53,636	27.9

* Estimated from bar graph.

current support of the company for freer trade between the United States and Mexico may mean that more Mexican production can be anticipated after NAFTA.)

In 1985 the company explained:

> The company cut its workforce 38% in the four years ending Dec. 31, 1985. The reasons for the reduction included: new techniques in our facilities; outsourcing; and the sale of Turbomach. (Hourly employees: -24,250 jobs (44%); salaried employees: -8000 (26%).[9]

If the common expression of the late 1980s was that companies needed to get "leaner and meaner," Caterpillar looked much leaner after 1985. The company had also become more international in terms of employment since there was less drop in international employment, than in domestic. However, the situation was not simply "exporting jobs" from the United States since there were fewer jobs everywhere, if we use the 1979 figures as a baseline.

II. HISTORICAL OVERVIEW—CORPORATIONS AND MULTINATIONAL CORPORATIONS

At the extremes of the legal imagination, it is conceivable that one or a handful of gigantic corporations could own and manage every economic activity on earth, and for all time. The limits to multinationals are not to be found in legal concepts—at least those found in the corporate law as now written and interpreted. The limits to enterprise size come from sources other than law: the physical and emotional impossibility of managing at all, let alone effectively, such large entities, even with the help of computers, instantaneous communication systems, and other commonplace adjuncts of modern business; political resistance in all the places where the mythical giants would

[8]Caterpillar Inc., Annual Reports.

[9]Caterpillar Inc., Annual Report, 1985, p. 20.

operate, as loss of self-determination and local control generate irresolvable resentments; and intraorganizational warfare—unruly egos, fights among subsidiaries, and fights between the divisions and headquarters.

These tensions might move the very large corporate networks from hyper-organization to disorganization and finally breakdown. There are also finite limits imposed by the carrying power of the earth—perhaps nature will one day wake up and shake the corporate giants off her back, leaving the megacompanies like Oklahoma farmers in the Dust Bowl of the 1930s, who looked out over barren ground and had to give up farming whether they wanted to or not.

Size may generate counterpressures toward disintegration and smallness, but the present movement toward greater and greater size has been underway for 100 years. If what is permissible under present legal constructs later proves unworkable, it must also be remembered that for the critical present there is no end to the intensified concentration of control in sight.

The evolution of corporate law can best be described as the gradual elimination of limits upon corporate purposes, size and capitalization, geographic scope, and longevity. Every limit had its origins in fear; every elimination of limits is the bypassing of the fear, through the buildup of legal and business practice to the point where the limit looks impractical and old-fashioned. Prior points in the history of corporations are like the archeological remains from business cultures that have disappeared.

The 1933 case of *Liggett Company* v. *Lee* before the United States Supreme Court occurred at one of the many historical break points. Justice Brandeis, in dissent, reviewed the history of the corporate form, up to the date of his decision, and the constitutional power of government to limit the size and scope of enterprise in the interest of the individual. As a scrupulous historian he records the past, and his intuitions about the future may speak more persuasively to audiences today than they did when he wrote the opinion. One commentator said that Brandeis had a great nineteenth-century mind, not a compliment about a judge of the twentieth century. Whether he was behind the times or ahead of his times can be considered as the opinion is studied.

The background of the case is simple enough to understand. The state of Florida had passed a tax law that imposed higher license fees on owners of many stores—chain stores—than on owners of one store or a few stores. Florida was among several states responding to the transformation of retailing that threatened the individually owned and operated store. A number of corporations with chain stores challenged the reasonableness of the classification of businesses under the Fourteenth Amendment, and the majority of the Supreme Court had little trouble ruling Florida's "anti-chain store" statute unconstitutional as an unreasonable classification.

The Brandeis dissent had three main elements: the relationship of the corporation to the state, the evolution of corporate law, and the reasonableness of the fear of the state of Florida which may have impelled it to want to make life more difficult for larger-scale enterprises.

Contemporary readers who take chain stores for granted might consider his opinion quaint, which in the mind of a contemporary corporate legal adviser it clearly is, but Brandeis records in great detail the transformation of enterprise from small, locally owned and operated ventures to larger nationally based ones, and the passion with which he states his disagreement with the Court's decision demonstrates that what people today take for granted was at one time the subject of sharp debate.

Small-scale farming and shopkeeping were not far from the American dream, and neither could be threatened without challenges like the anti-chain store legislation. After reading the *Liggett* case, the next trip to the shopping mall might be a little different; besides Muzak in the background there might be the more distant voice of the *Liggett* case which, Brandeis' dissenting opinion notwithstanding, helped legitimate the distribution system that is now thoroughly embedded in the culture.

LIGGETT CO V. LEE 288 U.S. 517 (1932)

Mr. Justice Brandeis, dissenting . . .

In my opinion the judgment . . . should be affirmed . . .

Florida Laws . . . Chapter 15,624 is legislation . . . popularly called Anti-Chain Store Laws. The statute provides for the licensing of retail stores by the State, the counties and the municipalities—a system under which large revenues may be raised. But the raising of revenue is obviously not the main purpose of the legislation. Its chief aim is to protect the individual, independently owned, retail stores from the competition of chain stores. The statute seeks to do this by subjecting the latter to financial hardships which may conceivably compel their withdrawal from the State. An injunction against its enforcement is sought on the ground that the law violates rights guaranteed by the Federal Constitution.

. . . [A]nnual license fees . . . are in part graduated. If the owner operates only one store the state fee is $5; if more than one, the fee for the additional stores rises by step increases . . . The highest fee is for a store in excess of 75 . . .

The plaintiffs are thirteen corporations which engage in Florida exclusively in intrastate commerce. Each (except one) owns and operates a chain of retail stores within the State . . . Several of the plaintiffs are organized under the laws of Florida; the rest under the laws of other States . . . The suit is brought as a class suit for the benefit of all merchants similarly situated who may desire to avail themselves thereof . . .

One who would strike down a statute, must show . . . that as it applies to him it exceeds the power of the State . . .

[T]he discrimination complained of, and held arbitrary by the court is, in my opinion, valid as applied to corporations. *First.* The Federal Constitution does not confer upon either domestic or foreign corporations the right to engage in intrastate commerce in Florida. The privilege of engaging in such commerce in corporate form is one which the State may confer or may withhold as it sees fit . . .

Florida might grant the privilege to one set of persons and deny it to others; might grant it for some kinds of businesses and deny it for others; might grant the privilege to corporations with a small capital while denying it for those whose capital or resources are large. Or it might grant the privilege to private corporations whose shares are owned mainly by those who manage them and to corporations engaged in cooperative undertakings, while denying the privilege to other concerns called private, but whose shares are listed on a stock exchange—corporations financed by the public, largely through the aid of investment bankers. It may grant the privilege broadly, or restrict its exercise to a single county, city or town, and to a single place of business . . .

Whether the corporate privilege shall be granted or withheld is always a matter of state policy . . . It may be granted as a means of raising revenue; or in order to procure for the community a public utility, a bank or a desired industry . . . Similarly, if the privilege is denied, it is denied because incidents of like corporate enterprises are deemed inimical to the public welfare and it is desired to protect the community from apprehended harm.

Here we are dealing with intrastate commerce . . . If a state believes that adequate protection against harm apprehended or experienced can be secured . . . by imposing . . . higher discriminatory license fees as compensation for the privilege, I know of nothing in the Fourteenth Amendment to prevent it from making the experiment . . .

Whether the citizens of Florida are wise in seeking to discourage the operation of chain stores is, obviously, a matter with which this court has no concern. Nor need it, in my opinion, consider whether the differences in license fees employed to effect such discouragement are inherently reasonable . . .

[A] review of the legislation of the several States by which all restraints on corporate size and activity were removed, and a consideration of the economic and social effects of such removal, will help to an understanding of Anti-Chain Store Laws . . . *Second.* The prevalence of the corporation in America has led men of this generation to act, at times, as if the privilege of doing business in corporate form were inherent in the citizen; and has led them to accept the evils attendant upon the free and unrestricted use of the corporate mechanism as if these evils were the inescapable price of civilized life and, hence, to be borne with resignation. Throughout the greater part of our history a different view prevailed. Although the value of this instrumentality in commerce and industry was fully recognized, incorporation for business was commonly denied long after it was freely granted for religious, educational and charitable purposes. It was denied because of fear. Fear of encroachment upon the liberties and opportunities of the individual. Fear of the subjection of labor to capital. Fear of monopoly. Fear that the absorption of capital by corporations and their perpetual life, might bring evils similar to those which attended mortmain. ["Mortmain" means "dead hand." In earlier days it was realized that property in the hands of the Church might never become available to others again—it would sit in a dead hand. Over time, since the Church exists in perpetuity and mere mortals live and die, more and more property would come under permanent church control unless limits were imposed. —Ed.]

There was a sense of some insidious menace inherent in large aggregations of capital, particularly when held by corporations. So, at first, the corporate privilege was granted sparingly; and only when the grant seemed necessary in order to procure for the community some specific benefit otherwise unattainable. [Corporations were once created by *special acts* of the legislature—one for each corporation. —Ed.] The later enactment of general incorporation laws does not signify that the apprehension of corporate domination had been overcome. The desire for business expansion created an irresistible demand for more charters; and it was believed that under general laws embodying safeguards of universal application the scandals and favoritism incident to special incorporation could be avoided. The general laws, which long embodied severe restrictions upon size and upon the scope of corporate activity, were, in part, an expression of the desire for equality of opportunity. (a) Limitation upon the amount of authorized capital of business corporations was long universal. The maximum frequently varied with the kinds of business to be carried on, being dependent apparently upon the supposed requirements of the efficient unit. Although the statutory limits were changed from time to time this principle of limitation was long retained . . .

(b) Limitations on the scope of a business corporation's powers and activity were also long universal. At first . . . only for a limited number of purposes—usually those which required a relatively large fixed capital, like transportation, banking and insurance, and mechanical, mining, and manufacturing enterprises. Permission to incorporate for "any lawful purpose" was not common until 1875; and until that time the duration of corporate franchises was generally limited to a period of 20, 30, or 50 years. All, or a majority, of the incorporators, or directors, or both, were required to be residents of the incorporating state. The powers which the corporation might exercise in carrying out its purposes were sparingly conferred and strictly construed. Severe limitations were imposed on the amount of indebtedness, bonded or otherwise. The power to hold stock in other corporations was not conferred or implied. The holding company was impossible.

(c) The removal by the leading industrial States of the limitations upon the size and powers of business corporations appears to have been due, not to the conviction that maintenance of the restrictions was undesirable in itself, but to the conviction that it was futile to insist upon them; because local restrictions would be circumvented by foreign incorporation [Corporations created in one state are considered "foreign" corporations by other states—for example, a Delaware corporation doing business in Connecticut is a "foreign corporation." —Ed.] Indeed local restrictions seemed worse than futile. Lesser states, eager for revenue derived from the traffic in charters, had removed safeguards from their own incorporation laws. Companies were early formed . . . where the cost was lowest and the laws least restrictive. The States joined in advertising their wares. The race was not of diligence, but of laxity . . . [T]he great industrial States yielded in order not to lose wholly the prospect of the revenue and the control incident to domestic incorporation.

The history of changes made by New York is illustrative. The New York revision of 1890, which eliminated the maximum limitation on authorized capital, and permitted intercorporate stockholding in a limited number of cases, was passed after a migration of incorporation from New York, attracted by the more liberal incorporation laws of New Jersey. But the changes made by New York in 1890 were not sufficient to stem the tide. In 1892, the Governor . . . approved a special charter for the General Electric Company, modelled upon the New Jersey Act, on the ground that otherwise the enterprise would secure a New Jersey charter. Later in the same year the New York corporation law was again revised, allowing the holding of stock in other corporations. But the

New Jersey law continued to be more attractive to incorporators . . . Of the seven largest trusts existing in 1904 . . . all were organized under New Jersey law; and three of these were formed in 1899. During the first seven months of that year 1,336 corporations were organized under the laws of New Jersey . . . The Comptroller of New York . . . in . . . 1899 complained that "our tax list reflects little of the great wave of organization . . . to which this state contributed more capital than any other state of the Union. It is time . . . that the great corporations having their actual headquarters in this State and a nominal office elsewhere, doing nearly all of their business within our borders, should be brought within the jurisdiction of this State not only as to matters of taxation but in respect to other and equally important affairs . . .

The history of other states was similar. Thus the Massachusetts revision of 1903 was precipitated by . . . possibilities of incorporation in other states . . . *Third.* Able discerning scholars have pictured for us the economic and social results of thus removing all limitations upon the size and activities of business corporations and of vesting in their managers vast powers once exercised by stockholders . . . They show that size alone gives to giant corporations a social significance not attached ordinarily to smaller units of private enterprise. Through size, corporations, once merely an efficient tool employed by individuals in the conduct of private business, have become an institution—an institution which has brought such concentration of economic power that so-called private corporations are sometimes able to dominate the State. The typical business corporation of the last century, owned by a small group of individuals, managed by their owners, and limited in size by their personal wealth, is being supplanted by huge concerns in which the lives of tens or hundreds of thousands of employees and the property of tens or hundreds of thousands of investors are subjected through the corporate mechanism to the control of a few men . . . The changes thereby wrought in the lives of the workers, of the owners and of the general public, are so fundamental and far-reaching as to lead these scholars to compare the evolving "corporate system" with the feudal system . . .

[T]wo thirds of our industrial wealth has passed from individual possession to the ownership of large corporations whose shares are dealt in on the stock exchange; that 200 nonbanking corporations each with assets in excess of $90,000,000, control directly one fourth of all our national wealth, and that their influence extends far beyond the assets under their direct control; that these 200 corporations while nominally controlled by about 2000 directors, are actually dominated by a few hundred persons—the negation of industrial democracy. Other writers have shown . . . a marked concentration of individual wealth . . . Such is the Frankenstein monster which States have created by their corporation laws.

Fourth. Among these 200 corporations . . . are five of the plaintiffs. These five have in the aggregate $820,000,000 of assets . . . and they operate . . . an aggregate of 19,718 stores . . . Against these plaintiffs . . . the individual retailers of Florida are engaged in a struggle to preserve their independence—perhaps a struggle for existence. The citizens of the State, considering themselves vitally interested in this seemingly unequal struggle, have undertaken to aid the individual retailers by subjecting the owners of multiple stores to the handicap of higher license fees. They may have done so merely to preserve competition. But their purpose may have been a broader and deeper one. They may have believed that the chain store, by furthering the concentration of wealth and of power and by promoting absentee ownership, is thwarting American ideals; that it is making impossible equality of opportunity; that it is converting independent tradesmen into clerks; and that it is sapping the resources, the vigor and the hope of the smaller cities and towns.

The plaintiffs insist that no taxable difference exists between the owner of multiple stores and the owner of an individual store . . . The fee is the compensation for carrying on intrastate business in corporate form. As this privilege is one that a state may withhold or grant, a State . . . may charge such compensation as it pleases . . . Moreover, since the authority to operate many stores . . . is certainly a broader privilege . . . there is . . . no basis for a finding that it is unreasonable to make the charge higher . . .

A more comprehensive answer should, however, be given. The purpose of the Florida statute is not . . . merely to raise revenue. Its main purpose is social and economic. The chain store is treated as a thing menacing the public welfare . . . [B]usiness must yield to the paramount interests of the community in times of peace as well as in times of war . . . Businesses may become as harmful to the community by excessive size . . . If the State should conclude that bigness in retail merchandising as manifested in corporate chain stores menaces the public welfare, it might prohibit the excessive size . . . as it prohibits excessive size or weight in motor trucks or excessive height in the buildings of a city . . .

The State's power to apply discriminatory taxation . . . is not conditioned upon the existence of economic need. It flows from the broader right of Americans to preserve, and to establish, from time to time, such institutions, social and economic, as seem to them desirable; and likewise to end those which they deem undesirable . . .

[A]mericans seeking escape from corporate domination have open to them under the Constitution another form of social and economic control—one more in keeping with our traditions and aspirations. They may prefer the way of the cooperation which leads directly to the freedom and equality of opportunity which the Fourteenth Amendment aims to secure . . . For the fundamental differences between capitalistic enterprises and the cooperative—between economic absolutism and industrial democracy—is one which has been commonly accepted by legislatures and the courts as justifying discrimination in both regulation and taxation.

There is a widespread belief that the existing unemployment is the result, in large part, of the gross inequality in the distribution of wealth and income which giant corporations have fostered; that by the control which the few have exerted through giant corporations, individual initiative and effort are being paralysed, creative power impaired and human happiness lessened; that the true prosperity of our past came not from big business, but through the courage, the energy and resourcefulness of small men; that only by releasing from corporate control the faculties of the unknown many, only by reopening to them the opportunities for leadership, can confidence in our future be restored and the existing misery be overcome; and that only through participation by the many in the responsibilities and determinations of business, can Americans secure the moral and intellectual development which is essential to the maintenance of liberty. If the citizens of Florida share that belief, I know of nothing in the Federal Constitution which precludes a state from endeavoring to give it effect . . . To that extent the citizens of each State are still masters of their destiny.

Notes and Questions

1a. At the center of the Brandeis dissent lies the question of where trust for the general or public welfare should be placed. Limiting the inquiry to only two places, should people encourage the state to delegate power to private businesses out of the belief that business practice will in the end maximize public welfare; or should people insist on the state's taking a more activist role in determining the kind of business enterprises to be conducted?

b. Once the legislature of Florida has made a choice, should the Supreme Court closely scrutinize it under its powers of judicial review, or should the Supreme Court resolve all cases of doubt in favor of the legislature's action?

c. In practice, states have deferred to business judgment by granting broad powers to corporations, continuing and extending the trend that Brandeis outlined. Evaluate.

2. The preferences of Brandeis are not hard to find; he refers to the corporate trend as an "insidious menace" and a "Frankenstein monster" arousing—as menaces and monsters do—"fear of encroachment upon the liberties and opportunities of the individual. Fear of the subjugation of labor to capital. Fear of monopoly. Fear of the absorption of capital by corporations, and their perpetual life . . ."

   Are these fears rational or irrational? If the fears are rational, are conditions more worrisome under multinational enterprise conditions?

3. Brandeis also finds a relationship between the aggregation of wealth and the decline of democracy. Are the two connected, or can there be wealth on the one hand and the preservation of democracy and democratic institutions on the other?

4. One of the corporations contesting the constitutionality of the Florida statute was a chain with 16,000 stores. Presumably it was operating in areas formerly served by owner-operated stores.

   a. Would the presence of a chain store enhance or restrict competition in the short and long runs?
   b. Which retailing system would be more responsive to local needs?
   c. Which more efficient?
   d. How would local or absentee ownership figure into the equation? Opportunity to enter and run one's own business? Maintenance of a local community?
   e. If local people didn't want chain stores, would there not have been a direct way to limit their spread—not buying? Where does the resourcefulness of the individual, whose virtues Brandeis extols, start and stop?

5. The deregulation under state law of enterprise size and corporate powers does not end the legal inquiry. There remains for consideration other regulatory systems, such as laws prohibiting restraints of

trade and monopolizing and attempting to monopolize trade. These will be taken up later.

6. Students may be surprised to learn that there is no national law governing the formation of corporations and may have wondered why most corporations are "Delaware" corporations, even when they do only a tiny fraction of their business there. Corporations can be created under the laws of any one of the 50 states and then do business as "foreign corporations" in other states.

   The practice of a business's seeking most favorable law has existed across much of United States history, and Delaware, as one of the favored places to incorporate, reflects this practice. Delaware maximized corporate options upon formation, and minimized legal restraints on corporate governance.

   Other states have surfaced from time to time as the favorite place, only to be outdone by other states' adopting even more accommodating corporate law, as the following excerpts from Brandeis' extensive footnotes reveal:

> The traffic in charters quickly became widespread. In 1894 Cook . . . described . . . "New Jersey is a favorite state for incorporation. Her laws seem to be framed with a special view to attracting incorporation fees and business fees . . . especially from New York . . . and [New Jersey] now runs the state government very largely on revenues derived from New York enterprises . . .
>
> Maine formerly was a resort for incorporators, but a recent decision of its highest court holding stockholders liable on stock which has been issued for property where the court thought the property was not worth the par value of the stock makes Maine too dangerous . . . especially where millions of dollars of stock are to be issued for mines, patents and other choice assortments of property. . .
>
> West Virginia for the past ten years has been the Snug Harbor for roaming and piratical corporations. The manufacture of corporations for the purpose of enabling them to do all their business elsewhere seems to be the policy of this young but enterprising state . . .
>
> In 1906 . . . Where and How—A Corporation Handbook . . . New Jersey . . . advertised . . . The policy of New Jersey proved profitable . . . And soon legislatures of other states began active competition . . .
>
> Delaware and Maine revised their laws, taking New Jersey as a model, but with lower organization fees and annual taxes. Arizona and South Dakota also adopted liberal corporation laws, and contenting themselves with the incorporation fees require no annual state taxes whatever.
>
> West Virginia . . . increased the rate of annual taxes. And . . . lost her popularity. On the other hand too drastic price cutting was also unprofitable. The bargain prices in Arizona and South Dakota attracted wildcat corporations . . . and both states fell into disrepute . . .
>
> [A] pamphlet, "Business Corporations Under the Laws of Maine" (1903) . . . enumerated . . . advantages . . . low organizational fees and annual taxes; the absence of restrictions on capital stock or corporate indebtedness; the authority to issue stock for services as well as property, with the judgment of the directors as to their value conclusive . . .[10]

[10]Brandeis Dissent, pp. 557–565.

The state "hustle" to gut any limits on corporate prerogatives proceeded to the point where the least restrictive law drove out the more restrictive. In the end, corporations were beyond any significant state control.

7. As complete as Brandeis was, he never included the strategies used to change corporate law to meet the needs of national corporations, although we cannot believe that the changes occurred spontaneously and without the intervention of lawyer-go-betweens. Brandeis puts no smoking gun into the hands of the actors who helped coopt the political process of state legislatures and make the world safer for enterprises wanting to eliminate unwanted controls, but the results make us wonder just who was behind the changes.

   Morton Horwitz, a legal historian, identifies William Cromwell as one of the corporate lawyers whose firm drafted the amendments to the New Jersey law. The amendments made it possible to escape the limits that states such as Ohio were imposing limits on such business trusts as Standard Oil. Standard Oil trust could "legally" flee from the state of Ohio to New Jersey once the New Jersey law was passed. After 1899, national companies could operate as holding companies, which allowed Standard Oil to hold stock in participating companies directly and not indirectly through trusts.[11]

8. We see in the history of the transformation of corporate law an example of the selective invocation and rejection of legal systems by those business organizations whose activities are large enough to make the search for the greatest legal advantages economical. To say that corporations invariably want to escape from law tells only half the story, since corporations create and invoke the "right" kind of law as well as avoid unwanted law. If Ohio law was disliked by Standard, New Jersey law was desired.

Throughout history larger enterprises have been semi-lawless and semi-law abiding, a characteristic which frustrates students looking for a consistent philosophy like "getting the government off the back of business."

By 1967, when the next reading appeared, the debate had shifted from the ability of one of the 50 states to regulate corporate activity to the propriety of the nation as a whole, or of other nations throughout the world, asserting control over businesses that had by this time outgrown their national limits. The same larger implications appear here as in the *Liggett* case.

Needed: an international companies law that will enable the world enterprise to pursue the true logic of the global economy without ceaseless interference from its puzzled parent, the sovereign nation.

[11]M. Horwitz, "Santa Clara Revisited," 88 *West Virginia Law Review*, 1986, p. 173.

COSMOCORP: THE IMPORTANCE OF BEING STATELESS[12]

George W. Ball

. . . In these twenty postwar years, we have come to recognize in action, though not always in words, that the political boundaries of nation-states are too narrow and constricted to define the scope and activities of modern business. This recognition has found some reflection, though not enough, in political action. Six countries of Western Europe have frontally attacked the stifling restrictions imposed on trade by shedding the ancient concept of nation-states. They have created a thriving common market.

In the summer of 1968 goods will move with full freedom throughout Western Europe to serve the needs of nearly two hundred million people. . . .

The importance of common markets and free trade areas rests not only on their economic efficacy but also on the seeds of political unity they carry with them. . . .

International trade, as everyone knows, is as old as time. International-ized production is less familiar. Businessmen in the United Kingdom are old hands at making their living in world markets and exporting capital to produce goods abroad. This has not always been true of the United States. Except in extractive industries, most U.S. enterprises until recent times have concentrated their activities on producing for the national market, exporting only their surplus. Many still do. However, this is no longer adequate for the requirements of the world we live in. In order to survive, man must use the world's resources in the most efficient manner. This can be achieved only when all the factors necessary for the production and use of goods—capital, labor, raw materials, plant facilities and distribution—are freely mobilized and deployed according to the most efficient pattern. And this in turn will be possible only when national boundaries no longer play a critical role in defining economic horizons.

It is a fact of great import, therefore, that, at a time when politicians have been moving to create regional markets to supersede national markets, businessmen have been making quiet progress on an even larger scale: The great industrial enterprises of the world are moving to recast their plans and design their activities according to the vision of a total world economy.

In this development, as is so often the case in history, commerce has been in advance of politics. In a thoroughly pragmatic spirit it has improvised the fictions needed to shake free from strangling political impediments. To make possible the global activities of modern business, it has extended the fiction of the corporation—that artificial person invented by lawyers to free entrepreneurs of personal liability in doing business and thus enable them to mobilize capital from diverse financial sources. The corporate form was originally conceived as a special privilege granted by states to some businessmen for attainment of the states' political purposes. But, over the years, the corporate form of business has become common everywhere and enabled business to roam the world with substantial freedom from political interference, producing and selling a multiplicity of national markets and creating corporate offspring of various nationalities.

[12]G. Ball, "Cosmocorp: The Importance of Being Stateless," *Columbia Journal of World Bus.* II 6 (1967). Copyright © 1967 by *CJWB*. Reprinted by permission.

. . . Today we recognize the immense potentials of the emancipated corporate person. For at least a half century, a handful of great companies have bought, produced and sold goods around the world. Since the Second World War the original handful has multiplied many fold. Today a large and rapidly expanding roster of companies is engaged in taking the raw materials produced in one group of countries, transforming these into manufactured goods with the labor and plant facilities of another group, and selling the products in still a third group. And, with the benefit of instant communications, quick transport, computers and modern managerial techniques, they are redeploying resources and altering patterns of production and distribution month to month in response to changes in price and availability of labor and materials.

This is an achievement of impressive magnitude and we are only beginning to know its implications. By no means all industries in the United States or elsewhere have comprehended the full meaning and opportunity of the world economy. But they will soon. Meanwhile we can detect the extent to which the concept shapes corporate thinking by the attitudes of management toward liberal trade.

By and large, companies that have achieved a global vision of their operations tend to opt for a world in which not only goods but all of the factors of production can shift with maximum freedom. Other industries—some of great size and importance in the United States, such as steel and textiles—which have confined their production largely or entirely to domestic markets, anxiously demand protection whenever a substantial volume of imports begins to invade national markets.

. . . American businessmen have become involved in world trade to an extent where they can no longer turn their backs on it. But trouble will always arise in some places as business continues to expand its horizons. Conflict will increase between the world corporation, which is a modern concept evolved to meet the requirements of the modern age, and the nation-state, which is still rooted in archaic concepts unsympathetic to the needs of our complex world.

. . . Even in economically advanced Western Europe the concern of local enterprises over the superior size and resources of the global company is being loudly voiced. European businessmen are worried because the measures taken to liberate the movement of goods have preceded adequate modernization of the structure of their own enterprises. They have not had time to build up their strength. They have not yet effected the across-boundary industrial concentration that is essential for European industry to stand on its feet and meet the competition of direct investment by the great global corporations.

The problem is perhaps even graver in Canada, where business and political leaders are deeply worried about how they can maintain their national integrity while living next to an economy 14 times the size of their own, and yet not jeopardize the inflow of investment capital on which their prosperity depends.

We see comparable phenomena in the developing countries. Hypersensitive to anything that suggests colonialism, they are afraid their economies will fall under foreign domination and, to prevent this, they impose obstacles to the entry of foreign firms, thereby blocking the inflow of the capital they desperately need. . . .

A greater menace may come from the actions of governments addicted to a regime of planning, who see in the global corporation a foreign instrumentality that may frustrate their economic designs. The basis for their concern is easy to understand, especially in countries where a world company, if allowed in, would become the largest employer of national labor and consumer of national materials. The problem is something like this: how can a national government make an economic plan with any confidence if a board of directors meeting 5,000 miles away can by altering its patterns of purchasing and production affect in a major way the country's economic life?

. . . The government of the United States is far from blameless in the corporation–state struggle. On more than one occasion it has sought to enforce its domestic legislation abroad by trying to extend its writ to actions of foreign subsidiaries of American companies. But, happily, there is a growing realization in the United States that we cannot use American-based world corporations as vehicles to export our own national psyche—our prejudices, whether with respect to trading with China or other communist countries or to controlling monopolies or concerning practices—without diminishing the utility of the corporate institution itself. And if we are going to be consistent in our encouragement of the world economy and the global company that inhabits it, we shall have to change our ways.

. . . [I]t is in the nature of things that the world company should frequently tread on hostile ground.

. . . The dilemma arises because neither the people nor the government of the country in question plays a part in selecting the directors or the management of world corporations. Since it is only through national legislation that managements can be made in any way responsible to the local people, there is bound to be frustration when the managements of world firms are out of reach of such legislation.

[T]here is an inherent conflict of interest between corporate managements that operate in the world economy and governments whose points of view are confined to the narrow national scene.

. . . One obvious solution is to modernize our political structures—to evolve units larger than nation-states and better suited to the present day. But that is going to take a long time. Meanwhile, many company managements, sensitive to the problem if not always to the full range of considerations that produce it, have developed corporate diplomacy to a high level of sophistication. Not only do they take great pains to ease pressures on national governments but many seek to attach a kind of national coloration to their local subsidiaries.

These commendable efforts take a variety of forms. For example, some world corporations associate themselves with local partners; others take only minority holdings in their local affiliates. In some cases they leave effective control of local subsidiaries to local managers while inserting only a minimum of direction.

While leaving control to the local managers sometimes works well, often it gives rise to additional problems. It is clear to me that national ownership in local subsidiaries impedes the fulfillment of the world corporation's full potential as the best means yet devised for utilizing world resources according to the criterion of profit: an objective standard of efficiency.

The obvious drawback of local ownership interests is that they necessarily think in national and not in world terms. Thus they are likely to impress their narrowly focused views on vital policies having to do with prices, dividends, employment, the use of plant facilities in one country rather than another, even to the source of component materials. In other words, once the central management of a global company is restricted to the divergent interests of national partners, it loses its ability to pursue the true logic of the global economy.

This leads me to suggest that we might do well to approach the problem at a different level, not by nationalizing local subsidiaries but by internationalizing or perhaps more accurately denationalizing the parent. Only in this way can we preserve the full economic promise of the world corporation as an institutional instrument of the world economy.

. . . The essence of this suggestion is that those artificial persons whom I have referred to as world corporations should become quite literally citizens of the world. What this implies is the establishment by treaty of an international companies law, administered by a supranational body, including representatives drawn from various countries, who would not only exercise normal domiciliary supervision but would also enforce antimonopoly laws and administer guarantees with regard to uncompensated expropriation. An international companies law could place limitations, for example, on the restrictions nation-states might be permitted to impose on companies established under its sanction. The operative standard defining those limitations might be the quantity of freedom needed to preserve the central principle of assuring the most economical and efficient use of world resources.

Obviously such an international company would have a central base of operations. It would not be like Mohammed's coffin, suspended in air. It is clearly unnecessary that there be a single profit center. The international company's operations in its home country would be subject to local laws, to the extent that they do not infringe the overriding regulations of the organic treaty.

I recognize, of course, that a company will not become effectively a citizen of the world merely by a legal laying on of hands. It requires something more than an international companies law to validate a company's passport: the company must in fact become international. This means among other things that share ownership in the parent must be spread through the world so that the company cannot be regarded as the exclusive instrument of a particular nation. Of course, in view of the underdeveloped state of most national capital markets, even in economically advanced countries, this is not likely to occur very soon. But eventually, as savings are effectively mobilized for investment in more and more countries, companies will assume an increasingly international character. At the same time, we can expect a gradual internationalizing of boards of directors and parent company managements.

. . . But let me be quite clear on one point. This proposal does not rest on the notion of world government or anything resembling it. I have lived far too long on the exposed steppes of diplomacy and practical politics to believe in such an apocalyptic development within foreseeable time. Nonetheless what I am suggesting necessarily has its political implications. Freeing commerce from national interference through the creation of new world instrumentalities would inevitably, over time, stimulate mankind to close the gap between the archaic political structure of the world and visions of commerce vaulting beyond confining national boundaries to exploit the full promise of the world economy.

Notes and Questions

1a. Brandeis identified fears that Floridians might have had about chain stores. What fears might the people of other countries have about multinationals being more extensively present as extractors of raw materials, traders, industrial producers, or financiers? How does George Ball dismiss those fears as unfounded?

b. Ball wrote at a time when the predominant critique of multinationals concerned the adverse impact of multinationals in Third World countries. What are the fears in First World countries, such as those that might be felt by workers at Caterpillar Inc., either about the free mobility of investment by United States-based multinationals in Third World countries, or about the influx of capital from multinationals based in other countries? How might Ball dismiss those fears?

2. Were Brandeis in the audience listening to George Ball's speech, what questions would he ask? What observations would he make?
3. What level of organization does Ball recommend for business—local, national, or world? What organization for law? For politics? Should there be parallel levels of organization across law, politics, and business, or should there be differences?
4. Ball seems to advocate the following positions:
   a. A decline in the usefulness of the nation state.
   b. The encouragement of common markets or free enterprise zones (Free enterprise zones are created by agreement between international producers and local governments. Goods are produced for export, using local labor, with a suspension of the application of local law in the zone).
   c. Free mobility of capital, raw materials, plant and facilities, and distribution networks.
   d. In cases of conflict, commercial interests being given preference to political- legal interests.
   e. Free trade given preference over "protectionism."
   f. Legal systems limited territorially, even if when so limited all commercial activity would not be reached.
   g. A world legal order providing a "domiciliary" for international businesses and freeing them from the law–government systems of nation states.

   With which of the following positions do you agree most? With which ones least?
5. Where does the rule of law fit into the thinking of George Ball?
6. Early corporate law was marked by the removal of state law as the primary locus of regulation of corporations. Ball advocates the removal of national regulatory structures on multinationals. Does the earlier experience tell what questions to ask about contemporary control of multinationals?

III. POWERS

No transfer of power from the state to private parties has been more extensive than the grant made to corporate enterprises. Two recent writers have stopped for a moment of meditation on the magnitude of this delegation:

> Consider the domain of . . . choice. The founders and managers of a firm choose whether to organize as a corporation, trust, mutual, or cooperative. . . . They choose what the firm will make or do and whether it will operate for profit, not for profit, or hold a middle ground, pursuing profit but not to the exclusion of some other objective . . . They choose whether to allow the public to invest or whether, instead, the firm will be closely held. They choose the kinds of claims (debt, equity, . . .) to issue, in what ratios, for what price, with what entitlements: not only the right to receive payments (how often, in what amounts) but also whether these investments allow their holders to vote—and if to vote, how many votes, and on what subjects. They choose where to incorporate . . . They choose how the firm will be organized (as a pyramidal hierarchy or a loose, multidivisional collective), whether central leadership will be strong or weak, or whether the firm will grow (internally or by merger) or shrink (by selling assets or spinning off divisions). Investors select the board of directors, who may be "inside" (part of the management team) or "outside" (often associated with investors, suppliers, or customers) . . . As a practical matter boards are self-perpetuating until investors become dissatisfied and a majority decides to redo everything to a new taste. With trivial exceptions all business decisions—including the managers' pay, bonuses, stock options, pensions and perquisites—are . . . under the supervision of this board, with no substantial inquiry by anyone else. Anyone who asks a court to inquire will be brushed off with a reference to the business judgment rule[13] . . .

A complete compendium of the latitude of business choice according to corporate law would be extensive. Some feel for the almost total legitimation of business discretion can be found in the Model Business Corporation Act.

> Each corporation shall have power:
> (a) To have perpetual succession by its corporate names unless a limited period is stated in its articles of incorporation.
> (b) To sue and be sued, complain or defend, in its corporate name.
> (c) To have a corporate seal which may be altered at pleasure, and to use the same . . .
> (d) To purchase, take, receive, lease, or otherwise acquire, own, hold, improve, use, and otherwise deal in and with real or personal property, or any interest therein, wherever situated.
> (e) To sell, convey, mortgage, pledge, lease, exchange, transfer and otherwise dispose of any or all or any part of its property and assets.
> (f) To lend money and use its credit to assist its employees.

[13]F. Eaterbrook et al., *The Economic Structure of Corporate Law* (Cambridge: Harvard, 1991), pp. 2, 3.

(g) To purchase, take, receive, subscribe for, or otherwise acquire, own, hold, vote, use, employ, sell, mortgage, lend, pledge, or otherwise dispose of, and otherwise use and deal in and with, shares or other interests in, or obligations of other domestic or foreign corporations, associations, partnerships, or individuals, or direct or indirect obligations of the United States or of any other government, state, territory, governmental district or municipality or of any instrumentality thereof.

(h) To make contracts and guarantees and incur liabilities, borrow money at such rates of interest as the corporation may determine, issue its notes, bonds, and other obligations, and secure any of its obligations by mortgage or pledge of all or any of its property, franchise, and income.

(i) To lend money for its corporate purposes, invest and reinvest its funds, and take and hold real and personal property as security for the payment of funds so loaned or invested.

(j) To conduct its business, carry on its operations and have offices and exercise the powers granted by this Act, within or without this state.

(k) To elect or appoint officers and agents of the corporation, and define their duties and fix their compensation.

(l) To make and alter by-laws, not inconsistent with its articles of incorporation or with the laws of this State, for the administration and regulation of the affairs of the corporation.

(m) To make donations for the public welfare or for charitable, scientific, or educational purposes.

(n) To transact any business which the board of directors shall find will be in aid of governmental policy.

(o) To pay pensions and establish pension plans, pension trusts, profit sharing plans, stock bonus plans, stock option plans and other incentive plans for any or all of its directors, officers, and employees.

(p) To be a promoter, partner, member, associate, or manager of any partnership, joint venture, trust, or other enterprise.

(q) To have and exercise all powers necessary or convenient to effect its purposes.[14]

One might wonder what business powers the corporation does not have, or why the statute did not simply read, "A corporation can exercise all powers necessary to accomplish its purposes." A corporation can do practically anything not manifestly illegal, and the list simply codifies the virtually unlimited range of business activities that may be undertaken using the corporate form.

Power can best be thought of as a relationship and not a mere capability. The expression "power over" leads to more insight than the expression "power to"; one expression takes the student toward interpersonal relationships, the other toward connection to the inanimate world or to a setting where there need not be occasions for conflict. A master controls a slave; the relationship is interpersonal and brims over with power questions. Contrast

[14]Model Business Corporation Act, quoted in John Moye, *The Law of Business Organizations*. (St. Paul: West, 1974), pp. 54, 57.

the "power" to climb a mountain or the "power of concentration" necessary to read a book from beginning to end.

The foregoing list of the powers of a corporation can be reconsidered by reference to the first meaning of power. What groups are made more powerful, and what groups are made more powerless under the foregoing provisions? Potential rivals in the power struggle could include suppliers, customers, creditors, shareholders, labor forces, and communities large and small which may be affected by corporate actions. If power settles everything, as the novelist Albert Camus once observed, who has greater power and the greater legal basis for settling doubts?

IV. NUTS AND BOLTS OF CORPORATE LAW

In modern commerce, the corporation is it. The multinational is first a corporation, and second an international holding company of subsidiary corporations. An understanding of the extensive implications of a corporations's being a legal entity with plenary powers, a "person" with constitutional rights, and a unique structure of internal governance needs to be considered before we can go further.

The idea that a corporation exists only in the legal imagination, separate and apart for its creators or present incumbents (shareholders, officers, and employees) takes some getting used to. For George Ball the legal invention of the corporation was an organizational breakthrough. Others parade a list of abuses done via the corporate form.

According to law, the corporation is both a "legal entity" and a "person," two conceptions which for all their mind-bending metaphysics, have enormous legal, ethical, economic, political, social, and cultural consequences. At the moment when corporations chafe at the prospects of being merely a "legal entity," and treated as such, they assert their being "persons" with full protection accorded to persons under the Constitution. This mixed character of corporations provides us with yet another example of businesses wanting the best of both worlds—to be a *legal* entity, with *personal* rights. Perhaps some cases can get us over the mental hump of having one's cake and eating it too.

Corporation as Legal Entity

The first case is an older one from Massachusetts. The corporate question originated with a dispute between labor and management over whether a union should exclusively control the labor supply (a closed shop) as an agreement between the union and the corporation provided. After unsuccessfully working at getting along, the management decided to form a "new" corporation to carry on the same business. If the court recognized the new corporation as a distinct entity, the labor agreement had been successfully jettisoned; if not, the agreement applied.

BERRY V. OLD SOUTH ENGINEERING CO. 283 MASS.441 (1933)

Pierce, Justice

This is a suit in equity brought by the plaintiffs (hereinafter called the union) against the Old South Engraving Company (hereinafter called the old company) and the Old South Photoengraving Company (hereinafter called the new company) to enjoin the violation of an agreement entered into between the union and the old company and for damages . . . The old company in January, 1930 entered into an agreement . . . "which regulated generally the conditions and prices to be paid employees". . . On April 29, 1932, the old company sent a letter to the union . . . which reads: "This is to notify you that one month from today the agreement between the Union and Old South Engraving Company will be terminated . . ." [T]he defendant officers and directors had decided to run a non-union shop and to terminate the . . . agreement . . .

. . . The directors of the old company consulted their attorney and were advised that . . . the agreement between the old company and the union was not binding on the individuals who composed the stockholders and directors of the old company; and that he (the attorney) saw no reason why the directors and stockholders, as individuals, could not start a business as a corporation. Thereupon the attorney was authorized to take the necessary steps to form a new corporation . . . under the name of the Old South Photoengraving Corporation. The incorporators of the new corporation are the same persons who are or were directors of the old corporation . . .

The new company was organized with a capital of twelve thousand shares of no par value. The old company had a capital of one hundred and twenty shares of the par value of $100 issued and outstanding, and all held by Huntsman, Balcom (the treasurer) and Paine (who was the clerk). Huntsman held one half, Balcom one third and Paine one sixth. The old company transferred its machinery, equipment and accounts receivable to the new company for nine thousand shares of its capital stock, The stockholders of the old company agreed to purchase stock of the new company as follows: Huntsman six hundred shares, Balcom four hundred shares and Paine two hundred shares. The cash held by the company . . . was used to pay its liabilities and the balance left, $529, was distributed one half to Huntsman, one third to Balcom and one sixth to Paine. The company also had a reserve . . . of bonds . . . of $3,500. . . . It was the purpose to . . . use the money as well as the proceeds of the sale of the bonds . . . for the purposes of purchasing stock in Old South Photoengraving Corporation . . . The old company surrendered its lease . . . and the new company took a lease on the same premises for the unexpired term on the same terms and conditions. A bank account was opened . . . and new stationery was procured . . . A new crew composed of nonunion workmen went to work . . .

. . . The master found [A master had been designated by the court as a factfinder in the case.—Ed.] "that the organization of the corporation . . . was for the purpose . . . to conduct its business as a non union or open shop; that . . . the officers and directors . . . did not propose to contest the question of the violation of the agreement but that acting under the advice of counsel they adopted the procedure of forming a new corporation believing that by so doing they could conduct their business as they planned . . . free from the obligations of the . . . agreement . . .

He further found the union is "able, willing and ready to supply members . . . in any numbers that the defendant [the old company] may require . . . and that said tender of services and employment have been rejected . . .

The motives of the officers, directors and stockholders of the old corporation, as individuals, that is the desire of these incorporators of the new corporation to secure through the instrumentality of a corporation authority to do business exactly like the business done by the old corporation, without the burden of the . . . agreement . . . cannot be regarded as fraudulent in fact or in law. Corporations like individual shareholders are distinct entities; neither can be treated as the agents of the other when openly contracting for themselves and in their own names . . . In absence of a fraudulent purpose in the organization of a corporation, it is settled law in this commonwealth that the ownership of all the stock and the absolute control of the affairs of a corporation do not make that corporation and that individual owner identical. Nor do such ownership and control make the property of the corporation subject to the payments of the stockholders' debts nor subject the corporation to liability upon contracts which neither executed nor assumed . . . The contention that the new corporation is but a continuance of the old company is without merit in fact or in law. . . .

The bill was rightly dismissed as against the old company. It did not break the contract by ceasing to employ either members of the union or anybody else. The bill was rightly dismissed as against the new company. It never contracted with the union or assumed the contract of the old company.

Notes and Questions

1. If a person transfers property to a relative to escape the claims of creditors, the transfer can be undone as a "fraudulent conveyance" designed to deprive creditors of assets that would otherwise be available. Compare the facts of the *Berry* case with this elementary rule of bankruptcy law.
2. The court rejected the argument that the new business was merely a continuation of the old one, saying that the argument was "*without merit in fact or law.*" Conceding the point about law, couldn't there be a *factual* basis for union's argument? Consider the theoretical implications of the conclusion that the argument had no merit in *fact*. (Warning: thinking about this could make your head hurt.)
3. The court enumerates some of the transactions that can be undertaken in the corporate form: making contracts of all types; holding property including cash, bonds, and leases; establishing bank accounts and operating businesses under chosen names. The case gives concrete examples of the exercise of some of the powers enumerated in the preceding section.

4. That each corporation is a "separate entity" has enormous importance in the field of multinationals, entities being sometimes a device to escape from or limit liability, and sometimes as a way to invoke advantages, especially for taxation that may be available by using a string of corporations rather than a single one with proliferate branches and divisions.

Returning to the example of Caterpillar Inc. for another moment, Caterpillar operates through at least 75 subsidiary entities owned in whole or part. These have been set up in 19 countries outside the United States. The countries range from the usual—United Kingdom, Japan, Australia, Brazil, Canada, and Belgium—to the mysterious—Switzerland, Bermuda, and the Netherlands Antilles. Some of these separate entities reflect the disparate activities of the multinational—production, distribution, finance, insurance, capital ventures, and so on, but not all. Since all of the foregoing activities could also be carried out using more straightforward organization, it is probable that it is the ability to float in and out of legal systems to avoid disadvantages and create advantages that motivates the extensive use of legal entities in an otherwise integrated company.

Caterpillar Inc. is in no sense unique in the use of separate corporate entities, as the cursory study of any multinational will reveal. There is a whole literature on the comparative advantages and disadvantages of "doing business" in particular places. The following two charts from a provocative text on the financing and taxation of multinationals tells how separate corporate entities can make a difference:

EXAMPLES OF FOREIGN TAX HAVENS[15]

Havens Imposing No Tax	Countries Taxing Local Income Only	Low Tax Countries with Treaty Benefits
Bahamas	Liberia	Netherlands Antilles (0.03)
Bermuda	Panama	British Virgin Islands Is. (0.15)
Cayman Islands	Costa Rica	Montserrat (0.20)
Nauru	Hong Kong	Jersey (0.20)
New Hebrides		Guernsey (0.26)
Turks and Caicos Islands		Isle of Man (0.2125)

In addition to the foregoing there are countries offering "special companies," usually of consequence for tax purposes: Luxembourg, Netherlands, Switzerland, Liechtenstein, Gibraltar, Barbados, and Grenada.[16]

[15]Julian Alworth, *Finance, Investment, and Taxation Decisions of Multinationals* (London: Basol Blackwell, 1988), p. 101. This text was written before the United States tax law changes in 1986 which made it more difficult to use "offshore" tax havens.

[16]Ibid., p. 102.

A second chart reflects the holding of assets by U.S. controlled corporations in tax havens in 1968 and 1976:[17]

	Assets in Havens (U.S. $ billions)	Assets in Havens % of Total Assets
1968		
Industries		
Manufacturing	1.8	3.7
Transportation	1.9	50.6
Insurance	.1	12.8
Holding and investment Companies	1.3	34.7
Other Finance	2.3	26.7
Other Industries	4.3	16.0
Total	11.7	12.1
1976		
Manufacturing	7.6	5.1
Transportation	9.0	74.2
Insurance	2.4	3.8
Holding and Investment Companies	8.3	51.6
Other Finance	10.2	19.5
Other industries	17.9	29.6
Total	55.4	17.6

For certain activities such as transportation and investment holding companies, the percentages of assets in havens is large. The foregoing figures probably understate the percentages, since one of the advantages of a tax haven is secrecy about transactions. For example, the private international grain companies involved in billions of dollars of trade to and from everywhere in the world are superbly situated for strategic placement of company assets, revenues, and expenses.

Corporation as Person

Just where the corporation fits on the spectrum between the animate and the inanimate has been a perplexing legal subject for almost two hundred years. In the 1819 United States Supreme Court case, *Dartmouth College* v. *Woodward*, Justice Marshall defined the corporation as an

> artificial being, invisible, intangible and existing only in contemplation of law. Being the mere creature of law, it possesses only those properties which the charter of creation confer upon it.

This conception came in handy for lawyers who desire to establish a corporation's ability to carry on business in its own name: making contracts,

[17]Ibid., p. 104.

holding property, to have its own commercial "life," and to shed the identity and human finitude of its founders and stockholders. But the notion of artificiality becomes singularly unhandy if the corporation wants to invoke constitutional protections which by their terms seem to apply only to *natural* as opposed to *artificial* persons.

The Fourteenth Amendment prohibits states from depriving a *person* of liberty and denying *citizens* equal protection of law. As we saw in the *Liggett* case, where corporations claimed that Florida had infringed their "right" to equal protection by imposing special taxes on chain stores, there are instances when a corporation wants to have the same constitutional rights as are generally available. Some deft legal maneuvering, over more than a century, has been required to qualify the corporation for some constitutional protections, while preserving the latitude that accompanies being a "legal" entity, independent of its creators.

Some cases concern the rights of a corporation under the First and Fourteenth Amendments, which provide:

> Amendment I
>
> Congress shall make no law respecting an establishment of religion, or prohibiting the free exercise thereof; or abridging the freedom of speech, or of the press, or the right of the people peaceably to assemble, and to petition the Government for a redress of grievances.
>
> Amendment XIV
>
> Section 1. All persons born or naturalized in the United States and subject to the jurisdiction thereof, are citizens of the United States and of the State wherein they reside. No state shall make or enforce any law which shall abridge the privileges or immunities of citizens of the United States; nor shall any State deprive any person of life, liberty, or property, without due process of law; nor deny to any person within its jurisdiction the equal protection of laws.

A straightforward reading of the Amendments raises the problem of a corporation's eligibility for constitutional protection. The wording seems to apply to natural persons: under the First Amendment, practicing a religion, speaking, assembling, grieving; or under the Fourteenth Amendment being "born or naturalized," a "citizen," residing, being deprived, or denied equal protection. The next case, which is part of a long line of cases establishing the political position of corporations, reveals that a "normal" definition of person does not necessarily apply.

The state of Massachusetts had passed a law limiting political contributions of corporations. The corporation argued that the combined effect of the above Amendments made the statute unconstitutional and unenforceable, that the corporation ought to able to contribute to political campaigns just as any other citizen would be entitled to do.

FIRST NATIONAL BANK OF BOSTON V. BELLOTTI 435 U.S.765 (1978)

Mr. Justice Powell

In sustaining a state criminal statute that forbids certain expenditures by banks and business corporations for the purpose of influencing referendum proposals, the Massachusetts Supreme Judicial Court held that the First Amendment rights of a corporation are limited to issues that materially affect its business, property or assets . . . We now reverse.

The statute . . . prohibits appellants, two national banks and three business corporations, from making contributions or expenditures "for the purposes of . . . influencing or affecting the vote on any question submitted to the voters, other than one materially affecting . . . the property, business, or assets of the corporation." The statute further specifies that "[n]o question submitted to the voters solely concerning the taxation of the income, property, or transactions of individuals shall be deemed materially to affect the property, business or assets of the corporation." A corporation that violates [the statute] may receive a maximum fine of $50,000; a corporate officer, director or agent who violates this section may receive a maximum fine of $10,000 or be imprisoned for up to one year, or both.

Appellants wanted to spend money to publicize their views on a proposed constitutional amendment . . . [which] would have permitted the legislature to impose a graduated income tax on the income of individuals . . . [T]hey brought this action [originally in Massachusetts courts. —Ed.] to have the statute declared unconstitutional . . . Appellants argued that [the statute] violates the First Amendment, the Due Process and Equal Protection Clauses of the Fourteenth Amendment, and similar clauses of the Massachusetts Constitution . . . [T]he court . . . viewed the principal question as "whether business corporations . . . have First Amendment rights coextensive with natural persons or associations of natural persons". . . [T]he court held that "only when a general political issue materially affects a corporation's business property or assets may that corporation claim First Amendment protection. . . .

If the speakers here were not corporations, no one would suggest that the state could silence the proposed speech. It is the type of speech indispensable to decision making in a democracy, and this is no less true because the speech comes from a corporation rather than an individual . . . Freedom of speech and the other freedoms encompassed by the First Amendment always have been viewed as fundamental components of liberty safeguarded by the Due Process Clause . . . and the Court has not identified a separate source for the right when it has been asserted by corporations . . . Nor do our recent commercial speech cases lend support to appellees' business interest theory. They illustrate that the First Amendment goes beyond protection of the press and the self-expression of individuals to prohibit government from limiting the stock of information from which members of the public may draw. A commercial advertisement is constitutionally protected not so much because it pertains to the seller's business as because it furthers the societal interest in the "free flow of commercial information" . . .

Appellee nevertheless advances two principal justifications for the prohibition of corporate speech. The first is the State's interest in sustaining the active role of the individual citizen in the electoral process and thereby preventing elimination of the citizen's confidence in government. The second is the interest of protecting the rights of shareholders whose views differ from those expressed by management on behalf of the corporation. However weighty these interests may be in the context of partisan candidates elections they are not [implicated . . . or . . . served by this prohibition].

Preserving the integrity of the electoral process, preventing corruption and "sustain[ing] the active, alert, responsibility of the individual citizen . . . are interests of the highest importance . . . Preservation of the individual citizen's confidence in government is equally important.

Appellee . . . arguments . . . hinge upon the assumption that [corporate] participation would exert an undue influence on the outcome of the referendum vote . . . and destroy the confidence of the people in the democratic process and the integrity of government. According to the appellee, corporations are wealthy and powerful and their views may drown out other points of view . . . [T]here has been no showing that the relative voice of corporations has been overwhelming or even significant in influencing referenda in Massachusetts or that there has been any threat to the confidence of the citizenry in government . . .

Finally, appellee argues that [the statute] protects corporate shareholders . . . Ultimately shareholders may decide through the procedures of corporate democracy whether their corporation should engage in debate on public issues. Acting through their power to elect the board of directors or to insist upon protective provisions in the corporate charter, shareholders are presumed competent to protect their own interests . . .

Mr. Justice Burger, concurring . . . [T]he First Amendment does not "belong" to any definable category of persons or entities; it belongs to all who exercise its freedoms.

Mr Justice White . . . dissenting

[T]he issue is whether a State may prevent a corporate management from using the corporate treasury to propagate views having no connection with the corporate business . . . The Court invalidates the Massachusetts statute and holds that the First Amendment guarantees corporate managers the right to use not only their personal funds, but also those of the corporation to circulate fact and opinion irrelevant to the business placed in their charge and necessarily representing their own personal or collective views about political and social questions . . .

By holding that Massachusetts may not prohibit corporate expenditures or contributions . . . the Court not only invalidates a statute which has been on the books in one form or another for many years, but also casts considerable doubt on the constitutionality of legislation passed by some 31 States restricting corporate political activity, as well as upon the Federal Corrupt Practices Act . . . The Court's fundamental error is its failure to realize that the state regulatory interests . . . are themselves derived from the First Amendment. The question posed by this case, as approached by the Court, is whether the State has struck the best possible balance . . . What is inexplicable, is for the Court to substitute its judgment as to the proper balance for that of Massachusetts where the State has passed legislation reasonably designed to further First Amendment interests in the context of the political arena where the expertise of the legislators is at its peak and that of judges is at its very lowest . . .

There is now little doubt that corporate communications come within the scope of the First Amendment. This, however, is merely the starting point of analysis, because corporate expression . . . is not fungible with communications coming from individuals and is subject to restrictions which individual expression is not. Indeed what some have considered to be the principal function of the First Amendment, the use of communication as a means of self-expression, self-realization, and self-fulfillment, is not at all furthered by corporate speech. It is clear that the communications of profit making corporations are not "an integral part of the development of ideas, of mental exploration and of the affirmation of self. They do not represent a manifestation of individual freedom of choice . . .

Of course it may be assumed that corporate investors are united by a desire to make money, for the value of their investment to increase. Since even communications which have no purpose other than that of enriching the communicator have some First Amendment protection, activities such as advertising . . . may be viewed as furthering the desires of individual shareholders. The unanimity of purpose breaks down, however, when corporations make expenditures or undertake activities designed to influence the opinion or general public on political and social issues that have no material connection with or effect upon their business, property or assets . . .

Ideas which are not a product of individual choice are entitled to less First Amendment protection. Secondly, the restriction of corporate speech . . . impinges much less upon the availability of ideas to the general public than do restrictions on individual speech. Even the complete curtailment of corporate speech concerning political or ideological questions not integral to the day-to-day business functions would leave individuals, including corporate shareholders, employees and customers, free to communicate their thoughts. . . . These individuals would remain perfectly free to communicate any ideas which could be conveyed by the corporate form. Indeed such individuals could even form associations for the very purpose of promoting personal or ideological causes . . .

Corporations are artificial entities created by law for the purpose of furthering certain economic goals. In order to facilitate the achievement of such ends, special rules relating to . . . limited liability, perpetual life, and the accumulation, distribution and taxation of assets are normally applied to them . . . It has long been recognized, however, that the special status of corporations has placed them in a position to control vast amounts of economic power which may, if not regulated, dominate not only the economy but also the very heart of our democracy, the electoral process. The interest of Massachusetts and . . . many other states . . . is . . . preventing institutions which have been permitted to amass wealth as a result of special advantages extended by the State for certain economic purposes from using that wealth to acquire an unfair advantage in the political process . . . The State need not permit its own creation to consume it . . .

The Court's opinion appears to recognize at least the possibility that the fear of corporate domination . . . would justify restrictions . . . but brushes this interest aside by asserting that "there has been no showing that the relative voice of corporations have been overwhelming or even significant in influencing referenda in Massachusetts . . . It fails to even allude to the fact, however, that Massachusetts' most recent experience with unrestrained corporate expenditures in connection with ballot questions establishes precisely the contrary. In 1972, a proposed amendment to the Massachusetts Constitution which would have authorized . . . a graduated income tax on both individuals and corporations was put to the voters. The Committee for Jobs and Government Economy, an organized political committee, raised and expended $120,000 to oppose the proposed amendment, the bulk of it raised through large corporate contributions . . . In contrast the Coalition for

Tax Reform, the only political committee organized to support the 1972 amendment, was able to raise and expend only $7,000.

The necessity of prohibiting corporate political expenditures in order to prevent the use of corporate funds for purposes with which shareholders may disagree is not a unique perception of Massachusetts. . . [O]ne of the purposes of the Corrupt Practices Act [passed by the U.S. Congress. —Ed.] was to prevent the use of corporate or union funds for political purposes without the consent of the shareholders or union members and to protect minority interests from domination by corporate or union leadership . . .

Mr. Justice Renquist, dissenting.

The question presented today . . . has never been squarely addressed by any previous decision of this Court. However, Massachusetts, The Congress . . . and the legislatures of 30 other States . . . have considered the matter, and have concluded that restrictions upon the political activity of business corporations are both politically desirable and constitutionally permissible. The judgment of such a broad consensus . . . is entitled to considerable deference . . .

Early in our history, Mr. Justice Marshall described the status of the corporation in the eyes of the federal law:

> A corporation is an artificial being, invisible, intangible, and existing only in contemplation of law. Being the mere creature of law, it possesses only those properties which the charter of creation confers upon it, either expressly, or as incidental to its very existence. These are such as are supposed best calculated to effect the object for which it was created. Dartmouth College v. Woodward (1819)

. . . There can be little doubt that when a State creates a corporation with the power to acquire and utilize property, it necessarily and implicitly guarantees that the corporation will not be deprived of that property absent due process . . . Likewise when a State charters a corporation for purpose of publishing a newspaper, it necessarily assumes that the corporation is entitled to the liberty of the press . . . Until recently it was not thought that any persons, natural or artificial, had any protected right to engage in commercial speech . . . Although the Court has never explicitly recognized a corporation's right of commercial speech, such a right might be considered necessarily incidental to the business of a commercial corporation.

It cannot be so readily concluded that the right of political expression is equally necessary to carry out the functions of a corporation organized for commercial purposes. A state grants to a business corporation the blessings of potentially perpetual life and limited liability to enhance its efficiency as an economic entity. It might reasonably be concluded that those properties, so beneficial in the economic sphere, pose special dangers in the political sphere. Furthermore, it might be argued that liberties of political expression are not at all necessary to effectuate the purposes for which States permit commercial corporations to exist . . . Indeed the States might reasonably fear that the corporation would use its economic power to obtain further benefits beyond those already bestowed. I would think that any particular form of organization upon which the state confers special privileges or immunities different from those of natural persons would be subject to like regulation, whether the organization is a labor union, a partnership, a trade association, or a corporation.

The free flow of information is in no way diminished by the Commonwealth's decision to permit the operation of business corporations with limited rights of political expression. All natural persons who owe their existence to a higher sovereign than the Commonwealth, remain as free as before to engage in political activity . . .

Comments and Questions

1. There seem to be distinct differences in the ways the justices conceive of a corporation: like a natural person with rights of a natural person; as an artificial entity open to limitations not properly imposed upon natural persons; or as the alter ego of the shareholders, so that political stances taken by a corporation will inevitably run counter to the will of at least some of the shareholders.
   a. What conception of the corporation seems most persuasive to you?
   b. Can the line that Justice White wishes to draw between political-ideological positions and what is materially related to business be maintained?
   c. In cases of doubt, how should courts rule on corporate speech questions?
2. Justice Burger's concurrence has the merit of simplicity: All speech from any source is protected. Why the aversion of the two dissenting judges for this simple position?
3. The Court ruled that corporate contributions on referenda questions cannot be constitutionally limited. What would be the effect of this ruling on the confidence of the general populace in government? (You might try an informal poll of people you know as to what rule of law on corporate political contributions they would prefer. If they hold stock in corporations, do they prefer political activism by corporations or not?)
4. All judges concede an area of "commercial speech" which, if advertising is taken as an example, means that wherever a corporation derives either a direct or indirect commercial benefit, its speech is protected. Isn't this sphere of constitutional protection large enough to cover lobbying at all levels of government, financing referenda, publicizing positions on such issues as trade, foreign relations, unionization, federal deficits, interest rates, crime in the streets, and national health care?

   Alexis de Toqueville in his early appraisal of America observed that most political questions eventually become legal ones. Is it not also difficult to think of a political question that is without economic implications and effects? If so, can there be any substantial limits that may be imposed on corporate political speech?
5. Justice Renquist seems to be on the edge of cutting back the constitutional protection available to corporations. Evaluate his position.
6. Justice White compares the dollar expenditures of corporations with the amounts spent by others on a given referendum, and finds what for him was a disturbing ratio.

   Make an inventory of corporate expenditures in your state on ballot questions, or on legislative hearings and processes (lobbying). Evaluate your results.

7. The committee whose financing was challenged was called the "Committee on Jobs and Government Economy." Does one get the idea from its name that the committee was designed to oppose a graduated income tax structure? Should there be disclosure requirements so that the general public can sort out what groups are supporting what, or would this notice requirement be an abridgement of free speech?
8. The Federal Corrupt Practices Act arose out of the Watergate scandal. Congressional hearings disclosed an illegal blending of corporate entities and politics. Corporate money for the campaign to elect Richard Nixon, after being laundered through foreign subsidiary corporations to assure secrecy, found its way back into the election.

V. CORPORATE GOVERNANCE

The states by enacting permissive legislation delegated substantial power to the business enterprise. Given this delegation, it is up to the student of corporations to follow the delegation of power into the enterprise to see just how corporations are in fact governed. What groups in and around a corporation participate in critical decisions, or limit the power being exercised by others? The answers to these questions have been different across history.

The older understanding was that the corporation simply aggregated shareholders in an artificial entity. The main movers in the corporation were the incorporators, who became the stockholders and ran the company. Stockholders were vastly fewer than those in a modern company, and since they held the key positions in the business, the careful delineation of duties and powers of directors and company officers that is found in later treatises on corporations would have been an unneeded exercise in legal niceties.

However, there did come a time when the following hierarchical order became a business reality:

Shareholders
Board of Directors
Officers and Managers

According to the letter of the law, this formal organization exists to the present day. Shareholders elect boards of directors, who select officers. They in turn select their subordinates. In a formal sense the corporation parallels representational government of the state at large, with voters and elected officials, but much has been written on whether the formal structure matches the way corporations are actually run.

During the 1930s, owing to a more careful analysis by Professors Berle and Means,[18] the textbook version of corporate governance was challenged

[18]*The Modern Corporation and Private Property* (New York: Harcourt Brace, 1932).

and discredited as a gross distortion of the real political life of corporations. When they did their empirical investigations, the stock of most corporations was widely enough dispersed so that blocks of stock/voting power—that is, far smaller than the 51 percent technically necessary to control a corporation—were the critical ones involved in the selection of boards of directors and principal officers. With the separation of ownership and control, Adolph Berle and Gardiner Means worried about corporate managers holding power without property, and losing their impulse for responsible action. John Galbraith, writing later, concurred that power had shifted to what he termed the corporate "technostructure," which consisted of technical people and managers of the business.[19] Returns to technostructure could displace returns to owners.

With stockholders largely transformed into "investors" rather than participants in corporate political affairs, managers set the corporate agenda in all but the most exceptional circumstances. The proxy process through which shareholders vote at corporate meetings is in most cases controlled by management, and proxy paperwork is usually considered so meaningless by small investors that it is thrown away along with junk mail. The ordinary investor became interested in dividends or the appreciation of stock value, and not in voting. This has led to what is called the Wall Street Rule: If stockholders like the results of a corporation, they keep a stock; if not, they sell. Getting involved is not usually considered a serious option.

Boards of directors, who are also in the chain of corporate command, have likewise come to be controlled by the top managers of a company. The CEO, or chief executive officer, usually chairs the board of directors, sitting with other high-level corporate officers, called "inside directors" because of their day-to-day connection with the actual operations of the company. The "outside directors" are often drawn from the boards of other corporations—large banks, key customers or suppliers—to which are added a sprinkling of women and academics to lend a veneer of alternative vision. Given their relative unfamiliarity with the corporate operations, the outside directors tend to defer to the judgment of the inside directors. (Incidentally, the inside directors have a hand in choosing the outside directors via their control of the proxy process, by which directors are formally elected by the shareholders who actually vote.)

The more realistic picture of the contemporary corporate hierarchy of governance would be the reverse of the textbook version:

CEO's and Top Managers
Boards of Directors
Shareholders

What difference does this make? It means that in the United States corporations can be the most autocratically run organizations that exist. Shareholders are not "sovereign" as is sometime piously proclaimed. Nor do

[19]*The New Industrial State* (Boston: Houghton Mifflin, 1978).

"outside" members of corporate boards exercise much surveillance over business affairs; they usually rubber stamp what line officers who sit with them on the boards have recommended for perfunctory board approval. Other constituencies that come to mind—labor, consumers, or communities whose welfare turns on corporate decisions—are likewise without significant say about either the overall direction of a corporation or the day-to-day operations.

Some people believe that the current state of corporate governance is the best imaginable. "You've got to have good leadership," or "Managers have to be able to manage" is a common way of rationalizing the practically complete non-involvement of groups affected by corporate decisions. However, choices of this magnitude should be made more consciously and mindfully than they are, given the large effects of this wholesale delegation of power. At the least, the delegation is undemocratic; at the most it puts the general welfare utterly put beyond any real control. If as Calvin Coolidge said the business of America is business, and business is what key executives say it is, then the fate of the country rests in the hands of very few people. Nothing has brought this point home more strongly than the increasing public consciousness of the policies of multinational corporations.

Stockholding patterns have changed since the time of the Berle and Means study. A critical precondition for the operation of their thesis was the dispersal of stock over a large group of *passive individual* investors. That pattern has been partially reversed by the growing importance of institutional investors—*public pension funds* for teachers and other public officials; *corporate pension funds* to cover company retirees, *union pension funds* for members, *mutual funds, banks and thrifts, insurance and annuity funds.* These "institutional investors" now hold more than 40% of the stock and the accompanying voting power of corporations. It is not clear what they will do with their voting power and how intimately they want to be involved in setting corporate policies. Will these huge funds hold their stocks for dividends and price appreciation and simply sell if they are unhappy with corporate management, or will they become more aggressive? It is clear that passivity can at times be costly.

Passivity bore obvious costs during the wave of mergers in the 1980s. Institutional investors preferred different outcomes from managers in critical instances. Managers can be more interested in the continuity of an enterprise under its direction than in selling off the entire business at a gain. For example, management might want to resist a "hostile" takeover of the firm by the enactment of "poison pill" provisions which make a corporation less desirable as a takeover candidate. (The hostile tender offer, if successful, aggregates voting power to oust those who previously controlled the corporation, but also dramatically changes the market price for shares, since a premium over market is usually offered on stock being sought. The "poison pill" preserves management, but kills the prospect of a shareholder windfall.) Disputes over mergers and buy outs have put managerial interests at odds with institutional investors.

The more extreme cases have aggravated an increasingly tense relationship. Management has sometimes preserved its place by paying "greenmail" to ward off a "raider" who has acquired a large block of stock. (Greenmail involves the payment of a premium for the stock held by a person or group threatening takeover. Where the premium paid to the greenmailer is funded by corporate debt, managerial success has come at the expense of those shareholders who were not part of the greenmail purchase, and sometimes at the cost of long term corporate solvency; more debt means more fixed charges against a corporation's earnings, amounting to the grant to creditors of an option to take over the company, should there be default on the debt. Thus greenmail can erode dividends, the prospects of stock appreciation, and at times company survival.)

Cases of conflict between managers and shareholders have produced a movement toward *shareholder advisory committees*. Institutional stockholders can assert more influence over corporate management through the creation of committees than has been customary.

In the popular press stockholder initiated proxies have concerned issues of war and peace, environmental proposals, or anti-apartheid investment strategies. These measures are usually voted down with dispatch at the annual meeting, or marginally tolerated because they have virtually no chance of passage, if management desires to resist them.

Not so with stockholder initiatives that have concerned investment issues such as the ones involving mergers. Admittedly this activism has been more interested in better belt for the investment buck, than ushering in a corporate utopia marked by peace, environmental sensitivity or racial harmony, worldwide. It would be an ironic twist if *more* shareholder activism could lead to *less* corporate social responsibility, or help justify the worst managerial impulses. For example, if a firm can invest in Mexico and triple its profits, but the investment requires the displacement of a well-paid United States-based workforce, the circumvention of environmental and workplace standards, and the payment of trifling wages and benefits to an impoverished Mexican workforce, what should the shareholder committee advise? Will it be conscience or pocketbook? Should fund managers act on their own evaluations or should they stick to maximizing investment returns of the fund?

More democracy is better than less, but both forms of corporate governance may turn out to be too limited to contribute to long-term general welfare. Speculations about the future aside, corporations are still governed by key managers, and institutional investors and shareholder advisory committees have yet to pose any serious challenges to managerial control.

CONCLUSION

This chapter can be ended where it began. At the outset it was observed that the multinational corporation both builds upon and transcends the corporate form as it has evolved under the law of the United States. The controversy which was introduced via the juxtaposition of the opinion of Brandeis, brimming over with fears about size and the perversion of democratic values, and the opinion of George Ball, extolling the great advances through the economic integration of the world through giant enterprise, still rages today.

The trend line is currently in favor of George Ball. No legal limits have replaced those originally imposed by the states. There have been no assaults on the main conceptual underpinnings which have enabled the corporation, and now the multinational corporation, to become the preeminent organizational form for business. The corporation as entity; with proliferate powers; status under the Constitution as a person; and with key insiders free from any substantial challenge from potentially rival constituencies, in or out of the corporation, is the law and practice of our day.

CHAPTER 6

Antitrust Law: Big Is Beautiful

INTRODUCTION

With the decline of state law limitations on the size and scope of corporate activity, potential problems arising from the aggregation of property and power devolved to the national antitrust laws. The Sherman Act of 1890 and the Clayton Act of 1914 had two principal purposes: to prohibit contracts, combinations, and conspiracies in restraint of interstate commerce; and to prevent monopolizing and attempts to monopolize. Considering only the wording and the manifest spirit of the antitrust laws, one would think that they would impose restrictions on the unlimited growth of corporations.

Multinational corporations, given their unprecedented size, the number and range of their business activities, and their geographic scope, would seem to be especially vulnerable to charges of antitrust violation. At some point their activities would be so momentous that they would be restraining trade, monopolizing, or attempting to monopolize, and hence subject to legal limitations. To make an observation before documenting it, there are reasons why the antitrust laws impose no serious impediments to international firms that have become the largest in history.

The parties who can bring antitrust actions fall into two major categories: agencies of the national government—the Justice Department and the Federal Trade Commission—and business competitors of an offending company who can bring private lawsuits.[1] In the case of government actions, the primary focus here, remedies range from fines to orders that anticompetitive practices be stopped; to orders breaking up an offending company into unoffending parts as was the case with AT&T's being broken into seven regional telephone companies.

In private antitrust actions, competitors who have been adversely affected by antitrust violations bring actions for injunctions and treble damages—offending practices ordered stopped, losses attributable to violations tripled. Recoveries can result in verdicts of hundreds of millions of dollars, as was the case in *Telex* v. *IBM*,[2] before the case was reversed on appeal. Telex had argued that the monopolistic practices of IBM had interfered with its ability to compete. In this chapter we consider several aspects of antitrust law that have rendered antitrust ineffective against multinationals:

[1]Lawrence White, ed., *Private Antitrust Litigation* (Cambridge, Mass.: Massachusetts Institute of Technology, 1988).

[2]510 F.2d 894 (1975)

1. Doctrines in antitrust law on size—whether large *size in itself* is actionable.
2. Doctrines on market definition, since for a company to be found guilty of antitrust, some *market* or *trade* must be "restrained" or "monopolized."
3. The law of mergers and large size through acquisition, a favored strategy, especially since 1980.

Cutting across all of the foregoing issues in antitrust law are the tactical and financial problems in bringing an antitrust suit to conclusion—antitrust suits are the most expensive and lengthiest of all cases to try.[3] Complexity of legal and factual issues, long delays, and the resulting costs are not neutral. The best-funded party to antitrust litigation can exploit the foregoing elements and thereby prevail, regardless of the overall rules or policies of antitrust law.

Surrounding the intricacies of antitrust law in theory and as enforced, there is also the business–political context of antitrust law. Over the 100 years since the passage of the Sherman Act, there have been different degrees of enthusiasm for zealous enforcement of antitrust law, to say nothing of different ideas about competition and acceptable business practices generated within law, imported from economics, or traceable to transformation of the United States economy.[4] Different attitudes about small retailers and chain stores, studied in the previous chapter, indicate shifting preferences about what enterprises should be, how big they should be, who should control them, and whether law ought to have any role at all in the matter.

At the present time antitrust law is in retreat, having been virtually abandoned during the Reagan-Bush years, with the support of some economists who regard antitrust laws as unnecessary and harmful to efficiency. Whether there will be a revival of antitrust is doubtful, since large size and extensive market power are now deemed by some to be necessary to firms headquartered in the United States when they encounter large multinationals based in other countries. Practices that once may have been ruled dangerous threats to open markets and competition have been reclassified as virtues indispensable to participation in a world economy.

This sentiment is not unprecedented. Cyclical shifts in the enthusiasm for antitrust law and enforcement have occurred across the entire history since 1890, although the law has rarely been as utterly lifeless as it now seems to be. To summarize the entire period, the doctrines of antitrust have attracted provisional rather than sustained support.

The focus in this chapter is on domestic applications of antitrust laws, since for the multinational corporation to succeed the antitrust law must fail; the mom and pop convenience store on the corner cannot set its sights on Latin America, but a very large enterprise with substantial domestic market power can consider such expansion as a logical extension of the firm.

[3]James Stewart, *The Partners* (New York: Warner, 1984), pp. 53–113.

[4]H. Hovenkamp, "The Sherman Act and the Classical Theory of Competition," 74 *Iowa Law Review*, 1989, pp. 1019-1065; L. Schwartz, "Cycles of Antitrust Zeal," *Antitrust Bulletin*, 1990, pp. 771–800.

Before getting down to some representative cases, as is the habit of hard-nosed lawyers to do, it might be useful to stand back from antitrust law and consider an early assessment of business development in the United States. In 1913, just twenty-odd years after the Sherman Act, there was already concern over the size and power of enterprises. Congressional hearings at that time established just how big big was becoming, who controlled critical enterprises, how supposedly competitive enterprises were connected through common stock ownership and interlocking boards of directors, and whether existing laws were imposing any appreciable limits on the ability to aggregate assets and market power.

THE "MONEY TRUST" HEARINGS

The Pujo Committee, convened by Congress in 1913 on "money trusts,"[5] had before it a problem that had not been manifest in the earlier days of business trusts. The first business trusts in oil, tobacco, or beef were easier to understand; a group got a corner on a critical commodity or market and maximized its profit at public expense. Not so with the activities investigated by the Committee—high finance and the interplay between finance and utilities, transportation, and industrial companies. The "money trusts," as they were called, were one step removed from the industrial or commodity-based companies, and their influence was more difficult for the public to see, just as it is difficult for the public today to comprehend high finance and its effects.

The banks of 1913 were powerful by virtue of being in the right place at the right time—when money changed hands—and benefited from knowing more about more businesses everywhere than the principals in any particular business could ever know. They placed stocks and bonds of a wide variety; coordinated voting trusts[6] through which otherwise competing corporations could be politically controlled; acted as critical intermediaries between companies and their sources of investment capital; managed other people's money in trust accounts; and held large amounts in deposits, corporate stock, and corporate indebtedness.

The committee found that five banks were not only the principal financiers of virtually all of the important corporations of the time, but were also involved in their management through stockholdings, voting trusts, fiscal agency contracts, or memberships on boards of directors. With regard to boards of directors, five principal banks had 134 directorships in 34 banks, 30 directorships in 10 insurance companies, 105 directorships in 32 transportation companies, 63 directorships in 24 producing and trading companies, and 25 directorships in 12 public utility companies. In all, banks held 341

[5]U.S. Congress, Committee on Banking and Currency, Investigation of Concentration of Control of Money and Credit (Pujo Committee Investigation), 62nd Congress, 3rd Session, (1913).

[6]A trustee aggregates the *voting power* of common stocks that would otherwise be voted by the shareholders. The voting power controls the Board of Directors, and the Board in turn selects the principal officers who run the day-to-day business of the corporation. Dividends are still received by the shareholders.

directorships in 112 corporations having aggregate resources of $22.24 billion.[7] (To get some feel for what $22 billion was at this time, note that *Harper's Weekly*, which carried an expose on the "money trusts," cost ten cents.) The above connections between banks with corporate finance and control do not include the influence that the banks could assert via the corporate investments of their wealthy customers.

J. Pierpont Morgan was called the "Jupiter of Wall Street" because he presided like a god over lesser financial gods. The New York banks had an intimate connection with corporations, and by virtue of stockholdings and interlocking directorates *they controlled one another*. The cartoons from *Harper's*, Figures 6-1 through 6-3, show Morgan at the center of things and may have helped propel the issue of antitrust law onto the agenda of President Wilson.

The relationship between finance and control is exemplified by Morgan's creation of U. S. Steel, the first billion-dollar corporation. When Louis Brandeis, later a Supreme Court justice, wrote a series for *Harper's* on the "money trusts," he concluded:

> Industrial trusts feed the money trust. Practically every trust created has destroyed the financial independence of some community and of many properties; for it has centered the financing of a large part of whole lines of business in New York, and this usually with one of a few banking houses. This is well illustrated by the Steel Trust, which is a trust of trusts; that is, the Steel Trust combines in one huge holding company the trusts previously formed in the different branches of the steel business. Thus the tube trust combined 17 tube mills, located in 16 different cities, scattered over 5 states and owned by 13 different companies. The wire trust combined 19 mills; the sheet steel trust 26; the bridge and structural trust 27; and the tin plate trust 36, all scattered similarly over many states. Finally these and other companies were formed into the United States Steel Corporation combining 228 companies in all, located in 127 cities and towns, scattered over 18 states. Before the combinations were effected, nearly every one of these companies was owned largely by those who managed it, and had been financed to a large extent, in the place, or in the state, in which it was located. When the Steel Trust was formed all these concerns came under one management. Thereafter, the financing of each of these 228 corporations (and some that were later acquired) had to be done through or with the consent of J.P. Morgan & Co. That was the greatest step in financial concentration ever taken."[8]

According to the Brandeis analysis, words like "growth," "creativity," and "improvement" had no place in the formation of United States Steel; *growth* implies an organic increase from forces within; *creativity*, real genius, and not simply financial reorganization; and *improvement*, something better. Financial reorganization was simply the aggregation of what was already in

[7]Pujo Committee Investigation, Exhibit 134 (c), December 18, 1912.

[8]L. D. Brandeis, "Big Men and Little Business," *Harper's*, January 3, 1914, p.14.

FIGURE 6-1 The cartoon caption reads: "The most potent single source of J. P. Morgan & Co.'s power is the $162,500,000 deposits including those of 78 interstate railroad, public-service and industrial corporations."(*Harper's*, 12/13/13)

existence when the combination took place. In fact, the bankers had inhibited creativity when it was financially expedient to do so.[9]

The formation of United States Steel was part of the first of four waves of mergers that have swept across the United States in different periods. Walter Adams and James Brock in *The Bigness Complex* make the following summary of the 1895 to 1904 merger wave and its impacts:

> Among the corporate giants created in this era were General Electric (a combination of eight firms controlling an estimated 90 per cent of the market); American Tobacco (162 firms controlling 90 percent of the market); DuPont (64 firms, 65–75 percent of the market); International Harvester. . . (4 firms, 75 percent) Nabisco (27 firms, 70 percent) Otis Elevator (6 firms, 65 per cent); U.S. Gypsum (29 firms, 80 per cent); International Paper (24 firms, 60 percent); American Smelting and Refining (12 firms, 85 percent); and . . . U.S Steel (. . . an amalgam of 180 formerly independent plants controlling 65 percent . . .); the giant combines. . . National Lead, U.S. Rubber . . . Pittsburgh Plate Glass . . . United Fruit . . . Allis–Chalmers, United Shoe Machinery, Eastman Kodak, International Salt, Pullman, and Corn Products Refining . . . All told, more than three thousand companies disappeared through merger during the decade 1895–1904. Three-quarters of these were absorbed in consolidations devouring five or more firms in a single gulp. Nearly half of the disappearing firms (and seven–tenths of the mergers and capitalizations) were involved in mergers that immediately attained market and industry domination.[10]

[9]Ibid., pp. 11-14.
[10]W. Adams, et al., *The Bigness Complex* (New York: Pantheon, 1986).

FIGURE 6-2 This cartoon reads: "The most harm-bearing incident of the trusts is their promotion of financial concentration. Industrial trusts feed the money trust." (*Harper's*, 1/3/14)

The number of firms involved and the practices across different industries demonstrate the pervasiveness of corporate concentration at this early time. The financial returns from corporate consolidation were highly stratified and largely unearned—some made a great deal of money and attained unprecedented market power. (The Morgan group made $62 million in fees for the U. S. Steel mergers, as depicted in the cartoon in Figure 6-4.) But some were left out—displaced entrepreneurs, some communities, customers, and labor.

The Democratic party and President Woodrow Wilson advocated stiffer antitrust laws and the result was the Clayton Act of 1914. The merger problem was addressed in Section 7 of Clayton, which provided:

> No corporation shall acquire, directly or indirectly, the whole or any part of the stock or other share capital of two or more corporations engaged in commerce where the effect of such acquisition or the use of such stock, . . ., may be to substantially lessen competition between such corporations or any of them, . . . or to restrain such commerce in any section or community, or tend to create a monopoly in any line of commerce.[11]

[11]Clayton Act, Section 7, 1914.

To Him That Hath

FIGURE 6-3 This cartoon has no caption other than the legend at the bottom. The picture says it all! (*Harper's*, 12/13/13)

Included in Section 7 was an ambiguous provision that said the new law would not "affect or impair any right heretofore legally acquired." What was the legal status of corporations like U. S. Steel that were formed prior to the Clayton Act?

When the foregoing provisions of the Clayton Act are read legalistically and without regard for the spirit of the law, the contours of later lawsuits can be predicted:

1. The statute covers acquisition of *stock*. What about the purchase of *assets* of a competing corporation? (For example, the acquisition of a railroad can be made either by buying the stock in the company or by buying the rail lines and equipment. Both have the same business results.)

FIGURE 6-4 The cartoon reads: "The syndicate which promoted the Steel Trust took, as compensation for a few weeks' work, securities yielding $62,500,000 in cash." (*Harper's* 12/20/13)

2. Does a merger have to affect commerce *immediately* or need it only create a condition where competition *may at some future time* be diminished?
3. What do the following phrases mean: "in any section of community"; "tend to create a monopoly"; and "line of commerce"?

The foregoing ambiguities can make for extensive legal strategizing, as the post–1914 period reveals, and were antitrust law a lively field today, litigation, with wave upon wave of legal and economic experts, could grind on almost endlessly interpreting the foregoing phrases. Businesses do not necessarily want efficient, expeditious outcomes, especially when wrong outcomes will interfere with business discretion.

The 1914 law also addressed the problem of interlocking directorates. The Pujo hearings revealed that corporations were linked by simultaneous memberships by the same people on the boards of multiple corporations. This network of shared directors facilitated communication and intercorporate dealings inimical to the antitrust laws (for example, price fixing, division of territories, and reciprocal dealings). Section 8 of the Clayton Act prohibited interlocking directorates between banks, and interlocking directorates between other "competing corporations." What may seem to be fairly straightforward—a prohibition of intimacy among corporations—did not come out that way, as we shall see later.

THE FIRST U. S. STEEL CASE

The case of *United States* v. *United States Steel*, which reached the United States Supreme Court in 1920, is interesting for several reasons. First, we have already encountered some of the background on the company through the material on J. P. Morgan and the Congressional hearings on financial networks, and we wonder whether the Congressional and popular fury over the creation of U. S. Steel was matched by an equivalent judicial response when the government sought dissolution of the company under the Sherman Act. Second, the case occurred after two big cases—*Standard Oil* and *American Tobacco*—which resulted in the breakup of those companies.

The case against United States Steel was delayed by World War I; war requires steel, and a government cannot simultaneously depend on a company for war material and sue it for antitrust violations. The almost twenty years that elapsed between the formation of the company and the final decision raised a number of unique problems: Had business conditions changed since the formation of the company? Did an original intent to monopolize, if it could be proved, warrant dissolution some years later? Did the company have market power at the time the suit was brought? Was the steel company cooperative with competitors rather than ruthless, as the Standard Oil and the American Tobacco companies had been shown to be? Was the size of the company *in itself* a basis for breaking up the company?

All of these questions were set against the largely intuitive estimation by the court as to whether the steel company, as aggregated, constituted industrial progress or an inhibition to progress. Was progress to come through dazzling size, or was progress best assured through the preservation of less impressive, smaller companies in competition with one another?

UNITED STATES V. UNITED STATES STEEL CORP. 251 U.S. 417 (1920)

Mr. Justice McKenna

. . . Suit against the Steel Corporation . . . charged as violators of the Sherman Anti-Trust Act . . .

It is prayed that it . . . be dissolved because engaged in illegal restraint of trade and . . . monopoly.

The case was heard in the District Court by four judges. They agreed that the bill should be dismissed; they disagreed as to the reasons . . . One opinion . . . by Judge Buffington . . . expressed the view that the Steel Corporation was not formed with the intention . . . to monopolize or restrain trade . . . The corporation . . . was an evolution, a natural consummation of the tendencies of the industry on account of changing conditions, practically a compulsion from "the metallurgical method of making steel and the physical method of handling it," this method . . . tending to combinations of capital and energies rather than diffusion in independent action. And the concentration of powers . . . was only such as was deemed necessary, and immediately manifested itself in improved methods and products and in an increase of domestic and foreign trade . . . Not monopoly, therefore, was the purpose of . . . the corporation, but concentration of efforts, with resultant economies and benefits.

The tendency of the industry . . . was expressed in . . ."integration" which signifies continuity in the processes of the industry from ore mines to the finished product . . .

The other opinion, by Judge Woolley, . . . was in some particulars in antithesis . . . [N]either the Steel Corporation nor the preceding combinations . . . had the justification of industrial conditions, nor were they . . . impelled by the necessity for integration . . . On the contrary . . . the organizers of the corporation . . . had illegal purpose from the very beginning, and the corporation became "a combination of combinations by which . . . 180 independent concerns were brought under one business control," which measured by the amount of production extended to 80 percent or 90 percent of the entire output of the country and that its purpose was to secure great profits . . . and . . . monopolize and restrain trade.

The organizers however . . . underestimated the opposing conditions . . . the testimony did "not show that the corporation . . . ever possessed or exerted sufficient power when acting alone to control prices of the products of the industry." Its power was efficient only when in cooperation with its competitors . . . in . . . pools, associations, trade meetings and finally in a system of dinners inaugurated in 1907 by the president of the company . . . called the "Gary dinners" . . .

The Corporation . . . did not at any time abuse the power . . . it possessed. It resorted to none of the brutalities or tyrannies that the cases illustrate of other combinations. It did not secure freight rebates; it did not increase its profits by reducing the wages of its employees . . .; it did not increase its profits by lowering the quality of its products, nor create an artificial scarcity of them; it did not oppress or coerce its competitors . . .; it did not undersell its competitors in some localities by reducing its prices there below those maintained elsewhere; or require its customers to enter contracts limiting their purchases or restricting them in resale prices; it did not obtain customers by secret rebates . . .; there was no evidence that it attempted to crush its competitors or drive them out of the market; nor did it take customers from its competitors by unfair means. [Abuses were found in the earlier *Standard Oil* and the *American Tobacco* cases—ed.] . . .

Both opinions were clear . . .that the power of the Corporation never did and does not now reach to monopoly . . . [W]e add no comment except . . . that they [the two legal opinions—ed.] underestimated the . . . tendency . . . to . . . integration, the appreciation of the necessity or value of the continuity of manufacture from the ore to the finished product . . . [I]t had certainly become a facility of industrial progress . . .

We have seen that it was the view of the District Court that size was . . . a circumstance and had no accusing or excusing influence. The contention of the Government is to the contrary. Its assertion is that the size of the Corporation being the result of a "combination of powerful and able competitors" had become "substantially dominant" in the industry and illegal . . . The companies combined . . . had already reached a high degree of efficiency, and in their independence were factors in production and competition, but ceased to be such when brought under the regulating control of the Corporation, which by uniting them offended the law; and that the organizers . . . "had in mind the specific purposes of the restraint of trade and the enormous profits resulting from that restraint."

It is the contention of the Corporation . . . that there was a necessity for integration, and rescue from the old conditions—from their improvidence and waste of effort . . . its purpose and effect being "salvage not monopoly" . . .

[T]he judges . . . unanimously concurred that the corporation did not achieve monopoly . . . [C]ompetitors had to be persuaded by pools, associations, trade meetings, and . . . dinners, all of them, it may be, violations of the law, but transient in their purpose and effect . . . They were . . . after instances of success and failure, abandoned nine months before the suit was brought . . .

What then can now be urged against the Corporation? . . . It is greater in size and productive power than any of its competitors, equal or nearly equal to them all, but its power over prices was not and is not commensurate with its power to produce . . .

The company's officers, and as well its competitors and customers testified that its competition was genuine, direct, and vigorous and was reflected in prices and production. No practical witness was produced by the Government in opposition. Its contention is based on size and the asserted dominance of the Corporation—alleged power for evil, not the exertion of the power . . .

[T]he Corporation . . . called 200 witnesses . . . [T]he balance of the 40,000 customers was open to the Government to draw upon . . . [N]ot one was called, but instead the opinion of an editor of a trade journal is adduced, and that of an author and teacher of economics . . . His deduction was that when prices are constant through a definite period, an artificial influence is indicated; if they vary, it is a consequence of competitive conditions . . .

We magnify the testimony by its consideration . . .

The Government, therefore, is reduced to the assertion that the size of the Corporation, the power it may have, not the exertion of the power, is an abhorrence to the law, or as the Government says "the combination embodied in the Corporation restrains competition by its *necessary effect* . . . and therefore is unlawful regardless of purpose" . . .

[S]hall we declare the law to be that size alone is an offense, even though it minds its own business . . .? The corporation is undoubtedly of impressive size, and it takes an effort of resolution not to be affected by it or to exaggerate its influence. But we must adhere to the law, and the law does not make mere size an offense, or the existence of unexerted power an offense. It, we repeat, requires overt acts . . . It does not require competition, nor require all that is possible.

[I]t is . . . a matter for consideration that there was no legal attack until 1911, 10 years after its formation and the commencement of its career . . . the many millions of dollars spent, the development made, and the enterprises undertaken; the investment by the public that have been invited . . . are not to be ignored . . .

[The court next considered the *Standard Oil* and *American Tobacco* cases and found them to be *abuse* cases and not *size* cases.]

Mr. Justice Day, dissenting

The record seems to me to leave no fair room for a doubt that the defendants . . . were formed in violation of the Sherman Act. I am unable to accept the conclusion which directs a dismissal . . . instead of . . . requiring a dissolution . . .

I agree with . . . Judges Woolley and Hunt . . . that the combinations were not submissions to business conditions but were designed to control them for illegal purposes . . . and "were made upon a scale that was huge and a manner that was wild," and "properties were assembled and combined with less regard to their importance as integral parts of an integrated whole than to the advantages expected from the elimination of the competition which theretofore existed between them."

[I]n the language of Judge Woolley . . . "it is clear to me that combinations were created by acquiring competing producing concerns at figures not based upon their physical . . . or business values, but upon their values in combination . . . upon their values as manufacturing plants and business concerns with competition eliminated. In many instances capital stock was issued in amounts vastly in excess of the values of the properties purchased, thereby capitalizing the anticipated fruits of combination . . . [T]he combination extended in some instances . . . from 80 percent to 95 percent of the entire output of the country . . ."

This record shows that the power obtained by the corporation brought under its control large competing companies which were themselves illegal combinations, and succeeded to their power . . .

For many years . . . this unlawful combination exerted its power to control and maintain prices by pools, associations, trade meetings and . . . so-called "Gary Dinners" . . .

It inevitably follows that the corporation violated the law in its formation and by its immediate practices . . .

These facts established . . . it follows that if the Sherman Act is to be given efficacy, there must be a decree undoing so far as possible that which has been achieved in open, notorious, and continued violation of its provisions . . .

I agree that the Act offers no objection to the mere size of a corporation, nor to the continued exertion of its lawful power when that size and power have been obtained by lawful means and developed by natural growth, although its resources, capital and strength may give to such a corporation a dominating place in the business and industry with which it is concerned. It is entitled to maintain its size and power that legitimately goes with it, provided no law has been transgressed in obtaining it. But I understand the reiterated decisions of this court construing the Sherman Act to hold that this power may not legally be derived from conspiracies, combinations, or contracts in restraint of trade. To permit this would be to practically annul the Sherman Law by judicial decree . . .

Nor can I yield assent to the proposition that this combination has not acquired a dominant position in the trade which enables it to control prices and production when it sees fit to exert its power. Its total assets on December 31, 1913 were in excess of $1,800,000,000; its outstanding capital stock was $865,583,600; its surplus 151,798,428. Its cash on hand ordinarily was $75,000,000; this sum alone exceeded the total capitalization of any of its competitors, and with a single exception, the total capitalization and surplus of any one of them. That such an organization thus fortified and equipped could if it saw fit dominate the trade and control competition would seem to be a business proposition too plain to require extended argument to support it . . . That the exercise of the power may be withheld, or exerted with forebearing benevolence, does not place such combinations beyond the authority of the statute which was intended to prohibit their formation . . .

Questions and Comments

1. Both the majority and dissenters reject the argument that size alone is enough to warrant the conclusion that a firm has market power. The requirement that the government show more than simply size made the future course of trade regulation far more complicated than it would have been had there been some readily proved standard—for example, dollar value of assets, volume of sales, phases of the industry in which a firm operates, and so forth.

a. Review the discussion of the majority and dissenting judge on size. In your judgment does large size usually carry market power, or is the court correct in demanding that more be shown? Does an "integrated company" (ore through finished steel) have undue competitive advantages? If so, what are they?

b. The court lists "abuses" that show wrongful extensions of enterprise power. Review the list of abuses and estimate whether a large company, by its size alone, has greater capacity to engage in them.

2a. The Sherman Act speaks of "intent to monopolize." How would intent to monopolize be proved? In most cases will a company be able to offer business explanations for what the government or competitors complain about to show "good intent"? How did U.S. Steel explain its behavior?

b. If a company has manifested an intent to monopolize, but has not accomplished what it intends for lack of economic power, is there any recourse that should be available to the government? What does the phrase "intent to monopolize" mean? Compare attempting, but failing, to rob a bank.

c. How would monopolistic intent be distinguished from regular competition, in which companies use aggressive strategies to get ahead at the expense of other companies? Review the practices that the court listed as abusive. What makes them offensive? Are these tactics unusually effective competition, or are they anticompetitive?

3. The steel company offered proof via 200 witnesses that there was price competition in steel, while the government called an economist to testify that the lack of price changes evidenced price fixing. Review the hostile commentary of the majority opinion on the use of an economist for expert testimony. (Economists have come up in the legal world, and are now used routinely by both sides in antitrust cases.)

4. The steel case opened many lines of proof in antitrust cases—intent, market power, market conditions across long periods of time, and so on. The more lines of proof that are available to those resisting antitrust enforcement, the longer and more expensive antitrust cases will be.

5. Walter Adams of Michigan State University has written extensively on the steel industry of the United States. His findings can be

found in his text, *The Structure of American Enterprise*, and they are not pleasant. He concludes that from the formation of U.S. Steel there has not been competition in steel, and that the lack of competition has produced higher prices, anticompetitive division of territories and markets, bizarre paperwork in shipping steel, a lack of innovation, and other wasteful characteristics. He argues that if Americans want to know why American producers lost their competitive edge in world markets they need consult only the history of steel. Loss of market position was a self-inflicted wound, or more accurately, a highly profitable strategy that turned into a near-fatal wound, once world competition began to take hold.[12]

THE ALCOA CASE, SIZE, AND MARKET DEFINITION

On the surface it would have appeared that the case against the Aluminum Company of America would be an easy one for the government to win. Alcoa was a fully integrated company—it controlled raw materials, cheap electric power for primary aluminum production, and almost all "virgin" aluminum manufacturing capacity. It also had its own plants for fabrication of aluminum into end products. The government charged the company with monopolization and sought dissolution.

How were the boundaries of the market to be defined? Should the market include only "virgin" aluminum—the production of ingot from ore—in which Alcoa had almost 100 percent, or should the market include the production of aluminum ingots from scrap, which Alcoa did not control? Should the virgin production for Alcoa's own use be included, since it never "reached" the market? If production from scrap were included and the production for its own processing were excluded, Alcoa's market share dropped to a less alarming percentage.

Another defense raised by Alcoa was that the company got to its large size by patents and, when the patents had expired, by "natural growth," rather than by monopolistic tactics. An additional problem in the case concerned the activities of Alcoa-affiliated companies located outside the United States, a matter that will be taken up later in Chapter 10 on the territorial limits of United States law. The following excerpts of the opinion concern market definition and size.

[12](New York: Macmillan, 1990), pp. 72–100.

UNITED STATES V. ALUMINUM COMPANY OF AMERICA 146 F.2D 416 (1945)

L. Hand . . . Judge
. . . Alcoa's Monopoly of "Virgin" Ingot

"Alcoa" . . . has always been engaged in the production and sale of "ingot" aluminum, and since 1895 also in the fabrication of the metal into many finished and semi-finished articles. It has proliferated into a great number of subsidiaries, created at various times between the years 1900 and 1929, as the business expanded. Aluminum is a chemical element; it is never found in a free state, being always in chemical combination with oxygen. One form of this combination is known as alumina; and . . . the most available material from which alumina can be extracted is . . . "bauxite." Aluminum was isolated as a metal more than a century ago, but not until about 1886 did it become commercially practicable to eliminate the oxygen . . . Hall discovered a process by which that could be done . . . and got a patent . . . which he assigned to "Alcoa," which thus secured a legal monopoly . . . until . . . 1906 when this patent expired. Meanwhile Bradley had invented a process . . . Bradley's improvement resulted in great economy in manufacture, so that . . . for practical purposes no one could compete with Bradley or with his licensees . . . until . . . 1909, . . . "Alcoa" was granted an exclusive license under this patent . . . Thus until . . . 1909, "Alcoa" had either a monopoly of the manufacture of "virgin" aluminum ingot, or the monopoly of a process which eliminated all competition.

The extraction of aluminum . . . requires a very large amount of electrical energy which is ordinarily . . . most cheaply obtained from water power. Beginning at least as early as 1895, "Alcoa" secured such power from several companies by contracts . . . binding the power companies not to sell . . . power to anyone else for the manufacture of aluminum. Alcoa . . . also entered into four successive "cartels" with foreign manufacturers . . . by which it secured covenants from the foreign producers, either not to import into the United States at all, or to do so under restrictions, which in some cases involved the fixing of prices. These "cartels" . . . were the subject of a suit filed by the United States . . . in which a decree was entered declaring . . . these covenants unlawful . . . "Alcoa" did not begin to manufacture alumina on its own behalf until . . . 1903. In that year it built a very large alumina plant in East St. Louis, where all of its alumina was made until 1939, when it opened another plant in Mobile, Alabama . . .

[T]he most important question in the case is whether the monopoly in "Alcoa's" production of "virgin" ingot, secured by the two patents until 1909, and in part perpetuated between 1909 and 1912 by the unlawful practices . . . continued for the ensuing twenty-eight years; and whether, if it did, it was unlawful under Section 2 of the Sherman Act . . . It is undisputed that throughout this period "Alcoa" continued to be the single producer . . . in the United States; and the plaintiff [the government—Ed.] argues that this without more was enough to make it an unlawful monopoly. It also takes an alternative position: that in any event . . ."Alcoa"consistently pursued unlawful exclusionary practices . . . "Alcoa's" position is that the fact that it alone continued to make "virgin" ingot in this country did not, and does not, give it a monopoly . . . ; that it was always subject to the competition of imported "virgin" ingot, and of what is called "secondary" ingot; and that even if it had not been, its monopoly would have been the result of a growth which the Act does not forbid, even when it results in a monopoly . . .

From 1902 onward until 1928 "Alcoa" was making ingot in Canada through a wholly owned subsidiary; so much of this . . . imported into the United States it is proper to include with what it produced here. In the year 1912 the sum of these two items represented nearly ninety-one percent of the total amount of "virgin" ingot available for sale in this country . . . and for the last five years 1934–1938 . . . it averaged over ninety percent . . .

[I]t will be necessary first to consider the nature and uses of "secondary" ingot . . . made from aluminum scrap . . . One of these is the clippings and trimmings of "sheet" aluminum . . . The other source of scrap is aluminum which has once been fabricated and the article, after being used, is discarded and sent to the junk heap . . .

There are various ways of computing "Alcoa's" control of the aluminum market . . . [The trial found thirty-three percent by including "secondary" and excluded what Alcoa used itself. —Ed.]. If on the other hand, "Alcoa's" total production, fabricated and sold, be included, and balanced against the sum of imported . . . "virgin" and "secondary," its share of the market was in the neighborhood of sixty-four percent . . . The percentage we have already mentioned—over ninety—results only if we both include all "Alcoa's" production and exclude "secondary" . . . That percentage is enough to constitute a monopoly; it is doubtful whether sixty or sixty-four percent would be enough; and certainly thirty-three per cent is not . . .

At any given moment, . . . "secondary" competes with "virgin" in the ingot market; further it . . . probably does set a limit or "ceiling" beyond which the price of "virgin" cannot go . . . It might seem for this reason . . . in estimating "Alcoa's" control we ought to include the supply of "secondary" . . .

In the case of a monopoly of any commodity which does not disappear . . . the supply . . . will be made up of two components: (1) the part which the putative monopolist can immediately produce and sell; and (2) the part which . . . can be reclaimed . . . "Alcoa" always knew that the future supply of ingot would be made up in part of what it produced . . . The competition of "secondary" must therefore be disregarded . . . it was as much within "Alcoa's" control as was the production of the "virgin" from which it had been derived.

We conclude therefore that "Alcoa's" control over the ingot market must be reckoned at over ninety percent . . .

It does not follow because "Alcoa" had such a monopoly, that it "monopolized" . . . monopoly may have been thrust upon it. If it had been a combination of existing smelters . . . it would certainly have "monopolized" the market . . .

. . . [F]rom the very outset the courts have at least kept in reserve the possibility that the origin of a monopoly may be critical in determining its legality . . .

This notion is usually expressed by the saying that size does not determine guilt; that there must be some "exclusion" of competitors; that growth must be something else than "natural" or "normal"; that there must be "wrongful intent" . . . or that some "unduly" coercive means must be used . . .

[P]ersons may unwittingly find themselves in possession of a monopoly, automatically so to say . . . they may have become monopolists by force of accident . . . A market may . . . be . . . limited . . . Or there may be changes in taste or in cost that drive out all but one purveyor. A single producer may be a survivor out of a group of active competitors, merely by virtue of his superior skill, foresight, and industry . . . The successful competitor, having been urged to compete, must not be turned upon when he wins . . .

It would completely misconstrue "Alcoa's" position in 1940 to hold that it was the passive beneficiary of a monopoly . . . Already in 1909 when its last lawful monopoly ended, it sought to strengthen its position by unlawful practices . . . in 1934 . . . its production had risen . . . eight-fold. Meanwhile not a pound of ingot had been produced by anyone else in the United States . . . This increase and this continued and undisturbed control did not fall undesigned into "Alcoa's" lap . . . There were at least one or two abortive attempts to enter the industry, but "Alcoa" effectively anticipated and forestalled all competition and succeeded in holding the field alone . . . It was not inevitable that it should always anticipate increases in the demand for ingot and be prepared to supply them. Nothing compelled it to keep doubling and redoubling its capacity before others entered the field. It insists that it never excluded competitors; but we can think of no more effective exclusion than progressively to embrace every new opportunity as it opened, and to face every newcomer with new capacity already geared into a great organization having the advantage of experience, trade connections and the elite of personnel . . . [Ruling against Alcoa]

Comments

1. In this case we see a new line of argument on market definition. Just what did Alcoa control? When the secondary aluminum was included and production not headed for market was excluded, Alcoa went from virtual control to control of only one-third. Arguments over market boundaries turned an open-and-shut case for the government into a near loss. Moreover, the case invited an enlarged role for economists in antitrust litigation, since they are the experts on markets.
2. The *Alcoa* case was eventually concluded after World War II, when plants owned by the government were disposed of in 1947 to create Reynolds Aluminum Company and Kaiser Aluminum Company. In 1950 Alcoa was ordered to sever its connection with Alcoa Ltd., its Canadian subsidiary. The structure of the industry had been changed from a monopoly to an oligopoly, with a few firms rather than only one setting prices and output, but Alcoa still held preponderant market power.

   The case had taken a long time to try, appeal, and work out final remedies. Begun in 1938 it was not wound up until the decree divesting Alcoa Ltd. in 1950. During the long pendency of the action, the company remained intact and functioned as it had done before the action was brought.

   Law students over the next several decades were amazed that the trial record ran 40,000 pages, graphic evidence of the length and complexity of antitrust litigation.

THE "DU PONT CELLOPHANE" CASE

Market definition was raised to the level of a legal art form over the next 50 years of antitrust law. Disputes about market definition and market share shifted the judicial focus from concern about the sheer size of enterprises to the consideration of what part of what market was controlled by a company charged with antitrust violations. One case where lawyers created the potential for endless legal journeys was *United States* v. *Du Pont* 351 U.S. 378 (1956). Du Pont was charged with monopolizing cellophane, a clear packaging material; at the time, it produced 75 percent of all cellophane used. The company argued that *cellophane* was not *the market*. Instead, they contended, the market included all "flexible packaging materials," since there was "cross elasticity" of demand between cellophane and other packaging materials.

The concept of *cross elasticity*, borrowed from economics, measures the interchangeability or substitutability of one product for another. To use a textbook example, when the price of pork gets too high, some people will switch to other meats, thereby limiting at least to some degree the market power of those who sell pork. Advocates for Du Pont contended that Du Pont's power to exploit its strong position in cellophane was limited by the substitutes for cellophane that packagers could use. The chart[13] indicated as Table 6-1 shows the percentage of market control by Du Pont after the array of substitutes was included.

The company also argued that the submarkets for packaging were different, depending upon what it was that was being wrapped. If Du Pont had 17.9 percent of the total market for "flexible packaging materials" it had more or less market share when particular products being wrapped were taken into account, for example 0.2 percent for cereal packaging and 47.2 percent for fresh produce. Ninety-six percent of regular bread was wrapped in paper or "glassine," while 48 percent of specialty breads were wrapped in cellophane. Tobacco, cake and baked sweet goods, snacks, meat and poultry, crackers and biscuits, frozen food (excluding dairy)—were all different as to the percentage of cellophane used.

The water of market definition having been sufficiently muddied, the court accepted the company's theory of the case:

[13]Du Pont opinion, p. 405.

TABLE 6-1

	Thousands of Square Yards
Glassine, greaseproof and vegetable parchment papers	3,125,826
Waxing papers (18 pounds and over)	4,614,685
Sulphite bag and wrapping papers	1,788,615
Aluminum foil	1,317,807
Cellophane	3,366,068
Cellulose acetate	133,982
Pliofilm, polyethylene, Saran and Cry-O-Rap	373,871
Total	14,720,854
Total Du Pont cellophane production	2,629,747
Du Pont cellophane percent of total United States production and imports of these flexible packaging materials	17.9%

> It may be admitted that cellophane combines the desirable elements of transparency, strength and cheapness more definitely than any of the others . . . Moistureproof cellophane is highly transparent, tears readily but has high bursting strength, is highly impervious to moisture and gases, and is resistant to grease and oils. Heat sealable, printable, and adapted to use on wrapping machines, it makes an excellent packaging material for both display and protection of commodities.
>
> Other flexible wrapping materials fall into four major categories: (1) opaque moistureproof wrapping *paper* . . . (2) moistureproof *films* of varying degrees of transparency . . . (3) nonmoistureproof transparent *films* and (4) moistureproof *materials* other than films . . . (foils and paper) . . .
>
> [D]espite cellophane's advantages it has to meet competition from other materials in every one of its uses . . .[14]
>
> The 'market' which one must study to determine when a producer has monopoly power will vary with the part of commerce under consideration. The tests are constant . . . reasonable interchangeability . . . price, use, qualities . . . While the applications of the tests remain uncertain, it seems to us that Du Pont should not be found to monopolize cellophane when that product has the competition and interchangeability with other wrappings . . .[15]

The foregoing discussion was not meant to flexibly wrap the reader in useless details. The discussion is included simply to show the early shaping of what would become almost irresolvable debates—economic and legal—about "relevant markets." The advocates for Du Pont and other companies charged with antitrust violations had converted disputes to endless fact finding and refinements of legal and economic theory. They contended that every case was unique, and hence unamenable to presumptions or conclusions of law that might limit proof and expedite enforcement.

[14]Ibid., p. 398.

[15]Ibid., p. 404.

Time, delays, and complexity are the abiding lesson from these cases, and not which side won or lost. Business firms have advantages in litigation; it is the government that must overcome the burden of changing business practices. Through lawsuits that are time consuming, burdensome, and expensive, businesses can postpone unwanted results for a long time.

BROWN SHOE CO. V. UNITED STATES 370 U.S. 294 (1962)

Chief Justice Warren

The government filed a civil action alleging that a contemplated merger between G.R. Kinney . . . and the Brown Shoe Company . . . through an exchange of Kinney for Brown stock would violate Sec. 7 of the Clayton Act.

> The Act as amended, provides . . .
> No corporation engaged in commerce shall acquire, directly or indirectly, the whole or any part of the stock or other share capital . . . of another corporation . . . where in any line of commerce in any section of the country, the effect of such acquisition may be substantially to lessen competition, or tend to create a monopoly."

The complaint sought injunctive relief . . . to restrain the consummation of the merger. . . . [T]he Government contended that the effect of the merger of Brown—the third largest seller of shoes by dollar volume in the United States, a leading manufacturer of men's, women's and children's shoes, and a retailer with over 1,230 owned, operated and controlled retail outlets—and Kinney—the eighth largest company, by dollar volume, among those primarily engaged in selling shoes, and a retailer with over 350 retail outlets—"maybe substantially to lessen competition or to tend to create a monopoly" by eliminating actual or potential competition in the production of shoes for the national wholesale shoe market and in the sale of shoes at retail in the Nation, by foreclosing competition from a "market represented by Kinney's retail outlets" . . . and by enhancing Brown's competitive advantage over other producers, distributors and sellers of shoes. The Government argued that the "line of commerce" is "footwear" or alternatively, . . . "men's", "women's" and "children's" shoes, separately considered . . . and the "section of the country" within which the anticompetitive effect . . . is to be judged, is the Nation as a whole, or alternatively, each separate city or city and its immediate surrounding area in which parties sell shoes at retail.

In the District Court, Brown contended that the merger would be shown not to endanger competition if the "line[s] of commerce" and the "section[s] of the country" were properly determined. Brown urged that not only were the age and sex of the intended customers to be considered in determining the relevant line of commerce, but that the differences in grade of material, quality of workmanship, price, and customer use of shoes established different lines of commerce. While agreeing with the Government that, with regard to the manufacturing, the relevant geographic market . . . is the country as a whole . . . with regard to retailing, the market must vary . . . from the central business district of a large city to a "standard metropolitan area" for a smaller community. Brown further contended that . . . at the manufacturing level and at the retail level, the shoe industry enjoyed healthy competition and that . . . competition would not . . . be diminished . . . because Kinney manufactured less than 0.5 percent and retailed less than 2 percent of the Nation's shoes.

For Discussion

Before continuing with the opinion, observe how the advocates for Brown shaped the questions in the lawsuit. Consider the many possible ways the market for shoes can be divided and subdivided and how Brown might derive advantages in litigation from the possibilities.

BROWN OPINION, CONTINUED

. . . The District Court found that although domestic shoe production was scattered among a large number of manufacturers, a small number of large companies occupied a commanding position. Thus while the largest 24 manufacturers produced about 35 percent of the nation's shoes, the top 4 . . . produced approximately 23 percent of the Nation's shoes or 65 percent of the production of the top 24.

In 1955, domestic production of nonrubber shoes was 509.2 million pairs, of which about 103.6 million pairs were men's shoes, about 271 million pairs were women's shoes, and 134.6 million pairs were children's shoes . . . normally produced in separate factories.

The public buys these shoes through about 70,000 retail outlets, only 22,000 of which derive 50 percent or more of their gross receipts from the sale of shoes . . .

The District Court found a "definite trend" among shoe manufacturers to acquire retail outlets . . . [B]etween 1950 and 1956 1,114 retail shoe stores, were found to have become subsidiaries of these large firms . . .

And once the manufacturers acquired retail outlets . . . there was a "definite trend" for the parent–manufacturers to supply an ever-increasing percentage of the retail outlet's needs, thereby foreclosing other manufacturers from effectively competing for the retail accounts . . .

Another "definite trend" . . . was a decrease in the number of plants manufacturing shoes . . . In 1947 there were 1,077 independent manufacturers of shoes, but by 1954 their number had decreased by 10% to 970.

Legislative History. The case is one of the first to come before us . . . upon allegations that the appellant has violated Sec.7 of the Clayton Act as . . . amended in 1950.

As enacted in 1914 . . . [t]he act did not . . . appear to preclude the acquisition of stock in any corporation other than a direct competitor. The dominant theme pervading congressional consideration of the 1950 amendments was a fear of a rising tide of economic concentration in the American economy . . . Other considerations cited in support of the bill were the desirability of retaining "local control" over industry and the protection of "small businesses." . . . Congress used the words "may be substantially to lessen competition" . . . to indicate that its concern was with probabilities, not certainties . . .

The Vertical Aspects of the Merger. Economic arrangements between companies standing in supplier–customer relationship are characterized as "vertical." The primary vice of a vertical merger . . . is . . . foreclosing the competitors of either party from a segment of the market otherwise open to them . . .

The Product Market. The outer boundaries of a product market are determined by . . . the cross elasticity of demand . . . However, within this broad market, well-defined submarkets may exist . . . [W]e conclude that . . . the relevant lines of commerce are men's women's and children's shoes. These product lines are recognized by the public; each line is manufactured in separate plants; each has characteristics peculiar to itself . . .; and each is . . . directed toward a distinct class of customers.

[Brown] . . . contends that the . . . definitions fail to recognize sufficiently "price/ quality" and "age/sex" distinctions . . . that the predominantly medium–priced shoes which it manufactures occupies a product market different from the predominantly low–priced shoes which Kinney sells. But agreement with that argument would be equivalent to holding that medium–priced shoes do not compete with low–priced shoes . . .

Brown's sharpest criticism is directed at the District Court's finding that children's shoes constituted a single line of commerce. Brown argues . . . "a little boy does not wear a little girl's black patent leather pump" . . . "[I]nfants and babies' shoes," "misses' and children's" shoes and "youths and boys'" shoes each should have been considered a separate line of commerce.

We agree with the District Court's conclusion that . . . to subdivide the shoe market further on the basis of "age/sex" distinctions would be impractical and unwarranted.

The Geographic Market. We agree with the parties . . . that insofar as the vertical aspect of this merger . . . the relevant market is the entire Nation.

Probable Effects of the Merger. . . . [T]he legislative history of Sec. 7 indicates clearly that the tests for measuring the legality of any particular economic arrangement . . . are to be less stringent than those used in applying the Sherman Act. On the other hand, foreclosure of a *de minimis* [trifling —Ed.] share of the market will not tend "substantially to lessen competition."

Between these two extremes . . . the percentage of market foreclosed by the vertical arrangement cannot itself be decisive. In such cases it becomes necessary to undertake an examination of the various economic and historical factors in order to determine whether the arrangement . . . is of the type Congress sought to proscribe . . .

A most important . . . factor . . . is the very nature and purpose of the arrangement . . .

The present merger involved neither small companies nor failing companies . . . [I]n this industry, no merger between a manufacturer and an independent retailer could involve a larger potential market foreclosure. Moreover, it is apparent both from past behavior of Brown and the testimony of Brown's President that Brown would use its ownership . . . to force Brown's shoes into Kinney's stores . . .

Another important factor to consider is the trend toward concentration in the industry . . . The existence of a trend toward vertical integration . . . is well substantiated . . . Moreover the District Court found a tendency of the acquiring manufacturers to become increasingly important sources of supply for their acquired outlets. The necessary corollary of these trends is the foreclosure of independent manufacturers . . .

Brown argues, however, that the shoe industry is at present composed of a large number of manufacturers and retailers, and that the industry is dynamically competitive. But remaining vigor cannot immunize a merger if the trend in that industry is toward oligopoly . . .

Where several large enterprises are expanding their power by successive small acquisitions, the cumulative effect of their purchases may be to convert an industry from one of intense competition among many enterprises to one in which three or four large concerns produce the entire supply . . .

The Horizontal Aspects of the Merger. An economic arrangement between companies performing similar functions in the production or sale of comparable goods and services is . . ."horizontal" . . .

The acquisition of Kinney by Brown resulted in a horizontal combination at both the manufacturing and retailing levels of their businesses. [The District Court found that the merger of manufacturing facilities was too insignificant, and the government did not appeal —Ed.]

The Product Market. Shoes are sold in the United States in retail shoe stores and in shoe departments of general stores. These outlets sell: (1) men's shoes, (2) women's shoes, (3) women's or children's shoes, or (4) men's, women's, or children's shoes. Brown and Kinney sold their shoes in competition with one another through the enumerated kinds of outlets . . .

Congress prescribed a pragmatic factual approach to the definition of the relevant market and not a formal, legalistic one. The geographic market selected must . . . correspond to the commercial realities . . . Thus although the geographic market in some instances may encompass the entire Nation under other circumstances it may be as small as a single metropolitan area . . .

The District Court found that the effects of this aspect of the merger must be analyzed in every city with a population exceeding 10,000 and its immediate contiguous surrounding territory . . . By this definition . . . less than one-half of all of the cities in which either Brown or Kinney sold shoes through such outlets are represented. [Brown] claims that such areas should, in some cases, be defined . . . to include only the central business districts of large cities and in others to encompass the "standard metropolitan areas," within which smaller communities are found . . .

We believe . . . the record . . . supports the . . . findings that shoe stores in the outskirts of cities compete effectively with stores in central downtown areas . . .

Brown . . . says the court erred in failing to enter findings with respect to each relevant city . . . for example, men's shoes in Council Bluffs . . . women's shoes in Texas City . . . children's shoes in St. Paul . . . Brown also objects that the . . . detailed analysis of competition . . . was limited to a single city—St. Louis— . . . While it is true that the court concentrated its attention on the structure of competition in the city in which it sat . . . it also heard witnesses from no less than 40 other cities . . .

We recognize that variations of size, climate and wealth as enumerated by Brown exist in the relevant markets. However, . . . the markets with respect to which evidence was received provide a fair sampling . . .

There is no reason to protract already complex antitrust litigation with a detailed analysis of peripheral economic facts . . . During 1955 in 32 separate cities . . . the combined share of Brown and Kinney sales of women's shoes exceeded 20 percent. In 31 cities . . . the combined share of children's shoe sales exceeded 20 percent. [I]n six cities their share exceeded 40 percent . . . In 118 . . . cities the combined shares . . . exceeded 5 percent . . . If a merger achieving 5% control were now approved, we might be required to approve future merger efforts by Brown's competitors seeking similar market shares. The oligopoly Congress sought to avoid would then be furthered and it would be difficult to dissolve the combinations previously approved . . . Testimony in the record from numerous independent retailers . . . demonstrates that a strong national chain can insulate selected outlets from the vagaries of competition . . . can set and alter styles . . . can market their own brands at prices below those of competing independent retailers . . .

Of course some of the results of large integrated or chain operations are beneficial to consumers . . . But we cannot fail to recognize Congress' desire to promote competition through the protection of viable, small, locally owned businesses. Congress appreciated that occasionally higher costs and prices might result from the maintenance of fragmented industries and markets. It resolved these competing considerations in favor of decentralization . . .

We cannot avoid the mandate of Congress that tendencies toward concentration . . . are to be curbed in their incipiency, particularly when those tendencies are being accelerated through giant steps across a hundred cities at a time . . .

UNITED STATES V. VON'S GROCERY 384 U.S. 270 (1966)

Mr. Justice Black . . .

On March 25, 1960, the United States brought this action charging that the acquisition by Von's Grocery Company of its direct competitor Shopping Bag Food Stores, both large retail grocery companies in Los Angeles, California, violates Sec. 7 of the Clayton Act . . .

On March 28, 1960, three days later, the District Court refused to grant the Government's motion for a temporary restraining order and immediately Von's took over all of Shopping Bag's capital and assets including 36 grocery stores in the Los Angeles area. After hearing evidence, the District Court . . . concluded . . . that there was "not a reasonable probability" that the merger would tend "substantially to lessen competition" or "create a monopoly" . . .

The record shows the following facts . . . The market involved here is the retail grocery market in the Los Angeles area. In 1958 Von's retail sales ranked third in the area and Shopping Bag's ranked sixth. In 1960 their sales together were 7.5 percent of the total two and one-half billion dollars of retail groceries sold in the Los Angeles market each year. For many years before the merger both companies had enjoyed great success as rapidly growing companies. From 1948 to 1958 the number of Von's stores . . . practically doubled from 14 to 27, while at the same time . . . Shopping Bag's stores jumped from 15 to 34. During the same decade, Von's sales increased four fold and its share of the market almost doubled while Shopping Bag's sales multiplied seven times and its share of the market tripled. The merger of these two highly successful, expanding and aggressive competitors created the second largest grocery chain in Los Angeles with sales of almost $172,488,000 annually. In addition . . . the number of owners operating single stores in the Los Angeles retail grocery market decreased from 5,365 in 1950 to 3,818 in 1961. By 1963, three years after the merger, the number of single store owners had dropped still further to 3,590. During roughly the same period, . . . the number of chains with two or more grocery stores increased from 96 to 150. While the grocery business was being concentrated into the hands of fewer and fewer owners, the small companies were continually being absorbed by the larger firms through mergers . . . [F]rom 1949 to 1958 nine of the top 20 chains acquired 126 stores from their smaller competitors . . . Figures . . . illustrate the many acquisitions and mergers . . . among the 10 leading chains of the area . . . These facts alone are enough to cause us to conclude contrary to the District Court that the Von's–Shopping Bag merger did violate Sec. 7. Accordingly, we reverse.

From this country's beginning there has been an abiding and widespread fear of the evils which flow from monopoly—that is, the concentration of economic power in the hands of a few. On the basis of this fear, Congress in 1890, when many of the Nation's industries were already concentrated into what it deemed too few hands passed the Sherman Act in an attempt to prevent further concentration and to preserve competition among a large number of sellers. Several years later, in 1897, this court emphasized the policy of the Sherman Act by calling attention to the tendency of powerful business combinations to restrain competition "by driving out of business the small dealers and worthy men whose lives had been spent therein, and who might be unable to readjust themselves to altered surroundings" . . . The Sherman Act failed to protect the smaller businessmen from elimination through the monopolistic pressures of large combinations which used mergers to grow ever more powerful. As a result in 1914, Congress, viewing mergers as a continuous pervasive threat to small business, passed Sec. 7 of the Clayton Act which prohibited corporations in most instances from merging by purchasing the stock of their competitors. Ingenious businessmen, however, soon found a way to avoid Section 7 . . . by purchasing their rival's assets . . . and mergers continued . . . until 1950 when Congress passed the . . . Anti–Merger Act now before us.

Like the Sherman Act in 1890 and the Clayton Act in 1914, the basic purpose of the 1950 . . . Act . . . was to prevent economic concentration . . . that . . . was rapidly driving the small businessman out of the market . . . Congress decided to clamp down with vigor on mergers. It both revitalized Sec. 7 by "plugging its loophole" and broadened its scope . . . Congress sought to preserve competition among many small businesses by arresting a trend toward concentration in its incipiency before that trend developed to the point that a market was left in the grip of a few big companies . . .

The facts of this case present exactly the threatening trend toward concentration which Congress wanted to halt. The number of small grocery stores in the Los Angeles retail grocery market has been declining . . . Von's and Shopping Bag, two of the most successful and largest companies in the area, jointly owning 66 grocery stores, merged to become the second largest grocery chain in Los Angeles. This merger cannot be defended on the ground that one of the companies was about to fail or that the two had to merge to save themselves from destruction by some larger and more powerful competitor. What we have on the contrary is simply the case of two already powerful companies merging in a way which makes them even more powerful than they were before . . .

Appellee's primary argument is that the merger . . . is not prohibited . . . because the Los Angeles . . . market was competitive before the merger, has been since, and may continue to be in the future. Even so, Sec. 7 "requires not merely an appraisal of the immediate impact of the merger upon competition but a prediction of the impact upon competitive conditions in the future; this is what is meant . . . to arrest anticompetitive tendencies in their incipiency" . . . [A] market marked . . . by a large number of mergers would slowly but inevitably gravitate from a market of many small sellers to one dominated by one or a few giants . . .

[We] not only reverse the judgment below but direct the District Court to order divestiture without delay.

Comments and Questions

1. The *Brown* case signalled both future hope and future trouble for the government in prosecuting merger cases; *hope* in that the case was won, and relatively small percentages of market foreclosure in retailing were brought within the Clayton Act; *trouble* in that the possible combinations of market definitions could make the cases endless. The Brown Corporation was still arguing for more refinements of market definition until the Court simply declared an end to the debate.
2. In reading the *Von's Grocery* case, you have encountered what is perhaps the cleanest, most straightforward approach to a merger case imaginable. It probably also marks the maximum enthusiasm for the enforcement of antimerger law in the more than one hundred years that have elapsed since the passage of the Sherman Antitrust Act.
3. Compare the commentary in the *Brown* and *Von's* cases to the commentary of Justice Brandeis in the *Leggett* case in the preceding chapter on the evolution of corporate law. Is small size a practical goal for law enforcement, or should the Congress and the courts allow businesses to grow or shrink as they themselves see fit?
4. Justice Black blames the failure of earlier antimerger law on "ingenious businessmen." Is it likely that businessmen dreamed up the "assets loophole" and dizzying definitions of markets, or is it more probable that their lawyers did?

   Did the lawyers practicing in the field owe any duty to see that the spirit of the antitrust laws were faithfully enforced? Or did their duties begin and end with zealous representation of their clients?

CONGLOMERATE MERGERS

Conglomerate mergers raised special problems under the antimerger provisions of the Clayton Act as amended. A *conglomerate* merger differs from either *vertical integration* or *horizontal integration* as found in the preceding cases. The creation of United States Steel had vertical aspects, the integration from raw materials—iron ore, coal, and limestone—through steel making and on to fabrication of steel products. United States Steel also had horizontal aspects; companies that were formerly in the same market as buyers or sellers of steel, producers of steel, or steel fabricators were merged out of existence. (The same was true in the Brown merger, which would have integrated manufacturing and retailing, but also had horizontal effects.)

The problem raised by conglomerate mergers can be introduced quite simply with a question: if a company desires to merge with a company arguably in another "line of commerce" can the merger be prohibited under the law? To stay with the steel industry, could United States Steel have been prevented from buying Marathon Oil since after the merger there would be just as many steel companies and just as many oil companies as there were before the merger? On the surface, it may look like there is no less competition in either steel or oil after the merger. Other examples: if a tobacco company buys a beer maker (Philip Morris buying Miller Brewing) or an electrical equipment manufacturer buys a securities firm (General Electric purchase of Kidder Peabody), can the mergers be challenged under Section 7 of the Clayton Act?

The answer to the foregoing questions is no, worked out in case law and regulatory practice, even though as a matter of horse sense an observer might conclude that the progressive enlargement of a company will have effects on competition either at the time of the merger or later, in a number of "lines of commerce." One of the reasons why a corporation wants to enlarge itself may be that there are market advantages to greater size and scope, some of which might not be perfectly predictable when a merger takes place.

The conglomerate merger problem is an offshoot of the general problem of size, which appeared many years earlier in the *U.S. Steel* case. The argument made by the government there—size in itself inhibits competition—was never accepted later; large size alone does not violate the antitrust law.

FTC v. *Procter and Gamble* (1967) was a conglomerate merger case. Procter and Gamble, a national powerhouse in detergent marketing, wanted to acquire Clorox, the leading national company in liquid bleach (48 percent of the national market; $40,000,000 in sales), a market in which Procter and Gamble was not engaged prior to the proposed acquisition. The merger was challenged under Section 7 and disallowed, the Supreme Court finding numerous ways that this "product extension" by Procter could have anticompetitive effects:

> In the marketing of soaps, detergents, and cleansers, as in the marketing of household liquid bleach, advertising and sales promotion are vital. In 1957 Procter was the Nation's leading advertiser, spending more than $80,000,000 on advertising and an additional $47,000,000 on sales promotion. Due to its tremendous volume, Procter receives substantial discounts from the media . . . [I]t can . . . feature several products in its promotions, reducing printing, mailing and other costs, for each product. It also purchases network programs on behalf of several products, enabling it to give each product network exposure at a fraction of the cost per product that a firm with only one product to advertise would incur.[16]

[16]368 U.S. 568, 573 (1967).

> The Commission found that the subsidization of Procter with its huge assets and advertising advantages for the already dominant Clorox would dissuade new entrants and discourage active competition from the firms already in the industry due to fear of retaliation by Procter. The Commission thought it relevant that retailers might be induced to give Clorox preferred shelf space since it would be manufactured by Procter . . . There was also the danger that Procter might underprice Clorox in order to drive out competition and subsidize the underpricing with revenue from other products.[17]
>
> Section 7 . . . was intended to arrest the anticompetitive effects of market power in their incipiency. The core question . . . requires a prediction of the merger's impact on . . . competition, present and future.[18]
>
> The anticompetitive effects with which this product-extension is fraught can easily be seen: (1) the substitution of the powerful acquiring firm for the smaller, but already dominant, firm may substantially reduce the competitive structure of the industry by raising entry barriers and dissuading the smaller firms from aggressively competing; (2) the acquisition eliminates the potential competition of the acquiring firm.[19]

In the *Procter and Gamble* case, the Supreme Court came close to finding that size in itself may warrant limits to preserve competition. This line of thinking, if extended, could have curtailed the vast numbers of mergers in the 1970s and 1980s, many of which were "conglomerate" in nature. If courts were to take into account *advertising budgets*, the possibilities of *reciprocal dealing* (formerly independent companies use one another's products and services and thereby take themselves out of the market) and *cross subsidization* (one company financing the acquired firm to secure a competitive advantage over nonsubsidized companies in the same line of commerce) then many mergers of the next two decades would have been prohibited.

The initial success in the *Procter and Gamble* case was not matched in other cases involving mergers, and eventually the courts accepted the merging companies' arguments based on the "lines of commerce" rules from the vertical and horizontal merger cases.

The growing toleration for conglomerate mergers did not mean that conglomerate mergers did not affect competition. As part of his extensive commentary on conglomerate mergers, Professor Mueller discusses the impact of the acquisition in 1970 by Philip Morris (a tobacco company) of Miller Brewing (a beer maker):

> Prior to its acquisition, Miller was the eighth largest U.S. brewer with only 4.5% of sales in 1969. Miller was a financially successful company, whose operating income . . . roughly equalled that of other national brewers. But in comparison with its acquirer, Philip Morris Inc., Miller was a financial midget. Philip Morris is a huge, powerful conglomerate firm, which overshadows all other U.S. brewers except for Anheuser-Busch . . .

[17] Ibid., p.575.

[18] Ibid., p.575.

[19] Ibid., p.578.

> When a conglomerate acquires a small factor in the market it has a strong incentive to engage in cross-subsidization to expand its position . . .
>
> In 1972, Philip Morris acquired the Meister Brau and Lite brands of Meister Brau . . . Immediately PM–Miller began accelerating advertising outlays for the Lite brand from $525,000 in 1973 to $33 million in 1980 and $83 million in 1987. The Lite advertising program has become a classic case study of how to blitz one's way into a market segment with advertising outlays . . .
>
> This is the environment in which other brewers struggled for survival. As PM–Miller and Anheuser–Busch increased advertising and further segmented the market with new brands, competing brewers were crowded out . . . The increased emphasis on advertising especially disadvantaged the regional brewers . . .
>
> The extent and significance of PM-Miller's cross-subsidization can be best appreciated if Miller is viewed as an autonomous profit center . . . Miller Division incurred losses every year during 1971–1975, totalling $120 million. In 1976 and 1977, Miller earned very modest profits. Since then its profits have continued to be submarginal . . .[20]

As a small aside, the conglomerate acquisitions of Philip Morris did not stop with Miller. In 1984, Philip Morris acquired General Foods with sales of $8.6 billion, and in 1988 it acquired Kraft Foods with sales of $11 billion. Through acquisitions Philip Morris had become the tenth largest corporation operating in the United States. Recalling the earlier antitrust standards, we see that none of these acquisitions involved companies that were about to fail, or smaller companies joining to become more competitive. On the contrary, what made the above acquisitions desirable was the gigantic size and profit ability of the acquired companies.

In the end, the *United States Steel* dictum that size alone is not an offense ruled, and the lawyer-economist–directed battles over market definition could proceed unabated, unless the government gave up the fight altogether, as was increasingly the case. Fewer and fewer enterprises, through "conglomerate" mergers, controlled greater and greater assets, sales, and profits.

THE 1980 SENATE STUDY OF CORPORATE CONCENTRATION

In the sixty-odd years that separate the Pujo Committee hearings from a 1980 Senate study on corporate concentration,[21] there were dramatic changes in the way Americans lived, worked, and did business: the horse gave way to the car; the telegraph to the telephone and the computer; the mechanical to the electronic; coal to oil; railroads to automobile and air travel; country living to urban living and then suburban living; small business and subsistence farms

[20]W. Mueller, "Conglomerates," in Adams, op. cit. (*Structure . . .*), pp. 331, 332.

[21]U.S. Senate, Committee on Governmental Affairs, "Structure of Corporate Concentration," 96th Congress, 2d Session (1980).

to large business and 500-acre spreads; and sole proprietorships to partnerships to corporations to multinational holding companies. Some of these changes were already underway at the turn of the century and were changes of degree rather than kind.

By 1980, when the Senate study was done, the degree of sophistication in collecting and interpreting corporate data had markedly improved, but the overall findings in 1980 were hauntingly similar to those reached in 1913. Computerization made it much easier to tabulate the largest stockholders and voting power in the 100 largest industrial and trading companies, the largest banks, and the largest insurance companies. Researchers could construct elaborate matrices mapping the tens of thousands of interconnections among the boards of directors of the leading industrial and financial institutions.

The results were not pleasant if one were hoping that ninety years of antitrust law had inhibited the ability to concentrate wealth and the control of American businesses. The Committee found no smoking guns, that is, concrete proof that power that was available was being used or abused, but the data showed a day-to-day potential for corporations' violating every prohibition found in the antitrust laws. Moreover, there were no identifiable villains, like an overstuffed J. P. Morgan surrounded by money bags, to render the structure of American enterprise intelligible at a glance; economic control had become more abstract. The Senate study sits in its drab green cover in the government documents section of the library, gathering dust, never having been brought to life by the pen of any cartoonist.

The study documented that large firms controlled a significant percentage in each critical sector of the economy. [Included in the study were New York banking, Midwestern banking, California banking, airlines, surface transportation (railroads, trucking), electric utilities, retailing, transportation equipment, steel, rubber, chemicals, energy (oil), electrical equipment, telecommunications, information processing and office equipment, aerospace and aircraft, food, and broadcasting.] Putting nominally "competitive" companies side by side, the researchers found "a pattern of dominance by the industry leader in sales, assets, net income and employees over its largest competitors... [T]he analysis showed that for most of the industries in the study, the number one company was twice the size of its next competitor and four times larger than the other major competitors." The study also found that the few largest companies in each sector controlled the sector.[22]

Many of the companies that had been among the biggest in the early part of the century continued to be so at the time of the study—for example U. S. Steel and Exxon (successor to Standard Oil of New Jersey) and other spin-offs from the Standard Oil Trust (SoCal, Mobil, Standard of Indiana, and Atlantic Richfield). Other companies that had been in their infancy when first put together, still dominated their field (G.E. in electrical equipment and AT&T in telecommunications).

[22]Ibid., pp12–28.

Some very large companies did not exist at all in 1903. In 1980, consequential automobile manufacturers were three, with General Motor substantially larger than Ford and both substantially larger than third–place Chrysler. Other very large companies had come onto the scene—IBM in information processing, United Technologies in aerospace, and United and American Airlines in air travel. Some of the names prominent in 1913 had disappeared, but the abiding phenomenon of size and relatively few companies being dominant in all important sectors of the economy still typified the industrial and financial structure. If out-and-out monopoly did not exist, oligopoly did.[23]

In banking, analyzed regionally, a few banks dominated each regional market. In New York six banks (Citicorp, Chase, Manufacturer's-Hanover, J. P. Morgan, Chemical Bank, and Bankers Trust) had overwhelming consequence in deposits, assets, and, as will be discussed later, in voting power and directorships in all of the largest corporations. Extensive banker involvement in all corporations, which had been so worrisome in 1913, was still present 67 years later.[24]

What about the ownership of the firms and the voting power in the firms? The 1980 study charted the consequential stockholders and their voting power in the largest enterprises. Banks and investment groups predominated as holders of stock and holders of voting power in the industrial giants. (Ownership by famous families, however, was not as visible in 1980 as it was in the TNEC study done in 1937 since the SEC rules did not require that families disclose their holdings; for example, the Rockefeller family and Rockefeller–created foundations still held substantial stock in the Exxon corporation.) The percentages of stock ownership and voting power in the charts that follow may look small, but it should be remembered that for the largest corporations, with stock widely held and not voted, a smaller percentage of the total stock in large blocks can be enough for the political control of the entire corporation.[25]

In addition to stock ownership and voting power, the 1980 study also considered direct and indirect interlocks. Section 8 of the Clayton Act prohibited direct interlocks between competitors, but did not cover *indirect interlocks*, which occur when directors from two competing companies sit on the board of a third corporation that is the competitor of neither. Thus while Citicorp and Chase could not have members on each other's board—a direct interlock—both banks furnished directors for the Exxon Corporation, thereby indirectly interlocking the two banks. Similarly, Exxon and Socal could not have interlocking directors, but each furnished directors for a third corporation, Caterpillar, indirectly interlocking them.[26]

The following figures and tables show the results of the stockholding-voting and the interlocking directorate tabulations. In Table 6-2 on electrical

[23]Ibid., pp.33-93.

[24]Ibid., pp.11–19.

[25]Ibid., pp.1–12.

[26]Ibid., pp.5-6; 18,19.

TABLE 6-2
ELECTRICAL EQUIPMENT

COMPANY Size		GENERAL ELECTRIC				WESTINGHOUSE		
Sales				$22,460,600,000				$7,332,000,000
Assets				$16,644,500,000				$6,821,500,000
Net income				$1,408,800,000				$73,900,000
Employees				405,000				145,254
Auditor				Peat, Marwick, Mitchell & Co.				Price Waterhouse & Co
Institutional Shareholders		*VOT%*	*COM%*	*CUM%*	*NAME*	*VOT%*	*COM%*	*CUM%*
Largest 6	‡J P Morgan & Co Inc	.19	1.68	1.68	Capital Group Inc	1.20	2.77	2.77
	TIAA/CREF	1.16	1.16	2.83	J P Morgan & Co Inc	2.63	2.74	5.50
	†Citicorp	.26	1.04	3.87	†Bankamerica Corporat	1.78	2.67	8.17
	†First Natl Boston Co.	.82	1.01	4.89	Lord Abbett & Compan	1.52	1.52	9.69
	National Detroit Cor	.86	.96	5.85	Marsh & McLennan Com		.87	10.56
	Bankers Tr New York	.91	.93	6.78	†Mfg Hanover Corporat	.61	.72	11.28
Summary	Top 6 holders	4.20	6.78		Top 6 holders	7.74	11.28	
	Next 18 holders	7.71	11.18		Next 18 holders	4.64	7.12	
	All 321 others	20.53	25.22		All 105 others	4.33	5.65	
Interlocks with firms in the study								
Direct				18				11
Indirect				747				409
Indirect interlocks within the group								
General Electric				-				9
Westinghouse				9				-

†Indicates the issuer shares exactly one director with the holder and/or its subsidiaries or affiliates.
‡Indicates the issuer shares two or more directors with the holder and/or its subsidiaries and affiliates.

equipment, the two leading companies, General Electric and Westinghouse, are profiled. The stockholding for General Electric shows that five of the top six shareholders are banks and that the top 24 holders of stock control about 18 percent of the voting power of the corporation. For Westinghouse, three banks and one investment company are the principal holders, and the top 24 holders also control about 18 percent of the stock.

Figure 6-5 shows the pattern of indirect interlocks between General Electric and Westinghouse. They each had indirect interlocks by simultaneous membership on the boards of nine banks, giving them connections that would have been illegal were they accomplished directly rather than through other corporations.

Table 6-3 and Figure 6-6 show the patterns for energy—oil. The seven largest companies were owned in largest part by banks and investment companies. Socal and Atlantic Richfield showed the greatest concentration of ownership-voting, with the top 24 holders holding 24 percent of the stock and

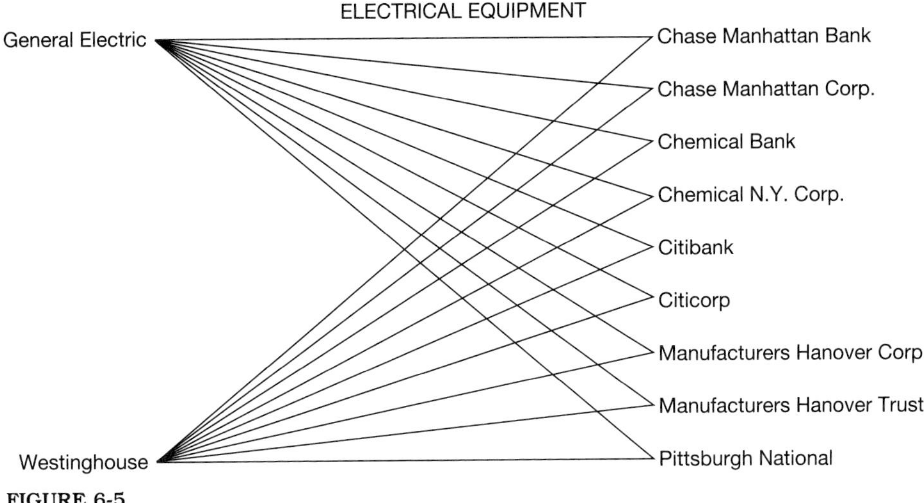

FIGURE 6-5

other companies showing concentrations of 15-20 percent. Figure 6-6 shows the direct interlocks among the oil companies, with oil companies simultaneously furnishing directors for the boards of many other corporations.

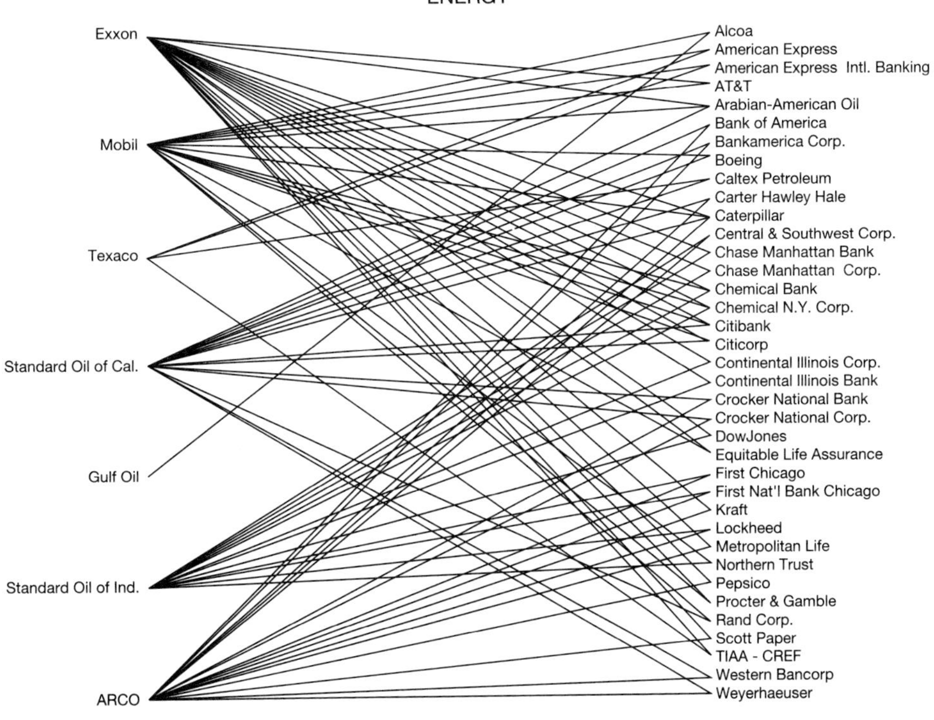

FIGURE 6-6

TABLE 6-3
ENERGY

COMPANY Size		EXXON			MOBIL				TEXACO			
Sales				$79,106,471,000				$44,720,908,000				$38,350,370,000
Assets				$49,489,964,000				$27,505,756,000				$22,991,955,000
Net income				$4,295,243,000				$2,007,158,000				$1,759,069,000
Employees				169,096				213,500				65,814
Auditor				Price Waterhouse & Co.				Arthur Young & Co.				Arthur Andersen & Co.
Institutional Shareholders		*VOT%*	*COM%*	*CUM%*	*NAME*	*VOT%*	*COM%*	*CUM%*	*NAME*	*VOT%*	*COM%*	*CUM%*
Largest 6	†Chase Manhattan Corp	1.57	1.71	1.71	†J P Morgan & Co Inc	1.94	2.43	2.43	Union National Bank	.96	.99	.99
	Mfg Hanover Corporat	.75	1.26	2.97	National Detroit Corp	1.46	1.57	4.00	National Detroit Cor	.84	.90	1.89
	J P Morgan & Co Inc	.38	1.14	4.11	Bancoklahoma Corpora	1.26	1.26	5.25	†TIAA/CREF	.87	.87	2.76
	†TIAA/CREF	1.02	1.02	5.13	Chase Manhattan Corp	1.07	1.21	6.46	Fayez Sarofim & Comp	.01	.79	3.54
	Fayez Sarofim & Comp		.86	5.99	Fayez Sarofim & Comp	.01	1.03	7.50	Continental Illinois	.37	.70	4.24
	Citicorp	.32	.81	6.80	Prudential Insurance	.97	.97	8.47	Mfg Hanover Corporat	.48	.65	4.89
Summary	Top 6 holders	4.04	6.80		Top 6 holders	6.70	8.47		Top 6 holders	3.52	4.89	
	Next 18 holders	7.88	9.99		Next 18 holders	5.60	8.55		Next 18 holders	6.21	7.49	
	All 355 others	19.61	24.80		All 299 others	14.92	18.75		All 286 others	12.96	16.54	
Interlocks with firms in the study												
Direct				13				19				3
Indirect				441				548				94
Indirect interlocks within the group												
Exxon				-				9				2
Mobil				9				-				4
Texaco				2				4				-
Standard Oil California				6				12				2
Gulf Oil				0				1				0
Standard Oil (Indiana)				8				5				0
Atlantic Richfield				5				2				0

†Indicates the Issuer Shares Exactly One Director with The Holder and/or its subsidiaries or affiliates.

TABLE 6-3 (cont.)
ENERGY

COMPANY		STANDARD OIL CALIFORNIA			GULF OIL				STANDARD OIL (INDIANA)			
Size												
Sales				$29,947,554,000				$23,910,000,000				$18,610,347,000
Assets				$16,102,632,000				$17,265,000,000				$17,149,899,000
Net income				$1,784,694,000				$1,322,000,000				$1,506,618,000
Employees				39,676				57,600				52,282
Auditor				Price Waterhouse & Co.				Coopers & Lybrand				Price Waterhouse & Co.
Institutional Shareholders		*VOT%*	*COM%*	*CUM%*	*NAME*	*VOT%*	*COM%*	*CUM%*	*NAME*	*VOT%*	*COM%*	*CUM%*
Largest 6	†Crocker National Corp	.64	10.72	10.72	‡Mellon National Corp	5.71	6.17	6.17	Fayez Sarofim & Comp	.01	1.23	1.23
	Chase Manhattan Corp	1.20	1.26	11.97	TIAA/CREF	1.43	1.43	7.60	Citicorp	.60	1.13	2.36
	Fayez Sarofim & Comp	.01	1.04	13.01	Prudential Insurance	1.28	1.28	8.88	†Chase Manhattan Corp	1.04	1.12	3.48
	Mfg Hanover Corporat	.33	.86	13.87	J P Morgan & Co Inc	.80	1.28	10.16	†Harris Bankcorp	.99	1.11	4.59
	Wells Fargo & Compan	.79	.81	14.68	First Tulsa Bancorp	1.09	1.09	11.25	National Detroit Cor	.92	.99	5.58
	J P Morgan & Co Inc	.63	.75	15.43	Fayez Sarofim & Comp	.01	.83	12.08	‡First Chicago Corp	.81	.87	6.46
Summary	Top 6 holders	3.60	15.43		Top 6 holders	10.31	12.08		Top 6 holders	4.37	6.46	
	Next 18 holders	6.70	8.98		Next 18 holders	5.37	8.60		Next 18 holders	7.69	9.78	
	All 288 others	13.83	17.02		All 244 others	9.64	13.05		All 299 others	18.11	22.66	
Interlocks with firms in the study												
Direct				13				5				11
Indirect				402				96				355
Indirect interlocks within the group												
Exxon				6				0				8
Mobil				12				1				5
Texaco				2				0				0
Standard Oil California				-				0				0
Gulf Oil				0				-				0
Standard Oil (Indiana)				0				0				-
Atlantic Richfield				12				0				6

†Indicates the Issuer Shares Exactly One Director with The Holder and/or its subsidiaries or affiliates.
‡Indicates the Issuer Shares Two or More Directors with The Holder and/or its subsidiaries or affiliates.

TABLE 6-3 (Cont.)
ENERGY

COMPANY		ATLANTIC RICHFIELD		
Size				
Sales				$16,233,959,000
Assets				$13,833,387,000
Net income				$1,165,894,000
Employees				50,341
Auditor		Coopers & Lybrand		
Institutional Investors		*VOT%*	*COM%*	*CUM%*
Largest 6	†Security Pacific Cor	.15	2.88	2.88
	Citicorp	.90	2.43	5.30
	Mfg Hanover Corporat	.90	1.96	7.27
	Marsh & McLennan Com	.57	1.25	8.52
	Prudential Insurance	.90	1.04	9.56
	Calif Pub Emp Ret Sy	.89	1.03	10.58
Summary	Top 6 holders	4.30	10.58	
	Next 18 holders	5.22	12.73	
	All 318 others	22.41	30.21	
Interlocks with firms in the study				
Direct				14
Indirect				382
Indirect interlocks within the group				
Exxon				5
Mobil				2
Texaco				0
Standard Oil California				12
Gulf Oil				0
Standard Oil (Indiana)				6
Atlantic Richfield				-

†Indicates the issuer shares exactly one director with the holder and/or its subsidiaries or affiliates.

Table 6-4 shows the stockholdings of the New York banks, and reveals that the banks had substantial stockholdings in each other. Figure 6-7 demonstrates the extensive connections among banks through the indirect interlock phenomenon already discussed. If the banks had been directly interlocked in 1913, they were just one step removed from direct interlocks in 1980.

The conclusion that could be drawn is that financial institutions had substantial stock and voting power in industrial corporations, and in each other. The banks also shared common public accounting firms. (We know from the Iran case in Chapter 2 that the lawyers for the largest banks know each other very well.)

What had happened to J. P. Morgan & Company? In 1980, Citicorp led the list of the corporate interconnections of the major banks with 49 direct

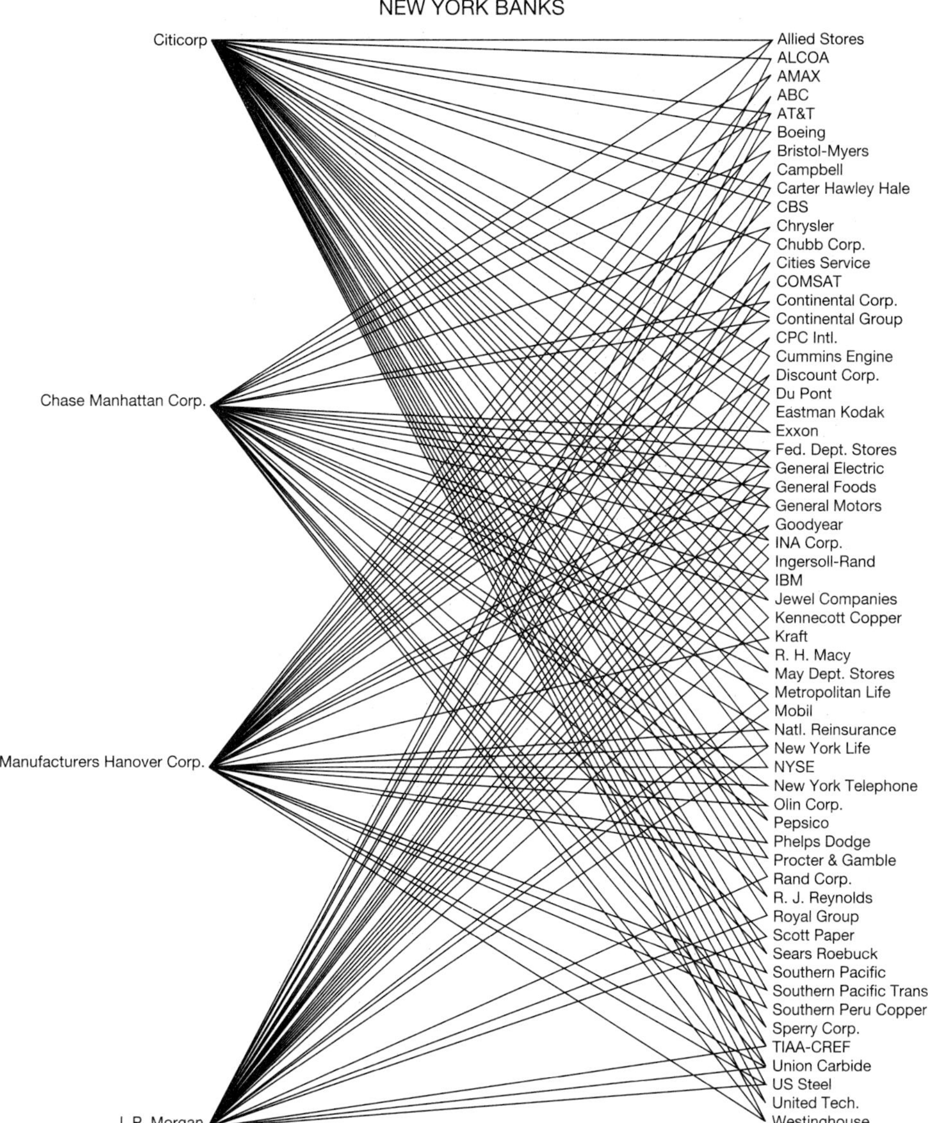
NEW YORK BANKS
Citicorp
Chase Manhattan Corp.
Manufacturers Hanover Corp.
J. P. Morgan
Allied Stores
ALCOA
AMAX
ABC
AT&T
Boeing
Bristol-Myers
Campbell
Carter Hawley Hale
CBS
Chrysler
Chubb Corp.
Cities Service
COMSAT
Continental Corp.
Continental Group
CPC Intl.
Cummins Engine
Discount Corp.
Du Pont
Eastman Kodak
Exxon
Fed. Dept. Stores
General Electric
General Foods
General Motors
Goodyear
INA Corp.
Ingersoll-Rand
IBM
Jewel Companies
Kennecott Copper
Kraft
R. H. Macy
May Dept. Stores
Metropolitan Life
Mobil
Natl. Reinsurance
New York Life
NYSE
New York Telephone
Olin Corp.
Pepsico
Phelps Dodge
Procter & Gamble
Rand Corp.
R. J. Reynolds
Royal Group
Scott Paper
Sears Roebuck
Southern Pacific
Southern Pacific Trans.
Southern Peru Copper
Sperry Corp.
TIAA-CREF
Union Carbide
US Steel
United Tech.
Westinghouse

FIGURE 6-7

TABLE 6-4
NEW YORK BANKS

COMPANY		CITICORP				CHASE MANHATTAN CORP				MANUFACTURERS HANOVER			
Size													
Assets					$106,370,619,000				$64,708,018,000				$47,575,446,000
Deposits					$70,290,725,000				$48,456,210,000				$38,156,078,000
Loans					$62,536,389,000				$39,749,569,000				$25,230,815,000
Net Income					$541,447,000				$303,019,000				$211,605,000
Employees					51,600				32,510				21,165
Auditor		Peat, Marwick, Mitchell & Co.				Peat, Marwick, Mitchell & Co.				Peat, Marwick, Mitchell & Co.			
Institutional Shareholders			*VOT%*	*COM%*	*CUM%*	*NAME*	*VOT%*	*COM%*	*CUM%*	*NAME*	*VOT%*	*COM%*	*CUM%*
Largest 6		J P Morgan & Co Inc	2.29	2.78	2.78	Citicorp	1.35	2.13	2.13	Delaware Management	2.82	3.08	3.08
		Prudential Insurance	2.38	2.38	5.16	First Intl Bancshare	1.76	1.77	3.90	‡Continental Corporat	2.71	2.71	5.79
		First Natl Boston Co	1.77	2.06	7.22	Teledyne Inc	1.23	1.23	5.13	J P Morgan & Co Inc	.11	2.63	8.41
		Price T Rowe Associa	.26	1.90	9.12	Mfg Hanover Corporat	.93	1.19	6.32	Citicorp	1.56	2.31	10.72
		†TIAA / CREF	1.86	1.86	10.98	Calif Pub Emp Ret Sy	1.19	1.19	7.50	TIAA / CREF	2.01	2.01	12.73
		Babson David L & Co		1.56	12.54	Boesky Ivan F & Comp	.98	.98	8.48	Ameritrust Corporati	1.86	1.98	14.71
Summary		Top 6 holders	8.56	12.54		Top 6 holders	7.43	8.48		Top 6 holders	11.06	14.71	
		Next 18 holders	11.84	14.66		Next 18 holders	9.42	12.07		Next 18 holders	12.20	16.99	
		All 207 others	19.08	23.59		All 115 others	10.88	14.40		All 109 others	9.39	13.34	
Interlocks with firms in the study													
Direct					49				24				21
Indirect					871				544				504
Indirect interlocks within the group													
Citicorp					-				33				26
Chase Manhattan Corp					33				-				22
Manufacturers Hanover					26				22				-
J. P. Morgan					35				19				23
Chemical New York					27				17				22
Bankers Trust					21				15				13

† Indicates the issuer shares exactly one director with the holder and/or its subsidiaries or affiliates.

‡ Indicates the issuer shares two or more directors with the holder and/or its subsidiaries and affiliates.

TABLE 6-4 (cont.)
NEW YORK BANKS

COMPANY		J. P. MORGAN			CHEMICAL NEW YORK				BANKERS TRUST			
Size												
Assets				$43,487,679,000				$39,375,293,000				$30,952,922,000
Deposits				$30,278,552,000				$28,986,820,000				$22,436,852,000
Loans				$22,158,171,000				$20,337,991,000				$15,975,911,000
Net Income				$288,127,000				$134,706,000				$113,738,000
Employees				10,831				17,494				12,671
Auditor				Price Waterhouse & Co.				Price Waterhouse & Co.				Price Waterhouse & Co.
Institutional Shareholders		*VOT%*	*COM%*	*CUM%*	*NAME*	*VOT%*	*COM%*	*CUM%*	*NAME*	*VOT%*	*COM%*	*CUM%*
Largest 6	National Detroit Cor	2.45	3.72	3.72	Connecticut General	.48	1.76	1.76	Citicorp	2.73	3.84	3.84
	Price T Rowe Associa	1.04	3.18	6.90	Teledyne Inc	1.60	1.60	3.36	American General Ins	1.69	1.69	5.53
	First Natl Boston Co	1.84	2.50	9.40	Gulf & Western Inds	1.46	1.46	4.82	FMR Corporation		1.66	7.20
	Chase Manhattan Corp	1.79	2.39	11.79	Bankers Life Company	1.35	1.35	6.17	Maryland National Co	1.49	1.49	8.69
	Bankamerica Corporat	1.07	1.62	13.41	Citicorp	.18	1.13	7.29	Institutional Cap Co	.28	1.14	9.83
	Continental Corporat	1.50	1.50	14.91	Firestone Pension Pl	1.08	1.08	8.37	†Continental Corporat	.88	.88	10.71
Summary	Top 6 holders	9.68	14.91		Top 6 holders	6.14	8.37		Top 6 holders	7.07	10.71	
	Next 18 holders	11.14	16.87		Next 18 holders	9.59	12.16		Next 18 holders	3.94	7.64	
	All 174 others	18.72	23.83		All 49 others	4.04	5.35		All 38 others	2.23	2.75	
Interlocks with firms in the study												
Direct				31				24				16
Indirect				625				588				476
Indirect interlocks within the group												
Citicorp				35				27				21
Chase Manhattan Corp				19				17				15
Manufacturers Hanover				23				22				13
J. P. Morgan				-				25				9
Chemical New York				25				-				26
Bankers Trust				9				26				-

† Indicates the issuer shares exactly one director with the holder and/or its subsidiaries or affiliates.

interlocks and 871 indirect interlocks. It was followed by J. P. Morgan with 31 directs and 625 indirects. The six New York banks had 165 direct interlocks and 3608 indirect interlocks—a list that parallels the one compiled by the Pujo Committee.[27] Among nonbankers, AT&T led with 39 direct and 938 indirect interlocks.[28] (This was before the breakup of AT&T by an antitrust decree in 1980.)

Far and away the leading investor was J.P. Morgan & Company with $18.5 billion worth of securities followed, by Capital Group ($7.7 b), Citicorp ($7.6 b), and Prudential Insurance ($7.4 b).[29]

The researchers for the study were clearly worried that despite the antitrust law there had been persistent concentration of control among the largest companies in each industrial sector and substantial voting power concentration in banks and financial institutions. Moreover, the network of shared directors showed that there was nothing left of Section 8 of the Clayton Act as a practical matter. The researchers called for more studies with their own as a starting place. They did not anticipate the utter abandonment of antitrust law in the Reagan years.

THE IBM AND AT&T CASES

The largest corporations of the United States have been compared to sovereign states due to their size, their geographic scope, their interconnections to governments around the world, and their ability to make their presence felt in all settings pertinent to their welfare. Anthony Sampson in his book, *The Sovereign State of ITT*[30] argued that the International Telephone and Telegraph Company (not to be confused with AT&T) could be better understood as a sovereign nation pursuing its own interests than as a company operating within regular governmental limits. ITT dealt with both fascist and non–fascist regimes in the World War II period.

Other writers have compared the earnings of the giant companies with the incomes of whole countries and find that some companies can dwarf the economic performance of entire nations. If the companies act like countries, then in the antitrust field they are countries at war with all of their legal forces mobilized to thwart any efforts to reduce their size and scope.[31] Their antagonists in warfare are either the government or rival businesses who sue for treble damages.

The *IBM* cases, which ended just after President Reagan took office, signalled the death of antitrust as a consequent counterforce to corporate power and size. The cases spanned a decade, involving government, business rivals of IBM, all levels of the federal court system, unprecedented pretrial

[27]Ibid., p. 12.

[28]Ibid., p. 25.

[29]Ibid., p. 12.

[30](New York: Stein and Day, 1973).

[31]For additional discussion of multinationals at legal war, see Chapter 9.

maneuvering, and the largest law firms in the country. Trials took place nationwide, and everyone—except IBM—lost.

What happens when giant corporations are threatened with serious antitrust charges that could lead to their dissolution? In one of the cases against IBM brought by Control Data in Minneapolis, Minnesota, Control Data was represented by a leading local firm, which was dwarfed by Cravath and Swaine from New York, the firm representing IBM. Someone wondered whether there was a funeral in town, seeing a stream of black Cadillac limousines. "No," the president of Control Data cracked, "that's the IBM legal department returning from lunch."[32]

The cortege was actually a funeral, but it might have been the lawyers representing IBM. The Control Data lawyers were outnumbered, outspent, and outmaneuvered in their lawsuit. Accepting their fate, Control Data settled, salvaging attorneys' fees and agreeing to destroy their computerized evidence files. In a related case, Telex Corporation won the first round against IBM, netting one of the largest recoveries in antitrust history, only to lose on appeal and wind up owing IBM for the theft of trade secrets. Telex went from being a big winner to facing bankruptcy, and settled the case for a small sum.

What made IBM so formidable an opponent against private litigants like Control Data, Telex, and even the Antitrust Division of the U. S. government? First there was the ability to hire a very large law firm and fully mobilize it for as long as necessary: establishing special offices for lawyers within the corporate headquarters; developing a vast IBM computer system for the classification and retrieval of millions of pertinent documents; providing an unlimited budget for expenses—travel, accommodations for lawyers, associates and secretaries (including, on occasion, summer homes for lawyers and associates working on the case); generating pretrial proceedings discovery all over the country, preparing and reproducing of mountains of documents under which opponents could be buried. (The trial transcript in the government case ran 114,000 pages, as compared to the once surprising record of 40,000 pages in the Alcoa case.) Legal fees to the Cravath firm ran to levels that were not exceeded until the 80's and the merger bonanza. One Cravath associate billed IBM for 27 hours of legal work in a single day, having gained three hours because of a New York to California flight!

The ability of IBM to spend has a corollary applicable to their adversaries. Opponents, including the government itself, faced costs and burdens of litigation that could be imposed largely at the discretion of IBM, leading in every facet of the litigation to an emotionally and financially spent opposition. One might think that the government with the whole treasury behind it would be exempt from the power traceable to the deep pockets of IBM. Not so. The government, although it spent $50 million, vastly underspent IBM and wound up accepting a dismissal of the case after years of litigation. One need say nothing about *the law* of antitrust against this background of tactics, expense, and time.

[32]The story is told in J. Goulden, *The Million Dollar Lawyers* (New York: Putnam, 1977)

Second, there was extensive use of expert witnesses from economics on the presence or absence of monopoly and monopoly power in the computer market. (IBM sent out 2700 questionnaires to companies on the computer industry, and the 1800 responses gave lawyers and economists practically infinite grist for theorizing on market definition and market power.) The applicability of economic theory created by the language of the antitrust law—"monopolize" or "attempt to monopolize"—made for a doubling of the usual theoretical refinements in an antitrust case. A dispute among rival economists might equal the disputes among lawyers, about which many a satirical story has been written.[33]

All cases against IBM by private litigants and the government were either lost or dropped. Everyone who opposed IBM must have been chastened by the experience, because the cases and their companion—AT&T—stand as the last significant monopoly cases.

The IBM loss was "matched" against a "victory" against AT&T. AT&T was settled in 1982 after the government had presented its evidence. AT&T, which had formerly held 22 companies for the provision of local and long distance service, was broken into seven regional compaines.[34] But the willingness of AT&T to settle rather than pursue the case further, leads one to wonder what AT&T got out of the settlement. (AT&T had more money than IBM if it had wanted to stretch out the lawsuit.)

It turns out that the gains from its "loss" were substantial: retention of its position in long distance service and telecommunications equipment manufacturing, deregulation of its activities, freedom to engage in businesses from which it had been foreclosed under prior consent agreements with the Justice Department—for example, international ventures. After the suit was settled, AT&T acquired National Cash Register to deepen its presence in computers and business data systems. AT&T has also established its own credit card system to rival Visa, Mastercard, and Discover. As a "loser" of an antitrust battle, AT&T in the early 1990s scarcely looks emaciated in size, scope, and power.

1980 ONWARD

Antitrust got off to less than a flying start in the first year of the Reagan administration. The winding up of the AT&T and IBM cases foretold the policy for the rest of the decade; no serious cases of antitrust would be brought. The 1980 Senate study had sounded warnings about corporate concentration, but they went unheeded. Moreover, many of the practices that were assumed by antitrust scholars to be clear-cut antitrust violations were embraced as positive virtues in the Reagan years.[35]

[33]M. Stewart, op. cit., pp. 53–113; see also Richard DeLemarter, *Big Blue: IBM's Use and Abuse of Power* (New York: Dodd Mead, 1986).

[34]M. Irwin, "The Telecommunications Industry," in Adams, op. cit. (*Structure*), pp. 245, 248–49.

[35]For a lament on the lack of antitrust enforcement after the IBM and AT&T cases, see H. Thorelli, et al., "Longer Live the Sherman Act!" *1990 Antitrust Bulletin,* pp. 537, 577-583.

Antitrust was swept away by deregulation, amplified by the official endorsement of the Chicago School of economists, who contended that antitrust law was ineffective, unnecessary, an impediment to economic efficiency, or all three. By the end of the decade, United States based multinationals offered additional justification for abandoning antitrust; what would otherwise amount to antitrust violations—for example, near-monopolistic size, agreements among competitors, and mergers establishing domestic market power—were essential if U. S.–based multinationals were to effectively "compete" with multinationals based elsewhere.

It was tricky logic, but what took competition away at one level—domestically—sustained it at another—in international trade. If dissenting observers thought that domestic competition and international competition are strung in the same key, they had simply missed an economic turning point; in some academic circles, the discourse had shifted from competition to efficiency. Political and business commentary becoming looser, competition and efficiency were casually intermixed, but the overall direction of the commentary was the same—the less antitrust the better, for everyone.[36]

Corporate mergers of the 1980s brought unprecedented size. At least ten of the corporations that were among the largest in 1980 no longer existed as independent companies, having been merged into another of the largest corporations. For example, Gulf Oil, one of the "seven sisters" (so named because of their almost familial relationship in international oil cartels) was acquired by Socal, its erstwhile sister, for $13.3 billion. Since the combination had vertical, horizontal, and conglomerate dimensions, it probably would not have been allowed under the antitrust standards of just a few years earlier.

Walter Adams and James Brock in their book, *Dangerous Pursuits*,[37] chart the 1980s merger wave. They argue that the mergers resulted in very large corporations, made some people very rich, and had no beneficial effect on efficiency, innovation, or the creation of "new value." (They contest the commonly heard claim that mergers uncover previously untapped corporate wealth. Instead, they contend that most of the mergers squandered corporate wealth.) When taken as a whole, the "merger craze" generated not much more than extortionate fees for lawyers and investment bankers, and quick profits by arbitrageurs (among whom the convicted felons Ivan Boesky and Michael Milkin were notorious, but not exceptional).[38] Whatever position one takes on the desirability of the 1980s' merger wave, an unduly intrusive antitrust law cannot be blamed for anything, since antitrust law prohibited nothing.

Too extreme? Table 6-5 shows the activity of the Antitrust Division of the Justice Department and the Federal Trade Commission in the Reagan years.

[36]For a contrary view on the continued need for zealous enforcement of antitrust, see W. Adams, et al., "The Sherman Act and the Economic Power Problem," *1990 Antitrust Bulletin*, pp. 25–55.

[37](New York: Pantheon, 1989).

[38]Ibid., pp. 31–66.

TABLE 6-5
MERGER POLICY UNDER THE REAGAN ADMINISTRATION

	Justice Department		Federal Trade Commission	
Year	Premerger Notifications Received	Cases Filed	Premerger Notifications Received	Administrative Complaints Filed
1981	993	3	996	6
1982	1,204	3	1,203	2
1983	1,101	2	1,093	1
1984	1,339	5	1,340	3
1985	1,604	5	1,603	2
1986	1,949	4	1,949	3
1987	2,533	4	1,346	0
TOTAL	10,723	26	9,530	17

Source: *Trial Lawyers for Public Justice,* Washington, D.C., November 22, 1988.

FIGURE 6-8
NUMBER OF MERGERS 1895–1987

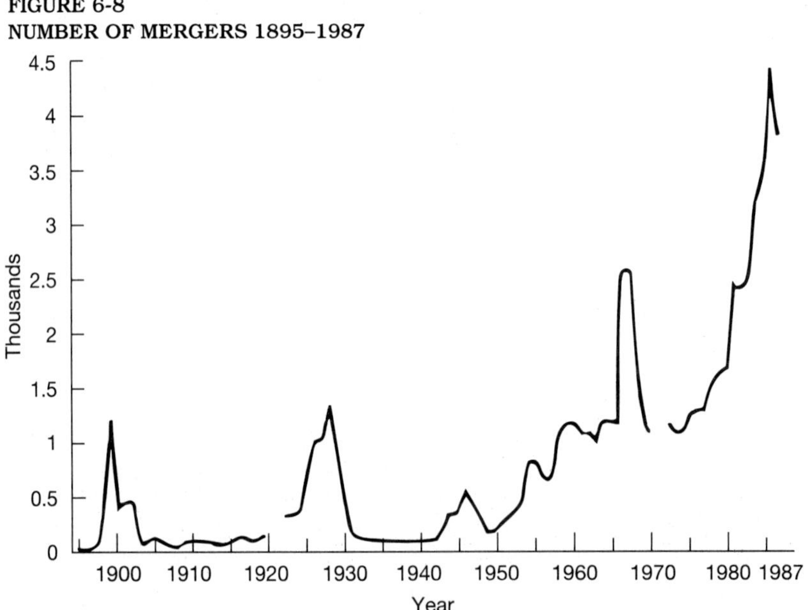

Source: Barrie A. Wigmore, "Speculation and the Crash of 1987." Paper delivered at the annual meeting of the American Economic Association, New York City, December 28, 1988.

TABLE 6-6
CORPORATE MERGERS AND ACQUISITIONS 1980–1988

Year	Number of Mergers and Acquisitions	Value ($ billions)	Number Valued in Excess of $1 billion
1980	1,565	$ 33.0	3
1981	2,326	67.0	8
1982	2,296	60.4	9
1983	2,387	52.8	7
1984	3,158	126.0	19
1985	3,428	145.4	26
1986	4,323	204.4	34
1987	3,701	167.5	30
1988	3,487	226.6	42
TOTAL	26,671	$ 1,083.4	178

Sources: Mergers & Acquisitions, May–June 1989; Walter Adams and James W. Brock, "Reaganomics and the Transmogrification of Merger Policy, "*Antitrust Bulletin,* Summer 1988, Table 1, p. 310; U.S. Congress, House, Subcommittee on Labor Management Relations, *Report: Pensions and Leveraged Buyouts,* February 7, 1989.

Under amendments to the antitrust law, premerger notification must be given to the government so that objections can be made before a merger goes forward. The trifling numbers on regulatory opposition to mergers speak for themselves.

But what if the anemic performance were traceable to a lack of need for the agencies to do more? Figure 6-8 shows the number of mergers from 1895 and the size of the 1980s wave relative to earlier waves of mergers. The year by year number and dollar volume for the 1980s are found in Table 6-6, and particular mergers by dollars involved and type are tabulated in Table 6-7. The most straightforward conclusion from the data would be that there were numerous opportunities for regulatory activism, but no inclination to invoke them.

The end of the decade found the largest corporations, all of them multinational in geographic scope, to be bigger, more in debt from the high–flying 1980s, and less competitive, in both the old and new senses of the word, than they had ever been historically. Size and market power were still present throughout the domestic American economy, antitrust law notwithstanding. Whatever limits there were originated in their own excesses rather than the rule of law.

By ironic twist, some of the speculative excesses of the merger wave produced divestitures and restructuring, and corporations were "spun out" from their erstwhile enthusiastic acquirers. Rather than by government decree of divestiture, sell offs, sometimes renamed "restructuring" "downsizing" or "rightsizing" were made, with this difference—enormous waste—despite Orwellian claims by CEOs, their financiers, and their lawyers that whatever was done was good, and what is now being done is even better—for now and evermore.

TABLE 6-7
TWENTY LARGEST CORPORATE DEALS IN U.S. HISTORY

Rank and Firms	Type of Deal	Value ($ billions)	Year
1. RJR–Nabisco	Leveraged buyout	$25.0	1989
2. Philip Morris–Kraft	Merger	13.4	1988
3. Chevron–Gulf	Merger	13.3	1984
4. Texaco–Getty	Merger	10.1	1984
5. Du Pont–Conoco	Merger	8.0	1981
6. British Petroleum–Standard Oil	Acquired half-interest not already owned	8.0	1987
7. Campeau–Federated Department Stores	Merger	7.4	1988
8. U.S. Steel–Marathon Oil	Merger	6.6	1982
9. General Electric–RCA	Merger	6.4	1986
10. Beatrice Foods	Leveraged buyout	6.2	1986
11. Royal Dutch Shell–Shell Oil	Acquired one-third interest not already owned	5.7	1985
12. Mobil Oil–Superior	Merger	5.7	1984
13. Philip Morris–General Foods	Merger	5.6	1985
14. Grand Metropolitan–Pillsbury	Merger	5.5	1988
15. Sante Fe–Southern Pacific	Merger	5.1	1983
16. Kodak–Sterling Drug	Merger	5.1	1988
17. Allied–Signal Companies	Merger	4.9	1985
18. R.J. Reynolds–Nabisco	Merger	4.9	1985
19. Burroughs–Sperry	Merger	4.8	1986
20. General Motors–Hughes Aircraft	Merger	4.7	1985

Source: Various business publications, various years.

CONCLUSION

From the time of the earliest aggregations of businesses that inspired the Sherman Antitrust Act, there have been three lines of inquiry worth following. The first, as evidenced by the 1913 Congressional hearings and countless others that have been held over the intervening years, concerns the trend toward fewer and larger firms with greater market power in all significant sectors of the American economy; some of the famous names in economic history have come and gone, but the structural elements of size and power have remained unchanged.

The second trend is a legal one; it has become virtually impossible, as a matter of expense, time, and energy to effectively control anticompetitive business activity through litigation. The IBM case, if an extreme one, makes the general point.

The third trend line is political. Since the high water mark of antitrust enforcement in the 1960s, there has been less and less enthusiasm for antitrust, a disenchantment reflected not only in the trifling number of cases brought since 1980 against mergers however large or consequential, but also in the severe reductions in budgeting for agencies charged with antitrust enforcement. This political disfavor undercuts the energy of government lawyers and pro-antitrust economists for zealous work in the field.

But what has all this got to do with the multinationalization of enterprise? Sanjaya Lall, an economist who has written extensively on multinational corporations, makes a critical observation on the relationship between a firm's size and market power, and its ability to multinationalize:

> Casual empiricism suggests that there is a good deal of common ground between internal oligopoly, export performance and overseas production. In advanced economies like the US, it is the large firms that grow to dominate their domestic industries which are also the main investors abroad, and it is these multinationals which account for some three-quarters of the country's total exports of manufactured products. It seems reasonable therefore to view the growth of firms within countries and their "involvement" abroad—by exports and foreign production—as closely linked processes, and to attempt to explain foreign involvement with reference to the factors that cause the emergence of large firms and, at the industry level, more concentrated market structures.[39]

Size and market power are the preconditions for multinationalization. Had the U.S. antitrust laws been completely successful in maintaining perfectly competitive markets and atomistic firm size across all industries, the multinational phenomenon could not have occurred, or at least could not have occurred on the scale currently extant.

Some economists mourn the demise of antitrust as a controller of enterprise. Walter Adams, long an opponent of the new Chicago School of econom-

[39]S. Lall, *The Multinational Corporation* (London: Macmillan, 1980).

ics, dedicated a recent book to the economists who have kept faith with the need for competition and control of market power:

> To the small but brave army of young economists who "prefer to see the truth imperfectly and obscurely rather than to maintain error, reached indeed with clearness and by easy logic, but based on hypotheses contrary to fact."[40]

This is Adams' way of encouraging the rejection of the new economics which has undercut the enforcement of the antitrust laws. Adams worries that if present thinking continues, we may find ourselves in a world where economic power settles all disputes, once and for a few.

Not all economists feel this way. In another recent book, an author recounts the demise of antitrust law that came via the rethinking of economics:

> Other economists... advanced the normative point that economic efficiency should be the principal—some said sole—objective for antitrust policy. Their position led them to careful examination of the microeconomics of various market structures and behavior. They found the received economic wisdom wanting and offered alternative theories and interpretations of economic evidence. They encountered a sympathetic audience, first in much of the business community, and subsequently in policy-making agencies and the courts themselves.[41]

The latter economists believe antitrust unnecessary, and welcome the decline of antitrust as the removal of an impediment to firm and market efficiency.

Whatever one's position in the antitrust debate, a critical fact appears to be irrefutable: antitrust law is dead. Some observers are happy about the demise of antitrust law, while others continue to throw fresh flowers on its grave, hoping for a rebirth. For purposes of this text, it need only be noted that antitrust law has not inhibited the trend toward larger and larger firm size, greater and greater concentration of power in the handful of firms that control each important sector of the economy, and, in the end, the multinationalization of enterprise.

[40]Adams, op. cit. *(Bigness)*, dedication.

[41]John Krowka, et al., eds., *The Antitrust Revolution* (Glenview: Scott, Foresman, 1989), p. 1.

CHAPTER 7

Labor Law and Multinationals—the Present as Past

INTRODUCTION

The 1992 strike at Caterpillar provides a provocative starting place for the study of labor, labor law, and the connection of both to multinationals. After six months the strike was lost by the United Auto Workers Union with all the ignominy that goes with a defeat after a long battle that both sides have identified as crucial. Some 13,000 workers were prepared to go back to work without a new contract after a threat by Caterpillar to hire permanent replacements.

Company officials claimed that they were doing no more than trying to preserve the company's international competitiveness against Japanese heavy equipment manufacturers, and that their actions had nothing to do with destroying the union. Union officials insisted that the fight was to break the union, and that the war had not been lost, but was simply "entering a new phase."

Onlookers knew better. The union had called off the strike. Workers were returning under the company's "final offer," which had earlier been rejected after a one-hour bargaining session. The union could not get terms comparable to what it got in previous negotiations with the John Deere corporation, and the returning work force would have less job security, a two-tiered wage system that looked like a pay cut, and more restricted health benefits. It was not even clear that all of the workers who had been on strike would be reemployed, meaning that an instant "downsizing" of the work force had taken place. Additional negotiations might remove some of the more offensive features of management's position, but the power seemed to have shifted dramatically away from organized labor.

The loss showed the relative powerlessness of labor in the face of corporations whose productive options and choices of work forces span the world; labor is almost strictly local, thinking locally and acting locally, while enterprise thinks globally and can act both locally and globally. Caterpillar was not only faced with global competition but also had global options. In fact, it knew it would not have to go abroad to continue production and get replacements. There was even some risk that former Caterpillar workers laid off in previous work-force reductions might replace strikers. To head off this possibility the union at one point announced that workers recalled from layoff could join the strike and receive strike benefits ($125/wk).[1]

The temptation in light of this current geographic-organizational-tactical mismatch might be to regard the decline of labor power as a very recent phenomenon, a decline that parallels the post-World War II rise of the multinational corporation. This temptation should be resisted. The power of labor with respect to enterprise has been an ongoing issue from the time of the disappearance of small-scale farming and craft-based production, beginning in the middle of the nineteenth century.[2] If labor has had its victories and "high-water marks" across history, the more constant trend has been the consolidation of power in owner-managers over all of the critical decisions concerning the direction of enterprise and control of the work process. The story of control over labor ends with multinationals controlling labor but begins far earlier with domestic companies controlling labor.[3]

Labor as a commodity—time and service in return for money—means that labor has been stripped of any consequential and political role in the contexts which affect its welfare most. Labor reduced to a commodity or a "factor of production" neither owns the enterprise nor has a voice in its direction. A political role would include a voice in what is produced, how it is produced, for whom, at what prices, and with what shares of return going to whom. Currently labor has very little say in any of the foregoing, and many people conclude that this allocation of power in the enterprise is appropriate, since the ownership of property ought to carry with it control over choices about production and distribution.[4]

But that conclusion is hardly "natural," judging from history and the bitter struggles fought to see just what the allocation of power should be. To state the result of a long struggle as a *natural* fact of life neglects at least a century of contest, sometimes in the courts and legislatures, sometimes at gunpoint. If there is truth to the proposition that control ought to accompany the ownership of property, such a truth has never been considered self-evident by all concerned parties, and will probably not be considered so in the future, the growing preeminence of multinationals and the recent results of the Caterpillar strike notwithstanding.

EARLY INDUSTRY AND LABOR LAW

The post-Civil War period saw the transformation of the economy of the United States from subsistence farming and craft production to industrial

[1]The details on the sequence of the strike come from the *Wall Street Journal*, UAW newsletters, and company and union press releases.

[2]For an account of the decline of labor power with industrialization, see Harry Braverman, *Labor and Monopoly Capital* (New York: Monthly Review Press, 1974).

[3]James Atleson, *Values and Assumptions of American Labor Law* (Amherst: U. of Mass. Press, 1983).

[4]In *NLRB* v. *Yeshiva University* 100 U.S. 856 (1980), the United States Supreme Court reaffirmed these assumptions about the appropriate governance of industrial production.

production. Representative of this change was shoemaking, an ancient craft that until the 1860s had been the same for centuries. One commentator said that a shoemaker from the Middle Ages would have felt totally comfortable hundreds of years later in a New England "ten footer"—the tiny shop, in the home, where a shoemaker at a cobbler's bench made shoes from start to finish, using eight simple hand tools.[5]

The early shop organization, with master, journeymen, and apprentices, making shoes to order, with very few labor-saving devices and minimum capital, yielded very quickly around 1860 to the shoe factory that made shoes "for market," and used the newest machinery. The machinery, while requiring more capital, allowed an extensive division of labor and deskilled many aspects of the trade. "Green hands" working for a fraction of what a journeyman would have earned could turn out parts of a finished shoe for less.[6]

The response of experienced shoemakers was the Knights of St. Crispin, a union formed in 1868 to meet the multifaceted crisis brought by industrialization. Its membership reached approximately 50,000, by far the largest of the early unions, but after 1874 it was virtually dead, having failed to save shoemaking either as it had been traditionally done, or as done in factories. Before they died as a union, the Crispins conducted many strikes that helped shape labor law for the next 100 years.

The overall goals of the Crispins can be readily inferred from the problems they faced: a need to control the knowledge about shoemaking to inhibit the use of inexperienced workers; to limit the supply of labor by working only with other members of the Crispins; to preserve hand labor (early and rare) and, alternatively, to limit the use of machines to members; and to organize workers for a joint confrontation with shoe manufacturers on wages and working conditions. The Crispins also promoted cooperatives among shoemakers to combine newer methods of production with ownership of them.

In 1871, when the next case, *Walker* v. *Cronin*, arose, shoemaking was at an in-between point in technological development and the Crispins were at full strength. Factories existed, but not all of the production occurred at the factory. Some of the work was still done at home—shoes by the box being "put out" into the ten-footers of individual workers—and when completed returned to the company that had commissioned the work. The Crispins in their strike–boycott wanted to disrupt production at the factory and to interrupt the flow of work from those working at home.

The labor law of the time was poorly defined. The earlier Massachusetts case of *Commonwealth* v. *Hunt*[7] had established that it was not a criminal conspiracy to form unions, but left open the legality of tactics that a union might use to gain its objectives. This meant that unions could not be prohibited outright, but certain tactics of unions could be. The *Hunt* case was a criminal action, and employers derive little benefit from the fines

[5] B. Hazard, *The Organization of the Boot and Shoe Industry in Massachusetts Before 1875* (Cambridge: Harvard University Press, 1921).

[6] The discussion of early unionization in shoemaking is based on D. Lescohier, *The Knights of St. Crispin 1867–1874* (Madison: U. of Wisconsin, 1910).

[7] 45 Mass. 4 (1842).

or imprisonment that the criminal law can impose. Some *noncriminal* legal remedy was needed by employers to bring unions under greater control, and the *Walker* case, which follows, was a move in that general direction.

In reviewing the noncriminal prospects for worker control, contract law offered practically nothing. According to the law then, as now, no one is required to contract with anyone. And even when under contract, the arrangements between employers and employees were "at will," and either party could get out of a relationship whenever so inclined. Work put out on piece rates was paid on completion: no completion, no pay; and as a corollary, if a person returned work unfinished, the "employer" might have no standing to complain—in contract. It was for this reason that the lawyers for the company chose "tort," the general legal category covering "wrongs."

The complaint in the *Walker* case charged that the defendant did "unlawfully and without justification . . . molest, obstruct and hinder the plaintiffs from carrying on . . . business" and also "willfully persuad[e] and indu[ce] a large number of persons, who were in the employment of the plaintiff as bottomers of boots and shoes and others who were about to enter into the employment of the plaintiffs to withhold their labor." What these allegations came down to was that the defendant had encouraged workers at home to return work to the factory unfinished, urged people to leave the factory, or if they were considering working at the factory, requested them to stay away. That the case fit the prior case law poorly is evident from the court's struggle to find applicable precedents.

WALKER V. *CRONIN* 107 MASS. 555 (1871) TORT.

Wells, J.

The declaration . . . alleges that the defendant did "unlawfully and without justifiable cause, molest, obstruct and hinder the plaintiff from carrying on" their business of manufacture and sale of boots and shoes, "with the unlawful purpose of preventing the plaintiff from carrying on their said business, and willfully persuaded and induced a large number of persons who were in the employment of the plaintiff and others who were about to enter into their employment to leave and abandon the employment of the plaintiffs without their consent and against their will; whereby the plaintiffs lost the services of said persons, and the profits and advantages they would otherwise have made and received therefrom, and were put to large expenses to procure other suitable workmen, and suffered losses in their said business."

This sets forth sufficiently (1) intentional and wilful acts (2) calculated to cause damage to the plaintiffs in their lawful business, (3) done with the unlawful purpose to cause such damage and loss, without right or justifiable cause on the part of the defendant (which constitutes malice), and (4) actual damage and loss resulting.

. . . [T]he intentional causing of such loss to another, without justifiable cause, and with the malicious purpose to inflict it, is of itself a wrong . . .

[The court next considered two English cases brought against a defendant for frightening ducks out of a plaintiff's decoy, or for driving ducks away from the plaintiff's decoy; the court concluded that the aggrieved hunter had a tort remedy for either act. The court also considered an early case in which a remedy was allowed when schoolboys were frightened away from a school and a schoolmaster lost income. Still another earlier case involved the right to recover lost profits after the defendants frightened natives away from the coast in Africa, where they would have traded with the plaintiff. —Ed.]

There are indeed many authorities which appear to hold that to constitute an actionable wrong, there must be some definite legal right of the plaintiff. But those are cases . . . where the defendants were themselves acting in the lawful exercise of some distinct right, which furnished the defense of a justifiable cause for their acts . . .

[E]veryone has an equal right to employ workmen in his business or service; and if, by the exercise of this right in such manner as he may see fit, persons are induced to leave their employment elsewhere, no wrong is done to him whose employment they leave unless a contract exists by which such other person has a legal right to the further continuance of their services. If such a contract exists, one who knowingly and intentionally procures it to be violated may be held liable for the wrong, although he did it for purpose of promoting his own business.

[The court next reviews cases where the use of one's property interferes with or destroys the property of an adjacent owner, as would be the case where one person's water well draws down the water of a neighbor. The court concluded that in these cases there is no actionable wrong, regardless of the motives of the "offending" party.]

Everyone has a right to enjoy the fruits and advantages of his own enterprise, industry, skill and credit. He has no right to be protected from competition; but he has a right to be free from malicious and wanton interference, disturbance, or annoyance. If disturbance or loss come as a result of competition, or the exercise of like rights by others, it is *damnum absque injuria* [a loss without a legal right to recovery.—Ed.], unless some superior right by contract or otherwise is interfered with. But if it come from the merely wanton or malicious acts of others, without justification of competition or the service of any interest or lawful purpose, it then stands on a different footing . . .

[Ruling that the employer's case should be heard and that damages might be recovered. —Ed.]

For Discussion

1. Labor lost substantial real and symbolic ground in the Walker case. First there was the elevation of a business to the status of a person such that a business, like a person, could be "molested," "interfered with," "annoyed" and "disturbed"—complaints we usually associate with real persons. These words made the business the victim of assault, and it is not accidental that the opinion reads like an assault case.

   At the same time, the interests of the workers in boycotting and striking the defendant were trivialized. Their acts are simply "wilful" or "wanton," not rational acts designed to produce a defensible purpose. Their will advances no "right or justifiable cause" and was thus reduced to a pointless intrusion upon the plaintiff's business.

As noted in the introductory commentary preceding the case, the contracts that were allegedly jeopardized were of the most evanescent kind, terminable at any moment by either party. They were so out of an impulse by employers to preserve flexibility in raising and lowering work-force levels and to otherwise control costs. The use of replacements from Maine and New Hampshire, and even as far away as California was a common practice.[8] By ironic twist, it was more security that the Crispins sought and not the precarious employment then extant. Yet the opinion is grounded on the unwarranted assumption that very stable work relationships offered by an employer had been mindlessly upset by the strike-boycott.

One is also struck by the cases on which the court drew for legal authority. Were workers on the job like ducks sitting on a pond until disturbed by an offending party, or did they choose to follow the strike–boycott?

Were workers who approached the factory of the plaintiff like ducks being frightened off from a decoy?

The willingness of the court to engage in loose reading of hunting cases to find a "wrong" attests more to the desire to reach a result and invent remedies than an impulse for ordinary legal reasoning from prior similar cases.

2. The opinion also required a deep revision of the notion of competition and other forms of economic rivalry. The law was well established that even though the success of a business might jeopardize the success of business rivals, the unsuccessful businesses could have no legal claims for damages against the successful one.[9] This seems to go without saying in a capitalist economic system premised on competition, and the early cases were consistent with this idea. The court in the *Walker* case also acknowledged the well-accepted rule that rival uses of property must be tolerated even though the burdens of the rival uses might fall more heavily on one party than another—this is the case where digging a well on one's property inhibits access to water by an adjacent owner.

   Here the case gets interesting. The court distinguished between the rivalry between owners of businesses and the rivalries between businesses and labor. Labor–owner conflict might have been considered competition for control of the market for labor, with labor, the "property" of the worker, subject to being withheld for the right prices, terms, and conditions, even if the withholding meant the ruination of prospective employers. In short, if labor conflict had been found to be a form of competition, workers and owners could have slugged

[8]Massachusetts Bureau of Labor Statistics, 11, (1886) p. 18; B. Hazard, op. cit. p. 150.
[9]C. Gregory and H. Katz, *Labor and the Law* (New York: Norton, 1979), Chapter 2.

it out economically like competing businesses or adjacent property owners pursuing incompatible purposes.

After the *Walker* case and in countless labor cases that followed, a stratified concept of competition was framed by the courts: (1) businesses could compete to the utter destruction of rivals without fear of lawsuits; (2) workers, like businesses, could freely compete *with each other* even where consequences might be ruinous to workers losing out; but (3) the justification of competition did not apply when workers were pitted against businesses for economic advantage. In the last category, courts would closely scrutinize tactics for legality along the lines first suggested by the famous *Hunt* case.

3. The *Walker* case helped to financially disrupt the Crispins, but there were other causes for the disarray that led to the demise of the union only a few years later. The industry continued to rapidly change technologically, and there was literally no way to coordinate the aspirations of the thousands of workers who had formerly been independent tradespeople. This along with a growing supply of "green labor" eager to work at jobs requiring little skill, helped undo the union after its brief surge of power around 1870.

   Moreover, labor had been put on the wrong side of important national symbols—technological progress and the efficiencies accompanying the factory system. Words like "molest" connoted violence rather than reasonable demands. Labor, or more specifically organized labor, had been defined as a force for disruption to a new and valuable industrial order.

THE GENERAL STRIKE OF 1877

For all of the current bewilderment over the lack of cooperation between owner-managers and labor, any student of labor history knows that the battles between labor and management are deep and long-standing. Notwithstanding the reputation of workers as troublemakers, being unduly demanding and just plain stubborn—an image which is itself a cultural product carefully developed by anti-labor propagandists—management has had its own role in making trouble, asserting demands, and being intractable. If the labor story has two sides, what are they?

1877 has been a most forgettable year for contemporary Americans, but probably it was the most important year in all of labor history.[10] Uncharacteristically, the people who lived at the time had a better sense of the importance of the moment than those who came later. They called the railroad strike *The Great Strike*, and it was. In our time, people do not know what was at issue, but those living at the time, whether oriented toward management or labor, knew, almost too intimately.

[10]This account of the 1877 general strike is based on Jeremy Brecher, *Strike*, (San Francisco: Straight Arrow, 1972).

The Great Strike tested the industrial order as it had taken shape after the Civil War. Railroads were the centerpiece of that order. Workers, at first railroad workers, and then workers in general, were asking a critical question: We know what *you* think is progress, but just where do we fit in? Workers at the time were only precariously organized. At the same time they were confronting business organizations which if not totally modern had been more completely transformed.

One has to begin to reverse the usual characterizations applied to labor and management; against history, management often looks more radical in the sense of injecting deeper changes, and labor looks conservative in attempting to slow down or moderate change. In many instances workers were trying to prevent the deterioration of their position rather than seeking positive improvements in it. Moreover, workers were not so far away from craft production and subsistence farming to be without contrasting models.

One railroad worker said, "We were tired of being treated like rolling stock or locomotives." If a ten percent pay cut set the railroad workers off on strike, the emotions ran far deeper. The 1877 strike raised conflicts in the raw, without known labels and well beyond wages and hours.

The Great Strike had an unlikely beginning in Martinsburg, West Virginia, when a crew for the B&O Railroad refused to take out a train after the railroad had ordered the pay cut. Other workers refused to replace them, began to uncouple cars, and occupy railroad property. The local mayor and police, called in by the company, were ineffective, and summoned still higher government officials and greater force, to bring the spreading strike under control. Finally, the governor of West Virginia asked President Rutherford B. Hayes to send help:

> Owing to the unlawful combination and domestic violence now existing at Martinsburg and at other points along the line of the Baltimore and Ohio Railroad, it is impossible with any force at my command to execute the laws of the state. I therefore call upon your excellency for the assistance of the United States military to protect law-abiding people of the state against domestic violence, and maintain the supremacy of the law.[11]

The president of the railroad seconded the motion, saying, "West Virginia had done all it could to suppress this insurrection" and added that "this great national highway can only be restored for public use by the interposition of U.S. forces."[12] Before turning to the spread of the strike to other cities, other industries, and to many workers across a variety of trades, it is important to note several critical assumptions implicit in this joint call for force: law was tacitly assumed to be on the side of the railroad; that the full force of the local, state, and national governments should be available when summoned on behalf of the company; and that *business* interests were synonymous with the *public* interest—hence the language describing a private railroad as a "great *national* highway" and the demand that it be restored for "*public* use."

[11]Ibid., p. 3.
[12]Ibid., p. 3.

Workers in refusing to work and engaging in direct action had again put themselves on the wrong side of important symbols—peace, good order, and business. They were on the wrong side of law at all levels, and also on the wrong side of force—the local police, the state militia, and the U. S. Army. The ability to call out the army in the name of property is one of the consequential rules of labor law.

The news from Martinsburg spread across the whole B&O system, to other railroads, and to many cities, including Pittsburgh, Baltimore, Chicago, Buffalo, and St. Louis. Miners, canal workers, coopers, steel workers, tanners, and many other skilled and unskilled workers joined the strike, partially out of sympathy with the railroad men, but as often out of their own grievances against their own employers; they too were caught in a new style of enterprise that was disempowering them. The strike had become *general*—all workers against all employers.

Industrial warfare had sparked class warfare. Conflicts of a variety of types and depth became visible and were well beyond the initial reasons for the strike—a pay cut. In the end, the Pittsburgh train yards of the Pennsylvania railroad were in flames, and all major cities had their own local incidents which when added up amounted to the Great Strike. The army eventually put down the strike, with more than 100 dead before "order was restored."

General strikes are rare. What instruction do they hold for contemporary students of labor? The general strike shows labor at full power, like a large engine being revved at maximum capacity, and also shows owner-managers at maximum weakness, when "business as usual" has been involuntarily suspended.

When labor is at full strength, what does it look like? What frightens owner-managers when general strikes are underway? What is the difference between labor in the streets, en masse, and labor at a bargaining table voicing its demands through elected spokespeople? What is the difference between the power of labor unchanneled, with the rule of law in abeyance and ineffective to control labor, and labor when it comes in from the streets and into the house of the law?

There are a number of peculiarities of a general strike, of which five stand out:

> *No parameters or boundaries to the conflict.* The "trouble" ranges across everything from hours, wages, and control of the work process to control of the workplace itself.
>
> *Means of conflict open.* The means can range from talking to seizure and destruction of property; all imaginable forms of "self-help" may be tried, many of which are clearly "illegal."
>
> *No parameters as to the parties involved.* Workers at a place of employment, other workers of other employers, and even unemployed workers are all active. All employers are also affected—this is what is meant by a *general strike*. Employment conflict becomes class conflict.

No authority recognized as legitimate source of finality for disputes. Workers have moved beyond "channels"; restoration of "order" means restoration of authority, but the legitimacy of the authority itself has been challenged and cannot be asserted while the strike is underway.

No predictable stopping points for the conflict. The general strike has within it both manageable "claims" such as better hours, wages, or working conditions but also raises questions of power and property. Such a strike can result in normal "gains," such as rescinding a wage cut or the establishment of safer working conditions, or can incite a revolution, permanently changing power and property relationships.

The unpredictability of events and outcomes under conditions of a general strike can be compared to conditions "according to law."

GENERAL STRIKE/RULE OF LAW

General strike	Law
No boundaries as to what is in conflict	Claims, issues
Means of conflict open	A case, argument, remedies
No limits on people involved	Parties
No legitimate authority acknowledged by the general strikers	Court, or other place for "dispute resolution"
Unknown stopping points	Legal decision and remedies

In their encounter with general strike conditions, owner-managers were drawn onto unfamiliar terrain, and with no stretch of language the order they wish to restore was their own sense of how things usually proceed.

The shock is no different for the workers who are striking. They have all the strength that mobilized numbers bring, but they cannot readily convert their power into concrete gains. Energy expended, the general strike ends, as it did in 1877. Unions are a way of routinizing otherwise volatile conditions to consolidate benefits. At times this routinization makes the union leadership more conservative than the membership, and at times makes management prefer unions when compared to work forces acting on their own (unruly).

What lasting consequences might be found in embryonic form after the Great Strike? Besides a general hope that such a strike never occur again, an *owner-managerial agenda* for future labor relations must have crossed the minds of many who experienced the psychic blitzkrieg of the strike. Upon the restoration of order, owner-managers might have wanted to see the following in place and enforced by law:

Workers kept atomized and not readily aggregated into large groups

Workers silent rather than communicating their grievance to others

Workers unable to withhold their services on a large scale

Workers unable to politicize their positions (to widen the issues beyond terms and conditions of employment and widen the constituencies that might be supportive of larger issues)

Workers unable to organize with other workers beyond a particular company, and beyond the industry where the dispute first arises

Workers kept away from power over product to be produced, methods of production, location of production, and prices to be charged

Workers kept on the wrong side of important national symbols—peace, progress, and prosperity

This managerial agenda could not be achieved overnight into thorough labor law, but these overall preferences are instructive, especially when charted alongside labor law developments over the next century:

MANAGERIAL AGENDA/LABOR LAW

Need	Law
Atomization	Right to work laws; individual contracts between workers and employers; strict rules governing just what workers can be involved in what union; rules preventing the spread of strikes, mass picketing, and worker boycotts of struck employers and the products of struck employers
Silence	Rules limiting picketing to make grievances public; rules limiting solicitation for union membership or the distribution of literature on company property
Workers working	Rules inhibiting striking, picketing, boycotting; rules permitting the hiring of permanent replacements for workers on strike; rules clearing the workplace of strikers who might want to occupy business premises to prevent the hiring of replacements
Workers depoliticized	Anti-syndicalist laws to inhibit anarchistic and marxist influences on the labor movement; noncommunist affidavits
Worker solidarity discouraged	Rules on the places where picketing can take place, and in what numbers, boycotts, secondary boycotts, sympathy strikes, outlawing unfair employer lists, outlawing "hot cargo" prohibitions (refusing to handle goods of a struck employer); rules against refusals to work on nonunion-made goods
Worker prerogatives limited	Rules limiting the scope of worker involvement in critical decisions about the enterprise; what is made, where it is made, to whom it goes, and with what allocation of the proceeds; grievance procedures with limited scope
Worker interests subordinated	An abiding policy that property is more important than persons; that labor actions are often "violent" and contrary to peace and good order

The foregoing list stretches the general strike to its limits as an instructional device, but it should be remembered that the righthand list of desirable labor law and policy is not at all far-fetched.[13] The list provides a rough guide to contemporary labor law. The general strike provides a measure of the overall decline of labor power according to law.

[13]Any primer on labor law will include as elementary principles the rules listed in the right-hand column. Douglas Leslie, *Labor Law* (St Paul: West, 1979); Sanford Cohen, *Labor Law* (Columbus: Merrill, 1964). For a thesis close to the idea that labor has derived far too little from labor law, see D. Trumka, "Why Labor Law Has Failed," *West Virginia Law Review*, 89 (1987), p. 871.

Workers have fared poorly in the house of the law, in the house of labor policy, and in the house of national symbols. But we are far ahead of the story. In the next pages some feel for the demise of labor as a countervailing power to the power of owner-managers will be partially illustrated.

THE LABOR INJUNCTION

The labor injunction was first used in the late 1870s as a judicial response to the Great Strike. The injunction had distinct advantages to employers over either criminal actions such as those undertaken in the 1840 *Hunt* case or tort actions like those in the 1871 *Walker* case. In criminal or tort actions, the defendant has a right to trial by jury, which might, given the makeup of the community, be more likely to produce a pro-labor rather than a pro-owner-manager result. In addition, the remedies—fines, imprisonment, or money damages—in additon to being of limited use against a whole work force, can be imposed only after trial.[14]

The *labor injunction,* as it evolved over more than fifty years of use in thousands of cases, was the answer. It was such a powerful weapon that it might have inspired Samuel Gompers, an early labor leader to pray: "God save labor from the courts." Through the injunction, the courts became singularly inhospitable to the cause of labor, a fact that could explain the resort of labor to courts on only very rare occasions.

When the injunction reached full development, a company, upon a sworn statement presented by their lawyer that damage to property was imminent, could get a court order prohibiting the behavior. Parties disobeying the court order could be found in contempt of court, and put in jail without trial.

The next case, *Sherry* v. *Perkins*, provided a critical element in this strategy, combining the idea of wrongfulness articulated in the Walker case with a court order to stop the behavior. Most labor tactics wrongfully interfered with the operation of a company, and the courts, using the threat of jailing without trial, could focus on the leadership rather than ordinary workers.

SHERRY V. *PERKINS* 17 N.E. 307 (MASS, 1888)

Bill in equity, by Patrick P. Sherry against Charles E. Perkins and Charles H. Leach, for an injunction to restrain the defendants, respectively president and secretary of the Laster's Protective Union, from causing to be carried in front of the plaintiff's shoe factory a banner on which was the following inscription: "Lasters are requested to keep away from P. P. Sherry's. Per order of L. P. U."; and also a banner on which was the following: "Lasters on a strike; all lasters are requested to keep away from P. P. Sherry's until the present trouble is settled. Per order L. P. U." The court at the trial, found as facts that members of the Lasters' Protective Union entered

[14]Felix Frankfurter et al., *The Labor Injunction* (Gloucester: P. Smith, 1930); Edwin Witte, *The Government in Labor Disputes* (New York: Arno, 1969).

into a scheme, by threats and intimidation, to prevent persons in the employment of the plaintiff, as lasters, from continuing in such employment, and in like manner to prevent other persons from entering into such employment as lasters; that the defendants participated in the scheme; that the use of the banner was a part of the scheme, and its use an injury to the plaintiff in his business and property.

W. Allen, J.

The case finds that the defendants entered, with others, into a scheme, by threats and intimidation, to prevent persons in the employment of the plaintiff from continuing in such employment, and to prevent others from entering into such employment; that the banners, with their inscriptions, were used by the defendants as part of the scheme, and that the plaintiff was thereby injured in his business and property. The act of displaying banners with devices, as a means of threats and intimidation, to prevent persons from entering into or continuing in the employment of the plaintiff, was injurious to the plaintiff, and illegal at common law and by statute. *Walker* v. *Cronin* . . . We think that the plaintiff is . . . entitled to relief by injunction. The acts and the injury were continuous. The banners were used more than three months before the filing of plaintiff's bill, and continued to be used at the time of the hearing. The injury was to the plaintiff's business, and adequate remedy could not be given by damages . . . The scheme, in pursuance of which the banners were displayed and maintained, was to injure the plaintiff's business . . . by intimidating workmen, so as to deter them from keeping or making engagements with the plaintiff. The banner was a standing menace to all who were or wished to be in the employment of the plaintiff, to deter them from entering the plaintiff's premises. Maintaining it was a continuous, unlawful act, injurious to the plaintiff's business and property, and was a nuisance, such as a court of equity will grant relief against. . . .

Comments

1. We see the same figurative use of words in the *Sherry* case as was found in the *Walker* case. The banner and the words on the banner were in themselves incapable of rendering anyone physical harm. However, the court found them to be "intimidation," a "threat" and a "standing menace."

   The primary justification for the injunction was interference with the company property, but the court also amplified the rationale by finding a need to protect workers who did not request the injunction. It is rare for a court to grant remedies to those not parties to a suit, and their inclusion in the court's discussion can only be because the "threats" to the company were symbolic.

2. In a later court case that has totally escaped most labor law scholarship—*Worthington* v. *Waring*[15]—workers who had been blacklisted by an employer association sought an injunction to prevent the inte-

[15] 157 Massachusetts 421 (1892).

ference with the pursuit of their "trade and occupation." The court found their case different from the *Sherry* case; their rights were *personal rights* as distinguished from *property rights* and could not therefore be protected by injunction.

In a still later case, which does make it to the labor law texts—*Plant* v. *Woods*[16]—workers in one union (favored by the company) sought an injunction to prevent interferences by a rival union with their ability to get employment. (Members of the rival union refused to work alongside members of the plaintiff's union and were pressuring the employer for their dismissal.) The rival union raised the defense that should have been available—the rights that the plaintiffs were asserting to employment were *personal* rights for which injunctions were not available according to the *Worthington* case. Nevertheless, the injunction was *granted.*

How can what appears to be contradictory judicial behavior be explained?

The *Plant case* also forced a departure from the common law rule that workers can compete among themselves for employment even where the competition is ruinous.

3. The *Sherry* case spawned many limitations upon tactics that workers might employ. In the famous *Vagelahn* v. *Guntner*[17] case the court extended the injunction to picketing by two members of a union in front of the plaintiff's company.

> The patrol was maintained as one of the means of carrying out the defendant's plan and it was used in combination with social pressure, threats of personal injury or unlawful harm, and persuasion to break existing contracts. It was thus one means of intimidation indirectly to the plaintiff, and directly to the persons employed, or seeking to be employed by the plaintiff, and of rendering such employment unpleasant and intolerable to such persons.

Judge Oliver Wendell Holmes dissented in part on the ground that there was "no proof of any threat or danger" from the pickets. He was objecting to the loose use of language regarding intimidation begun in the *Walker* and *Sherry* cases, and extended in the *Vagelahn* case.

INJUNCTIONS UNLIMITED

For many years after the *Sherry* case, virtually every aspect of union organization and tactics became a fit subject for the issuance of an injunction: the internal affairs of a union—rules for maintaining discipline, levying fines and expulsion; external activities—for example, strikes for a shop closed to nonunion members; to secure or prevent union membership of foremen; to

[16] 176 Massachusetts 492 (1900).
[17] 167 Massachusetts 92 (1896).

prevent the use of labor-saving devices, to prevent less skilled workers from making inroads at the borders of "the trade." Similarly, courts routinely enjoined picketing and boycotting an employer.

In most cases the bills for injunction were sought by employers, but in some cases, as in *Plant* v. *Woods* discussed above, the fight—at least for the record—was between workers. The temporary restraining orders issued in a labor case were eventually reduced to a form that could be filled in by the most unimaginative lawyer:

> . . . the respondents individually named in said bill and the members of _(name of union)_ and each and every of them, their agents, their attorneys, from interfering with the complainants' business, by obstructing, threatening, intimidating, or interfering with any person or persons who are now or may hereafter be in the employment of the complainant or desirous of entering the same, or by inducing or attempting to induce any person now or hereafter in the employment of the complainant to break any contract of employment with the complainant, and from interfering with the complainants' business by picketing and patrolling or causing others to picket or patrol in the streets in the vicinity of the complainants' place of business, or by following persons now or hereafter in the employment of the complainant to or from their work, or their places of abode, for the purpose of inducing such persons to leave the employment of the complainants. (This sample dated 1907.)[18]

LABOR LEGISLATION OF THE DEPRESSION

That labor did not fare well at common law can be readily inferred from the foregoing cases and other labor cases that reached the Massachusetts Supreme Court from 1840 to 1920—labor lost all but one head-to-head contest with owner-managers (the exception being an 1867 case that allowed full "competition" between employers and employees, a rule abandoned four years later in the Walker case).[19]

Employers benefited not only directly from those cases in which they were parties but also indirectly from cases where workers sued unions and union officials for damages or injunctions based on the interference with free access to work. Those cases helped assure employers of uninterrupted labor by making it impossible for organized labor to control the labor supply.

The use of injunctions against labor had become so notorious and coercive that by the end of the 1920s what little legitimacy labor law had left was rapidly petering out, and by the 1930s there was growing political pressure to limit the availability of injunctions in labor cases.

At the federal level, the Norris-LaGuardia Anti-Injunction Act of 1932 provided that federal courts could not issue injunctions in cases involving

[18]The growth and expansion of the labor injunction in Massachusetts is explained by J. de Sloovere, Massachusetts Statistics of Labor (1916). The form injunction was included in his monograph.

[19]Ibid.,1 ff.

"labor disputes." This Act curtailed the remedy in situations like those already considered in the Massachusetts cases, and also limited the uses of the Sherman Antitrust Act against labor. (Even though one thinks of businesses as the principal target of the Sherman Act, the Act was in the early years more frequently applied to organized labor as combinations or conspiracies in restraint of trade than it was to businesses.) Many states passed laws called "little Norris-LaGuardia Acts" limiting the use of injunctions in state courts.

The real opening to labor for organizing, collectively bargaining, and engaging in concerted tactics came with the Wagner Act of 1935. Two facts seemed to coalesce to make the Wagner Act possible; labor had gained in political strength and had been a factor in the election successes of the Democratic Party; and the claim that owner-managers of businesses were the best guardians of progress and prosperity had been discredited by the Great Depression and 16,000,000 people out of work.

Whether the Act was a "radical" step designed to profoundly change labor relations or was intended to leave unaffected the underlying assumptions dating back to the common law has been long debated in the courts and by labor commentators.[20] Looking at the policy statement of Congress found in the Act, it might be inferred that a dramatic change was envisioned by Congress with the passage of the Act:

> It is hereby declared to be the policy of the United States to eliminate the causes of certain obstructions to the free flow of commerce . . . by encouraging the practice and procedure of collective bargaining and by protecting the exercise by workers of full freedom of association, self-organization and designation of representatives of their own choosing, for the purpose of negotiating the terms and conditions of their employment or other mutual aid and protection.

Other Congressional statements of policy and experience made the Wagner Act appear to be a significant departure from labor relations at common law:

> The inequality of bargaining power between employees who do not possess full freedom of association or actual liberty of contract, and employers who are organized in the corporate or other forms of ownership association substantially burdens and affects the flow of commerce and tends to aggravate recurrent business depressions, by depressing wage rates and the purchasing power of wage earners in industry and by preventing the stabilization of competitive wage rates and working conditions within and between industries.
>
> Experience has proved that protection by law of the right of employees to organize and bargain collectively safeguards commerce from injury, impairment, or interruption, and promotes the flow of commerce by removing certain recognized sources of industrial strife and unrest, by encouraging practices fundamental to the friendly adjustment of industrial disputes arising out of differences as to wages, hours, or other working conditions, and by restoring equality of bargaining power between employers and employees.[21]

[20] See for example Cletus Daniel, *The ACLU and the Wagner Act* (Ithaca: Cornell, 1980); K. Klare, "Deradicalization of the Wagner Act," *University of Minnesota Law Review* (1978), p. 62.

[21] National Labor Relations Act, Section 1 (1935).

A dissection of the foregoing explains why labor found great promise in the Wagner Act. Congress had acknowledged:

1. That workers had no real freedom of association.
2. That there was no equality of bargaining power between labor and owner-managers despite the assumption that all parties could freely contract.
3. That the corporate form of business enterprise had no parallel form of worker association.
4. That lack of association, and freely made contracts had worsened the depression by reducing the purchasing power of wage earners.
5. That lack of organizations of work forces increased instability.
6. That collective bargaining was in the public interest to remove industrial strife, and for the friendly adjustment of disputes.

Labor for the moment had some powerful national symbols of its own—labor organization as a positive good rather than a conspiracy or an "interruption" to business; wages and improved wages as critical elements in economic growth and stability, and labor peace through negotiation and greater economic-political equality in the workplace, where it might count most. Labor responded to what it believed to be a new direction in national policy. A wave of organization of labor swept the country in the 1930s, bringing unions to the highest levels of membership in history.

Critical questions nevertheless remained after the Wagner Act, which required answering before labor could know whether the Wagner Act had mandated a revolution in labor–management relationships. Returning to ideas presented earlier in this chapter, had the Wagner Act made it more possible for labor through organization and collective bargaining—that is, according to law—to implement labor's agenda, which had been present ever since the Knights of St. Crispin and the general strike of 1877? Or was the legal realm still to be oriented toward the preservation of private property?

The assessment of the Wagner Act can follow the principal chambers of the Act itself: organization into unions, collective bargaining, and "concerted activities" or "tactics." However, one point must be made first: employers did not accept the Wagner Act and make a good-faith attempt to comply with its provisions. Instead they resisted the Act on advice of legal counsel that the Act was unconstitutional. It was not until the *Jones and Laughlin*[22] case, decided in 1937, that the Wagner act was declared constitutional. Until then, employers continued their prior practices of maintaining "open shops" (workers to be hired without regard to their union affiliation), promoting "company" or "inside" unions which were set up by employers to preempt "outside" unions, resisting the organization of workers into independent unions, and refusing to recognize and bargain with successfully organized unions.[23]

[22]301 U.S. 1 (1937).

[23]Harry Millis et al., *From the Wagner Act to Taft-Hartley*. (Chicago: U. of Chicago Press, 1950) pp. 33–39.

Meanwhile, labor was hampered by the prolonged Depression, which made for a chronic overabundance of workers ready and willing to take any job. Labor's response to employer resistance and the chronic oversupply of labor was the "sit-down strike"—a form of strike where strikers refused to leave the workplace. Owner-managers could not continue production, using unemployed workers as replacements, so long as workers occupied the factory.

The next case provides an instance of an employer's unwillingness to voluntarily accept what the Wagner Act seemed to require—recognition of an employee-chosen union and collective bargaining. By calling a sit-down strike, labor challenged their employer's recalcitrance. The case contains both the reasoning of the newly created National Labor Relations Board and the United States Supreme Court.

NLRB V. FANSTEEL CORPORATION 306 U.S. 247; (1939)

Mr. Chief Justice Hughes:

. . . [T]he principal question presented relates to the authority of the Board to require the respondent to reinstate employees who were discharged because of their unlawful conduct in seizing respondent's property in what is called a "sit-down strike."

Respondent, Fansteel Metallurgical Corporation, is engaged at North Chicago, Illinois, in the manufacture and sale of products made from rare metals . . .

The findings of the board show that in the summer of 1936 a group of employees organized Lodge 66 . . . Amalgamated Association of Iron, Steel and Tin Workers of North America; that respondent employed a "labor spy" to engage in espionage within the Union and his employment was continued until about December 1, 1936; that on September 10, 1936, respondent's superintendent was requested to meet with a committee of the union and the superintendent required that the committee should consist only of employees of five years' standing; that a committee, so constituted, presented a contract relating to working conditions; that the superintendent objected to "closed-shop and union check-off provisions" and announced that it was respondent's policy to refuse recognition of "outside" unions; that on September 21, 1936, the superintendent refused to confer with the committee in which an "outside" organizer had been included; that meanwhile, and later, respondent's representatives sought to have a "company union" set up but the attempt proved abortive; that from November, 1936, to January, 1937, the superintendent required the president of the union to work in a room adjoining the superintendent's office with the purpose of keeping him away from the other workers; that while in September, 1936, the Union did not have a majority of the production and maintenance employees, an appropriate unit for collective bargaining, by February 17, 1937, 155 of respondent's 229 employees in the unit had joined the Union and had designated it as their bargaining representative; that on that date a committee of the Union met twice with the superintendent who refused to bargain with the Union as to rates of pay, hours, and conditions of employment, the refusal being upon the ground that respondent would not deal with an "outside" union.

Shortly after the second meeting in the afternoon of February 17th the Union committee decided upon a "sit-down strike" by taking over and holding two of respondent's "key" buildings. These were thereupon occupied by about 95 employees. Work stopped and the remainder of the plant also ceased operations. Employees who did not desire to participate were permitted to leave and a number of Union members who were on the night shift and did not arrive for work until after the seizure did not join their fellow members inside the buildings. At about six o'clock in the evening, the superintendent, accompanied by police officials and respondent's counsel, went to each of the buildings and demanded that the men leave. They refused and respondent's counsel "thereupon announced in loud tones that all of the men in the plant were discharged for the seizure and retention of the buildings." The men continued to occupy buildings until February 26, 1937. Their fellow members brought them food, blankets, stoves, cigarettes, and other supplies. On February 18th, respondent obtained from the state court an injunction order requiring the men to surrender the premises. The men refused to obey the order and a writ of attachment for contempt was served on February 19th. Upon the men's refusal to submit a pitched battle ensued and the men successfully resisted the attempt by the sheriff to evict and arrest them. Efforts at mediation on the part of the United States Department of Labor and the Governor of Illinois proved unavailing. On February 26th the sheriff with an increased force of deputies made a further attempt and this time, after another battle, the men were ousted, and placed under arrest. Most of them were eventually fined and given jail sentences for violating the injunction.

Respondent on regaining possession undertook to resume operations and production gradually began. By March 12th the restaffing was approximately complete. A large number of the strikers, including many who had participated in the occupation of the buildings, were individually solicited to return to work with back pay but without recognition of the Union. Some accepted the offer and were reinstated; others refused to return unless there was union recognition and mass reinstatement and were still out at the time of the hearing before the Board. New men were hired to fill the positions of those remaining on strike.

Meanwhile the union was not inactive. On March 3rd and 5th there were requests, which respondents refused, for meetings to consider the recognition of the Union for collective bargaining. There was no collective request for reinstatement of all the strikers. The position of practically all the strikers who did not go back to work, and who were named in the complaint filed with the Board was "that they were determined to stay out until the union reached a settlement with the respondent."

Early in April a labor organization known as the Rare Metal Workers of America Local No. 1 was organized among respondent's employees. There was a meeting in one of the respondents buildings on April 15th which was attended by about 200 employees and the balloting resulted in a vote of 185 to 15 in favor of the formation of an "independent" organization. Another meeting was held soon after for the election of officers. Respondent accorded these efforts various forms of support. The Board concluded that the Rare Metals Workers of America Local No. 1 was the result of the respondent's "anti-union campaign" and that respondent had dominated and interfered with its formation and administration.

Upon the basis of these findings and its conclusions of law the Board made its order directing respondent to desist from interfering with its employees from their right to self-organization and to bargain collectively . . . to bargain collectively with Amalgamated Association . . . to the employees who went on strike February 17 "immediate and full reinstatement to their former positions," with back pay, dismissing, if necessary, all persons hired since that date . . .

First—The unfair labor practices. The Board concluded that by "anti-union statements and actions" of the superintendent on September 10, 1936 and September 21, 1936, by "the campaign to introduce into the plant a company union" by "the isolation of the union president from contact with his fellow employees" and by the employment and use of a "labor spy," respondent had interfered with its employees in their right of self-organization guaranteed in Section 7 of the Act [Section 7 provided: Employees shall have the right to self-organization, to form, join, or assist labor organizations, to bargain collectively through representatives of their own choosing, and to engage in concerted activities, for the purpose of collective bargaining or other mutual aid or protection. —Ed.] and thus had engaged in an unfair labor practice under Section 8 (1) of the Act. [Section 8(a) of the Act provides: It shall be an unfair labor practice for an employer (1) to interfere with, restrain, or coerce employees in the exercise of the rights guaranteed in section 7; (2) to dominate or interfere with the formation or administration of any labor organization or contribute financial or other support to it . . .; (3) by discrimination in regard to hire or tenure of employment or any term or condition of employment to encourage or discourage membership in any labor organization; (4) to discharge or otherwise discriminate against an employee because he has filed charges or given testimony under this Act; (5) to refuse to bargain collectively with the representatives of his employees. —Ed.] . . . the Board found . . . a refusal [to collectively bargain under 8(5). —Ed.] on February 17th when the union did have a majority of the employees. . . .

These conclusions are supported. . . .

Second—The discharge of the employees for illegal conduct in seizing and holding respondent's buildings. The Board does not now contend that there was not a real discharge on February 17th when the men refused to surrender possession. . . .

Nor is there any basis for dispute as to the cause of the discharge . . . for the seizure and retention of the buildings . . .

Nor is it questioned that the seizure and retention of the respondent's property were unlawful. It was a high-handed proceeding without shadow of legal right. It became the subject of denunciation by the state court . . . resulting in fines and jail sentences for defiance of the court's order. . . .

This conduct . . . manifestly gave good cause for . . . discharge unless the National Labor Relations Act abrogates the right of the employer to retain in his employ those who illegally take and hold possession of his property.

Third—The authority of the Board to require reinstatement of the employees thus discharged. The contentions of the Board in substance are these: (1) That the unfair labor practices led to the strike and thus furnished grounds for the reinstatement of the strikers; (2) . . . employees . . . on strike because of unfair labor practices retain their status as employees . . . despite their discharge for illegal conduct; (3) that the Board was entitled to order reinstatement or reemployment to effectuate the purposes of the Act.

For the unfair labor practices of the respondent the Act provided a remedy . . . But reprehensible as was that conduct of the respondent, there was no ground for saying that it made the respondent an outlaw or deprived it of its legal rights to the possession and protection of its property. The employees had the right to strike but they had no license to commit acts of violence or to seize the employer's plant . . . [I]n its legal aspect the ousting of the owner from lawful possession is not essentially different from an assault upon the officers of an employing company, or the seizure and conversion of its goods, or the despoiling of its property . . . to force compliance with its demands. To justify such conduct because of the existence of a labor dispute or of an unfair labor practice would put a premium on resorting to force instead of legal remedies and to subvert the principles of law and order which lie at the foundations of society. . . .

We are unable to conclude that Congress intended to compel employers to retain persons in their employ regardless of their unlawful conduct—to invest those who go on strike with an immunity from discharge for acts of trespass and violence. . . .

It was not a mere quitting of work . . . they took a position outside the protection of the statute and accepted the risk of the termination of their employment . . .

Comments and Questions

1a. Review the behavior of the employer as described by Justice Hughes in the Supreme Court opinion, and compare the behavior to the requirements of the Wagner Act, which are set out in the bracketed material in the opinion. Would the employer's behavior have inclined the workers to "take the law into their own hands" rather than resort to their legal remedies?

b. The Labor Board looked more sympathetically upon the behavior of the workers than did the courts. What would have impelled the Board to rule against the employer and order reinstatement of the workers?

c. Some of the scholarly commentary after the decision of the case was less critical of the behavior of the workers than one might have imagined. In an article appearing in the Harvard Law Review, the authors observed:

> . . . [E]xperience discloses the sit down strike as a product not of exuberance over enforcement of the National Labor Relations Act but of resentment at its non- enforcement. Sit down strikes first appeared as a major phenomenon in 1936 when employers and employers' lawyers were widely asserting that the act was invalid—and when litigation over the validity of the Act was bringing the effort to enforce it to a standstill.[24]

[24]H. Hart and E. Pritchard, "The Fansteel Case," *Harvard Law Review* 52 (1939), p. 1322.

Other commentators on the early years of the National Labor Relations Board found that the Board was fighting for its own survival which, of course, turned on a court ruling that the Wagner Act was constitutional, and that work on behalf of labor often "came to a standstill." Their own struggles robbed them of energy to cope with serious labor problems:

> In the early years . . . Board case records were full of instances where . . . employers violated the Act blatantly, violently, using spies to report on activities of union adherents and to undermine union organizations, discriminating against employees for union activities, instigating violence, establishing and maintaining company-dominated unions, refusing the right to collective bargaining to legitimate organizations representing a majority of the employees and interfering with the rights guaranteed by the Act.[25]

1. The foregoing, along with labor's disenchantment over the courts and 50 years of the labor injunction, helps explain why labor sat down. But what do these observations say about the fidelity of employers to the rule of law? If as a group they doubted the constitutionality of the Wagner Act, should they have obeyed the law pending final court ruling, just as a labor union would have been expected to obey a preliminary injunction, pending final disposition? When employers flouted the Act, were they "taking the law into their own hands?" Being socially irresponsible?
2. There is no explicit statement in the Wagner Act that property rights under the common law are to be carried along and preempt the federal law mandating free organization, collective bargaining, and concerted action in support of them.

   If there are whole areas of law which remained untouched by remedial labor acts, would this make workers jittery about rights according to federal labor law? Less inclined to resort to law and instead to take the law into their own hands?
3. Today many agree with Justice Hughes that occupation of a plant is a totally inappropriate response to nonrecognition of a union, or the refusal by an employer to collectively bargain. The workers were faced with a difficult dilemma. If they resorted to law, they feared being replaced while waiting for *possible* legal vindication at some unknown time, possibly in the distant future. If they occupied the building, the police would be called and they could jeopardize the remedies that the Wagner Act provided.

   What do you think you would have done had you been in their position?

   As their lawyer, how would you have recommended that they resolve the dilemma?

[25]Millis, et al., op. cit., p. 95.

4. The case shows the multiple levels of decision and review of decisions in the labor field after the Wagner Act; first there are the administrative investigation and decision by the National Labor Relations Board and then there is a round of federal court review of the administrative decisions, including the possibility of review by the United States Supreme Court.

   How would the two principal parties to the labor–management conflict view this prospect of administrative-judicial thoroughness? Compare the material in the antitrust chapter on delays, and the length and costs of trials and appeals and which party stands to benefit most from them.

   What would either party be able to do pending the final disposition of a given labor case? Are the parties equally desirous of a quick resolution of questions?
5. The sit-down strike, which had been so effective in organizing the rubber and automobile industries, fell into disuse after the Wagner Act was declared constitutional in 1937.

HIRING REPLACEMENTS FOR STRIKERS

If *Fansteel* assured that there could be no disruption in the use of plant properties, the case of *NLRB* v. *Mackay Radio*[26] assured that production could be continued during a strike by using replacements for striking workers. The ruling not so subtly undercut the ability of organized labor to call strikes and maximize the economic pressure on employers, especially in periods when high unemployment made the availability of replacements highly likely.

The *Mackay* case was a relatively simple one, which the Supreme Court could have decided on narrow grounds. A strike had occurred among telegraphers, and when the employer called in replacements, the strikers realized that the strike was doomed and offered to return to work. The employer offered reinstatement to a list of 36 of the strikers, but said that 11 others would have to reapply for employment. Of the eleven, five who had been very active in the union were eventually denied reinstatement. The Supreme Court found the discriminatory callback a violation of the Wagner Act, but went on to declare the right of an employer to permanently replace striking workers:

> Nor was it an unfair labor practice to replace the striking employees with others in an effort to carry on the business. Although section 13 . . . provides, "Nothing in this Act . . . shall be construed so as to interfere with or impede or diminish in any way the right to strike," it does not follow that an employer, guilty of no act denounced by the statute, has lost the right to protect and continue his business by supplying places left vacant by strikers. And he is not bound to discharge those hired to fill the places of strikers, upon the election of the latter to resume their employ [The Court next found discrimination in the employer's refusing to take back union activists] . . .[27]

[26]304 U.S. 336 (1938).
[27]Ibid., p. 345.

> [T]he respondent was not bound to displace men hired to take the strikers' places in order to provide positions for them. It might have refused reinstatement on the grounds of skill or ability, but the Board found it did not do so. It might have resorted to any one of a number of methods of determining which of its striking employees would have to wait because five men had taken permanent positions during the strike, but it is found that the preparation and use of the list, and the action taken by the respondent was with the purpose to discriminate against those most active in the union . . .[28]

The *Mackay* case is still the law despite organized labor's perennial opposition to the case since it was decided more than 50 years ago. The *Mackay* was critical to Caterpillar's breaking the 1992 strike of the UAW. The case ranks among the handful of most influential decisions in all of labor law history, and despite extensive Congressional hearings in 1992 on the need to modify the *Mackay* result, no changes were ever made. Organized labor is trying to get President Clinton to press for legislation to overturn the *Mackay* case.

The Wagner Act, despite its limitations, nevertheless significantly affected the level of union membership, bringing membership to 14.8 million members or 35.5 percent of the entire work force in 1945, excluding agricultural workers. However, there were a number of impediments that inhibited the full use of union power as it emerged in the period: open employer resistance to the Act from 1935 until it was declared constitutional in 1937; incomplete organization of work forces at critical employers like Ford Motor until almost the onset of World War II; and a moratorium on strikes after Pearl Harbor for the duration of the war. Labor did assert itself in a massive round of postwar strikes, but after two years came Taft–Hartley and deep amendments to the Wagner Act. Labor's Golden Age was not free from serious problems, and was very short.

This was the opinion of Millis, who chaired the Labor Board until 1945:

> It has been said truly that the Board never had a chance to operate in a 'normal' period with adequate staff and speed and efficiency in handling of cases, and to show what it might have done for the elimination of strife. Instead it had first the bitter opposition of most of industry and the fight on constitutionality; then the deluge of cases after the establishment of the constitutionality of the Act and the increase of membership following the organization of the CIO; then before it would get its work on a current basis the hampering Congressional investigations; next the war; and finally the postwar avalanche and the renewed attack upon the Act. And through most of the twelve years' history, appropriations and staff were inadequate, and the backlog of cases grew.[29]

Millis's commentary is instructive on the many lines of resistance to law that are open to a determined and well-financed party:

1. Opposing the enactment of law.

[28]Ibid., p. 347.
[29]Millis, op. cit., p. 34.

2. Resisting the enforcement of the law by pressing all contested cases to their bitter ends administratively and in the courts.
3. Keeping enforcers in fear of their own existence, and busy on procedural matters.
4. Pressing Congress to underfund and understaff enforcers, and to beseige enforcers with inquiries that required special preparation and appearances.
5 Mounting an ongoing campaign for amendment or repeal of the unwanted law.

TAFT–HARTLEY AND RELATED LABOR LAW DEVELOPMENTS

The Taft–Hartley Act of 1947 was a special disaster for organized labor.[30] Owners-managers, chafing at some of the advantages accruing to labor under the Wagner Act, demanded a "balance" in the labor law, meaning a restoration of pre-Wagner Act advantages, even though labor had not had much of a chance to cash in on the advantages that might have been realized under a fully enforced Wagner Act.

Taft–Hartley was only part of what has come to be a six-way squeeze on organized labor that has led to the continued economic and political weakness that persists today. The main lines of the squeeze on labor have involved:

1. The restoration of the tactical advantages of owner-managers .
2. The legitimization of *internal runaways* of companies from regions of the country with stronger unions and pro-union legal environments to areas weak in unionization and with weaker labor laws–herein of the flight of businesses from the Northeast to the Southeast and the Sunbelt.
3. No legal impediments to *external runaways* from all areas of the country including the South, to foreign sites for production, which are totally beyond the reach of domestic law, of whatever strength or leniency.
4. Opening the internal workings and finances of unions to outside scrutiny and control, (Labor Management Reporting Act of 1959).
5. The mergers and acquisitions movement that thinned out organized labor power with respect to some companies.
6. The overall decline of the political power of labor, traceable to the decline in the percentage of the work force organized into unions, and the inability of organized labor to act cohesively.

Since labor pinned most of its hopes on organizing and collective bargaining these topics will be considered in more detail here. (In passing, however, it should be remembered that *unorganized* labor, which now comprises

[30]Cohen, op.cit., pp. 167–185; K. Stone, "The Post-War Paradigm in American Labor Law," *Yale Law Journal* 90 (1981), pp. 1509–1580.

almost 85 percent of the work force in the United States, has probably fared worse, being left to individual contracts with employers not distinguishable from labor contracts of the nineteenth century.)

The Taft–Hartley law came as a result of two pressures, the first, an ongoing managerial resistance to the Depression legislation, which intensified immediately after the War. The second pressure was produced by a wave of postwar strikes which in some cases, most notably railroads and coal, had irritated the President, the Congress, and the general public; the strikes and media coverage of them helped shift the symbolic edge that labor briefly held in the Depression and war years. It is from this Taft-Hartley period that the one liner—"Labor is too powerful"—may have come. Labor was clearly more powerful than it had been under common law, and the percentages of unionization were at all-time high levels.

At the center of Taft–Hartley is a set of unfair labor practices of organized labor to "protect" employers against union excesses, just as the list of unfair labor practices in the Wagner Act had done for unions. These included coercion of employers regarding workers' joining unions; pressure on employers to discriminate against certain employees to enforce union rules; refusal by a union to bargain collectively; prohibition of labor boycotts; excessive initiation fees for union membership; eliminating "featherbedding" (the perpetuation of unneeded or obsolete work); and picketing to secure recognition of a union.

These provisions gave employers many lines of tactical action in labor cases, adding levels of complexity analogous to those considered in connection with antitrust cases in Chapter 6. In the end, labor law on the books and in practice became as complex as antitrust law, and a litigious employer could hang up a union for long periods by resisting organizing, collective bargaining, and union tactics.

The most infamous provision of Taft–Hartley from labor's perspective was the so-called "right to work" provision under 14(b) of the Act. It provided:

> Nothing in this Act shall be construed as authorizing the execution or application of agreements requiring membership in a labor organization as a condition of employment in any State or Territory in which such execution or application is prohibited by state or Territorial law.[31]

What may look simply unintelligible to the lay person comes down to a federal rule that *workers need not join a union where state laws have exempted them from joining*. This would be true even where a union had been voted in and authorized by law to be the collective bargaining representative.

Some states, most notably in the South, that wanted to create a "favorable business climate" passed "right to work" statutes authorized by the Taft–Hartley exception to the national labor law. The "right to work" proviso has been characterized in many ways for many purposes: the protection of the right of all workers to join or not join a union, the impairment of the abili-

[31]Labor Management Relations Act of 1947 (Taft–Hartley), Section 14 (b).

ty of organized labor to effectively represent a work force nationally in face of legally protected dissenters and "freeloaders," and the granting of a distinct advantage to employers, who can run away from areas that provide higher levels of union security to areas promoting non-union labor and more tractable work forces. All three characterizations can be supported, but there is little doubt that 14(b) has exacerbated the problem of domestic runaway employers.

In the post-World War II period, the multinationalization of enterprise accelerated, adding an international runaway shop problem to the internal runaway problem discussed above. Even the South, with relatively less unionization and more lenient labor legislation of all kinds, has not been immune from a decision of an employer to move production overseas. After the South had attracted "low end" production from the Northeast, such as in cotton spinning and weaving, it in turn has become vulnerable to the transfer of production overseas for cheaper labor.

The LMRA, passed in 1959, produced similar symbolic and practical effects. The law was passed after a series of Senate hearings exposing the presence of racketeering, sweetheart contracts (instigated by corrupt labor leaders who favored employers to the detriment of other employers and, in some cases, the union members themselves); gross abuses of union finances and pension funds; and near-dictatorial systems of union governance. The hearings were carried on television, and viewers came away with the idea that *all* labor leaders were a "bunch of bums," even though the hearings had focused primarily on the Teamsters.[32]

The 1959 law provided for much greater external surveillance of unions, ranging from their officers to their finances, and included a bill of rights for union members giving them a basis for challenging their unions in the federal courts. The opening of the internal workings of unions created a new front to limit the freedom of action of unions. There were good reasons for the passage of the law—especially assuring financial reporting and promoting democracy within unions—but the law was not without serious side effects on the labor–managerial power relationships.

The mergers and acquisitions movement also affected labor relations. Employers could choose as places of production from among the companies and locations in their newly aggregated networks. Some might be unionized, some not. In critical instances like automobile parts and assembly, "multiple-sourcing" possibilities were international as well as domestic. The diversification of companies meant multiple "profit centers," rendering labor tactics directed at a single profit center less effective. For example, were the United Mine Workers to call a strike, it would not be striking against a *coal company*; it would be striking an "*energy company*," not necessarily dependent upon continued coal production for its overall profitability.

One commentator rating industrial countries according to the strength of unionization used three criteria: the percentage of unionization, the degree

[32]H. Pelling, *American Labor* (Chicago: U. of Chicago Press, 1960), pp. 181–209.

of solidarity and cooperation among unions, and the ability of a given union to control the activities of its subunits. By all measures, organized labor in the United States ranks weak among industrialized countries. This weakness has corresponded to growing political weakness, so that even the Democratic Party, which traditionally depended upon block voting by labor for election success, has been increasingly casual about listening to the demands of labor.

Despite perennial protest, no changes have been made in the most undesirable features of Taft–Hartley. In 1976 a "Labor Reform Bill" sponsored by the Carter Administration died despite both the House and Senate being under Democratic control. Congressional hearings conducted in connection with the bill revealed gross abuse of labor law processes by such companies as J. P. Stevens, which had continuously frustrated efforts of textile workers to organize and collectively bargain. Their use of every nook and cranny of labor law and procedure bordered on abuse of legal process.

COLLECTIVE BARGAINING

Collective bargaining between unions and employers comprises the center of American labor law. In order to bargain, a union must be in place, having been elected and certified to bargain. This step has turned out to anything but a lithe and quick one, since every aspect of organization and certification can be challenged. There can also be challenges to the "appropriateness" of the bargaining units: which employees are eligible to join a union and which ineligible under the federal definitions? (For example, supervisors or other "managerial" employees are not eligible.) Where the employees are eligible, are they joined with the right workers in the right unit?

Does the union have a majority of the work force? What kind of campaign can be conducted by either a union or management to secure or resist unionization? If a union has secured a majority, does it still have a majority when it proposes to act as bargaining representative of the work force? If not, the union can be challenged.

It must be remembered that employers gain more from delays and complexity in labor law and process than do unions. The employer does not lose the ability to act pending the resolution of controversy, whereas a union often does. Where there are delays, unions must deal with the claim by workers that they are ineffective, and run the risk of being voted out by the membership, even though not all of the blame for the union's immobilization can be laid exclusively on it.

Some labor law commentators envisioned grand changes in the politics of labor–management relations after the Wagner and Taft–Hartley Acts. The government was committed to stay out of the relationship between management and unions and let the parties make their own arrangements. The collective bargaining process was compared to a constitutional convention or a legislative session, drawing up a government and making the detailed rules for their *mutual* governance. Grievance and arbitration procedures provided "a judiciary" to settle disputes with a minimum of strife.

This extension of the democratic political ethos into the labor–management sphere was embraced by a leading labor law commentator, Archibald Cox:

> In annual conferences, the employer and the union representing the employees, in addition to fixing wage rates, write a basic statute for the government of an industry or plant, under which they work out together through grievance procedure and arbitration the day-to-day problems of administration . By this "collective bargaining" the employee shares through his chosen representatives in fixing the conditions under which he works, and a rule of law is substituted for absolute authority. With these roots in the ideals of self-rule and government according to law, the institution seems certain to grow, at least as long as there survives the political democracy on whose achievement it has followed.[33]

The alternatives to this democratic vision were not pleasant to consider. There was a long history of labor conflict in which the public as well as the immediate parties had lost. But there was also the antipathy to autocratic rule about which World War II had been fought and a cold war begun. An autocratic work place would be incongruous with the general claims about the democratic imperative.

In the late 1970s the critical issues for organized labor moved from wages and hours to job security, and demonstrated the distinct limits of collective bargaining. Job security was being undercut by the capital flight of companies domestically and internationally, hardly business-as-usual subjects. In a total or partial close-down, jobs no longer existed, rendering work forces—and their union—irrelevant. Placement of work that had been formerly done by an inside work force with outside companies, "contracting out" or "outsourcing," also threatened job security. The next case concerns the refusal of an employer to collectively bargain with a union when work formerly done by union members was to be put out on contract to an outside company.

FIBREBOARD PAPER PRODUCTS CORP. V. N.L.R.B. 279 U.S. 208 (1964)

[Fibreboard Products Company had a manufacturing plant in California, where it had employed members of a local of the United Steel Workers of America to do maintenance work. When the last of a series of collective bargaining agreements was about to expire, the union gave the agreed notice to Fibreboard that it wanted to modify the contract. The union prepared its requests for modification and the parties met.

At the meeting the company informed the union that it was concerned with the high cost of maintenance and had undertaken a study of cost savings

[33]A. Cox, "Some Aspects of the Labor–Management Relations Act, 1947," *Harvard Law Review* 61 (1947), p. 1.

from hiring an independent contractor for maintenance, and presented a letter to the union containing the following: "For some time we have been seriously considering the question of letting out our Emeryville maintenance work to an independent contractor, and have now reached a definite intention to do so . . . In these circumstances we are sure you will realize that negotiation of a new contract would be pointless. However, if you have questions we will be glad to discuss them with you."

By the time the parties next met the company had selected Fluor Maintenance, Inc. to do the maintenance work for costs plus a monthly fee. At the meeting the company pointed out that maintenance work "was creating quite a burden" and stated that other unions representing company employees "had joined hands with management in an effort to bring about an economical and efficient operation" but that the company "had not been able to attain that . . .with this particular Local."

The union filed a charge of unfair labor practices, alleging Fibreboard's refusal to bargain with the local before contracting out the work formerly done by the union. The Labor Board agreed with the union, as did the lower federal court.]

Chief Justice Warren:

. . . Was petitioner required by the National Labor Relations Act to bargain with a union representing some of its employees about whether to let to an independent contractor for legitimate business reasons the performance of certain operations in which those employees had been engaged?

. . . We agree . . . that on the facts of this case, the "contracting out" of the work previously performed by the members of an existing bargaining unit is a subject about which the National Labor Relations Act requires employers and the representatives of their employees to bargain collectively. We also agree . . . that the Board did not exceed its remedial powers in directing the Company to resume its maintenance operations, reinstate the employees with back pay, and bargain with the Union.

I. Section 8(a)(5) of the National Labor Relations Act provides that it shall be an unfair labor practice for an employer "to refuse to bargain collectively with the representatives of his employees" . . . "to meet at reasonable times and confer in good faith with respect to wages, hours and other terms and conditions of employment"

. . . [T]hese provisions establish the obligation of the employer and the representative of the employees to bargain with each other in good faith with respect to "hours, wages, and other terms and conditions of employment . . ." The duty is limited to those subjects, and within that area neither party is legally obligated to yield . . . As to other matters, however, each party is free to bargain or not bargain . . . the subject about which the employer allegedly refused to bargain—contracting out of plant maintenance work . . . which the employees were capable of continuing to perform—is covered by the phrase "terms and conditions of employment". . .

The facts of the present case illustrate the propriety of submitting the dispute to collective negotiation. The Company's decision to contract out the maintenance work did not alter the Company's basic operation. The maintenance work still had to be performed in the plant. No capital investment was contemplated; the company merely replaced existing employees with those of an independent contractor to do the same work under similar conditions of employment. Therefore to require the employer to bargain about the matter would not significantly abridge his freedom to manage the business . . .

[A]lthough it is impossible to say that a satisfactory solution could be reached, national labor policy is founded upon congressional determination that the chances are good enough to warrant subjecting such issues to the process of collective negotiation . . .

While the Act does not encourage a party to engage in fruitless marathon discussions at the expense of frank statement and support of his position . . . it at least demands that the issue be submitted to the mediatory influence of collective negotiations . . . [I]t is not necessary that it be likely or probable that the union will yield or supply a feasible solution but rather that the union be afforded an opportunity to meet management's legitimate complaints that its maintenance was unduly costly . . .

We are thus not expanding the scope of mandatory bargaining to hold that this type of "contracting out" . . . is a statutory subject of collective bargaining . . .

[We make a first break from the opinion here to raise the following: Suppose the lawyers for Fibreboard were to have had the foregoing opinion available to them when they were giving their original advice to the company? Assume that the company wanted to save money and eliminate the need to deal with a difficult union. They approach their lawyers with a simple request: "We want to contract with an outside company, but we don't want to be accused of an unfair labor practice by the union—tell us how." Draw up a memorandum of legal advice based on the Supreme Court opinion.

In a separate small writing, discuss the larger implications of your advice. We now return to the *Fibreboard* opinion.]

Justice Stewart, Concurring

. . . [T]he Court's opinion radiates implications of such disturbing breadth that I am persuaded to file this separate statement of my views . . .

The question posed is whether the particular decision sought to be made unilaterally by the employer in this case is subject to mandatory collective bargaining within the statutory phrase "terms and conditions of employment." That is all the Court decides. The Court most assuredly does not decide that every managerial decision which necessarily terminates an individual's employment is subject to the duty to bargain. Nor does the Court decide that subcontracting decisions are as a general matter subject to the duty. The Court holds no more than that this employer's decision to subcontract this work, involving "the replacement of employees in the existing bargaining unit with those of an independent contractor to do the same work under similar conditions of employment" is subject to the duty to bargain collectively. Within the narrow limitations implicit in the specific facts of this case, I agree with the Court's decision . . .

The basic question is whether the employer failed to "confer in good faith with respect to . . . terms and conditions of employment" . . .

It is important to note that the words of the statute are words of limitation. The National Labor Relations Act does not say that the employer and employees are bound to confer upon any subject which interests either of them; the specification of wages, hours, and other terms and conditions of employment defines a limited category of issues subject to collective bargaining . . .

The phrase "conditions of employment" is no doubt susceptible to diverse interpretations. At the extreme, the phrase could be construed to apply to any subject which is insisted upon as a prerequisite to continued employment . . . [T]here are passages in the Court's opinion which suggest just such an expansive interpretation, for the Court's opinion seems to imply that any issue that may reasonably divide an employer and his employees must be the subject of compulsory collective bargaining.

Only a narrower conception of "conditions of employment" will serve the statutory purpose . . . What one's hours are to be, what amount of work is expected during those hours, what periods of relief are available, what safety practices are observed, would all seem conditions of one's employment. There are less tangible but no less important characteristics of a person's employment—most prominently . . . the security of one's employment. On one view of the matter, it can be argued that the question whether there is to be a job is not a condition of employment, but the more fundamental question of whether there is to be employment at all . . .

Many decisions made by management affect the job security of employees. Decisions concerning the volume and kind of advertising expenditures, product design, the manner of financing, and sales, all may bear on the security of the workers' jobs. Yet it is hardly conceivable that such decisions so involve "conditions of employment" that they must be negotiated . . .

[T]here are . . . areas where decisions by management may quite clearly imperil job security, or indeed terminate employment entirely. An enterprise may decide to invest in labor-saving machinery. Another may resolve to liquidate its assets and go out of business. Nothing the court holds today should be understood as imposing a duty to bargain collectively regarding such managerial decisions, which lie at the core of entrepreneurial control. Decisions concerning the commitment of investment capital and the basic scope of the enterprise are not in themselves primarily about conditions of employment, though the effect of the decision may be necessarily to terminate employment . . . [T]hose management decisions which are fundamental to the basic direction of a corporate enterprise or which impinge only indirectly upon employment security should be excluded from that area . . .

This kind of subcontracting falls short of the larger entrepreneurial questions as what shall be produced, how capital shall be invested in fixed assets, or what the basic scope of the enterprise shall be . . .

I am fully aware that in this era of automation and onrushing technological change, no problems in the domestic economy are of greater concern than those involving security and employment stability. Because of the potentially cruel impact upon the lives and fortunes of working men and women of the Nation, these problems have understandably engaged the solicitous attention of government, of responsible private business, and particularly of organized labor. It is possible that . . . Congress may eventually decide to give organized labor or government a far heavier hand in controlling what have until now been the prerogatives of private business management. That path would mark a sharp departure from the principles of a free enterprise economy . . .

Questions and Comments

1. Under Stewart's understanding of collective bargaining, what is to be the connection between collective bargaining and the establishment of industrial democracy?

   What are the powers granted to managers in the Stewart opinion?
2. Justice Stewart's concurrence has become the rule on the scope of collective bargaining.

   Plant closings and partial discontinuance of businesses have become an increasingly visible area of conflict between workers and owner-managers. In 1981, the Supreme Court reaffirmed and expanded Stewart's concurring opinion in a case that involved the refusal to bargain about a partial closedown:

> In establishing what issues must be submitted to the process of bargaining, Congress had no expectation that the elected representatives would become an equal partner in the running of the business enterprise . . . Despite the openness of the statutory language there is an undeniable limit to the subjects about which bargaining can take place . . .
>
> The decision (to terminate a portion of the business) involving a change in the scope and direction of the enterprise is akin to the decision as to whether to be in business at all . . . and not primarily about conditions of employment, although the effect of the decision may necessarily be to terminate employment.[34]

a. In your judgment, should the phrase "wages, hours, and other terms and conditions of employment" be broad enough to require collective bargaining about total or partial plant closings?

b. If there is to be no "equal partnership" between unions and owner-managers, what is the relationship to be? Without more equality, what are the prospects for collective bargaining in promoting a lasting peace?

c. After cases like *Fibreboard* and the *First National Maintenance* cases, is it fair to say that the *more important* a question is to the long-run welfare of labor, the *less likely* it will be a mandatory subject for collective bargaining?

d. The Court in the *Fibreboard* case did not seem to have in mind the multinationalization of enterprise, which has often involved dramatic shifts in investment strategies and relocation of all or parts of an enterprise. Consider the applicability of the *Fibreboard* case to decisions of multinationals on the allocation of production worldwide.

e. When a firm decides to close, how does it fulfill its legal obligations? Under the *Fibreboard* case, the *decision* to close or relocate need not be bargained, but the *effects* of the decision must be. In a recent case involving the sell-off of a business during the time a collective agreement was in place, a federal court stated:

[34]*First National Maintenance Corp.* v. *N.L.R.B.* 452 U.S. 666 (1981).

Coca Cola was not under an obligation to notify the Union of the decision to sell its sales department assets . . . Coca Cola fully complied with its only obligation under the law which was to bargain over the effects of the sale. Likewise the union did not breach its duty of fair representation when it bargained over the effects of such sale and obtained the most favorable terms and conditions for the plaintiffs, in view of the inevitable sale and layoff.
[In this case the union negotiated severance pay.][35]

f. Are there any legal rights apart from collective agreements that would impose limits on companies closing plants? Are there general obligations to work forces who have devoted their most productive years to a company or an industry? And what of communities who have called themselves "steel cities," "rubber cities" or "Motown" and have built an infrastructure—roads, water systems, sewers—and established school programs in support of a company or industry? Can a company simply pick up and leave, and let the consequences be what they may?

In a unique case, *Local 1330 of the United Steelworkers* v. *United States Steel*,[36] a union joined with the city of Youngstown arguing that the company owed something to workers and a city that had been oriented exclusively around steel production. Their theory was that long practice must have given rise to property and community rights that were violated when the company abandoned the area.

The court offered consolation, but no remedy:

. . . [T]he lives of 3500 workers and their families and the supporting Youngstown community cannot be dismissed as inconsequential. United States Steel should not be permitted to leave the Youngstown area devastated after drawing from the lifeblood of the community for so many years. Unfortunately the mechanism to reach this ideal settlement, to recognize this new property right is not now in existence . . .

Whatever the future may bring, neither by statute nor by court decision has appellant's property right been recognized in this country . . .

[F]ormulation of public policy on the great issues involved in plant closings is clearly the responsibility of the legislatures of the state or of the Congress . . .

We find no basis for judicial remedy.[37]

To add extra irony, while the plants were too unprofitable to require the company to operate, they were still the property of the company, and displaced workers and their communities could not necessarily buy the plants and operate them themselves.

g. No substantial remedy for plant closings has been enacted. In 1986 a companion statute to the Omnibus Trade Bill required 60-day notice of intention to close a plant. The ability to unilaterally make the decision to close was left unaffected.

[35]*Cruz-Capella* v. *Coca Cola Bottling Co.* 677 F. Supp. 65 (1987).
[36]631 F.2d 1264 (1980).
[37]Ibid., p. 1266, 1281, 1282.

CONTEMPORARY COLLECTIVE BARGAINING AND LABOR-MANAGEMENT TACTICS

In cases where there are "mature" relationships between companies and unions, there is still an unpredictable blend of conflict and conciliation. The problem is that each side bargains like poker players, including upping the antes, bluffing, and calling. And as in poker, sometimes bargaining can be a zero sum game with clear winners and losers. There follows a chronology of the 1991–1992 Caterpillar strike, based on *Wall Street Journal* accounts, with some comments added in brackets.

September 30, 1991. Contract expires at midnight and Union gives company a 5-day strike notice. Company refuses to accept "pattern bargaining" based on the agreement reached between the UAW and John Deere Corporation.

November 4. Union on strike in two cities [At this point about 15 percent of the UAW at Caterpillar is out. The union does not want to call a complete strike because it would take all 17,000 workers off the payroll and more rapidly deplete its strike fund—benefits for strikers are $100/week from the union treasury plus $25/week from workers still on the job.]

November 8. Caterpillar "locks out" 5600 workers at two sites previously not on strike. [This put added pressure on the strike funds and the personal finances of the affected workers, but company claims that its response was based on the union's selectively striking places that would maximize harm to the company.]

November 14. Caterpillar lays off 320 hourly workers at parts facilities.

November 26. Caterpillar lays off an additional 680 workers; 200 members of the machinists union, and 480 UAW members at York, Pennsylvania; 10,000 idled at this point.

December 27. Wall Street Journal records commentaries on the strike and the issues dividing the parties:

An AFL–CIO official: "This is a big one."

Caterpillar executive: "We are not out to break the union."

Harley Shaiken, of the University of California–Berkeley, says the company's message is "[T]he better we do internationally, the lower the wages we're going to need at home."

Audrey Freeman, an economist at the Conference Board: "[G]lobal competition makes pattern bargaining an anachronism."

Striking worker: I just wish the company and the union would do some serious talking."

Douglas Frazer, former head of the UAW during the long 1982–1983 strike at Caterpillar: "I think it's going to be a long, bitter strike."

The issues dividing the work force and the company were wages, wage structures, health care, automation (job security). Wages demanded were $37.50 per hour (13 percent increase over 3 years), of which one-half was the hourly wage and the other half benefits including health care. The wage structure debate was over the company's demand for a two-tier wage system which would have downgraded the pay on a number of jobs. The company wanted employees to pay 30 percent of their health care costs when they did not go to designated doctors and hospitals. [Job security in the Deere agreement involved a commitment by the company to maintain the same number of jobs—as workers left through retirement or other causes they would be replaced by workers on layoff.]

January 23, 1992. Caterpillar set aside $325 million for the "probable" closing of Caterpillar in York, Pennsylvania and consolidation of its Brazilian operations into one factory. [This message must have sent terror into the hearts of York workers and the city where they live. An elaborate bluff or the real thing?]

February 10. Caterpillar ends lockout at two plants, announces "important modifications in its contract proposal" and asks the union to resume bargaining on February 17.

February 12. Union has said it will strike the two plants the company had locked out. Company spokespeople are said to be disappointed that the union was maintaining its "hard line" position [There was commentary all through the time of the strike–lockout regarding the impact of the strike on the ability of the company to supply and keep customers. After the initial backlog of inventories of parts and machines were worked off, it was believed that the company would have difficulty in meeting orders. Was the company at last feeling the pinch, or was it desirous of resuming serious bargaining, or both? Or neither?]

February 19. Workers previously locked out join the strike.

February 20. Union has rejected what Caterpillar says is its "final offer" in a brief bargaining session.

February 24. Union has struck Mossville Illinois diesel engine factory, which competes with Cummins and Detroit Diesel; 2700 more workers are now out.

March 9. Company has announced that it has made its final offer and that it will hire replacements. It will not accept the bargain made at Deere. Gets an injunction in the Illinois state courts to prevent threats of bodily harm, blocking gates, and having more than 10 pickets at any gate.

March 30. UAW files unfair labor practice charges to try to protect strikers in the event of replacement. [Under the *Mackay* case ruling economic strikers can be permanently replaced, whereas "unfair labor practice" strikers may be entitled to reinstatement with back pay. The filing may be a formality here.]

April 8. Caterpillar files unfair labor practice charges against the union for harassing workers desirous of returning to work.

April 10. UAW strikes 1800 more workers at four more plants making a total of 12,600 workers out.

April 14. Union calls off strike. After two days of mediation, with a federal mediator, the company implements its final offer and withdraws its threats to hire replacements. 12,600 workers are to start returning to work on April 20. Company says 1350 jobs will be cut.

April 21. Company says it will recall all strikers, but cut 1350 through attrition.

Very little bargaining took place between the parties, because the company refused to accept the terms of the Deere bargain and the union refused to abandon its demand for "pattern bargaining." A fact that did not escape anyone's notice who was close to the negotiations is that the average age of a Caterpillar union worker is 47 with 28 years of service. With only two years remaining before becoming eligible to retire, these workers were especially vulnerable to a threat of permanent replacement. A second fact stands out: no matter how the collective bargain had come out, the work force at Caterpillar would be far smaller than it had been a little more than a decade earlier. The work force had a retirement prospect, but no solid future. A third fact is that after the devastating confrontation between Caterpillar and the UAW, it will be unlikely that the work force will be as cooperative in improving productivity and quality control. If workers see themselves on a slow phaseout with no prospects for their sons and daughters with the company, it is hard to make them interested in the long term.

Business Week, in its story on April 27, thought a great victory had been won by the management at Caterpillar:

> It didn't take long for the United Auto Workers to crack after Caterpillar Inc. Chief Executive Donald V. Fites rolled out his big guns on April 6. Fites warned Cat's 13,000 striking workers that if they didn't return on that date he would find replacements for them. Just eight days later, union leaders agreed to send the strikers back on Cat's terms while the two sides keep bargaining.
>
> The union's move is no less than a clear victory for Fites. If he ultimately prevails with his contract demands, as now seems likely, Cat may not save much more in wages and benefits than the profits it lost during the six month strike. But it could steal a march on its rivals by reaping large productivity gains...

Novelists know that what is past is prologue and stories do not really end, but simply take new, and sometimes unpredictable, turns. So too with the Caterpillar conflict. The following article appeared in the *Wall Street Journal* almost two months after workers had returned to work "on Cat's terms."

CATERPILLAR MAY FACE SLOWDOWN BY THE UAW

Wall Street Journal, June 5, 1992

In a move to pressure Caterpillar Inc. at the bargaining table, the United Auto Workers union is training local union officials in tactics that could lead to a work slowdown at the construction-equipment maker.

Under the so-called in-plant strategy, employees would do such things as work strictly to rules, slow or stop production to correct even minor defects and consult foremen about even the smallest of details.

Union officers already have been trained in some locations, and the goal is to train every union member, local union officials said.

"We're not going to be at rest until we can get a contract we can live with," said Al Weygand, a UAW official in Aurora, Ill.

Although company officials have been worried about such a slowdown, a Caterpillar spokesman in Peoria, Ill., said the company hasn't seen "any evidence" that one has started.

"Rather than expending energy trying to hurt Caterpillar employees and communities," the spokesman said, "we would hope the union would focus on coming up with a new [contract] proposal."

The UAW and its members have warned about such moves ever since strikers returned to work without a contract April 20, under the threat that they would be replaced if they didn't return. Individuals on both sides say little progress has been made in bargaining since then with federal mediators.

The Caterpillar situation is being carefully watched by Detroit's Big Three auto makers, who fear the UAW may use the same in-plant strategy when their UAW contracts expire next year. The most likely target: General Motors Corp., which has been feuding with the UAW ever since GM announced plans to close 21 plants. GM has 270,000 employees who are represented by the UAW, including some on the company's layoff rolls.

However, a GM spokesman said he would be puzzled if the union should want to employ a slowdown strategy against GM, which suffered record losses last year. "Losing $4 billion a year is enough for any company to take," he said." "I don't know why [workers] would want it to be any higher."

A UAW official in Detroit said: "We see the Big Three as quite different from the situation at Caterpillar." But if the auto makers decide to play hardball with UAW bargainers, he added, then in-plant strategy would not be ruled out.

There are 15,000 UAW members working at Caterpillar. Not all agree with the union, and some would refuse to take part in such a strategy. But because the union has the allegiance of many members, analysts and dealers fear that a concerted effort could disrupt production.

Indeed, if successfully implemented, the strategy could be debilitating for Caterpillar. It would be hard for managers to discipline workers abiding by the rules, even if production does suffer. Workers taking part, meanwhile, would continue to collect pay and benefits.

The training is done basically in a few hours, though follow up sessions are possible. Among other things, local union officials are being encouraged to conduct rallies before and after work, or during lunch breaks.

The strategy involves "anything that's legal and applies pressure on the corporation to come to the bargaining table." . . .

Among those training local union officials is Doug Womack, president of a UAW local in Marshalltown, Iowa, that doesn't represent Caterpillar workers . . .

Ironically one of the strongest backers of the in-plant strategy is the UAW's New Directions dissident movement. "It grinds the process of production to a much slower pace, but without being the kind of slowdown that's in violation of the rules," said Jerry Tucker, a former UAW executive who heads New Directions.

Comment and Question

1. The coverage of the Caterpillar strike ends here. The conflict seemed to hover somewhere between a strike and a sit-down strike.
2. Give your final reflections about the Caterpillar strike, the relationship between the strike and the prior labor law, and the possible futures of collective bargaining in an era of multinationalization of enterprise.

CONCLUSION

We began and ended this chapter with the strike of Caterpillar Corporation, asking how well-organized and experienced labor could have been unable to win a long strike. Our tendency might have been to say that the weakness of labor is of recent origin, or was brought on exclusively by the ability of United States-based corporations to simply pick up production and go abroad. There is no doubt that the multinationalization of enterprise has exacerbated the adverse position of organized labor by making workers competitive with all other workers everywhere, but this phenomenon, though true, is not the sole cause.

Labor at common law, later under the Wagner and Taft-Hartley statutes, and under the current law has been *systemically* disadvantaged; this makes the general strikers' preference in 1877 *for the streets* rather than *the courts* not so stupid, if they could have figured out a way to translate their hard-hitting activism into concrete changes in their work lives.

Across time workers have been pitted against other workers by rules inhibiting organization, effective bargaining, and tactics. In the Caterpillar case, the strikers were up against unemployed workers who were lined up to replace them. This tactic of dividing and ruling has appeared all across labor history, with the force of law to make it an effective option. Experienced shoemakers stood against "green hands" in the 1870s; picketing strikers against potential replacements in the 1888 *Sherry* case, independent unions versus captive company unions in the 1900 *Plant* and 1939 *Fansteel* cases, strikers against replacements in the 1938 *Mackay* case; workers in one region of the United States against workers of other regions after the 1947 Taft-Hartley Act, and its "right to work" provision; organized workers against outside contractors in the 1964 *Fibreboard Products* case.

Space has not permitted discussion of all of the episodes of division and rule across all of American history: "native" work forces against immigrants, one group of immigrants against other immigrants, women against women, women against men, blacks against whites, southern and "sun belt" workers against northern workers, and other divisions that have kept workers divided and ruled. Workers acting by class has been rare but not totally unknown as the general strike of 1877 and the consensus developed in the Depression attest. In the Depression, no amount of self-hatred or soul searching could have led workers to blame themselves or their brethren for the total collapse of employment.

Employers, without the strength of numbers, have stayed, with rare exceptions, on the right side of symbols: innovation and progress; peaceful production as opposed to disruption, nonviolence (except that done indirectly through private detectives, plant guards, the police or, on occasion, the army or the national guard), efficiency of production rather than boondoggling-featherbedding, and so on.

Labor law across over one hundred years has performed a significant role in implanting and augmenting these symbols to the point where what ought to be a highly debatable statement about labor goes unexamined: "American workers are lazy, have become too demanding, and it is no wonder that employers will no longer tolerate labor's abuse of power." Such commonplaces cannot stand up against the historical record, which is itself dismissed as a useless gloss on practical wisdom.

The study of labor must be integrated with the two preceding chapters. In Chapter 5 on the evolution of the corporate form of doing business, it was demonstrated that the corporation became free of state control over its size, scope, longevity, and purposes. By the end of this evolution, the corporation had become a person, able to make contracts and own all types of property. The corporation got the best of two worlds: treated as "an entity" for business flexibility and taxation, and as a "person" for the assertion of constitutional rights. According to law, the corporation was really a *superperson* with unlimited power and immortality.

In Chapter 6 on antitrust, the point was made that the antitrust law has asserted no limits upon corporate size and market power, two preconditions to corporation's assuming national power, establishing a platform for international expansion, and asserting an even more unassailable bargaining position with respect to labor.

In this chapter we have seen that labor from the inception of industrialization has not been an effective countervailing power to corporate power, and labor is even more anemic when matched against multinational corporate power. If ordinary wisdom says, "Labor has become too powerful," a study of history would probably reveal that labor, according to law, is not now, nor has it ever been, very powerful—except sporadically. History would also reveal that labor is getting weaker rather than stronger, as the failure of the Caterpillar strike and opposition to NAFTA demonstrate.

So what? What if one takes the position that labor interests ought to be subordinate to the prerogatives that go with the ownership of productive facilities? It can be argued against this generally held belief that a country is only so free as its labor movement is free, that democracy requires that greater numbers ought to count more wherever possible.

But there are additional reasons for choosing people over property. Most remedial legislation—social security, health care, occupational safety, public education, free libraries, and affordable transportation—have come with the help of political pressure from labor and organized labor; most workers know that they will not hit the lottery, and cannot individually bankroll everything they need. And it is not coincidental that we list among the atrocities of totalitarian regimes the outlawing of labor unions, free collective bargaining, and tactics to make them effective. Totalitarian rules on labor are cited as serious intrusions upon human freedom because they are. And this wisdom applies in the United States as well as abroad, even though international lessons are rarely applied domestically.

PART 3

Multinational Networks and Legal Networks

CHAPTER 8

Intersections—World Business Networks

This chapter opens consideration of the many ways that multinationals have business dealings across countries. The term *multinational* itself indicates that company activities span two or more countries. The open term *intersections* raises the prospect that there are many possible forms that the multinationalization of enterprise can take with different implications. They range from the quite trivial and transient intersection—a single international trade that links a buyer and a seller—to substantial and long-lasting relationships—the outright ownership by a multinational of land, facilities, and companies in another country, or the control of a country's principal export, as was the case for years with crude oil production.

There are a number of possible relationships that fall somewhere in between, for example, setting up production in an industrial processing zone for export only, joint ventures with local companies for production or sales, or joint ventures with local governments covering a variety of stages of production or distribution. The sample profiles described in this chapter are not exhaustive of all possibilities, but they each carry with them representative legal problems and political-economic implications.

These examples can do at least two things necessary to an understanding of contemporary international business: give a sense of the history of international intersections, some of which have persisted to this day; and second, they tell us what elements of enterprise intersections to watch for in business news. If, as we are frequently warned, history does not repeat itself, history nevertheless reveals themes that are perennial.

Some of the themes considered in greater detail here were first introduced in Chapter 2 through the material on business allocation decisions and the inevitable involvement of multinational enterprises in political life. There we asked about the degree of control exercised by multinationals over local political systems, or, to take the flip side, the degree of control over multinational activities exerted by the local law–government system or "host country." The desire for profitable relationships across the world impels businesses to become politically active and to gain places in an economic system rather than to accept political contexts as they find them.

In Chapter 3, where the John D. Rockefeller and J. P. Morgan dynasties were considered, the companies in which the men were principals outgrew their domestic bases and came to be involved in business worldwide. To make the world safe for these businesses so enlarged, the boundaries between business and political activity were so frequently crossed that political strategizing became an integral part of the business.

Similarly, Chapter 4 showed that the power that had been amassed in worldwide business networks required the rebirth of the subject of political economy, an academic effort to bring academics up to the speed and scope of the business networks that had rendered compartmentalized study a quaint distortion. The companies involved in the grain trade or in the ocean shipment of oil by supertanker operated in networks that were historically unprecedented.

In Chapter 5 the profile of the Caterpillar Corporation demonstrated that the company had many worldwide connections for production, marketing, finance, and service. Some of the related enterprises of the Caterpillar network are owned outright, some are partially owned, and some are joint ventures with other companies.

This chapter deepens the coverage of worldwide intersections, beginning with some classical ones and ending with some of recent origin. The classical examples are important, since commentators critical of multinationals contend that present business practices replay the past with only superficial differences, that colonialism thought dead reappears in qualitatively similar forms of commercial domination and dependence.

The contemporary configuration of multinationals is defended on the ground that there has been a break with dismal economic pasts. In place of exploitative relationships, there are now worldwide efficiencies that contribute to development everywhere; a world that is unified commercially is both universally prosperous and universally peaceful. Once the phenomenon of multinationals has run its course, defenders of the multinational ethos contend, the cornucopia of products and services that was once the exclusive privilege of people in the industrialized nations will be accessible to countries and people everywhere.

A. CLASSICAL CONTROL SYSTEMS

The first round of intersections concerns those that are well developed in business histories: straight trade, colonialism and companies operating in colonial systems, direct control of indigenous production by international companies, indirect control by international companies of indigenous production, and finally the concession system, which presents a special case of control.

International trade is the oldest intersection and reaches back to the ancient world. Legal texts carrying titles like "International Business Transactions" trace the many problems that can result from such trade in goods and services: nondelivery, nonpayment, defective goods, goods lost in transport, unsatisfactory services, and so on. Students interested in chapter-

and-verse discussion of these problems in finance, sales, and transport will find ample coverage in legal treatises and primers on the commercial contingencies of international trade, but they will not find them here.

When the word *empire* is used, thoughts run to historical exemplars in the western world: the Roman or Greek empires in the ancient world, or the Byzantine, Spanish, Portuguese, Ottoman, and Russian empires that came later. Preeminent among the modern empires are the British, Dutch, and French colonial regimes. These usually entailed physical control of indigenous territory and political systems of force or cooptation—that is, rule by the military or rule via allegiances with local people who would thereafter act on behalf of the empire.

Empires also connote captive trade, and domination of economies by the colonizer over the colonized, a dimension sometimes missed when historical coverage is preoccupied with personalities, dates and places of battles, or political and cultural transformations divorced from economic transformations.

If one thinks about it, the pride accompanying "having an empire" would probably play out as a motivation were it not for the economic gains that accrue from controlling other places. The British empire was often said to be "burdensome" to Great Britain, but that persistent complaint masks the fact that the empire offered an outstanding opportunity structure to British entrepreneurs. While the sun was never setting on the British empire, it was also never setting on British businesses.

A relatively neglected piece of the history of empires is United States imperialism. It came late and was piddling alongside others, once the purchases and conquests that established what is presently the United States were complete. But the United States had its "colonies," the most notable of which was the Philippine Islands, taken from Spain in 1898 and held until after World War II. It is to the Philippines that the United States continues to claim a "special relationship," including, although it is not mentioned first, the relationship between the two economies.

Sometimes, even in absence of the out-and-out control characteristic of empires, companies have *direct control* of indigenous production. The most notable example of this form of control would be United Fruit in Central America, where the company owned land and transportation systems to produce and export bananas for sale in other countries.

In earlier chapters there has been some discussion of *indirect control systems*. The Standard Oil trust in its early days controlled transportation, refining, and distribution of oil, but not production. J. P. Morgan and other banks controlled railroads and industrial companies through finance and stock voting power, but otherwise engaged in no "industry." Cargill and the other five companies who control most phases of the world commodity trade do no farming; they concentrate on transportation, trading, and the linkages forward to their own processing companies, or other end users of commodities. A little-known historical example—the early sisal trade between the Yucatan in Mexico and the United States, discussed later in this chapter, outlines the paridigm of an indirect control system.

A final classical relationship concerns *concessions*, the principal way that international oil companies operated in the Middle East and in other countries where oil might be found and brought into production. Through concessions, a company, or consortium of companies, received exclusive rights to future oil production, in return for the development of oil properties and royalty payments. Concessions have been a large and special type of control that is technically indirect (since the country granting the concession "owns" the resource), but border on direct control, since the concessionaire companies organized the production. OPEC, the organization of petroleum exporting countries, was formed in 1960 to eliminate the concession system and bring at least a measure of control of oil back to the producing countries.

American Empire in the Philippines

In 1898, the Spanish Empire collapsed after the Spanish–American War, and the United States confronted the question of an overseas empire.[1] Democratic principles and inherent rights of self-determination notwithstanding, the United States chose empire and began extensive economic relationships between the United States and the Philippines that still exist despite Philippine independence.

It took years of bloody fighting—termed America's first Vietnam by one writer[2]—to pacify the Philippines. Up to a million people were killed. The ethic of intervention was to save the Philippines from worse colonizers such as Europeans, or from herself, as is implicit in Senator Beveridge's speech in 1900 urging colonization:

> It would be hard for Americans who have not studied them to understand the people. They are a barbarous race, modified by three centuries of contact with a decadent race. The Filipino is the South Sea Malay, put through a process of three hundred years of superstition in religion, dishonesty in dealing, disorder in habits of industry, and cruelty, caprice, and corruption in government. It is barely possible that 1,000 men in all of the archipelago are capable of self government in the Anglo-Saxon sense.[3]

A few sentences later:

> But Senators, it would be better to abandon this combined garden and Gibraltar of the Pacific, and count our blood and treasure already spent a profitable loss, than to apply any academic arrangement of self government to these children.

[1]For a general introduction to the Spanish–American War period and Philippine pacification, see Stanley Karnow, *In Our Image*, (New York: Random House, 1989).

[2]L. Francisco, "The First Vietnam: The Philippine–American War, 1899–1902," in *The Philippines: End of an Illusion* (London: AREAS, 1973).

[3]Beveridge is quoted in Daniel Schirmer et al., eds., *The Philippines Reader*, (Boston: South End, 1987), p. 25.

> They are not capable of self government. How could they be? They are not a self-governing race. They are Orientals, Malays . . .
>
> What alchemy will change the oriental quality of their blood and set the self-governing currents of the American pouring through their Malay veins? How shall they, in the twinkling of an eye, be exalted to the heights of self-governing peoples which required a thousand years for us to reach, Anglo-Saxons though we are?[4]

Kindness and humane concern, leavened by racism, required that the United States go slow in granting independence. In the meanwhile, the Philippines could pay for civilization in kind—Beveridge once more:

> No land in America surpasses in fertility the plains and valleys of Luzon. Rice and coffee, sugar and coconuts, hemp and tobacco, and many products of the temperate as well as the tropic zone grow in various sections of the archipelago . . . the wood of the Philippines can supply the furniture of the world for a century to come. At Cebu the best informed man in the island told me that 40 miles of Cebu's mountain chain are practically mountains of coal.
>
> I have a nugget of pure gold picked up in its present form on the banks of a Philippine creek. I have gold dust washed out by crude processes of careless natives from the sands of a Philippine stream. Both indicate great deposits . . .
>
> And the wood, hemp, copra, and other products of the Philippines supply what we need and can not ourselves produce. And the markets they will themselves afford will be immense . . . Ultimately our trade, when the islands shall be developed, will be $125,000,000 annually, for who believes we can not do ten times as well as Spain?[5]

The speech characterizes the almost 50 years prior to independence. After pacification there was no disruption of the Philippine elite classes under Spanish rule. This group controlled the agricultural sector and assumed nominal control of the national legislature (a process called Filipinization, with a U.S.-appointed Governor General possessing veto power and an American-controlled Supreme Court). The Filipinos would be slowly schooled—literally, and in English, by a volunteer teacher corps recruited in the United States. The United States gave assurances that independence would eventually be granted, but not until the necessary acculturation to the requirements of self-government could be safely assumed.[6]

What was the United States to get in return? Along with a military presence in the Far East (oriented toward China at first), an assured supply of raw materials according to the list ticked off by Beveridge in the Senate debates, and a monopoly for United States manufacturers of the Philippine market.

[4]Ibid., p. 26.

[5]Ibid., p. 25.

[6]See Karnow, op. cit., pp. 196–226. Also, Renato Constantino, *The Filipinos in the Philippines*, (Quezon: Filipino Signatures, 1966), pp. 39–65.

This overall plan for the Philippines ran into less trouble in the Philippines than it did in the United States. The Philippine market for U.S. exports was secured by high tariffs on imports to the Philippines from other countries, and no duties on imports from the United States. On the commodity side there had to be duty free imports into the United States, a sticking point for some U.S. interests. The Tariff Act of 1909 was passed in the United States over the opposition of U.S. sugar beet growers who did not want competition from Philippine sugar.

Policy debates in the U.S. Congress suggest that whatever limits there were upon economic planning for the Philippines did not come from Philippine resistance to the country's being made an adjunct to the American economy. They came from political rivalries in the United States, which became especially intense during the Great Depression.[7] The line between international and domestic business, and the accompanying politics, can never be sharply drawn.

The foregoing is the early part of the United States–Philippine story. The Philippines were of interest because of their fit with the needs of the United States economy. The elites of the Philippines were left in place politically and economically, obviating the need to make the Philippines a perpetual theater of war; the lives of the Philippine peasant (*tao*), after the pacification of the Philippines, did not change appreciably with the changing of the guard from Spain to the United States.

Critical legislation both in the Philippines and the United States facilitated the United States–Philippine relationship: protective tariffs in the Philippines were enacted into law to ensure the monopoly for U.S. manufacturers, and in the United States legislation granted duty-free importation of Philippine commodities. Later statutes affected currency transfers, assuring risk-free mobility of capital between the two countries. Taken as a whole, the relationship typifies dependency—commodities out, manufactured goods in, and capital flowing between the countries without unwanted state interference.

Direct Control by Multinational Companies—Honduras

In the rare instances when the country of Honduras surfaces in our consciousness, the image of a general comes to mind. He wears an ambiguous uniform, with a chest full of medals; the gold-braided visor of his hat is pulled down to the top of his dark glasses. We might think he ought to have one hand on his gun to be perpetually ready for violence. He seems eminently corruptible, and with a country as poor as Honduras, corruption ought to come pretty cheap. His life expectancy might range from a few minutes to a few months, depending on the aim of the next head of state.

The actual history of Honduras comes precariously close to the stereotypes of the dictator-general in the pocket of foreign businesses. Between the years 1821 and 1876, 85 different presidents ruled Honduras, and General

[7]Karnow, op. cit., pp. 220–226

Jose Maria Medina is said to have taken control eleven different times! Richard Lapper and James Painter tell the early story of Honduras, bananas, and companies as well as it can be told.[8]

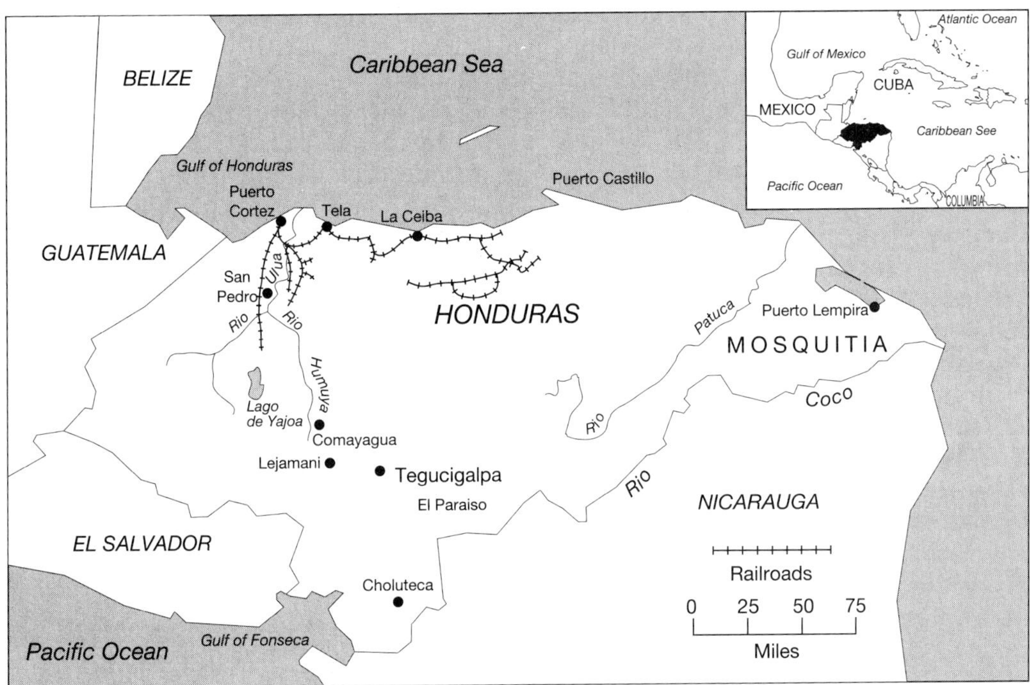

THE ARRIVAL OF THE BANANA COMPANIES

Britain had been the major foreign power in Central America since Independence. Its merchant fleets, backed by a powerful navy, won considerable advantage from the expansion of trade which accompanied Independence, and during the first half of the nineteenth century the British consolidated their hold over the Atlantic side of the isthmus. British Honduras (Belize) became the major entrepôt for Central American trade. While the British military occupied the Bay Islands off Honduras' Atlantic coast and Greytown in Nicaragua, British investors made loans to Honduras and other Central American states on ruinous terms which the British government was often prepared to protect by force.

However, from the mid nineteenth century Britain found itself faced with growing problems in Europe, and its influence began to wane as that of the US grew. The American Civil War greatly strengthened the economic power of

[8]R. Lapper and J. Painter, *Honduras: State for Sale*, (London: Latin American Bureau, 1985), pp. 21–28.

northern manufacturers who were able to take advantage of the foreign concessions offered by Liberal governments throughout Central America. Britain remained the major foreign investor in Central America during the nineteenth century, but US investment gradually increased and by the end of the century equalled that of the British. At the same time, US naval power in the Caribbean and Pacific grew to match British strength. The construction of the Panama canal in 1914 and a series of military interventions throughout Central America (including Honduras in 1911 and 1912) confirmed US control of the area. The US succeeded in replacing Britain as the dominant power in the region.

The growth of US influence in Honduras was closely related to the expansion of a number of fruit companies which at the turn of the century were attracted to the rich agricultural belt along the country's north coast. In the last three decades of the nineteenth century, local farmers had found American traders eager to buy their bananas. Trade was limited by the difficulties of transporting a fruit which rots relatively quickly, but the introduction of refrigeration at the end of the century revolutionised the industry, opening up huge new markets in the US and Europe. Demand grew enough to make direct investment in production attractive to US entrepreneurs, who were soon able to buy out local Honduran rivals and win an increasing share of a growing trade. Honduran governments welcomed these developments and, in the belief that an influx of foreign capital would have beneficial spin-offs for the whole of the economy and society, extended generous concessions to the banana companies. Companies were exempted from paying custom duties, were given mineral and other rights over land and were allowed to build and control railways, canals, ports, finance centres and import/export houses.

Two companies took centre stage: in the east around the port of La Ceiba, it was the Vaccaro brothers (who were subsequently to become Standard Fruit), and to the west, along the banks of the Cuyamel river and near the port of Tela, Samuel Zemurray (commonly known as "Sam the banana man") set up the Cuyamel Fruit Company. From 1912 onwards a third force emerged. The United Fruit Company, through its two subsidaries the Tela and Trujillo Railroad Companies, took over some of Zemurray's properties to the east of Cuyamel and then totally swallowed up Zemurray's creation in 1929. The banana industry grew rapidly. Bananas accounted for 11 per cent of total exports in 1892, 42 per cent in 1903 and 66 per cent in 1913. Production increased from around six million branches in 1910 to 30 million in 1929. Foreign control of the industry was virtually complete—by 1918, 75 percent of banana lands were owned by the three companies.

The companies were zealous in their attempts to secure the most favourable concessions. They promised to build railways linking the capital to the banana growing areas, but the mileage actually laid was little more than what was strictly necessary for the smooth running of their operations. The railways tended to run parallel to the sea and not towards Tegucigalpa. In addition, in return for each kilometre of railway built, the companies received huge land concessions in lots adjacent to the railway. The terms of the concessions also included a provision that local farmers should own alternate lots of land as a way of retaining a certain degree of local control over the industry. But companies soon found that they could by-pass these provisions by buying off local landowners. It was not long before they owned northern Honduras.

The banana boom did provide the export-led growth so desired by the Liberals. But whereas the coffee boom and the rise of the coffee bourgeoisies elsewhere in Central America had brought some semblance of national development, in Honduras the banana boom actually impeded development. In Guatemala and El Salvador, strong state institutions had emerged and the Pacific coastal ports were integrated with the capital cities and centres of agricultural production. In Honduras, investment was concentrated on the northern Atlantic coast, which remained geographically and economically isolated from the argricultural zones of southern and central Honduras. The effect of economic growth in the north on these backward areas was minimal, as the banana economy functioned virtually autonomously.

An excellent network of roads and railways—owned by affiliates of the banana companies—linked San Pedro Sula, Tela and La Ceiba, but all three towns still remained isolated from the capital. The result was that it [was] easier to travel from Tela to New Orleans than from Tela to Tegucigalpa. The banana companies imported almost everything, including equipment for their ports and railways, and consumer goods for company shops. A large part of the labour demand was met by bringing in workers from the labour surplus countries of the Caribbean, Mexico and El Salvador. Workers were made dependent on the company for all their provisions by a system of company tokens to be used only at company shops. So the north of Honduras functioned as an enclave economy. The banana lands were held purely as a source of wealth for the banana companies, and, with little or no customs or tax requirements, central government could gain little revenue. The nearest thing Honduras had to a state was the mini-version created by the companies in and around the plantations.

Company Power

The banana companies soon developed a level of political influence commensurate with their economic power. For this, they took advantage of the fact that the country's political system was as vulnerable as its underdeveloped economy. After the overthrow of Aurelio Soto in 1883, constant civil wars between liberals and conservatives lasted for 50 years until 1933. The endemic political instability was accentuated by the rivalry between the major banana companies who sought Honduran allies in the political parties in order to extract the best concessions.

Honduras' two political parties reflected the weakness of the local ruling elite. . . .

Membership of either party depended on a complex mix of regional and personal loyalties, not on ideological or economic differences. Nationalists were every bit as in favour of foreign investment as their Liberal rivals, and both parties were equally conservative on social issues. The two-party system was simply a vehicle in a spoils system and parties used their control of government to bestow patronage often in the form of jobs, to their supporters. This tradition has lasted to the present day.

A political crisis between 1911 and 1912 demonstrated the power the companies soon wielded over the two parties. In 1911, President Dávila's government had foolishly shown too much favour towards United Fruit, so Zemurray's Cuyamel company organised a mercenary force, led by a soldier of fortune named Lee Christmas, to oust him. The invasion failed, but in order to restore stability, the US stepped in to negotiate Dávila's replacement. The new president, Manuel Bonilla, soon granted Zemurray more concessions, while Zemurray showed his gratitude by negotiating a loan to help Bonilla pay the bill for the invasion that had brought him to power. Lee Christmas also received his reward—he later became US consul in Honduras.

After 1912, internal Honduran politics became virtually indistinguishable from the activities of the fruit companies, in particular the rivalries between Cuyamel and United Fruit. Zemurray and Cuyamel developed close links with the Liberal Party while United Fruit allied with the National Party. Politicians were kept on company payrolls and arms were shipped and financed for rival groups of insurgents. Presidents came to power and fell from grace depending on the favours and money of the fruit companies. The companies' political and economic clout made the Honduran elite even weaker. . . . As early as 1920, United Fruit's H.V. Rolston showed remarkable vision in describing its essential characteristics. In a letter to his lawyer, he wrote that of " . . . this privileged class, whom we need for our exclusive benefit . . . none of them has any convictions or character, far less patriotism."

The Doctor and General

Following the Wall Street crash in 1929, commodity prices tumbled and markets contracted sharply. In Central America both the coffee planters and banana growers rationalised their operations, creating rapid increases in unemployment and imposing wage cuts. In El Salvador, Guatemala, Nicaragua and Honduras, the agrarian oligarchies turned to a series of ruthless—and eccentric—dictators to maintain the economic and social status quo and resolve the crisis of the 1930s. . . .

Honduras too had its dictator. *El Doctor y General*, Tiburcio Carias Andino, had earned the first half of his title when the Liberal government of 1907 rewarded him with an honorary law degree for his part in the rebellion that had brought them to power. The length of his legal career—one case fought and lost—was soon outstripped by his 16 years of dictatorship.

In Honduras also, the depression was initially accompanied by an increase in working-class militancy on the banana plantations. In 1932 a strike among the banana workers organised by the Communist-dominated Honduran Union Federation (FSH), threatened social unrest. But although Carias was soon to kill and jail a number of labour leaders and destroy all labour organisations, popular organisation was very weak and posed no real threat to the establishment.

Gradually, the ending of the rivalry between the banana companies opened up the possibility of greater political stability in Honduras. In 1929 Zemurray sold Cuyamel to United Fruit for US $32 million, and thus brought to an end to the company-backed civil wars that had plagued Honduras through the 1920s. Revolts continued after 1929, but they no longer had a fruit company behind them to give them muscle. With the near-complete monopolisation of the banana industry by United Fruit after 1929, Carias' National Party was able to rely on the company for its political dominance and source of patronage.

Government officials were on United's payrolls and the country's political elites saw United Fruit as the main source of finance for the national budget. The Liberals inevitably declined without the financial support from Cuyamel.

The most serious threat to Carias' rule came with the Liberal revolt in November 1932 after Carias' electoral triumph. But helped by arms from the Salvadorean government and two planes from a New Zealander named Lowell Yerex, the rebels were soon routed. Carias immediately took the offensive, exiling Liberal leaders and closing down the opposition press. After 1933 elections were abolished and Carias had his presidential term extended until 1939 and subsequently until 1948. . . .

A recent first person account by a Honduran activist woman named Elvia Alverado updates conditions in Honduras:

The land here is rich, but it doesn't belong to us. Large parts of it are controlled by the banana companies and all their profits are taken out of the country. The same with our forests. The government just sold off a whole chunk of our forest to a gringo, even though the law says you can't sell state land to foreigners. They just put some Honduran's name on the paper, but everyone knows the real owner is the gringo.

The same with our minerals. Honduras has lots of minerals—gold, copper, silver. We have these big mining companies like the Rosario Mining Company. They take all these minerals and ship them out of the country, and they don't leave anything for us Hondurans.

Honduras isn't poor, but our riches leave the country. Most of it goes to the United States. And then we have to go back to the gringos and beg to get some of it back. What a racket! They get rich off our wealth, and then we get down on our knees begging for help . . .

When you think about it we campesina women are terrific administrators. With a measly dollar a day the men give us we buy corn, beans, sugar, salt, rice, oil and coffee. If we can run our homes on a dollar a day, we'd surely do a better job of running our country than these rich guys can . . .

We'll spread the wealth. We'll distribute the land, we'll get the banana companies in line, we'll take good care of our minerals and forests. And we won't depend on the United States or anyone else. We women like our independence.[9]

. . . [T]he law only applies to the poor.

Look what happened to CONADI, a government corporation that lends money to big business. The heads of CONADI took money from the government and stuffed it in their own bank accounts or loaned it to their friends, who never paid the money back. So now we're told that CONADI is missing $300 million and has gone bankrupt. Can you imagine that? . . .

What about these corrupt politicians? Look at Osvaldo Lopez. When he was president he took a million dollar bribe from the banana companies ... do corrupt politicians ever go to jail? The worst that happens to them is that they leave the country and live like kings somewhere else . . .[10]

[9]M. Benjamin, ed., *Don't Be Afraid, Gringo* (New York: Harper, 1989), pp. 101–102, 105-106.

[10]Ibid., pp. 118,119.

Alverado's commentary dates from the 1980s, attesting to a perverse continuity in Honduras which spans the entire modern period. But what has been the role of law in Honduras? At times it has been nonexistent. At others, law is whatever the companies say it is, either by delegation of state power to them, or through company collaborators in government and the courts.

The next excerpt from a recent *Wall Street Journal* (June 7, 1990) reports large companies tangling over the control of bananas, a battle that brings law, government, and business into visibility.

BANANA WAR

Jose de Cordoba

Puerto Cortes—Honduras.

. . . [I]n this usually placid tropical port, war has broken out.

A banana war.

On one side is the Honduran subsidiary of the U.S. company Chiquita Brands . . . formerly United Brands, earlier United Fruit Co. On the other is an upstart ex-subsidiary of Chiquita's Fyffes Group Ltd, now owned by the big Irish–British fruit importer Fyffes, PLC. Fyffes precipitated hostilities by ordering bananas from a grower that Chiquita says has an ironclad contract to supply Chiquita.

The outside world's appetite for bananas is strong, and demand will grow with Europe's economic integration and Eastern Europe's developing ability to import. But the supply of green gold, so called by the banana men because it is cut and shipped green, is limited. It greatly disturbs Chiquita that a major supplier has defected to Fyffes. Chiquita says it will enforce compliance with its contract, but strictly by legal and ethical means.

Awaiting the Outcome

"We can't afford to let Fyffes get that fruit," says Manuel Rodriguez, a Chiquita vice president . . . in his temporary office in the old company town of La Lima. Fyffes Chairman Neil McCann counters: "We will stay here as long as necessary."

In Honduras, Chiquita's 80 or 90 other independent growers are following the war with great interest. The independents account for nearly one-third of the 34 million boxes of bananas Chiquita shipped from Honduras last year. "This is [Chiquita's] biggest and best division," says Lawrence Swan, a Fyffe's marketing executive. "Lose it here and that's it." Independent growers in Ecuador, Panama, Costa Rica and Colombia would love to see more competition from buyers and are watching the fight too. "If people realize Fyffes can induce producers to break contracts then everybody will do it," says Chiquita's Mr. Rodriguez.

"It's the most serious threat the U.S. banana companies have had to their privileged position, perhaps since the beginning of the century," says Mark Rosenberg, a Honduras expert at Florida International University.

For the moment Chiquita—whose United Fruit predecessor was called "the Octopus" by Hondurans—has prevailed. El Tiempo, Honduras's most influential newspaper, has editorialized acidly that the "banana republic system" is alive and well in Honduras, if nowhere else. The main casualties of the war have been bananas. Chiquita has obtained a court order that has empowered officials to confiscate about 300,000 boxes of Fyffes-bound bananas, worth about 3.6 million dollars abroad.

Divided Courts

Some of the seized fruit has been pilfered and some has spoiled. Most has been sold for small change in Honduras, where the demand for bananas is not exactly insatiable. This strikes Fyffes partisans as tragic. "As a professional banana man, I'm appalled," says Tim Stickney, a Fyffes agricultural specialist in Belize.

At the heart of the war is a contract dispute between Chiquita and the Echeverri family, Honduras's largest independent banana growers. Chiquita accuses Fyffes of paying the Echeverris $2.5 million to break their company's long-term contract with Chiquita in order to sell to Fyffes, which offers higher prices and pays in dollars rather than the shaky Honduran lempira.

The Echeverris assert that the contract has expired and that, in any case, Chiquita itself has violated certain provisions thereby voiding it. Fyffes says that the Echeverris are free to sell to whom they please and that it has done nothing wrong.

One Honduran judge has ruled for Chiquita. In a different legal action, another judge has ruled that the Echeverris can sell their fruit to Fyffes. Chiquita's judge, however, seems to have more muscle.

Dockside Drama

Through legal maneuvering—and Chiquita men say, the intimidating presence of hundreds of banana workers at the port—Fyffes and the Echeverris were able to ship three boatloads of bananas . . . in early spring. Since May 11, however, a Fyffes freighter, the *Frost Cetus*, has bobbed fruitlessly at the harbor at a cost of $5,000 a day.

Court officials, accompanied at times by soldiers in combat gear, have confiscated truckload after truckload of fruit. Chiquita's Mr. Rogriguez says the Honduran government and the military, initially confused by the legal maneuvering, now are fully aware of Chiquita's superior legal position.

In March and April, court officials supervised the unloading of more than 2,000 tons of bananas from two vessels chartered to Fyffes by Seatrade Goningen N.V., a Dutch concern. In one instance the ship company says, the captain reported that the ship was unloaded at gunpoint—although a judge on the scene denied in an affidavit that any force was used. More recently, three trainloads and 68 truckloads of green gold were confiscated. On the way to port, one fruit-laden train was derailed when its locomotive, crewmen said, hit a spike that someone had jammed into the space between two lengths of rail. At a press conference two days later, lawyers for Chiquita's subsidiary denied any responsibility for the incident.

On a recent night at the port, a police lieutenant, toothpick firmly planted in his jaw, orders the confiscation of three truckloads bound for the *Frost Cetus*. A woman in a flaming pink dress, Marta Moran, who is the lawyer for the Echeverris, suddenly appears on the scene and waves a court paper in the officer's face. "Show me *your* order," she barks. "My paper against your paper!"

Sullen stevedores press in on the lieutenant and his four men, who carry rifles. "Load the bananas!" one of the dockworkers shouts. "I have four cubs at home who have to eat." The police retreat, but the Fyffes-Echeverri victory is short-lived. The judge on Chiquita's side has been found partying at Studio 54, a discotheque, and again approves seizure of the bananas. The lieutenant returns to the dock with a court order and a dozen soldiers in battle gear. The three truckloads of bananas are impounded.

In another recent incident, witnesses say, police with automatic rifles, accompanied by at least two Chiquita employees and a Chiquita lawyer who is an alternate member of the Honduran supreme court, burst into a hotel here. They sought to detain for questioning a Fyffe's official and the Fyffe's agent who arranged the Echeverri agreement.

Confronted by the hotel manager, the raiding party was unable to produce proper warrants. The Fyffes men had escaped anyway; one had ducked out a back entrance. But a visiting Fyffes director who resembled one of the wanted men was almost arrested . . . Chiquita says its lawyer was there to identify the Fyffes men, for whom there were valid arrest warrants.

Peace Talks

Some Fyffes officials now travel with bodyguards and mask their identities. Two executives carry . . . stun guns bought in Miami . . .

Peace talks have begun. Last week, about eight security guards from both sides waited in the lobby of a hotel in San Pedro Sula, their guns discreetly hidden from view, as lawyers from Chiquita and Fyffes held what a Fyffes man called a "tense" three hour meeting. Both sides pledged to seek ground on which to resolve their dispute.

There are diplomatic pressures to do so. The two sides met this week after gentle prodding from the American and British ambassadors here; They had responded to a request from the president of Honduras. Ireland ... has no representation here. But the Fyffes group subsidiary is headquartered in London. The British ambassador to Honduras is Peter Streams, a heavy-set cigar-smoking diplomat given to wearing pale pink safari outfits on his visits to Puerto Cortes. He say he has "expressed concern" over the dispute many times to the Honduran government.

Also on the diplomatic front, Fyffes officials have met with officials of the European Community in Brussels. Chiquita officials, Mr. Stream says, have explained their position to the British Foreign Office in London. U.S. Ambassador Cresencio Arcos says the dispute has become a "lose–lose" situation for Honduras with total victory by one side or another damaging the nation's reputation either in the U.S. or in Europe. He is counselling the antagonists to reach a "mutually acceptable agreement."

As a Chiquita subsidiary, Fyffes Group had acquired most of its bananas from former British colonies—Belize, Jamaica, the Windward Islands—and from Surinam and sold them in the British market. In 1986, FII PLC bought Fyffes Group. As part of the deal, United Brands (now Chiquita) got a minority interest in FII Fyffes . . . Then last September, United Brands sold its interest in Fyffes . . .

Mr. Swan says Fyffes never meant to start a war with Chiquita. But it needed an additional source of bananas, and to enter Honduras—next door to Belize, where Fyffes had long sent ships—"was a logical geographic decision." . . .

Fyffes is the fifth-largest company whose shares are traded on the Dublin stock exchange. But with total sales of $600 million a year it is dwarfed by Chiquita whose banana sales alone last year were $1.4 billion.

If Chiquita has been winning the legal side of the war, the affair has been a public relations disaster. The spectacle of Chiquita squashing a Honduran grower that had managed to get better terms from Chiquita's much smaller competitor has rekindled Honduras's historical resentment of "the Octopus." In the bad old days, Hondurans say, the company made and unmade presidents.

Some U.S. diplomats are irritated by all this. One says the tactics . . . have exploited the negative side of the U.S. firm's history in Honduras and "sparked a smear campaign."

As recently as 1974, during the last banana war (which was set off by a fight for market share between United Brands and Castle and Cooke . . . Standard Fruit . . .) United Brands paid $1.25 million to Honduran government officials to lower a banana export tax . . . The Honduran government later collapsed.

Big Guys Win

In the green fields and tin-roofed packing stations of the Echeverri farm, the sympathies of sweat-drenched banana workers clearly lie with the Fyffes. Since the Echeverris have begun dealing with Fyffes, wages have jumped, in some case doubling to $10 for a 12-hour day from $5. Sunday overtime at double pay has become common. Fyffes accepts even the smaller bananas at the bottom of a bunch for which Chiquita had no use . . .

Workers say that for years, under the Chiquita contract, the Echeverris were strapped for cash and could not meet some of their obligations they had agreed to in labor negotiations . . . But if Fyffes money keeps flowing in, the workers expect more benefits, including housing . . .

But in Puerto Cortes, Simon Templeman, Fyffe's bearded shipping manager, sits slumped on the dock watching as another truckload of confiscated bananas is driven away. "This is what happens in a banana republic . . . The big guys win."

Questions and Comments

1. Chiquita says that it will enforce its contract only by legal and ethical means. What do these terms mean in this context?
2. Examine the position of the independent growers and their power vis-a-vis Chiquita and how it might be affected by the presence of Fyffes.

   Stephen Hymer, whose career as a political economist was introduced in Chapter 4, believed that multinationals would come to agreements rather than engage in mutually destructive rivalries. Evaluate his contention against this account of this Honduran "banana war."
3. It is said that the judge who ruled for Chiquita had "more muscle" than another judge who made a contrary ruling. What is this all about? Where did the judge get his "muscle"?
4. Diplomats become involved in the dispute. What is their role? When the American ambassador calls the situation a lose–lose situation for Honduras, what is he talking about? What is the reputation of Honduras that he says might be put in jeopardy?

5. What is a "banana professional," a position claimed by one of the Fyffes officials?
6. In some particulars the account is a farce, but in some respects it is dead serious. Sort out the laughable from the dismally instructive.

Indirect Control Systems—International Harvester in the Yucatan

Today when we think of rope or cord, we think of the yellow polyester or white nylon coils in a hardware store. These petroleum derivatives were not the source of roping at earlier times in history, when natural fibres were woven into the necessary products. Manila rope is made from plant fibers and gets its name from the Philippines, where the raw material for the rope originates. So too with *sisal* twine, a natural product which gets its name from the port of Sisal in the Yucatan region of Mexico.

Henequen, the desert plant from which the sisal fibers are extracted, made many people rich and many people abjectly poor in the areas where, until just after World War I, it was king. As the world prices of sisal rose and fell, so went the fate of the Yucatan.[12] Sisal had its greatest days when binding twine for grain harvests could not be made without the commodity, and since the Yucatan was the sole source to meet world demand, the makings of an agricultural boom were in place.

The near panic in the United States over the high prices of sisal is reflected in President Woodrow Wilson's 1915 message to his Secretary of State on how to deal with President Caranza of Mexico:

> Go into Yucatan rather fully with Caranza and explain how indispensable the sisal is . . . as the food supply of the world may be said in large measure to depend on it, and that we are justified, as friends of Mexico, in keeping her out of the deep trouble that would ensue if he interfered with the trade.[13]

What . . . the "deep trouble" would be is not stated. In the same year, International Harvester Corporation, which until that time had controlled the trade through its monopolistic buying power, wanted the U.S. Navy to send an American warboat to the Yucatan "at least until provision can be made to protect the supply of binder twine for the coming harvest . . . [W]ithout the moral influence of an American naval vessel, the situation of American interests is unsafe."[14] The Navy refused to assert its "moral influence," not out of a sense of impropriety, but because vessels were needed elsewhere.

These episodes occurred around the time of World War I, when monoculture in henequen was well along. One would not expect that a little-known commodity could cause diplomatic concern or near acts of "gunboat diplomacy." By this time the Yucatan had come to rely totally on sisal, and the dis-

[12]For excellent accounts with extensive bibliographies see Allen Wells, *Yucatan's Gilded Age: Haciendas, Henequen and International Harvester 1860-1915* (Albuquerque: U. of New Mexico Press, 1985) and G. M. Joseph, *Revolution From Without* (New York: Cambridge University Press, 1982).

[13]Joseph, op. cit., p. 154.

[14]Ibid., p. 343.

pute was not over its availability—there was plenty to more than meet demand—but over the price to be charged. At that point International Harvester's control over the trade had broken down.

We drop back from the World War I period to outline the structure of indirect economic control by International Harvester, and the law, politics, and finance that made the indirect control system possible. It should be remembered that the appearance of a gunboat would have been only one of many instances of the use or threat of force; the story of sisal is a story of power—naked power, subtle power, and sometimes secret power—and a story of economics, with all people locked into a single crop that yielded both riches and pure misery.

As is true of other agricultural ventures, land, labor, and capital were critical to henequen monoculture. In the latter part of the nineteenth century some profound changes were occurring in the Yucatan. Prior to this period the Yucatan was largely self-sufficient, with cattle, corn, and daily staples the principal agriculture. Henequen was an indigenous plant, but with limited local uses beyond matting and hammocks, it had never taken over either the imagination, or all of the land, as it eventually came to do.

The henequen boom generated by outside demand aroused new interest in land accumulation. Land at the time was held in haciendas, in small parcels (pequenos properterios), and communally (ejidos), or was vacant (baldios). Owners of haciendas moving toward henequen monoculture acquired adjoining small tracts (and their accompanying work force). Some of these small parcels were derived from land that had once been communally held and distributed under an 1856 law which required distribution of communal lands to individual families. The resulting small pieces (lotes) were purchased for trifling sums and added to the hacienda-becoming-plantation.

A grower could also petition for ownership of land that was "vacant." As can be imagined in a land system that had once been communal with sparse written documentation, disputes proliferated. What land was owned; what was in use, what was vacant; who, if anyone, might own particular tracts; and what the dimensions of parcels were became the province of those with financial ability to legally contest ownership and force cash settlements.

In the later stages of henequen monoculture, the less powerful and undercapitalized growers went broke and their lands and work forces were incorporated into still larger units of production.[15]

At the bottom of the hierarchy of henequen were the work forces required to grow the crop and prepare it for shipment. The difference in human relations on a hacienda and on a plantation are noteworthy. On a hacienda, production had been primarily for subsistence, not trade. The hacienda may not appear especially humane to modern eyes since it was "an agricultural estate operated by a dominant landowner and a dependent labor force organized to supply a small-scale market by means of scarce capital in which the factors of production are employed not only for capital accumulation but also to support the status aspirations of the owner."[16]

[15]Wells, op. cit., pp. 119–126.
[16]Ibid., p. 115.

But as socially problematic as the hacienda was, the plantation system was many cuts worse, since the work force lost its claim to any reciprocal duties beyond wages, including plots of land to grow food for subsistence (milpas). The plantation was "an agricultural estate operated by dominant owners (usually organized into a corporation) and a dependent labor force organized to supply a large scale market by means of abundant capital in which the factors of production are employed to further capital accumulation without reference to the status needs of the owners."[17] In the plantation system the owner runs a business driving toward a bottom line determined solely by monetary costs and revenues, with subsistence taking a subordinate place.

Henequen was shipped at whatever price prevailed, since it had no extensive local use and would simply pile up on docks if not sold. With a fickle market, work forces were secured for as little as possible and expendable within the outside limits of necessary labor.

The henequen plantation has been justifiably compared to a slave plantation of the antebellum South, without formal ownership of the work force. The control mechanism was debt, and the system was debt peonage. The law required that debts be paid under penalty of imprisonment. Debts of two types were run up at the plantation store: the small debts for food, supplies, or liquor, payable out of weekly wages, and the large debts run up for marriages or at fiestas. Workers never could pay off their debts, and given the legal sanctions available to growers, "employment" was forever.

The word *peon*, which today means the utter bottom, had a different meaning in the Yucatan: there were three levels of workers *beneath* the peones: contract laborers, who signed on for a period (inevitably extended by debt), Indians transported from other parts of Mexico (usually a death sentence, since they did not have any indigenous base whatever), and a small number of oriental contract laborers. All workers were in the same unenviable position of debt servitude, and the above gradations among captive work forces simply fine tune levels of disadvantage rather than privilege.

When the brutal uses of law against runaways was criticized as barbaric by outside critics, a different technique of control was enforced by law. Each Yucatecan, was subject to conscription in the military unless excused by permission of the owner of the plantation where he worked. Workers suspected of being runaways were asked for identification papers to prove their exemption from military service. These immediately showed the name of the employer, and the runaway was forced to return to the plantation.[18]

At the top of the hierarchy of henequen was a multinational, International Harvester, based in the United States. After the formation of the farm implement trust in 1902 by J. P. Morgan, International Harvester controlled virtually all production of grain binders and mowers in the United States, and over 60 percent of the business for sisal twine that was used with the equipment.

[17]Quoted in Wells, pp. 114,115.
[18]Ibid., pp. 151–182.

Harvester had the financial strength to *directly* control land, production, and transport of sisal in the Yucatan, but deemed such control unnecessary. Instead it made a secret deal in 1902 with two powerful brokerage houses in the Yucatan, the Molina and Montes, and the Peabody companies, to act as their agents for the purchase of sisal at prices determined by Harvester. These double agents, or *collaboratores* as they were called when the agreement became publicly known in 1915, occupied the critical place in the trade—between the growers in the Yucatan and their principal buyer in the United States.

The business done by these brokers and the prices of sisal measure the success of the Harvester system of indirect control. The brokers in 1914 controlled 93 percent of the trade, and prices were half in 1910 what they had been in 1902, before beginning to rise in the pre-World War I period.

Like their indebted work forces, the growers could not run away. Molina was politically powerful, having assumed the position of governor of the Yucatan in 1902. But more important, the brokers, using lines of credit from the United States, controlled the finance of the henequen growers, whose capital needs for land, land preparation, processing equipment, rail transportation to port, and imported food grew faster than their income. This says nothing about their personal consumption, which also cut into earnings. With only two forms of security for credit—land and crops—the brokerage houses by controlling credit controlled land, crops, and eventually the heavily indebted growers themselves.[19]

As profits of growers were squeezed by those above them in the sisal trade, the growers in turn squeezed their work forces, reducing pay and otherwise extorting more to cover revenue shortfalls. The following diagram of hierarchical control shows the relationships and what held people into a system with which they did not always agree.

INDIRECT CONTROL SYSTEM
INTERNATIONAL HARVESTER
SISAL—YUCATAN (1902–1915)

International Harvester
(Buyer and financier)
↓
Molina & Co
Peabody & Co
(Brokers-financiers)
↓
Henequen growers
(Indebted)
↓
Peons and contract laborers
(Indebted)

[19]Joseph, op. cit., pp. 41–65.

Why was there no rebellion by the work forces? They had no land or alternatives for ready exit. They had no say in law or government, which was controlled by grower-financiers who circulated into and out of office. They had no access to state force and were emotionally and physically exhausted. But as we learned very early, the most effective form of control is in the minds of oppressed peoples themselves. The wage laborers on henequen plantations might no longer have believed in their own capabilities. It took four years for the 1911 Mexican Revolution to reach the Yucatan region, and even then the revolution did not come from workers and peasants, as it did in other regions of Mexico. The common use in the Yucatan of two phrases, "casta divina" and "gente decente"—the divine group and the decent people—defined not only the statuses of the Yucatan elite but, by exclusion, the agricultural laborers, who were neither divine nor decent.

What about the indebted growers? They saw no alternatives once henequen was established and absorbed all their capital and more. Instead of breaking out, they simply transferred the pressures from the undependable trade downward, maintaining what prosperity they could. The system of sisal production eventually collapsed not by human intervention, but by the precipitous decline in the world demand for sisal after World War I.[20]

The story of sisal is the story of leverage traceable to market power and finance. International Harvester had power in the United States through the formation of the implement trust and as the principal buyer of Yucatan's one and only export crop. It extended its power in the Yucatan by financing local brokerage houses who used debt to control local growers. Moreover, these houses had power in the law-government system of credit and collections. The lower-level participants—growers and their work forces—were not always perfectly content, but they were nevertheless locked into a system that had its own economic dynamics with state force in the not too distant background.

Concessions—The Seven Sisters and International Oil Production

The subject of multinational oil companies and their connections to all parts of the world presents unique difficulties. In studying them we could become like the seabirds covered with crude oil after the *Valdez* oil tanker disaster in Alaska—never able to fly away from the topic. Oil is a subject with its own law and political economy, which, if studied from end to end, would provide a complete education in multinational business.[21]

For most of history there has been too much oil, and the only way to control markets and profitability was for companies to control oil shipping, refining, and distribution. This was John D. Rockefeller's strategy with Standard Oil, and it worked like a charm for over fifty years.[22] The opening up of new

[20]Ibid., pp. 172–182.

[21]For excellent examples see Robert Engler, *The Politics of Oil*, (Chicago: U. of Chicago Press, 1961) and *The Brotherhood of Oil* (Chicago: U. of Chicago Press, 1977).

[22]For an excellent account of John D.Rockefeller and the development of the oil monopoly of Standard Oil, see Peter Collier and D. Horowitz, *The Rockefellers* (New York: Signet 1976).

fields—in the United States, Mexico, Venezuela, Russia, the East Indies and the Middle East—threatened the ability of the major oil companies located in the United States and Europe to control the oil business from a strictly national base. Companies internationalized, and rationalized the control of oil production regardless of where it might occur.

A significant dimension of control of production was at the wellhead, by getting concessions from the countries where the new oil fields might be discovered and brought on line. The concession agreements are easy to understand, even if they were difficult to administer and enforce. (They were renegotiated from time to time, and countries which had granted concessions that they later considered excessively generous, sometimes taxed corporations over and above the concession royalties.[23]) The agreement made between Saudi Arabia and Standard Oil of California in 1933 eventually opened the richest oil fields in the world. It followed the pattern of earlier concession agreements that had been made in Latin America and other parts of the Middle East:

> . . . [T]he company agreed to loan the government of Saudi Arabia 30,000 (British pounds) in gold . . . The government would also receive an annual sum of 5,000 (pounds) in rental, payable in advance, until the discovery of oil. If the agreement were not terminated in eighteen months the company would make a second loan, this one of 20,000 pounds in gold . . . The two loans were to be repaid by deductions from one half of the royalties due the government. In deference to Moslem practice, the loans carried no interest. On the discovery of oil in commercial quantities, Standard Oil of California contracted to advance the government an additional 50,000 pounds gold and a similar amount to be paid later, both loans to be repaid by deductions from royalties. On all the oil produced, the Saudi Arabian government would receive royalty of four shillings gold per ton of oil produced and saved. The initial concession was for sixty years and covered roughly 360,000 square miles (the mileage was not specified in the concession, only the boundaries . . .) The concession gave the company "preference rights" to acquire an oil concession covering the balance of eastern Saudi Arabia . . . [Standard Oil of California formed an operating company, California Arabian Standard Oil, to develop its concession."[24] The original 35,000 British pounds at $5/pound was equivalent to $175,000. At that rate of exchange, the 4 shillings per ton royalty would be 80 cents. —Ed.]

Socal through this agreement had made what upon discovery of the Saudi fields would be the biggest oil bargain in history. The territorial coverage of the concession was increased in 1939 to 440,000 square miles (one-sixth the size of the United States). Socal was first joined by Texaco, and in 1948 the two were joined by Esso (Exxon) and Mobil, who bought into Aramco, the production company. When the Saudis later cut a fifty-fifty deal on the profits of Saudi production, the payments were considered "taxes" by a

[23]The Venezuelan evolution is discussed in J. E. Hartshorn, *Politics and World Oil Economics* (New York: Praeger, 1967), pp. 301–307.

[24]M. Wilkins, *The Maturing of Multinational Enterprise*(Cambridge: Harvard University Press, 1974), pp. 214–215.

foreign government and credited against taxes owed by the companies in the United States. Thus, despite these new terms improving the position of Saudi Arabia, the oil companies were still benefiting in at least two ways: by keeping access to the cheapest oil on earth, and by gaining favorable tax treatment in the United States for the amounts paid in "tax" (royalties) to Saudi Arabia.[25]

As will be developed later in this chapter, cross-company joint ventures and other forms of cooperation helped ensure that none of the companies would suffer unduly from overproduction, overloaded markets, or depressed prices. This system of cooperation did not work perfectly, as sporadic price and territorial wars attest, but the principal companies, as oligopolists with the same products and services, realized that cooperation would mean more profits to each company than aggressive rivalries.

The companies who were the prime movers in this development were the Seven Sisters: Exxon, Mobil, Texaco, Gulf, Socal, Royal Dutch, and BP (British Petroleum). They were not all based in the same countries but had a common interest in not allowing the oil market to be overwhelmed with the abundant supplies that new fields might contain.[26]

With two exceptions—Mexico in 1938 and Iran in 1951—seven major oil companies (plus a French company) controlled 100 percent of the crude oil production until the succession of nationalization of oil fields, which began in Venezuela in 1972. The distribution of concession agreements across the principal oil companies assured each "major" of its share of "foreign oil." The following pre-OPEC chart shows the participation in concessions by the seven-plus sisters:[27]

MIDDLE EAST JOINT VENTURES

	Aramco	Kuwait Oil Company	Iranian Consortium	Iraq Petroleum Company
Exxon	30%		7%	11.875
Texaco	30		7	
Gulf		50%	7	
Chevron	30		7	
Mobil	10		7	11.875
Royal Dutch/Shell			14	23.75
British Petroleum		50	40	23.75
CFP			6	23.75
Others			5	5

Note: CFP-Compagnie Française de Pétroles

Source: S.A. Schneider, *The Oil Price Revolution.* Baltimore: Johns Hopkins, 1983, p. 40. ©1983 by S.A. Schneider. Reprinted by permission of Johns Hopkins University Press.

[25]Tax aspects of the fifty–fifty arrangement are discussed in Albert Danielsen, *The Evolution of OPEC* (New York: Harcourt Brace, 1982), pp. 140–142.

[26]Blair, *The Control of Oil,*. (New York: Vintage, 1978).

[27]Quoted in W. Adams, ed., *The Structure of American Industry* (New York: MacMillan, 1990), p.43.

What would impel a country to grant sweeping concessions for what in retrospect seem to be inconsequential shares in the proceeds from oil? No capital and no technological expertise to find and bring their underground resources into production. No methods of transmission or shipment. No refineries to convert crude oil into usable product. And finally, no access to markets where petroleum products are sold.

To jump ahead in the ongoing story of oil, readers can follow the current efforts of OPEC countries to liberate themselves from each of these constraints on their control of oil. In the end the producing countries will try to replicate the practices of the seven-plus sisters to whom they originally gave concessions, and be fully integrated from the wellhead, through shipping and refining, and on to the ultimate customers of oil.

Where was the law while all of these near-monopolistic activities were taking place? The logical place to look for legal activism in the face of extensive limits on competition by price and output would be the antitrust laws. There have been occasional lawsuits brought against the oil companies—for example, the antitrust case against the Standard trust, which resulted in a "breakup" in 1911 of Standard into its constituent companies (quotations are used around the word breakup because the stock of the companies into which Standard was "broken" was distributed to the Standard shareholders; common shareholding facilitated cooperation across the network of "new" companies after the "breakup"). There were also antitrust cases involving price fixing in gasoline distribution and the forcing of products on retail stations.

Nothing touched the activities of the principal United States oil companies in their international operations, of which the concession agreements were a critical part. In the international sphere, there were no legal limitations on free-wheeling cooperation among the companies, which had extensive "effects" within the United States and elsewhere. Moreover, the U.S. State Department actively cooperated with the largest U.S. oil companies in their struggles with British-based companies for control of Mexican and Venezuelan concessions and concessions in the Middle East.

Decades after the Mideast concessions, when cooperation and not competition had become the abiding business practice, the U.S. Federal Trade Commission found that there was an international cartel in oil:

> Control of the industry by these seven companies extends from reserves through production, transportation, refining, and marketing. All seven engage in every stage of operations, from exploration to marketing. The typical movement of petroleum from producer until acquired by the final consumer is through intercompany transfer within a corporate family. Outright sales, arms-length bargaining, and other practices characteristic of independent buyers and sellers are conspicuous by their absence. Control is held not only through direct corporate holdings, by parents, subsidiaries, and affiliates of the seven but also through such indirect means as interlocking directorates, joint ownership of affiliates, intercompany crude purchase contracts, and marketing agreements.[28]

[28]Ibid., p. 137.

However, no legal action was effectively taken by the Commission or the Justice Department to interdict the cartel. The strategic importance of oil to "national security" had for practical purposes exempted the oil companies from monopoly laws.[29]

The end of the *complete* supremacy by the major oil companies in crude production came from a different source than the rule of law—the decline of oil supplies in the United States, which increased the bargaining power of other producing countries; the rise of independent oil companies, which gave producing countries alternative customers for their crude; and finally the cooperation among the producing countries through OPEC.

However, the transfer of ownership upon nationalization did not end relationships between OPEC member countries and the major oil companies. Venezuela is instructive in this regard because it had the earliest and most aggressive policies with respect to the oil companies. Upon assuming ownership of its oil, Venezuela still needed technical services from the majors to bring the oil into production; these were contracted for at so much per barrel of crude. The producing countries also needed markets for oil, and the concession agreement was replaced by the long-term supply contract pursuant to which the oil companies were assured of the supplies formerly covered by concessions. Nationalization, as dramatic as it may sound, brought evolutionary rather than revolutionary changes in oil and the returns therefrom.[30]

Even after the formation of OPEC, which seemed to be premised on aggressive nationalism, OPEC producers and the multinationals jointly controlled enough of the production and sale of oil to find it mutually advantageous to act as duopolists. Their joint control could not be complete given the presence of independent oil companies and non-OPEC producers, and the oil business would not be as "smooth" as it had been in the 1950s, when the FTC found the presence of an oil cartel, but the majors and OPEC were still the prime movers of oil.[31]

Two tidbits printed side by side in the *Wall Street Journal* (3/16/93) give a bird's eye view of stability and change in oil since the king of Saudi Arabia, strapped for money, negotiated the first concession back in 1933.

SAUDI ARABIA DISCOVERS OIL AND GAS ON RED SEA COAST

HOUSTON—Saudi Arabia announced its first oil and gas discovery on the Red Sea coast in the northwestern part of the kingdom.

The new field, which was found by Saudi Arabian Oil Co., or Aramco, is in the Median region some 350 miles northwest of the Red Sea industrial city of Yanbu on the western side of the kingdom.

With output of some eight million barrels a day, Saudi Arabia is the world's largest oil producer. But the bulk of production is in eastern Saudi Arabia, on

[29]Anthony Sampson, *The Seven Sisters* (New York: Bantam, 1976), pp. 149–157.

[30]Daniel Yergin, *The Prize* (New York: Simon & Schuster, 1991), pp. 648–650.

[31]Danielsen, op. cit., pp. 154–155, 270–271.

the Persian Gulf side, although some fields have recently been found in the central part south of Riyadh.

The Saudi announcement of the Red Sea discovery provided few details. But Hisham Nazer, the Saudi oil minister and chairman of Aramco, said further seismic surveys and drilling will be carried out to determine the size of the field's reserves.

UNIT, SAUDI GROUP INTEND TO BUILD A CHEMICAL PLANT

Chevron Corp.'s Chevron Chemical Co. said it signed a letter of intent with a consortium of Saudi investors to build a $400 million chemical plant in Jubail, Saudi Arabia.

The agreement calls for design and feasibility studies to be completed by the end of the year. Assuming approval by the partners, construction would begin early next year and operations would begin in mid-1996.

The plant would produce 420,000 tons of benzene and 270,000 tons of cyclohexane annually. Benzene is a hydrocarbon and cyclohexane is a feedstock for nylon.

The facility would be operated by a proposed new company to be owned on an equal basis by Chevron and the Saudi group. The company would market products inside Saudi Arabia and Chevron would market them elsewhere.

Chevron Chemical said it has a $250 million benzene plant under construction in Pascagoula, Miss., that uses Chevron's same patented technology. The Saudi facility would cost more because of its cyclohexane plant and the need to construct loading facilities and other infrastructure.

The articles show Aramco, now completely nationalized, as the developer of Saudi oil prospects. The second article shows Chevron (Socal) in a business relationship with the Saudis, not as concessionaire but as a joint venturer on a project that makes forward linkages for the Saudis from production to petroleum derivatives.

The new oil discovery is itself of interest, since the oil fields developed to date in Saudi Arabia and elsewhere in the Middle East have been primarily on the Persian Gulf. One can only wonder at the future implications of oil production on the Red Sea.

For Discussion

1. What characteristics do you find in common across the examples drawn from colonialism, direct control systems, indirect control systems and the concession system?

   What held people into such systems which in retrospect look one-sided?

   Could there have been alternative strategies for economic systems in the places where these systems took hold, or did the countries take the only opportunity open to them?

   How are each of the systems connected with law and government? What holds the systems together?

2. As a class project, other colonial systems might be studied, such as those listed in the introduction to the Philippine materials. Investigators might watch for the connection between colonial control and the economic system that emerges. It might also be useful to note what alternative economic systems are bypassed or discarded as a colonial regime takes hold.
3. A number of Middle Eastern countries can be studied for the relationship between the country's natural resources and multinational companies: Iraq, Kuwait, and Iran come to mind first, but there are other smaller oil-producing countries that can be considered.
4. Some commodities are especially instructive, since they have been associated with particular countries: copper and nitrates from Chile, tin from Bolivia and Malaysia, sugar from the Dominican Republic or Cuba, rubber from Brazil, Malaysia, Liberia, and Vietnam, gold and diamonds from South Africa, wool from Australia and New Zealand, and so on. Commodities lead to countries where they are produced. Production and distribution lead to companies, often multinational ones. Both lead to the law-government system of the country, which will have a special character based upon critical economic activities. Using the materials included here as models, researchers can prepare reports showing the connection among commodities, companies, and countries and the effect of all on the government and the people of the place.
5. The persistent question derived from historical study of this type is whether early relationships continue, if in sometimes slightly different forms, or whether they cease at a point. Do we find political-economic systems comparable to colonialism after colonialism officially ceases to exist? Do direct and indirect control systems over production continue, or do they cease once the controlled group asserts itself politically?

   Such questions call for ongoing assessments and carefully following news stories with a sense of history and a knowledge of how countries and their economies have traditionally been connected to the world economy. With this sensitivity and knowledge, the nightly news will never be quite the same again.
6. Using business periodicals or newspapers, find other contemporary accounts like the ones on Saudi oil developments and trace current events back to their historical origins.

B. OTHER MULTINATIONAL NETWORKS

Of the modern networks, a few more are singled out for special coverage here: (1) joint ventures between private companies, (2) joint ventures between private enterprises and governments, and (3) operations of international companies in enterprise processing zones. The private joint venture links two otherwise independent companies for a limited purpose, for example, exploring and producing oil under a concession agreement; these joint ventures may be thought of as limited-purpose mergers. Oil concessions are a type of public-private joint venture. The enterprise processing zone is a place where manufacturers can set up in another country with minimal commitments of capital and little or no investment in land and facilities, for example renting space in a building on the island of St. Lucia for the assembly of board games for shipment back to the United States. More substantial investments by U.S.-based multinationals in other countries, and the investments in U.S. assets by multinationals headquartered in other countries will be considered in later chapters.

Joint Ventures

We have already had a glimpse of joint ventures among oil companies in the discussion of concessions with producing countries. Of course, in an integrated oil company production is only one phase of the process, and joint ventures have existed in a number of phases of the business. For integrated multinationals the line between international cooperation and domestic cooperation is meaningless, since they consider the oil business on a world scale and all "domestic" activities related to the world system.

John Blair, in *Control of Oil*,[32] found it highly misleading to think of the oil companies as "separate and independent" or "free from any influence through intercorporate relationships that would affect their competitive behavior." Instead of competition he found:

> . . . through interlocking corporate relationships and joint ventures of every conceivable form, the opportunities for substituting collective judgment for independent judgment are legion.[33]

Beginning with Blair's analysis undertaken in the early 1970s, we can move to an updating on the current variety of joint ventures of a multinational, using the 1992 annual report of the Exxon Corporation.

Blair focused on two types of joint ventures that gave the integrated oil companies substantial advantages. The first was joint ownership of pipelines through which 75 percent of the oil produced in the United States was transported. The second was cooperation in bidding for offshore leases that became critical to the supplies of crude oil once technological changes permitted undersea exploration and production.

Pipelines While technically an oil pipeline is by law a "common carrier" and as such open to use by independent oil companies, the major integrated companies can use their joint ownership of pipelines to control independents through informal methods: (1) requiring a minimum size for shipments; (2) granting independents irregular shipping dates; (3) limiting available storage at the pipeline terminals; (4) imposing unreasonable product standards . . . and (5) other harassing or delaying tactics.

[32]Op. cit.
[33]Ibid., p. 136.

Blair's chart of joint ventures in pipelines shows the numerous opportunities for control of independents and occasions for cooperation among the majors:[34]

COMPANY SHARES OF TOP EIGHT IN SELECTED PIPELINES

	Colonial	Plantation	Dixie	Laurel	Texas N. Mex.	Wolverine	Four Corners
Exxon		48.8%	11.1%				
Mobil	11.5%		5.0			26.0%	
Texaco	14.3		5.0	33.9%	45.0%	17.0	
SoCal							25.0%
Shell		24.0	5.5				25.0
Gulf	16.8		18.2	49.1		7.0	20.0
Standard (Ind.)	14.3		12.1				
ARCO	1.6		7.4		35.0	25.0	10.0
Total	58.5	72.8	64.3	83.0	80.0	75.0	80.0
Assets ($ million)	$480.2	$176.2	$46.4	$35.9	$30.5	$21.8	$20.9

Source: Compiled from testimony by John W. Wilson before the Senate Subcommittee on Antitrust and Monopoly, *Hearings on the Natural Gas Industry*, Pt. 1, pp. 456 ff.

A later inventory of the joint ownership of pipelines found:

> Concentration in major crude oil transport corridors (i.e. specific pipeline markets) is extremely high. In Texas–Cushing, Oklahoma corridor, for example, the four largest pipeline companies together account for 76% of total crude carried. Three pipeline companies control all crude oil shipments in the Gulf Coast–Upper Mid Continent corridor . . . In 1979, the four-firm concentration ratio for pipeline shipments in the nation's major crude carriers averaged 91%.
> A pipeline rate set above the competitive cost of transporting crude oil . . . imposes no burden on the majors who own the pipeline. For them the high price is simply a transfer of funds from the refinery operation to the pipeline operation. To the non-integrated refiner, however, an excessive pipeline charge is a real cost increase that he cannot recoup elsewhere and that places him at a competitive disadvantage vis-a-vis his integrated competitors.[35]

Among the majors there were dual advantages: another occasion for mutual cooperation, and a means for the control of potential competitors. They could assure their own profitability through price and market allocation and, when necessary, discipline the independent producers and refiners of oil.

The control of pipelines was not limited to lines in the United States. Historically, there have been comparable control systems covering foreign pipelines. Blair reported ownership of the 753-mile pipeline from Saudi Arabia to the Mediterranean by Exxon, Socal, Texaco, and Mobil as part of

[34]Ibid., p. 139.

[35]W. Adams, ed., *The Structure of American Industry* (New York: Macmillan, 1990), pp. 57, 58.

the Aramco joint venture; and of the 143-mile pipeline running from Lake Maricaibo in Venezuela to the Caribbean by Exxon and other multinationals.[36]

Offshore Oil Leases The exploration and production of oil offshore expanded rapidly after federal legislation in 1953. Under the Submerged Lands Act and the Outer Continental Shelf Lands Act, states were given the leasing power over lands that were "tidelands"—the words are in quotes because states took different positions as to the mileage out to sea that their offshore claims extended (for example, 3, 10, 30), and the federal government was given leasing power over lands beyond the areas reserved to the states. The federal areas are administered by the Interior Department.[37]

Control of offshore oil is as important to a multinational as control of oil anywhere else, and they made the same efforts to control this huge potential source of oil as they had made in negotiating the concession agreements in other countries. The submission of joint bids for oil leases violates the letter of the Sherman Antitrust Act as a combination in restraint of trade, since the joint bids eliminate competition among the majors, and foreclose independents from making substantial inroads into offshore sources of oil. However, no antitrust actions were brought.[38]

Robert Engler in *Brotherhood of Oil* quotes the sworn testimony of the chairman of Socal on the organization of a joint bid with Atlantic Richfield and Humble:

> You just put the number on the table—that is on this parcel we want to bid $32 million. They come in and say "No, we want to bid 34." This one comes in and says "No, we want to bid 60." And then we look at the geology jointly. Not all of it. And the experts will talk to the likelihood of finding $20 million or $40 million, or $250 million or a billion. And this is not too precise, obviously. If we decided we wanted to bid 32 [million], we tried to bring them down. If they are below us, bring them up. And sometimes they bring us up, and we try to reach a concurrence. If we can't then the one who wants to bid the high number is free to come out and bid completely by himself. That is part of the procedure.[39]

Cooperation in bidding led to a higher degree of concentration of control with respect to offshore oil than for other phases of the business. The practices made for joint ownership and single ownership by the largest companies. According to Blair:

> Much of the offshore output is produced by joint ventures, thus affording the majors still another opportunity for the development of commonalities of interest. Exxon shares ownership of federal offshore leases with Gulf and Mobil; Shell shares ownership with SoCal; Gulf with Mobil; SoCal with Mobil and

[36]Blair, op. cit., p. 138.
[37]Engler, *Brotherhood of Oil*, pp. 86–95; Politics of Oil, pp. 93–99.
[38]Blair, op. cit., p. 138.
[39]Engler, *Brotherhood of Oil,* p. 160.

> ARCO; and Standard (Ind.) with Texaco and Mobil. But an analysis of the data reveals something else. By and large, the companies with the greatest financial resources . . . have little need to spread the costs or share the risks. Hence it is not surprising to find most of the leases held by these companies are individually owned, without participation by other firms. Forty-three out of 52 leases held by Exxon . . . 64 of 68 by Shell . . . 34 of 51 held by Gulf; . . . 86 of 105 held by SoCal . . .

By either joint venture or individual ownership, then, the production by the majors of offshore crude showed higher concentration in the largest companies than land-based production. (The top eight controlled 64.5 of offshore production as compared to 50.5 of land-based production; the top three companies controlled half of the offshore production.)

Exxon

A walk through the 1992 annual report of Exxon reveals the importance of joint ventures to the company's overall position and growth. The report opens with a linguistic clarification that has the unintended consequence of reminding us of the size and spread of the largest oil company headquartered in the United States:

> The terms *corporation, company, Exxon, Esso, our, we, and its* as used in this report refer not only to Exxon Corporation or to one of its divisions but collectively to all of the companies affiliated with Exxon Corporation or to any one or more of them. The shorter terms are used merely for convenience and simplicity.[40]

Financial	**1992**	**1991**
Net income, *billions of dollars*	4.8	5.6
Net income, *dollars per common share*	3.79	4.45
Dividends, *dollars per common share*	2.83	2.68
Shareholders' equity, *dollars per common share*	27.20	28.12
Revenue, *billions of dollars*	117.1	116.5
Capital and exploration expenditures, *billions of dollars*	8.8	8.8
Research and development costs, *millions of dollars*	624.0	679.0
Return on average shareholders' equity, *percent*	13.9	16.5
Retun on average capital employed, *percent*	11.0	12.8

Operating	**1992**	**1991**
Net liquids production, *thousands of barrels daily*	1,705	1,715
Natural gas production available for sale, *millions of cubic feet daily*	5,661	5,497
Petroleum product sales, *thousands of barrels daily*	4,811	4,770
Refinery crude oil runs, *thousands of barrels daily*	3,303	3,333

[40]Exxon Annual Report, 1992 cover.

1992 HIGHLIGHTS

EXPLORATION

A New Worldwide Exploration Division

A new division, Exxon Exploration Company (EEC), became operational January 1, 1992, with responsibility for Exxon's exploration activities throughout the world . . .

EEC operates through four geographically organized business units. It also has technology and computing departments that ensure that the best geological, geophysical and computing technology is applied . . .

Establishment of EEC has enhanced the deployment of modern technology, such as the applaction of three-dimensional seismic, the exploration for hydrocarbon reservoirs deposited in ancient deepwater environments and the search for potential reservoirs in geologically complex areas, such as those beneath thick salt formations.

New discoveries in 1992

During 1992, Exxon participated in the discovery of 48 new oil and gas fields, with net resources totaling over 500 million oil-equivalent barrels believed to be commercial eventually.

In conjunction with the Malaysian national oil company, Exxon announced four oil discoveries in blocks PM-5 and PM-8 off peninsula Malaysia's east coast. With this year's finds, Exxon has made a total of nine discoveries in the area since the beginning of the current Malaysian exploration program in July 1989. Exxon, as operator of the blocks, recently obtained a three-year extension on its exploration rights to the acreage.

In the Netherlands, Exxon holds interests in two substantial gas discoveries: Munnekezijl (24 percent) and Anjum (20 percent). The finds are on a trend with previous Exxon-interest discoveries made in 1990 and 1991.

In the Norwegian sector of the North Sea, a discovery was made on Block 34/7, in which Exxon has a 10.5 percent interest. Eight discoveries have been made in this block since it was awarded in 1984.

Seeking New Opportunities . . .

In December, the Dutch Ministry of Economic Affairs awarded (NAM)—a major Dutch oil- and gas-producing company in which Exxon holds a 50 percent interest—12 licenses covering 13 blocks (1,100 square miles) in the eighth offshore licensing round. These blocks complement NAM's strong existing acreage position in the Netherlands.

The company secured a 15 percent and a 20 percent interest in two blocks offshore Angola in west Africa. Each block covers about 1,900 square miles. Water depths range from 1,000 to 5,000 feet.

Exxon increased its interest to 40 percent in the large exploration block (26 million gross acres) it operates in Chad, following acquisition of a portion of Chevron Chad's interest.

New exploration opportunities are emerging in areas that for years have not been available to private companies. Projects are being considered, for example, in China, Venezuela and several countries that comprise the Commonwealth of Independent States (C.I.S.), formerly the Soviet Union.

In 1992, a new company, Exxon Ventures (C.I.S.) Inc., was formed and an Exxon office was opened in Moscow. The office will represent Exxon's upstream interests—including exploration for and production of oil and natural gas . . .

Exxon and Mobil Oil Corporation have entered into an agreement to jointly identify economically attractive exploration and development opportunities in an 86-million-acre region in western Siberia. Located about 1,100 miles northeast of Moscow, the region is a part of one of the largest hydrocarbon-producing areas in the world.

After an absence of nearly 30 years, Exxon has reentered Algeria with a 27.5 percent interest in a 2,800-square-mile block . . .

PRODUCTION

Europe

Production from the Snorre Field in the Norwegian North Sea began in August. When Snorre is fully developed, Exxon's $700 million investment is expected to yield the company about 20,000 barrels of oil per day.

Cost-effective development of the Snorre Field, which lies in water more than 1,000 feet deep, involves the use of a tension leg platform (TLP). . . —only the third such platform in use in the world.

Also in the Norwegian North Sea, construction is on schedule for an October 1993 start-up of the Sleipner East gas field.

In December, the Norwegian Storting (Parliament) approved plans . . .

Exxon has a working interest of about 30 percent in the $7 billion industry investment in the Sleipner area developments.

The NOGAT pipeline system ($50 million Exxon investment) began bringing gas ashore from a previously undeveloped area of the Dutch North Sea. Production from fields feeding NOGAT supplements that from other Exxon-interest fields, including the Groningen Field (30 percent interest), the largest source of gas in the Netherlands.

In the U.K. sector of the North Sea, the Gannet multi-field development started up in October. It is one of the company's largest projects in the U.K. North Sea, with an estimated final Exxon investment of over $750 million. . . .

The Achim–Salzwedel natural gas pipeline started up in December, providing a major new supply link between western and eastern Germany. Through its interests in German gas distribution companies, Exxon is a 36 percent participant in the new pipeline. Exxon-interest gas will help supply the growing gas markets of eastern Germany.

Asia-Pacific

In April, the Malaysia Phase II gas project was started up, and the first natural gas was brought ashore from the Jerneh Field, the largest gas field Exxon has discovered off Malaysia. The development positions Exxon to be the major supplier of gas to Malaysia's domestic markets and to Singapore. Production reached 150 million cubic feet per day at year-end 1992. . . .

Agreement was reached with the Government of Malaysia on new production-sharing contract arrangements for the existing oil fields. These arrangements extend Exxon's production rights in these fields until the year 2012. . . .

Exxon is the largest oil producer in Malaysia, operating 32 offshore platforms.

Agreement was reached with the Government of Indonesia and with Pertamina, the Indonesian national oil company, on key terms for development of the Natuna gas field, largest known undeveloped hydrocarbon resource in Southeast Asia. . . . If commercialized, Natuna would represent Exxon's largest offshore development project in the world . . .

United States

Faced with flat energy demand, weak prices and costly government regulations, Exxon continued to emphasize cost-management measures to improve profitability.

Production costs in the upstream were reduced by $176 million from 1991, and unit costs were lowered by $0.33 per oil-equivalent barrel (6 percent).

Exxon's domestic petroleum operations were consolidated from six production divisions into three, yielding a reduction in office personnel and over $50 million in annualized cost savings.

Upgrading the production asset portfolio continued, with a focus on improving efficiency by consolidating operations around substantial properties with long-life reserves. Since 1990, low-return properties with a book value of $560 million have been divested. . . .

In May, Exxon and the other owners of the Point Mclntyre Field on Alaska's North Slope approved its development at a cost of approximately $1 billion. Gross hydrocarbon reserves are estimated to exceed 300 million oil-equivalent barrels. . . . The oil will move to market via the Trans-Alaska Pipeline System.

In the Prudhoe Bay Field, the first phase of a $1.9 billion gas-handling expansion project was completed in 1992 at a cost of $435 million (Exxon working interest: 23 percent).

The two phases of the project combined will raise overall gas-handling capacity to 75 billion cubic feet per day, making it the largest gas-cycling plant in the world. . . . In addition to increasing reserve recovery, the expanded gas handling will help slow the production decline from the giant oil field, which currency produces more than 1.2 million barrels per day (gross).

The $1.2 billion Mobile Bay Project to develop over 1 trillion cubic feet of long-life natural gas reserves off the coast of Alabama continues toward start-up in late 1993. . . .

In California, the $2.1 billion Santa Ynez Unit expansion is progressing toward start-up by early 1994 (100 percent Exxon working interest). Topside facilities are being installed on two new deepwater platforms.

Off Louisiana, the *Alabaster* platform in 470 feet of water at Mississippi Canyon Block 397 was started up in April. The platform will process production from Exxon's 100 percent owned Alabaster and Zinc fields. . . .

Thc Zinc Field is being developed from a subsea multi-well production system that will be operated remotely from the *Alabaster* platform. The Zinc satellite subsea template, installed in December, is the largest such system in the Gulf of Mexico. . . .

Canada

In a very difficult business climate, Imperial Oil Limited continued to pursue vigorous cost-containment measures in 1992. Production costs in the upstream were reduced by $208 million from 1991, and unit costs were lowered by $1.63 per oil-equivalent barrel (26 percent).

Since 1989, a program to focus operations in major producing areas has resulted in the divestment of properties with a book value of about $650 million.

Imperial continues to invest selectively in this environment. Exploration expenditure was refocused and reduced by more than 50 percent from 1991 levels.

As a result of improved prices for bitumen (very heavy oil), Imperial has initiated the start-up of two more phases of the Cold Lake development in northern Alberta. . . .

Record production levels and lower unit operating costs improved profitability at the Syncrude oil sands plant in northern Alberta, where Imperial has a 25 percent share. . . . The plant accounts for more than 10 percent of Canada's total daily requirements for crude oil.

REFINING AND MARKETING

WORLDWIDE downstream (refining and marketing) earnings were $1.6 billion—a decline from last year's record earnings of more than $2.5 billion. . . .

Exxon continued to upgrade its refineries in Europe and the Asia–Pacific region, increasing their capacity to manufacture high-value fuel products, such as motor gasoline, jet fuel and diesel fuel. Demand for these products is expected to grow rapidly when regional economies improve. . . .

Exxon's worldwide lubricants business made further gains. In the U.S., margins remained strong as industry manufacturing capacity was fully utilized. Exxon continues to be the largest manufacturer of lubricants worldwide . . .

The growing integration of Exxon's refineries with its adjacent chemicals manufacturing plants achieves important economies of scale, lowers unit costs and enhances product value.

In the U.S. and Canada, faltering economies and mature markets required major programs to improve productivity and reduce costs. In both countries, Exxon's downstream businesses have been restructured, less attractive assets have been divested, selective investments have been made in areas of strong representation and close attention has been directed to all aspects of cost management. . . .

Europe

Although marketing margins remained strong during 1992, refining margins were down substantially, resulting in earnings below 1991 levels...

At Augusta, Italy, a new 18,000-barrel-per-day Hydrotreater unit was brought on-stream in 1992. It removes sulfur and other undesirable substances from low-value distillate streams, thus upgrading fuel oil components to more valuable products...

At Port Jerome, France, a new alkylation unit is being built to convert petroleum gas streams into high-octane components for the manufacture of unleaded gasoline.

At Rotterdam, the Netherlands, construction of a 36,000-barrel-per-day Hydrocracker is well under way. The unit will produce low-sulfur automotive diesel fuel and also supply Exxon's chemical plant at Notre-Dame-de-Gravenchon, France, with premium feedstock.

At Ingolstadt, Germany, an expansion project is geared to supplying growing demand for petroleum products in eastern Germany. . . .

At year's end, Exxon's retail network in the former East Germany had grown to 47 all-new, high-volume service stations equipped with state-of-the-art environmental controls and protection systems, car washes and convenience stores.

In addition to eastern Germany, Exxon is marketing at selected locations in Hungary and Poland.

In April, an Esso service station—one of the largest in Europe—was opened at Euro Disneyland near Paris as part of Exxon's long-term participation agreement with Disney. Most Exxon affiliates in Europe have launched special promotions tied to Euro Disney under the umbrella theme "The Magic Begins at Esso." . . .

United States

Ample product supplies put downward pressure on prices in 1992, lowering refinery margins. Exxon continued to concentrate on reducing unit costs, streamlining business operations and high-grading its assets.

Agreement has been reached to sell the Bayway Refinery in Linden, New Jersey, to Tosco Corporation for $175 million. . . . Better utilization of existing capacity at the Baton Rouge, Louisiana, and Baytown, Texas, refineries will permit Exxon to serve customers more efficiently.

In markets within the Gulf Coast, Middle Atlantic and Northeastern states, Exxon is well positioned. . . .

A new methyl tertiary-butyl ether (MTBE) plant was started up at the Baton Rouge Refinery. It produces low-cost oxygenate for blending reformulated gasoline. A similar MTBE facility is under construction at the Baytown Refinery. Cost advantages result from capturing the refineries' by-product . . .

Filtration improvements to the dewaxing plant at the Baytown lubricants facility will reduce solvent losses, lower refinery emissions and increase the yield of lubricants.

Pumping capacity at many Exxon service stations has been increased . . . A key feature of the new dispensers is Express Pay, an automated payment system that allows customers with credit or debit cards to pay for purchases directly at the pump.

About 100 stations in the Los Angeles and Seattle areas were divested. Also, steps were initiated to exchange some 60 Exxon service stations in southern Florida for service station properties in Maryland, Virginia and Washington, D.C. . . .

Asia–Pacific

Exxon has a well-established presence in the rapidly growing markets of Southeast Asia, particularly Thailand, Singapore and Malaysia. The company has 22 percent of refinery capacity and an average 18 percent market position in these three countries . . .

The company is also well represented in Japan, whose economy continues to grow, although at a slower pace. Exxon affiliates have approximately a 9 percent position in the attractive clean products market.

Construction is progressing on expanding the Sriracha Refinery in Thailand from 75,000 to 145,000 barrels per day in several phases between 1993 and 1995. . . . Exxon is the only major fully integrated refiner/marketer in Thailand and has a 25 percent market position.

Capacity at Exxon's Singapore Refinery was increased by 15 percent to meet increasing demand for petroleum products in Asia-Pacific markets.

Canada

Imperial's five major refineries implemented wide-ranging job reorganization and cost reduction programs that reduced cash operating costs by 1.5 cents per gallon.

Retail marketing expenses were reduced by 12 percent. More than 200 of Imperial's least-productive service stations were closed, but with a total network of 3,800 stations, that company remains the largest marketer in Canada.

Exxon Expands Lubricants Business

New Facilities: Lube oil blending plants were built, modernized or expanded in Japan, Taiwan, Singapore, Tunisia and the U.S.

A modernized plant near Tokyo supplies over 300,000 barrels per year of lubricants to Exxon's two Japanese marketing affiliates, Esso Sekiyu K.K. and General Sekiyu K.K.

A new joint-venture plant in Taiwan will blend and package 160,000 barrels per year of automotive, industrial and marine lubricants.

White oils are highly purified specialty products used in the food processing, pharmaceutical, cosmetics, textile, rubber and plastics industries. . . .

New Products:

TERESSO SYNTHETIC HP, an industrial oil intended for use in lubricating industrial equipment exposed to very high and/or very low temperatures.

UNIREX RS 300, a premium grease designed to survive the extremely high temperatures encountered on papermaking machines.

New Markets: Exxon's presence in four emerging markets—the People's Republic of China, eastern Europe, Mexico, and Taiwan—provided further sales and earnings growth during 1992.

In Mexico, first-year results after Exxon's 1991 acquisition of a privately owned lubricants blending and distributing facility were well above expectations.

New Standards: The company's continuing emphasis on all facets of quality was further recognized in 1992 when it was awarded additional customer and International Standards Organization (ISO) quality certifications. . . .

CHEMICALS

United States

Higher operating efficiency and reliability will result from completion of a five-year program to upgrade computer control systems at Exxon Chemical facilities in Baton Rouge, Louisiana. A similar project has been launched at Baytown, Texas.

Also at Baton Rouge, construction is under way on a major ester plant that will increase U.S. plasticizer production by 50 percent. . . .

Commercial sales of EXACT resins . . . began in 1992. The catalysts allow polymer resins and compounds to be tailored to precise quality and performance specifications required by makers of film packaging, adhesives, sealants, textiles and healthcare products.

Europe

At Exxon's Notre-Dame-de-Gravenchon petrochemical complex in France, new units to produce 140,000 tons per year of polypropylene (100 percent Exxon) and 220,000 tons per year of linear low-density polyethylene (50 percent Exxon) came on-stream. . . .

[A] new facility was commissioned at Augusta, Italy, to recover propylene from refinery units.

Asia-Pacific

In Korea, production of plasticizers and solvents to supply rapidly growing regional demand was expanded with the completion of two joint-venture plans to make those products.

Exxon Chemical and Mobil merged the operations of their joint-venture companies—Altona Petrochemical, Australian Synthetic Rubber and Commercial Polymers—into a single organization, Kemcor Australia. The new company is the largest center for the production of plastics, rubber and petrochemicals in Australia.

COAL, MINERALS AND POWER

Exxon's coal, minerals, electric power and other operations earned $254 million in 1992. Profits from electric power investments in Hong Kong continued to be a major contributor.

Although coal and copper prices declined, the earnings impact was lessened somewhat because copper production increased to record levels.

Asia–Pacific

Through its 60 percent interest in power-generating stations serving Kowloon and the New Territories, Exxon has shared in Hong Kong's economic growth. . . .

Electricity sales increased 11 percent for the year, reaching almost 24,000 gigawatt hours. This was the 18th consecutive year of increased electricity sales. New gas turbines at Penny's Bay (300 megawatts) were commissioned in May. Government approval was received for a plan for four 625-megawatt, gas-fired combined-cycle generators to be commissioned in 1996–1999. The project investment totals $3 billion.

The Government of Hong Kong approved a new Scheme of Control that will provide the regulatory framework for Exxon's Hong Kong power investments through the year 2008. The People's Republic of China has confirmed the Scheme of Control's continuing validity after the 1997 sovereignty transfer.

Exxon's coal production in New South Wales, Australia, increased 10 percent to 4 million metric tons. . . .

South America

The $440 million expansion of the Los Bronces copper mine in Chile was completed in 1992, tripling annual production capacity to 130,000 metric tons and providing significant economies of scale that will reduce operating costs.

The $176 million expansion of the Chagres copper smelter, which will nearly triple production of blister copper, is proceeding on schedule. Emissions of sulfur dioxide from the smelter will be reduced further. The smelter already is a leader in environmental performance in the Chilean mining industry.

Sales of coal from the Cerrejon mine in Colombia were 12 million metric tons, down 10 percent from the prior year due to weak market conditions in Europe. . . . Exxon has a 50 percent interest in the mine.

United States

At the Monterey No. 1 Mine near Carlinville, lllinois, a new block of lower-sulfur coal is being developed under a 20-year contract signed with Central Illinois Public Service Company (CIPS). Engineering is progressing on a new longwall mining system . . .

At Carter Mining's Caballo surface mine near Gillette, Wyoming, a $35 million Bucket Wheel Excavator system has enhanced the efficiency of overburden removal. . . .

Comments and Questions

1. What appears to be the role of joint ventures in Exxon's recent activities?
2. Where is Exxon now, and where does it seem to be headed in the future? How does one make the determination as to whether or not Exxon is an American company?
3. Some of the items mentioned in the annual report can be amplified by using *Wall Street Journal* accounts:

Alyeska, the Alaskan Pipeline which runs from the North Slope to the port of Valdez, Alaska, is jointly owned by Exxon, BP, Arco, Amerada Hess, Unocal, Phillips, and Mobil. (*Wall Street Journal*, July 30, 1992)

The Prudhoe Bay oilfield in Alaska is owned 50% by British Petroleum, 22% by Exxon, 22% by Arco and 6% by Unocal, Amerada Hess and Mobil. (*Wall Street Journal*, November 21, 1991)

For the European market the Norwegian natural gas fields in the North Sea are the largest source of natural gas outside OPEC and the old Soviet Union. Norway retains the ownership of substantial interests in the North Sea oil and natural gas fields that are developed in joint ventures with private companies. (*Wall Street Journal*, September 30, 1991)

The agreement between Exxon, Mobil and Russia for oil exploration in Siberia covers 86,000,000 acres of land, but does not include drilling rights. (*Wall Street Journal*, July 11, 1992)

The exploration project on the Sakhalin peninsula will be a joint venture between Exxon, the Japanese Oil Company and Itoh Corporation. (*Wall Street Journal*, October 21, 1991)

Exxon's natural gas agreement with Malaysia gives Exxon a majority interest in five fields and a minority interest in seven fields; the other stakeholder is Petroleum National Bhd, a Malaysian state company. (*Wall Street Journal*, July 27, 1992)

Exxon has consolidated its oil exploration into an international division which will employ 1600 people, with 200 fewer jobs in the United States. (*Wall Street Journal*, October 9, 1991)

Exxon and British Petroleum have a joint venture covering a deep water discovery off Mexico. (*Wall Street Journal*, December 10, 1991)

The foregoing shows the range of Exxon's activities that use the joint venture. As a class project students can begin with an annual report of a multinational oil company and update or amplify the leads provided in the report through the *Wall Street Journal* or other business periodicals. Most libraries have computerized finding aids which make this exercise easy to do.

Alternatively, a week's worth of *Wall Street Journals* may be surveyed for news about international joint ventures.

4. How big is big? *Europa*, a fact book on world production, sets the gross domestic product of Honduras at $4.5 billion in 1989. (Revenues for Exxon in 1989 were $95.2 billion.) It is not totally accurate to say that Exxon produces 21 times what Honduras does, because some Honduran production goes unrecorded. Nevertheless, the scale of this single multinational does dwarf the Honduran economy.

VALCO—A Multinational–Developing Country Joint Venture

The following case from Ghana in Africa profiles the many connections between companies and a developing country that are required for aluminum production: cheap electricity, extensive transport systems for bulk commodities, and product, port facilities, and production sites. The extensive investments require long-term relationships rather than the more transient ones of narrow scope in an enterprise zone. Countries have much more at stake when projects of this scale are undertaken, as the conflicts in the case reflect.

The case[41] typifies the "big project" that involves the home countries of the multinationals, and multilateral international agencies, such as development banks, commercial banks, and host country governments.

RESUME OF THE VOLTA RIVER PROJECT

The Valco Master Agreement was signed by the government of Ghana and the management of Kaiser Chemicals, Inc., in January 1962. It ushered in the Volta River Project—compromising a hydroelectric power (HEP) dam at Akosombo; a Volta River Authority (VRA), which distributes HEP, monitors the Lake Volta (the largest man-made lake in the world by volume), and serves as a local authority of the township of Akosombo; and an aluminum smelter at Tema, the Volta Aluminum Company (Valco)—the dam and the smelter came into full operation in 1967.

The feasibility of the Valco project had been established by a series of technical studies conducted between 1920 and 1950 in the basin of the Volta River; and it was known that there were vast deposits of bauxite, the basic raw material for aluminum, in that region, as well as a gorge along the river valley that offered natural advantages for the construction of a HEP plant. With the abundance of bauxite and the potential for a HEP plant, the Volta basin proved to be ideal for the aluminum industry. (The smelting of alumina into aluminum requires plentiful and cheap power.)

This finding proved enticing. Ghana (then the Gold Coast, until independence in 1957) was convinced of the potential benefits of the project: electrification of the country for industrial development and domestic consumption; the development of an integrated aluminum industry, with all the stages from bauxite mining to aluminum smelting being undertaken domestically, as well as aluminum-utilizing industries (such as those making foils, pans, roofing sheets, etc.) being established; gains in employment, income, and trade and tax revenues; and other benefits such as lake transport, fishing, and irrigation. Foreign investors, too, found the project attractive: the presence of vast bauxite deposits and HEP potential in the same region was itself attractive enough, not to mention the high world market prices then for aluminum, coupled with the cheap power and presumably cheap labor that the investors hoped to obtain.

In 1951, Kwame Nkrumah, then leader of (the Gold Coast) government business appointed a special commissioner to coordinate activities of the project. In 1956, a reappraisal of the costs of the project was undertaken, and it was estimated at £309 million. This was very expensive, indeed prohibitive, for a single project, especially then, and even by the standards of rich aluminum TNCs, [In British texts on international businesses, TNC is used instead of MNC.—Ed.] multilateral lending agencies, and influential

41P. Bondzi-Simpson, *Legal Relationships between TNCs and Host States,* (New York: Quorum, 1990) pp. 78–85.

governments like that of the UK and United States. In 1957, when Ghana became independent and as the United States was courting the former colonies, President Eisenhower promised to offer what assistance the United States could.

The understanding, tacit and expressed, was to secure an integrated aluminum industry using Ghana's resources and potential (in extraction, HEP, and smelting); the required capital was to be obtained from Ghana and abroad; and the integrated aluminum industry was to serve the international market as a technically and financially viable operation at current rates and for the mutual benefit of the host and the foreign investors. This was the original understanding.

In line with the government's offer of assistance, Kaiser Inc., a U.S. firm and one of the world's six largest aluminum firms, went to Ghana to examine the technical and financial feasibility of the Volta project. And its report, which formed the basis of the present project, in which Kaiser has a very major involvment, made three changes to the pre-existing design. . . .

> First, the site of the dam was moved, which made it constructable in four years instead of seven, and improved the capacity of the hydro-electricity generation. Secondly, the site of the aluminum smelter was changed from the river to the harbour at Tema. The third proposal made was extremely unwelcome to President Nkrumah: the middle stage of the project, namely the alumina plant which would change Ghana's bauxite into alumina, was omitted. As Kaiser presented it, for a preliminary period of ten years, the scheme would involve the importation of alumina while Ghana's bauxite would continue to be mined and exported.

With the feasibility of the project confirmed by the Kaiser report, subject to the proposed changes, Ghana gave necessary approval for its construction. Ghana bore half (50 percent) of the costs for the dam, power station, and transmission lines, and the other half was borne jointly by the IBRD, [World —Ed.] U.S. Export Import (Exim) Bank, and the British government. The bulk of the financing for the smelter, however, came from U.S. governmental sources and the little that the investors put in was guaranteed by the U.S. government under a political risk program. [The United States has a program covering United States-based companies for the risk of expropriation of foreign property and investments. —Ed.] Therefore, in truth, the foreign investors bore little of the capital contributon or the risk, but they stood to gain considerably.

The HEP dam at Akosombo was and is owned and run by Ghana. The major customer was intended to be Valco. Valco owned the aluminum smelting plant at Tema. Valco is a consortium of two American firms, Kaiser holding 90 percent ownership therein, and Reynolds, holding the remaining 10 percent. Valco was incorporated under the laws of Ghana in 1962. It is notable that by the arrangements that were conceived, Kaiser/ Reynolds were made the exclusive *shareholders* and *customers* of Valco.

Highlights of the 1962 Valco Master Agreement

The Master Agreement between the government of Ghana and Valco, signed on January 22, 1962, governed relationships between them. The Valco Agreement, as it is known, actually comprises more than twenty related agreements. Valco is a Ghanaian firm (since it is incorporated under the laws of Ghana), but its owners, Kaiser and Reynolds, are American. The rights that the shareholders have in Valco are in

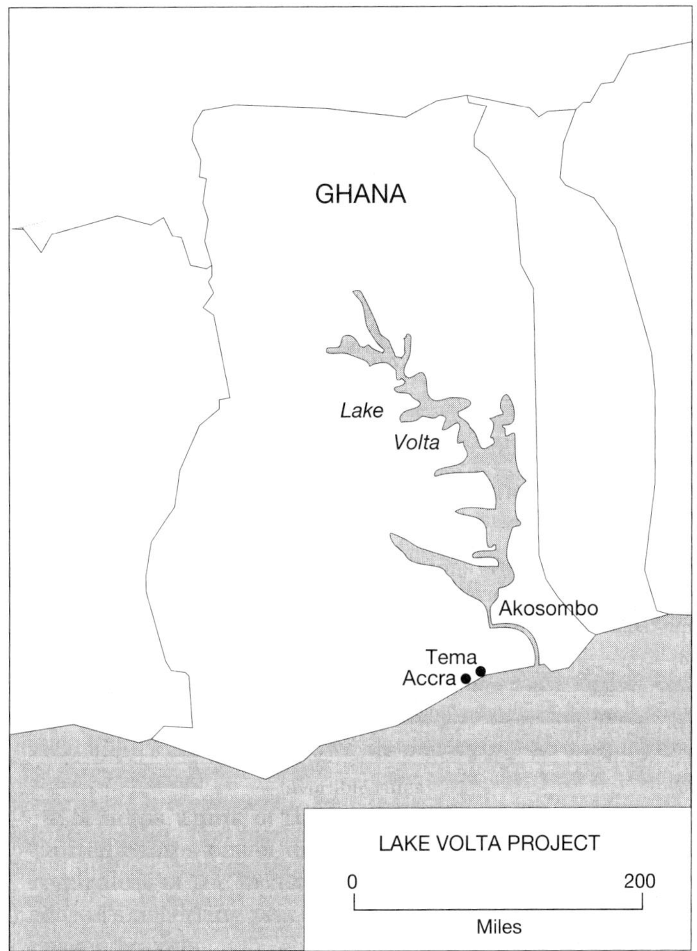

proportion to their shareholding therein (i.e., 90:10 for Kaiser and Reynolds respectively).

Smelter. Valco was set up as a tolling service [company charges for alumina processed into aluminum. —Ed.] owned by and serving exclusively Kaiser and Reynolds. It was to smelt alumina (aluminum oxide) imported by the shareholders in proportion to their shareholding . . . The alumina that Valco smelted was imported notably from Jamaica and Guyana from plants affiliated with its shareholders. But neither the alumina nor the aluminum was owned by Valco. In the same vein, Kaiser/Reynolds were to pay Valco a penalty for not utilizing the capacity allotted for smelting alumina on their behalf. This penalty, too, was payable by the owners of Valco on a 90:10 ratio. For their services, Valco was to charge a fee—the tolling fee—which was set as a percentage (56 percent) of the price per ton of aluminum produced by Valco.

There were at least five unique—indeed, anomalous—features of the smelting arrangements. First, although Ghana had vast deposits of bauxite and indeed exported that mineral and although the whole idea for setting up the project was to utilize to the maximum the resources and potential that Ghana had, the alumina that was smelted at Valco was actually imported. Second, the fee charged for the smelting was determinable as a percentage of the value of the aluminum (the smelted product of alumina): 56 percent of the value in the first ten years, and thereafter raised to 60 percent if Valco was not by then using alumina made from Ghanaian bauxite. This provision apparently sought to encourage the use of domestic alumina if some of comparable quality was found, but in 1990 it still is not the case. Third, it is to be noted that out of the tolling fees that Valco charged, the shareholders retained a significant portion. At tolling rates of 56 percent (i.e., within the first ten years of operation) that Valco was to receive from its customers, the shareholders were to retain 40 percent thereof for such expenses as obtaining and marketing the alumina/aluminum and for payment of the management and technical services obtained; and at rates of 60 percent (i.e., after the ten-year period if Ghanaian alumina was still not used), the shareholders were to retain 44 percent thereof. Fourth, although it would have been supposed that Valco would seek to maximize its earnings from the tolling fee, it did not necessarily do so. (Ghana had a tax interest in higher Valco receipts, and the latter's creditors would be more secure if Valco maximized its earnings.) The tolling fee was set by using the lower of two values—one computed in pounds sterling and the other in U.S. dollars. Fifth, the tolling charge was determinable by the price of metal on the date Valco shipped the aluminum to the customers rather than on the date it rendered the tolling service. One would have thought that the value of services rendered would have been determined by the rates at that time.

The picture for the smelting operations then was this: The shareholders took the profits of Valco. Valco was to smelt alumina for its *customers*. The customers of Valco were, exclusively, its *shareholders*. The smelting was done in proportion to the shareholding in Valco. For the smelting, Valco received payment. From these Valco receipts, the shareholders retained 44 percent for management, etc. By a separate management contract, Valco did not manage itself but was managed by an arrangement with the shareholders. Therefore, the major shareholder of Valco was its *manager*. In payment for smelting alumina for its customers, Valco was to receive the lower of two sums in tolling values. But Valco was to pay an increased share for management, etc. If Valco was prompt with the production and shipping of its customers' alumina it was certain to receive current market rates, but with manipulation of production and shipping schedules Valco's receipts could be varied.

This discussion shows some of the intra-corporate schemes adopted by the TNC. Valco qua autonomous profit-making enterprise was expected to maximize its profits, but Valco qua TNC unit was bound to seek the maximization of the global corporate profits of the TNC, even at the expense of some loss. Note again some of the implications of this arrangement. "Loss" to Valco (i.e., shareholders) might be gain to customers (i.e., shareholders), or charge to Valco for management was gain to managers (i.e., shareholders). This arrangement is a typical corporate scheme, sanctified by contract, of intracorporate transactions that secure global profit-maximization even at the expense of unit profit maximization. And through such devices, the few benefits that host states seek, such as tax revenues, become illusory. (One does not even here mention the employment of domestic natural and human resources.)

Management. As provided by a Management and Technical Assistance Agreement, Valco was to be managed (not by itself but) by another subsidiary of Kaiser, the Kaiser Aluminum Technical Services, Inc. (KATSI). Reynolds entrusted the management of Valco to Kaiser. The agreement stipulated that Valco (1) pay KATSI a monthly management fee of $17,000 and (2) reimburse KATSI for any and all expenses expended by KATSI on behalf of Valco or otherwise in the performance of services rendered. It also provided that in the event that USAID assumed management of Valco under the contract of guarantee, KATSI was still to be paid a fee (of 3.5 percent of the UK or U.S. metal price, whichever was higher)! In effect, this provision meant that even when the ownership of Valco changed from Kaiser/Reynolds to USAID, (1) KATSI would still manage Valco and (2) a higher management fee would be charged. Consequently, . . . the fee payable to KATSI in the circumstances described was really a way of transferring funds out of Ghana's control to Kaiser and Reynolds when they no longer owned the company.

Services Obtainable from and Rates Payable to Ghana.

1. Hydroelectric power. By the Power Agreement, the VRA was to supply Valco at least sufficient power to run five out of its six potlines. This amounted to over 60 percent of the output of the huge Akosombo Dam. It was also provided that in the event that the water level of the dam diminished to such as extent as to necessitate the reduction of power output from the dam, Valco was to receive a pro rata share of power. That is, at all times Valco was to receive over 60 percent of Ghana's HEP or sufficient power to run five potlines, whichever was less. The price of power was fixed a 2.265 mills per kilowatt hour of energy for a duration of thirty years, with Valco maintaining an option to extend the term another twenty years. Valco was also exempted from power uses taxes.
2. Water. By the Water Agreement, the Ghana Water and Sewerage Corporation was to supply Valco water at a rate of three schillings per thousand gallons. This, too, had a duration of thirty years, with an option to Valco to extend for another twenty.
3. Port and Wharfage. Because of the import/export operations that Valco undertook—smelting imported alumina and exporting the aluminum (Valco neither used domestic resources nor served the domestic market)—Valco had to establish terms with the Ghana Ports Authority, also fixed for thirty years with an option to extend for twenty more. Valco had its dock at the Tema harbor, as well as railway lines between the harbor and the plant, both at Tema.

Mining. Although there were plentiful bauxite in Ghana and infrastructure and resources to support all aspects of an integrated aluminum industry—from bauxite mining to aluminum smelting and the aluminum-utilizing industries (such as the manufacturing of foils, pots, and roofing sheets)—the Kaiser Report did not advise the establishment of the integrated industry, ostensibly because of costs, but apparently because of Kaiser's operations elsewhere. Consequently, the mining of Ghana's bauxite or its processing into alumina was of no priority to Kaiser. Kaiser's main interest was in Ghana's cheap HEP. However, the 1962 Agreement provided that if after ten years the shareholders were still importing alumina for smelting, the tolling fee for its smelting that Valco was to charge was to be raised from 56 percent to 60 percent. But even then, the shareholders were to retain an increased share of the Valco fee—44 percent, whereas before they could retain 40 percent—for management and miscellaneous purposes.

Applicable Law. The Valco Agreement contained a clause that purported to "freeze" the applicable law to that of Ghana on January 22, 1961 (the date that the Valco Agreement was signed). The effect of the clause was to preclude or oust the capacity of the legislative authority of Ghana over it. Nor was the agreement to be reviewed within the first thirty years, after which date Valco could continue to enjoy the same terms if it so opted, in effect giving the Agreement a non-reviewable life of fifty years. The tax provisions (indeed concessions) were also to apply for thirty years, but thereafter the Ghana government could impose a new fiscal regime, so long as it was not discriminatory. Finally, there was the right of unrestricted access to international arbitration in respect of any dispute arising from the agreements.

Catalogue of Ghana's Objections to the 1962 Agreement

The objections selected and enumerated here are those raised by the government of Ghana against the text of the Agreement itself. Indeed, since the Agreement was considered unfair by Ghana but fair by Valco and Kaiser, it was only Ghana that could have [raised], and did raise, substantial objections to it. The objections that Ghana raised formed the bases of the renegotiations that commenced in the early 1980s, culminating in the conclusion of an amended Valco Agreement in 1985. Some of these objections have been alluded to already.

1. The exclusion of Ghanaians from the Valco Board of Directors. In spite of Ghana's heavy commitment, financial and otherwise, in the whole Volta River Project, it did not have even a single member on the Valco Board of Directors.
2. The duration of the non-reviewable clauses. The power, water, and wharfage rates were all fixed for thirty years with an option to extend for another twenty.
3. The pittance rates. At the time the rates were set, even though at below world market rates, they were less unjustified than they came to be years later—with global fuel and (primary and manufactured) commodity prices escalating and with global and domestic inflation, the Valco rates lost all meaning, in fact, they became simply exploitative. By 1982, Valco was paying one-third the average global rates for HEP; one-twentieth the rates for water that the ordinary Ghan-

aians (who are far poorer than Valco) paid; and one-forty-fifth the rates that the ordinary users of the port facilities paid!

4. The power floor/ceiling. The minimum amount of power that the VRA was to supply to Valco amounted, in effect, to over 60 percent of the Akosombo Dam's output or sufficient power to run five potlines, whichever was less. This fact meant that there was only a proportionally small amount of power left for industrial and household consumption in Ghana, and for exports to neighboring states. Consequently, Ghana felt that (a) the power ceiling should be reduced from sufficient power to run five potlines to something below that level and (b) in case of power shortages, Valco should take more than proportional reductions (because the amount of power to run one potline could serve thousands of households!).
5. Valco's maximizing its earnings from tolling operations, so that Ghana's tax stake therein, however modest, is increased. Ghana felt that the maximization of Valco's profits could be done by (a) requiring the use of a higher metal price index and (b) changing the reference point at which prices were made for the payments from the point of shipment to the point of production.
6. Requiring, or at least encouraging, the development of a local alumina sector, which alumina would be smelted by Valco into aluminum.
7. Increasing the taxes payable to Ghana, as the days of the liberal tax concessions given were long over.
8. Defreezing the supposed standstill clauses that purported to limit the applicable laws of Ghana to those in force in 1962.
9. Ghana's wanting the right to periodic general reviews of the agreement with Valco.

These were the core objections that Ghana raised against the Valco Agreement, especially as it stood in the 1980s. During the 1980–81 period, under the civilian government of Dr. Hilla Limann, initiatives were commenced to renegotiate the Agreement, but the government was ousted before long. The Provisional National Defence Council, which took over power, followed up on this initiative, however, and in December 1982, the incumbent government invited Valco to renegotiate the Agreement. The Ghana team, comprising lawyers, accountants, economists, and engineers, was assisted by [international agencies]. . . .

Highlights of the 1985 Renegotiated Agreement

. . . What follow are highlights of the agreement as a whole (comprising the essentially agreed upon points of . . . three documents).

1. The government of Ghana was allowed representation on the Valco Board of Directors although for two seats only and as non-voting members.
2. The Agreement was made subject to general reviews every five years. Therefore the purported freeze on revisions was neutralized. The governing law was to comprise (a) the contract, subject to the five yearly reviews, and

(b) the laws of Ghana . . . ". . . The parties hereto acknowledge and agree that the legislative competence of Ghana as a sovereign state is defined by its applicable constitutional instruments and can be exercised only in the limits ordained by established International Law."

3. The rate (price) of power sold by the VRA to Valco was raised; the power ceiling was lowered, sufficient to run four instead of five of the potlines (so that more electricity would be available for other industrial and household consumption in Ghana); and it was provided that in the event of the HEP dam's producing under capacity, Valco was to take proportionately greater, pro rata, cuts . . .
4. The rates for water and wharfage were raised to compare more favorably with domestic and international rates. These rates were subject to five yearly reviews.
5. The tolling fee was pegged at 68 percent of the London Metal Exchange (LME) metal price, whereas before it was 60 percent of the lower of two prices, one quoted in pounds sterling and the other in dollars.
6. The reference point at which Valco was to receive payment for smelting done for its customers-cum-shareholders was changed from the point at which shipment was made at the Tema harbor to the time it produced the aluminum.
7. In a bid to encourage the utilization of Ghanaian resources and the integration of an aluminum industry, it was stipulated that Ghana could impose duties on imported alumina if alumina of comparable quality was available there.
8. The tax rates paid by Valco were increased: income tax was raised from 40 percent to 46 percent, to equal that otherwise payable by the United States and a dividend withholding tax set at 15 percent . . .

The renegotiated agreement between Ghana and Valco served mutual benefits. Although the operating costs of Valco increased compared to its previous operating costs, the rates agreed upon were comparable to the current global rates, including the rates and taxes that subsisted in Ghana (the home state of Valco) and the United States (the home state of the shareholders). Therefore, Valco suffered neither discriminatory treatment nor above-market costs. Its hitherto privileged—indeed superior—status was revised, and it enjoyed national, as well as globally comparable, treatment. Yet Valco was assured a plentiful supply of electricity and the opportunity to smelt alumina exclusively for its shareholders, and control remained in the hands of Kaiser as before.

The renegotiations, therefore, served to reflect market transactions rather than the subsisting exploitative rates. Nor were they instituted to demonstrate host state whim or power.

The renegotiation secured an equitable *quid pro quo* that reflected contemporary economic realities in both domestic and global terms. Thereby, the law was made to correspond with the times, without its being rendered unduly otiose, exploitative, or capricious.

Questions and Comments

1. Review the financing of the project, where the funds were coming from, and the risks being taken by the various parties.
2. What stake did the United States have in the project? The government of Ghana? The multinationals? The people of the United States? The people of Ghana?
3. Examine the principal features of the project as first contemplated. As first agreed. As it first operated. As it was modified. What were the advantages and disadvantages of the project at each time mentioned above?

   What do you predict for the future under the modified agreement?
4. What tactics does the company use to control business arrangements? As an adviser to Ghana, what would you advise to prevent overreaching by the multinationals?
5. The compiler of this case, Professor Bondzi-Simpson, in his closing paragraph, concludes that the agreement as renegotiated "served mutual interests." Evaluate his conclusion and the basis he gives for it.

Enterprise Processing Zones

Cheap labor and the ability to shop the world for the most favorable "business climate" have been the appeal of "enterprise zones," "offshore assembly" zones, or "industrial processing zones," as they are variously called in the literature on international trade. The popularity of these zones among business groups has inspired proposed legislation in Washington that would establish processing zones in large cities and in rural areas of the United States that have experienced chronic unemployment. Given this new round of enthusiasm for zones, it is especially timely to consider them at greater length.

Enterprise processing zones also came into the news through debates over NAFTA (North American Free Trade Agreement between the United States, Mexico, and Canada). Much of the discussion concerned the *maquiladoras*, enterprise zones located all along the thousand-mile border between the United States and Mexico. These maquila factories of Northern Mexico are only one group from among hundreds that are located everywhere in the Third World.

The idea behind zones is easy to grasp even though the many effects of zones are not. A country offers international companies a place or zone where they can set up factories, import factory machinery and other inputs duty-free, employ locals, and export the product from the zone. On the other end of the line—the final destination of the products—there is either no import duty imposed, or the duty imposed is limited to the value added in the export zone, as it is under Section 807 of the U.S. Tariff Code, which will be discussed in detail later.

Decisions about production are controlled by the international company. The "home" country (for example the United States) where the multinational company is "based" sometimes gets the benefit of employment from companies' making inputs for export to the zones for further processing—parts to an electronic game, components for electrical equipment for a car, or cloth cut for sewing. In addition there may be some import duties collected by the "home" country when finished products are brought back.

However, the government of the "home" country may furnish direct and indirect subsidies—sometimes low-visibility subsidies—to the companies going abroad. For example, the "home country" may make grants or extend loans to the "host country" to pay for the infrastructure necessary to make the processing zone usable by companies. Or perhaps some food aid might be allocated to the cooperating country that opens itself to processing zones.

The "home" country loses "labor intensive" work; hence the current proposals in the United States to keep assembly work in urban and rural areas of chronic unemployment. (This policy runs counter to the simultaneous support to companies moving production "offshore"!) The "host" country contributes what it must to attract industry to the zone. Where the "host" country gets a loan to build infrastructure to support the zone, the loan eventually must be paid. In addition, "host" country support can include assistance in finance, free factory space, roads, harbor and transportation improvement, water and sewage systems, job training, public transportation, housing, health facilities, and so on.

The "host" country also usually abdicates most of its rights to impose legal regulations in the zone either by express grant, that is, "on the law books," or by the nonenforcement of law that would, strictly speaking, be applicable in the zone. Rigorous or lax law enforcement affects the costs of doing business. Despite the general endorsement in business of good organization and precise control, when it comes to some aspects of law, businesses prefer lawlessness, usually termed "deregulation."

There are then at least two categories of public subsidy applicable to the creation and operation of processing zones—one set in the "home country," which often provides loans or grants, using taxpayers' money raised in the "home" country, to get the zone established, and reduces import duties on the products from the zone; and a second set of subsidies in the "host country," which provides institutional support for the zone that commonly includes, in addition to the items mentioned above, a police and security force and other prerequisites to keep the zone running smoothly.

Those in favor of zones defend them as a great way to promote growth, create employment, and generate badly needed investment in poor countries. Those more skeptical of zones look upon them as publicly subsidized enclaves for gain that accrues primarily to the multinational corporate participants, and leaves zone work forces as a permanent underclass. Whatever growth is counted is usually accompanied by uncounted losses: the employment is marginal and often below subsistence, the infrastructure is pushed beyond environmentally sound limits, and countries are caught in endless rounds of debt from which they can never seem to extricate themselves.

The following description of an industrial zone in Indonesia offers an introduction to offshore assembly. A Korean company acts as a subcontractor of Nike Inc. for athletic shoe assembly.

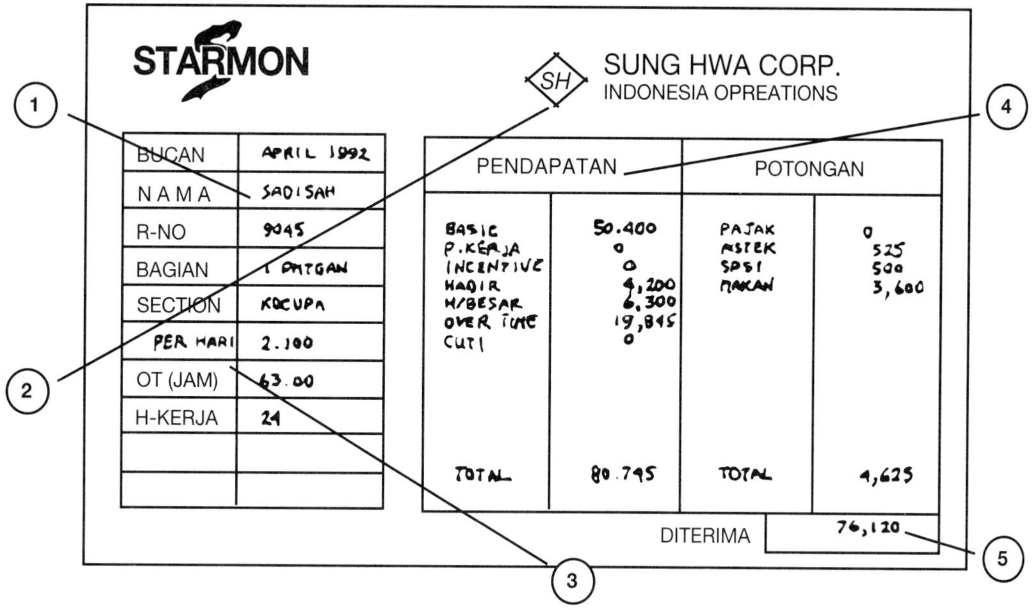

STARMON

SH SUNG HWA CORP.
INDONESIA OPREATIONS

BUCAN	APRIL 1992
NAMA	SADISAH
R-NO	9045
BAGIAN	I PMTGAN
SECTION	KOCUPA
PER HARI	2.100
OT (JAM)	63.00
H-KERJA	24

PENDAPATAN		POTONGAN	
BASIC	50.400	PAJAK	0
P.KERJA	0	ASTEK	525
INCENTIVE	0	SPSI	500
HADIR	4,200	MAKAN	3,600
H/BESAR	6.300		
OVER TIME	19,845		
CUTI	0		
TOTAL	80.795	TOTAL	4,625
		DITERIMA	76,120

THE NEW FREE TRADE HEEL

Jeffrey Ballinger

1. Her only name is Sadisah, and it's safe to say that she's never heard of Michael Jordan. Nor is she spending her evenings watching him and his Olympic teammates gliding and dunking in prime time from Barcelona. But she has heard of the shoe company he endorses—Nike, whose logo can be seen on the shoes and uniforms of many American Olympic athletes this summer. Like Jordan, Sadisah works on behalf of Nike. You won't see her, however, in the flashy TV images of freedom and individuality that smugly command us to JUST DO IT!—just spend upward of $130 for a pair of basketball shoes. Yet Sadisah is, in fact one of the people who is doing it—making the actual shoes, that is, and earning paychecks such as this one in a factory in Indonesia.

2. In the 1980s, Oregon-based Nike closed its last U.S. footwear factory, in Saco, Maine, while establishing most of its new factories in South Korea, where Sung Hwa Corp. is based. Sung Hwa is among many independent producers Nike has contracted with. Nike's actions were part of the broader "globalization" trend that saw the United States lose 65,300 footwear jobs between 1982 and 1989 as shoe companies sought non-unionized Third World workers who didn't require the U.S. rubber-shoe industry average of $6.94 an hour. But in the late 1980s, South Korean laborers gained the right to form independent unions and to strike. Higher wages ate into Nike's profits. The company shifted new factories to poorer countries such as Indonesia, where labor rights are generally ignored and wages are but one seventh of South Korea's. (The Sung Hwa factory and others like it are located in Tangerang, a squalid industrial boom-

town just outside Jakarta.) Today, to make 80 million pairs of shoes annually, Nike contracts with several dozen factories globally, including six in Indonesia. Others are in China, Malaysia, Thailand, and Taiwan. By shifting factories to cheaper labor pools, Nike has posted year after year of growth; in 1991 the company grossed more than $3 billion in sales—$200 million of which Nike attributes to Jordan's endorsement—and reported a net profit of $287 million, its highest ever.

3. The words printed on the pay stub are in Bahasa Indonesian, a language created by fusing Roman characters with a dominant Malay dialect. The message, however, is bottom-line capitalism. "Per hari" is the daily wage for seven and a half hours of work, which in Sadisah's case is 2,100 Indonesia rupiah—at the current rate of exchange, $1.03 per day. That amount, which works out to just under 14 cents per hour, is less than the Indonesian government's figure for "minimum physical need." A recent International Labor Organization survey found that 88 percent of Indonesian women working at Sadisah's wage rates are malnourished. And most workers in this factory—over 80 percent—are women. With seldom more than elementary-school educations, they are generally in their teens or early twenties, and have come from outlaying agricultural areas in search of city jobs and a better life. Sadisah's wages allow her to rent a shanty without electricity or running water.

4. "Pendapatan" is the earnings column, and five lines below the base pay figure for the month (50,400 rupiah) is one for overtime. Sadisah and the other workers in this factory are compelled to put in extra hours, both by economic necessity and by employer fiat. Each production line of 115 workers is expected to produce about 1,600 pairs of Nikes a day. According to the column at left, next to "OT (JAM)," Sadisah worked 63 hours of overtime during this pay period, for which she received an extra 2 cents per hour. At this factory, which makes mid-priced Nikes, each pair of shoes requires .84 manhours to produce; working on an assembly line, Sadisah assembled the equivalent of 13.9 pairs every day. The profit margin on each pair is enormous. The labor costs to manufacture a pair of Nikes that sells for $80 in the United States is approximately 12 cents.

5. Here are Sadisah's net earnings for a month of labor. She put in six days a week, ten and a half hours per day, for a paycheck equivalent to $37.46—about half the retail price of one pair of the sneakers she makes. Boosters of the global economy and "free markets" claim that creating employment around the world promotes free trade between industrializing and developing countries. But how many Western products can people in Indonesia buy when they can't earn enough to eat? The answer can't be found in Nike's TV ads showing Michael Jordan sailing above the earth for his reported multiyear endorsement fee of $20 million—an amount, incidentally, that at the pay shown here would take Sadisah 44,492 years to earn.

Notes and Questions

1a. In some ways Nike is "well known" in the United States, but in some ways it is not. Tell a friend about Nike in Indonesia, Sadisah, and "offshore assembly." Record your friend's reaction to the story, and your discussion.

b. Nike is only one example of the many companies that have chosen to manufacture overseas. Nike's response to criticism of employment practices might be a narrow one—Nike does not own or control the companies doing the assembly; or a broader one—Nike operates in an internationally competitive market that is not of its own making.

If one is upset over the exploitation of workers in Indonesia, how would one refute these claims?

2. The identification of benefits and detriments, and beneficiaries and victims, requires a careful assessment. In the Nike case, can it be said that the United States as a whole gained, or that Indonesia as a whole gained, or must there be a determination of just what groups or social strata we are talking about in both countries?

Did the owners of Nike gain? Did the workers in Saco, Maine, lose? Do consumers of Nike footwear in the United States and Europe gain? The shareholders of Nike? The principals of the South Korean subcontractor? Do the workers in Indonesia gain? Are there other people in Indonesia who gain through their allegiances with international companies or their willingness to deliver a tractable work force?

3. It might be assumed that the author of the Nike case study had picked the perfect point of comparison to measure the dismal fate of Sadisah—Michael Jordan and the need for Sadisah to work 44,000 + years to catch up with Jordan's earnings from endorsements. Closer study will reveal that Michael Jordan, as lucrative as his contract might seem to an impoverished college student, is really not a very big fish once the Nike Corporation and its management are considered.

Michael Jordan makes no production decisions for Nike; he is simply part of its sales force. Philip Knight, the Nike president and CEO, does. He owns enough stock, about 25 million shares, to control the board of directors. If he converted his shares and sold them on the stock exchange, they would bring about $1.4 billion (Aug. 10, 1993 closing price was $56 per share). In addition to his stock, Knight makes almost $1 million per year, plus perks. If students have a talent for high numbers, they can calculate how long Sadisah would have to work at $37 per month to amass the fortune that Knight already has.

4. Nike has no labor problems of its own, because it has very little labor in the usual sense of the word. Footwear and apparel are manufactured by subcontractors, and Nike is essentially a marketing company. All of the Nike footwear and 50 percent of Nike apparel is made overseas. (The other 50 percent is made by subcontractors in the U.S. South.)

As you learned in the chapter on labor law, there are no limits on the discretion of U.S.-based companies to close plants, move production overseas, or to use subcontractors rather than their own work forces.

Industrial Processing Zones and Imports under U.S. Tariff Code 807

Tariffs in the United States and elsewhere are the taxes levied against imports. Anyone who has traveled internationally knows that the cheapest answer to the question, "Anything to declare?" is always no. So too with businesses who would like to bring product into the United States with as little duty on it as possible.

The politics surrounding tariffs can be difficult to unravel. Free market enthusiasts, who could not always count the largest corporations in their ranks (for many years U.S. enterprises and the Republican Party wanted high tariffs to protect the domestic market from "cheap imports") are generally in favor of the elimination of tariff barriers that can inhibit the movement of goods. Protectionists, on the other hand, advocate tariffs primarily to protect the American industrial base with its accompanying labor forces from foreign manufacturers.

The politics of trade are further complicated by the interests of the largest United States-based enterprises importing from their own manufacturing facilities overseas; some of the so-called "foreign competition" is from the offshore production enclaves of the largest corporations headquartered in the United States!

Still another source of tension comes via international debt repayment. If countries are to repay their international loans, especially those owed to the largest international commercial banks of the world, they must be able to have economic activity and generate foreign exchange. The largest financial institutions favor free trade and the accompanying capital flows so that indebted countries will pay their debts.

In addition, there has been a fear comparable to that which was associated with the U.S. Food for Peace Program. If countries cannot provide employment for their growing populations, many of whom are unemployed, then the people might move leftward and rebel. To "preserve stability," "development strategies" were devised to make the world safer for friendly regimes, and for international capitalism generally. The words are in quotations to indicate that there has not been universal agreement on what long-run stability means, how it might best be achieved, or who should define development.

One piece of the strategy, that in its total reach was far wider, was Section 807 of the Tariff Code. which allowed U.S.-made products or components to be shipped abroad for assembly and then brought back into the United States with import duties charged only on the value added by the offshore assembly.

Title 19, Sec. 1202 of the U.S. Revised Tariff Schedule provides:

> 807- Articles assembled abroad in whole or part of fabricated components, the product of the United States, which (a) were exported in a condition ready for assembly without further fabrication, (b) have lost their physical identity in such articles by change in form, shape, or otherwise, and (c) have not been advanced in value or improved in condition abroad except by operations inciden-

tal to the assembly process such as cleaning, lubricating, and painting . . .
A duty upon the full value of the article, less the cost or value of such products of the United States . . .

What 807 comes down to is that import duties on reentry are assessed on the total value of the finished product *less* the value of United States inputs.

There is a compromise built into the law; the offshore company cannot go beyond simple assembly. A part of the production process can been done overseas, but not so much of it that there will be a total reduction of employment in the United States. Of course, this does not preclude manufacturing overseas entirely if a firm is willing to pay more duty than would be owed when the production process is broken into stages, as envisioned under Section 807.

To put the legislation in its kindest light, from the standpoint of the welfare of the United States, it was believed that the higher end of manufacturing would remain in the United States, whereas the "lower end"—simple assembly—would be overseas. Everyone would win.

Organized labor has always opposed Section 807 on the ground that assembly jobs are needed in the United States, not only in themselves, but also because they increase the demand for local inputs of all types through backward and forward linkages. Labor has always believed that when assembly is lost, it is only a question of time before job losses move backward to employment on inputs and forward to related employment.

The enthusiasm of the largest manufacturers for NAFTA attests to the reasonableness of the earliest concerns of labor about Section 807. Under NAFTA there would be no limits to the ability of companies to make backward and forward linkages with the assembly process, and more manufacturing will probably go to Mexico. NAFTA may be seen as 807 made unnecessary; the importation of all products from Mexico would be duty free.

The growing volume of imports under 807 suggests the impacts that the law has had on assembly work in the United States. With Mexico alone, the trade under 807 grew from $145 million in 1969 to $8.6 billion in 1987. The rate of growth in the period from 1978 to 1987 was almost sixfold, from $1.54 billion to $8.6 billion.

The types of products being imported under 807 also changed over the period. In the early years it was apparel; cloth would be manufactured and cut in the United States and sent to Mexico for sewing. Later electronic assembly predominated, and most recently transportation equipment (read cars and trucks) have been the principal products. The transformation of the types of production feeds the argument of trade unionists that offshore assembly will not stay at low-end jobs and simple products but will eventually include all jobs. (*Note:* The foregoing discussion does not include all of Mexican manufacturing that is United States bound, but only that manufacturing imported under 807.)

Mexican, Caribbean, and Other Processing Zones

The organization of assembly work in Indonesia typifies low-wage, export-oriented assembly everywhere. In the Indonesia story, the factory where Sadisah works was said to be located in "a squalid industrial boomtown just outside Jakarta." In other countries there have been more clearly identified zones set aside for the establishment of factories, but conditions are comparable.

The *maquiladora* zones of Mexico cannot be considered in isolation, since they compete with zones in the Caribbean and elsewhere for assembly work. An inventory of the principal features of the zones reveals their fundamental similarities rather than their differences. In not so subtle ways, workers in all these zones are reminded of their place in a competitive world economy, a reminder not different from that now being given to workers in the United States.

In 1989, in the Dominican Republic there were 18 zones with 220 employers, mostly in apparel, but also in shoes, leather and furs, electronic components, cigars, jewelry, and kitchen hardware. They employed 90,000 people, approximately 70 percent women. Under the constitution and the Dominican labor law there is a right to form unions and to strike, but in practice there is discrimination against union sympathizers, and the zones are kept union-free. Frequently workers are "sweated" (required to work overtime to make quotas) and are paid on piece rates that yield about 40 cents per hour.[42] Beyond the zones, approximately 50 percent of the work force is employed in producing sugar for export. Other alternative paid employment to that found in the zone does not exist.

The situation in the Dominican Republic on the legal status of workers and the de facto elimination of unions is not unique. The U. S. Labor Department found:

> In general, unions have not had a high success rate in organizing EPZ workers . . . Jamaica's labor laws, for example, apply equally to EPZ and non EPZ operations. And yet, while many domestic Jamaican firms are unionized, . . . only 1 of the 16 firms in the Kingston Free Zone [had] union representation. Similarly, while 20% of Sri Lanka's non EPZ workers are represented by unions, not a single EPZ firm is unionized. Mexico's nearly 400,000 *maquiladora* workers have the same legal right to form and join unions as other Mexican workers, but only 10–20% belong to unions as compared to over 90% of workers in similar *non maquiladora* industrial enterprises . . .
>
> Sometimes there are economic reasons for this. High unemployment and competition for scarce jobs . . . In a number of cases, however, . . . [researchers found] examples of efforts by governments and employers to restrict or discourage [organization] which do not comply with internationally recognized worker rights concerning freedom of association and collective bargaining.[43]

In 1988, according to the U. S. Labor Department, the Dominican Republic stood near the bottom in wages and "fringe benefits." The salaries per hour in the survey were \$.84 per hour in the Mexican *maquiladora*, \$1.00 in Costa Rica, \$.61–.88 in Guatemala, \$.44–.48 in the Dominican Republic, and \$.36 in Jamaica.

[42]United States Labor Department, "Worker Rights in Export Processing Zones" (1989).
[43]Ibid., pp. 6,7.

When the U. S. International Trade Commission compared the cost of sewing garments in the West Indies with costs in the United States and the Far East, it found that women's blouses were . . . "$4.75 per unit in the United States, $2.20 in Hong Kong, and $1.66 in the Caribbean. For men's sport coats, the assembly and overhead costs were $15.66 per unit in the United States, $7.24 in Hong Kong, and $5.24 in the Caribbean."[44]

Women make up the greatest percentage of workers in export processing zones, not only in Mexico and the Caribbean basin, but everywhere in the world, as the following U. S. Labor Department figures show:

PERCENTAGE OF WOMEN IN EPZ WORKFORCE[45]

Country	
Barbados	90
Belize	90-95
Dominican Republic	60–70
Honduras	72
Indonesia	89
Jamaica	90
Korea	77
Malaysia	70
Mauritius	66
Mexico	66
Morocco	84
Philippines	74
Taiwan	75
Tunisia	88

The report continues: "In most cases EPZ workers are also young. In Taiwan the average EPZ worker is 27 years old, while in Indonesia 78 percent are under age 25. In Jamaica, Mexico, the Dominican Republic, and Haiti, most women are also under age 25." The report then adds that some countries are losing EPZ employment to countries where labor costs are lower.[46]

The social, cultural, and psychic effects of this grand transformation of the world labor force must be put to one side. They would have to be revolutionary, in the sense that the lives of many people in many places will have been involuntarily and perhaps irretrievably changed; few will be able to live their lives as they customarily did. Without being an incurable romantic, seeking "the good old days" or a nostalgic return to simple living, any reasonable person would pause at the changes being made in the lives of so many people everywhere.

From a more limited perspective—mere business, economics, or law—the inescapable conclusions seems to be that there is an interest worldwide in using nonunion, young, female labor under conditions that maximize employer discretion. Second, the competition among the enterprise zones of differ-

[44]G. Schoepfle and J. Perez-Lopez, "Export Assembly Zones," *Journal of Interamerican Studies* 31 (1989), p. 131.

[45]U. S. Labor Department, op. cit., p. 6.

[46]Ibid., p. 6.

ent countries anchors wages, hours, and other terms and conditions of labor and may create in their work forces a group of permanent outcasts.

This competition among countries for assembly work undercuts the impulse of governments, regardless of any good-faith desire to conscientiously protect their citizens, to enact law, enforce stringent controls, or do anything else that will be contrary to the maintenance of a "good business climate." Legal limits being unavailable as a practical matter, the more ethereal realm of "corporate social responsibility" becomes the only, and, at best, modest limit on complete corporate discretion.

Questions and Comments

1. The class might begin with the list of countries included in the U.S. Labor Department survey and study the industrial systems of the countries mentioned in greater detail. Such study will eventually lead to processing zones and the role of international companies and governments in their operation.

2a. Would the repeal of the 807 provision eliminate the advantages of locating offshore for assembly?

b. Should high tariffs be assessed against the products from offshore assembly to cover the hidden costs associated with their establishment and maintenance?

c. Would high tariffs hurt working people in countries offering low-cost manufacturing?

3. When we see a "cheap shirt" at a shopping mall, should we add all of the costs that are not necessarily reflected in the ticket price?

4. The Congressional debate over the establishment of NAFTA replayed the debate that has surrounded 807 of the Tariff Law from its inception. The NAFTA debate was complicated by the fact that the treaty will have different effects on different socio-economic strata in Mexico, Canada, and the United States.

CONCLUSION

There are many variations on the theme of intersections between multinationals and other countries where they carry on business. Here some of them have been selected not out of a compulsion to cover all aspects of multinational history, but because early forms never completely die; they provide a checklist for the evaluation of contemporary relationships. The economy of the Philippines is still dominated by the United States and Japan, despite its independence. Honduras remains a country directly controlled by multinationals. Though sisal is no longer king in the Yucatan, indirect control systems like that which controlled the sisal trade still exist wherever countries have raw materials without production and distribution systems.

If no longer being made by OPEC countries, concessions are still made and honored by countries. The joint venture has become a principal vehicle for linking companies to companies and companies to countries in every economic sector, covering all phases of production and distribution. At present these extensive linkages encounter no consequential resistance from the legal orders of the United States and elsewhere.

Enterprise zones, promoted on the strength of their lack of legal restrictions and the abundant state subsidies that surround them, grow in number each day. A simple extension of the logic of the enterprise zone would be render the entire world an enterprise zone, an idea not far from the scope of the trade agreements already negotiated.

If one has only a very little time to make predictions about the industrial arrangements of the next century, a shortcut might be found in using the industrial processing zone as the future world political economy in embryo. The kind of order the world will keep or fail to keep might be found in the present-day processing zones.

Such a prediction suffers from all the infirmities of any simple projection of the present into the future—a risky practice. Who could have predicted at the end of the last century that the multinational corporation would emerge into a place of utter preeminence in a world economic order? But the projection is nevertheless worth at least passing attention.

CHAPTER 9

Elite Law Firms, Legal Ethics, and Multinational Litigation

Which comes first, the chicken or the egg? In law, do lawyers work according to legal systems, or is a major part of their work devoted to the creation and transformation of the legal systems themselves? If legal systems are lawyers' products rather than limits on what they do, then lawyers are the chickens laying the eggs, or the eggs from which the future chickens spring. From the standpoint of practical affairs it would make no difference. The philosophical question about chickens and eggs concerns *causes* rather than ongoing systems of chicken and egg production. A farmer who serenely gathers up eggs or methodically plucks chickens rightly says that the question of what causes what is academic.

So too with lawyers and legal systems: whether lawyers shape systems or systems shape lawyers can be put to one side, since the interaction occurs simultaneously in real lawyering and real legal systems. Once a legal system is underway, lawyers, and more particularly elite lawyers who practice in the largest firms, shape systems and also bring the behavior of their clients within, around, over, under, or away from systems that could limit the discretion of their clients. This flexibility in law work may be a revelation to those who believe that lawyers look up "the law," and "follow it," by recommending compliance with law to their clients. If plain reading, straightforward interpretation, and direct application of law are expected, that expectation will fail.

The common assumption of practice according to law departs from reality at all stages of elite law practice, as the following materials show in detail. But what makes the elite lawyer the most suitable focus when in terms of numbers they do not comprise more than eight percent of all lawyers? For a long time it has been observed that the best legal talent from the most prestigious law schools has been attracted to this single stratum of legal practice. As Karl Llewellyn once put it:

> . . . [M]ost legal energies have been expended on the furtherance of the business and financing side, from the angle of the enterpriser and the financier. It has been focused on organizing their control of others, and on blocking off control of them by others.[1]

[1]Quoted in J. Ladinsky, "Impact of Social Backgrounds of Lawyers on Law Practice and the Law," *Journal of Legal Education*, 16 (1963), p. 143.

He made a more consequential prophecy with greater implications now than when he made it in the late 1930s:

> . . . courts are made and shaped more by the character of the bar before them than by any other single factor. Courts over the long haul, tend in their standards and in their performance to fit the character of the bar with whom they deal.[2]

The elite lawyers make up in consequential work for the major industrial and financial multinationals what they lack in total numbers. Law practice on their behalf becomes the right place to assess the impact of multinationals and their lawyers upon courts and upon the law itself.

In Chapter 2, via the Iran hostage case, we got some feel for the educational and social origins of elite practitioners and the sometimes alarming assignments they get from their elite corporate clients. The lawyers representing the money center banks (all multinationals) virtually displaced the U. S. State Department of the United States as the principal spokespeople in the hostage negotiations. It was also noted earlier that the elite lawyers who circulate in the often ambiguous international realms are more accurately described as thinkers in an environment that blends the strictly legal with economic and political concerns. Even if one would balk at this sweeping definition of their work, and resist the idea that the legal domain is bounded only by what the clients of prestigious lawyers require, one would still be stunned by even a cursory inventory of the work of they do.

In Chapter 5 on corporations, we saw early and ongoing examples of lawyers shaping rule structures in which their clients could prosper. If corporate law presents an instance of using law *to facilitate* business planning, the field of antitrust law discussed in Chapter 6 presents one where lawyers once expended great energy and money *to prevent* unwanted regulatory control on size and market power. Those chapters demonstrated the two halves of elite law work: "organizing control" and "blocking off control by others."

A. THE STRUCTURE OF LITIGATION

The ins and outs of high-level legal work are not the easiest of subjects to make manageable for study. If the work were all that easy, more lawyers would do it at far lower fees. The plan here is to begin with an essay by Mark Galanter on the nature of legal practice and the way large and well-funded litigants have the advantage in law suits. This will be followed by a run-through of a case brought by an injured worker against a multinational corporation. The law firms in that lawsuit were not giants by law firm standards, but their tactics are representative of those of the largest law firms. A second excerpt from Galanter concerns lawyers, and other materials that follow will enlarge the discussion of elite lawyers, from their legal training to their post-graduate careers.

[2]Ibid., p. 143.

The *contested case* on which Galanter focuses is but one corner of legal representation, and, relatively speaking, a small one when compared to legal strategizing, shaping transactions, drawing documents, and other low-visibility, day-to-day, corporate legal work in "the office." And office work does not encompass the lawyer as go-between before legislatures or administrative agencies at the federal and state level of the United States or before foreign governments. To get a more realistic understanding of the professional rounds of the contemporary elite practitioner, one would need to extend Galanter's model to include other settings besides courts where elite lawyers advance the interests of their clients.

Galanter tells why the haves come out ahead in lawsuits. How they come out in other settings—legislative, regulatory-administrative settings and anywhere else where benefits or detriments may be imminent for the clients they represent—will be variations on the same themes that are found in litigation.

According to Galanter, the legal profession is highly stratified; this finding runs counter to the popular conception that all lawyers are alike. In the legal system as a whole there is a top-to-bottom ordering based on the *parties* to lawsuits, the *lawyers* who represent parties, on the ability to develop and use *rules of law*, and on the way *courts* process legal cases. Lawyers have status by the kind of clients they attract and keep.

The "haves" experience a greater probability of winning over the long run by adroitly exploiting all of these hierarchically ordered dimensions. Presenting the central findings of Galanter before reading his work heightens the suspense in learning just how it is that a system premised on equality before the law yields advantages that pervert the goal of equality. The last thing a party with an advantage wants is a fair fight.

WHY THE HAVES COME OUT AHEAD

Marc Galanter[3]

. . . For purposes of this analysis let us think of the legal system as composed of these elements:

RULES . . .

COURTS . . .

LAWYERS . . .

PARTIES . . .

It is a society in which actors with differing amounts of wealth and power are constantly in competitive or partially cooperative relationships in which they have opposing interests.

This society has a legal system in which a wide range of disputes and conflicts are settled by court-like agencies which purport to apply pre-existing general norms impartially (that is, unaffected by the identity of the parties).

The rules and procedures of these institutions are complex; wherever possible disputing parties employ specialized intermediaries in dealing with them.

[3]*Law and Society Review* (Fall 1974), pp. 95ff. Copyright © 1974 by the Law and Society Association; reprinted by permission.

The rules applied by the courts are in part worked out in the process of adjudication . . .

I. *Typology of Parties*

Most analyses of the legal system start at the rules end and work down through institutional facilities to see what effect the rules have on the parties. I would like to reverse that procedure and look through the other end of the telescope. Let's think about the different kinds of parties and the effect these differences might have on the way the system works.

Because of differences in their size, differences in the state of the law, and differences in their resources, some of the actors in the society have many occasions to utilize the courts . . . to make (or defend) claims; others do so only rarely. We might divide our actors into those claimants who have only occasional recourse to the courts (one-shotters or OS) and repeat players (RP) who are engaged in many similar litigations over time. The spouse in a divorce case, the auto injury claimant, the criminal accused are OSs; the insurance company, the prosecutor, the finance company are RPs . . . Typically the RP is a larger unit and the stakes in any given case are smaller (relative to total worth). OSs are usually smaller units and the stakes represented by the tangible outcome of the case may be high relative to total worth, as in the case of injury victim or the criminal accused). Or, the OS may suffer from the opposite problem; his claims may be so small and unmanageable . . . that the cost of enforcing them outruns any promise of benefit . . .

Let us refine our notion of the RP . . . We would expect an RP to play the litigation game differently from an OS. Let us consider some . . . advantages:

(1) RPs, having done it before, have advance intelligence; they are able to structure the next transaction and build a record. It is the RP who writes the form contract, requires the security deposit, and the like.

(2) RPs develop expertise and have ready access to specialists. They enjoy economies of scale and have low start up costs for any case.

(3) RPs have opportunities to develop facilitative informal relations with institutional incumbents.

(4) The RP must establish and maintain credibility as a combatant. His interest in his "bargaining reputation" serves as a resource . . . With no bargaining reputation to maintain the OS has more difficulty committing himself in bargaining.

(5) RPs can play the odds. The larger the matter at issue looms for OS, the more likely he is to adopt a minimax strategy (minimize the probability of maximum loss). Assuming these stakes are relatively smaller for RPs they can adopt strategies calculated to maximize gain over a long series of cases, even where this involves the risk of maximum loss in some cases.

(6) RPs can play for rules as well as immediate gains. First it pays an RP to expend resources in influencing the making of the relevant rules by such methods as lobbying . . .

(7) RPs can also play for rules in litigation itself, whereas an OS is unlikely to . . . [T]here is a difference in what they regard as a favorable outcome. Because his stakes in the immediate outcome are high and because by definition OS is unconcerned with the outcome of similar litigation in the future, OS will have little interest in that element of the outcome which might influence the disposition of the decision maker next time

around. For the RP, on the other hand, anything that will favorably influence the outcomes of future cases is a worthwhile result. The larger the stake for any player and the lower the probability of repeat play, the less likely that he will be concerned with the rules which govern future cases of the same kind. Consider two parents contesting the custody of their only child . . . On the other hand, the player with small stakes in the present case and the prospect of a series of similar cases . . . may be more interested in the state of the law.

Thus, if we analyze the outcomes of a case into a tangible component and a rule component, we may expect that in case 1 the OS will attempt to maximize tangible gain. But if RP is interested in maximizing his tangible gain in a series of cases 1 . . . *n*, he may be willing to trade off tangible gain in any one case for rule gain (or to minimize rule loss). We assumed that the institutional facilities for litigation were overloaded and settlements were prevalent. We would then expect RPs to "settle" cases where they expected unfavorable rule outcomes. Since they expect to litigate again, RPs can select to adjudicate (or appeal) those cases which they regard as most likely to produce favorable rules. On the other hand, OSs should be willing to trade off the possibility of making "good law" for tangible gain. Thus we would expect the body of "precedent" cases—that is, cases capable of influencing the outcome of future cases—to be relatively skewed toward those favorable to RP.

Of course it is not suggested that the strategic configuration of the parties is the sole or major determinant of rule development. Rule development is shaped by a relatively autonomous learned tradition, by the impingement of intellectual currents from outside, by the preferences and prudence of the decision makers. But courts are passive and these factors operate only when the process is triggered by parties. The point here is merely to note the superior opportunities of the RP to trigger promising cases and prevent the triggering of unpromising ones . . .

(8) RPs, by virtue of experience and expertise are more likely to be able to discern which rules are likely to "penetrate" and which are likely to remain merely symbolic commitments . . . They can trade off symbolic defeats for tangible gains.

(9) Since penetration depends in part on the resources of the parties (knowledge, attentiveness, expert services, money) RPs are more likely to be able to invest the matching resources necessary to secure the penetration of rules favorable to them.

It is not suggested that RPs are to be equated with "haves" (in terms of power, wealth, and status) or OSs with "have-nots." In the American setting most RPs are larger, richer, and more powerful than are most OSs . . .

We may think of litigation as typically involving various combinations of OSs and RPs. We can construct a matrix . . . with some well-known if approximate American examples. [See Figure 9-1.]

Box I: OS v. OS

The most numerous occupants of this box are divorces and insanity hearings. Most (over 90 percent of divorces, for example) are uncontested. A large portion of these are really pseudo-litigation, that is, a settlement is worked out between the parties and ratified in the guise of litigation. When we get real litigation in Box 1, it is often between parties who have some intimate tie with one another, fighting for some unsharable

FIGURE 9-1
A TAXONOMY OF LITIGATION BY STRATEGIC CONFIGURATION OF PARTIES

Defendant \ Initiator, Claimant	One-Shotter	Repeat Player
One-Shotter	Parent v. Parent (Custody) Spouse v. Spouse (Divorce) Family v. Family Member (Insanity Commitment) Family v. Family (Inheritance) Neighbor v. Neighbor Partner v. Partner **OS vs OS** **I**	Prosecutor v. Accused Finance Co. v. Debtor Landlord v. Tenant I.R.S. v. Taxpayer Condemnor v. Property Owner **RP vs OS** **II**
Repeat Player	Welfare Client v. Agency Auto Dealer v. Manufacturer Injury Victim v. Insurance Company Tenant v. Landlord Bankrupt Consumer v. Creditors Defamed v. Publisher **OS vs RP** **III**	Union v. Company Movie Distributor v. Censorship Board Developer v. Suburban Municipality Purchaser v. Supplier Regulatory Agency v. Firms of Regulated Industry **RP vs RP** **IV**

good . . . The law is invoked *ad hoc* [only for the moment. —Ed.] There is a strong interest in vindication, but neither party is likely to have much interest in the long term state of the law . . . There are few appeals, few test cases, little expenditure of resources on rule-development . . .

Box II: RP v. OS

The great bulk of litigation is found in this box—indeed every really numerous kind except personal injury cases, insanity hearings, and divorces. The law is used for routine processing of claims by parties for whom the making of such claims is a regular business activity . . . The state of the law is of interest to the RP, though not to the OS defendants . . .

Box III: OS v. RP

All of these rather infrequent types, except for personal injury cases which are distinctive in that free entry to the arena is provided by the contingent fee [The lawyer on contingent fee agrees to take fees from a financial recovery and to forego them if the case is unsuccessful. —Ed.] . . . The OS claimant generally has little interest in the state of the law; the RP defendant, however, is greatly interested.

Box IV: RP v. RP

Let us consider the general case and then several special cases. We might expect that there would be very little litigation in Box IV because to the extent that RPs play with each other repeatedly, the expectation of continued mutually beneficial interaction would give rise to informal bilateral controls . . . Units with mutually beneficial relationships do not adjust their differences in court. Where they rely on third parties in dispute resolution it is likely to take a form (such as arbitration . . .) detached from official sanctions . . .

However there are several special cases. First there are those RPs who seek not furtherance of tangible interests, but vindication of fundamental cultural commitments. (An example . . . organizations which sponsor much church–state litigation). . .

Second, government is a special kind of RP. Informal controls depend upon the ultimate sanction of withdrawal and refusal to continue beneficial relations. To the extent that withdrawal of future association is not possible in dealing with government, the scope of formal controls is correspondingly limited. The development of informal relations between regulatory agencies and regulated firms is well-known. And the regulated may have sanctions other than withdrawal which they can apply; for instance, they may threaten political opposition . . . [G]overnment parties may be more willing to externalize decisions to the courts. And opponents may have more incentive to litigate against government in the hope of securing a shift in its goals.

A somewhat different kind of special case is present where plaintiff and defendant are both RPs but do not deal with each other repeatedly . . .

Where there is litigation in the RP v. RP situation we might expect that there would be heavy expenditure on rule-development, many appeals and rapid and elaborate development of the doctrinal law . . . Litigation appears when the relationship loses its future value; when its "monopolistic" character deprives informal controls of sufficient leverage and the parties invoke outside allies to modify it; and when the parties seek to vindicate conflicting values . . .

Comments and Questions

1. Galanter provides a way of classifying all types of lawsuits, from those in the fictional People's Court on television to the hospital trying to collect an unpaid bill, to the government bringing criminal charges, to the government suing a company for antitrust violations, to giant multinational corporations fighting one another. Use his table of litigation to classify the foregoing disputes. How would each type of dispute differ?
2. In this text we are concerned with multinational corporations. If Galanter is right, we can expect that multinationals will be markedly advantaged in litigation, since they are no strangers to the legal system and have the financial and nonfinancial resources to improve their chances of winning, including but not limited to lawyers. Run down the list of advantages which he argues that the regular participants in litigation have. The following cases and the cases throughout the text can be studied with reference to his classifications.
3. People who are unschooled in law might think that it would be most important for a lawyer to understand the rules of law. What important modification would Galanter make to this commonplace assumption? He says that he is looking through the opposite end of a tele-

scope. What does he see from this odd vantage point? If he turned the telescope around, what would he see? It remains to be seen which end imparts the more accurate image of law as it is practiced.

We are now ready to try our learning out on a case. The case is simple enough on its facts, but complex as it procedurally unfolds. A person working on a barge off the coast of Africa was injured. Upon his return home to the United States he brought suit against his employer, a multinational corporation, charging negligence that resulted in his injuries. Hang onto your chairs as complexities pile up in the case, and try to bear with the case through to the end. The snarls will eventually be combed through, and offer a good test of Galanter's theory.

POWELL V. MCDERMOTT INTERNATIONAL, INC. 588 SO.2D 84 (LA., 1991)

Marcus, Justice

The issue in this case is whether foreign law or American law governs in a personal injury suit arising from an accident on the high seas.

In August of 1982, Clinton Powell was injured while working aboard the Derrick Barge 14 . . . on the high seas off the West African Coast. Powell is a citizen of the United States. He was hired by McDermott International, Inc. to serve as a barge foreman in the West Africa area pursuant to an employment contract executed at McDermott International's corporate offices in New Orleans, Louisiana. At the time of the accident, the D/B 14 was operated by McDermott International. McDermott International is a foreign corporation chartered and based in Panama; however, at the time of the injury, it was a wholly-owned subsidiary of McDermott, Inc., a Delaware corporation. The executive corporate offices of both McDermott International and McDermott Inc. are located at 1010 Common Street in New Orleans. Additionally the D/B 14 is registered in Panama and flies the Panamanian flag.

Following the accident, McDermott International arranged for Powell to be transported to this country for treatment at Ochsner Hospital in Jefferson Parish, Louisiana. During his stay, McDermott International paid maintenance and cure pursuant to the laws of the United States [maintenance and cure is a right under admiralty law, which provides compensation for an injured seaman without regard to fault—Ed.] After treatment, he again signed on with McDermott International in September of 1983 for continued work in the West Africa area. He was re-injured in October of 1983 while working in a heavy machinery yard in Nigeria and again went to Ochsner Hospital for treatment. Maintenance and cure payments were reinstated and continued until they were terminated in January, 1989, when McDermott International learned from Powell's treating doctor that Powell had reached maximum cure.

Powell filed suit against McDermott International in [a state court of Louisiana] under the Jones Act and the general maritime laws of the United States [these are national laws providing for recoveries in cases of negligence—ed.] McDermott International . . . assert[ed] that Panamanian law governed Powell's claims. The trial court . . . [held] that Panamanian law governed the case, not the Jones Act or general maritime law. Subsequently, the trial court issued [an order] stating that it did not intend to dismiss the suit, but rather to try it under the law of Panama. Powell [appealed] arguing that the Jones Act and general maritime law governed his claim. The court of appeal denied [his appeal] . . . Upon Powell's application to this court we granted [his appeal] and remanded the case to the court of appeal [La. has two appeal court levels —Ed.] . . . On remand, the court of appeal affirmed the trial court's ruling and held that the law of Panama governed Powell's claim. Upon Powell's application, we granted a writ . . . to review the correctness of that decision.

The sole issue for our determination is whether Powell's claim is governed by the laws of Panama or the laws of the United States.

At the outset we note that this court is governed by federal substantive admiralty law . . . At the time of Powell's accident [United States Code—the Jones Act—Ed.] . . . provided that "any seaman who shall suffer personal injury in the course of his employment may, at his election, maintain an action for damages . . ." Up until the Supreme Court decision in *Lauritzen* v. *Larson* . . . (1953) it was unclear whether this act applied to any seaman, regardless of his nationality, injured in the course of his employment. In Lauritzen, a Danish seaman was injured while aboard a Danish vessel in Havana, Cuba. The vessel, registered in Denmark, was owned by a Danish citizen. The seaman filed suit in New York, asserting that the Jones Act governed his claim. His only connection to the United States was that his employment contract was executed in New York. The Court held that the Jones Act did not apply . . . [T]he Supreme Court ultimately concluded that Congress did not intend for the Jones Act to apply in every case where a seaman, regardless of his nationality, was injured.

The Court recognized several traditional choice of law factors that would determine whether American or foreign law would apply in a case where both the United States and a foreign nation could claim some connecting factor to a maritime tort suit. These factors include place of the wrongful act, law of the flag, allegiance or domicile of the injured party, allegiance or domicile of the defendant shipowner, place of contract, inaccessibility of the foreign forum [court—ed.] and the law of the forum [the law of the place where the suit is brought—Ed.] . . . The Supreme Court in . . . *Rhoditis* (1970) added the base of operations of the shipowner as an additional factor. In Rhoditis, the Court stated:

[T]he decisional process of arriving at a conclusion on the subject of the application of the Jones Act involves the ascertainment of the facts or groups of facts which constitute contacts between the transaction involved in the case and the United States, and then deciding whether or not they are substantial. Thus, each factor is to be "weighed" and "evaluated" only to the end that, after each factor has been given consideration, a rational and satisfactory conclusion can be arrived at on the question of whether the factors present add up to the necessary substantiality. Moreover, each factor, or contact, or group of facts must be tested in light of the underlying objective which is to effectuate the liberal purposes of the Jones Act . . .

The *Lauritzen–Rhoditis* test is not a mechanical one; moreover, the list of factors is not exhaustive . . . Not all of the factors are treated equally, some factors carry greater weight than others. The law of the flag (meaning the country where a vessel is registered) is perhaps the most important factor because it "is deemed to be a part of the territory of that sovereignty (whose flag it flies), and not to lose that character when in navigable waters within the territorial limits of another sovereignty." However, *Lauritzen* does not stand for the proposition that the law of the flag controls in every instance. The flag overbears most other connecting events in determining applicable law "unless some heavy counterweight appears"...

The allegiance or domicile of the injured plaintiff, especially if an American on a foreign-flagged vessel has been considered an important "counterweight" to the law of the flag . . . In the instant case, Powell was an American citizen who resided in Alabama. Furthermore every member of the crew working on the D/B 14 when Powell was injured was an American citizen. Powell was compensated with American currency; McDermott International deposited his paychecks in an American bank. His retirement plans were handled by McDermott, Inc., an American corporation. When Powell was injured, both times he was transported to the United States for medical treatment, and both times he was paid maintenance and cure under federal maritime law. Additionally, Powell's contract with McDermott International was executed in the United States in . . . the corporate offices in New Orleans.

Another important factor is the allegiance (domicile) of the defendant shipowner. The Supreme Court in *Lauritzen* stated:

> But it is common knowledge that in recent years a practice has grown, particularly among American shipowners, to avoid the stringent shipping laws by seeking foreign registration eagerly offered by some countries. Confronted with such operations our courts on occasion have pressed beyond the formalities of more or less nominal foreign registration to enforce against American shipowners the obligations which our law places on them . . .

The courts have often disregarded a nominal foreign registration or a "flag of convenience" in maritime tort cases . . . Additionally, the courts are reluctant to recognize the importance of the flag where a shipowner inserts an additional nominal foreign corporation between the flag and the true beneficial ownership of the vessel . . . McDermott International is a foreign corporation, organized and chartered under the laws of Panama. The D/B 14 is a Panamanian vessel, flying the Panamanian flag, and registered under the laws of Panama. However, at the time of the accident, McDermott International was a wholly owned subsidiary of McDermott, Inc. Many of the corporate officers held identical roles in both corporations. The shareholders of McDermott, Inc. were primarily American citizens. The stockholders meetings were regularly held in New Orleans. The principal executive offices are located in . . . New Orleans; whereas McDermott International's offices in Panama measured only one thousand square feet and employed 3–5 employees. Moreover the office in Panama did not exercise any control over the operations . . . in fact D/B 14 has never worked the waters of Panama; the base of operations . . . was Nigeria . . . The D/B 14 was constructed in Amelia, Louisiana, presumably according to American standards. Following a brief stint in U.S. waters, the vessel was transported to the East Atlantic ocean off the coast of Africa where it has remained ever since.

We have evaluated those factors relevant to the case; namely the allegiance of the injured plaintiff, the allegiance of the defendant shipowner, the place of contracting, and the law of the flag. The remaining factors need not be discussed in detail . . .

CONCLUSION

While the D/B 14 was registered and flagged in Panama, and owned by a Panamanian corporation, we do not find that these facts are controlling here because of the substantial contacts with the United States. Powell was an American citizen who executed his employment contract with McDermott International in the United States. McDermott International, although a Panamanian corporation was wholly owned by McDermott Inc., an American corporation. The executive corporate offices of both McDermott Inc. and McDermott International are located at 1010 Common Street in New Orleans. The D/B 14, an American built vessel, was stationed off the coast of West Africa and had never been in Panamanian waters. Additionally, McDermott International's office in Panama . . . never exercised any control . . . Clearly these factors are strong counterweights to the law of the flag . . . Therefore we conclude that the law of the United States, not that of Panama, should govern in this case . . . [T]he case is remanded to the district court for further proceedings . . .

Questions

1. Did the "haves" (the McDermott corporations) come out ahead? Who won the case?

2a. Galanter contends that the advantages of a repeat player start well before a case is ever brought. Which party to this case had advantages traceable to "the law" applicable to *choice of law* questions in international tort claims? Is the prior law generally advantageous to claimants like Powell or to defendants like McDermott?

b. Galanter also says that repeat players structure their affairs in advance to improve their chances of succeeding if trouble later arises. What evidence of prelitigation structuring do you see on the part of McDermott to limit the corporation's exposure to liability for tort claims arising from their international operations?

3. Galanter also contends that rules of procedure and tactics can eat up substantive rules of law, that is, fussiness about the right time, place, and manner of bringing lawsuits, can displace concerns about coming to a proper result—in this case the determination of responsibility for safety and assessing harms done. Do you find his prediction present or absent in the Powell case?

4. The problem of choosing what law governs involves *at least* eight factors or "contacts" as outlined in the *Lauritzen* and *Rhoditis* cases. If each of the eight factors can be present or absent, entitled to no special weight, and influential by itself or in combination with other factors, then the possible combinations in a choice of law case is 2 to the eighth power, or 256.

Who benefits in litigation with the foregoing myriad possibilities for legal argument and evidence?

Another rule of law rule compounds the possible combinations, if that is imaginable. An appeal court is not necessarily bound by what a trial court has concluded to be the most appropriate law to apply. The appeal court can evaluate the eight factors for itself. Applying this rule, the number of combinations is 2 to the eighth power again!

Who benefits from the rule that permits a reconsideration of the choice of law factors on appeal?

5. The plaintiff has been in the Louisiana courts five times so far. Where does his case now stand? Compare question 1, above.
6. In a footnote to the case, the court reports that the once *parent* corporation of McDermott Inc. had become the *subsidiary* of the McDermott International of Panama. (During the suit, parent and subsidiary changed legal places.) What might be the purpose of this change in the corporate structure?
7. Galanter states that repeat players will use their experience in litigation to plan for the future. Imagine yourself as an advocate for a company with an international business comparable to Mc Dermott. How would you use the decision in the *Powell* case in guiding your client's future affairs?
8. What would impel McDermott International to resist settlement of this injury case? The numerous trips to court cost the corporation as well as the plaintiff, and we might wonder what could be motivating them.

9a. The *Powell* case is not an unusual one in the field of multinationals; multinationals by definition operate across national lines and hence across the lines of legal systems. There are always at least two sets of laws that might be applicable to conflicts involving multinationals and sometimes there are more than two, as there could have been here if the accident had occurred in Nigerian waters. The multiple systems of law, domestic and international, are the subject of the next chapter.

10. Later in his article, Galanter noted additional pressure on the non-RP in litigation that is traceable to most court's having more cases than they can handle:

    "(a) . . . delay

    (b) . . . raising the cost of keeping the case alive . . ."

While it may be generally assumed that delay and costs are neutral—both parties want cases to be brought to an end as quickly and as cheaply as possible—Galanter wants us to pause and look more deeply at the differential impacts of time and expense. Are these factors neutral, or do they impose more burdens on one party to litigation than another?

b. The questions can be raised about *complexity*. One might think that both parties to a lawsuit have a common interest in keeping matters as simple and clear as possible to expedite decisions. But is complexity neutral? Does one party tend to benefit more from complexity than others? If one party benefits from complexity, will there be a universal desire to eliminate it? Should courts do anything about this?

11. Where do legal ethics fit in? What legal outcomes are lawyers duty bound to try to obtain? What limits are there in arguing a case for a client? Use the *Powell* case as a basis for discussion about legal ethics, legal systems, and zealous advocacy.

WHY THE HAVES COME OUT AHEAD (CONTINUED)

Marc Galanter,[4]

LAWYERS

What happens when we introduce lawyers? Parties who have lawyers do better. Lawyers are themselves RPs. Does their presence equalize the parties, dispelling the advantage of the RP client? Or does the existence of lawyers amplify the advantage of the RP client? We might assume that RPs . . . who can buy legal services more steadily, in larger quantities, in bulk (by retainer) and at higher rates, would get services of better quality . . . Not only would the RP get more talent to begin with, but he would on the whole get greater continuity, better record-keeping, more anticipatory or preventative work, more experience and specialized skill . . . more control over counsel.

One would expect . . . RP advantage would be related to the way in which the profession was organized . . . The more close and enduring the lawyer–client relationship, the more the primary loyalty of lawyers is to clients rather than to courts or guild, the more telling the advantages of accumulated expertise and guidance . . . [Galanter notes that lawyers have multiple allegiances: to clients, to courts or other institutions committed to promoting systemic justice, and to the profession itself. These mixed allegiances could take lawyers away from no-holds-barred advocacy for clients. Yet, as one moves up the hierarchy of careers–prestige, Galanter contends that lawyers look more exclusively after the interests of their clients.—Ed.]

What about the specialization of the bar? Might we not expect the existence of specialization to offset RP advantages . . . ? We may divide specialists [See Figure 9-2.] into (1) those specialized by field of law (patent, divorce, etc.), (2) those specialized by the kind of party represented (for example, house counsel [lawyers on the payroll of businesses—Ed.]) and (3) those specialized by field of law and "side" or party (personal injury plaintiff, criminal defense, labor). Divorce lawyers do not specialize in husbands or wives, nor real-estate lawyers in buyers or sellers. But labor lawyers . . . do specialize not only by the field of law but in representing one side. Such specialists may represent RPs or OSs.

[4]Ibid., pp. 114 ff.

FIGURE 9-2
A TYPOLOGY OF LEGAL SPECIALISTS

Client	Lawyer: **Specialized by Party**	**Specialized by Field and Party**	**Specialized by Field**
RP	"House Counsel" or General Counsel for Bank, Insurance Co. etc. Corporation Counsel for Government Unit	Prosecutor Personal Injury Defendant Staff Counsel for NAACP Tax Labor/Management Collections	Patent
OS	"Poverty Lawyers" Legal Aid	Criminal Defense Personal Injury Plaintiff	Bankruptcy Divorce

Most specializations cater to the needs of particular kinds of RPs. Those specialists who service OSs have some distinctive features:

First, they tend to make up the "lower echelons" of the legal profession. Compared to the lawyers who provide services to RPs, lawyers in these specialties tend to be drawn from lower socioeconomic origins, to have attended local, proprietary, or part-time law schools, to practice alone rather than in large firms, and to possess low prestige within the profession (of course the correlation is far from perfect; some lawyers who represent OSs do not have these characteristics and some representing RPs do. However, on the whole the difference in professional standing is massive).

Second, specialists who service OSs tend to have problems of mobilizing a clientele . . .

Third, the episodic and isolated nature of the relationship with particular OS clients tends to elicit a stereotyped and uncreative brand of legal services . . .

Fourth, while they are themselves RPs, these specialists have problems in developing optimizing strategies . . .

For the lawyer who services OSs with his transient clientele, his permanent "client" is the forum, the opposite party, or the intermediary who supplies clients. Consider . . . the dependence of the criminal defense lawyer on maintaining cooperative relations with . . . the "criminal court community". . .

The existence of a specialized bar on the OS side should overcome the gap . . . [b]ut this is short of overcoming the fundamental strategic advantages of RPs . . .

We arrive at Figure 9-3 which summarizes why the haves come out ahead . . .

Questions and Comments

1. Reread the *Powell* case. How would the lawyers for Powell and McDermott be fitted into the classifications of lawyers by Galanter? Does it look like one or the other side was especially advantaged in the lawsuit, or do the two lawyers look about even?

FIGURE 9-3
WHY THE "HAVES" TEND TO COME OUT AHEAD

Element	Advantages	Enjoyed by
PARTIES	— ability to structure transaction — specialized expertise. economies of scale — long-term strategy — ability to play for rules — bargaining credibility — ability to invest in penetration	— repeat players large, professional
LEGAL SERVICES	— skill, specialization continuity	— organized professional wealthy
INSTITUTIONAL FACILITIES	— passivity — cost and delay barriers	— wealthy, experienced, organized — holders, possessors — beneficiaries of existing rules
	—favorable priorities	— organized, attentive
RULES	— favorable rules	— older, culturally dominant
	— due process barriers	— holders, possessors

2. Would the pressures on Powell's lawyer be different from those on the lawyers for McDermott?
3. Is it likely that the lawyer for Powell will care about the rules regarding choice of law so long as the case at hand is not dismissed? Are there longer-term interests that can be identified for McDermott or their insurers that transcend the particular case?
4. Some of the elements contributing to the lower status of some lawyers have changed since Galanter first wrote, for example, solos are now in small firms, but the substance of Galanter's characterization of lawyers still holds.
5. Martindale–Hubbell, a directory for lawyers, shows that the lawyer for Powell, William Rutledge, is a member of a 13-lawyer firm specializing in plaintiff's claims for "maritime personal injury, general personal injury, and products liability law." Vance Ellefson, the lawyer for McDermott, is in a nine-person firm that has a number of insurance companies as clients as well as McDermott.

B. THE ETHICS OF ADVOCACY

Lawyers generally do not care two straws if a drug addict in a vomit-stained shirt goes to jail for knocking off a package store. There is much lawyer posturing to the contrary, and it is true that the ethics of advocacy are most visible in the criminal context. When a lawyer is asked, "Would you be able to defend someone whom you know is guilty?" the lawyer will usually reply, "Of course," adding, "Everyone is entitled to representation."

Better reasons for the enthusiastic support of the right of every person *or group* to have aggressive legal representation will be found outside the criminal law. Entitlement to a well-argued case comes much closer to the representation of advantaged clients than to the representation of "common criminals."

Can you defend a corporation that you know has polluted Lake Erie? That marketed an intrauterine device for birth control, knowing that its use was dangerous? That continued manufacturing or installing asbestos, knowing its dangerous effects? The latter questions would take the inquiry toward the largest corporations and the domain of elite lawyers practicing in the largest firms. They are better questions to ask about professional ethics, but they are rarely asked.

How does one expose the sources and core tenets of legal ethics? A first stop would seem to be the law school. Most beginning law students, while perhaps having dreams of more power, prestige, or income, of the options that more schooling might create, or, in rarer cases, of a greater capacity to "help," have no clear idea of the ethics of the profession, aside from the fragments picked up from popularizations of professional life on television or in newspapers. It is during the course of their professional study that they will learn what the law school values, what the legal profession values, and what careers in law are preferred and create "success."

This is not to say that the curriculum in professional education formally includes these themes in explicit courses. This learning, like other learning that has the most telling effects, is part of a subterranean curriculum. One wonders why the questions that need to be exposed, discussed, and made as clear as possible are relegated to the intuitive realm or are "extracurricular." It could be that talking about them is like talking about air breathed, or the chemistry of dirt. The ideas may be so basic and generic that they become part of "an understanding" that can be "felt," and "known," but not readily articulated.

The second stop is law practice. The ethics of the profession can be teased out of the relationship of lawyers to clients: do lawyers maintain an independent moral stance based on their membership in the profession of law, their duty to courts and other settings where they practice, and their commitment to the pursuit of the public good, democracy, and justice? Or do lawyers uncritically accept the values of their clients? The latter role for lawyers causes the least emotional bother, since almost any activity can be rationalized as ethical when a lawyer simply "represents" another and stays at least one step removed from choice. The former role—lawyer as moral actor— requires soul searching; the latter role—lawyer as advocate—requires doing a competent job.

The homespun question about defending "the guilty" criminal cuts across all of the foregoing conflicting duties, and also whether the lawyer is a merely a mouthpiece or *personally* accountable. Beyond this useful function of raising all of the important questions about the ethics of advocacy, the most common question about criminal representation obscures more about law practice than it reveals, as we shall see.

At the "highest" level of law practice, far away from rapes, armed robbery, and murder, there has been relatively little ethical scrutiny. Camus once observed that having wealth and power grants immunity from judgment, even where "silk hides eczema." Camus's wisdom applies to law and lawyering. Galanter has told that us that the legal profession is stratified according to the kind of clients lawyers can get and keep. The more large businesses, on retainer, in consequential commercial transactions, the higher the lawyer's place in the power and wealth hierarchy of the profession. In addition, the further away from criminal law, family law, and personal injury law—the areas of practice accessible to "public" knowledge—the less a lawyer's work will be subjected to outside scrutiny.

Concern about legal ethics is therefore as socially stratified as the practice of law itself. When one hears the word "shyster," thoughts run to the bottom of the status hierarchy of the legal profession. At the "lowest end" of practice, lawyers must crawl for crumbs falling from the legal table and in doing so cannot always be genteel. This is the realm of the "ambulance chasers," or the criminal lawyer in the bad suit who needs the bailbondsman to bring business. That this stratum has borne most of the criticism can be proved by the inability to come up with unkind remarks that apply to a lawyer on Wall Street. Average people don't know what Wall Street lawyers do, and have no pet words for them. Wall Street lawyers seem to get the benefit of the ethical doubt. When an undergraduate states as a career aspiration "corporate law," the notion of the lawyer as unscrupulous shark seems to fall away. Perhaps fear and awe take its place.

There are ways to bring professional values as found in schooling and practice into visibility. A few authors have articulated the values dilemmas that they found in their legal education. Turow's account of his first year at Harvard (*One L*) is one such effort; portions of Patricia Williams's *The Alchemy of Race and Rights* is another, and the author's own record of his experience as a beginning student is still another. And on rare occasions, law school professors have assisted, by putting into words what usually goes without saying.

Law School and Ethical Training

Law students seem to be much happier about getting into law school than they are about staying there any longer than they absolutely must. The typical student may go from fear in the first year to sullen boredom in the second and third year. Turow defined upper-class law students as "stoic," "frozen," "alienated," and "cowed."[5] They grimly bear up, assuming a tired austerity, and notch sticks to record the time served on their three-year sentence.

The fear of the first year can be traced to learning to think like a lawyer, a taxing assignment that mixes the case method of study and adjusting to the socratic method of teaching. The learning requires long days and nights poring over legalisms, and adjusting to the classroom method—the everyday prospect of being made an utter fool in front of a hundred people.

The troubles with law school are usually put in terms of the "unbelievable workload" and classroom terror. The troubles are rarely put in terms of the values that students are being asked get rid of or to embrace, or the unwillingness of many students to wholeheartedly accept some of what is said to be necessary for effective lawyering—for example, aggressiveness, meanness, and even ruthlessness. Although virtually never squarely faced, these difficulties could be a major part of the decline of enthusiasm students feel once the warm glow of being admitted to a school and the excitement of getting started in a new field have worn off.

In his book about Harvard, Turow records the value tensions in beginning students at Harvard:

> . . . [T]here was a subtler difficulty in our education, one which went to the basis of legal thinking itself . . . We were learning more than a process of analysis or a set of rules. In our discussion, with the professors, as they questioned us and picked at what we said, we were also being tacitly instructed in the strategies of legal argument, in putting what had been analyzed back together in a way that would make our contentions persuasive to a court. We all quickly saw that that kind of argument was supposed to be reasoned, consistent, progressive in its logic. Nothing was taken for granted; nothing was proven just because it was strongly felt. All of our teachers tried to impress upon us that you do not sway a judge with emotional declarations of faith [one teacher referred to these responses as "sentimental goo]."
>
> "Why," [another teacher] asked one day, "is the right to bargain and form contracts granted to all adults, rather than a select group within the society?"
>
> "Because that was fundamental," one student suggested, "basic: all persons are created equal."
>
> "Oh *are* they?" [the teacher] asked. "Did you create them, Mr. Vivian? Have you taken a survey?"
>
> "I believe it," Vivian answered.
>
> "Well hooray . . . that proves a great deal. How do you *justify* that, Mr. Vivian? . . ."

[5]S. Turow, *One L* (New York: Penguin, 1977), p. 67.

Many of the deepest beliefs often seem inarticulable in their foundations . . . I thought, for example, that wealth should be widely distributed, but there were many instances in class which involved taking from the poor, for whom I felt that property rights should be regarded as absolute.

Yet, with relative speed, we all seemed to gain skill in reconciling and justifying our positions . . .

[In] a class debate on various schemes for regulating prostitution . . . I noticed the differences in the style of argument from similar sessions we'd had earlier in the year. Students now spoke about crime statistics and patterns of violence . . . They pointed to evidence, and avoided emotional appeals and arguments based on the depths and duration of their feelings.

But to Gina the process that had brought that kind of change about was frightening and objectionable.

"I don't care if [the teacher] doesn't want to know how I *feel* about prostitution . . . I *feel* a lot of things about prostitution and they have everything to do with how I *think* about prostitution. I don't want to become the kind of person who tries to pretend that my feelings have nothing to do with my opinions . . ."

I heard similar comments, all to the effect that they were being limited, harmed, by the education, forced to substitute dry reason for emotion, to cultivate opinions that were "rational" but which had no roots in the experience, the life they'd had before. They were being cut off from themselves . . .

"Legal thinking is nasty," I said to Gina . . . thinking like a lawyer involved being suspicious and distrustful. You reevaluated statements, inferred from silences, looked for loopholes and ambiguities. You did everything but take a statement at face value . . .[6]

It might have been simpler for Turow and others if the training regime had consistency in abiding disbelief. This would have made going to law school analogous to an abused child's learning the structure of abuse; when the behavior of an abusive parent follows a pattern, the child can minimize the occasions of violence. However, according to Turow, the law school required uncritical acceptance of wild beliefs—such as a business being a person—*while at the same time* it demanded that nothing ought to be uncritically accepted. Given contradictions like the foregoing, the law student can devise no sensible way to minimize the harmful intrusions of the training regime upon personal values. Resolution of the conflict may be reached in a dangerous way: no idea of anyone is worth anything; no lasting sense can be made of anything.

A few more accounts of the value tensions can be recorded to see whether Turow is alone. Patricia Williams, who also writes about Harvard, recalls:

[6]Ibid., pp.93.

> My abiding recollection of being a student at Harvard Law School is the sense of being invisible. I spent three years wandering in a murk of unreality. I observed large, mostly male bodies assert themselves against one another like football players caught in a gauzy mist of intellectual slow motion. I stood my ground amid them, watching them deflect from me, unconsciously, politely, as if I were a pillar in a crowded corridor. Law school for me was like another planet, full of alienated creatures with whom I could make little connection. The school created a dense atmosphere that muted my voice to inaudibility. All I could do to communicate my existence was to posit carefully worded messages into hermetically-sealed, vacuum-packed blue books, place them on the waves of that foreign sea, and pray that they would be plucked up by some curious seeker and understood.[7]

Women studying at Yale Law School in the mid-1980s reported four levels of alienation: "from themselves, from the law school community, from the classroom, and from the content of legal education."[8]

The author of this text attended the University of Chicago in the late 1950s. Still trying to make sense of the experience, I wrote in 1973:

> "Most lawyers have at some point felt themselves to be at the edge of law. In my own case since my entry into law school was more a matter of chance than design and my post-law school activity somewhat deviant, I wonder if I ever entered the realm of law more than provisionally. As a neophyte in law school I was reluctant to subject myself to legal ways of thought—although the full implications of this reluctance were admittedly only dimly perceived. I can recall my first impressions of the early cases; most seemed to be unjustly decided; law seemed to be overly technical and neglectful of matters of substance. Most importantly, the ways of thought and the content of the thought in law seemed destructive of what I had developed prior to law school, and I often wondered about the value of the "law school experience."
>
> "But the tug of law school, as reinforced by family, friends, and classmates, is very strong and what I now look upon as a healthy distrust of law ways withered in the boot camp atmosphere that is law school. I continued with study, explaining my fundamental doubts as a kind of personal lunacy . . .[9]

On rare occasions law school professors have explored the values on which legal education is premised. Instead of regarding the transformation as necessary, or a necessary evil, they sometimes inventory the out and out losses that go with professional training. One such essay is by Roger Cramton, entitled the "The Ordinary Religion of the Law School Classroom," so named because the law school does espouse beliefs that approach the orthodoxies of religion, even though law schools usually see themselves as secular places where training and not indoctrination is the rule of the day.

[7]Patricia Williams, *The Alchemy of Race and Rights* (Cambridge: Harvard, 1991), p. 55.

[8]C. Weiss and L. Melling, "Legal Education of Twenty Women," *Stanford Law Review* 40 (1988), p. 1299.

[9]J. Bonsignore, "At the Edge of Law," *American Business Law Journal* 11 (1973), p. 11.

THE ORDINARY RELIGION OF THE LAW SCHOOL CLASSROOM[10]

Roger Cramton

A sophisticated observer of the typical classroom in most American law schools would hear a variety of views, and see many differing methods. But he could also detect certain fundamental value assumptions unconsciously presupposed by most faculty and student participants. This intellectual framework is almost never openly articulated . . .

The "ordinary religion . . ." serves as a shorthand expression for this value system. It includes . . . the unarticulated value assumptions communicated to the students by example or by teaching methods, by what is *not* taught, and by the student culture of law schools.

The essential ingredients of the ordinary religion . . . are: a skeptical attitude toward generalizations; an instrumental approach to law and lawyering; a "tough-minded" and analytical attitude toward legal tasks and professional roles; and a faith that man, by the application of his reason and the use of the democratic processes, can make the world a better place . . .

A SKEPTICAL ATTITUDE TOWARD GENERALIZATIONS, PRINCIPLES AND RECEIVED WISDOM

. . . [T]he foremost task of legal education is to inculcate a skeptical attitude toward principles, concepts and rules. When the universe is looked at honestly, without the preconceptions that emanate from childish yearnings for security, it is apparent that "concepts" and "interpretations" and "methodological premises" are simply our man-made, custom-built tools for organizing facts . . .

Since it is apparent that people differ in the values they hold and that there is no rational way to resolve these differences, a practical person will not waste time worrying about unanswerable questions. In short the good lawyer develops a skeptical attitude . . .

AN INSTRUMENTAL APPROACH TO LAW AND LAWYERING

A second basic feature . . . is that . . . law is instrumental only, a means to an end, and is to be appraised only in light of the ends it achieves . . .

Since the lawyer is engaged in the implementation of the values of others—a client, or a government agency or the general society—he need not be concerned directly with value questions. His primary task is that of the craftsman or skilled technician who can work out the means by which the client or the society can achieve its goals. He should concern himself with the choice of means, and the relationship of means to ends, not to the choice of ends . . .

A "TOUGH MINDED" AND ANALYTICAL ATTITUDE . . .

. . . The law teacher must stress cognitive rationality along with "hard" facts and "cold" logic and "concrete" realities. Emotion, imagination, a sense of wonder or awe at the inexplicable—these soft and mushy domains of the "tender-minded" are off limits for law students and lawyers.

Two models of professional behavior are presented to law students: the "hired

[10]*Journal of Legal Education* 29 (1978), p. 247.

gun" and the "social engineer." The former is the skilled craftsman of the discrete controversy, while the latter is the technician and applied scientist of the use of legal tools for broader social change. Both are technicians in the dispassionate use of legal skills . . .

A FAITH THAT MAN BY THE APPLICATION OF HIS REASON AND THE USE OF DEMOCRATIC PROCESS CAN MAKE THE WORLD BETTER

. . . In a pluralistic and tolerant society it is impossible to expect that individuals or groups will agree about many basic values. What we do agree on is a mechanism for handling social conflict and resolving disputes ... representative democracy to establish priorities ... an independent judiciary to adjudicate particular disputes . . .

If we use our heads and follow these . . . mechanisms, the ordinary religion concludes, society will get better and better . . .

THE INSTRUMENTAL NATURE OF LAW

Today law tends to be viewed in solely instrumental terms and as lacking values of its own, other than . . . "process values" [ways] of doing things . . . Substantive goals come from the political process or from private interests . . . The lawyer's task in an instrumental approach to law, is to facilitate and manipulate legal processes to advance the interests of his client . . .

The instrumental approach to law also implies a dependent relationship of law to society. In this view, the conscious, creative power of change comes from social needs and pressures; law is a responsive instrument lacking a conscious, creative power of its own . . .

The instrumental approach also involves technocratic perspective which elevates power and control at the expense of other values . . .

THE TWO MODELS OF PROFESSIONAL CONDUCT . . .

The two abstract models of professional conduct—the "hired gun" and the "social engineer"—are specialists in manipulation . . . But they present serious moral difficulties for many law students.

If reasons are merely rationalizations for hidden motives, and if there is no way to choose one set of reasons over another, "then the purpose of offering reasons . . . cannot be to change men's minds in the sense of showing that one view is genuinely superior to another. It can only be a trick or sway or condition or force to woo men to believe or to do what the persuader desires." Reasons, then, become instruments in the service of warring preferences, and legal training involves arming advocates with the aggressive and defensive skills . . . in persuading others. Suspicion, distrust, and skepticism are appropriate attitudes.

The role of the "hired gun" forces the potential lawyer to visualize himself as an intellectual prostitute. In law school he may argue both sides of many issues. It is common for a student to respond to the question, "How do you come out on this case?" with . . . "It depends on what side I'm on." If the lawyer is going to live with himself, the system seems to say, he can't worry too much about right and wrong. Many sensitive students are deeply troubled by the moral implications of this role . . .

The "social engineer" model is cast on a larger scale, dealing with issues and interests rather than with individuals, but this role has a somewhat lifeless, bureaucratic and technocratic flavor . . . [the lawyer is still caught between domination and subservience, depending on whether he creates direction or simply accepts direction.]

THE NEGLECT OF NONCOGNITIVE ASPECTS...

"Law students," Griswold [former dean at Harvard—Ed.] stated, "bring a larger measure of idealism to law school than they leave with . . . Imagination in a broad sense is stifled rather than encouraged. And the emphasis of the curriculum on business and finance, the areas in which there are the greatest opportunities for remunerative private practice, conveys the impression, intended or not, that law students' future success and happiness will be found in the traditional areas of law" . . .

A growing literature supports the thesis that law students are more "tough-minded" and less "tender-minded" than other nonlawyer groups, and that law school tends to accentuate this bias . . .

The utility of "tough-minded" characteristics in many settings is not an issue. The question is whether the selection and training of law students does not neglect humane aspects of personal development and experience, the emotional aspect of the professional relationship, and the development of capacities of imagination, empathy, self-awareness and sensitivity to others. Are law students encouraged to be indifferent to character, insensitive to human problems, lacking in human concerns? Are they educated in accordance with an unreal professional model of detachment, noninvolvement, and insensitivity? . . .

Questions and Comments

1. According to Cramton, what is deficient about the "ordinary religion"? How does his inventory of deficiencies compare with the deficiencies noted in the autobiographical accounts of law students which preceded the excerpts from his essay?
2. What might be the appeal of the style and ethics of law training that Cramton criticizes? Would the espousal of the "ordinary religion" make a better professional, if not necessarily a better person? Would some law students welcome "the challenge" implicit in the training Cramton criticizes, especially after the relative leisure of undergraduate life?
3. In the *Powell* case do you see in kinds of arguments made by the lawyers authentication of the Cramton thesis, or do you see refutation of it?

   We also see in *Powell* the work of judges. Do judges have a peculiar way of looking at the world that is traceable to their own legal training?
4. Cramton seems to concur with former Dean Griswold of Harvard that law training is especially conducive to business law practice. Does the "ordinary religion" fit well with the practice of law on behalf of multinational corporations? Would other possible law school belief systems fit worse with the legal representation of multinationals?
5. Compare the materials from Galanter on the structure of litigation and stratification of lawyers with the essay from Cramton. Is the representation of RPs made more defensible, given the orthodoxies of the ordinary religion?

6. Sensitive students in law school seem to be presented with unenviable choices: (1) leave, (2) adapt and accept, (3) provisionally adapt and accept, hoping they can reconstruct their "true selves" after graduation and being admitted to the bar. Appraise these choices, imagining, if it helps, that you are their lawyer recommending a course of action.
7. Cramton ends his article on an optimistic note that is outside the excerpted material. He does not think that the attributes he finds in legal education are inevitable or unchangeable:

> The aim of education, even in law school, is to encourage a process of continuous self learning that involves the mind, spirit, and body of the whole person. This cannot be done unless larger questions of truth and meaning are directly faced.[11]

Cramton envisions a time when the legal profession will be called "to a covenant of faith and moral commitment that it has forsaken" and will "start doing the truth."

We can now sense what makes the article of Cramton such an unusual one— "being called," "a covenant of faith," "moral commitment," and his contention that lawyers need to "do the truth."

If some students chafe at the lawyer as "hired gun" or "intellectual prostitute," would they also rebel at Cramton's near mystical vision for professionals? Do his recommendations come too close to mixing the sacred and the secular? Would he make law as studied and practiced too "moralistic" and open to dogmatism?

Does Cramton's idea of what lawyers should do match the incoming sentiments of law students? The expectations of lawyers in practice?

In the latter connection, would large law firms accept or reject a proposal to put Cramton's reforms into effect?

Large Law Firms and the Ethics of Advocacy

It would be foolish to suppose that while the dominant form of enterprise changed from small businesses to multinationals, law firms would have remained the same as they were at the turn of the century. The solo law practitioner is to the corner store what the very large law firm is to the multinational corporation. And just as small business has become "vestigial" in terms of holding consequential assets, engaging in the bulk of production and sales, and being the prime movers in national and world economies, so too the solo lawyers have yielded to the large firm lawyers in relative shares of a growing market for legal services. There are still many lawyers working outside the largest law firms, but the big law firms have an influence vastly disproportionate to the numbers of lawyers working in them, and as a group, they set the terms of the relationship of law to political economy.[12]

[11] Ibid., p. 267.

[12] For the best discussion of the largest law firms and their transformation since the turn of the century, see Richard Abel, *American Lawyers* (New York: Oxford, 1989); Robert Nelson, *Partners With Power* (Berkeley: U. of California Press, 1988); and Marc Galanter, *Tournament of Lawyers* (Chicago: U. of Chicago Press, 1991).

Large-firm influence begins with the recruitment of the most able graduates of the most prestigious schools, and to the extent that law schools want to see their graduates gain preferred placements, these firms provide the basis for the ordinal ranking of law school courses and programs: courses on tax law and commercial transactions beat out family law and criminal procedure in the rivalry for law school time, energy, attention, and respect. The fields of law where the large firms practice, the way they practice, and the places they practice affect the training models used in law schools, and establish the style that the practicing profession values most highly.

Galanter's recent book on large law firms opens with a quick profile of that level of practice:

> . . . large numbers, relatively easy entry, intensive specialization, organization into large firms, strong ties to clients, weak controls by the state and by professional bodies, extraordinary prominence in public life, a protean entrepreneurial quality, and unparalleled scope of professional activity.[13]

A few sentences later he reiterates the thesis from his earlier essay, "Why the Haves Come Out Ahead . . .":

> Lawyers nominally form a single profession. But the profession is highly stratified. The upper strata . . . consist mostly of large firms whose members are recruited mainly from elite schools and who serve corporate clients; the lower strata practice as individuals or small firms, are drawn from less prestigious schools and serve individual clients . . . "the two kinds of practice are the two hemispheres of the profession. Most lawyers reside in one hemisphere or the other and seldom, if ever, cross the equator."[14]

About the relative social importance of the elite strata Galanter notes:

> The big law firm has been with us for almost a century. It is, in a Darwinian sense, a success story: big firms are flourishing; there are more of them, they are bigger, they command a bigger share of the expanding legal market. The big law firm is also a success in the deeper sense, as a social form for the organizing of comprehensive, continuous, high quality legal services. Like the hospital as a way to practice medicine, the big firm provides the standard for delivering complex services . . . [S]pecialization, teamwork, continuous monitoring on behalf of clients, representation in many forums, have been emulated . . . The specialized boutique firm [a firm working in one or a few narrow specialties.—ed.], the public interest law firm, the corporate law department—all model themselves on the style of practice developed in the large firm.[15]

Galanter and others have charted the transformation of the firms, just how big they are, where they are, what branches they have opened, and so on. In 1950, there were only 36 law firms with more than 50 lawyers; in 1985 there were 508 firms with 51 or more lawyers. In addition, large meant larger

[13]Galanter, op. cit., p. 1.
[14]Ibid., p. 1.
[15]Ibid., p. 2.

than had historically been the case; in 1960 there were less than a dozen firms of more than one hundred lawyers, but in 1986 there were 251. The largest law firm in 1968 had 169 lawyers, while the largest in 1988 had more than 900 lawyers, and there were 149 firms whose size was larger than the largest firm in 1968.[16]

The largest firms are now located in more cities than New York, which if it still has the greatest number of the largest firms, now shares the scene for large-firm practice with other major cities such as Chicago, Washington, DC, Philadelphia, San Francisco, Houston, Cleveland, and Los Angeles. Many of the largest firms have branches in several cities, and what is noteworthy for students of multinationals, some firms have branch offices outside of the country to serve United States-based multinationals doing business abroad and to serve foreign-based companies that do business in the United States.[17]

Of special interest here is whether this historical transformation of firms has altered professional ethics as officially espoused and practiced. The key question can be asked in several ways. Have lawyers, once idealized as learned free lances or "independent cusses," become integers in a legal service delivery system whose values are dominated by clients? Has the profession as organized on this scale to serve leviathan clients retained professional independence, or does the large law firm function like a prestigious branch office of the business clients it represents? Who sets what goals for the law firm, and what is the role of the lawyer in setting the goals for the multinational in times of corporate peace and in times of corporate warfare? Is the corporate lawyer a "hired gun" who shoots at the client's bidding, or does the corporate lawyer have independent anchoring points and retain sensitivity to interests greater than those of the corporate clients?

If the practice of law did not have any airs about it, lawyers could settle into the role of selling legal services just as any other commodity is sold. The airs about law can be traced to the mixed duties that all lawyers are trained to acknowledge: (1) to the system of law, which they are committed to uphold, (2) to the courts of which they are deemed "officers," and (3) to the clients who have retained them. If lawyering were a matter only of client representation, the tensions in modern law work would disappear; the lawyer as mouthpiece comes closest to rank commoditization of law which most professionals will at some level of their thinking resist, even where their daily rounds appear to be almost entirely client-determined. It is the first two duties—to law and order and to the court or other institutions where they appear—that could complicate the lives of modern lawyers. The cash nexus takes the lawyer toward the client, while other aspects of professionalism pull the lawyer away from strictly client service. Lawyer as moral actor grows out of the duty to society or legal institutions; lawyer as hired gun grows out of client servicing, an orientation that routinizes moral questions out of existence.

[16]Galanter, *Tournament of Lawyers*, pp. 37–86; 139–145.
[17]Ibid., Chapter 4.

Theoreticians on the transformation of law firms study the differing orientations of lawyers across time. Their overall finding is that lawyers have increasingly resolved all value dilemmas in favor of client service. Size, the financial pressures that go with size, and the need to fully utilize a firm's high-priced capacity requires the maximization of cash flow. Given this abiding imperative, large-firm practitioners can grant little more than passing endorsement to broadly defined ethical responsibilities. If one would think that the low end of the bar, practicing for the OSs, would have less room for independent judgment, the exigencies felt by large firms for revenue make the larger firms even more prone to "sell out" professional responsibilities than their lower-status brethren.

This ethical compromise was not always required. Earlier versions of law firm work, traceable in part to anecdotes and some self-serving histories, support the image of lawyer as a free lance, an autonomous professional answering to internal demands as often as client demands. The lawyer was frequently of higher status than the businesses they represented. Measured by who goes to whose office for a meeting, at the turn of the century the client might go to the lawyer's office rather than vice versa. Quantitative change in the numbers of lawyers in an office eventually produced a qualitative change in firm organization.[18]

Law firms get large in two major ways: either by rendering *general services* for a client as is the case where a large firm represents a money center bank and can count on a steady flow of business on a variety of legal matters, many of which border on the routine; or by *specialized services*, nonroutine business of a more sporadic nature, for example, difficult litigation or problems that transcend the ability of a corporation's in-house legal staff. The advantage of general service over specialized service should be obvious; it is more dependable, and the firm rendering it is less subject to wild swings in volume of business and revenues. The problem in getting *general services* work is that since it borders on the routine, clients can use in-house lawyers at less expense. An additional problem arises even in those cases where house counsel choose to refer matters to outside firms. Corporate counsel are much more sophisticated purchasers of legal services than regular officers of a corporation would be, and can more effectively monitor costs. Moreover, when outside counsel deal with the corporation via in-house corporate counsel, they have much less opportunity to build personal relationships with the principals of the corporation than they had in earlier periods.

What effects have the foregoing business pressures had on lawyers being able to function as independent professionals? The shortest answer is that the more the law firm is caught between its budget and sporadic business and other client discretions, (including the decision not to use the law firm at all), the less the large firm can be high-minded about broad ethical responsibilities. In the contemporary pinch, the firms will fall back to the tenet that their primary ethical obligation is to the client.[19]

[18]Paul Hoffman, *Lions in the Street* (New York: Saturday Review Press, 1973) pp. 4–11; Galanter, *Tournament of Lawyers*, pp. 4-19; Nelson, *Partners With Power*, pp. 7–12.

[19]Nelson, *Partners With Power,* pp. 51–62; Galanter, *Tournament of Lawyers,* pp. 48–55.

Room for ethical choice is further constrained by the pattern of organization that now characterizes the largest law firms. In earlier times law firms were aggregations of individual lawyers who acted like solo practitioners under one roof. They were more highly charismatic and inclined to a personalized style in their law work. It was about this era that Elihu Root said, "about half the practice of a decent lawyer consists of telling would-be clients that they are damned fools and should stop."[20] Several decades later Felix Frankfurter, once a professor at Harvard and later a United States Supreme Court judge, said, "A lawyer is a counsellor, an adviser. He isn't just a hired man to do the bidding of his clients, but he must exert the independence of mind and understanding upon the conduct of his client's business."[21]

One of the great gains that the large law firms made was to do work in teams, an absolutely indispensable requirement for long and complicated litigation or complex client problems, but right next to the gain was the jettisoning of the older collegial, informal office organization; bureaucratic efficiency replaced personal flair. In the law firm as bureaucracy, higher-level participants (senior partners) allocated parts and subparts of work to subordinates (associates), who despite their being lawyers in their own right, are less inclined to think beyond the craftsmanlike completion of assigned tasks. The end point is not necessarily pretty, but it meets the new imperatives of the firms. Returning to Galanter:

> Growth changes the character of the firm. Informality recedes; collegiality gives way; notions of public service and independence are marginalized, the imperative of growth collides with notions of dignified passivity in obtaining business. Eventually the firm faces the necessity of reorganizing to support ever larger increments of growth, or reorganizes to suppress growth. Either way collegiality, independence and public service are likely to be jeopardized.[22]

It is practically impossible, given the confidential nature of lawyer–client relationships to know just how often lawyers are torn between personal choice and client demands. It is well-known that the longer the association between lawyer and client, the more likely there will be a convergence of values rather than conflict. The closest the empirical data come on convergence and divergence of choices can be found in a survey of large firm lawyers in Chicago, which recorded the number of lawyers who had refused to carry out a client's requests because of a conflict with personal values. Of 222 respondents 186 had never refused an assignment; of the 36 who did, the reasons were divided between personal values and the code of professional ethics.[23]

Whatever lip service is still paid to broad-based ethical tenets, modern researchers have found them to be virtually nonexistent in practice. Big law firms hustle to get and keep clients. They would like to convert special-service clients into general-service clients, but this runs smack into larger and larger inhouse legal staffs. In the end they do what they feel economically constrained to do, being both unable to go back to a golden age, or forward with a reconstituted professionalism. They become hired guns and chase after business.

[20]Quoted in Martin Mayer, *The Lawyers* (1967) p. 6.
[21]Ibid., p. 6.
[22]Galanter, op. cit., p. 3.
[23]Nelson, *Partners With Power*, pp. 252–259.

Ethics and Advocacy in Other Multinational Cases

The next two cases, *Chambers* v. *Merrell* and *Dow* v. *Alfaro,* are representative of the many cases where persons from other countries alleging injuries from products of multinational companies, or their foreign subsidiaries, bring actions in the United States. In the first case, the plaintiffs, who were from Great Britain, brought suit in Ohio against a pharmaceutical company for birth defects from the drug Debendox. In the second case an action was brought in Texas by agricultural workers from Costa Rica against multinational manufacturers of pesticides. These cases anticipate the themes of the next chapter, where the many systems of law with which multinational corporate activities intersect will be developed more fully. For the present, the cases will be used to analyze the way very large law firms, on the defense against claims, represent their corporate clients. The cases test the theory about "haves" coming out ahead, and they also give concrete instances when large law firms put professional ethics into practice.

The cases, like many others in the multinational field where complexities abound, may be difficult to read on several counts which need to be cleared up as much as possible. The first case was brought in the state courts of Ohio, and the second was brought in the state courts of Texas. There is no doubt that both these courts have *jurisdiction* over the defendant corporations, because the corporations *do business* in the states where the actions are brought and are therefore *present*, and subject to the state court's power to render a decision.

We soon learn that a court's having jurisdiction in a case may be just the start of debate. Even where a court can decide a case, the court may nevertheless decide that it *ought not* to hear a case; this is where the doctrine of *forum non conveniens* comes in. A court having jurisdiction may nevertheless decide that the court, or forum, selected by the plaintiffs is "not convenient." In such cases, the court is saying, sometimes in complex ways, that another court would be a better one to hear the case.

The alternative places for trial of the drug and pesticide cases were Great Britain and Costa Rica. These were the places where the drugs were taken or where the agricultural workers used the defendant's pesticides and lived and worked. In the cases the place of injury is being balanced against the place where the defendant multinationals have their headquarters.

Forum non conveniens is a doctrine that will be raised only by defendants, since the plaintiff in choosing to bring an action would not later challenge the court as "inconvenient." Second, it should be remembered that the appropriateness of a court is a *preliminary* question that is raised before the merits of a case are taken up. Be patient with these cases; they are technical, but highly representative of the litigation of international tort claims. If you can successfully bash your way through them without losing sight of the underlying realities, you will be on your way to joining the tiny fraction of people who understand a main dimension of international law.

CHAMBERS V. MERRELL-DOW PHARMACEUTICALS 519. N.E.2D 370 (OHIO, 1988)

[B]y the Court

The common-law doctrine of *forum non conveniens* is committed to the sound discretion of a court and may be employed . . . to achieve the ends of justice and convenience of the parties and witnesses . . .

This case involves fifteen substantially identical actions filed separately in the Hamilton County Court of Common Pleas between September 20, 1984 and July 5, 1985. Each of the plaintiff–appellants is a citizen of Great Britain . . . Fourteen of the appellants are minor children and their parents . . . Each of the children experienced multiple birth defects, allegedly as the result of ingestion by their mothers of the drug Debendox during pregnancy.

Sole defendant . . . Merrell-Dow Pharmaceuticals is a Delaware corporation, with its principal place of business in Hamilton County, Ohio. In the late 1950's, Merrell-Dow designed, developed, tested, and marketed the drug Bendectin in the United States, to be used for the relief of nausea and vomiting during pregnancy. The British counterpart of the drug, Debendox, was marketed and distributed in the late 1950's and 1960's by a wholly-owned British subsidiary of Merrell-Dow . . . Merrell-Dow Pharmaceuticals Ltd. Debendox was approved by the Department of Health and Social Security in the United Kingdom, and was manufactured and assembled in the United Kingdom by Boots Pure Drug Company Ltd . . .

Each of the actions herein seeks compensatory and punitive damages against Merrell-Dow under theories of negligence, fraudulent misrepresentation and strict products liability . . . Merrell-Dow filed motions to dismiss each action on the basis of *forum non conveniens*. The trial court . . . dismissed . . .

Holmes, Justice

[T]he sole question raised upon appeal is whether the trial court erred in dismissing these actions utilizing the common law doctrine of *forum non conveniens* . . .

The criteria set forth in *Gilbert* and other United States Supreme Court decisions are to be applied flexibly, with each case turning on its own facts . . . These factors may be divided into the private interests of the litigants and factors of public interest . . . Important private interests include: the relative ease of access to sources of proof, availability of compulsory process for attendance of unwilling . . . witnesses . . . and all other practical problems that make a case easy, expeditious and inexpensive . . . The *Gilbert* court noted that "the plaintiffs' choice of forum should rarely be disturbed" . . . particularly when the plaintiff has chosen his home forum . . . However, in *Piper Aircraft* . . . the court held . . . "a foreign plaintiff's choice deserves less deference."

Public interest factors . . . include the administrative difficulties and delay to other litigants caused by congested court calendars, the imposition of jury duty upon the citizens of a community which has very little relation to the litigation, a local interest in having localized controversies decided at home, and the appropriateness of litigating a case in a forum familiar with the applicable law . . . Essentially "the ultimate inquiry is where the trial will serve the convenience of the parties and the ends of justice" . . .

[The court next discusses whether the doctrine is part of the law of Ohio and concludes that it is. —Ed.]

Our final task is to determine whether the trial court below properly employed the doctrine . . . considering all the relevant private and public interest factors and the weight given to each. We will not independently assess and reweigh each factor as our review is limited to the narrow determination of whether the trial court abused its discretion . . .

The trial court considered the following private interest factors: if the suit were maintained in Ohio, the foreign plaintiffs would benefit from this country's practice of allowing counsel to operate on a contingent fee basis, a practice whose absence in Great Britain makes it difficult for many plaintiffs to bring suit; in Ohio, plaintiffs are not burdened by paying their opponent's legal fees should they lose, as they would in Great Britain; in Ohio, unlike Great Britain, plaintiffs would be entitled to a jury trial and could utilize depositions rather than live witnesses at trial, would likely be entitled to punitive damages, and would benefit from far more liberal law regarding strict products liability; and the documents and witnesses relating to the initial development of Bendectin in defendant's Cincinnati laboratories are located in this state, which to that extent would benefit both parties. However, plaintiffs would have to travel at great expense to Cincinnati, as would several witnesses located in Great Britain, also at plaintiff's expense. These foreign witnesses relating to the personal and family medical history of the plaintiffs, and relating to the preparation, testing, and distribution of Debendox in Great Britain are located throughout Great Britain. Finally, the Ohio courts would be unfamiliar with applying British law, which would inure to neither party's benefit.

The public factors considered were the burden on Ohio courts in applying foreign law in a difficult case; the lack of subpoena power to compel cooperation of foreign witnesses; the "near certainty" that allowing this suit would result in the filing in Cincinnati of one thousand or more similar Debendox cases from various countries; and the tremendous burden upon the jury system of Hamilton County should such a flood of litigation occur, coupled with the equally tremendous burden on the limited resources of the Ohio judiciary and the potential denial of our own citizens of access to Ohio courts.

The court then balanced these considerations in light of the fact that Debendox was manufactured almost exclusively in Great Britain by a British corporation; its contents were somewhat different from the drug developed by the defendant in the United States; Debendox was tested and licensed under British law, promoted and sold by British firms to citizens and residents of Great Britain; the injuries all occurred there; and the information on the initial development and testing of Bendectin . . . was still available to the plaintiffs . . .

The court determined the balance weighed in favor of the defendant, as "Great Britain has the overwhelming greater interest in this matter.". . .

A viable alternative forum exists in the United Kingdom, and the possibility that these foreign appellants' recoveries may be smaller in the United Kingdom is not of paramount concern. Second, appellants argue that we should protect our interest in regulating drug testing and promotion occurring in this state by subjecting appellee to the deterring effect of strict products liability litigation here . . . The incremental deterrence that would be gained if this trial were held in an American court is likely to be insignificant . . . Judgment affirmed.

Douglas, Justice, dissenting:

[Douglas discusses whether the doctrine is part of the law of Ohio and concludes that it is not. —Ed.]

[T]hose of us who are charged with being too judicially progressive would now seem to have free rein as we continue to move the law of Ohio into the twentieth century . . .

[I]t is a sad day for Ohio when the highest court . . . holds that *our* Constitution . . . which provides for our courts to be open to "every person," does *not* include aliens. This is akin to the outrageous and outmoded holdings of yesteryear when blacks and women were not "persons" under the law. Therefore, I would . . . permit appellants' litigation to continue.

Questions and Comments

1. At the center of the doctrine of *forum non conveniens* are said to be the "ends of justice." Think of yourself as a judge. What do the *ends of justice* require were a case of this type to be before you?
   Is there some tension between the way you would define the ends of justice and the procedural doctrine of *forum non conveniens*?

2a. Can the lawyers who represent the defendant Merrell-Dow afford to think about the *ends of justice*? What about the 1000 other claimants which the court says are awaiting the outcome of this lawsuit? Should the defense lawyers feel some breach between their duty, to their client, Merrell-Dow, and their duty to uphold law that deters the distribution of unsafe pharmaceuticals? If they recognize the latter duty, would they have to stop practicing law?

   Can they defend a corporation if they "know" that corporation is guilty? Could Merrell-Dow be "getting off on a technicality" here?

b. Return to Professor Cramton's exhortation to lawyers—that they start "a new covenant" and begin "doing the truth." How would his recommendation apply in cases like *Chambers*?

c. Return to the comment of Scott Turow about a central lesson of law school—that legal thinking is nasty. How would his idea play out in cases like *Chambers*?

3a. Some other issues suggested by this case seem noteworthy: (1) The court says that it would be expensive *for the plaintiffs* to try the lawsuit in Ohio. Haven't the plaintiffs taken these expenses into account before deciding to bring their lawsuits in Ohio?

   (2) Should a suit that is brought in the place where the defendant company has its home office ever be considered "inconvenient"?

   (3) The court notes a number of "contacts" between Great Britain and the alleged injuries. Do some of these contacts collapse, given the fact the British corporation marketing Debendox, Merrell-Dow, Ltd., was a wholly owned subsidiary of the United States-based Merrell-Dow, Inc?

b. Still another question arises: is the effect of the doctrine of *forum non conveniens* fundamentally incompatible with its stated purposes of deciding cases "expeditiously" or "inexpensively"

4. Cases like *Powell* on choice of law, or *Chambers* on *forum non conveniens* can make the head hurt from thinking about complexities. The temptation might be to slough off cases like these, and get down to matters of "substance." But alas, cases like these cannot be bypassed as long as they remain so common in the courts. Procedural issues are raised in virtually every case involving claims brought against international companies for their foreign operations.

DOW CHEMICAL CO. V. CASTRO ALFARO 786 S.W.2D. 674 (TEXAS, 1990)

Ray, Justice:

Domingo Castro Alfaro, a Costa Rican resident and employee of the Standard Fruit Company, and eighty-one other Costa Rican employees and their wives brought suit against Dow Chemical Company and Shell Oil Company. The employees claim that they suffered personal injuries as a result of exposure to dibromochloropropane (DBCP), a pesticide manufactured by Dow and Shell, which was allegedly furnished to Standard Fruit. The employees exposed to DBCP allegedly suffered several medical problems, including sterility.

Alfaro sued Dow and Shell in Harris County district court [Texas—Ed.] in April 1984. The amended petition alleged that the court had jurisdiction . . . Following an unsuccessful attempt to remove the suit to federal court, Dow and Shell contested the jurisdiction of the trial court almost three years after the filing of the suit, and contended in the alternative that the case should be dismissed under the doctrine of forum non conveniens. Despite a finding of jurisdiction, the trial court dismissed the case on the ground of forum non conveniens . . .

We conclude that the legislature has statutorily abolished the doctrine of forum non conveniens . . .

[Case remanded to the trial court for further proceedings]

Doggett, Justice concurring

Because its analysis and reasoning are correct I join in the majority opinion without reservation. I write separately, however, to respond to the dissenters who mask their inability to agree among themselves with competing rhetoric. In their zeal to implement their own preferred social policy that Texas corporations not be held responsible at home for harm caused abroad, these dissenters refuse to be restrained by either express statutory language or the compelling precedent, previously approved by this very court, holding that forum non conveniens does not apply in Texas. To accomplish the desired social engineering, they must invoke yet another legal fiction with a fancy name to shield alleged wrongdoers, the so-called doctrine of forum non conveniens. The refusal of a Texas corporation to confront a Texas judge and jury is to be labeled "inconvenient" when what is really involved is not convenience but connivance to avoid corporate accountability.

The dissenters are insistent that a jury of Texans be denied the opportunity to evaluate the conduct of a Texas corporation concerning decisions it made in Texas because the only ones allegedly hurt are foreigners. Fortunately Texans are not so provincial and narrow-minded as these dissenters presume. Our citizenry recognizes that a wrong does not fade away because its immediate consequences are first felt far away rather than close to home. Never have we been required to forfeit our membership in the human race in order to maintain our proud heritage as citizens of Texas.

The dissenters argue that it is inconvenient and unfair for farmworkers allegedly suffering permanent physical and mental injuries, including irreversible sterility, to seek redress by suing a multinational corporation in a court three blocks away from its world headquarters and another corporation, which operates in Texas this country's largest chemical plant. Because the "doctrine" they advocate has nothing to do with fairness and convenience and everything to do with immunizing multinational corporations from accountability for their alleged torts causing injury abroad, I write separately.

I. THE FACTS

Respondents claim that while working on a banana plantation in Costa Rica for Standard Fruit Company, an American subsidiary of Dole Fresh Fruit Company, headquartered in Boca Raton, Florida, they were required to handle dibromochloropropane ["DBCP"], a pesticide allegedly manufactured and furnished to Standard Fruit by Shell Oil Company ["Shell"] and Dow Chemical Company ["Dow"]. The Environmental Protection Agency issued a notice of intent to cancel all food uses of DBCP on September 22, 1977 . . . It followed with an order suspending registrations of pesticides containing DBCP on November 3, 1977 . . . Before and after the E.P.A.'s ban of DBCP in the United States, Shell and Dow apparently shipped several hundred thousand gallons of the pesticide to Costa Rica for use by Standard Fruit.

The Respondents, Domingo Castro Alfaro and other plantation workers, filed suit in a state district court in Houston, Texas, alleging that their handling of DBCP caused them serious personal injuries for which Shell and Dow were liable under the theories of products liability, strict liability and breach of warranty.

Rejecting an initial contest to its authority by Shell and Dow, the trial court found that it had jurisdiction ..., but dismissed the cause on the grounds of forum non conveniens. The court of appeals reversed and remanded, holding that Section 71.031 provides a foreign plaintiff with an absolute right to maintain a death or personal injury cause of action in Texas without being subject to forum non conveniens dismissal . . . Shell and Dow have asked this court to reverse the judgment of the court of appeals and affirm the trial court's dismissal.

Shell Oil Company is a multinational corporation with its world headquarters in Houston, Texas. Dow Chemical Company, though headquartered in Midland, Michigan, conducts extensive operations from its Dow Chemical USA building located in Houston. Dow operates this country's largest chemical manufacturing plant within 60 miles of Houston in Freeport, Texas. The district court where this lawsuit was filed is three blocks away from Shell's world headquarters, One Shell Plaza in downtown Houston.

Shell has stipulated that all of its more than 100,000 documents relating to DBCP are located or will be produced in Houston. Shell's medical and scientific witnesses are in Houston. The majority of Dow's documents and witnesses are located in Michigan, which is far closer to Houston (both in terms of geography and communications linkage) than to Costa Rica. The respondents have agreed to be available in Houston for independent medical examinations, for depositions and for trial. Most of the respondents' treating doctors and co-workers have agreed to testify in Houston. Conversely, Shell and Dow have purportedly refused to make their witnesses available in Costa Rica.

The banana plantation workers allegedly injured by DBCP were employed by an American company on American-owned land and grew Dole bananas for export solely to American tables. The chemical allegedly rendering the workers sterile was researched, formulated, tested, manufactured, labeled and shipped by an American company in the United States to another American company. The decision to manufacture DBCP for distribution and use in the third world was made by these two American companies in the corporate offices in the United States. Yet now Shell and Dow argue that the one part of this equation that should not be American is the legal consequences of their actions.

II. FORUM NON CONVENIENS—"A COMMON LAW DOCTRINE OUT OF CONTROL"

. . . A. USING THE "DOCTRINE" TO KILL THE LITIGATION ALTOGETHER

Both as a matter of law and of public policy, the doctrine of forum non conveniens is without justification. The proffered foundations for it are "considerations of fundamental fairness and sensible and effective judicial administration." . . .

In fact, the doctrine is favored by multinational defendants because a forum non conveniens dismissal is often outcome-determinative, effectively defeating the claim and denying the plaintiff recovery. The contorted result of the doctrine of forum non conveniens is to force foreign plaintiffs "to convince the court that it is more convenient to sue in the United States, while the American defendant argues that . . . [the foreign court] is the more convenient forum."

A forum non conveniens dismissal is often, in reality, a complete victory for the defendant. As noted in *Irish Nat'l Ins. Co.*v. *Aer Lingus* . . .

> [i]n some instances, . . . invocation of the doctrine will send the case to a jurisdiction which has imposed such severe monetary limitations on recovery as to eliminate the likelihood that the case will be tried. When it is obvious that this will occur, discussion of convenience of witnesses takes on a Kafkesque quality—everyone knows that no witnesses ever will be called to testify.

In using the term forum non conveniens, "the courts have taken refuge in a euphemistic vocabulary, one that glosses over the harsh fact that such dismissal is outcome-determinative in a high percentage of the forum non conveniens cases . . ."

Empirical data available demonstrate that less than four percent of cases dismissed under the doctrine of forum non conveniens ever reach trial in a foreign court. A forum non conveniens dismissal usually will end the litigation altogether, effectively excusing any liability of the defendant. The plaintiffs leave the courtroom without having had their case resolved on the merits. [After concluding that Texas has an interest in such lawsuits because of the impressive presence of Shell and Dow in Texas, and rejecting the idea that Texas will be overwhelmed by litigation, Judge Doggett proceeds to a discussion of comity. —Ed.]

JUDICIAL COMITY

Comity—deference shown to the interests of the foreign forum—is a consideration best achieved by rejecting forum non conveniens. Comity is not achieved when the United States allows its multinational corporations to adhere to a double standard when operating abroad and subsequently refuses to hold them accountable for those actions. As S. Jacob Scherr, Senior Project Attorney for the Natural Resources Defense Counsel, has noted:

> There is a sense of outrage on the part of many poor countries where citizens are the most vulnerable to exports of hazardous drugs, pesticides and food products. At the 1977 meeting of the UNEP Governing Council, Dr. J.C. Kiano, the Kenyan minister for water development, warned that developing nations will no longer tolerate being used as dumping rounds for products that had not been adequately tested "and that their peoples should not be used as guinea pigs for determining the safety of chemicals."

Comity is best achieved by "avoiding the possibility of 'incurring the wrath and distrust of the Third World as it increasingly recognizes that it is being used as the industrial world's garbage can."

PUBLIC POLICY AND THE TORT LIABILITY OF MULTINATIONAL CORPORATIONS IN UNITED STATES COURTS

The abolition of forum non conveniens will further important public policy considerations by providing a check on the conduct of multinational corporations (MNCs) . . . The misconduct of even a few multinational corporations can affect untold millions around the world.[1] For example, after the United States imposed a domestic ban on the sale of cancer-producing TRIS-treated children's sleepwear, American companies exported approximately 2.4 million pieces to Africa, Asia and South America. A similar pattern occurred when a ban was proposed for baby pacifiers that had been linked to choking deaths in infants. Hazardous Exports, supra, These examples of indifference by some corporations towards children abroad are not unusual.[2]

[1]As one commentator observed, U.S. multinational corporations adhere to a double standard when operating abroad. The lack of stringent environmental regulations and worker safety standards abroad and the relaxed enforcement of such laws in industries using hazardous processes provide little incentive for [multinational corporations] to protect the safety of workers, to obtain liability insurance to guard against the hazard of product defects or toxic tort exposure, or to take precautions to minimize pollution to the environment. This double standard has caused catastrophic damages to the environment and to human lives.

Note, "Exporting Hazardous Industries: Should American Standards Apply?" *Int'l L. & Pol.* 20 (1988), pp. 777, 780–81.

[2]A subsidiary of Sterling Drug Company advertised Winstrol, a synthetic male hormone severely restricted in the United States since it is associated with a number of side effects that the F.D.A. has called "virtually irreversible", in a Brazilian medical journal, picturing a healthy boy and recommending the drug to combat poor appetite, fatigue and weight loss. . . . The same company is said to have marketed Dipyrone, a painkiller causing a fatal blood disease and characterized by the American Medical Association as for use only as "a last resort," as "Novaldin" in the Dominican Republic. "Novaldin" was advertised in the Dominican Republic with pictures of a child smiling about its agreeable taste. . . . In 1975, thirteen children in Brazil died after coming into contact with a toxic pesticide whose use had been severely restricted in this country.

The allegations against Shell and Dow, if proven true, would not be unique, since production of many chemicals banned for domestic use has thereafter continued for foreign marketing.[3] Professor Thomas McGarity, a respected authority in the field of environmental law, explained:

> During the mid-1970s, the United States Environmental Protection Agency (EPA) began to restrict the use of some pesticides because of their environmental effects, and the Occupational Safety and Health Administration (OSHA) established workplace exposure standards for toxic and hazardous substances in the manufacture of pesticides . . . [I]t is clear that many pesticides that have been severely restricted in the United States are used without restriction in many Third World countries, with resulting harm to fieldworkers and the global environment.

McGarity, *Bhopal and the Export of Hazardous Technologies*, 20 *Tex.Int'l L.J.* 333, 334 (1985). By 1976, "20 percent, or 161 million pounds, of all the pesticides exported by the United States were either unregistered or banned for domestic use." McWilliams, *Tom Sawyer's Apology: A Reevaluation of United States Pesticide Export Policy,* 8 *Hastings Int'l & Comp.L.Rev.* 61,61 & n. 4 (1984). It is estimated that these pesticides poison 750,000 people in developing countries each year, of which 22,500 die. . . . Some estimates place the death toll from the "improper marketing of pesticides at 400,000 lives a year." . . .

Some United States multinational corporations will undoubtedly continue to endanger human life and the environment with such activities until the economic consequences of these actions are such that it becomes unprofitable to operate in this manner. At present, the tort laws of many third world countries are not yet developed. An Economic Approach, supra, . . . Industrialization "is occurring faster than the development of domestic infrastructures necessary to deal with the problems associated with industry." . . . When a court dismisses a case against a United States multinational corporation, it often removes the most effective restraint on corporate misconduct. . . .

The doctrine of forum non conveniens is obsolete in a world in which markets are global and in which ecologists have documented the delicate balance of all life on this planet. The parochial perspective embodied in the doctrine of forum non conveniens enables corporations to evade legal control merely because they are transnational. This perspective ignores the reality that actions of our corporations affecting those abroad will also affect Texans. Although DBCP is banned from use within the United States, it and other similarly banned chemicals have been consumed by Texans eating foods imported from Costa Rica and elsewhere. See

[3]Regarding Letophos, a powerful and hazardous pesticide that was domestically banned, S. Jacob Scherr stated that:

> In 1975 alone, Velsicol, a Texas-based corporation, exported 3,092,842 pounds of Leptophos to thirty countries. Over half of that was shipped to Egypt, a country with no procedures for pesticide regulation or tolerance setting. In December 1976, the Washington Post reported that Leptophos use in Egypt resulted in the death of a number of farmers and illness in rural communities... But despite the accumulation of data on Leptophos' severe neurotoxicity, Velsicol continued to market the product abroad for use on grain and vegetable crops while proclaiming the product's safety.

D. Weir & M. Schapiro, Circle of Poison 28-30, 77, 82–83 (1981).[4] In the absence of meaningful tort liability in the United States for their actions, some multinational corporations will continue to operate without adequate regard for the human and environmental costs of their actions. This result cannot be allowed to repeat itself for decades to come.

As a matter of law and of public policy, the doctrine of forum non conveniens should be abolished. Accordingly, I concur.

Gonzalez, Justice, dissenting

Response to J. Doggett's Concurrence

When you strip Justice Doggett's concurring opinion of its fiery rhetoric, it is clear that he has twisted my dissent to such an extent that ordinarily I would feel compelled to respond at length. Deprived of rhetorical flourishes, however, his concurring opinion contains only the following conclusions:

(1) The legislature has abolished forum non conveniens . . .

(2) As a matter of law and of public policy," the doctrine "should be abolished." . . .

(4) The legal systems of many countries of the world are not as generous as ours, and the doctrine of forum non conveniens is a barrier to holding greedy, irresponsible multinational corporations accountable. The doctrine is therefore invalid on public policy grounds. (We are a court, not a legislative body. We do not have the power or authority to make this public policy decision.)

Justice Doggett also criticizes the doctrine of forum non conveniens as "yet another legal fiction" and assumes that by calling it such he has challenged its validity. Taking this line of reasoning to its logical conclusion, it appears that Justice Doggett opposes the use of such legal fictions as corporations . . . and numerous others. . . .

In conclusion, I have no intent, much less "zeal" to implement social policy as Justice Doggett charges. That is not our role. It is clear that if anybody is trying to advance a particular social policy, it is Justice Doggett. I admire his altruism, and I too sympathize with the plight of the plaintiffs. However, the powers of this court are well-defined, and the sweeping implementations of social welfare policy Justice Doggett seeks to achieve by abolishing the doctrine of forum non conveniens are the exclusive domain of the legislature . . . I dissent.

Comments and Questions

1. Compare the *Chambers* and the *Alfaro* cases.
2. Use this case to review the themes of the chapter—litigation, legal ethics, and the application of ethics in cases where large firms and multinational corporations are involved.

[4]Less than one percent of the imported fruits and vegetables are inspected for pesticides. General Accounting Office, Pesticides: Better Sampling and Enforcement Needed on Imported Food GAO/RCED-86-219 (Sept. 26, 1986), at 3. The GAO found that of the 7.3 billion pounds of bananas imported into the F.D.A.'s Dallas District (covering Texas) from countries other than Mexico in 1984, not a single sample was checked for illegal pesticide residues such as DBCP. Id. at 53. Even when its meager inspection program discovers illegal pesticides, the F.D.A. rarely sanctions the shipper or producer.

3. As early as 1908 Roscoe Pound anticipated the effects of large law firms' skewing contested cases toward procedure and away from substance:

> The leaders of the American bars . . . devote themselves to the study of the interests of particular clients, urging and defending interests in varying forms . . . Their interest centers wholly in an individual client or set of clients, not in the general administration of justice.[24]

4. The *Alfaro* case was one of a series of cases brought to get the claims of the Costa Rican banana workers to trial in the United States. There were earlier unsuccessful attempts beginning in 1983 in the state and federal courts in Florida and California against the chemical companies and the Standard Fruit Company (a subsidiary of Dole, which used the pesticide in its Central American banana production).

   Two judges in the Alfaro case who voted for dismissal picked up on the earlier failed attempts to get the case to court:

> *Judge Cook:* Like the turn of the century wildcatters, the plaintiffs in this case searched all across this nation for a place to make their claims. Through three courts they moved, filing their lawsuit on one coast and then on the other. By each of those courts the plaintiffs were rejected, and so they continued their search ... Their efforts are finally rewarded. Today they hit pay dirt in Texas.
> *Judge Hecht* [O]ne federal court in California and *two* in Florida have already dismissed essentially the same lawsuit which the court now welcomes in Texas . . .

   The judges seem to be saying that the injured workers have been unwilling to take no for an answer or that they might even be harassing the defendants through the pressing of frivolous claims.

   Evaluate the judicial comments and whether the plaintiffs have been too pushy.

5. In late 1992, settlement discussions were taking place.[25]

CONCLUSION

Franz Kafka wrote a parable entitled "The Problem of Our Laws," which opened:

> Our laws are not generally known; they are kept secret by a small group of nobles who rule us . . . it is an extremely painful thing to be ruled by laws that one does not know.[26]

[24]Pound is quoted in Galanter, *Tournament of Lawyers*, p. 7.
[25]*Multinational Monitor*, (August, 1992), p. 38.
[26]F. Kafka, *Parables and Paradoxes*, (1974), p. 155.

Now that we know more, and have a map of litigation as it operates in cases where the largest business firms are in court, we may have a different source of pain. If we are headed toward law school, we might wonder whether our soul will be in good hands, or whether the method of instruction and the premium put on "bread and butter" courses relevant for commercial practice will undercut the very reasons why we might be drawn toward law study or a legal career. The solution of holding deep questions until after graduation and licensure will not work if after schooling and passing the bar, ethical problems take on only slightly different forms, and, what may be worse, are more inextricably tied to earning a living.

We may be aggrieved for courts whose judges are tied to procedural rules or general passivity which inhibit their activism towards justice. If, according to tradition, parties are to shape their own lawsuits, a prospect that appears to be democratic, what is to happen when parties are not equally positioned for a number of reasons to get disputes litigated in a fair way? If the parties cannot open the right options for decision for courts, and the problem is chronic, not transient, what must courts do?

Looking across the three cases presented in detail, it might be hard to see how any court, pursuing an independent course, would have chosen to expend so much energy on preliminaries. If litigation is to become more than a cruel hoax, should courts become more activist and undo the structural advantages now experienced by well-financed and well-represented business organizations? Such a proposal runs smack into the self-imposed limits that courts have recognized. Many courts see their role as subordinate to federal and state legislatures, which are deemed to be in a more legitimate position to take aggressive political action to regulate the affairs of multinationals.

The claimants against multinationals also come to mind. In two of the three cases the plaintiffs were "successful" in getting the rulings they advocated. But in the *Powell* case it took five tries and in the *Alfaro* case it took coast-to-coast persistence to get *preliminaries* settled. In the case lost, *Chambers*, the claimants failed to get the cases tried in the United States.

Where is the most appropriate place for a multinational to be held accountable for practices that cause trouble? Which legal order or orders will be likely to be most effective in eliminating unwanted behavior? It seems hard to believe that such questions will be best answered via the doctrines surrounding choice of law questions or *forum non conveniens*, but for the moment these are the chambers of legal discourse where these momentous matters are debated.

CHAPTER 10

Legal Systems, Their Reach and Nonreach

In a number of the preceding chapters we have been at the edge of the question of legal systems and their reach. In the immediately preceding chapter it was evident that since multinationals operate in and across multiple legal jurisdictions there is always the issue of what law governs what behavior, that is, *from what* legal system rules can originate, and *in what* system legal rules can to be applied. In the *Powell* case an injury occurred on the high seas, and the court found enough "contacts" between the United States and the event to justify the application of United States law. In the drug and pesticide cases that followed, the doctrine of *forum non conveniens* produced nonapplication of United States court power in one case, and the application of that power in the other.

The likelihood of disputes over jurisdiction, choice of law, and *forum non conveniens* in virtually every case where multinationals are parties means more opportunities for lawyers to make intricate arguments than would be present in strictly domestic cases. (Domestic cases can themselves be quite technical at times due to there being in the United States 50 systems of state law as well as a national law system superimposed on top of them.) The overriding implication of so many legal systems, both foreign and domestic, may already be apparent; the more legal systems *potentially applicable*, the more difficult it may be to make *any system actually applicable!*

The reach and nonreach of legal systems was a consideration in other preceding chapters. In Chapter 4 on political economy, the point was raised about nationalism and whether nationalism is out of date, given the worldwide scope of economic systems. The mismatch between legal-political organization and economic organization means that national systems are less effective because of their limited scope at the very time when they are deemed most necessary to control multinational behavior. There was also some discussion of international regimes for the resolution of conflicts on a worldwide basis to eliminate this mismatch between worldwide economic systems and national regulatory systems. For the critical present it must be acknowledged that what "international regimes" there are do not reach the level of full-scale legal systems with rule-making and enforcement powers.

For want of alternatives, national legal systems, whether they are creaking from obsolescence or not, will remain the foreseeable future of legal action and control. When national systems fail, observers must face the stark realization that international business is largely lawless.

In the chapter on corporations some reference was made to the ability of multinationals such as Caterpillar Inc. to establish worldwide networks using separate legal entities to hold and use property. Not only do these networks bring activities *within* legal systems but also, in sometimes telling respects, take corporate activity *outside* legal systems, thereby rendering undesirable law inapplicable.

Multinationals have also used tax havens to shelter income, jurisdictions in which corporate and financial affairs can be kept secret, and countries offering "flags of convenience" for ships. All of these corporate strategies serve the dual purpose of getting out from under restrictive law and coming within less restrictive legal orders.

Other advantages of coming *within* legal systems, the dimension usually overlooked, include access to state subsidies—for example, state contracts, interest-free loans, or qualifying for such benefits as police protection. The different motivations that impel moving into or out of legal systems make for more complexity in a field that is already complex. No multinational with its prolific networks of legal entities will ever fit squarely within or totally outside a legal system. And there is, of course, a distinct third possibility—where multinational activities fall *between* rather than *under* legal systems.

The *Alcoa* case, which was included in the antitrust materials in Chapter 6, had a dimension not previously considered. One of the charges of monopolization against Alcoa concerned the participation by Alcoa in an international cartel to control the worldwide production and distribution of aluminum. Because the alleged participation was done via Alcan, Ltd., a Canadian corporation in which Alcoa shareholders held enough stock for control, the question arose as to whether U. S. antitrust law applied to the participation by the "foreign" corporation (Alcan) in the aluminum cartel. The court ruled that activity undertaken "outside the United States might be subject to U. S. law if the behavior had *effects* in the United States."

In this chapter a sample of cases on the application of court power is considered. While the discussion gets technical and might seem to be designed to make old people out of young ones, they nevertheless can be moderately intriguing once one gets beyond the surfaces. With luck, the cases will be as irritating as bits of popcorn stuck between the teeth. If you keep rolling your tongues over them, some understanding of the extent of state control over international business will be dislodged.

Because the cases are essential, especially if law is to be integrated with political economy, these technical areas cannot be bypassed in favor of material closer to the heart. Like the cases in the last chapter, they give further illustration of the cat-and-mouse game between businesses and political-legal systems, but in some instances the mice are much larger than the cats.

A TOUCH OF HISTORY

In the *Powell* case in the previous chapter, we learned that one of the factors a court can consider in determining what law governs a maritime case is the flag a ship flies. The utter randomness with which flags can be hoisted or hauled down makes the inquiry about flags appear to be an odd way to determine what law should apply in a case. It appears odd because it *is* odd. However, across the history of court power, the law of the flag might have had a more defensible purpose, since in many cases it was either the law of the flag or nothing.

Earlier courts were trying to bring criminal behavior within a court's power when crimes were committed on the high seas; the high seas being beyond the territorial limits of any nation, the usual territorial justification for the application of national law was absent. In some cases citizenship of a party might be used to extend the power of a country beyond territorial limits, but citizenship might itself have limits, as would be the case where criminal behavior occurred on the ship of one country, on the high seas, by a citizen of another country. For example, a trial for murder by an American sailor on a British ship off the coast of France, before a British court, would make jurisdiction based on the flag important.[1]

Courts sometimes fleshed out the legal fiction of the flag. In the words of an English court speaking in 1868,

> A ship on the high seas, carrying a national flag is *part of the territory* of that nation whose flag she carries; and all persons on board her are to be considered as subject to the jurisdiction of the laws of that nation as much so as they had been on land within that territory.[2]

Other courts balked at the fiction of a ship being regarded as a part of a country, especially where regarding it so would produce the wrong result:

> A ship is a movable chattel, it is not a place; when on a voyage it shifts from hour to hour and when in dock it is a chattel ... the jurisdiction over crimes committed on a ship at sea is not of a territorial nature at all. [T]he country of the flag [could have jurisdiction] provided that if the offender is of a nationality different from that of his ship, the prosecution may alternatively be in the courts of his own country."[3]

Several ideas can be teased out of the foregoing quotations before we go on to more contemporary cases:

1. Even where courts had physical control of people or property, they were sometimes ill at ease about the propriety of making decisions.
2. The primary bases for the proper exercise of jurisdiction were either territory or citizenship.

[1]The early history of national courts in cases on the high seas is discussed in William Bishop, *International Law* (Boston: Little Brown, 1953), Chapter 7.

[2]Ibid., p. 578.

[3]Ibid., p. 549.

3. Conflicts over applicable law could occur where not all factors fit squarely within one legal system, as would be true in the foregoing cases where the ship as territory could lead to one result, while citizenship might lead to another. (The *Lauritzen* factors considered in the Powell case in Chapter 9 are a full-blown example of the factor mix.)
4. The application of state power or its legal rules was not automatic, but open to debate.

Courts developed rules of deference for cases that touched multiple legal systems; a court that could hear a case might nevertheless choose not to hear it out of "comity," meaning respect for the sovereignty of another nation and the desire another state might have to manage its own legal affairs.

The idea of comity was present in the following famous case where one U.S.-based corporation challenged another U.S. corporation in the courts of the United States, for antitrust law violations that took place in Costa Rica.

AMERICAN BANANA COMPANY V. UNITED FRUIT 213 U.S. 347 (1908)

Mr. Justice Holmes

This is an action to recover threefold damages under the act to protect trade against monopolies.[Sherman Antitrust Act–ed.] . . .

The plaintiff is an Alabama corporation, organized in 1904. The defendant is a New Jersey corporation, organized in 1899. Long before the plaintiff was formed, the defendant, with intent to prevent competition and to control and monopolize the banana trade, bought the property and business of several of its previous competitors, with provisions against their resuming the trade, made contracts with others . . . regulating the quantity to be purchased and the price to be paid, and acquired a controlling amount of stock in still others. For the same purpose it organized a selling company . . . By this and other means it did monopolize and restrain trade and maintained unreasonable prices . . . One McConnell, in 1903, started a banana plantation in Panama, then part of . . . Columbia, and began to build a railway (which would afford his only means of export) . . . in accordance with the laws of . . . Columbia. He was notified by the defendant that he must either combine or stop. Two months later, it is believed at the defendant's instigation, the governor of Panama recommended to his national government that Costa Rica be allowed to administer the territory through which the railway was to run, and this although that territory had been awarded to Columbia . . . The defendant, and afterwards . . . the government of Costa Rica, it is believed by the inducement of the defendant, interfered with McConnell . . . Panama revolted and became an independent republic, declaring its boundary to be that settled by the award. In June, 1904, the plaintiff bought out McConnell and went on with the work . . . under the laws of Panama. But in July, Costa Rican soldiers and officials, instigated by the defendant, seized a part of the plantation and a cargo of supplies and have held them ever since, and stopped construction and operation of the plantation and railway. In August one Astua . . . got a judgment from a Costa Rican court, declaring the plantation to be his, although, it is alleged, the proceedings were not within the jurisdiction of Costa Rica, and were contrary to its laws and void. Agents of the defendant then bought the lands from Astua. The plaintiff has tried to induce the government of Costa Rica to withdraw its soldiers and also has tried to persuade the United States to intervene, but has been thwarted in both by the defendant and has failed . . .

As a result of the defendant's acts the plaintiff has been deprived of the use of the plantation and the railway . . . The defendant also, by outbidding, has driven purchasers out of the market and has compelled producers to come to its terms and it has prevented the plaintiff from buying for export and sale . . .

. . . [T]he plaintiff's case depends on several rather startling propositions. In the first place, the acts causing the damage were done, so far as appears, outside the jurisdiction of the United States, and within that of other states. It is surprising to hear it argued that they were governed by the act of Congress.

No doubt in regions subject to no sovereign, like the high seas . . . such countries may treat some relations between their citizens as governed by their own law . . . They go further, at times, and declare that they will punish anyone, subject or not, who shall do certain things, if they catch him, as in the case of pirates on the high seas. In cases immediately affecting national interests they may go further still and may make . . . similar threats as to acts done within another recognized jurisdiction . . . And the notion that English statutes bind British subjects everywhere has found expression . . . But the general and most universal rule is that the character of an act as lawful or unlawful must be determined wholly by the law of the country where the act is done . . . For another jurisdiction, if it happen to lay hold of the actor to treat him according to its own notions rather than those of the place where he did the acts, not only would be unjust, but would be an interference with the authority of another sovereign, contrary to the comity of nations, which the other state concerned justly might resent . . .

Law is a statement of the circumstances in which public force may be brought to bear upon men through the courts. But the word commonly is confined to such prophecies or threats when addressed to persons living within the power of the courts . . . It is true that domestic corporations always remain within the power of the domestic law; but in the present case, at least, there is no ground for distinguishing between corporations and men.

The foregoing . . . would lead, in cases of doubt, to a construction of any statute as intended to be confined in its operation and effect to the territorial limits over which the lawmaker has general and legitimate power. "All legislation is prima facie territorial" . . . Words having universal scope, such as, "every contract in restraint of trade," "every person who shall monopolize". . . will be taken . . . to mean only everyone subject to such legislation not all that the legislator subsequently may be able to catch ... [W]e think it entirely plain that what the defendant did in Panama or Costa Rica is not within the scope of the statute so far as the present suit is concerned . . .

For again, not only were the acts of the defendant in Panama or Costa Rica not within the Sherman Act, but they were not torts by the law of the place, and therefore were not torts at all, however contrary to the ethical and economic postulates of that statute. The substance of the complaint is that . . . Costa Rica . . . took and [kept] possession . . . by virtue of its sovereign power . . .

The fundamental reason why persuading a sovereign power to do this or that cannot be a tort is not that the sovereign cannot be joined as a defendant or because it must be assumed to be acting lawfully . . .

The fundamental reason is that it is a contradiction in terms to say that, within its jurisdiction, it is unlawful to persuade a sovereign to bring about a result . . . [F]oreign courts cannot admit that the influences were improper and the results bad. It makes the persuasion lawful by its own act . . . The injuries to the plantation and the supplies seem to have been the direct effect of the acts of the Costa Rican government . . .

Comments and Questions

1. Justice Holmes refused to apply the antitrust laws of the United States to anticompetitive acts that occurred in another country. Evaluate the decision and its implications upon international companies.
2. In the case of *U.S.* v. *Alcoa*, Judge Hand reconsidered the rule on applicability of antitrust law outside the United States. Alcoa had been charged with participation in "the Alliance," a worldwide cartel to control prices and markets for aluminum, but it had done so through Alcan Ltd, a Canadian corporation in which the main shareholders of Alcoa had controlling interest.
   Judge Hand first acknowledged that Alcoa and Alcan Ltd were separate legal entities and that Alcoa could not be said to be in control of what Alcan Ltd did:

Except when there [is] evidence that those in nominal control of one of the two corporations, exercised no independent decision, but followed the directions of the other, they [are] treated as juridically separate . . . For these reasons we conclude that Alcoa was not a party to the "Alliance."[4]

After reviewing the terms of two cartel agreements entered into between Alcan Ltd. and companies in France, Britain, Germany and Switzerland, Judge Hand continued:

[W]e are concerned only with whether Congress chose to attach liability to the conduct outside the United States of persons not in allegiance to it . . .

We should not impute to Congress an intent to punish all whom its courts can catch, for conduct which has no consequences within the United States [citing *American Banana*] On the other hand, it is settled law . . . that any state may impose liabilities even upon persons not within its allegiance for conduct outside its borders that has consequences within its borders . . .

Both agreements would clearly have been unlawful had they been made within the United States; and it follows . . . that both were unlawful, though made abroad, if they were intended to affect imports and did affect them.[5]

[4]*U.S.* v. *Alcoa* 146 F.2d 416, 442 (1945).
[5]Ibid., 443, 444.

What modifications has Judge Hand made to the rule laid down by Justice Holmes? Which rule is to be preferred? Were the rules outlined by Hand to have been applied to the facts of the *American Banana* case, would a different result have been reached?

3. In both the Holmes and Hand opinions there is the requirement that Congress express an intention that United States law apply extraterritorially. Only after this incoming requirement has been established, will a court go on to determine whether acts done outside the country have violated United States law.

   An earlier case which failed to meet the incoming requirement of Congressional intention involved a U. S. citizen who was working overseas for a U. S. company in Iraq and Iran. The worker claimed that he was entitled to overtime pay under the United States Eight Hour Law. The United States Supreme Court, citing the *American Banana* case, ruled that there was a presumption *against* applying United States law extraterritorially:

> An intention ... to regulate labor conditions which are the primary concern of a foreign country should not be attributed to Congress in absence of a *"clearly expressed purpose"* [The emphasis is the Court's.] *Foley Bros.* v. *Filardo*[6]

   The *Foley* case may appear to be a small fight—overtime pay or straight time. What are the more far-reaching consequences of a rule that hours and labor laws do not apply to employment outside the United States?

   If it helps, think of the implications of applying U. S. labor laws to United States-based multinationals and their controlled subsidiaries regardless of the location of operations. This would be analogous to a nation's asserting power based on citizenship regardless of where the citizen travels.

   How would business location decisions, first introduced in Chapter 2, be affected by such a rule?

4. In an antitrust case begun in 1974, *Matsushita Elect. Indus.* v. *Zenith Radio* 475 U.S.574 (1986), a number of United States-based manufacturers of consumer electronic products brought an action for treble damages against 21 Japanese electronic goods manufacturers and their United States subsidiaries, arguing that the firms engaged in selective price cutting designed to drive the American manufacturers out of the U. S. market. They claimed that the Japanese companies had charged high prices on goods sold in Japan, its exclusive market, and low prices on goods exported to and sold in the United States, where the companies had competitors, thereby making it impossible for United States manufacturers to compete against the Japanese companies in the United States.

[6]336 U.S. 281 (1949).

The United States Supreme Court decided that the case should be dismissed. The case was interesting in that it sat at the intersection of two competing doctrines potentially applicable to the lawsuit: (1) under the *Alcoa* decision behavior, although outside the United States, may be actionable in the United States if it "affects" competition in the United States [behavior of the Japanese companies in Japan can affect competition in the United States]; and (2) according to the *American Banana* case, behavior authorized or ordered by a foreign state cannot be made the subject of legal action in the United States courts [behavior by the Japanese electronics firms if done by order of the Japanese government to coordinate Japanese electronic production would not be actionable].

The case never went to trial, but more than a decade of litigation involving many parties and many lawyers attests to the applicability of Galanter's thesis of RPs opposing each other in protracted litigation.

The case also presents a not very well-known dimension of the "loss" of the electronics industry to Japan. The contention of the United States-based manufacturers was that the industry was *not lost* so much as it was *taken* through antitrust violations begun in Japan and carried out in the United States.

Since many acts of multinationals occur with the complicity, if not the order, of foreign governments, the *act of state* defense can present a substantial impediment to the application of United States law, as later cases in this chapter illustrate.

CONTEMPORARY CASES

The tensions over the limits of the United States legal system have continued to this day. In this section some cases have been selected from a number of areas to illustrate the persistence of the problem and the contexts where problems arise. Besides charting the scope of legal systems, the cases also provide additional factual information about international business practices.

Were it not for changes in business and the way it is now carried on, it might be thinkable to get along on rules tied strictly to territory, as Justice Holmes preferred in the *American Banana* case. The compelling clarity of the territorial criterion has been rendered obsolete by a growing chasm between law and business practices. The territorial rule has been extensively modified, as will be apparent from the cases, but the principle of territoriality is by no means dead.

1. Employment

The *Foley* case noted in the previous section establishes the rule that the labor laws of the United States do not apply to employment overseas, absent explicit Congressional intention. In the next case a United States citizen sued under the Civil Rights Act for alleged violations arising from employment in Saudi Arabia by a U.S.-based multinational.

BOURESLAN V. *ARAMCO, ARABIAN AMERICAN OIL CO.* 892 F.2D. 1271 (1990)[7]

Davis, Circuit Judge

I

In his Title VII suit, Boureslan charged that while he was working in Saudi Arabia his employer, Arabian American Oil Co. (Aramco), discriminated against him because of his race, religion and national origin. Aramco's motion to dismiss for lack of jurisdiction squarely raised the question whether Title VII's protection extends to U.S. citizens employed abroad by U.S. employers.

II

A. The respect for the right of nations to regulate conduct within their own borders is a fundamental concept of sovereignty that is not lightly tossed aside.

. . . From this concept the established presumption against extraterritorial application of a statute developed. The critical question that governs this appeal is whether Congress included language in Title VII that reflects a clear congressional intent to overcome the presumption against extraterritorial application of the Act.

The Supreme Court described this presumption in *Foley Bros., Inc.* v. *Filardo* (1949), a case closely analogous to [the] case at hand. In that case, Filardo, a U.S. citizen, argued that the Federal Eight Hour Law entitled him to overtime pay for work he had performed while in the employ of Foley Brothers, a U.S. government contractor operating in Iran and Iraq. . . . The Court's scrutiny of the Eight Hour Law's statutory language and structure revealed no congressional intent to cover workers such as Filardo—a conclusion bolstered by the legislative history's focus on domestic wage and unemployment problems. . . . [T]he Supreme Court set out the standard by which we must measure Boureslan's arguments: "An intention so to regulate labor conditions which are the primary concern of a foreign country should not be attributed to Congress in the absence of a *clearly expressed purpose.*" . . .

B. Boureslan's argument that Title VII reflects a clear congressional intent to extend its reach outside this country chiefly rests on Title VII's alien exemption provision, . . . This provision which expressly establishes an exemption from coverage under the Act provides: "This title shall not apply to an employer with respect to employment of aliens outside of any state." Boureslan finds the necessary clear expression of congressional intent to apply Title VII abroad by drawing a negative inference from that provision, and concluding that Congress meant to *include* citizens working abroad when it excluded aliens abroad. We disagree, and for the reasons that follow conclude that this single negative inference falls short of the required clear expression of congressional intent necessary to extend the reach of the Act outside this country.

1. Boureslan argues first that if we do not attach his negative inference to the alien exemption provision, we strip the provision of all purpose. This is simply not accurate. As we noted in the panel opinion, "no one disputes that the provision excludes coverage to aliens employed outside the states." [T]he Supreme Court in *Espinoza* v. *Farah*

[7]The case was later affirmed by the U. S. Supreme Court. *E.E.O.C.* v. *Arabian American Oil Co.* III. Supreme Court Reporter, 1227 (1991)

Mfg. Co., determined that this provision reflects a congressional intent to provide Title VII coverage to aliens employed *within* the United States. . . .

3. The Act is also curiously silent in a number of areas where Congress ordinarily speaks if it wants to extend its legislation beyond our borders. First, the Act fails to address venue problems [where actions are to be brought. —Ed.] . . . that arise with foreign violations. Next, the Equal Employment Opportunity Council's investigatory powers are limited to evidence obtained in the United States and its territories. . . .

Finally, if we give extraterritorial reach to Title VII, the plain language of the Act would necessarily extend that title to govern the employment relationship between foreign employers, and their American employees anywhere in the world . . . We doubt that Congress ever intended to impose Title VII on a foreign employer who had the grace to employ an American citizen in its own country.

4. As the Court stated as recently as January 1989, when it desires to do so, Congress knows how to give extraterritorial effect to one of its statutes. . . .

A good example is the Age Discrimination and Employment Act which was amended in 1984 to give the Act extraterritorial application. . . . ("The term 'employee' includes any individual who is a citizen of the United States employed by an employer in a workplace in a foreign country.") See also The Comprehensive Anti-Apartheid Act of 1986. . . .

Congress demonstrated in the above acts its awareness of the need to make a clear statement of extraterritorial application, address the concerns of conflicting foreign law, and provide the usual nut-and-bolts provisions for enforcing those rights.

C. In essence, Boureslan asks this court to conclude that Congress balanced Title VII's important goals against the foreign sovereignty concerns that underlie the presumption against extraterritoriality, considered the implications of application abroad and then addressed these concerns by inviting courts to read between the lines. For the reasons stated above, we cannot accept this conclusion . . .

King . . . dissenting

I agree with the majority that the sole question presented is whether Congress acted to extend the protections of Title VII to United States citizens employed in other countries by United States employers. I believe that a fair and reasonable reading of this civil rights statute compels the conclusion that Congress did, in fact, intend Title VII's broad remedial goals to encompass, and eradicate, an American employer's discriminatory employment practices against a United States citizen, even if the acts constituting such discrimination were carried out on foreign soil.

. . . The Alien Exemption Clause

It is undisputed that Congress has the power to extend the protection of its laws extraterritorially when it is regulating the conduct of a United States national. . . .

A clear expression of Congress's intent regarding the extraterritorial reach of Title VII is found ... the alien exemption clause . . . This section provides that Title VII "shall not apply to an employer with respect to the employment of aliens outside any State." . . . If Congress had not envisioned an extraterritorial application of Title VII, a specific provision exempting only aliens from such coverage would not have been needed . . .

The logical and necessary interpretation of section 702 is that, by specifically providing an exemption for employers regarding the extraterritorial employment of "aliens," without providing a similar exemption as to the corresponding category of "citizens," Congress intended that American employees would be covered under Title VII . . .

Conclusion

In enacting Title VII of the Civil Rights Act of 1964, Congress expressed its determination that all Americans are entitled to be free of the intolerable barrier of discrimination in employment based on race, color, religion, sex or national origin. Under the majority's holding, however, Congress's commitment represents merely an empty promise to the thousands of American women and minorities employed in other countries by American multinational firms. Such individuals face the dilemma of accepting an assignment abroad, often considered to be a lucrative opportunity and, in many such multinational enterprises, a prerequisite for career advancement at home, only at the cost of relinquishing the protections and remedies of Title VII upon crossing the territorial borders of the United States. Employment discrimination by American employers against American citizens—wherever practiced—has devastating effects both on the economy of this country and on the dignity and livelihoods of Americans who have come to rely over the past quarter of a century on achievements made possible, in part, by civil rights legislation. The salutary goals of Title VII cannot be fully realized if the fortuitous location of an American employee at the overseas office of an American firm could mean the difference between equal opportunity and discrimination at will.

Congress certainly recognized the potential for abuse represented by American multinational concerns when it enacted Title VII, which must explain its inclusion of section 702 of the Act, the alien exemption clause. Balancing the broad remedial goals of this civil rights statute against the potential conflicts that would arise in attempting to regulate the employment of aliens outside the United States, Congress followed the reasoning of the Supreme Court in *Foley Bros.* and drew an extraterritorial line based on nationality.

There is no justification for disregarding the clear evidence of congressional intent to apply Title VII to United States citizens employed in other countries by American enterprises. Congress made the judgment in 1964 in Title VII, just as it did again in 1984 in the ADEA amendments, that American nationals employed by United States employers are entitled to the same protection from employment discrimination abroad as they enjoy at home . . .

Notes and Questions

1a. If the laws against discrimination do not apply outside the United States, how might this affect multinational practices? Should different legal rules apply *inside* and *outside* the United States regarding discrimination in employment?

b. What would be the effect upon a U.S.-based multinational if United States Civil Rights legislation were to apply wherever multinationals operated, or to all employment regardless of the citizenship of the employee?

2. Management texts sometimes speak of corporate social responsibility, which means that managers feel an ethical imperative even where strictly legal obligations do not apply. Would cases like the one brought by Boureslan be compelling ones for the assumption of corporate social responsibility? Even apart from legal obligation, ought the corporation to take the initiative to eliminate discrimination wherever it occurs?

   Once the lawsuit got going, should Aramco have raised the argument about the inapplicability of the statute, or should it have concentrated on proving that it had not discriminated against the employee? (Should the corporation have gotten "technical," or should it have stuck to substance—that is, whether there was any merit to the discrimination claim?)
3. The United States Supreme Court affirmed the *Boureslan* decision, but the Civil Rights Act of 1991 included the following amendment:

Section 109 (a) DEFINITION OF EMPLOYEE

With respect to employment in a foreign country, such term includes an individual who is a citizen of the United States...

If the foregoing would be the basis of a suit by a U. S. national, Section 109 (b) of the 1991 Act seems to express an intention to defer to the sovereignty of other countries in some cases:

It shall not be unlawful . . . for an employer . . . to take any action otherwise prohibited . . . , with respect to an employee in a workplace in a foreign country if compliance . . . would cause such employer . . . to violate the law of the foreign country in which such workplace is located.

The Act also addresses the problems of corporate subsidiaries which may be incorporated in foreign countries:

If an employer controls a corporation whose place of incorporation is a foreign country, any practice . . . shall be presumed to be engaged in by such employer . . .

The Act then deals with "control" of foreign subsidiaries and bases control on the following:

(A) the interrelation of operations

(B) the common management

(C) the centralized control of labor relations

(D) the common ownership or financial control, of the employer and the corporation

The Act does not speak about whether all of the factors need to be present or whether only one or some of the factors need to be present for a business unit to be "the employer." Without being incurably cynical, one could wonder whether there will be a whole round of cases giving weights to the individual factors (along the lines of the choice of law cases excerpted in Chapter 9). With four factors, the possible combinations of factors are 2 to the fourth power or 16 (minus 1 for the case where no factor is present).

After the enactment of the Civil Rights Act of 1991, what about discrimination against U. S. citizens by U. S.-based multinationals or their subsidiaries? Discrimination against aliens? Make a small outline showing the present law governing employment discrimination by multinationals.

In the next case we have the increasingly common situation of a *foreign-based* multinational operating in the United States through subsidiaries incorporated here. We learn that some rules of United States law apply, but some may be displaced by treaty provisions between the United States and the country of origin of the multinational.

SUMITOMO SHOJI AMERICA, INC. V. AVAGLIANO 102 S.CT.2374 (1982)

Chief Justice Burger

We granted certiorari to decide whether Article VIII(1) of the Friendship, Commerce and Navigation Treaty between the United States and Japan provides a defense to a Title VII employment discrimination suit against an American subsidiary of a Japanese company.

I

Petitioner, Sumitomo Shoji American, Inc., is a New York corporation and a wholly owned subsidiary of Sumitomo Shoji Kabushiki Kaisha, a Japanese general trading company or *sogo shosha*.[1] Respondents are past and present female secretarial employees of Sumitomo. All but one of the respondents are United States citizens; that one exception is a Japanese citizen living in the United States. Respondents brought this suit as a class action claiming that Sumitomo's alleged practice of hiring only male Japanese citizens to fill executive, managerial, and sales positions violated both 42 U.S.C. Sec. 1981 and Title VII of the Civil Rights Act of 1964.

. . . Respondents sought both injunctive relief and damages. Without admitting the alleged discriminatory practice, Sumitomo moved . . . to dismiss the complaint. Sumitomo's motion was based on two grounds: (1) discrimination on the basis of Japanese citizenship does

[1]General trading companies have been a unique fixture of the Japanese economy since the Meiji era. These companies each market large numbers of Japanese products, typically those of smaller concerns, and also have a large role in the importation of raw materials and manufactured products to Japan. In addition, the trading companies play a large part in financing Japan's international trade. The largest trading companies—including Sumitomo's parent company—in a typical year account for over 50 percent of Japanese exports and over 60 percent of imports to Japan. . . .

not violate Title VII and Sec. 1981; and (2) Sumitomo's practices are protected under Article VIII(1) of the Friendship, Commerce and Navigation Treaty between the United States and Japan, Apr. 2, 1953. ...

The court refused to dismiss the Title VII claims, ... ; it held that because Sumitomo is incorporated in the United States it is not covered by Article VIII(1) of the Treaty.

...

II

Interpretation of the Friendship, Commerce and Navigation Treaty between Japan and the United States must, of course, begin with the language of the Treaty itself. The clear import of treaty language controls unless "application of the words of the treaty according to their obvious meaning effects a result inconsistent with the intent or expectations of its signatories."

Article VIII(1) of the Treaty provides in pertinent part: *"[C]ompanies of either Party* shall be permitted to engage, within the territories of the other Party, accountants and other technical experts, executive personnel, attorneys, agents and other specialists of their choice." (Emphasis added.)[2]

Clearly Article VIII(1) only applies to companies of one of the Treaty countries operating in the other country. Sumitomo contends that it is a company of Japan, and that Article VIII(1) of the Treaty grants it very broad discretion to fill its executive, managerial, and sales positions exclusively with male Japanese citizens . . .[3]

[T]he definition section of the Treaty . . . provides:

"As used in the present Treaty, the term 'companies' means corporations, partnerships, companies and other associations whether or not with limited liability and whether or not for pecuniary profit. Companies constituted under the applicable laws and regulations within the territories of either Party *shall be deemed companies thereof* and shall have their juridical status recognized within the territories of the other Party." (Court's emphasis.)

Sumitomo is "constituted under the applicable laws and regulations" of New York . . . it is a company of the United States, not a company of Japan. As a company of the United States operating in the United States, under the literal language of . . . the Treaty, Sumitomo cannot

[2]Similar provisions are contained in the Friendship, Commerce and Navigation Treaties between the United States and other countries.

...

These provisions were apparently included at the insistence of the United States; in fact, other countries, including Japan, unsuccessfully fought for their deletion. ...

According to Herman Walker, Jr., who at the time of the drafting of the Treaty served as Adviser on Commercial Treaties at the State Department, Article VIII(1) and the comparable provisions of other treaties were intended to avoid the effect of strict percentile limitations on the employment of American abroad and "to prevent the imposition of ultranationalistic policies with respect to essential executive and technical personnel."

[3]The issues raised by this contention are clearly of widespread importance. [T]reaty provisions similar to that invoked by Sumitomo are in effect with many other countries. In fact, some treaties contain even more broad language. . . . ("Nationals and companies of either party shall be permitted to engage, within the territories of the other Party, accountants and other technical experts, executive personnel, attorneys, agents and *other employees of their choice* . . .") As of 1979, United States affiliates of foreign corporations employed over 1.6 million workers in this country. . . .

invoke the rights provided in Article VIII(1), which are available only to companies of Japan operating in the United States and to companies of the United States operating in Japan.

The Governments of Japan and the United States support this interpretation of the Treaty. Both the Ministry of Foreign Affairs of Japan and the United States Department of State agree that a United States corporation, even when wholly owned by a Japanese company, is not a company of Japan under the Treaty and is therefore not covered by Article VIII(1).

The Ministry of Foreign Affairs stated its position to the American Embassy in Tokyo with reference to this case:

"The Ministry of Foreign Affairs, as the Office of [the Government of Japan] responsible for the interpretation of the [Friendship, Commerce and Navigation] Treaty, reiterates its view concerning the application of Article 8, Paragraph 1 of the Treaty: For the purpose of the Treaty, companies constituted under the applicable laws . . . of either Party shall be deemed companies thereof and, therefore, a subsidiary of a Japanese company which is incorporated under the laws of New York is not covered by Article 8 Paragraph 1 when it operates in the United States."

The United States Department of State also maintains that Article VIII(1) rights do not apply to locally incorporated subsidiaries . . .[4]

III

Sumitomo maintains that although the literal language of the Treaty supports the contrary interpretation, the intent of Japan and the United States was to cover subsidiaries regardless of their place of incorporation. We disagree . . .

The Friendship, Commerce and Navigation Treaty between Japan and the United States is but one of a series of similar commercial agreements negotiated after World War II. The primary purpose of the corporation provisions of the Treaties was to give corporations of each signatory legal status in the territory of the other party, and to allow them to conduct business with domestic firms. Although the United States negotiated commercial treaties as early as 1778, and thereafter throughout the 19th century and early 20th century, these early commercial treaties were primarily concerned with the trade and shipping rights of individuals. Until the 20th century, international commerce was much more an individual than a corporate affair.

As corporate involvement in international trade expanded in this century, old commercial treaties became outmoded. Because "corporation[s] can have no legal existence out of the boundaries of the sovereignty by which [they are] created," . . . it became necessary to negotiate new treaties granting corporations legal status and the right to function abroad. A series of Treaties negotiated before World War II gave corporations legal status and access to foreign courts, but it was not until the postwar Friendship, Commerce and Navigation Treaties that United States corporations gained the right to conduct business in other countries. The purpose of the

[4]Determining the nationality of a company by its place of incorporation is consistent with prior treaty practice. The place-of-incorporation rule also has the advantage of making determination of nationality a simple matter. On the other hand, application of a control test could certainly make nationality a subject of dispute.

Treaties was not to give foreign corporations greater rights than domestic companies, but instead to assure them the right to conduct business on an equal basis without suffering discrimination based on their alienage.

The Treaties accomplished their purpose by granting foreign corporations "national treatment" in most respects and by allowing foreign individuals and companies to form locally incorporated subsidiaries. These local subsidiaries are considered for purposes of the Treaty to be companies of the country in which they are incorporated; they are entitled to the rights, and subject to the responsibilities of other domestic corporations. By treating these subsidiaries as domestic companies, the purpose of the Treaty provisions—to assure that corporations of one Treaty party have the right to conduct business within the territory of the other party without suffering discrimination as an alien entity —is fully met.

We are persuaded, . . . that under . . . the Treaty, Sumitomo is a company of the United States; we discern no reason to depart from the plain meaning of the Treaty language. Accordingly, we hold that Sumitomo is not a company of Japan and is thus not covered by Article VIII(1) of the Treaty.

[The case was sent back to the lower courts.]

Notes and Questions

1. In this case the court has applied the rules on priority of law which govern multinational transactions: treaties have priority over national statutes, and national statutes have priority over state or local law. Since there can be differences up and down these lines of legal authority, as is evident in this case, this hierarchical ordering of legal authority can add yet another complication to lawsuits.
2. Sumitomo has lost its case to this point; equal employment law of the United States cannot be avoided altogether, despite the treaty. The corporation can still, however, make arguments *within* the equal employment laws, such as contending that the requirement of Japanese citizenship is a "bona fide occupational qualification" for high-level employment with a Japanese-owned subsidiary. The Supreme Court did not reach this question.

   A related case also involving a Japanese-based multinational concerned the firing of three American executives from its United States subsidiary. The Court of Appeals ruled that the Friendship Treaty between United States and Japan permitted discrimination based on citizenship. The court applied the usual rule of giving precedence to treaties over national statutes [Here Title VII of the Civil Rights Act of 1964 was preempted by the treaty], when there is conflict between the language of a treaty and the language of a statute. The court found "foreign businesses clearly have the right to choose citizens of their own nation as executives . . . Title VII would be taking back with one hand what the treaty gave with the other. This collision is avoided by holding national origin and citizenship separate . . .

Lest the *Sumitomo* and *Matsushita* cases feed anti-Japanese sentiments, also known as "Japan bashing," readers should be aware that the Friendship Treaty was negotiated at the instance of the United States, which set terms designed to prevent interference *by Japan* with the operation of United States-based businesses there. These cases fit the maxim of turnabout being fair play. The Japanese have gone to school on the practices of United States-based multinationals that have been reluctant to relinquish control of operations to foreign nationals.

In the words of the Court in the *Matsushita* case:

> If the conclusion seems callous toward Americans who lost their jobs at Quasar, we remind that the rights granted by the treaty are reciprocal. There are Americans employed abroad by foreign subsidiaries of U.S. companies who, but for the treaty, would lose their jobs to foreign nationals. Indeed the treaty was inserted at the instance of the United States. Japan was opposed to it.

It should also be remembered that the subsidiaries of Japanese corporations are represented by the same elite law firms that represent United States-based multinationals, and one should expect therefore the same no-holds-barred style of advocacy.

The combined effect of the *Sumitomo* and the *Matsushita* cases produces an ironic outcome. The *Friendship* treaties legitimate discrimination by U.S.-based firms when they operate elsewhere and discrimination by foreign-based multinationals when they operate in the United States. As the saying goes, "With friends like these . . ."

3. Sumitomo lost the case, an indication that there may be some disadvantages in using subsidiaries incorporated in the United States, traceable to the application of unwanted domestic law. Are there offsetting advantages to using them? Reconsider some of the material found in Chapter 5 on corporations, which discusses a corporation being equivalent to a natural person under the United States Constitution.

   Could Congress or a state legislature enact laws that discriminate against the U.S.-incorporated subsidiaries of foreign-based multinationals in such areas as defense contracting, or the ownership of businesses, commercial real estate, and farmland?

A last important intersection between labor and international business concerns the applicability of United States labor laws to companies whose activities are both within and outside the United States. As was observed in the last chapter on "flags of convenience," one of the inducements of shipping companies to register their vessels in other countries was to escape the necessity of hiring American crews at higher prices and under more stringent working conditions than would be applicable elsewhere. The next case introduces this perennial conflict between international shipping companies and organized labor.

MCCULLOCH V. *SOCIEDAD NATIONAL* 372 U.S. 10 (1963)

Justice Clark . . .

These cases . . . question the coverage of the National Labor Relations Act . . . A corporation organized and doing business in the United States beneficially owns seagoing vessels which make regular sailings between United States, Latin America and other ports transporting the corporation's products and other supplies; each of the vessels is owned by a foreign subsidiary of the American corporation, flies the flag of a foreign nation and has other contacts with the nation of its flag. The question is whether the Act extends to crews engaged in such a maritime operation. The National Labor Relations Board on application of the National Maritime Union held that it does and ordered an election . . . [A board-ordered election would determine whether the crew members desired a union and representation by the National Maritime Union. —Ed.]

The National Maritime Union . . . filed a petition . . . seeking certification . . . as representative of the unlicensed seamen employed by certain Honduran-flag vessels owned by Empressa Hondurena de Vapores . . . a Honduran corporation. The petition was filed against United Fruit Company, a New Jersey corporation which was alleged to be the owner of the majority of Empressa's stock. Empressa intervened and on hearing it was shown that United Fruit owns all of its stock and elects its directors, though no officer of Empressa is an officer or director of United Fruit and all are residents of Honduras. In turn the proof was that United Fruit is owned by citizens of the United States and maintains its principal office at Boston. Its business was shown to be the cultivation, transporting, and sale of bananas, sugar, cacao and other tropical produce raised in Central and South America and sold in the United States.

United Fruit maintains a fleet of cargo vessels . . . A portion of the fleet consists of 13 Honduran registered vessels operated by Empressa and time chartered to United Fruit [under contract for use by United Fruit for a period of time—ed.], which vessels were included in National Maritime Union's representation proceeding. The crews on these vessels are recruited by Empressa in Honduras. They are Honduran citizens and claim that country as their residence and home port. The crew are required to sign Honduran shipping articles, and their wages, terms and conditions of employment . . . are set by a bargaining agreement between Empressa and a Honduran union, Sociedad Nacional of Marineros de Honduras . . . [U]nder Honduran law, recognition of Sociedad as the exclusive bargaining agent compels Empressa to deal exclusively with it . . .

United Fruit, however, determines the ports of call of the vessels, their cargos and sailings . . . While the voyages are for the most part between Central American and South American ports and those of the United States, the vessels each call at regular intervals at Honduran ports for the purposes of taking on and discharging cargo . . .

II.

The Board concluded from these facts that United Fruit operated a single, integrated maritime operation . . . reasoning that United Fruit was a joint employer with Empressa of the seamen . . . It therefore ordered an election . . . [T]he Board's assertion of power to determine the representation of foreign seamen aboard vessels under foreign flags has aroused vigorous protests from foreign governments and created international problems for our Government.

Since the parties all agree that the Congress has constitutional power to apply the National Labor Relations Act to crews working foreign vessel ships at least while they are in American waters . . . we go directly to the question of whether Congress exercised that power . . . The Board has evolved a test relying on the relative weight of a ship's foreign as compared to its American contacts . . .

[H]ere there is a fleet not temporarily in the United States but operating in a regular course of trade between foreign ports and those of the United States; and second, the foreign owner of the ships is in turn owned by an American corporation. We note that both of these points rely on additional American contacts and therefore necessarily presume the validity of the "balancing of contacts" theory of the Board. But to follow such a suggested procedure to the ultimate might require that the Board inquire into the internal discipline and order of all foreign vessels calling at American ports. Such activity would raise considerable disturbance not only in the field of maritime law but in international relations as well. In addition this would project the courts into application of the sanctions of the Act to foreign-flag ships on a purely ad hoc weighing of contacts basis. This would lead to embarrassment in foreign affairs and be entirely infeasible in actual practice. The question . . . appears to us more basic . . . whether the Act as written was intended to have any application to foreign-registered vessels employing alien seamen.

[W]e find no basis for a construction that would exert United States jurisdiction . . . Sociedad, currently the exclusive bargaining agent of Empressa under Honduran law would have a head-on collision with N.M.U. should it become the exclusive bargaining agent under the Act . . . thus even though Sociedad withdrew from such an intramural labor fight . . . questions of such international import would remain as to invite retaliatory impact from other nations as well as Honduras.

[U]nder such conditions in this "delicate field of international relations" there must be present the affirmative intention of Congress . . . [W]e hold that the Board was without jurisdiction to order the election . . .

Comments and Questions

1. The court seems reluctant to interfere with Honduras, its corporations, and a recognized Honduran union which is the exclusive bargaining agent of the crew members on board the ships of Empressa. Through the *American Banana* case we were made aware that the "acts of state" in certain Latin American republics may be either much less (or much more) than "acts of state," given the extensive interaction between government officials there and the go-betweens of international companies. Should the United States courts allow proof of these interconnections that make the independence of governments suspect, or should it accept the policies and laws of such countries at face value?

Does the court seriously believe that NLRB elections will disrupt the international relationships between Honduras and the United States? On what are these "relationships" now based?

2a. There is provision in the labor law of the United States that disallows "company unions," that is, unions that are formed under the auspices of the company and are therefore not independent. Does the suspicion about the authenticity of company unions extend to unions like Sociedad? If a court does not know whether a union is independent or not, should it check?

b. In this connection the Court warns that the acceptance of the National Maritime Union of America as the union for Empressa crews might spark an "intramural fight." Does this phrasing tacitly recognize the independence of the Honduran union (an intramural fight is a fight "within the same walls")? If the Honduran union is a shell, then the fight is "extramural," that is between United Fruit and the union, and not among unions.

c. Would these ambiguities of the independence of the Honduran union have been resolved by a free election of the crews of Empressa, as provided under the procedures of the NLRB? Would crew members know best whether they have the union they want in Sociedad or not?

3. The Court also says that the recognition of Board power would require an *ad hoc*, or case by case, determination of the contacts between international companies and the United States. We learned from the cases in the last chapter on injuries that the courts appear to be willing to look at up to 256 combinations of factors to determine which law governs an injury case. Why the reluctance to engage in extensive inquiry in the area of elections of unions while there is no reluctance to engage in very extensive efforts in the injury cases?

   Would there be any reasons why multinational companies would want very limited judicial inquiry in one context and very extensive inquiry in another?

4. The *McCulloch* case is part of a long and losing battle fought by American trade unionists against the avoidance of the use of American crews. A common practice of the NMU and other unions was to picket ships entering U. S. ports, to discourage longshoremen from crossing picket lines to unload the ships. In one case the picketers carried the following placards:

ATTENTION TO THE PUBLIC

THE WAGES AND BENEFITS PAID TO SEAMEN ABOARD THIS VESSEL . . . ARE SUBSTANDARD TO THOSE OF AMERICAN SEAMEN. THIS RESULTS IN EXTREME DAMAGE TO OUR WAGE STANDARDS AND LOSS OF OUR JOBS. PLEASE DO NOT PATRONIZE THIS VESSEL. HELP THE AMERICAN SEAMEN. WE HAVE NO DISPUTE WITH ANY OTHER VESSEL ON THIS SITE.

The United States Supreme Court found that the picketing could be forbidden under Texas law without interfering with national labor relations law passed by Congress.

Justice Brennan in dissent sympathized with the efforts of the American unions to challenge the use of foreign-flagged vessels to circumvent both American workers and United States labor laws:

> Ninety-five percent of our export trade has already fled American-flag vessels for cheaper foreign-registry shipping . . . In holding [against the picketing of the ships—ed.] the Court effectively deprives American seamen among all American employees in commerce of any federally protected weapon with which to try to save their jobs . . .[8]

An article from the *Wall Street Journal* provides a partial update of the ongoing problems associated with foreign-flagged vessels.[9]

UNSAFE OIL TANKERS AND ILL-TRAINED CREWS THREATEN FURTHER SPILLS

By Wall Street Journal *Staff reporters Ken Wells, Daniel Machalaba, and Caleb Solomon*

LONDON – British Petroleum Co. inspectors spent hours crawling over a 550-foot Maltese-registered tanker in Amsterdam last year. They came away appalled.

BP found 73 deficiencies, some of them mind-boggling. Many of the navigation charts aboard the Greek-owned vessel, which had been offered to the oil company for charter, hadn't been updated for 20 years. Two of its engineers were unlicensed. Its anticollision radar was out of whack. The crew was Greek and Filipino, but the ship's safety and mechanical manuals were written in Serbo-Croatian. Even worse, the tanker, brimming with 22,000 tons of gasoline, had a hopelessly inadeqate fire-control plan while most of its crew went about blithely ignoring no-smoking regulations, BP inspectors noted. Not surprisingly, the oil company, which flunked nearly a third of the 1,000 vessels it inspected last year, rejected this one, too. Yet the ship continues to ply international waters for others.

Getting a Bad Name

BP's concern is one shared by major oil companies and governments around the world. Aging, poorly run ships, ill-trained crews and poor navigation are giving the world's tanker industry a bad name. While world-wide tanker losses dipped slightly in 1992 from 1991 levels, 1993 is off to a terrible start; tanker-related oil spills in the Shetland Islands, Indonesia and Estonia, along with one in Spain in December, have prompted inquiries and calls for stiffer regulation. Three of the accidents were believed caused by navigation errors.

Britain's transport secretary, John MacGregor, after a recent cursory look at the state of the global tanker fleet,

[8]*Windward Shipping* v. *American Radio Assn.* 415 U.S. 104. 116 (1974).

[9]Reprinted by permission of the *Wall Street Journal*; February 12, 1993, pp. 1, A6.

declared: "Substandard shipping is an international disgrace."

Statistics are on his side. Twenty percent of the world's tankers are considered unsafe, yet they continue to operate in vast and busy global sea lanes that remain largely unpoliced. Cutthroat market conditions, shoddy operators and scant international regulation add to the strain on a system that moves two billion tons of oil and petroleum products annually. With the exception of the U.S., where punishing liability laws imposed after the 1989 Exxon Valdez disaster seem to have shocked shippers into tougher safety standards, the world's tanker lanes are growing more perilous.

Expanding Fleets

Many of the seafaring states with the worst safety records over the past five years—Panama, South Korea, Malta, Cyprus and the island nation of St. Vincent among them—are the very flag states whose total fleets, tankers included, are expanding. The proliferation of these "flags of convenience"—ships registered in Third World countries by owners seeking to avoid the higher taxes and more stringent regulations of most Western maritime powers—implies "a continued deterioration" of world-wide ship-accident rates, says the Institute of London Underwriters, a marine-insurance consortium. Furthermore, the quality of international seamanship has slipped markedly in the past decade, in part because there is no global oversight of the accreditation of the world's seafarers. "Considering the very sophisticated navigational aids now available," the number of tanker collisions points to "poor crew standards and lack of training," an institute report says.

The nominal traffic cop of the seas, the United Nations' International Maritime Organization, has spent decades promulgating tanker standards and safety regulations now endorsed by 99% of the world's seafaring nations. Yet the IMO concedes it has no real power to punish member states that chronically flout the law. "The flags," says IMO spokesman Roger Kohn, "are our bosses."

U.S. as Outcast

The U.S., despite perceptions left over from the disastrous Exxon Valdez spill, is viewed as the bright spot in an otherwise gloomy global picture, and it could prove to be the model for other accident-weary nations contemplating an assault on tanker accidents. In 1990, dissatisfied with the IMO's progress in raising the liability limits for tankers involved in oil spills, the U.S. pushed ahead with the Oil Pollution Act.

The act raises the liability for owners of an average-size supertanker operating in U.S. waters to around $100 million from about $14 million under IMO regulation. In addition, it authorizes unlimited liability if the spill results from a violation of federal law—operation of a ship while intoxicated, for example. It's not coincidental, some experts think, that the U.S. hasn't had a major spill in the past two years. In 1991, its total-spillage was 55,000 gallons, the lowest in 14 years.

Luck plays a part in this. Tanker wrecks, like car or plane crashes, will never be completely avoidable. But the Oil Pollution Act has unquestionably improved "the quality of tankers coming to the U.S.," says Arthur McKenzie of the Tanker Advisory Center, a tanker rating service in New York. David Melville, manager of MRC Marine, an Oxford, England, consulting concern, agrees. While the law's passage raised an outcry in the world shipping industry, where it remains thoroughly unpopular, "it's caused tanker owners to take navigation more seriously in the U.S. than in the rest of the world he says.

Its liability section, in fact, is but one of a number of the act's reforms scheduled to be implemented in U.S. waters over the next several years. One of the most-publicized requirements, that tankers operating in U.S. waters be equipped with doublehulls, won't take full effect until 2015. Other provisions—establishing tanker-free zones in environmentally sensitive areas and requiring tug escorts in certain busy tanker lanes — are expected to come sooner.

Common Market Considerations

Environmentalists complain that the U.S. Coast Guard, charged with implementing these regulations, is dragging its feet, thus exposing some of the nation's fragile marine ecosystems to unnecessary danger. (The Coast Guard says the matter is complicated and it is moving with due speed.) But many of the Oil Pollution Act's notions are getting a fresh look from other IMO-member nations concerned about the recent rash of accidents. The 12-nation European Community is considering strict new safety rules, including a requirement for double-hull tankers in line with the U.S. timetable and provisions that could put certain areas important to fishing, wildlife and tourism off limits to tankers.

The EC is also considering establishing its own tanker registry to keep tabs on the quality of ships using EC waters while weighing an outright ban on ships older than 15 years. The ban, should it be adopted, would keep about 40% of the EC's own ships from Common Market ports. The IMO says it isn't necessarily opposed to tougher rules but has discouraged nations from acting unilaterally, as the U.S. did.

With 35% of the world's tanker traffic eventually calling at U.S. ports, American officials can't afford to be complacent about the dangers of unsafe ships. Global statistics are sobering:

- At least 20% of the world's tankers are what one London maritime consultant calls "floating garbage—ships simply not fit to be plying the trade." While BP flunked 30% of the ships it inspected last year, other major oil companies fret that the number could be even higher. Societe Nationale Elf Aquitaine, the French oil concern, says two-thirds of the tankers it put through its own rigorous risk-analysis in 1992 flunked the test.
- Owners are reluctant to scrap unworthy ships. The Institute of London Underwriters says it refused to insure 85% of 133 ships it inspected in 1992 after finding serious structural problems. Yet few of those vessels underwent repairs, and only three were sent by owners to the scrap yard. Oil companies say they often see tankers at sea that they themselves have declined to hire for safety reasons.
- The glut of aging and substandard tankers is continuing to depress charter rates. This in turn deprives the industry of the necessary return on capital to rebuild the aging fleet. The underwriters' institute estimates that 54% of the world's 3,200 tankers were more than 15 years old in 1991; those same tankers accounted for 70% of all tanker losses that year. Meanwhile, the current spot charter rate for a 280,000-deadweight-ton tanker is about $20,000 a day. Yet industry analysts estimate that rates of $50,000 to $60,000 a day are needed to justify spending the $100 million it costs to build a new tanker of that size.

The prime movers in this rate cutting "are the oil companies," complains

Paul Slater, chairman of First International Financial Corp., a Naples, Fla., ship finance company. "It's the old adage, if you don't pay enough, you will get lousy service."

• Most of the world's busiest tanker passages are unguarded by tug escorts that could rescue a tanker in trouble. The causes: squabbling among countries, industry resistance and the vagaries of international maritime law. As experience in the crowded Strait of Malacca, between Indonesia and Malaysia, recently showed, this often leads to disaster. The collision between the fully-laden oil tanker Maersk Navigator, registered in Singapore, and an empty Japanese tanker last month was but one of numerous recent accidents. Last September, the fiery collision of a Liberian-registered supertanker and a Panamanian-flag cargo ship killed 44 of the 46 crew members. Critics say some other spots—the English Channel, the Strait of Gibraltar and the Bosporus Strait in Turkey–are disasters waiting to happen.

• Flags of convenience, with notable exceptions, often are flags of danger. Seven of them—Panama, South Korea, Honduras, Malta, Turkey, Cyprus and Indonesia—account for 60 of the 111 total ships lost last year, according to statistics compiled by the Institute of London Underwriters. Their losses, expressed in percentages of total tonnage afloat, were almost three times higher than the worldwide average.

• More than a decade of cost-cutting, spawned by depressed oil prices, has left ships undermanned and the pool of qualified international seafarers depleted. Moreover, the number of sailors coming from flag states with wildly uneven standards of maritime training is growing, as the pay differential between seamen from traditional maritime powers and the Third World widens. By one estimate, wage rates for a Filipino crew aboard a standard 40,000-ton tanker are about one-third that of a British crew. While the best of the Philippines' 60-odd maritime schools produce first-rate seamen, the country—among others—is known to have a number of "diploma mills" where standards are less than rigorous. The IMO encourages member states to model their schools upon its own World Maritime University, but it has no authority to impose those standards or to verify graduates' credentials.

Inspections for a Fee

If some governments have been keen to respond to these concerns, tanker operators and charterers around the globe have also taken them to heart. As BP's tough inspection system shows, major oil companies don't always trust the traditional policing of the tanker industry by flag countries or "classification societies," which inspect ships for a fee.

Royal Dutch/Shell Group last year conducted more than 3,500 tanker inspections on its own, flunking about 20% of the class. Chevron Corp. carried out 600 inspections and spares no expense in investigating ships for long-term charter, says David Powell, the company's fleet manager. "We visit the vessel, whether it be in Singapore, Europe or any place else," he says.

For single-voyage charters, Chevron uses its own computer databank of 10,000 vessels, as well as word of mouth to determine whether an inspection is necessary; about a third of the time it is. "In today's climate you're risking your corporation when you put your cargoes on board the vessels of others," says Mr. Powell.

OMI Petrolink Corp., a Houston company that operates tankers in the Gulf of Mexico, recently phased out all ships except those of 1989 vintage or newer, says Wynn Wyman, the company's chief executive officer. "Our customers . . . are getting to the point that they aren't very interested in early-1980s ships."

Chevron, among others, doesn't stop at the hull. More and more companies are asking questions about the quality of the crew and officers. Chevron fears having crew members of too many nationalities aboard one ship, because communication problems can arise in a crisis.

Tanker safety concerns are also prompting overhaul of classification societies, which have been the primary inspectors of ship construction and maintenance for more than 100 years. The London underwriters' institute's 1992 inspections of 133 ships, for example, were part of an insurance-industry trend to dispatch its own inspectors to high-risk ships rather than rely solely on the societies' investigatlons.

As a result, major societies are phasing in new inspection procedures this year that will increase the extent of tanker surveys.

And while there is little talk at the moment of imposing the U.S. Oil Pollution Act's unlimited liability provisions abroad, players in the global marine-insurance trade display every sign of clamping down on substandard shipping themselves. With a long shakeout in the marine-insurance industry having shrunk the pool of casualty and liability underwriters, "we are in a position to be incredibly ruthless" with ship owners with a poor safety history says Roger Nixon, an official of the London underwriters' institute. He cites London hull rates that are already 25% higher, and cargo rates 10 times higher, for identical new policies written on similar ships.

"The differential will continue to grow between what the good owners pay and what the bad owners pay," says Mr. Nixon.

OTHER COURT TESTS OF RULE-MAKING POWER

A. Securities Law

One of the reasons given for the Great Crash of the stock market in 1929 and the Great Depression which followed was speculative excesses in the stock and bond markets by banks and investment houses. Sharp business practice, sometimes crossing over into fraud and illegality, wrecked individual investors, and eventually brought down the system as a whole. President Roosevelt declared a bank "holiday" to prevent runs on insolvent banks; speculators jumped from windows rather than face financial ruin; and many people lost their jobs and "everything they had."

The Securities Exchange Act of 1934 was designed to restore order and honesty to the securities markets. Understandably there was a domestic preoccupation around the 1934 law, since the financial markets were not as international as they now are. Accordingly, Congress expressed no intention about the effects of U. S. securities law on international transactions.

Over the years, with accelerating volume, federal courts have had to determine the reach of United States securities law, especially in securities fraud cases where a party claims losses traceable to misrepresentations of fact about the financial condition of a company. It became manifestly naive for courts to try to pin down transactions by territory or exactly where effects were felt.

The securities cases fulfill the prophecies made by some political economists that there would be increasing tensions between business systems organized on a world scale, and political-legal systems still conducted on a national scale. In finance, "deals" know no national boundaries. Places like New York City or London operate as near-perfect financial markets, where virtually anything of value located anywhere can be bought or sold to anyone, anywhere. The traditional effort to locate causes and effects by territory becomes a manifestly silly undertaking, given the contemporary activities of money markets. At some point in most deals, all villains and victims will have "passed through" the principal money centers in person or by telecommunication.

Courts, in sorting through securities fraud cases, have felt most directly the difficulty of making national legal rules fit international transactions. United States courts sit at this unenviable intersection between the international and domestic securities business. Their work has been complicated by high-powered law firms on *both* sides of securities litigation, and labyrinthine corporate networks that are sometimes designed to put a securities transaction beyond the scope of national legal systems.

In 1991, the body of Robert Maxwell, who had been a major player in worldwide mergers and acquisitions in publishing, was found in the Atlantic Ocean off his yacht. He had either suffered a heart attack and drowned, or he had committed suicide. Shortly after his death, his financial empire collapsed, and upon inventory was found to be grossly less than the huge debts the Maxwell Group had run up.

The next case came 20 years earlier, when Maxwell was emerging as a mover in international publishing ventures. The plaintiff corporation, Leasco, argued that it had been bilked of $22,000,000 in connection with their purchase in London of stock in Pergamon Press, a British corporation controlled by the Maxwell group. If Maxwell had perpetrated a fraud, just where had the fraud occurred, and was it an appropriate dispute for an American court to decide according to American securities law?

LEASCO DATA PROCESSING EQUIPMENT CORP. V. MAXWELL 468 F.2D 1326 (C.A. 2, 1972)

Friendly, Chief Judge . . .

I. The Facts Claimed by Leasco

The gist of the complaint is that the defendants conspired to cause Leasco to buy stock of Pergamon Press Limited . . ., a British corporation controlled by defendant Robert Maxwell, a British citizen, at prices in excess of its true value in violation of Section 10 (b) of the Securities Exchange Act . . . According to Leasco . . . the first contact occurred early in 1969 when Maxwell came to Great Neck, N. Y., where Leasco then had its principal office, and proposed to Saul Steinberg, Chairman of Leasco, that Pergamon and Leasco engage in a joint venture in Europe. Maxwell falsely told Steinberg that Pergamon had a computerized typesetting plant in Ireland and gave Steinberg the most recent Pergamon report, which contained untruthful and misleading statements of Pergamon's affairs. Steinberg telephoned Maxwell in London to decline the joint venture; Maxwell invited him to come there to discuss areas of possible cooperation.

Steinberg and Robert Hodes, a director of Leasco, met Maxwell at the latter's London office in late April, 1969; Maxwell made various false and exaggerated statements of Pergamon's performance and prospects. When he suggested that Pergamon could acquire Leasco's European operations, Steinberg responded that Leasco would be interested only in acquiring Pergamon and its related companies. Clark, a director of Pergamon, entered the room, Maxwell having left for a short time, and whetted Leasco's interest by falsely touting the profitability of International Learning Systems Company (ILSC). Pergamon was a 50% owner and had an option to acquire the other 50% of ILSC. When Maxwell rejoined the group, he told Steinberg and Hodes that Ladislaus Majhtenyi, an official of Pergamon Press, Inc., an American subsidiary . . . , would provide Leasco with all financial data necessary to evaluate the worth of Pergamon and the Maxwell-related companies.

In late April or early May, Michael Gibbs, Leasco's director of corporate planning, met in New York with Majhtenyi. The latter said that the Pergamon and Maxwell operations were very profitable. He added that Pergamon was in the process of acquiring MSI Publishers . . . and falsely spoke in glowing terms of the profitability of that company's operations in selling Pergamon back issues in Canada, Mexico, and South America. This was followed by telephone calls between Maxwell and Steinberg; in some (or perhaps all) of the calls, one (or perhaps both) of the participants were in the United States. Maxwell reported enthusiastically, and falsely, about sales of ILSC encyclopedias in Australia . . . [H]e said he would meet Steinberg in New York City.

The meeting occurred at a hotel in early May; Maxwell, with Majhtenyi present, made various misrepresentations about the sales and earnings of Pergamon and ILSC. Around May 17 Maxwell mailed a letter from London to Leasco in New York enclosing a dozen documents. Among these were a false report of ILSC's profits; a draft of Pergamon's 1968 annual report, certified by defendant Chambers, Impey, and Co., containing false reports of profits; and a misleading report on Pergamon's affairs prepared by Whinney, Murray and Co., accountants retained by Fleming and Co., Ltd., a London banking firm whose clients were large holders of Pergamon stock and which also acted as financial adviser to Pergamon. Late in the month, Maxwell, in London, called Steinberg, in New York; he said that any contract for the takeover would have to be signed before the Pergamon annual meeting . . . As a result, Gibbs and Schwartz went to London around May 30 and met for four days with Maxwell, Clark, Kerman (a director of Pergamon and Pergamon Press, Inc., and a senior partner of a large London firm of solicitors which represented Pergamon and the Maxwell family . . .) . . .

The meetings were followed by telephone conversations between Maxwell in London and Steinberg in New York, in

. . . which Maxwell is claimed to have made further false statements . . . Around the same time Richard Fleming, Chairman of Fleming, Ltd., and Lawrence Banks, president of its American subsidiary . . . visited Leasco's offices in New York and told Schwartz and Hodes that Pergamon was far more valuable than the price Leasco was proposing to pay; in effect they vouched for the correctness of the Whinney Murray and Co. report.

Later Maxwell telephoned from London that the contract would have to be signed on or before June 17. He and Paul DiBiase, a member of Kerman's firm, arrived in New York shortly thereafter. In the course of a series of meetings he told Leasco that the condition of Pergamon and its related companies could accurately be determined by relying on the public financial statements certified by Chambers, Impey, and Co. Allegedly these statements misrepresented the profits of Pergamon and ILSC and . . . a large payment from MSI. Banks, who was present during some of these meetings, repeated that the proposed price was too low and that Fleming Ltd. might oppose the offer . . . The upshot was an agreement between Leasco and Maxwell signed in New York on June 17, 1969. [Leasco was to buy a controlling interest in Pergamon, and Maxwell was to give best efforts to get the deal consummated with shareholders of Pergamon and its board of directors. —Ed.] Leasco was permitted to cause the offer to be made by a wholly owned subsidiary (or a wholly owned subsidiary of such subsidiary), providing Leasco remained responsible for the due performance of its obligations.

Apparently Steinberg and Hodes accompanied Maxwell back to England. There he told them on June 18 that it would be in Leasco's interest to purchase Pergamon stock on the open market as soon as possible . . . Later in June, Maxwell, from London, called, Steinberg, in New York, and said that there were rumors of a counter-takeover bid and that it would be in Leasco's interests to purchase Pergamon stock to prevent this. [Leasco later claimed that if there was a rumor, Maxwell had started it. —Ed.] On June 20 Leasco operating through the London banking firm of N. M. Rothchild . . . began buying Pergamon stock on the London Stock Exchange. By July 24 it purchased 5,206,210 such shares, expending some $22,000,000; later it learned that some 600,000 of these shares had been secretly sold by one or more of the defendants. The stock was paid for in cash furnished by a wholly owned subsidiary, Leasco International N. V., a Netherlands Antilles corporation, which had recently sold to a group headed by two New York underwriters $40,000,000 of 5% debentures and $20,000,000 of 7% notes for offering only outside the United States and to purchasers not nationals or citizens thereof or resident or normally resident therein. Both the debentures and the notes were . . . guaranteed by Leasco . . .

Investigation of Pergamon's affairs by Leasco . . . caused Leasco's representative to make further inquiries of Maxwell in England . . . Leasco was provided with data indicating that the previous representations . . . had been misleading. As a result . . . Leasco declined to go forward with the tender offer [to buy more of the Pergamon stock —Ed.] However it was left with the $22,000,000 of Pergamon stock acquired . . . Leasco seeks damages . . .

II. Subject Matter Jurisdiction

. . . [J]urisdiction depends on the applicability of the Securities Exchange

Act . . . [This] case deals . . . with the problem considered in Restatement's Section 17, Jurisdiction to prescribe with Respect to Conduct, Thing, Status or other Interest within Territory . . . Conduct within the territory alone would seem sufficient from the standpoint of jurisdiction . . . It follows that when, as here, there has been significant conduct within the territory, a statute cannot properly be held inapplicable on the grounds that, absent the clearest language, Congress will not be assumed to have meant to go beyond the limits [that is, to cover behavior wholly outside the United States—Ed.] . . . [C]ritical misrepresentations, if such they were, were made in England during the four days of meetings in early June . . . [T]here were abundant misrepresentations in the United States. Maxwell's initial misrepresentations were made here, although then in a context of seeking to interest Steinberg in a joint venture. Further misrepresentations were made by Majhtenyi in late April or early May. These were elaborated by Maxwell and Majhtenyi and Maxwell at the hotel meeting in early May. There was the visit by Fleming and Banks in late May. Finally there was the meeting preceding the signature of the June 17 contract . . . On what is now before us it is impossible to say that conduct in the United States, was not "an essential link" in leading Leasco into the contract of June 17, 1969 . . . And that contract, signed in the United States, was "an essential link" in inducing Leasco to make the open-market purchases, whether these were triggered by a call from London to New York, as Leasco contends, or by a conversation in England, as defendants assert. Putting the matter another way, if defendant's fraudulent acts in United States significantly whetted Leasco's interest in acquiring Pergamon shares, it would be immaterial . . . that the damage resulted not from the contract whose execution Maxwell procured in this country but from interrelated action which he induced in England, or, for that matter, which Leasco took there on its own . . . In order to establish a coherent chain of causation, it is not necessary that the precise details leading up to the accident [here the loss] should have been reasonably foreseeable . . .

Up to this point we have established only that because of the extensive acts alleged to have been performed in the United States considerations of foreign relations law do not preclude our reading of 10(b) [of the Securities Exchange Act —Ed.] as applicable here. The question remains whether we should . . . Appellants have three lines of defense: . . . (1) that Section 10(b) has no application to transactions in foreign securities not on an organized American market; (2) that if it does, it has no application when such transactions occur outside the United States; and (3) that, in any event, it can have no application when the purchaser is not a citizen of the United States . . . [The court found an intention by Congress to include under the fraud provisions of the Act sales of stock issued by foreign companies. —Ed.]

Since Congress meant . . . to protect against fraud in the sale or purchase of securities whether or not these were traded on organized United States markets, we cannot perceive any reason why it should have wished to limit the protection to securities of American issuers. The New Yorker who is the object of fraudulent misrepresentations in New York is as much injured if the securities are of a mine in Saskatchewan as in Nevada . . . We likewise cannot see any sound reason for believing that in a case like that just put, Congress would have wished protection to be withdrawn merely because the fraudulent promoter of the Saskatchewan mining security took the buyer's check back to Canada and mailed the certificate from there.

Our case, however, is not as simple as the one just hypothesized . . . Here it was understood from the outset that all the transactions would be executed in England. Still we must ask ourselves whether, if Congress had thought about the point, it would not have wished to protect an American investor if a foreigner comes to the United States and fraudulently induces him to purchase foreign securities abroad . . . While . . . we doubt that impact on an American company and its shareholders would suffice to make the statute applicable if the misconduct had occurred solely in England, we think it tips the scales in favor of applicability when substantial misrepresentations were made in the United States.

This brings us to the appellants' third line of defense, namely, that the purchaser was not an American but a Netherlands Antilles corporation.

The instructions to Rothchild to proceed with the open market purchases came from Leasco, and Rothchild began its purchases on June 20, 1969, for that company's account. The permission granted by the Bank of England also ran to Leasco. Just who decided that the cash should be supplied by Leasco N. V., and when this was decided, are not clear . . .

It seems quite arguable . . . that Leasco N. V. is holding the shares as trustee for Leasco, which has the beneficial interest and is bound to reimburse Leasco N. V. for the latter's expenditures. If that were so, defendants' contention that the true purchaser was a foreigner would be drained of force. But even if Leasco N. V. is the beneficial owner it would be elevating form over substance to hold this entails a conclusion that the purchases did not have a sufficient effect in the United States . . .

We see no need to enter into the debate whether, as defendants contend and plaintiffs deny, Leasco obtained substantial tax and other advantages through the incorporation of Leasco N. V. and the use of the latter to acquire the Pergamon shares . . . [T]he defendants themselves recognized that Leasco, the United States company remained at all times intimately involved . . . [Decision that the United States courts have jurisdiction —Ed.]

Comments and Questions

1. The business background was recounted by the court to show the critical representations alleged by the plaintiff to be fraudulent, and where they took place. Before turning to the question of court power, follow the steps the parties took in negotiating an international acquisition to get a feel for business dealings that you will probably never witness.

   From a business angle, where did Leasco make its mistakes?
2. What would have been the implications of the court's finding that the U. S. Securities Act did not apply?
3. It might be useful to think of two polar cases, one where there would be little debate about the applicability of U. S. law and another where a court would most likely find the law inapplicable:

Case 1. U. S. law applicable where securities of an American corporation which are registered and listed on a national exchange and a deal adversely affects either foreign or U. S. citizens. [Plaintiffs Canadian, United States corporation, stock registered in the United States and traded on the American Stock Exchange]. *Des Brisay* v. *Goldfield* 549 F2d 133. (1977).

Case 2. U. S. law not applicable where plaintiffs are foreign and the claim is based on foreign "securities" and any activity in the United States "clearly secondary." *Fidenas* v. *Compagnie Internationale* 606 F2d 5 (1979).

One can imagine a number of possible cases, some "solely" foreign, some "solely" domestic, and many in the mucky middle.

There will be many cases in the "gray area," with mixtures of U. S. and foreign elements (place of issuance of securities, place of registration of securities, citizenship of plaintiff or defendant buyers and sellers, place where transaction was negotiated, place of contracting, place of performance, and so on). With the securities business now unified worldwide, regardless of the origin of securities, or of the places where deals are made in whole or in part, or of where buyers and sellers have citizenship, should federal courts presume that all transactions "take place" in the United States or "affect" the United States, even where there are some "foreign" factors present?

What are the consequences upon international dealings in securities of the decision to bring or not to bring a case within U.S. law?

The argument that there has been a de facto merging of the United States and Canadian securities markets which makes fine tuning of jurisdictional questions unnecessary was rejected in *Kaufman* v. *Campeau* 744 F. Supp. 808 (1990).

4. One of the complications in *Leasco* case was caused by the plaintiffs themselves. Apparently, Leasco had set up its Netherlands Antilles corporation, Leasco N. V., a "foreign" corporation, to get "tax and other advantages." Technically therefore, the purchase of the Pergamon stock by Leasco N. V. was by a "foreign" corporation, making it less entitled to protection in the U. S. courts than would be accorded to a U.S. citizen, as the securities law was then interpreted.

   How does the court get around this obstacle to jurisdiction?

   Should the court have simply said that Leasco must take all of the consequences of shopping for the best place to incorporate its subsidiaries, including if it so happens, losing the ability to make a claim in the United States courts when their subsidiaries wind up with the "wrong" citizenship?

   If neither the Maxwell group nor the principals of Leasco Inc. are ready for canonization as saints, and both are experienced business people, how should a court respond to their dealings?

   What about cases where the issuer of securities tries to take a deal "offshore" [outside U.S. law] with such stipulations as Leasco used in connection with debt securities floated through its Netherlands

Antilles subsidiary? [The debentures and notes were offered "to persons not nationals or citizens" of the United States "or resident thereof"]. Should courts honor such stipulations designed to escape U. S. securities regulations?

Even in those cases where the connections to the United States have been thin, the courts have expressed fear that the United States might become a "base" for fraud in a era where international wheeler dealers enter and exit legal systems with the speed of light. A court in one case voiced the concern this way:

> We do not think Congress intended to allow the United States to be used as a base for manufacturing fraudulent security devices for export, even when these are peddled only to foreigners. This country would certainly look askance if one of our neighbors stood by silently and permitted misrepresented securities to be poured into the United States. By the same token it is hard to believe Congress meant to prohibit the SEC from policing similar activities within this country . . . *IIT* v. *Vencap Ltd* 519 F.2d 1001,1017 (1975)

5. It is not always easy to find the center of securities transactions since they involve stages that can take place in multiple locations, in, out and between the United States and other countries.

   One court outlined some of the possibilities:
   (1) . . . negotiations;
   (2) execution of . . . investment contracts;
   (3) utilization of . . . instrumentalities . . . (telephones and mails);
   (4) incorporation of defendant companies in the United States or . . . corporate offices;
   (5) use of the New York office of a Swiss bank as conduit for moneys;
   (6) other activities—books and records, drafting of agreements, transmittal of proceeds. *SEC* v. *Kasser* 548 F.2d 109, 111 (1977)
6. In the securities cases the courts have been concerned with financial base and financial extensions from that base. To avoid gross breaches between business realities and legal realities, courts take cases. If this approach were extended to other aspects of multinational networking, what principal advantages of multinational networking through separate legal entities would be undercut?

   In multinational cases of a number of types—for example, labor cases, products liability cases, and so on—how far should U. S. courts go in placing "substance over form" and getting to the bottom of international fraud, evasions of law, or other problems arising from international business?

   When substance takes precedence over mere form, would all "offshore" operations of a multinational become subject to United States court's surveillance?
7. In comparing securities cases with cases from the previous chapter, where injured persons were trying to get the United States courts

into action, one is struck by the overall willingness of courts to take on international securities fraud and the overall unwillingness of courts to take on international injury cases.

How can this disparity in willingness to hear cases be explained? Is the preservation of a fair and honest securities market and protecting investors from financial loss a more compelling goal than promoting safety and the adequate compensation of accident claimants? Compare also the difference between concern about honest dealings in securities markets and purging discrimination from employment.

B. Acts of State

Justice Holmes in the *American Banana* case justified the nonapplication of U. S. antitrust law in part upon a reluctance to interfere with *acts of state* and the exercise of sovereignty by another country; what Costa Rica might choose to do about its internal affairs ought not be subject to second-guessing by outsiders. *Acts of state* can include everything from genocide and the Holocaust to apartheid in South Africa, or commercial favoritism, as was the situation in the *American Banana* case.

Without considering major atrocities done in the name of the state, what are contemporary applications of the act of state doctrine that can inhibit a United States court's making decisions in cases? The next two record a conflict that arose almost by accident. It was never anticipated that countries indebted to the commercial banks of the United States would default on their international obligations, and declare, *under national law*, suspensions (moratoria) on the payments of principal or interest on their debts.

Before we turn to the case a little background is in order. When a country imports, it must either pay or get credit. The trade must be paid or financed in currency that is acceptable, and this usually means "hard" currency rather than "local" currency. In that event, local currency must be exchanged for the required hard currency. In crisis, when exchange or loans become difficult to secure, countries usually assess all of their import needs to see which can be sacrificed and which cannot. If it comes down to a dire need for food and spare parts for buses, international debt payments may be suspended. This form of resolution of the exchange crisis threatens losses for foreign creditors.

In 1982 Mexico nearly defaulted on its international obligations, and lending that had been a boon to U. S. money center bank earnings turned to cold fear that interest and principal on billions of dollars of Third World debt would never be paid. Almost overnight what was first referred to as the "third world debt crisis," had become a "first world debt crisis" since massive defaults would have threatened the solvency of the entire U.S. banking system.

The case involved a New Jersey bank that was insisting that the debt it held from a Costa Rican bank be paid as agreed. The defense to the action was that the Costa Rican bank was not paying because the government of

Costa Rica had ordered it not to pay. A straightforward application of the *act of state* doctrine would mean that the U. S. court would dismiss the suit out of deference to the inherent power in Costa Rica to make its own laws.

The amounts involved in the Costa Rican loans were not especially large, and this is what might have put the U.S. district court to sleep on the enormous implications of allowing the "act of state" defense to apply: just outside this case were hundreds of billions in international debt of many countries that were similarly situated to Mexico and Costa Rica and who could declare for themselves a moratorium. It did not take long for the U. S. banking establishment to mobilize and wake the federal courts up.

ALLIED BANK INTERNATIONAL V. BANCO CREDITO AGRICOLA 566 F. SUPP.1440 (1983)

Griesa, District Judge

This is a suit against three Costa Rican banks which are wholly owned by the government of Costa Rica . . .

The essential facts are not in dispute. Plaintiff Allied Bank International (Allied) is a bank chartered in the United States with its principal place of business in New York. Allied is the designated agent to prosecute this action on behalf of a syndicate of 39 banks. [In international lending it is common for loans to be made by a syndicate of banks rather than by a single bank. —Ed.] As a result of certain banking transactions . . . the three defendant Costa Rican banks in 1976 executed a series of promissory notes payable to the syndicate banks. Payments under the notes were due every six months . . .

Payments were made on schedule until 1981. In that year Costa Rica was encountering a serious economic crisis. In response, the Costa Rican government imposed restrictions on foreign exchange transactions. [In a financial crisis, a country may not be able to generate enough foreign currency to pay its external obligations. Typically, restrictions on exchanges from local currency to foreign currency are designed to conserve and ration foreign exchange. —Ed.] One of these restrictions was to require approval by the Central Bank of Costa Rica of any foreign exchange transaction on the part of Costa Rican banks.

On July 2, 1981 defendant Banco Cartago applied to the Central Bank for authorization to accomplish the foreign exchange transaction necessary to make the payment due on July 1 to the syndicate . . . On August 27, 1981, the Central Bank's Board of Directors passed a resolution prohibiting public sector entities, such as defendant banks, from paying any interest or principal on debts to foreign creditors denominated in foreign currency. On November 6, 1981 the President of Costa Rica and the Ministry of Finance published Executive Decree 13103-H preventing any institution in Costa Rica from making payment on an external debt without prior approval of the Central Bank in consultation with the Ministry of Finance. On November 9, 1981 the Central Bank denied Banco Cartago's pending application for foreign exchange. Subsequently, the Central Bank notified each of the defendant banks that they would not be permitted to make external debt payments pending resolution of the entire Costa Rican external debt situation. This effectively blocked all future payments . . .

Conclusions

There is no question about the fact that defendant banks have defaulted on debts due to Allied and the other syndicate banks. However, various defenses are raised . . .

[T]he act of state doctrine is a meritorious one . . .

[T]he payment of the notes *was prevented* by certain directives of the Central Bank of Costa Rica and of the President and Ministry of Finance of that country . . .

The act of state doctrine is designed to avoid judicial action which would impinge upon the foreign relations of the United States . . . The doctrine ultimately derives for the separation of powers provided in the Constitution . . .

The crucial factor . . . was that the conduct of the Costa Rican government which *prevented payment* of the notes was public in nature, rather than commercial, and its purpose was to serve a governmental function. The record demonstrates that the actions of the Central Bank . . . and the President and the Ministry of Finance . . . were undertaken in response to a serious national economic crisis, and that these actions were of the type which some governments undertake to try to assist in such a crisis—i.e., restrictions upon foreign currency transactions. There is no doubt that the actions of the Costa Rican government here were intended to serve a public, rather than a commercial purpose. They were clearly an exercise of governmental function . . .

A judgment in favor of Allied . . . would constitute a judicial determination that defendants must make payments contrary to the directives of their government. This puts the judicial branch of the United States at odds with policies laid down by a foreign government on an issue deemed by that government to be of central importance. Such an act by this court risks embarrassment to the relations between the executive branch of the United States and the government of Costa Rica . . .

[The U.S. banks' motion for judgment was refused.]

Comments and Questions

How would United States bankers with extensive loans to other countries, to foreign banks, and to non-financial companies across the globe, react to the decision in the foregoing case?

ALLIED BANK INTERNATIONAL V. BANCO CREDITO AGRICOLA 757 F. 2D 516 (1985)

Meskill, Circuit Judge

. . . We reverse . . . the denial of . . . Allied Bank International's . . . motion for . . . judgment.

I

[The facts as stated by the District Court in the preceding case were repeated. —Ed.] While the action was still pending before the district court, the parties began to negotiate a rescheduling of the debt. In July 1982 the suit was dismissed by agreement . . . Fidelity Union Trust Company of New Jersey, one of the members of the Allied syndicate, did not accept the agreement [Fidelity wanted its money as promised in the original agreement. Allied appealed on behalf of Fidelity, the lone syndicate holdout. —Ed.]

II

In our previous decision we affirmed the district court... We... concluded that principle of comity compelled us to recognize as valid the Costa Rican directives.

Our interpretation of United States policy . . . arose primarily from our belief that the legislative and executive branches of our government fully supported Costa Rica's actions and all of the economic ramifications. On rehearing, the Executive Branch of the United States joined this litigation . . . and respectfully disputed our reasoning. [D]ebt resolution procedure . . . operates through the auspices of the International Monetary Fund (IMF). Guided by the IMF, this long established approach encourages the cooperative adjustment of international debt problems. The entire strategy is grounded in the understanding that, while parties may agree to renegotiate conditions of payment, the underlying obligations to pay nevertheless remain valid and enforceable. Costa Rica's attempted unilateral restructuring of private obligations, the United States contends, was inconsistent with the system of international cooperation and negotiation and thus inconsistent with United States policy.

The United States government further explains that its position on private international debt is not inconsistent with either its own willingness to restructure Costa Rica's intergovernmental obligations or with continued United States aid to the economically distressed Central American country . . .

In light of the government's elucidation of its position, we believe our earlier interpretation of United States policy was wrong . . .

III

The act of state doctrine operates to confer presumptive validity to certain acts of foreign sovereigns . . .

The classic statement of the doctrine was delivered in *Underhill* . . . (Sup Ct.,1897):

> Every sovereign state is bound to respect the independence of every other sovereign State, and the courts of one country will not sit in judgment on the acts of the government of another done within its own territory. Redress of grievances by reason of such acts must be obtained through the means open to . . . sovereign powers as between themselves . . .

[T]he act of state doctrine has been described as arising out of the basic relationship between branches of government in a system of separation of powers . . . The policy concerns . . . focus on the preeminence of the political branches, and particularly the executive, in the conduct of foreign policy . . . Therefore the application of the doctrine depends on the likely impact on international relations that would result from judicial consideration of the foreign sovereign's act . . .

The doctrine demands a case by case analysis . . .

This analysis must always be tempered by common sense . . . The doctrine does not necessarily "preclude judicial resolution of all commercial consequences" that result from acts of foreign sovereigns performed within their own borders . . .

The extraterritorial limitation [of a country's lawmaking power —Ed.] . . . depends upon the situs of the property at the time of the . . . taking. The property, of course, is Allied's right to receive payment from the Costa Rican banks in accordance with the agreements ... The act of state doctrine is applicable to this dispute only if, when the decrees were promulgated, the situs [place —Ed.] of the debts was in Costa Rica. Because we conclude that the situs of the property was in the United States, the doctrine is not applicable . . .

In this case Costa Rica could not wholly extinguish the Costa Rican bank's obligation to timely pay United States dollars to Allied in New York. Thus the situs of the debt was not Costa Rica . . .

The Costa Rican banks conceded jurisdiction in New York and they agreed to pay the debt in New York City in United States dollars. Allied, the designated syndicate agent, is located . . . in New York; some of the negotiations between the parties took place in the United States. The United States has an interest in maintaining New York's status as one of the foremost commercial centers of the world. Further, New York is the international clearing center for United States dollars. In addition to other international activities, United States banks lend billions of dollars to foreign debtors each year. The United States has an interest in ensuring that creditors entitled to payment in the United States in United States dollars under contracts subject to the jurisdiction of the United States may assume that, except under the most extraordinary circumstances, their rights will be determined in accordance with recognized principles of contract law.

In contrast, while Costa Rica has a legitimate concern in overseeing the debt situation of state-owned banks and in maintaining a stable economy, its interest in the contracts . . . is essentially limited to the extent to which it can unilaterally alter the payment terms. Costa Rica's potential jurisdiction over the debt is not sufficient to locate the debt there for purposes of the act of state . . . analysis . . .

IV

Acts of foreign governments purporting to have extraterritorial effect . . . should be recognized by the courts only if they are consistent with the law and policy of the United States.

We have now come full circle to reassess whether we should give effect to the Costa Rican directives. We now conclude that we should not.

The Costa Rican government's unilateral attempt to repudiate private, commercial obligations is inconsistent with the orderly resolution of international debt problems. It is similarly contrary to the interests of the United States, a major source of private international credit. The government has procedures for resolving intergovernmental financial difficulties . . . With respect to private debt, support for the IMF resolution strategy is consistent with both the policy and the best interests of the United States . . .

[Decision for Allied]

Questions and Comments

1a. What has happened here? Compare the opinion in the district court with the opinion rendered here on appeal. This court calls for "common sense"; what does common sense require? Looking across the whole field of multinational corporate relationships, does common sense get enough recognition?

b. The court says that debts cannot be suspended unless the "most extraordinary circumstances" warrant it. Has not Costa Rica already made such a determination by stepping in to control foreign exchange?

c. The first opinion in the Costa Rican bank cases seems to take the perspective of Costa Rica and its struggle to work out its exchange problems. The second opinion seems to take the perspective of United States banks trying to collect loans put in jeopardy by Costa Rica's actions. Compare the two opinions, keeping in mind the assumptions implicit in the act of state doctrine.

2. Decode the opinion on appeal. Strip away the legal jargon and reduce the decision to a few sentences. If it helps, break into a small group for the discussion of the two preceding cases, and compare notes on the implications of the cases and the way they can be reduced to a few sentences.

3. Between the time of the district court decision and the appeal, the case took on far greater importance than what would seem to have been warranted based on the amount in dispute (roughly $4.5 million). The two law firms originally on the case were joined on the appeal by *amicus curiae* ["friends of the court"—groups which file briefs in a case even though they are not parties—ed.] from the New York Clearing House Association (where interbank balances are settled); the United States Department of Justice; the U.S. State Department; the U. S. Treasury Department, the Federal Reserve, the Rule of Law Committee, and the National Foreign Trade Council, Inc. To put it mildly, the first decision had brought a number of pro-creditor "friends" out of the woodwork.

   Virtually all of the participants were worried about Costa Rica wriggling out of its debt which if by no means the largest of Third World debts, was representative of billions more.

C. Acts of State and the Foreign Corrupt Practices Act

The next two act of state cases arose under the Foreign Corrupt Practices Act passed in 1977. Through this Act Congress intended to prevent the corruption of foreign officials by commercial bribery, even when the bribery occurs outside the United States. In a sense, the Foreign Corrupt Practices Act was designed to promote more honest acts of state, by making it a U.S. federal crime for businesses to exert improper influence upon foreign public officials.

There are not many reported cases under the Foreign Corrupt Practices Act, but it is unlikely that students will find a more explicit occasion of the interconnection of law and political economy than one where companies literally buy "acts of state." In the cases, United States-based businesses tried to sue the bribing companies for losses said to be caused by the bribes.

W.P. KIRKPATRICK V. ENVIRONMENTAL TECTONICS 110 S.CT.701 (1990)

Justice Scalia . . .

In 1981, Harry Carpenter, who was then Chairman of the Board and Chief Executive Officer of . . . W. S. Kirkpatrick . . . learned that the Republic of Nigeria was interested in contracting for the construction and equipment of an aeromedical center at Kaduna Air Force Bases in Nigeria. He made arrangements with Benson "Tunde" Akindele, a Nigerian citizen, whereby Akindele would endeavor to procure the contract for Kirkpatrick. It was agreed that, in the event the contract was awarded to Kirkpatrick, Kirkpatrick would pay to two Panamanian entities controlled by Akindele a "commission" equal to 20% of the contract price, which in turn would be given as a bribe to officials of the Nigerian Government. In accordance with this plan, the contract was awarded to . . . W. S. Kirkpatrick & Co., international . . . a wholly owned subsidiary of Kirkpatrick; Kirkpatrick paid the promised "commission" to the appointed Panamanian entities; and those funds were disbursed as bribes. All parties agree that Nigerian law prohibits both the payment and receipt of bribes in connection with the award of a government contract.

Respondent Environmental Tectonics Corporation, International, an unsuccessful bidder for the Kaduna contract, learned of the 20% "commission" and brought the matter to the attention of the Nigerian Air Force and the United States Embassy in Lagos. Following an investigation, the United States Attorney . . . brought charges against both Kirkpatrick and Carpenter for violation of the Foreign Corrupt Practices Act . . . and both pleaded guilty.

Respondent then brought this civil action . . . against Carpenter, Akindele, petitioner, and others seeking damages under the Racketeer-Influenced and Corrupt Organizations Act (RICO) . . . The defendants moved to dismiss . . . on the ground that the action was barred by the act of state doctrine . . .

The District Court concluded that the act of state doctrine applies "if the inquiry presented for judicial determination includes the motivation of a sovereign act which would result in embarrassment to the sovereign or constitute interference in the conduct of foreign policy of the United States . . . [T]he court held that respondent's suit had to be dismissed . . .

This Court's description of the jurisprudential foundation for the act of state doctrine has undergone some evolution over the years. We once viewed the doctrine as an expression of international law, resting on "the highest considerations of international comity and expediency . . ." We have more recently described it, however, as a consequence of domestic separation of powers, reflecting "the strong sense of the Judicial Branch that . . . passing on the validity of foreign acts of state may hinder" the conduct of foreign affairs . . . Nothing in the present suit requires the court to declare invalid . . . the official act of a foreign sovereign.

. . . [E]very case [where] we held the act of state doctrine applicable . . . would have required a court in the United States to declare invalid the official act of a foreign sovereign performed within its own territory . . . (The issue in this litigation is not whether [the alleged] acts are valid, but whether they occurred.)

In support of their position that the act of state doctrine bars any factual findings that may cast doubt upon the validity of foreign sovereign acts, petitioners cite Justice Holmes' opinion . . . in *American Banana* . . . "a seizure by a state is not a thing that can be complained of elsewhere in the courts" . . .

Whatever Justice Holmes may have had in mind, his statement lends inadequate support to petitioner's position here . . . It was a brief aside, entirely unnecessary to the decision. *American Banana* was squarely decided on the ground . . . that the antitrust laws had no extraterritorial application . . . [According to the court this rule was overruled in a later case. —Ed.]

In some future case, perhaps, litigation based on alleged corruption in the award of contracts or other commercially oriented activities of foreign governments could sufficiently touch on "national nerves" that the act of state doctrine . . . would . . . bar the suit . . .

The short of the matter is this: Courts in the United States have the power and ordinarily the obligation, to decide cases and controversies properly presented to them. The act of state doctrine does not establish an exception for cases and controversies that may embarrass foreign governments, but merely requires that, in the process of deciding, the acts of foreign sovereigns taken within their own jurisdiction shall be deemed valid . . . That doctrine has no application to the present case because the validity of no foreign sovereign act is at issue.

[Case sent back for trial.]

Questions and Comments

1. It might be useful to compare this 1990 decision to the decision in *American Banana*. Under the 1990 rule would American Banana have won its case against United Fruit?

   Compare the *Kirkpatrick* case with the Costa Rican bank cases. In the bank cases is the act of state defense more persuasive, since a ruling for the U. S. bank syndicate appears to countermand the Costa Rican decrees?

   In the second Costa Rican case, the court was very careful to say that the property (the debt) was located in New York and not Costa Rica. Does this careful use of language over the "situs" of the debt become more understandable after reading the *Kirkpatrick* case?

The final case of this chapter occurs at the intersection of act of state, the Foreign Corrupt Practices Act, and antitrust law.

LAMB V. *PHILLIP MORRIS* 915 F.2D 1024 (1990)

In this antitrust action, plaintiffs Billy Lamb and Carmon Willis appeal from the dismissal of their claims . . . against Phillip Morris. Because we find the act of state doctrine presents no impediment to . . . the . . . antitrust claims . . . we reverse the . . . dismissal . . .

Since we find no private right of action is available under the Foreign Corrupt Practices Act . . . we affirm the dismissal of the plaintiff's FCPA claim . . .

Plaintiffs Lamb and Willis, along with various other Kentucky growers, produce burley tobacco for use in cigarettes and other tobacco products. Defendants Phillip Morris and B.A.T. routinely purchase such tobacco not only from Kentucky markets serviced by the plaintiffs, but also from producers in several foreign countries. Thus, tobacco grown in Kentucky competes directly with tobacco grown abroad, and any purchases from foreign suppliers necessarily reduce defendants' purchase of domestic tobacco.

On May 14, 1982, a Phillip Morris subsidiary known as C.A. Tabacalera National and a B.A.T. subsidiary known as C.A. Cigarrera Bigott, SUCS, entered into a contract with La Fundacion Del Nino (The Children's Foundation) of Caracas, Venezuela. The agreement was signed . . . by the organization's president, the wife of the then President of Venezuela. [T]he two subsidiaries were to make periodic donations to the Children's Foundation totalling approximately $12.5 million dollars. In exchange, the companies were to receive price controls on Venezuelan tobacco, elimination of controls on retail cigarette prices in Venezuela, tax deductions for the donations, and assurances that existing tax rates applicable to tobacco companies would not be increased. According to the plaintiff's complaint, the defendants have arranged similar contracts in Argentina, Costa Rica, Mexico, and Nicaragua.

In the plaintiffs' view, the donations . . . amount to unlawful inducements designed and intended to restrain trade. The plaintiffs assert that such arrangements result in artificial depression of tobacco prices to the detriment of domestic tobacco growers, while assuring lucrative retail prices for tobacco sold abroad . . . [T]he plaintiffs seek . . . treble damages and injunctive relief . . .

The plaintiff . . . sought . . . to add a claim under the FCPA. [T]he district court dismissed the antitrust claims as barred by the act of state doctrine, and dismissed the FCPA claim . . .

II

The act of state doctrine . . . is based on the notion that "every State is bound to respect the independence of every other sovereign State . . ."

The Court explained in *Kirkpatrick* that the act of state doctrine in its present formulation "does not establish an exception for cases and controversies that may embarrass foreign governments, but merely requires that . . . the acts of foreign sovereigns taken within their own jurisdiction shall be deemed valid" . . . Justice Scalia . . . held that the act of state doctrine does not bar a court in the United States from entertaining a cause of action that . . . requires[s] imputing to foreign officials an unlawful motivation (the obtaining of bribes) in the performance of . . . an official act. Like the bribes . . . in *Kirkpatrick*, the payments made by the defendants in this case to induce favorable action in Venezuela may support the plaintiff's antitrust claims . . . [T]he district court erred in applying the act of state doctrine to dismiss . . .

Although the Foreign Corrupt Practices Act was enacted more than a decade ago, the question of whether an implied private action exists under the FCPA is one of first impression. [Here the court is asking whether a criminal statute creates a basis for a civil suit for damages by private parties. —Ed.] . . .

[T]he FCPA . . . generally forbids [businesses —Ed.] to endeavor to influence foreign officials by offering, promising, or giving "anything of value."

[O]ur central focus is on congressional intent . . . : (1) whether the plaintiffs are among "the class for whose *especial* benefit" the statute was enacted; (2) . . . the legislative history . . . ; (3) whether . . . a remedy . . . would be "consistent with the underlying purposes of the legislative scheme . . . .

The defendants contend, and we agree, that the FCPA was designed . . . to aid federal law enforcement agencies in curbing bribes of foreign officials . . . [W]e find that the FCPA was primarily designed to protect the integrity of American foreign policy and domestic markets, rather than to prevent the use of foreign resources to reduce production costs. The plaintiffs, as competitors of foreign tobacco growers and suppliers of the defendants, cannot claim the status of intended beneficiaries . . . The plaintiffs have identified only one reference in a House report to a private cause of action: "The committee intends that courts shall recognize a right of action based on this legislation as they have in cases involving other provisions of the Securities Exchange Act, on behalf of persons who suffer injury as a result of prohibited corporate bribery" . . . The availability of a private right of action apparently was never resolved . . . [N]either the FCPA nor the conference report mentions such a cause of action . . . [W]e infer that Congress intended no such result . . .

Recognition of the plaintiff's proposed private right of action . . . would directly contravene the carefully tailored FCPA scheme . . . [T]he introduction of private plaintiffs . . . would hinder congressional efforts to protect companies and their employees concerned about FCPA liability . . . [FCPA claim dismissed. —Ed.]

Questions and Comments

It seems clear that to allow the act of state defense in bribery cases would virtually eliminate the Foreign Corrupt Practices Act, since the act of state was instigated by what Congress prohibits. Yet, according to the *Lamb* case, an action for money damages is not automatic against the bribing company.

A long-standing argument by international companies for the repeal or narrowing of the FCPA contends that the Act foists American business values [—honesty—] on other countries where other values [—dishonesty—] are a way of life. At the furthest extreme, it is sometimes said that business cannot be done in some places without bribery and that the corrupt practices act imposes totally unrealistic standards upon international companies doing business in those places.

There are no reported criminal cases under the Act. Perhaps the Act is more a symbol than a threat. Or perhaps, the Justice Department efforts to bring about voluntary compliance, if there have been such efforts, have been so effective that the stream of bribery cases that inspired the passage of the Act has virtually dried up. This position runs counter to the commonly heard business contention that bribes are a way of business life in some places (outside the United States).

CONCLUSION

This chapter has no doubt been a rough ride for students unschooled in the technicalities of overlapping legal systems. The cases were simplified a bit, but for the most part they were presented in a way that professional law students who are more accustomed to case reading would study them.

There was a method to presenting this technical madness. As was true of the preceding chapter, the cases could not be boiled down to the point where technicalities were eliminated without losing a grasp of the difficulty of making national-territorial systems fit international transactions. As a bonus for their efforts, readers will have gained additional knowledge of international corporate networking and a variety of international business practices.

In biology lab amoebas are sometimes examined under microscopes. The amoeba has no fixed shape as it sends its “false feet” out in unpredictable directions and seems to let the rest of itself catch up. Like the amoeba, the reach of the United States legal system remains unpredictable, fluid, and with no easily determined boundaries. Sometimes its membranes reach out and encompass cases, but in others, like the amoeba that picks up the presence of acid, it pulls back.

There may be a deep structure that explains the relative aggression of the courts in securities cases and the relative passivity in antitrust, accident, discrimination, and Foreign Corrupt Practices Act cases. The unreflective observer might suspend investigation after concluding that the cases turn on Congressional intent and judicial acceptance of its place in a government of separated powers. Where the unreflective observer stops the reflective observer begins, and joins the political economists in charting the larger implications of the cases.

PART 4
Contemporary Issues in Multinationals

CHAPTER 11

Debt—The Ultimate Control System

INTRODUCTION

Leo Tolstoy, the Russian novelist, said that all happy marriages are the same and all unhappy marriages are different. So too with debt. All debts that are paid off are ho hum, but all debtors who are in trouble tell somewhat different stories; borrowing too much; changing costs of borrowing; too little income, too late; borrowing for the wrong purposes, and so on. Ask a friend who is in over her head.

Getting into debt, like getting married, is an optimistic statement about the present and the future. Unless the borrower is a deadbeat from the outset, incurring debt says the borrower will be able to pay, and trading a future commitment for a present purpose will be advantageous at both times.

In the current period, the debt story has had unhappy outcomes for many people, countries, and institutions in many places. But a bit different from Tolstoy's unhappy marriages, there are some structural similarities across unhappy debt stories regardless of the place in the world where they have occurred that are worth bearing in mind.

We have already had materials on the impact of debt on economy and political economy. In Chapter 8, the system of debt peonage in the Yucatan was considered—low-level peonage, which tied work forces to landowners, and higher-level "peonage" that in turn bound landowners to broker–financiers who were even more powerful than the landowners in the network of henequen and sisal. Debt being a not-so-subtle means of social and personal control unifies the Yucatan story. People can be stuck in a cycle of debt-repayment that makes them only semi-willing participants in their systemic fate, but they nevertheless often participate for far longer than they may prefer.

In Chapter 10 there were several cases concerning the debt crisis in Costa Rica and the near panic among banker–creditors in the United States when Costa Rica declared a moratorium on debt service. The Costa Rican decree that suspended international payments was eventually made unnecessary when overdue debts were rescheduled, but readers can tell from the bankers' panic how in a matter of days a third-world debt crisis can become a first-world debt crisis.

When prospects for payment grow dim, debtor and creditor are joined in a mutual problem rather than one that is exclusively the debtor's. The episode also could have demonstrated how the line between international finance and domestic finance has been obliterated, for the same reasons that lines had been obliterated in the securities business. The largest banks operate both domestically and internationally; mass defaults in any sector of a bank's operations can impair the solvency of the bank as a whole.

Debt turns out to be one of the most ecological subjects of all. Ecology is the study of how everything in nature is connected to everything else; as the songbird goes, so goes the level of insect population, so goes grain production, so goes nutrition, so goes hunger and survival. Debt has the same kind of potential in the world economy and everything connected to economy, even though debt seems a much more pedestrian subject than songbirds. Debtors are linked to creditors, and both are linked to the political economies in which they are found. As political economies go, so goes the welfare of people.

One way to raise the ecological dimensions of debt is to ask why a financial rock thrown into Brazilian waters can make a New York banker soaking wet, and what the banker does to dry off can affect life in both countries: push a Brazilian peasant off the land, help swell Brazilian slums, spur industrialization in Brazil, or contribute to the decimation of the Amazon rain forest. In the United States, Brazilian debt measures can put price pressure on U.S.-grown agricultural commodities, contribute to an adverse balance of trade for the United States, raise U. S. taxes, and reduce the number of industrial jobs.

The foregoing causal sequence of events is, of course, heroic and has been pushed to extremes for illustrative purposes, since there are joint causes for the foregoing problems. But there is a kernel of reality in the effects of debt on all sectors of the economies of Brazil and the United States, as should be clearer once the discussion of debt has unfolded.

For the present, the rundown of debt implications concerns what happens when a country cannot pay its debts in whole or in part. Brazil's debt problems were comparable to Costa Rica's, but on a much larger scale. Some banker–creditors based in the United States and elsewhere had loaned money and stood to lose billions (and approach insolvency) if their Brazilian loans were rendered worthless through nonpayment. Their salvaging operations, sometimes conducted with pressures from international agencies such as the International Monetary Fund and the World Bank, affected the welfare of people of Brazil and the people of the United States in ways only dimly perceived in the United States. (People in Third World countries are vastly more sensitive to the impacts of the policies of the United States in their country than people in the United States are of international events on theirs. If this book is successful, this differential literacy will be at least partially eliminated.) Extensive and sometimes low-visibility effects of debt *everywhere* are what make debt an ecological subject.

A. THE NATURE AND LIMITS OF DEBT

We begin coverage with a primer on debt: household debt, real estate debt, farm debt, business debt, and government debt; getting into debt and getting out of it, becoming a debtor and becoming a creditor, and the conditions in which parties regret having assumed either role. We have all known people who have become enslaved to their credit cards, must struggle to get out from under accelerating debt, reluctantly accept debt as the organizing principle to their lives, either file bankruptcy (repudiate is the harsher word for it), or finally pay off the debts at great personal discomfort for longer than they want to remember. Judging from frantic calls they get from their creditors, problem debt always cuts at least two ways.

When overextended credit card debtors finally pay off, they may cut their credit cards in half, and say, "Never again." The old Household Finance Company advertisement went something like:

> Never borrow money needlessly—
> But when you must—
> Borrow confidently,
> From folks like us
> At HFC.

It contained both a warning and an encouragement. From the late 1970s onward, the warnings were heard far less often than the encouragements, and debt has caused persistent and growing trouble for debtors and creditors alike.

Improvident householders have not been alone in the current period. Tim Congdon in *The Debt Threat*[1] provides a comprehensive introduction to debt, and discusses the many sectors of the economy where debt has put debtors and their creditors in trouble. He believes that the key elements of debt and repayment are the same for all debtors. His analysis will be presented through six brief excerpts.

THE MAIN ARGUMENT

T. Congdon, The Debt Threat, *pp. 5–9*

[W]e need to ask whether there are any general determinants of the growth of debt. Perhaps because debt enables the borrower—at least for a time—to enjoy something for nothing, the subject invites moral homilies. David Hume, the eighteenth century Scottish philosopher . . . considered government borrowing not just practically unwise but a sign of human inadequacy . . . In the end, whenever a "government has mortgaged all its revenues . . . it necessarily sinks into a state of languor, inactivity, and impotence . . ." [T]he countless moral diatribes on this subject over the centuries contribute little to understanding . . .

[1](London: Basil Blackwell, 1988). Copyright © 1988 by Tim Congdon. Reprinted by permission of Basil Blackwell, Ltd.

A natural approach is to consider the effect of interest rates on the growth of debt. The common-sense approach is that the higher are interest rates, the slower will be the increase in debt. It seems obvious that the more expensive it is to have the use of borrowed money, the less people will want to borrow. In practice, the relationship between interest rates and debt is more complicated . . .

Strange as the thought may seem on first acquaintance, many debts are very old. The British national debt exemplifies the point in an extreme, but not misleading way. As the British government has not repudiated any of its obligations since 1672, part of today's national debt is over three hundred years old . . .

In general, and disturbing though it may be to common sense, relatively few debts are altogether extinguished at the first repayment date. Most debts are repaid, then renewed, and subsequently repaid and renewed many times . . .

The purpose of emphasizing the longevity of debt is to show that the behavior of debt in total depends more on what is happening to old debt than on decisions about new debt. It may be that the higher are interest rates, the less new debt is incurred. But the effect of higher interest rates on old debt is quite different. If a borrower has a loan with variable interest rates, an increase in rate implies an increase in interest charges. The higher interest charges will by themselves cause an *acceleration* in the growth of debt. Even with a fixed-rate loan, an increase in interest rates can result in faster debt growth. The reason is that, when the loan matures, the borrower faces the choice of renewal or repayment. If for some reason he opts for renewal, the growth of his future debt will in the future be quicker than it would have been at the previous lower level of interest rates. The message seems to be that the relationship of interest rates and debt growth is ambiguous. A rise in interest rates discourages the incurral of new debt, but it may cause old debt to expand more rapidly . . .

Suppose that a borrower is facing an interest rate that is above the growth rate of his income. Unless he makes an effort to service his loan, either by repaying some principal or meeting interest payments as they fall due, the loan increases every year by the addition of interest charges. If there is no debt servicing whatever, the growth rate of the debt is the interest rate. It follows that, because the interest rate is above the growth rate of income, debt increases faster than income and the debt/income ratio rises.

This is an extremely important and powerful result . . . [W]hen we survey the evidence from many countries, it is the changed relationship between interest rates and income growth which is the root cause of the debt explosion of recent years. In the 1970s interest rates were beneath the growth rate of incomes, and debt/income ratios tended to fall; in the 1980s interest rates have been above the growth rate of incomes and debt/income ratios have, with few exceptions, increased . . .

The only way that a borrower can make a debt service payment is to keep his expenditures on items other than interest lower than his income. In other words, he has to run a "budget surplus" (note this is not a traditional surplus concept, but one exclusive of interest) . . . But the line of reasoning . . . is valid for any economic agent. It applies to companies, governments, and countries as well as persons . . .

So far we have talked about the dynamics of the debt/income ratio of a particular borrower . . . How do we extend the argument to the national level? Let us put the question of external debt to one side for the time being. [External debt is debt owed to people outside a country as opposed to a country's own citizens. —Ed.] . . . [W]e can divide a nation into the two categories of debtors and creditors . . . [I]f no one runs a budget surplus and interest rates are . . . above the growth rate of national income, the liabilities of the debtors to the creditors must be increasing faster than national income and the debt/income ratio must be rising. To the extent that debtors achieve budget surpluses, a brake is imposed on the increase in the debt/income ratio. But if they have budget deficits an extra twist is added to the spiral in the debt/income ratio. The broad conclusion is that debts will grow very rapidly in relation to national income when interest rates are in excess of the growth rate of income and when debtors are unable to live within their means.

The argument has the same structure if it is applied to external debt but, instead of thinking in terms of a "budget surplus," we have to talk about the current account of the balance of payments. The increase in a country's external debt is driven, like the individual's, by two components—the addition of interest to the existing debt and the incurral of new debt. If there is an exact balance on the noninterest transactions between the debtor country and its creditors, its external debt will grow faster than national income when the interest rate is above the growth rate of national income. An extra dimension is introduced by the possibility that the debt is expressed in terms of a foreign currency, as an adjustment then needs to be made for changes in the exchange rate . . .

There is a frightening implication of this central theme. We have shown that, when the interest rate exceeds the growth rate of a borrower's income and the borrower fails to run a budget surplus, his debt/income ratio increases. Is there any limit to this tendency? The answer is that, as long as the two conditions relating to the interest rate/income growth mix and his budgetary position remain as assumed, there is no limit at all. The debt/income ratio increases indefinitely.

The borrower can soon find himself in a sad predicament. If he makes no effort to service his debt, interest is added to his old debts in the first year. In the second year because the debt is larger, his interest payments are heavier. If he again does nothing about debt servicing, a large interest payment is added to his debt. In the third year, because his debt is larger again, his interest payments are even heavier . . . and so on . . .

Questions and Comments

1. Imagine how a person on a fixed or even declining income would make headway in eliminating balances outstanding on credit cards. Compare what would have to be done to Congdon's idea of running a "surplus" in *noninterest areas* of expenditure. Speculate on some of the personal costs that might be attendant to these "austerity measures." What should the debtor give up first?

   If you can do so with appropriate courtesy and confidentiality, gather information from someone you know who has become hopelessly behind on credit cards. Ask how he or she got behind, and what was done to make inroads into the debt.

2. Toward the last part of the excerpt, Congdon talks about the *current account* of countries. The current account is part of a country's balance of payments which tabulates what a country exports in goods and services and what it imports. There are two primary elements in a country's *balance of payments:* trade movements and capital movements. What has been expended on imports by a country must be offset by merchandise (exports) or capital inflow (debt or foreign investment).
3. When the external debt is in a different currency from the local currency, as is true for Brazilian debt, the indebted country must first convert local currency into the required currency according to the *exchange rate.* More loans in "hard currency" loans may ensue, the proceeds going to pay off older loans, with the new loans added to total indebtedness. When this practice exceeds the ability of a country to export or attract capital, the country is in debt crisis.

Commercial Real Estate Debt

The next excerpt from Congdon expands the discussion from individual debtors, to real estate developers, farmers, and corporate financiers, all participants in the debt boom of the 1980s in the United States.

T. Congdon, The Debt Threat, *pp. 166–168*

[W]e can consider the position of a real estate developer who depends on bank credit.

The developer intends to build an office block on a plot of land at a cost of \$10 m. Suppose that he is not prepared to put up any money of his own and so makes no investment in the development, even though he intends to own the equity in it outright. He therefore borrows the full \$10 m from a bank. Suppose the rent on the building is \$1 m a year, that annual management expenses are nil and that, with interest rates of 10 percent, interest charges each year are also \$1 m . . .

He may . . . be a flamboyant, high-spending individual. So he takes the \$1 m [from rents] away for his own consumption. As he does not apply it to servicing of the debt, the bank adds the \$1 m interest to the original loan, which becomes \$11 m after the first year. Will the bank protest about the developer's failure to service his debt? The answer, which may seem surprising, is "not necessarily." What the bank needs . . . is an assurance that the loan is backed up by collateral. It must be confident that, if it calls for repayment, the borrower can sell the asset for a price equal to or above the value of the loan. If the price of the office building is rising by 10 percent a year, it is worth \$11 m at the end of the first year. It remains exactly equal to the loan, just as at the beginning of the transaction. If the bank was happy then it should still be happy now.

The real estate developer is, of course, even happier. Without putting up any funds of his own, he takes an income of \$1 m from the building. If rents increase consistently by 10 percent a year, supporting the same rate of appreciation in office prices, his income also grows steadily . . . [I]n this stable environment of 10 percent interest rates and 10 percent a year rental growth— both the developer's debt/income ratio and the ratio of debt to the bank's collateral are constant . . .

Now consider the implications of changing the balance between interest rates and the growth rate of rental income. Let the change be drastic, with interest rates going to 15 percent and the annual growth rate slowing to 5 percent . . .

At the end of the first year the debt has become $11.5 m, while the developer's prospective income is $1.05 m and (assuming that the building appreciates in line with rents) the value of the building is $10.5 m. At the end of the second year the debt is $ 13.225 m, prospective income 1.1025 m and the value of the building is 11.025 m. It is quite clear that the developer is bust. His debts exceed his assets by over $2 m, and—even if [he] . . . devotes all the rental income to servicing the loan—he will never be able to eliminate the deficiency. As long as interest rates exceed the growth rate of rents, the bank is in an equally helpless position. It may step in, take control of the building and insist that the rental income be used to service the debt. But the arithmetic is remorseless. At the end of the third year, prospective rents of little more than $1.15 m remain altogether inadequate to bridge the gap between the value of the building, which will move toward $11.6 m over the next 12 months, and the loan of over $15 m. Moreover, just as the developer had to pay interest to the bank, the bank has to pay interest to its depositors. If its interest costs exceed its interest receipts, it may quickly find itself in the same predicament as the developer . . .

In our example the $10 m loan was equal, at the beginning of the development, to the value of the building. In practice no bank manager would expose his institution to such a high degree of risk. He would instead require that the developer put up some capital of his own to protect the bank against potential difficulties. The bank might also ask for a charge on some of the developer's other assets so that if the developer's equity interest [in the building—Ed.] had been wiped out, it still had means of avoiding loss.

The viability of the loan therefore depends not only on the relationship between interest rates and rental growth, but also on the adequacy of the bank's "margin" of collateral and the strength of the debtor's other assets . . .

Clearly, the behavior of asset prices as well as the relationship between interest rates and growth rate of incomes is important to understanding the dynamics of private debt in the USA. The key assets in this context are the various forms of real estate. Because they have the great advantage from the lender's viewpoint that they are highly visible and physically stuck in a particular location, land, buildings, and houses are used as collateral in loans . . .

Comments and Questions

1. How does a real estate developer and the bank that finances the developer get into trouble? What relationship among building values, interest costs, rental income, and borrower's other "worth," get the borrower and the lender in greatest trouble?
2. How realistic is the example that Congdon selected to demonstrate the frailties of the 1980s real estate boom in the United States? His

prediction of trouble was correct; in the early 1990s many banks experienced more and more problem loans in commercial and residential real estate (see Figure 11-1).

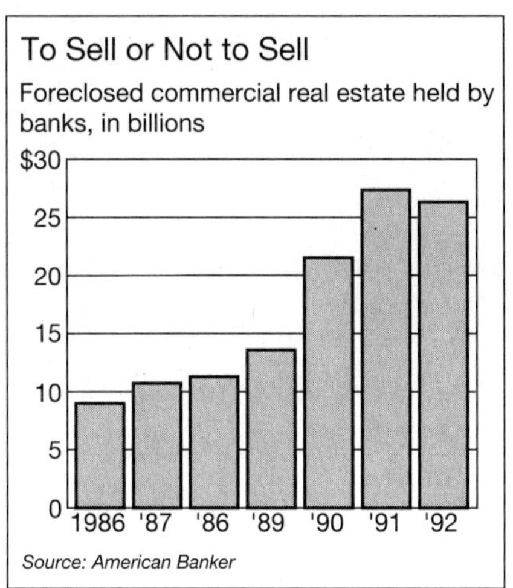

FIGURE 11-1
***Wall Street Journal*, June 7, 1993.**

As will be discussed in the postscript, Citicorp, the largest bank headquartered in the United States, went from difficulties in collecting on foreign loans to difficulties in collecting on commercial real estate loans. What it had done to "solve" one problem led to another.

In mid-1993, interest rates were low rather than high as in Congdon's illustration, but so were rental incomes. Vacancy rates were also high, putting more pressure on income streams and the values of commercial properties. Savings and loan associations (S&Ls) were the first casualties as the boom faded, with commercial banks and insurance companies following close behind.

3. As a class project, review the relationship of the lending of a particular bank (for example Chase Manhattan, Chemical Bank, or Wells Fargo) in the area of commercial real estate, noting the level of "loan losses" that occur when a bank must "write down" the value of assets to reflect loans that have become uncollectible in whole or in part.
4. What are the ABCs of commercial real estate lending doing in a book on multinationals? The shortest answer is that debt is of a single piece. Large banks have loan portfolios that include a variety of types of domestic and international lending—personal, real estate, commercial, and governmental. The worst eventuality for a multinational commercial bank occurs when all the loan categories are delinquent at the same time, or in close succession.

Farm Debt

Congdon also discusses farm lending. Willie Nelson's Farm Aid concerts were part of the effects, but what were the causes of the farm debt crisis?

T. Congdon, The Debt Threat, *pp. 183,184.*

While Texas suffered in the mid-1980s from the fall in the oil price, the Midwest was hit by the decline in food prices. Although in both cases the dependence on commodity production seemed to be largely to blame, high real interest rates were more directly responsible for the turmoil in regional financial systems. Their impact in the Midwest was different from that in Texas. Whereas in Texas and . . . the rest of the Sun Belt, the most obviously affected asset was office real estate, in the Midwest it was farmland. As the value of farmland fell, banks had no alternative to foreclosure for thousands of small farmers unable to make payments on their debts . . .

[S]harply higher . . . interest rates caused an appreciation of the dollar on the foreign exchanges, which undermined the competitiveness of US farm exports. The rise in farm prices decelerated markedly from the 8.1 percent annual rate enjoyed between 1972 and 1981. In 1982 and 1985 they actually fell. Farmland values reflected the change in market conditions. They continued in advance through sheer momentum in 1980 and 1981, but in 1981—for the first time in over a decade—they increased at less than the rate of interest. Clearly, farmland had dwindling attractions to nonfarm investors . . . In 1982 farmland prices reported their first fall since the 1930s. It was only a trifling drop of less than 1 percent, but it gave the signal for more disinvestment. In 1983 the value of farmland went down by 6 percent, in 1984 by 1 per cent and by 1985 by 12 1/2 percent. With prime rates remaining at over 10 percent until the summer of 1985, any farmer who had borrowed heavily against land collateral was in an impossible financial position ... [J]ust as the crisis in real estate hurt the banks who had supported heavy real estate development in the 1970s, so the financial stress in farming damaged the credit institutions which specialized in the rural sector.

At the end of 1985 total farm debt stood at $212 b. As with the debt in so many other contexts, it had continued to rise after the initial onset of trouble not because there were willing borrowers and lenders, but because of the addition of interest charges to old loans . . .

Questions and Comments

1. Loans in the southwestern part of the United States were made by both S&Ls and commercial banks. When S&Ls became insolvent, the United States government had to embark on the well-known bailout, since it had insured the deposits of S&Ls up to $100,000 per *account* (not per person). This bailout, while technically not part of the U.S. national debt, has been guaranteed by the United States government, and the agency that is liquidating insolvent thrifts gets periodic cash infusions from Congress that are part of the federal budgetary deficit.

Commercial banks also made loans in the Southwest. Continental Illinois, based in Chicago, was the subject of the largest federal deposit insurance "rescue" ever undertaken, to avoid a run on the bank by its largest depositors, some of whom were based in other countries.

2. The farm loan crisis shows the structural similarities across the various types of debt. For farmers, interest is an expense that is either offset or not offset when crops are harvested and sold. The income stream from farming, whether flowing abundantly or at a trickle, affects not only the ability of a farmer to pay loans, but also the value of farmland, which is the main collateral on which a farmer can borrow, and a bank can foreclose.

Corporate Debt

Corporate finance presents another part of the debt story. Flamboyant real estate speculation had its counterpart in corporate speculation and the takeover game, already discussed in Chapter 6. Both had the same underlying debt dynamics as commercial real estate and farm finance.

T. Congdon, The Debt Threat, *pp. 185–187.*

A company's vulnerability to unforeseen adversity depends largely on the ratio of equity to debt. If for any reason cash flow suddenly weakens, and turns negative, it has to continue to service its debt, until the condition improves. If it cannot service the debt, it has to close down. The purpose of equity is to give it the resources to see it through such periods of negative cash flow . . . [T]he lower the ratio of debt to equity, the greater is the corporate sector's resilience when confronted by untoward economic fluctuations . . .

[T]here have been many individual cases of financial adventurism which have resulted in an excessive build-up of debt. Financial deregulation in the early 1980s encouraged a rash of innovative practices in venture capital and the financing of mergers and acquisitions. Their purpose was to increase the potential reward to the players involved, but their drawback was that they involved more debt and more risk.

The leveraged buyout was one of the best examples of the new techniques. Typically a venture capital company would lend a large sum of money to a group of individuals, often former management, to buy up and run the subsidiary of a large industrial company. The loan would be repaid from future profits, leaving ownership in the hands of the management . . .

[B]uyouts . . . lead to an increase in the ratio of debt to income . . . [J]unk bond issuance creates particularly onerous debt. There are many junk bonds in existence with coupons of 14, 15, or 16 percent. It is hardly credible that in an economy with an inflation rate of less than 5 percent, industrial profits can rise at this rate for any extended period of time. So we have another instance of interest rate on debt much in excess of the rate of growth of borrower's income.

The banking system has facilitated some of the most imaginative maneuvers of the takeover raiders . . . Drawn by profit, bankers are channelling their limited liquidity into high risk areas of the financial sector which offer higher yields. Never in the course of monetary history has there been a scheme which attracted lenders into economically nonproductive enterprises at rates of return in excess of the prevailing market rates that has not come to a bad end. . .

Questions and Comments

1. We have not yet considered what created the mad scramble by commercial banks for higher yields on more speculative loans—consumer credit, commercial real estate, or corporate financing. What made the bankers throw caution to the wind will be discussed in connection with Citicorp and its abysmal experiences with international loans. The banks might have been trying to "grow" their way out of Third World problem loans through the gains on domestic loans, including the highly speculative loans made in connection with mergers and acquisitions.
2. Ivan Boesky and Michael Milkin, who were both convicted for violations of the securities laws, typify the buccaneer corporate finance of the 1980s. Their story can be found in the book *Den of Thieves,* by James Stewart. The award-winning film "Wall Street" also captures the speculative fervor that was general in the period, and might have more meaning when seen a second time with a better understanding of debt.
3. A leveraged buy-out may sound more complicated than it actually is. The buy-out of a corporation is leveraged when it is financed by debt (sometimes through "junk bonds"). Stockholders sell out, and the purchase price is paid for out of the proceeds of a loan. The loan, in turn, must be paid out of the earnings of the acquired corporation. Loans in connection with leveraged buy-outs go bad when the income stream of the acquired corporation is inadequate to service the debt.

   Some particular leveraged buy-outs and mergers can be studied with an eye on the role of debt. R.J Reynolds was the largest of the period. Campeau-Federated Stores was a highly leveraged merger in retailing.

Domestic Governmental Debt

The next facet of the debt story is governmental debt, which can be both domestic and international (external). Domestic governmental debt is payable in a country's own currency, while international indebtedness may or may not be. United States debt of both types is, for the present, payable in its own currency. Brazilian domestic debt is payable in its own currency, but its external debt is not.

T. Congdon, The Debt Threat, *pp. 98–100*

We shall . . . focus on the USA because of the clarity with which it illustrates the issues at stake as well as its importance to the world economy . . . Public debt held by private investors increased by 10.7 percent a year between 1977 and 1981, but by 18.6 percent between 1981 and 1985. In this purely numerical sense, budgetary policy under President Reagan can be blamed for the break in the trend in the debt/income ratio in the early 1980s. Indeed the indictment is more extensive. The deterioration of fiscal responsibility lay behind the increase in real interest rates . . . and . . . added another twist in the spiral in the debt/income ratio.

In view of the over $1,000 b of new debt incurred by the Reagan administration, it is hardly surprising that the public debt ratio increased in the 1980s, reversing the decline which had characterized the first three postwar decades. Gross public debt was 37.1 percent of GNP in 1981, but rose to almost 48.5 percent in 1985 and is projected to exceed 50 percent in the next two or three years. This larger debt has to be serviced at more onerous rates than those prevailing in the late 1970s . . . Interest payments on public debt are estimated to have been 5.0 percent of GNP in 1986, compared with 2.7 percent in 1979. Strong emphasis has to be placed on the eventual need to charge higher taxes on the American people to cover the costs of interest payments. This paradoxical and unfortunate outcome is, of course, implied by the logic of the debt trap . . .

The outpouring of new government debt has been on such a scale that domestic savings have not been able to absorb it in full. Foreign investors have had to fill the gap by substantially increasing their holdings of American government debt. These investments are the counterpart to a trade deficit which has grown continuously since 1982. The excess of imports over exports, which was $114.1 b in 1984, $124.3 b in 1985, and $147.7 b in 1986, is by far the largest the world has ever seen. The current account of the balance of payments has also been in the red. So far the deficit has not been on quite the same scale as that of the trade account because... [of] receipts of capital income on its foreign assets. Nevertheless, its foreign liabilities are now greater than its foreign assets, and within the next two or three years, the USA's payments of interest, dividends and profits to foreigners will become larger than foreigners' payments to it. Eventually the USA will have to run a trade surplus to service its external debt properly. To move from massive deficit to surplus will need a switch in resources to produce more exports and cause a major structural upheaval in the economy. In broad terms, the trade deficit is now 4 percent of GNP, whereas a surplus of perhaps 1 percent will be needed to satisfy foreign investors and to stop the debt growing further . . .

Questions and Comments

1. Many Americans are confused about the government debt. There is no doubt that Americans know there is trouble, as was evident in the presidential debates in 1992. But the *national debt* is sometimes confused with the *budgetary deficit*, and there is also confusion between the budgetary deficit and the *trade deficit*. (All three are

troublesome.) The national debt, now $4 trillion, is not the *budgetary deficit,* which President Clinton has promised to "bring down" over the next five years. The budget deficit is the amount by which the *current* budget is not in balance. The *national debt,* which is already twice what it was when Congdon warned of a debt threat, will grow even larger (by a trillion more dollars), since President Clinton is attempting deficit *reduction* and not deficit *elimination*. To make inroads into the national debt the budget would have to be in surplus.

In addition to what is already part of the national debt, the U. S. government has guaranteed a variety of obligations—everything from home mortgages to student loans to the S&L bailout; it may or may not have to make good on its guarantees, but if it does have to, the amounts guaranteed must be funded in the annual budget or added to the national debt.

Meanwhile the *trade deficit* is still present, adding indebtedness year by year, as the United States imports more than it exports.

To get a better understanding of the kinds of debt and their impacts, read material from the *Wall Street Journal* on the national debt, the budgetary deficit, and the trade deficit. The government reissues new indebtedness frequently and in larger and larger blocks, and trade figures appear once a month. Also, by paying close attention to presidential and congressional commentaries on the national debt, budget deficits, and trade deficits, readers will eventually be able to keep the three aspects of U.S. indebtedness straight, and also will be in a position to evaluate the consequences of each. Readers should be prepared for high numbers.

2. The interest rates at mid-1993 were quite low, making the governmental debt servicing bill lower than it would have been at the higher interest rates of the preceding decade. But the debt itself has been steadily growing, and lower interest rates, when applied to higher numbers, yield large amounts. Upward movement in the interest rates will make debt service more difficult.
3. The United States' owing its debt in its own currency presents the temptation to print money to get out of debt fast. This move has grave consequences, as will be discussed in the postscript to the chapter. Among the consequences are inflation, higher interest rates, the dollar as a worthless currency for trade, discouragement of saving, movement of capital out of the country (capital flight), pulling of capital by foreign investors, or their moving from financial assets to non-financial assets (for example, from government bonds to farmland, real estate, and factories, and so on). In effect, all the things that have happened in many other countries caught in the debt trap, including runaway inflation, could happen in the United States.
4. Some writers[2] have correlated increasing U. S. indebtedness with the growth of *foreign direct investment* in the United States. If the rate

[2]For example, Martin Tolchin et al., *Buying Into America* (New York: Times, 1988).

of exchange for U.S. currency falls by 20 percent (the dollar "losing value"), this drop in effect reduces the price of all dollar-denominated assets—farmland, commercial real estate, corporate stock, and whole companies, by 20 percent. Currency devaluations, until price levels catch up, reduce the price of all forms of property and cut the wage bills of foreign-based multinationals producing in the United States.

Sovereign Lending

Sovereign lending is the name given to loans to countries on the strength of the country's promise to pay. The term is usually associated with Third World debt, but it applies to the debt of any country. Walter Wriston, former CEO of Citicorp, once said that sovereign loans were the very best kind, since the assets and income-generating potential of an entire country were pledged to repayment. A few years later, Wriston was out of corporate power, and his successor was scrambling to reduce the impact of increasingly worthless sovereign loans on the solvency of the bank.

T. Congdon, The Debt Threat, *pp. 111-114.*

[I]f the *Pax Americana* of the 1950s and 1960s ushered in the lending boom of the 1970s, it still does not explain why the banks should have wanted to lend to Latin American countries rather than to their traditional customers in the USA and other industrial countries. Although many conjectures have been made about other political motives, profit maximization was the most important inducement. For some time after the disasters of the Depression years, American banks kept very high ratios of capital to assets to protect them against future loan losses. In the more tranquil conditions of the 1950s and 1960s they came to believe that loan losses would never again be on the scale of the 1930s. As perceptions changed, they decided to reduce their capital/asset ratios. But within the USA, business was extremely competitive, with numerous small and medium-sized banks trying to increase market share. The large banks therefore sought to expand their lending abroad . . . In part, they could achieve their objectives by setting up operations in other industrial countries, but . . . they were confronted by regulatory obstacles and stiff local competition. A warmer welcome came from the governments of developing countries. These governments were typically in constant need of finance, but had access only to backward and small-scale domestic capital markets.

In the mid-1970s the developing countries' demand for external finance became insistent because of the damage to their balance of payments from the first oil shock. The decision of the Organization of Petroleum Exporting Countries to triple the oil price caused the collective payments surplus of Middle Eastern oil exporters to increase from $6.5 b in 1973 to $55.9 b in 1974, with corresponding damage to the payments positions of the industrial and developing countries . . . In 1975 the industrial countries moved back into surplus. In consequence, the only possible deficit area remaining was the oil-importing Third World. Over the four years to 1978 the average annual surplus of the Middle Eastern Oil exporters was $33.8 b and the average deficit of the developing countries $39.5 b. The international banks came in as useful intermediaries between these two groups. They received much of the oil exporters' surplus in the form of deposits and were able to on-lend or "recycle" them to the developing countries . . .

With the banks playing a key role in recycling, their new loans to LDCs rose from negligible figures in the 1960s to $9.7 b in 1973 and to $12.0 b in 1975 . . . [I]n 1976 they amounted to 29.1 percent of the debt of $220 b and in 1978 to 30.4 percent of debt of $345 b. They were encouraged in their activities by governments and central banks in the main industrial countries who, in general, regarded recycling to the Third World as the best answer to the global payments imbalance caused by the oil shock.

The banks had no previous experience of lending on this scale across frontiers. They were not sure how to assess risks nor what rules they should be following on the size of the exposure . . . First, bond finance was minimal. In 1973 bond issues raised a mere $0.6 b for LDCs and in 1975 only $0.4 b . . . [T]he main obstacle to bond finance was that investors were more skeptical about LDCs' ability to pay than bankers. This contrast between the ready availability of bank loans and the virtually complete absence of bond finance is intriguing. It is also crucial to understanding why, at a later stage, the governments of developed countries became so anxious about the debts. Losses by bondholders are unfortunate, but they are restricted to the individuals concerned. As such they are not a policy problem for government or other official bodies. But losses by banks and possible bank failures have wider ramifications and do raise major questions of public policy.

Secondly, the bank lending rate was nearly all at variable rates of interest. The typical arrangement was to set a rate equal to the London inter-bank offered rate (LIBOR) plus a margin . . . As LIBOR measured the banks' costs of funds they make a profit so long as the margin (or spread) exceeded their administrative costs and overheads. . . . The acceptance of interest rate risk by developing country borrowers in the 1970s should be emphasized as it explains their vulnerability to the violent interest rate swings of the early 1980s. In earlier phases of LDC lending, bond issues . . . had carried fixed rates of interest.

Thirdly, the loans were predominantly to governments or public sector bodies with government or central bank guarantees. This is, of course, the meaning of the term "sovereign lending." Banks did not have to assess in detail the viability of investments being financed with their money or even have to check that the money was being invested. Instead they had only to appraise the credit worthiness of countries—such as the debt/export ratio and debt servicing ratios . . . As long as the various ratios appeared satisfactory, the banks thought they did not need to worry over the uses and misuses to which their loans were being applied. This characteristic had an important advantage [in] that the administrative costs of making sovereign loans were very low. It was necessary to have only a small number of people in the head office, usually in London, working out the ratios, preparing reports and making occasional trips . . . Implicit [was] the belief that the geographical areas which nations occupy cannot vanish and that every government will recognize a responsibility for the financial obligations of its predecessors. However, a deep knowledge of the twentieth century is not required to appreciate that size, shape, form and attitudes of political entities can be changed radically by warfare and revolution . . . [T]hey placed their trust in *Pax Americana*. After the 25 years of growth worldwide after the Second World War this was not a silly idea. It seemed to receive confirmation from the presence of airports, Sheraton hotels, Coca Cola tins and other imagery of market capitalism in the most backward Third World countries. In . . . Latin America it was also supported by the absence of significant intraregional military conflict for many decades and the pervasiveness of the USA's influence.

Comments and Questions

1. The distinction between financing by bonds and financing by bank loans should not be lost. Historically *individuals* held the bonds of other countries and suffered losses *personally* when there was a default. (There have been many defaults across history.) The post-1970s round of country indebtedness was held in *bank* portfolios, not *individual investor* portfolios. Upon default, losses would go straight to the net worth of the banks that had made the loans. Since all money center banks were overexposed, nonpayment would jeopardize the whole banking system of the United States.

   Private banks are not the only lenders to the Third World. Governments make loans (called "bilateral") and multilateral lending agencies such as the International Monetary Fund and the World Bank also make loans. The principal difference is that when government loans are not paid, it is the taxpayers of the lending country who will eventually pay. (The fate of the debts owed multilateral lending agencies such as the IMF and World Bank are also of interest to taxpayers, since these multilateral banks are funded from quotas assessed against member countries, and those quotas eventually come from taxation.)
2. Banks recycled money coming in from the Middle East to Third World countries that needed credit. Banks always recycle—transferring money on deposit to loans, making a profit on the "spread" between what it costs the bank for the money and what the bank can get as interest on the loan. When loans are not repaid, the bank loses the income on the loan (interest) *and loses the principal.* Meanwhile the bank is itself obligated to pay interest and principal to its depositors and other creditors.
3. The banks "protected" themselves in their sovereign lending through *variable rates of interest*, meaning that the rate of interest on the loans would fluctuate with world market rates.

   Variable rates are an attempt by lenders to shift the risk of market fluctuation in interest rates to the borrower. (This is equally true of now common variable-rate home mortgages.) So long as the loans were good, the variable rates assured income in excess of the bank's borrowing costs. Interest rate protection works only when interest and principal are paid. When countries default, interest risk protection through variable rates is irrelevant.

4. Should the banks have been more careful to monitor how the proceeds from their sovereign loans were used? If they had chosen to investigate, what uses of the money would they have preferred, and which ones might have offered more long-term safety to the banks?
5. The debt/export ratio is the sovereign loan counterpart of the debt/income ratio applicable in other forms of lending. Exports generate the foreign exchange necessary to pay interest and principal on debts denominated in foreign currencies. The higher the level of the debt, the less is the prospect that export revenues will be large enough to service the debt.

   The debt/export ratio also suggests the likely focus of external pressure upon debtor countries when debt becomes problem debt. Any measure that improves the prospect of export revenues—regardless of the domestic effects or ecological impacts—will be promoted by creditors. Money is money, and sources may be less consequential than money being available, on time, and in the requisite amounts. If it is to be either the Amazon rain forest or massive defaults, banks might not be thoroughgoing environmentalists.

Law and Debt

The foregoing material on the various types of debt and its cumulative effects presents debt as it occurs in real life, and not as it fits the disciplinary preferences of the scholar who wants to study it. Lawyers have traditional ways of approaching debt, but debt has a way of slipping out from under legal efforts to keep it under control. Lawyers usually represent creditors, since debtors as financial beggars cannot be choosers of the terms of indebtedness. (As observed above, by ironic twist, the debtor actually gains power as debt increases toward unmanageability, because at that time the *creditor's* financial fate has become inextricably tied to the fate of the debtor.)

Lawyers have less trouble with domestic settings and private debt. Debt is usually secured by collateral and upon default in debt service, credit agreements provide for "foreclosure," sale of assets, and the application of the proceeds to the debt. Cars, residences, commercial real estate, farms, railroad locomotives, goods, stocks, bonds, or other assets can be seized and sold. As bankers say, "Collateral doesn't pay off debts," but at least collateral may offer a way to avoid complete losses.

Governments, while they have the advantage of being able to draw on the entire tax base for payments, cause special problems because of the inability of a bank to foreclose on a country and sell it off to satisfy creditors. Gunboat diplomacy mixes debt collection with warfare, but in the modern period that method is too crude and, more important, achieves less success than other expedients.

The "freezing" of a foreign government's assets in the country where its creditors are located has been one way to circumvent the problem of collecting on debt. (For example, at one time or another, the assets of the Soviet Union, Germany, Vietnam, Cuba, and Iran in the United States have been frozen.) The disruption such freezes cause on diplomatic relationships with the country in which assets are frozen, to say nothing about making other sovereign depositors jittery about their own futures, explains why freezes are used sparingly. Perhaps an even more important reason would be the fact that there may be too few assets to freeze, and other measures create greater prospects of debtor control. (The freeze of Iranian assets, discussed in Chapter 2, worked because Iran had more on deposit in U.S. banks than it owed.)

Just as the political, economic, and legal aspects of sovereign debt are inseparable at the time of the creation of debt, they are also inseparable when debts go bad. If problem debts were simple to resolve, they would not have created a decade plus of deep worry in both debtor and creditor countries. Massive problem debt involuntarily places economists, politicians, and lawyers in an environment that has outstripped the thought patterns with which each feels most comfortable.

Life and Times with the World Bank: Equatorial Guinea, Africa

In the last two decades the IMF and World Bank have become far more active in sovereign lending and monitoring debt service. They make loans to countries like Equatorial Guinea in Africa, but as a condition to the loans will require "austerity measures" and "structural adjustments" to maximize the prospect of debt repayment of the new loans and outstanding old loans. The following is a first-person account[3] by an economist who worked on assignment in Africa for the World Bank.

R. Klitgaard, Tropical Gangsters, *pp. 7-12*

I had first learned of Equatorial Guinea early in 1985 from an economist at the World Bank. Heinz knew I was interested in a field assignment in a very underdeveloped area of Africa.

"As a matter of fact we have a project coming up that might be suitable for a person with your skills," he said. "But it is in *Equatorial Guinea*."

Heinz paused, as if three seconds of silence were mandatory after pronouncing that name.

"We would never assign anyone to Equatorial Guinea who had not visited first," he went on. "Not even people who have spent their lives in Africa. A very difficult country. Equatorial Guinea is the worst of the worst."

Though I had never heard of the place, Heinz's attitude did not faze me. In the end I spent two years . . . I wanted to work in Africa. I had been teaching economic development at Harvard and had been a consultant in sixteen countries around the world, mostly in Latin America and Asia. I had become convinced that Africa is where the toughest

[3]Robert Klitgaard, *Tropical Gangsters,* (New York: Basic, 1990).

challenges are—and also where the action is, because, like Equatorial Guinea, many African countries are undertaking radical economic reforms.

Africa has been at the vanguard of a worldwide movement away from state-controlled economies and toward the free market. For years the prevailing wisdom concerning economic development advocated an interventionist state. Government should be the mobilizers and managers of resources. In contrast, the new movement says that the private sector is the key to economic growth, and downplays the state's role as mobilizer and manager.

Africa's reforms are taking place in the context of poverty and disarray. Consider a few statistics. Already the poorest region of the world in 1970, Africa has grown still poorer. (By Africa I mean black Africa, excluding the Republic of South Africa.) The total income of the 450 million citizens of sub-Saharan Africa is today equal to that of Belgium, which has a population of only 10 million. From 1980 to 1987 alone, real income per person dropped 20 percent. Over the same period, real per capita investment fell by half, and Africa's terms of trade with the rest of the world deteriorated by almost one-third. The value of exports dropped by almost half. Africa's international debt is not large in global terms: it came to about $134 billion in 1988, a little more than Brazil's, or about 10 percent of all debt owed by developing countries. But compared with Africa's means, the debt burden is immense. Debt servicing—that is, simply the interest owed annually—averaged 47 percent of export earnings in 1988.

These miserable economic data have social counterparts. Only about one black youngster in five will go to secondary school, and only one in a hundred will get any higher education. The life expectancy in black Africa is about fifty years, compared with seventy-six in the industrialized countries. One African child in five dies before reaching the age of five from diseases that could be prevented by improved diet, immunization and health precautions. At the same time, the African population is growing faster than any population in human history.

Africa's underdevelopment also has political dimensions. A generation ago, the new African nations made proud promises of democracy and freedom of expression. In most countries these promises have drowned in dictatorship and censorship. One-party states like Equatorial Guinea's are now the norm. In most of Africa, corruption is widespread, and sexual and tribal discrimination flourish. In words applicable to much of the continent President Obiang writes of the need to "overcome first the savage aspects of our aboriginal ethic, ill suited for breaking the isolation of the tribes and organizing them in large states or broader societies ruled by common laws. Because of these tribal customs, political organization, instead of developing toward a more open and universalist human integration, has tended to consolidate personal power, identifying it with the leader's own horde, ethnic group, clan, or tribe."

Faced with these grave and worsening problems, most African countries are experimenting with radical economic reforms that can be compared to Eastern Europe's. (Few however, are emulating Eastern Europe's move toward democracy.) Why the sudden upheaval in economic strategy? Bluntly put, most African countries have gone broke. Private banks will no longer lend to them, so they need the financing of the

International Monetary Fund and the World Bank. The IMF and the bank are the preachers of free market economic reforms. To get their blessing, the African countries are converting.

The influence of the Fund and the Bank has grown tremendously over the past decade. The two institutions work closely together—their headquarters are on adjacent streets in Washington... Today both concentrate on the developing countries, to whom they offer low interest loans with strings attached. But the two institutions tend to differ in their economic concerns. Although the lines have been blurring, the IMF tends to worry about economic stability in the short run—say over a year or two—while the World Bank struggles with economic growth in the medium run—say three to five years. The IMF tends to focus on money supplies and budget balances, whereas the Bank homes in on public investment and pricing policies. Both the Fund and the Bank emphasize exports as the key to growth, as opposed to the old strategy of import substitution, which promoted industries producing goods for domestic consumption. And both stress the move toward free markets.

For a developing country an agreement with the IMF has become something like a Good Housekeeping Seal of Approval. Unless the IMF says your economic strategy is sound, many aid donors and commercial lenders will not ante up. The World Bank is less dramatic, but having a structural adjustment program with the Bank is frequently a facilitator if not a prerequisite for aid from other sources.

An agreement with the IMF and a structural adjustment program with the Bank typically contain common elements. The country devalues its currency, cuts government spending, frees up domestic and international trade, and turns public enterprises over to private management or joint ventures. In the parlance of the World Bank

> The objective of structural adjustment programs is to restore rapid economic growth while simultaneously supporting internal and external financial stability. As such, these programs have macroeconomic and microeconomic aspects. The major macro objectives are to improve the external balance and domestic fiscal balance. An adjustment program thus commonly includes a combination of (1) fiscal and monetary policies to bring about overall demand reduction and (2) trade policies (mainly the exchange rate and import/export taxes and subsidies) to alter the relative incentives between tradable and non tradable goods. On the micro side, the major objective is to improve efficiency in the use of resources by removing price distortions, opening up more competition, and dismantling administrative controls (deregulation). Such programs include those for government expenditures and the management of public enterprises, including reductions in the government's presence in areas where private enterprise can operate more efficiently.

Structural adjustment means less government, freer trade, and more private enterprise. But the change can be painful. It is often accompanied by a recession. Public spending on schooling and health collapses, while prices rise for food and housing and transport. Foreigners begin to play a greater role in the economy. And the shift is ideologically traumatic; free market reforms overthrow the gamut of socialist and nationalist policies of Africa's founding fathers, men like Ghana's Kwame Nkrumah, Guinea's Sekou Toure, Tanzania's Julius Nyerere.

Since so many countries are bankrupt and up to their eyes in debt, they virtually have to do what the IMF and the Bank say. Consequently, the Fund and the Bank often play the role of the outside heavies. They insist on reform, design it, monitor its implementation. No wonder such foreign aid is controversial; to many it smacks of neo-imperialism. And there is controversy over the adequacy of the IMF–World Bank recipe. Not only politicians but also academicians and even bank staff have qualms.

"I just don't have confidence in the formulas we prescribe," . . . an old friend, who had worked at the World Bank for years on various African nations, told me in 1985. "It's fine to praise export-led growth, but the experience is that it doesn't work for a lot of countries. The Bank has terrible morale now, as you have noticed. One reason is that many of us doubt what we are doing."

Especially in Africa . . .

My job was as the administrator–economist of a large project funded by the World Bank. Working with a team of three government ministers, I would help design a strategy for economic reform. Our team would also decide how to spend $13 million to rehabilitate the country's crumbled infrastructure and get the economy moving. What the project would become was largely what our team would make of it.

Officially, I was employed by the country of Equatorial Guinea and was not the official representative of the World Bank or any other foreign agency. This was good: I wanted the Guineans to perceive me as someone on their side. But the situation was complex. Equatorial Guinea was paying me with funds loaned by the World Bank. I was a foreigner. And so, even though I was working inside the Equatoguinean government, I was worried that I might be perceived an instrument of outside interference in the country's internal affairs. Nowadays international aid is infringing on the sovereignty and sensitivities of countries like Equatorial Guinea in new and poorly fathomed ways. Would my own desire to help and to learn contain the same contradictions?

Most societies share certain fundamental moral principles. Two such, I think, are the principles of beneficence and autonomy. Being *beneficent* means doing or producing good, specifically performing acts of kindness and charity . . . Autonomy comes from the Greek word for independence and means the quality or state of being self-governing. Sometimes the benefactor's role—his prescription—reduces the recipient's autonomy—as can occur, for example, in a medical setting. The physician wants to help, and the patient wants to be helped. But sometimes help becomes prescription, is required. The doctor may end up making and enforcing the decisions—in the process violating the patient's autonomy.

In the case of conditions imposed by multinational agencies, the conflict between beneficence and autonomy is pervasive and severe. To the proud people of newly freed nations, conditionality recalls colonialism. What justifies such dictating to sovereign states?

First of all the IMF and World Bank do not exactly dictate. A country has to ask for loans . . . It is in a strict sense voluntary that a nation submit to some impingements on its autonomy—as private companies sometimes do when they are in financial trouble and allow bankers to sit on their boards . . .

On the other hand, do bankrupt countries have a real choice?

Leverage can restrict sovereignty. Benevolence can undermine autonomy. Fundamental dilemmas like these often drive people to extremes. We seem to need to find bad guys, someone to blame, and put ourselves on the other side . . .

"Look," says one extreme . . . "these countries want to borrow money and the only way they will be credit-worthy is if they follow this advice. We've seen our recipes work elsewhere. And by imposing these conditions, by using our leverage, we are doing good. Not least we are saving the people of these countries a little bit from their corrupt and inefficient governments."

"The governments in places like Equatorial Guinea are composed of predatory figures who cloak themselves in concepts of 'African socialism' and 'poorest of the poor,' but spend their time with their hands in the till. Those beating the drum of sovereignty loudest are often ... the truest tropical gangsters."

But consider another extreme . . .

"So-called 'foreign aid' and 'help in economic reform' are nothing more than neo-imperialism, the transgression of sovereignty, and the imposition of the dictates of international capitalism. The standard advice does violence to our country's realities. It also foments domestic monopolies as allies to international monopolies, who wish again to tell the old colonies what to do."

"The real tropical gangsters are the capitalists, both domestic and foreign, and the aid agencies who promote them. Perhaps even the expatriate so-called experts qualify—such as you . . ."

Which side is right? Or are both? In most poor countries . . . the governments tend not to work well . . . So-called free markets do not work well . . . either. Nor does the machinery of international credit and foreign aid. Given Africa's poverty, ignorance, disease, and dictators, we should not be surprised to find rampant opportunism, deceit, distrust; and these in turn foster . . . corrupt institutions—public, private, and international. The harsh conditions of underdevelopment encourage tropical gangsters of every variety—government, business and international aid giver . . .

In these difficult circumstances, how can the outside world help without hurting, apply leverage without trampling sovereignty . . . ? How can we work for change while respecting what exists? How can we exercise analytical skills and make critical judgments while still affirming the imperfect people and situations we encounter? And how can we extend our limits in order to receive from the people to whom we are trying to give? These questions haunted me . . .

Questions and Comments

1. President Obiang wants to establish a strong central state. What would impel some people to reject this policy? Who stands to gain in power and wealth from a state so constituted?

   Do the Equatoguinean subgroups not know what is in their own best interest, or might they have reasons for avoiding the centrist tendencies implicit in the President's speech?

   If the country is broke, what do the average Guineans gain from stronger allegiances to the central government? What might they lose?

   What are the advantages of "common" laws as distinguished from tribal laws?

   Would a strong central government have more appeal to lenders like the IMF and World Bank? To multinational corporations?

2. There are a number of seemingly contradictory ideas which cause trouble in evaluating the role of the IMF and World Bank in Africa. For example:

   a. Do the countries get "aid" which seems to connote a gift, or are they taking out loans?

   b. Can a *reform* call for *radical* economic strategies or are reforms usually more modest in scope and gradual?

   c. If the international agencies are worried about democracy, must they use democratic methods in their economic planning, or can they insist that certain "recipes" be followed?

   d. If "recipes" have "worked elsewhere," what is destroying the morale of some economists at the World Bank?

   e. If the IMF and the World Bank want to make gifts, why are there any conditions imposed?

   f. If Africans do not know what to do with their economies, what warrants "respect for what already exists"? Or is the mention of respect just a cover for unilateral decisions?

3. The IMF is said to be focused on the next few years and the World Bank on three to five years. When we speak about a country, are these time perspectives adequate? What about the long term?

   In whose interests is a time focus that is limited to five years? Consider various possible time perspectives by reference to land and land use, conservation of natural resources or expenditure of them, industrialization or nonindustrialization, and rural and urban demographics.

4. Review the central concerns of the IMF and the Bank in the economic area. By reference to the prior discussion of debt and repayment, in whose interest is an "export led economy"?

   The IMF and the Bank discourage "import substitution," the practice of making domestically those products that are needed domestically, rather than importing them. (Import substitution is sometimes supported by high tariffs on imported goods to protect domestic producers.) What makes this practice suspect for the IMF and the Bank when it seems to make sense as a way to conserve scarce foreign exchange?

   What import–export policy would multinational manufacturing companies favor?

   When some people in the United States, including prominent CEOs of major corporations, say "Buy American" are they misguided? *Buy American* seems to be saying buy something made in the United States rather than something that is imported, to help the U.S. balance of payments, and preserve employment.

5a. Later there will be additional material on the impacts of the IMF and the World Bank in particular countries. For the present, unpack the statement of objectives of the World Bank, keeping the following in mind:

(1) What is the relationship between "rapid economic growth" and stability?

(2) In whose interest is it for a country to "improve the external balance" (run international surpluses in trade)?

(3) What are the effects of lowering the exchange rate (*more* local currency will purchase *less* hard currency; *less* hard currency will purchase *more* local currency)?

(4) Who benefits from lowering import duties on goods brought into a country, and lowering export taxes on goods sent out?

(5) *Tradable* goods are goods that are of interest to those outside a country, while *nontradable* goods are not of interest to outsiders. What are the effects of lowering the incentives to produce nontradable goods? (If it helps, think back to the story of the basket maker in "Assembly Line" in Chapter 1, who until he encountered an outsider did not know about *tradable* goods.)

(6) Efficiency seems to be defined as an economy run by multinational corporations. From a country's own perspective, what gains and losses might occur when multinationals run its economy? Or are the IMF and World bank implicitly saying that the economy is not exclusively theirs?

(7) Does it make any difference to the well-being of citizens of a country what government services are cut to save money? Does it make any difference to the welfare of a multinational operating in a country which services are cut?

b. More questions need answering:

(1) Should a country decide for itself under the principles of national sovereignty what economic policies it desires to pursue, or should the decision be made by outside experts? When a country agrees to debt, has it simultaneously agreed to less sovereignty?

(2) When an "agreement" is entered into between a country and the IMF or the World Bank, do the "parties to the agreement" have equal bargaining power? In contract law, a *contract of adhesion* is one where on the surface it appears that both parties are equally free to bargain for terms, but in fact only one party has the power to set the terms. Are agreements calling for austerity or structural adjustments analogous to contracts of adhesion?

(3) Is there a tacit assumption in the World Bank statement as to where *efficiency* lies in economic systems? Does the persistent complaint in 1992 that General Motors and IBM, two of the largest U. S. corporations, were paralyzed by inefficiency undercut the general presumption that private companies are by definition efficient, and that larger not only means more efficient, but also produces "economies of scale"?

Could it be that neither large government nor large businesses are efficient? If so, then what?

7. When there is to be more "private enterprise" as opposed to "state-owned enterprises" in a country, who is to own the private enterprises? Does it make any difference?
8. At one point Klitgaard mentions the cooperation between local monopolies and international monopolies. What will be the likely effect of "structural adjustments" on these arrangements?
9. Apparently some economists working for the World Bank wonder whether the prescriptions for growth and development of African countries really work. At the risk of appearing as cynical as the Bank insiders, does it make any difference from an external perspective whether the policies "work" for Equatorial Guinea or not?
10. The author seems to advance three positions on tropical gangsters—gangsters inside, gangsters outside, and gangsters inside and outside. Who are the victims of the gangsters' criminality? Does the victim's perspective clarify the apparently divergent views on just who the gangsters are?
11. The author seems to settle for using his analytical skills as effectively as the forbidding circumstances permit. Is this the only alternative open to a conscientious economist?

Cocoa, Clans, and World Financiers: Equatorial Guinea

From an external perspective, Equatorial Guinea and cocoa have often been synonymous. Along with timber and some coffee, cocoa is the primary export. If things had gone as planned, which they didn't, cocoa exports were to create exchange from which Equatorial Guinea's external debts could be serviced.

From an internal perspective, cocoa clearly means more to some than it does to others. Those who run the export sector in cocoa can get rich in an otherwise poor country. Taxes on cocoa exports have been a main source of government revenues. For the vast majority of the population, however, were it not for subsistence agriculture carried on principally by women, they would die. Subsistence—producing for home use or local sale—is of little interest to planners whose concerns are exports and foreign exchange.

The following excerpts tell us about cocoa, about those who direct its cultivation and export, and the approaches of outside experts whose advice eventually always seems to get around to cocoa.

R. Klitgaard, Tropical Gangsters, *pp. 42–43, 61–62, 73–77.*

Cocoa

Historically, cocoa has been the motor of growth in Equatorial Guinea . . .

The World Bank had funded a cocoa rehabilitation project. Three people of an eventual five-person advisory team had arrived . . . I struck up a friendship with Morton, a cocoa grading and marketing expert, who had worked with a cocoa import firm in London before taking this assignment. He and I tried to work through the costs and prices from production on the farm through the various stages of fermenting, drying, shipping, exporting, and so forth. He was a good teacher. After quite a while, Morton reached into his satchel and took out a typewritten paper.

"I haven't let anyone here see this . . ."

The document was a confidential November 1984 trip report written by two members of another English cocoa importing firm. This company did business with one of the two private Guinean companies that dominated the cocoa exporting business. The document Morton showed me was amazing in its frankness and detail. It referred to price fixing, and other scams between exporters and importers, such as pretending that so much cocoa of such-and-such quality was shipped when actually the quality and quantity were much higher. It described bribes to several Equatoguinean ministers. Most remarkably it detailed the company's corrupt deals with President Obiang and his lawyer.

Reading the document was like a kick in the gut. Even though I had written a book about Third World corruption, seldom had I seen such blatant, almost casual evidence of graft. Morton said earnestly that he hoped to do something in his grading and quality control job to break up the possibilities for such corruption. He wanted more money to go to the producers . . .

Since almost all the cocoa is on Bioko [one of the Equatoguinean islands—ed.] I thought I could learn firsthand about the sector's problems and prospects. One afternoon at six, I met Aurelio, one of the leading Guinean cocoa producers . . .

Aurelio thought I should visit a cocoa farm, and so the next afternoon we went to his own farm . . .

"See why we need manpower?" Aurelio asked, pointing to the cocoa fields we were passing. "Look at the suckers on the trees. Look at all the weeds. There are squirrels all over here. These orchards are no longer worked ... The trees need care, and spraying, and trimming. The old trees need to be replaced with new ones. We need people . . ."

Laborers worked in rubber boots and monkey suits, wielding machetes and machete sharpeners. They lived alongside the hacienda and cocoa drying machine in group housing that appeared designed for horses instead of humans—a series of connected stalls with walls and a roof. In addition to a wage of about $35 per month, laborers received a supply of basic food. If you had a large cocoa plantation of over 400 acres, you would ideally like to employ 1 worker for every 5 acres. But labor was in short supply in the cocoa sector. The imported Nigerians of Spanish times had gone home. Macias [prior dictator—Ed.] had responded by forcibly bringing some 35,000 people . . . to work the cocoa orchards. After Macias' overthrow, most of them forsook the occupation and many returned to the mainland. Consequently, perhaps half of all of the cocoa orchards on the island had been simply abandoned—and those under cultivation had 1 worker for every 8 or 9 acres.

The luscious, wet foliage gleamed in the late afternoon sunlight. The cocoa pods were about the size of avocados. Now they were green; at harvest time in the fall, they would be reddish orange. The pods would be picked and then for quality's sake the beans would be fermented in large piles for a few days.

Often nowadays the fermentation step was skipped. Then came drying, in huge cement basins the size of a basketball court with a wide courtwide mechanical rake moving back and forth to sift the beans, and wood fires burning under the cement to dry (but not roast) them . . .

The Clan

Casa Nota is one of Equatorial Guinea's largest cocoa exporters. It was here long before independence, remained during Macias' ruinous reign, and was now continuing in the post-1979 regime of President (and colonel) Obiang . . . That's staying power. Nineteen eighty-five had been a terrible year for Casa Mota and the cocoa business . . . Overall production . . . dropped from about 8,000 tons to about 5,000 . . .

When the World Bank's cocoa project was approved in late 1983, top government officials had foreseen a gold mine. "The World Bank will be giving credit to those with cocoa farms. Let's get cocoa farms." And so in 1984 there were . . . nationalizations of farms that had not been continually occupied during the Macias terror. Most had been owned by Spaniards and Portuguese; now government ministers held title to the choicest farms. The prime minister had a beauty . . . and the President himself seized nearly four thousand acres . . . The new "farmers" . . . demanded loans and got them. Often the money they received was squandered on cars and video recorders, not on lime and copper sulfate for the cocoa trees. Yields plummeted. When the harvest came a cropper, the ministers couldn't pay their loans—nor could many other debtors. Casa Mota itself was out . . . bad debts . . . Another large cocoa-exporting group . . . had extended almost a million dollars in unpaid loans . . . This was "the weak loan portfolio" mentioned in the economic reports; and in this way the country's credit system had been paralyzed.

The Casa Mota people asked me back . . . Now the topic was politics.

The government is dominated by the Mongomo clan one of them said . . . The president is the nephew of Macias himself . . . The power of the country is held in the major families of Mongomo and has been since independence. They say that the elders make a lot of big political decisions, in ways no outsider understands. The objective of the Mongomo clan in government is to take care of their family, their clan, and later the broad world of the Fang people. The rest of the peoples . . . may as well be foreigners . . .

The Financiers

[W]hen I had met Gabriela [from the IMF] in Washington, she had unloaded frank impressions . . .

"It's a remarkable place, there's no other like it. All the power is in the hands of a clique from Mongomo. The country is very corrupt. The leaders are shrewd, if not highly educated. You can't give them an inch, or they will sneak away from you. You have to treat them just like little children. You must be very strict with them. Don't discuss or show a lack of resolve, just tell them exactly what to do . . ."

The Bank's visiting agricultural expert . . . Renee said . . . "They won't understand analysis, they don't have the ability for that. They will seize on the alternative that is most favorable to their private interests . . . You have to tell them what to do, and do it in the simplest and most direct terms possible.

I had experienced an example of such telling in the final meeting of our mission . . . our mission's leader had sternly lectured a group of ministers in a classroomlike setting . . . He had simply laid down the law, and the leaders of the country had taken it—sullenly, arms crossed—like so many recalcitrant schoolboys. In order to receive the loan for the economic rehabilitation project, Equatorial Guinea had been obliged to agree to a number of conditions. The government promised to charge higher prices for electricity, water, and telecommunications. It agreed that the World Bank would have to approve of its public spending program. It agreed to establish a monitoring office for water supplies, to promulgate a health policy based on prevention, and to enunciate a transport policy that gave first priority to repairing existing vehicles and machines rather than buying new ones. These measures made sense, but I recalled how some of them were invented; in a suite at the Impala fifteen months ago, in something of the fashion of "Let's see, what else would be a good idea . . ."

The outcomes of such three-week visits—parachutings in by Washington-based officials of various backgrounds and training—would perforce become national policies. Or, if not, the country would not get another IMF agreement or World Bank loan.

The IMF–Bank medicine is potent stuff. In the short run, it can drive an economy to its knees and foster political unrest. In the long run, it presumably leads to greater economic efficiency but, as one World Bank vice president put it, "with yet unknown side effects." And even if long-run growth results, there are dangers. If expatriates and the already rich are the ones who take over privatized state-owned enterprises, the ones who have access to credit and international markets, therefore the ones who really profit from competition—then do we have a recipe not only for a kind of economic growth but also, in a few years' time, for a resentful backlash? . . .

For the IMF–Bank visit—as well as for the country's economic strategy—a key issue was the export tax on cocoa. This tax was the number one domestic source of revenue in a badly imbalanced budget. But world cocoa prices were falling. If the cocoa tax remained high, producers' prices would have to come down or exporter's margins would have to be reduced, or both; and it was logical to expect an adverse effect on production and exports. Here was a classic trade-off between revenues and production—in a sense, between short-term economic stabilization and long term economic growth . . .

I thought that government officials would be able to make better decisions about the cocoa tax if they had a memorandum . . . So I prepared one. The memorandum reviewed and analyzed studies of production costs, examined the elasticity of supply from studies elsewhere, guessed at how much production would increase if the tax were lowered, and summarized the effects of various tax–world price combinations in terms of government revenues. The memo included tables and illustrative charts. I analyzed the trade-offs and uncertainties, but made no recommendations... I was pleased with the result.

But others were not.

Morton brought up my memo. "Bob, your recommendation to keep the export tax at thirty percent will ruin the industry."

Surprised, I told him to read again: the memorandum contained no recommendations . . .

"But that's how the government is going to take it . . . They will look at the revenue side and decide to keep the tax."

"The exporters will shut down with a thirty-percent tax," Renee said. "It won't be profitable to export. And cocoa production won't increase in the future."

Everton said, "We won't know the effect of lower taxes on production until we try . . ."

I found the conversation baffling. Then Horace spoke. The previous day he had called the memo "a monumental piece of work." Now he said, "It's dangerous for the government to get a recommendation from Renee, from the World Bank, and then have another person from the World Bank to give contradictory advice.

Aha! It turned out that Renee had recommended a drastic reduction in the cocoa export tax. She was supported by the cocoa project's people. As agricultural people they vividly perceived the tax's adverse production effects; the loss of tax revenue and the increase in the budget deficit were for them a distant concern . . .

Later Everton, the head of the cocoa project, said, "Listen, we don't give a damn about government revenues. They just waste the money anyway. We want to raise cocoa production" . . .

Question and Comments

1. What is going on among the experts?
2. What is the political economy of cocoa and who are the principal actors in it?
3. The world price of cocoa continued to fall from the dates referred to in the excerpt to 1993:

1983	$2060 (price for 2,204.6 pounds)
1984	$2869
1985	$2480
1986	$2034
1987	$2240
1988	$1939
1989	$1543
1990	$1486
1991	$1215
1992	$1108
1993	$1164

Source: Wall Street Journal (prices on or about May 2 for each year)

What does the above price data say about making cocoa or any other single commodity a "motor of growth"? A basis for the floating of more and more "adjustment loans"?

4. Workers were said to be scarce for cocoa plantations, and apparently they left for the mainland as soon as they were no longer coerced into staying by Macias, the predecessor of President Obiang. Were they voting with their feet on cocoa as a "motor of growth?" Were they "experts" in the economics of cocoa, or did they simply not know any better?

5. Do economists have special discomfort in working with regimes known to be dictatorial? The concern seems to be more about the willingness of a regime to accept advice than its ideological preferences.

   A telling example can be found in Chile, where a political regime which by all standards was a pure dictatorship, found willing economic advisers trained at the University of Chicago:

   > In Chile a group of economists known as the Chicago boys ... came to power with Augosto Pinochet . . . Espousing conservative political doctrines, most of them had few scruples in working with an authoritarian government, and in fact, favored a military–technocratic alliance that could rule without adapting its policies to the demands of politicians.[4]

6. It is hard to repress a sardonic grin when reading a 1993 report on Equatorial Guinea compiled by the Economic Intelligence Unit of *The Economist* in London:

   > The prospects for transition to democracy hang in the balance. A successful transition could lift aid and investment. . . Arrears in external debt have mounted . . .[5]

B. EFFECTS OF INDEBTEDNESS

The remainder of the chapter concerns the effects of debt and its overall implications internationally and domestically. Klitgaard's account of the World Bank in Africa tells of IMF and World Bank interventions into the management of whole economies when indebtedness reaches precarious levels. Were financial collapses confined to a single indebted country, such as Equatorial Guinea, the world might little note or long remember them. There would be no need for multilateral institutions like the IMF and the Bank to intervene. But nonpayment has effects everywhere, either because of the amounts involved or as a precedent for the handling of other problem debtors.

Whatever the IMF and the World Bank say to the contrary about "helping" indebted countries get back on their feet, they act for international creditors whose own solvency will be impaired by nonpayment of outstanding loans.

Cheryl Payer, in her 1974 text *The Debt Trap,* outlined the typical *austerity* measures that the IMF has imposed as a condition to further borrowing by an indebted country. Her list and commentary on the effects of austerity are still worth consideration, despite the fact that almost two decades have elapsed since the appearance of her book. The IMF measures:

[4]S. Branford, et al., *The Debt Squads* (1988).

[5]London: Economic Intelligence Unit, *The Economist* Report #1, (1993).

(1) Abolition or liberalization of foreign exchange and import controls.
(2) Devaluation of the exchange rate.
(3) Domestic anti-inflationary programmes, including:
  (a) control of bank credit; higher interest rates and perhaps higher reserve requirements;
  (b) control of the government deficit: curbs on spending; increases in taxes and in prices charged by public enterprises; abolition of consumer subsidies;
  (c) control of wage rises, so far as within the government's power;
  (d) dismantling of price controls.
(4) Greater hospitality to foreign investment.[6]

A country in worsening financial condition will have trouble paying for essential imports. To cope with this shortfall many countries ration foreign exchange (hard currency), to ensure that essential imports can be covered. The same is true for overall limits on imports by type and quantity; the less a country imports, the less will be the current account deficiency. The IMF disfavors these rationing measures despite their seeming to make common sense. It does so out of its policy of eliminating governmental interference with the "free market."

Devaluation of the exchange rate reprices all of the goods and services of a country, making them more attractive for purchase by outsiders. *Less* of a hard foreign currency buys *more* in the soft local currency, making it attractive, until local price levels catch up with the devaluation, for outsiders to purchase local goods or to make investments in the debtor country. Wage bills financed out of foreign currency are also cut.

Since much of the problem debt is sovereign, the IMF insists that fiscal and monetary measures be taken by the government to improve the prospects of repayment: on the fiscal side, the cutting of government spending and deficits and improvement of government revenues through taxes or the sale of state services at higher prices; on the monetary side, the control of money supply and credit and the imposition of wage controls. Price controls, on the other hand, are rejected.

Shortfalls in hard currency for imports or debt service can be offset by foreign investment. In the short term foreign investment provides hard currency, but in the longer term can lead to an outflow of capital when interest and principal fall due, or when the investor repatriates profits from direct investments,

Government expenditures are cut, sometimes with a disastrous impact on even minimum social services, and consumer subsidies are eliminated. The overall effect of austerity is an immediate reduction in the standard of living in the indebted country, a result implicit in the word "austerity." As Payer puts it,

[6]Payer, p. 33.

In the "micro" view of inflation which is that of the common citizen as consumer and wage earner the Fund policies certainly make things worse rather than better. When wages are held down but the price[s] of utilities and government services are raised, this seems like a very curious attack on inflation, since all of these measures depress the real income of the ordinary citizen.[7]

The repricing of exports downward and the repricing of imports upward increase external demand, while internal demand is decreased. Inflation in consumer prices and cuts in government services to the poorest people are the two cruel faces of austerity.

The IMF austerity is tolerated by the officialdom because it is known that the measures will have stratified impacts—the poor will pay more; the better off will feel it less. Additional bitterness in the general population comes from the fact that the least advantaged probably never received much benefit from the debt in the first place.

Besides the devastating effect on consumers through increased utility rates, cuts in food subsidies, and increased public transportation costs, Payer identifies the disastrous effect on *domestic business* that IMF austerity measures bring:

> The programmes result, typically, in the take-over of domestically owned businesses by their foreign competitors. The stabilization programme puts the squeeze on domestic capitalists in several ways. The depression which it causes cuts deeply into their sales. Devaluation raises the costs, in local currency, of all imports needed for their business, and of all unpaid debts resulting from past imports... compounded by the fact that contraction in bank credit makes it more difficult than before to get . . . loans. Finally, the liberalization of imports robs them of the protected markets they had enjoyed before.
>
> Liberalization of imports tends to benefit the foreign-owned firms, which are dependent upon foreign inputs—raw materials, machinery, and spare parts—imported from another branch of the same multinational corporation . . .[8]

In 1989 Payer reiterated her earlier finding on the stratified effect of austerity measures and predicts their ultimate failure:

> The poor people, of many debtor countries, are worse off than they were before the borrowing spree began . . . The debtor countries are unwilling to deliver a net transfer to the North in perpetuity . . . Therefore defaults, repudiations, write-offs and forgiveness in some mixture are the way the debt crisis will be "solved."[9]

The older litany of austerity measures has been supplemented by newer recommendations which intensify the penetration of an economy by foreign investors. This "new orthodoxy" of the IMF–World Bank includes:

[7]Ibid., p. 36.

[8]Ibid., p. 41.

[9]C. Payer, "Causes of the Debt Crisis" In Bade Onimode, ed., *The IMF, the World Bank and African Debt* (London: Zed, 1989).

- the improved mobilization of domestic saving through higher interest rates and capital market development
- measures to discourage capital flight, such as improved interest rate, investment incentive and demand management policies
- privatization or reform of public enterprises, including better pricing policies
- the elimination of trade and exchange controls, and reduction of excessive tariffs[10]

This list adds "privatization," the movement away from state ownership or control of economic enterprises, about which more will be said later. The above also addresses *capital flight,* which occurs when people of a country move out of their own currency into the currency of other countries. "Improving the local climate" for business and investment by privatizing state enterprises, tax policies, interest rates, and so on might hold capital in a country which might otherwise wind up in a bank account in London, New York, or Geneva. (The proceeds of many international loans often found their way back to the lending countries as deposits from the elite in the Third World borrowing countries!)[11]

The stratified effects that cut across both the old and new-style IMF–World Bank interventions appear irrefutable: external concerns displace local concerns; external investors enjoy free movement of capital and goods into and out of a country; local elites take precedence over other locals—hence there is less concern about the regressive effects of import and export policies; and local government, either as employer or provider of services, yields control to home-based elites, international investors, and combinations of the two.

Comments

1. The IMF and World Bank are in the news practically every day with respect to one or another country. Most notably in the last few years the IMF is setting the terms for the reentry of the old Soviet Block into the world economy. (Not the least of Russia's economic problems is the fact that the ruble is not an internationally acceptable—convertible—currency. A more substantial problem concerns just who is going to own and manage the vast resources of the countries once part of the East Block.)

   It would be instructive to study any one of the East-Block countries to review the conditions that the IMF requires as a prerequisite to that country's getting international loans. Since these countries had state-run economies, the form and pace of privatization of what were once state-owned enterprises can be observed.

[10]G. Bird, ed., *Third World Debt* (Aldershot: E. Elgar, 1989), p. 86.

[11]C. Payer, *Lent and Lost* (London: Zed, 1991), pp. 85, 119, 124.

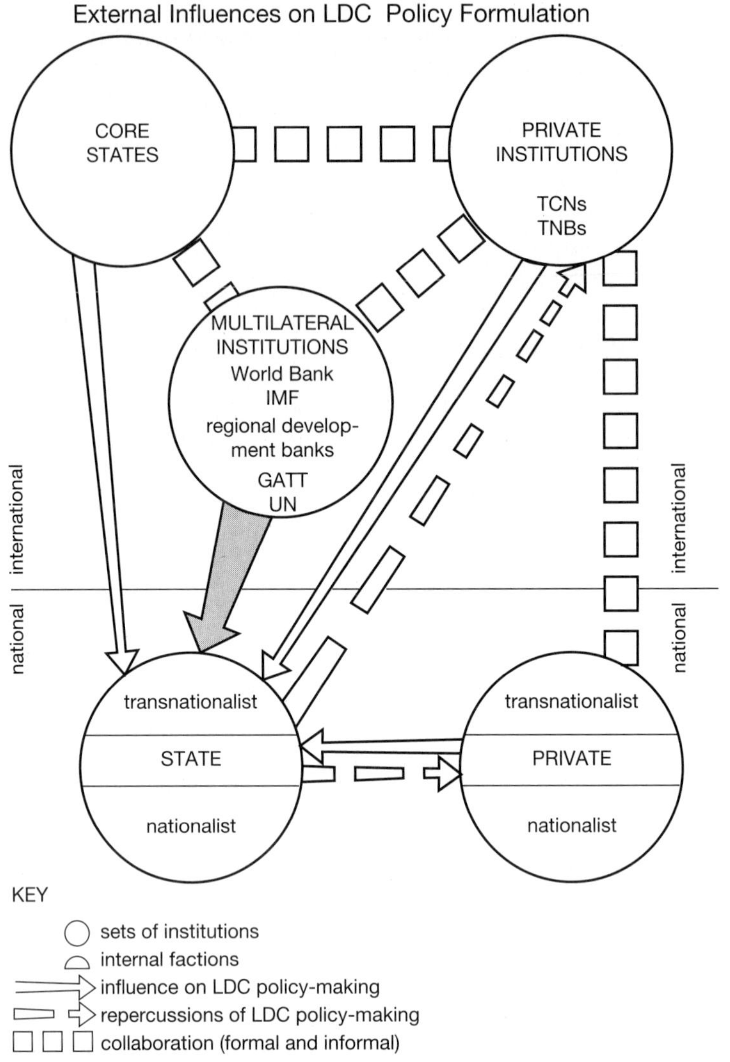

FIGURE 11-2

***Source:* R. Board, *Unequal Alliance* (1988).**

Most Third World countries have experienced successive IMF–World Bank "austerity measures" and "structural adjustments." Pick a country and follow its financial history over the last 20 years. You will probably find a pattern, even though it is the practice of experts to say that each country is unique.

2. Robin Broad in her book *Unequal Alliance*[12] charts the flow of influence on a country's economy from outside to inside. (See Figure 11–2.) In the Philippines the "motor of growth" was to be light industry in processing zones to supplement the traditional reliance on commodities.

[12](Berkeley: University of California Press, 1988), p. 8.

Core-periphery analysts trace the origin of economic policies to core countries and the interaction of transnational corporations and banks with government in the core country. These policies are transmitted via austerity measures of the IMF and World Bank. Local elites in and around government in the peripheral country are coopted by the prospect of loans, the proceeds of which they partially control. In the case of the Philippines, for many years the IMF and World Bank dealt with the government of Ferdinand Marcos and the coterie of his followers in government and the private sector. When he was deposed the same pattern of influence continued, leading one to conclude that economic power continues to preempt local political power there.

Brazil

Brazil has been the most heavily indebted of the Latin American countries. Despite having the largest economy and the most abundant land and natural resources in Latin America, it nevertheless became hopelessly behind in its ability to repay its external loans. In 1987 it declared a moratorium on debt service, which precipitated yet another round of negotiations between Brazil and international creditors. The next excerpt is an interview with a Brazilian activist on debt and its impacts in Brazil.

DROWNING IN DEBT[13]

AN INTERVIEW WITH MARCOS ARRUDA[14]

Multinational Monitor: What is the origin of Brazil's debt crisis?

Marcos Arruda: During the 1970's there was an enormous flow of petrodollars seeking easy investments throughout the world. The Northern countries sent ambassadors offering very cheap loans to finance investments in Southern countries . . . [I]t was also the decade of military regimes all over the world, many of them sponsored by the CIA. During the 1970's 18 out of 21 Latin American nations were under military dictatorships. So the bankers actually dealt with our dictators on the big loans that created our countries' overwhelming indebtedness.

The military dictatorship in Brazil used the loans to invest in huge infrastructure projects—particularly energy projects—that were useful to the private sector. After the government investments cleared the path, private capital was drawn in with subsidies, fiscal investment incentives, even co-investments with state companies, and private investors reaped the profits.

[13]*Multinational Monitor*, November 1992, pp. 18–21. Used by permission.

[14]Marcos Arruda is coordinator of the Institute for Alternative Policies for the Southern Cone of Latin America (PAC–PRIES, based in Brazil, Chile, Uruguay, and Argentina. He is professor of philosophy of education at the Institute of Advanced Studies in Education in Rio. Arruda is also a member of the international economy division of the Workers Party shadow government.

The state projects were intended to serve as radiators of development. The idea behind creating an enormous hydroelectric dam and plant in the middle of the Amazon, for example, was to produce aluminum for export to the North. The project involved the use of subsidized energy from the hydroelectric facility, minerals from Para (a state in northern Brazil) and a plant set up by transnational companies, including Alcan and Alcoa, in connection with a Brazilian state company. The government took out huge loans and invested billions of dollars in building the Tucurui dam in the late 1970's, destroying native forests and removing masses of native peoples and poor rural people who had lived there for generations.

The government would have razed the forests, but deadlines were so short that they used Agent Orange to defoliate the region and then submerged the leafless tree trunks under water. Now the trees are rotting, and we are having to pay millions of dollars to clean up the excessive amount of organic matter that is decomposing under water.

The hydroelectric plant's energy is sold at $13 to $20 per megawatt when the actual price of production is $48. So the public sector of Brazil—meaning taxpayers—is providing subsidies of $28 to $35 per megawatt. We are financing cheap energy for transnational corporations to sell our aluminum in the international market, often to themselves; Alcoa in the United States or Alcan in Canada buy what Alcoa sells from Brazil, a product with very little value added.

We think that these sorts of projects are destructive to the environment and financially irrational . . .

MM: What has been the overall effect of debt on the Brazilian economy?

Arruda: Let's take the decade of 1980–1989, which is now being called a lost decade—as I am sure the 1990's will be. From 1980 to 1989, Brazil paid a total of $148 billion as service on its debt— $90 billion in interest and the rest in principal. In 1980 the debt was $64 billion. Ten years later, having paid $148 billion . . . Brazil now owes $121 billion. This illustrates the vicious cycle of the debt which has a simple logic: the more we pay, the more we owe . . . there is no way out.

The way to break the cycle is to cancel the debt. But even cancellation will not solve the whole problem . . . [I]t is the very model of development that we have adopted in Brazil that is at the root of the process of indebtedness. And this holds true for all of the South. Our government and the rich of our country have talked us into the idea that the more we imitate the North, the more we will develop. The International Monetary Fund (IMF) and the World Bank have come up with the same recipe for the development of the entire South . . . But we've done it for thirteen years now and the results have been devastating.

The main component of the adjustment process . . . involves restructuring our economy so as to drive all savings to investments in exports. The logic was: exports are the main source of foreign currency; sell your products abroad and you will have currency to pay the debt. So everywhere in the South there has been a massive effort to produce enough goods for export at the expense of the internal economy.

Let us think of our economy as divided between the domestic economy and the external economy that produces for other countries. How can you drive investments in the internal economy to the external sector . . . ? By reducing the effective demand of the internal economy, reducing the real purchasing power of wage earners and using the surplus investment to produce for exports. This has meant 10 years of impoverishment and decapitalization of the domestic economy . . .

The GDP figures show that we have had fair results because our exports did very well. Brazil alone averaged exports between $25 and $30 billion every year.

However, what counts in paying the debt is not how much you export. What matters is the trade surplus . . . So the other mechanism to gain international currency to pay the debt was to compress imports. Since most of our industries still have to buy equipment and technology from abroad, the primary method of import compression involved deindustrialization, the cutting-down of internal production. For the most part our industry could not replace its equipment . . . so it is worse off now than it was 10 years ago.

Through the various adjustment measures, we were actually able to produce a trade surplus of approximately $69 billion in the 1980's. But we paid $148 billion to service the debt. How did we cover that deficit? First, we depleted our international reserves . . . Second, we took out new loans to pay old loans. That is the crucial element of the vicious cycle of indebtedness; you stop borrowing to invest in production, and you borrow to pay the former debt. The money does not even come in; it goes from one banker's book to another, in the process becoming a liability of the Brazilian government.

MM: What is your argument for the cancellation of the debt?

Arruda: Many loans were illegal according to our countries' existing constitutions . . . requiring, for example, that a country give up its sovereignty and accept a biased court to decide contractual disputes. They were also often secured without any knowledge of Congress . . . We believe there should be an audit of our debt and we should decide how much of it is legal . . .

There are other important reasons why the debt should not be paid in full. First the creditors knew who they were lending to. The banks should be responsible for their irresponsible loans. They were lending money to unaccountable governments. The bankers knew that sooner or later the governments would be taken down and those loans would be called into question . . .

Second, our debt increased sharply as a result of the unilateral U.S. decision at the end of the 1970's to increase interest rates. Those interest rate increases, multiplied the amount of Third World debt— . . . under flexible term interest rates—three or four times . . . Third, there is a secondary market for debt, in which the free market establishes how much any given Third World country's debt is worth. Why don't we use the free market rule to evaluate how much we should be paying as interest on the debt? . . . [T]he market value of our debt titles is 30 cents per dollar, the country should have to pay interest on only $36 billion . . .

But the Brazilian government is not interested in confronting the creditors because it continues to cling to the myth that we cannot grow without foreign capital . . . If we decide that the existing model of development is not desirable, then we can go another way. Each part of the world can go a people's way: a Latin American way, an African way, a Hindu way, instead of a Western way of conceiving development.

MM: What elements have made up the imposed Northern method of development?

Arruda: . . . These included opening up their economies, bringing down tariff and nontariff barriers, facilitating international investment in their countries, reducing the size of their governments, privatizing state companies and accepting debt-for-equity and debt-for-nature swaps . . .

Southern governments have reshaped the economy of their countries to the priorities of the North. The deal offered by the North was that it would help Third World diminish the size of their debt if they continued to pay. We argue that we cannot continue to pay. We have to use the surplus we are producing to invest in the internal economy. We have to redistribute wealth . . .

MM: What has been the effect of privatization in Brazil?

Arruda: Brazil has sold some of the most productive state companies to the private sector at very low prices. If the government prices the companies too low, it ends up giving out public assets that were the results of investments over decades.

Who buys these discounted companies? Usually the companies of the same industry which already have oligopolistic power. Take the steel sector, which is run by a small number of companies. State investment in that sector was very important in regulating the market as well as not allowing it to be totally controlled by a cartel. Now we are selling the state companies and increasing the oligopolistic power of the cartel . . .

By criticizing the privatization policy, we are not saying that we reject all privatization. I belong to the Workers Party, which argues that we need a deep restructuring of the state of Brazil. But that restructuring does not involve transferring the best and most productive assets of the state to the private sector. Rather, we advocate democratizing the state.

MM: What do you mean when you talk about a Latin American model of development, or about democratizing the state?

Arruda: [W]e want to move away from the logic of the free market, which is not truly free. The United States and Japan protected their economies when they were in the process of industrialization. Now we have the same right to protect our economies.

The second element is to submit capital to the rule of human needs, putting human beings and their needs at the center of our projects. We have to give people the power to manage, control, and participate in decision making about the direction in which their companies, factories, and farms are going to move. There must be more collective ownership and co-management of production . . .

We argue against an economy centered on capital and based on the logic that the main purpose of economic activity is to produce more and more. That means depleting nature, destroying natural resources and using up nonrenewable sources of energy.

We have to use the economy of enough as the criterion to plan the economies of the South and the North. There has to be a redistribution of wealth and resources from North to South. The North is using most of the world's energy resources. The North is the cause of most of the world's pollution, natural destruction and waste precisely because of its compulsive drive to always produce more. The North has to give up some of its excessive consumption. The world is one and its resources are limited. One of the conditions necessary for structural transformation of the South is structural transformation of the North.

At this time, the world is moving in the opposite direction. In 1960 and 1970, the richest 20 percent of the world controlled 70 percent of the world's income. By 1980, the figure rose to 76 percent, and, by 1989, to 82.5 percent. So there is an acceleration of income concentration on a world scale which means fewer people have greater wealth, and more people are in need, everywhere on the globe . . .

MM: Do you view the creation of Mercosur, a planned common market for the Southern cone of South America, as an example of a "Latin American model of development?"

Arruda: We do need a subregional arrangement that prepares the ground for more extensive integration. Countries of the subregion need to organize themselves to not submit so quickly to the strongest power in the region, which is the United States. But even that benefit is undercut by the existing role of Northern corporations in our economies.

The Mercosur treaty sets January 1, 1995 as the date for the economic and commercial integration of Brazil, Paraguay, Uruguay, and Argentina. Tariffs on between 400 and 900 products, ranging from agro-industrial goods to cars, are to be gradually reduced until they are eliminated altogether in five years . . .

There were many mistakes in setting the 1995 date . . . The treaty was agreed upon without any serious study of the reality of trade between these countries. There was no research about how each of these products will be affected by the creation of a free trade zone. How are these products' markets structured? How do the products flow? How many people and what sectors do they involve? What will be the social, environmental, political and economic impact of creating a commercially integrated zone for each of these products? . . .

The treaty process has been almost totally improvised. Private companies are mostly in the front line of this process, because the governments don't have all the information . . .

MM: What are the main forces pushing Mercosur, and pushing it so quickly?

Arruda: Companies that have already been working in this direction like Autolatina, which is a joint venture of the Brazilian subsidiaries of Ford and Volkwagen formed to face the competition of GM, Fiat, and Mercedes Benz in the region. Autolatina was formed long before the Mercosur treaty was signed in 1991, and now it is one of the companies most prepared to take a prevailing role in the process of integration. Other strong proponents include grain companies and chemical companies like the German Bayer and BASF.

MM: So foreign multinationals that invest in the Southern Cone are well positioned to take advantage of Mercosur's free trade zone?

Arruda: Absolutely. There is a growing trend toward creating export processing zones, which are completely free of controls and regulations. This gives transnational corporations the right to move in and produce without abiding by any rules . . .

The fact is that these companies are already penetrated by northern corporations . . . So the idea that we are in the process of integrating the Southern Cone is, in part, a lie. The governments are not interested in protecting the economy of the region from outside actors or in allowing the subregion to develop its own industrial infrastructure to produce and export with sovereignty or capacity to compete . . .

[The current leaders of Brazil] have decided that the politics of indebtedness—and Brazil's relationship with international creditors—will continue . . . If these hypotheses are borne out, I foresee a new inflationary surge, deeper recession, and growing masses of unemployed people. Without a deep change in the rhythm of debt repayment, and our relations with creditors and transnational capital, we will never overcome the crisis, nor escape the position of being subordinate to priorities that are not our own.

Questions and Comments

1. Arruda makes a separation between those who benefit from the creation of debt and those who bear the burdens of paying it off. One usually thinks of the benefits and burdens residing in one party— the original debtor—for all time. Compare his position to the position of Cheryl Payer on the stratification of debt burdens.
2. Arruda gives several reasons why Brazil should not have to pay part of its debts: (1) a prior dictatorial government made illegal debts on behalf of Brazil; (2) the country ought not be bound to pay that part of the debt traceable to flexible interest rates which suddenly boomed the amount of debt service; and (3) the market value of Brazilian debt is at heavy discount, and the interest charged should be based on the discounted value rather than the face value of the loans.

   Review these arguments and evaluate their implications.
3. Arruda advocates each country or region finding its own way rather than being fitted to a world plan. There might be a substantial number of people in agreement in the United States. One commonly hears that the United States should go its own way, become more self-determining, and "take care of our own people."

   Is there an explanation why there might be agreement between average Americans and a left-leaning activist from Brazil? Are average people in both places similarly situated when it comes to their assessment of power and powerlessness in the international economic order?
4. Arruda advocates more voice for workers concerning the directions of companies. Compare U.S. labor law on this subject of worker involvement in decisions that affect the location, scope, and the direction of enterprises (Chapter 7).
5. What is an *economy of enough*? Arruda argues that the United States and other developed countries have taken far more from Brazil and other Third World countries than they have given. How does this square with the popular belief in the United States that the United States has been ruined by "foreign aid" to countries like Brazil?
6. Arruda is skeptical of the rapid unification of the Southern Cone countries of South America (Mercosur) if that regional economy, like the economies of constituent countries, continues to be dominated by multinationals. Review his argument. Is his thesis equally appli-

caple to U.S., Canada, and Mexico after NAFTA? Who will be the principal managers and beneficiaries of the economies aggregated by the treaty? Who will run the U.S.– Canadian–Mexican economy and for whose benefit?

Later Collection Measures

Austerity measures reach their limit when necessary debt service can no longer be extracted in the ordinary course of events. It became apparent in the mid-1980s, if not earlier, that new loans, and optimistic projections of more exports, greater growth, import reductions, and government cutbacks were not going to materialize to a degree that would enable creditors to collect. New strategies were initiated to minimize creditors' absorbing the loan losses themselves.

One strategy was the advocacy of *debt swaps* of various types. The swaps—debt-for-exports, debt-for-equity and even debt-for-nature swaps—have a structural similarity. With the exception of debt-for-nature swaps, creditors wanted to move away from holding bad sovereign debt—worthless *financial* assets—to *real* assets in debtor countries—products, land, businesses, mines, or whatever else can generate cash or a reliable income stream to replace the increasingly empty obligations they held. Banks sometimes did this directly by swapping their debt claims for local currency and using the currency to buy assets. Or they did it indirectly by selling the debt to others who in turn would trade the debt for local currency and use the proceeds for purchases in the indebted country.

The direct method went roughly as follows:

1. Debt (denominated in hard currency, but selling in the secondary market at a discount, given the diminished prospects of repayment) is traded for the soft currency of the indebted country.
2. Soft currency is used to buy assets (equity) in the indebted country.
3. The income stream from the purchased assets enables the bank to recoup at least some of its original investment. The banks were hoping that through the debt–equity swap they would be acquiring assets with better prospects, in return for loans of declining worth. (One of the more extreme examples of sovereign debt gone bad was Bolivian debt which traded on the secondary market at 11 cents to the dollar.)

Raul Madrid describes the debt–equity strategy of banks:

> "Equity is a better place to be than debt right now, even if you don't plan to hold these investments forever," said a senior vice president . . . The banks had faith that they would find a way to sell their equity investments and remit the funds back to their home countries. By moving their exposure closer to the actual sources of foreign currency in the debtor nations—export oriented companies—the banks hoped that they would increase their opportunities to take funds out of the country.[15]

[15]Raul Madrid, *Overexposed; U.S. Banks Confront the Third World Debt Crisis* (Boulder: Westview, 1992), pp. 153-54.

Readers will not fail to see the analogy between the debt–equity swap and foreclosure and sale of any debtor's assets. Lenders prefer to sit back and get debt service in cash, but when that fails they need to recoup whatever can be salvaged by taking control of assets of the debtor—the diamond ring, the car, the house, the farm, the office building, the hotel and gambling casino. Bankers prefer pure and simple money, but in abnormal circumstances the diamond ring has to do.

Madrid records the bankers' preferences from among nonfinancial assets:

> Banks made their swap investments in a variety of companies. Most banks preferred to make their debt–equity investments in financial companies because they felt best qualified to select and manage these types of investments, but they found relatively few opportunities in this area. Laws barred banks from entering some of the domestic financial markets . . .
>
> As a result, banks frequently were forced to make investments in industrial corporations. They concentrated these investments in export-oriented or tourist industries—paper and pulp companies were a favorite . . . Because of their lack of experience in these areas, banks tended to purchase minority participations where they exercised no management role. Banks often went into these ventures in conjunction with large multinational corporations. Citicorp, for example, teamed up with Royal Dutch Shell in a number of ventures in Chile.[16]

The banks could also participate indirectly in the debt-for-equity swap by selling loans (at a discount) to multinational companies desirous of making investments in the debtor country. These would be exchanged for local currency, which could be used either for expansion of exiting operations or to buy companies. Again, Raul Madrid:

> Multinational companies based in the industrialized world continued to be the largest purchasers of Third World loans on the secondary market during this period [1986–1989]. . .
>
> The appetite of the multinational companies for debt-equity swaps was also whetted by the drop in loan prices on the secondary market. The large discounts available on Third World loans made debt-equity swaps an even cheaper source of financing for the multinationals . . .[17]

Chrysler Corporation used Mexican debt to extend its Mexican production capabilities by $100 million. A multinational like Chrysler might prefer this method to finance expansion over simply changing dollars for pesos at the prevailing exchange rate:

> In a typical debt–equity swap, a multinational corporation would buy a $10 million Mexican loan from a bank for $6 million. The multinational would next redeem the loan at the Mexican central bank for $8 million in pesos. The multi-

[16]Ibid., p. 153.

[17]Ibid., pp. 149–50.

national would then use the pesos to expand its Mexican subsidiary or purchase an interest in a new company in Mexico.[18]

Using the secondary market instead of direct exchange netted $2 million more in pesos.

The indebted countries were doing at least several things in these transactions: (1) partially reducing their interactions with foreign bankers as creditors, but substituting therefor a relationship to the banks or to other multinationals as *direct* investors; and (2) transforming external debt to internal debt (or other external debt) to finance the equity swap. In terms of national control over the economic system, there seemed to be either no change in the locus of control—the controlling party was simply a new one that bore a different label—or there was *more loss* of local control as the degree of penetration of control over the country's economy intensified.

The debt-for-nature, or debt-for-environment swaps have a different purpose. It has been contended that if heavily indebted countries are to press their economies harder to generate foreign exchange, they cannot simultaneously conserve environmentally sensitive areas. The debt-for-nature swap involves the purchase of foreign debt, and arriving at understanding with the indebted country that natural resources will be conserved, or environmental projects undertaken. While this type of debt swap has widespread appeal, especially when one thinks of disappearing tropical rain forests, such swaps have not been large enough to have an appreciable impact upon the direction of economies or sound uses of natural resources. Nor have they dramatically reduced debt.

Privatization

Privatization has been near the center of both domestic and international policy since the beginning of the Reagan Administration. It is premised on the virtues of private ownership and control and the devaluation of public ownership and control. The collapse of the old East Block has sometimes been considered proof positive that privatization is now and always will be the way for all countries, everywhere, to proceed.

The claims of superior virtue of private decision making, and the efficiency that is said to accompany private ownership can be put to one side, since they can obscure the relationship between privatization and unpayable public debt. While privatization does affect all aspects of an economy, and the economic welfare of the people who live where privatization occurs, in the context of debt, privatization has a different purpose—salvaging what can be salvaged from bad public debt. The best evidence of this contention would be the fact that when sovereign loans were first made, the international bankers did not fuss about who owned and managed enterprises in the borrowing countries.

[18]Ibid., pp. 137, 139.

Privatization, while it can take a number of forms—transfer of the *ownership* of state assets, or transfer of the *management* of state assets—always involves the reduction of the public sector and the enlargement of the private sector of an economy.[19]

The connection between privatization and debt can best be understood by observing what happens when private debt becomes unpayable. Modern finance texts regard a company's incurring debt as the grant by the company of an option to the creditor to buy the company. This is true because upon default in the promise to pay, the creditor can, through legal action, take the company. The same is true of a home buyer or farmer who gives a mortgage to a bank; the bank, upon default, can take the home or farm through foreclosure proceedings. When Donald Trump became "overextended," his creditors took greater ownership in the assets that were the collateral for Trump's loans; they went from holding debts to owning interests in gambling casinos and hotels.

Privatization is to a country's foreign indebtedness what foreclosure is to a private borrower's indebtedness. Through privatization, as with debt–equity swaps, banks and other creditors move from financial assets—the loans— to nonfinancial assets—state-owned enterprises. After privatization, instead of looking to the loan and debt service, the creditors look to the income stream from the state assets acquired. Creditors-turned-owners can cash out by transferring ownership of the acquired state assets to other investors.

In the strict economic sense, privatization might make no difference, since an income stream does not get larger or shrink simply by the transfer of ownership; an oil well is an oil well.[20] But there are enormous political consequences of the shift, as anyone who thinks about it can see. Yellowstone, Inc. as a nature theme park subsidiary of Walt Disney, will differ from Yellowstone National Park. The primary difference, besides the private claims to the income from the park, is the public's loss of control over the asset for the foreseeable future. A geothermal steam plant at the site of Old Faithful, with the old Old Faithful on video in a Visitor's Center, might not be what the public would have in mind for Yellowstone.

When state assets are privatized, the story is not over. Socialism of various types may be rediscovered at a later date, and some reversal of wholesale privatization may ensue. Few people would have predicted the abandonment of the belief in state ownership in the East Block as recently as five years ago, and based on this turnabout, people should be slow to conclude that privatization will be the prevailing property law and policy for now and evermore.

The reassumption of control of assets by the state—renationalization—can occur as it does every day through eminent domain proceedings. Lest this appear too radical or left-leaning, one need only imagine the popular response in the United States to a situation where all property right down to the sidewalks became privately owned. Political pressures would no doubt build for the

[19]For a general guide to privatization, see Christopher Adam et al, eds. *Adjusting Privatization* (London: J. Currey, 1992).

[20]Ibid., p. 9.

use of state power to recapture some control over property, and to ensure the use, control and product of at least some property for the general welfare.

Two illustrations can provide beginning information on the types of privatization now underway. The first concerns Estonia, a small Baltic country that was once a part of the East Block. The second concerns the transformation of Mexican law on investments to facilitate more foreign control of both public and private assets in Mexico.

Privatization in Estonia The following excerpt on Estonia speaks for itself. It is an advertisement from the *Wall Street Journal* of May 25, 1993, by an Estonian governmental agency for the sale of what were formerly government owned and operated companies.

ESTONIA

International Tender for the sale of
INDUSTRIAL ENTERPRISES
by the Estonian Government Agency
for Privatization of State Property

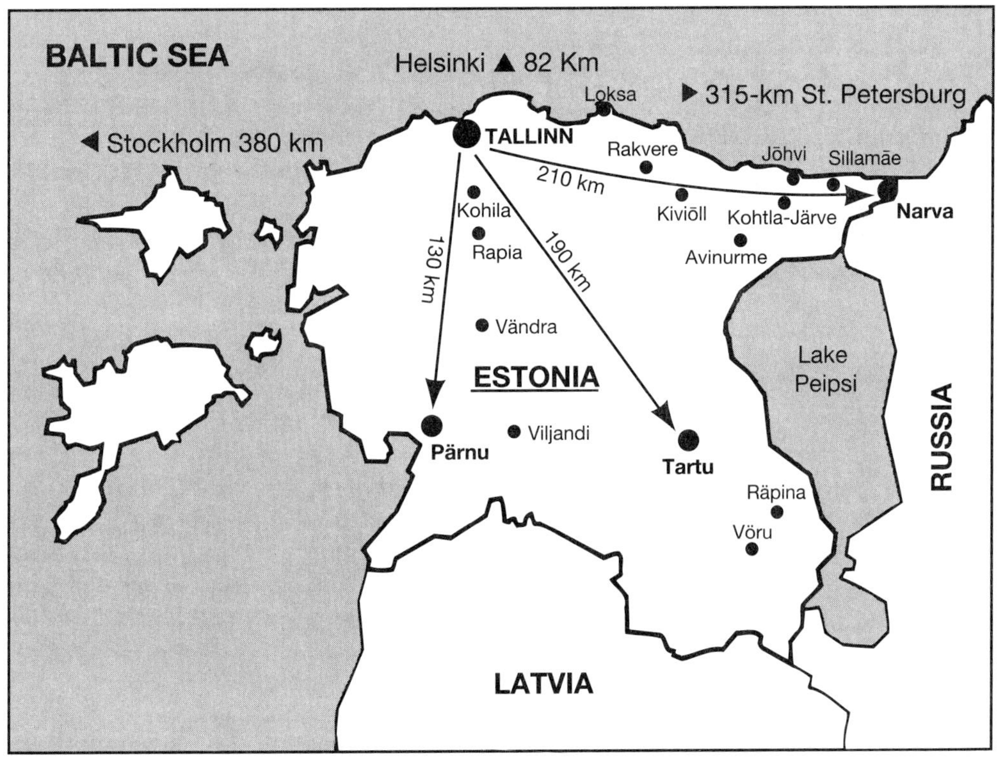

Food/Beverages

(EE-61) RAS "Leibur"
EE0026 Tallinn
(Bread and bakery products 42,000 tons per year; macaroni, noodles 4,000 tons per year; food concentrates 200 tons per year / 894)

(EE-62) RE "Tartu Leivakombinaat"
EE2400 Tartu
(Bread 64 tons per day; pastry 5 tons per day / 274)

(EE-65) RAS "Kohtla-Järve Leivatehas"
EE2020 Kohtla-Järve
(Bread 870 tons per month; pastry and biscuits 100 tons per month / 260)

(EE-71) RAS "Tartu Õlletehas"
EE2400 Tartu
(Beer 130,000 hl per year, soft drinks 30,000 hl per year; mineralwater 15,000 hl per year; malt 2800 tons peryear / 330)

Paper/Paper Products

(EE-38) RAS "Koil"
EE3420 Kohila
(Paper, wallpaper, note-books 4 million per year / 110)

(EE-96) RAS "Mehis"
EE0102 Tallinn
(Packages, plastic boxes, printing / 195)

(EE-161) RAS "Räpina Paberivabrik"
EE2611 Räpina
(Cardboard / 67)

Furniture/Wood Products

(EE-143) RAS "Viljandi Metsakombinaat"
EE2900 Viljandi
(Timber logging, sawn timber, matches, furniture / 550)

(EE-144) RAS "Parnu Metsatööstus"
EE3600 Pärnu
(Timber logging, wooden chips, sawn timber, metal frames for fumiture / 502)

(EE-146) RAS "Nordek"
EE2045 Jõhvi
(Timber logging, sawn timber / 134)

(EE-148) RAS "Avinurme Metsatööstus"
EE2055 Avinurme
(Sawn timber, wooden products / 112)

Textiles/Clothing

(EE-10) RAS "Pärnu Linakombiaat"
EE3600 Pärnu
(Linen cloth, linen products 25,000 tons per year / 600)

(EE-165) RAS "Klementi"
EE0026 Tallinn
(Men's wear; women's wear 540,000 pieces per year; children's wear; pillow-cases 220,000 pieces per year / 1,311)

(EE-168) RAS "Sõtke"
EE2010 Sillamäe
(Women's, men's and children's wear, sportswear and bed linen / 215)

(EE-169) RAS "Elf"
EE2040 Kiviöli
(Men's wear; women's wear 190,000 pieces per year; children's wear 370,000 pieces per year; curtains; underwear / 451)

Leather/Shoes

(EE-15) RAS "Kommunaar"
EE0108 Tallinn
(Shoes, boots and footwear / 2 million pairs per year / 1,630)

(EE-181) RAS "Nakro"
EE2000 Narva
(Trannery, chromatized leather 150 million sqdm per year / 972)

(EE-182) Assets of "Rakere Jalatsivabrik" (leased)
EE2100 Rakvere
(Lady shoes / 100)

(EE-183) RAS "Vöru Jalats"
EE2710 Vöru
(Shoes 600,000 pairs per year / 317)

Machines/Metal Products

(EE-31) RAS "Tallinna Masinatehas"
EE0017 Tallinn
(Air coolers, oil shale industry equipment, reservoir tanks, welded construction, steelcastings, forgings / 900)

(EE-121) Assets of RE "Pioneer" (leased)
EE0006 Tallinn
(Tools and moulds, metal ceramic / 277)

(EE-122) RAS "Valumehaanika"
EE2400 Tartu
(Cast iron and welded metal constructions / 207)

Electrotechnical

(EE-127) RE "Tööstusaparaat"
EE0107 Tallinn
(Electromagnetical water meters 3,500 pieces per year; calorimeters 50,000 pieces per year: position indicators, switches 170,000 pieces per year / 540)

(EE-128) RAS "Volta"
EE0110 Tallinn
(Electric motors 100,000 pieces per year; electric radiators 70,000 pieces per year / 1,584)

(EE-138) RAS "RET"
EE0100 Tallinn
(Electric and electronical parts, radios, tape recorders, turntables, Ioudspeakers / 1,151)

Chemicals

(EE-113) RAS "Flora"
EE0006 Tallinn
(Household chemicals, detergents candles, perfumes / 467)

EE-114) RAS "Polümeer"
EE0109 Tallinn
(Plastics fabrication, household articles sportballs, latex foam, calandered products, coated wallpaper / 633)

(EE-116) Plant "Fertiliser Complex" of RE "Põlevkivikeemia"
EE2020 Kohtla-Järve
(Ammonia 195,000 tons a year, urea 180,000 tons a year / 960)

Others

(EE-33) RAS "Tarbeklaas"
EE0110 Tallinn
(Glass and glassware 3 million pieces per year / 410)

(EE-159) RAS "Tallinna Klaverivabrik"
EE0004 Tallinn
(Pianos 300 pieces per year; other musical instruments / 120)

(EE-179) RAS "Uku"
EE0001 Tallinn
(Souvenirs from textiles, metal, wood, leather, national costumes / 574)

(EE-199) RAS "Viru Geoloogia"
EE2020 Kohtla-Järve
(Geological and hydrogeological surveys, drilling / 45)

(EE-200) RAS "Tartu Geoloogia"
EE2400 Tartu
(Geological and hydrogeological surveys, drilling / 30)

(EE-215) RAS "Tehnoprojekt"
EE0105 Tallinn
(Engineering, consulting / 42)

(EE-220) RAS "EPRE"
EE0102 Tallinn
(Construction work, engineering / 89)

(EE-280) RAS "Hotel Viru"
EE0105 Tallinn
(Hotel 428 rooms, 800 beds; restaurant 950 places [leased land 12,750 sqm] / 706)

Tender Conditions

1. In accordance with its legal mandate, RE Eesti Erastamisettevõte (Estonian Government Agency for Privatization of State Property, "EERE") intends to sell the aforementioned enterprises by means of a tender in the following manner:
   a) bids for a state owned joint stock company (organized as "RAS" under Estonian law) must be for the majority of the company:
   b) bids for a state owned enterprise (organized as "RE" under Estonian charter) must be for its total operations:
   c) bids for a plant must be for its total assets (e.g., buildings, leasehold, equipment and inventory), with inventory finally to be valued as of the time of acquisition.
   d) bids for assets or parts of an enterprise must be for a separable unit of a RAS, RE or plant, with inventory finally to be valued as of the time of acquisition.
2. The tender is public and anyone is entitled to bid.
3. In deciding among the bids, EERE will take into consideration, among other things, the bid price, the business plan submitted, promises to maintain or create jobs, and pledges to invest, each of which will be considered part of the bid. Upon signing a contract, the successful bidder will be required to post a bond in order to guarantee these pledges.
4. Interested parties can obtain enterprise and plant profiles without charge from EERE. EERE is not responsible for the accuracy and completeness of this information. Prospective bidders will receive written authorization from EERE to visit the enterprises or plants on the basis of which additional information will then be provided by the enterprise or plant management.
5. Bids must be in writing and should be submitted in a sealed envelope marked only with the name of the enterprise or plant for which the bid is submitted.
6. Bids must be received at EERE, Rävala 6, EE0105 Tallinn, Estonia, no later than 2:00 p.m. (local time), on July 8, 1993 (the "closing date"). Bids will thereafter be opened immediately. Bids must be denominated in Estonian Kroon (EEK) orDeutsche Mark (DM), and must remain valid for one hundred and twenty (120) days after the closing date.
7. Bids must be accompanied by a bond of five (5) percent of the bid price in the form of an irrevocable bank guarantee valid for one hundred and twenty (120) days after the closing date. The bid bond must be payable on first demand and will be forfeited if the bidder either fails to hold its bid open for the required period or refuses to sign a contract in accordance with its bid.
8. EERE will decide on the bids within one hundred and twenty (120) days after the closing date. Bidders will be invited to present their bid within this penod. EERE is not bound to accept any bid and may accept a bid other than the highest. Several bidders for one and the same object will have an additional opportunity to improve their bid. All other criteria being equal, ERRE will conclude a contract with the bidder that offered the highest bid price.
9. To the extent that a previous owner has submitted a claim seeking return (in whole or in part) of a company, enterprise or a part tendered, a sale will require a decision in accordance with applicable Estonian law.
10. Processing the tender and payments will be carried out according to applicable Estonian law.

EERE (RE Eesti Erastamisettevõte)

J. Manitski	Dr H. B. Schmidt
Chairman	Chief Consultant

Office hours for the EERE are Monday through Friday from 9 a.m. until 4 p.m. (local time).

Questions and Comments

1. What is the most striking fact in the notice of sale of properties now owned by the government?
2. Does this advertisement offer proof positive of the overall worth of a privately owned businesses, and an economy with minimal government involvement in the ownership and management of enterprises?
3. Study the tender conditions as if you were a potential buyer of one of the enterprises being offered. What would you be getting and what would you be expected to give, besides the price?

   What is Estonia worried about?

Privatization and the Demexicanization of the Economy of Mexico The Mexican Constitution of 1917[21] limited foreign ownership of Mexican assets of all types. Article 27 granted original title to Mexico of all property, water, and resources and gave the state expropriation and distribution powers. In addition, there was set aside from the possibility of foreign ownership land along the Mexican frontiers and the coastlines.

The 1917 Constitution was by its terms, if not its consistent implementation across postrevolutionary history, hostile to foreign investment in anything Mexican. Later limitations on foreign control included the "Calvo" clause, which provided that those foreigners who did acquire Mexican property took the legal status of Mexican citizens for purposes of government regulation, and any challenge they might later make to the regulatory power of Mexico via their home governments would result in an automatic forfeiture of their Mexican holdings.[22] It is from this organic baseline that subsequent law and policy on investment can best be appraised.

The general investment law of Mexico has changed dramatically since the debt crisis of 1982. Under the 1973 law, foreign investors could own notmore than 49 percent of new Mexican enterprises, and were limited in the acquisition of existing Mexican businesses. The law also prohibited both foreign investment and private Mexican investment in certain businesses such as petroleum, some mining activity, electricity, and railroads. A second category of businesses were open only to Mexicans—radio and television transmission, transportation, forestry, and gas transmission. This category has undergone marked erosion since the Salinas government took office, as evidenced by joint ventures between Mexicans and foreign investors in television production and distribution.

Remaining sectors were open to foreign investors subject to the 49 percent rule. A governmental agency, the Foreign Investment Commission, could, however, grant permission for investments in excess of the statutory limits.[23]

[21]Albert Blaustein, ed., *Constitutions of the Countries of the World* (Dobbs Ferry: Oceana, 1971).

[22]J. Landa, "The Changing Times: Foreign Investment in Mexico," *International Law and Politics* 23 (1991), pp. 801, 808.

[23]Ibid., pp. 841–851. And see J. Kepner, "Mexico's Foreign Investment Regulations," *Syracuse Journal of International Law* 18, pp. 42–73.

The logic behind the foregoing limitations seems reasonably clear; the more vital a sector of enterprise to Mexico's welfare, the less it was to be open to outside investment and control, a logic not unlike that embraced by people in the United States, who fear foreign investment in farmland, banking, commercial real estate, and industrial corporations. The limitations were also traceable to the bitter experience of Mexico with foreign investors prior to the Revolution of 1911. Petroleum and mining were among the sectors where foreign investors, in complicity with the corrupt Diaz dictatorship, took more from Mexico than they ever gave.

These earlier limitations on the ownership of Mexican assets disintegrated in the 1980s, and a greater and greater encouragement of foreign investment typified Mexican policy. In 1984 "guidelines" issued by President de la Madrid provided for the acceptance of foreign investment where it would be "beneficial to the Mexican economy." For some projects automatic approval was provided, and under the guidelines, 100 percent foreign ownership was allowed.[24] (For example, Caterpillar Inc. owns 100 percent of its four Mexican facilities).

The 1989 regulations issued by President Salinas were designed to extend the liberalizations under the 1984 guidelines, and allowed 100 percent ownership without prior approval provided six criteria were met:

1. Less than $100,000,000 is involved.
2. Finance for the project comes from abroad.
3. Industrial facilities are not in Mexico City, Monterrey, or Guadalajara.
4. Foreign exchange flows must be balanced over the first three years of the project.
5. The project will provide jobs and training.
6. The project will use adequate technology and comply with environmental law and regulations.[25]

The virtual disappearance of the historical policy against foreign investment can be readily observed from the foregoing. The 49 percent restriction on the acquisition of existing companies was relaxed, and more investments that had been limited to state ownership or to Mexicans were opened to foreign investors who had received governmental approval. For all but a shrinking list of the most sacrosanct areas of investment, the probability of either direct access, or access after government approval was dramatically greater. Mexico has traded control over foreign investment for foreign exchange and jobs. Debt service was never very far in the background of these changes in the investment law and policy. The dates of the successive and intensified transformations of Mexican investment law and policy match the intensification of outside pressures regarding debt.

[24]Ibid., p. 51.

[25]Ibid., p. 51.

The *maquiladora* program, which dates from 1965, about which more needs to be said in connection with the NAFTA agreement, violates a number of the general rules on foreign investment. The *maquiladora* zone was established all along the 2000-mile U. S.–Mexican border within the areas that had been declared off limits to foreign ownership in the Constitution. The original zone for *maquilas* ran 20 kilometers from the border into the interior, but this limit was relaxed in 1972 to allow companies to locate anywhere in Mexico under the same terms as could be had in the border zones, with prior government approval.[26]

The successive evolutions of the law covering *maquila* enterprises has reached a simple endpoint. In a *maquiladora* there can be 100 percent ownership of the assets of an enterprise by foreign companies, and all prohibitions regarding the ownership of land, and the standard requirement of Mexican participation in business ventures in which foreigners invest, are inapplicable. Other related national policies to promote the Mexicanization of the economy, such as those promoting the transfer of technology, or requiring progressive upgrading of worker skills to take them beyond assembly, are similarly inapplicable, sometimes through the tacit understanding that restrictions still found in the policies and law as written will not be taken seriously through zealous enforcement.[27]

The *maquiladora* policy, although a subset of Mexican investment and trade law, is a revealing one, in that all investment law has taken on the attributes of the law that once applied exclusively in the *maquiladora* zone. To put it most succinctly, Mexico has moved, and is moving further, toward an investment law that makes Mexico *as a whole* a *maquiladora,* a dramatic change from a condition where the *maquiladora* program was an exception to the rule rather than the rule itself.

Mexican investment law, if present policies run their course, will transform the ownership of the Mexican economy in two ways: first it will dramatically shrink the scope of government control and management of enterprises, and second, it will enhance the position of foreign investors vis-a-vis Mexican investors. The effect will be an economy that is less public, and less Mexican, two outcomes that can be explained as an outcome of debt, but not squared with the constitutional premises of revolutionary Mexico.

C. OVERVIEWS AND PROPHECIES

The most critical and largely unanswerable question concerns the future of the debt crisis and its implications. Here we look at two assessments: the first was made in 1986 in *Multinational Monitor*, at the time when the

[26]G. Schoepfle, et al., "Export Assembly in Mexico and the Caribbean," *Journal of Interamerican Studies* 31 (1989), p. 136.

[27]Testimony of A. Zinser, U. S. Congress, H.R. Subcommittee on International Economics, House Foreign Affairs, March 6, 1991.

largest U. S. banks were most imperiled by the prospect of sovereign debt defaults; the second was made in 1992 by World Bank economists on capital flows up to the year 2000 between the North (developed countries) and the South (less developed countries). By looking across these two overviews we can get a better understanding about what has been constant and what has been variable as the debt crisis has unfolded.

1986 Appraisal and Prophecy

The first assessment follows herewith:

INDEMNIFYING THE DEBT: A SPECIAL KIND OF FRAUD[28]

. . . The only serious question about the "debt crisis" worth discussing is the distribution of losses. The presumable gains will presumably remain with the lending banks, so only the losses are in question. First, there is no serious doubt that the bankers of this country from 1973 on have made a lot of incredibly stupid loans. These loans are never going to be repaid. The debtor developing countries now owe a staggering $2 trillion . . .

There now exists a real possibility that these loans will be lost. The issue is who the loss is going to fall on. The list of possible losers includes: (1) the people of the poor countries; (2) the international banks and their shareholders; and (3) the people of the United States.

The list narrows down very quickly. The people of the poor countries have already paid through the nose and don't have much, so forget them. The bankers are sure they should pay nothing and they make no apologies. They only made such loans, they say, to help out the U. S. government which could not send the needed money overseas because Congress wouldn't vote the loans or aid directly. The bankers, of course, never considered sharing the profits from these loans with the general public, but now that things have gone bad they think the public should shoulder the losses.

The bank's strategy is to defer recognition of the losses until some way is found to put the burden on the taxpaying public. In 1983 the Reagan administration pushed through a reluctant Congress an $8.4 [b]illion appropriation for the IMF so it could loan money to poor countries so they could pay interest to the bankers . . .

Since the Mexican bankruptcy of 1982, The Reagan administration has pursued what it calls a muddling through or a "case by case" approach. Treasury Secretary James Baker [said] that the administration had no policy at all ... This is false. The Reagan administration has in fact pursued one clear policy. The policy is that, at all costs, the debtor countries must appear to be paying the interest on their loans . . .

Government regulators can then pretend that the loans are still good . . . They can still balance the books. The administration policy is to maintain that fiction.

In reality, administration and Federal Reserve projections of Third World debt show it getting bigger and bigger in perpetuity. Mexico, at the time of its first bankruptcy (August, 1982), owed $86 billion in foreign debts; it now [1986] owes upwards of $103 billion. Contrary to official government policy and the banks' philosophies, more debt is not a solution to a debt crisis.

Maintaining this absurd fiction imposes enormous costs on U. S. employment and on the people of the indebted countries as well. The real economies of

[28]W. Quirk, et al., *Multinational Monitor*, July 11,1986, pp. 3, 4. Used by permission.

both the U. S. and the poor countries have been twisted to conform to a program by which the administration aids the banks.

The only way to squeeze cash out of the poor countries . . . is for them to somehow run a trade surplus. They must accordingly slash imports and boost exports. Any resulting profit, which should go to assist development, goes to pay interest . . . The U.S., as the major trading partner with Latin America, must respond by providing the cash. We must run deficits, boost imports and slash exports. And in the process, lose U. S. jobs.

Thereby the administration shifts revenue from the productive economy to the payment of the bank's . . . claims. Wharton Econometrics estimates that 800,000 U. S. jobs have been lost due to declining merchandise shipments to Latin America . . .

About 50 percent of Latin America's savings . . . goes to service foreign debt.

[A] reversal of the flow of resources—so that poor countries are now transferring their wealth to the rich—is having a strangling effect on the developing world . . .

The [creditor] claims are a paralyzing burden on trade, investment, and production, both in the United States and Latin America. The administration policy—based on keeping the U.S. and Latin American economies in a contorted position indefinitely— will surely fail. By their previous record, the administration has shown that when this failure comes, they will help the banks to transfer their liabilities to the public domain. The middle class taxpayer will bear the cost.

Comments

Return to the introduction to this chapter and the image of a rock being thrown in Brazilian waters making a New York banker soaking wet and what the banker does to dry off having an amazing variety of effects. Reconsider the image in light of foregoing essay.

1992 Appraisal

The abiding preoccupation of political economists concerns the effectiveness of economic arrangements to meet human needs. It is repulsive from this perspective when whole economies are made servomechanisms of other economies at the expense of the welfare of local people. The intersection of this question with the creation and discharge of debt is whether debt has "fostered development" or "destroyed development."

From a strict economic perspective, a measure of outside contribution to local welfare is the flow of capital to countries that are capital-short from countries that have capital. Liberal commentators, who have been the chief proponents of development strategies, are compelled to argue that capital flows have conferred benefits upon the people in developing countries.

The average American probably believes that the United States has given huge "foreign aid" to other countries. Putting this estimation in terms of capital flows, it is widely believed that there has been a flow of capital to the Third World with precious little return.

Many people in Third World countries believe that they have been victims of the worst ripoff since colonials exercised outright control over colonized countries. As proof, they point to urban squalor, emaciated children, and people scrounging through trash for food or salable junk where resources ought to be abundant enough to sustain all. In capital terms they contend that there has been very little *new* capital flowing to the Third World since the early 1980s, and, on the contrary, huge outflows have gone to service debt.

Is the First World an all-weather benefactor or an incurable parasite upon the Third World? Some World Bank economists have provided data and analysis on the directions of capital flows in recent history and have provided estimations of flows for the future based on the various debt-reduction strategies that have been advanced over the last few years. Their analysis gives a critical part of the answer to the benefactor–parasite question.

Their analysis carries the ambitious title, "Debt Reductions and North–South Transfers to the Year 2000."[29] The authors want to know whether capital has moved to or from the Third World (the South) and what the foreseeable future of financial flows will be. Past flows, if negative, demonstrate that the Third World has given up more than it received. Negative financial flows in the future support the argument that economic conditions will worsen in the Third World. The findings are summarized as follows:

1. Prior to 1982, commercial banks and official lenders regularly provided developing nations with a net transfer of external finance.
2. Beginning in 1984, resource transfers from North to South reversed.
3. Between 1984 and 1989, the negative net financial transfer averaged $24 billion per year.
4. This negative transfer will persist, if at declining rates, until the year 2000 "draining developing nations of $263 billion during the decade 1991–2000."
5. This negative net transfer has occurred "at the most inopportune time" for many borrowers, who are experiencing constraints at the very time they need more investment. Moreover, the transfers operate contrary to the strategies simultaneously said to be necessary for longer-term resolution of debt problems—"investment intensive, outward-oriented strategies."
6. Lending from private banks has decreased (banks are exiting) relative to official lending. (In the future, more creditors will be public and not private.)
7. Under the most "generous" debt reduction plans now offered, Latin America will experience a net negative transfer of $137 billion between 1992 and the year 2000.

Some transfers must be expected; debts in one period call for repayment in others. However, the more than two decades of net negative transfers from heavily indebted countries discredits the commonly heard contention that an abiding and one-way benefit has been conferred upon them.[30]

[29]Overseas Development Council (1992).

[30]Ibid., pp. 6-31.

Questions

1. Evaluate the common contention that the Third World is bleeding the First World financially in light of the World Bank economists' assessments of financial flows.
2. In the Quirk assessment of Third World debt and who will ultimately pay for it, he contended that the taxpaying public would pay. Do the economists support Quirk's position?
3. It should be noted that the economists have not measured other very consequential gains which have accrued to the North at the expense of the South. Real resource usage of the type discussed by Arruda regarding Brazil—raw materials, commodities, cheap manufactures—are not fully reflected in the numbers that find their way in flow analysis. But flow analysis does give us at least a reading on the net gains and losses, North and South.

CONCLUSION

The discussion of debt is not ended here—it has been ruthlessly stopped. Every time one aspect of debt is opened for discussion, it creates another loose end. Tying off that end leaves still another. New terms only half understood keep cropping up, and one always wonders about time; does what one has found out about debt still hold true? Yet all efforts expended to understand the subject are worth it. The best introduction to law and political economy would be through debt and its transforming power, everywhere.

Old timers used to warn their children: "Remember, it's better to have a penny of your own than two of someone else's." For creditors the maxim was, "Don't throw good money after bad." For everyone the maxim was, "Live within your means." Put ecologically: "Use it up, wear it out, make it do or do without." To an American Indian: "Live so that you will leave an opportunity for people to live seven generations from now." Debt destroys all of the conservative maxims that people espouse as abstract principles, and creates its own reality and demands within which people live—and die.

Debt is a subject that cannot be left to the experts, since it affects the welfare of people everywhere too much. At the microscopic level, debt and repayment can change bus fares or reprice tortillas or rice. At the macroscopic level, it can transform economies, undo political revolutions, incite revolutions, create employment, destroy employment, change land uses, build whole industries, destroy whole industries, stabilize governments, destabilize governments, change price levels, undercut national sovereignty, and redistribute wealth in both debtor and creditor countries. Debt arouses anger, as it should, and qualifies as a "hot topic" or an "emotional subject" once one penetrates surfaces.

Sovereign lending brings the subject of debt within the field of law and multinationals. Multinational banks were the principal lenders, and their getting into trouble enlarged the role of multilateral lending institutions like the IMF and World Bank. Multinational industrial companies extended their influence when the IMF and World Bank insisted that economies everywhere be "open to foreign investment"; multinational corporations are the foreign investors.

Postscript on Debt

In the United States, the most pressing question over the last decade has been the foreign debt held privately by money center banks like Citicorp. To what extent has chronic and unpayable debt affected these banks, and how have the banks become more active in setting U.S. banking law and policy to alleviate their inability to collect on their sovereign loans?

The banks were simultaneously creditors to countries who could not pay and debtors to their depositors and those who held the bank's own debt. Citicorp, now the largest bank in the United States, is the best case to consider, since their portfolio contained so many loans which after 1982 became precarious.

The United States government over the last two decades has assumed an unenviable dual position. It has been a principal creditor to many of the countries that have experienced debt problems and *at the same time* has become the largest debtor nation in the history of the world. Unfortunately the debts it holds may be uncollectable, while the debts it owes must nevertheless be paid.

Will the United States as a country experience the same fate as Brazil or Mexico: Having an export-oriented economy, with foreign ownership of any assets worth holding—whether they were publicly held or privately held before the onset of unmanageable debt? Having inflation, distorted economic priorities, disappearing social services, declining standards of living, and whatever other miseries accompany collection of debt and the destruction of the prospects of business as usual? These issues transform mere financial questions into questions of political economy.

This is a postscript to a chapter, and not a chapter in itself. As such, these giant themes will have to be broached and partially developed rather than exhaustively presented. They become excellent themes for further study through contemporary publications, since they are never very far from the discussion of the future of U. S. banking and the future of the United States.

I. CITICORP

Citicorp, headquartered in New York, had the heaviest exposure of any U. S. bank in problem Third World loans. Its mixed fortunes since 1982 support the thesis that debtors in trouble create creditors in trouble. Citicorp was the largest lender and owed most (to its depositors and other creditors).

In the annual report for 1992, Citicorp's CEO announced that the troubles of Citicorp were at last either behind the bank or rendered manageable. This is not the first time that the bank has issued optimistic prophecies, and only time will tell whether previous fixes for older problems have generated new ones. (Citicorp's activities are also worth following in business publications; to understand Citicorp is to understand major United States banks. And their common crisis made them continuously active on political–legal fronts.)

Citicorp has participated in all of the efforts to get more debt service from heavily indebted countries. In many instances Citicorp headed creditor committees put in place by the many bank lenders in indebted countries to monitor measures to secure debt repayment. It also maintained close relationships with the IMF, in which the United States has virtual veto power over what measures are to be put in place in the economy of an indebted country.

Three successive phases mark Citicorp's efforts to cope with problem debt: (1) loaning additional money in proportion to the loans it held, with proceeds used to service old debts; (2) reducing the effects of bad loans on its overall solvency by slow writedowns and transfers of some of debt to public lenders—the World Bank, the IMF, and the United States government; (3) exiting from Third World debt altogether by debt–equity swaps or other deals which enabled them to come closer to cashing out their Third World loans.

Their position could not be pure and simple flight when it became known that the prospects for debt repayment were poor, since alongside unpayable debt Citicorp had many profitable lines of business in indebted countries—banking in local currency, investment services, and credit cards for individuals.

The first phase was marked by a breezy optimism much like what a family member projects when a loved one is suspected of having a terminal illness. Walter Wriston, who had earlier claimed that sovereign loans were the very best kind, was very slow to eat his words:

> Two issues which have been receiving a good deal of public notice are the debt burden of developing countries and the increasing level of nonperforming loans. Certainly in the current world environment many governments, as well as businesses, have faced liquidity problems. But already a number of borrower countries have made the difficult but essential decisions necessary to strengthen their balance-of-payments programs, demonstrating their resolve to implement corrective action and build future growth on a solid economic foundation. History has demonstrated again and again, that if a country follows proper policies its economic situation can be rectified over time.[31]

Calling the problem a liquidity problem rather than utter insolvency conveyed the hope that the debtor countries would eventually be able to service their loans. The nonrecognition of insolvency premises a statement made later in the same annual report:

[31]*Citicorp Annual Report*, 1982, p. 6.

> Repudiation is rare as such action is seldom seen as a viable alternative because of the consequences to a country's future ability to access international capital markets. Repayment problems related to cyclical balance of payments difficulties are more common, but even in cases of severe payments problems, governments usually give priority to servicing public sector debt in order to protect their international creditworthiness . . .
> Citicorp expects to maintain its role in international lending to governments and believes that any losses in this area will continue to be below those on commercial and industrial loans . . . [32]

In addition to simple optimism on the part of Citicorp executives, there were pragmatic reasons for the unwillingness of Citicorp to acknowledge the distinct possibility of repudiation. Immediate recognition of the depth of the problem—which had to be done in 1987 when Brazil suspended debt service—would have meant that billions of dollars worth of loans carried *at face value* on the books of the bank were worthless. If written off, the bank would have had no net worth. (In the early 1980s, the outstanding problem debt exceeded by at least half the total net worth of the bank.)

Citicorp needed time and was forced to dance a while longer with a drooping partner. It was itself a dance partner about to do some sagging of its own. The dancing took the form of more loans with participation of other banks *and* the IMF. These loans could be used to service old debts and keep them "performing," under bank regulatory rules.

Citicorp was buying time, but who was managing its efforts? LEAG (Legal and External Affairs Group) of Citicorp took on a larger role, as one would expect, in what had become a solvency-threatening crisis:

> . . . LEAG coordinated the efforts of Citicorp's business groups and those of other commercial bank creditors to extend further credits to tide them [the indebted countries] over their difficulties. During 1983, Citicorp took a leadership role in fostering cooperation among the parties involved: the authorities in the troubled countries, the International Monetary Fund and the world's commercial banking system. While many issues remain to be settled, the perceived threat of an imminent global financial collapse has been substantially reduced.
> At the same time LEAG was also active in focusing the efforts of the major U. S. commercial banks in support of Congressional passage in late 1983 of the 8.3 billion U. S. IMF quota increase bill. This increase would augment the resources of the IMF and permit it to continue to play its vital role in proposing and monitoring adjustment programs for the troubled nations.[33]

In Chapter 2 we first noted the emergence of the legal-lobbying staff as thinkers in business–legal–political environments rather than simply practicing "law." Second, it is a bit confusing to determine from the foregoing quotation just who it is that is in trouble. The bank conveys the idea that it is "helping," but just who needs the help, and what form does the "help" take?

[32]Ibid., p. 26.

[33]*Citicorp Annual Report*, 1983, p. 24.

As noted earlier the austerity measures of the IMF are designed to improve the prospects of creditors' being paid and are not oriented to alleviating the problems of "troubled nations." To put it differently, the "troubled nation" was the United States, since the Third World loans jeopardized the solvency of the entire banking system of the United States. The private banking system, of which Citicorp was the largest and most vulnerable part, needed the help.

The $8.3 billion IMF quota bill then in the U. S. Congress is also worth closer scrutiny. Additions from the U. S. government to IMF funding raised a number of contradictions as it was debated in Congress. To conservatives it looked too much like "foreign aid," and in some instances foreign aid to "communist" countries, paid for by U. S. taxpayers and dispensed through the IMF. To liberal members of Congress, the bill looked like downside socialism—banks that had reaped substantial profits on the upside of their Third World lending were seeking an indirect U. S. government bailout when their lending later foundered.

The right wing was wrong: the IMF quota was going to domestic aid, not foreign aid. The liberal Democrats were silenced by the understanding that the banking system might collapse if the funding to the IMF were not approved. In the end, the U. S. taxpayers funded the partial bailout of U. S. banks via the IMF. Hence Citicorp's and LEAG's interest in lobbying for the IMF refunding bill that was eventually passed by Congress.

The next phase saw Citicorp and other money center banks slowly extricating themselves from Third World debt. The Reagan administration advanced the Baker Plan, although it barely justified being called a plan. It involved more bank lending on a proportional basis by banks that had extended loans to the countries with participation by the IMF and the World Bank. (As noted earlier, virtually all of the new loans went to service old loans.) In this period debt–equity swaps and increasing privatization of economies, discussed in the main chapter, were proposed.

Citicorp, with less choice than it may have wanted in the matter, approved:

> [W]e . . . have developed several new investment banking products such as debt–equity swaps to assist our customers in these countries while simultaneously helping the countries lower their total debts ... Our immediate focus is to work with these countries to help bring them back to the markets. As mentioned in the Chairman's letter, we have been supporting the Baker initiative with new funding as required, and with a focus on motivating structural changes likely to facilitate return to markets and greater support of private sector initiatives.[34]

When it later became apparent that the indebted countries were getting so little out of their cooperation with creditors and the IMF that total repudiation offered them a better option (Brazil declared a moratorium on debt service to private banks in early 1987), the *Brady Plan* was advanced, which involved banks' writing down a portion of their debt, with more public money and guarantees injected into debt restructurings. In plain words, the banks were agreeing to take less rather than nothing at all.

[34]*Citicorp Annual Report*, 1986, p. 17.

There was less charity in the partial writedowns under the Brady Plan than met the eye. The debt remained but on different terms, and more debt was held or guaranteed by public lenders, thereby reducing the exposure of the private lenders. The Plan let the banks exit, but did not drastically reduce the debts owed.

Citicorp wanted more than it got from the Brady Plan. More, in Citicorp's definition, meant the injection of more public money to replace privately held debt. The mixed reaction to the Brady Plan for debt reduction is reflected in Citicorp's 1989 Annual Report:

> In response to the Brady proposals, the International Monetary Fund and World Bank agreed to offer certain resources to back debt reduction ... This backing includes loans from those institutions that the restructuring countries can use to buy back debt from commercial banks at a discount or to guarantee principal and partial interest payments on new obligations exchanged for debt through voluntary debt-reduction programs . . .
> However the resources made available by the public sector to support debt reduction are proving insufficient to meet the expectations of various borrowing countries and, generally, to resolve the debt problem . . .[35]

In 1987, Citicorp had to take a huge loss in connection with the Brazil moratorium. But the effects of the ongoing debt crisis had other effects as well. Part of the overall plan of Citicorp was to grow its way out of the debt crisis by expanding other lines of business to offset the losses that it would eventually have to take in its country loans. But this resolution created problems of its own, since the areas it chose for expansion—consumer credit, commercial real estate, and corporate merger and takeover financing—were themselves not free of loan loss risk. For example, in the early 1990s with the Third World debt crisis largely behind it, Citicorp was struggling with a very bad commercial real estate loan portfolio. What it had done to alleviate one threat to its solvency had created another.

Raul Madrid provides a summary financial picture of Citicorp from 1985 to 1989, the critical years of the debt crisis:

CITICORP
I. SUMMARY DATA (DOLLAR FIGURES IN MILLIONS)

	1985	1986	1987	1988	1989
Total Assets	$177,000	$200,099	$207,749	$211,657	$230,643
Net income	959	1,028	(1,182)	1,858	498
Primary capital	10,710	13,308	16,545	17,386	18,109
LDC loans*	15,000	14,900	13,300	12,100	11,100
LDC reserves	763	929	3,275	2,876	3,285
LDC loans/assets	8.5%	7.4%	6.4%	5.7%	4.8%
LDC loans/capital	140.1%	112.0%	80.4%	69.6%	61.3%
LDC reserves/LDC loans	5.1%	6.2%	24.6%	23.8%	29.6%

*All cross-border outstandings to the refinancing countries.
Source: R. Madrid, *op. cit,* p. 201.

[35]*Citicorp Annual Report*, 1989, p. 26.

What does Madrid's chart tell us?

1. Citicorp's strategy was to get bigger (net assets), thereby attempting to reduce the percentage of total assets in problem debt.
2. In 1985, if all of the loans to LDCs had been declared uncollectible, they would have exceeded the total capital of the bank [the bank solvency crisis].
3. There was a slow reduction of the loans/capital ratio over the period, but the loans were still a significant percentage of primary capital in 1989.
4. Citicorp was slowly exiting from its Third World loans, cutting them from $15 billion to $11.1 billion.
5. Reserves against the loans had to be increased as the prospects of repayment grew more doubtful.
6. The overall earnings of the bank became more volatile.

   In the years following some of the same trends continued.

	1990	1991	1992
Total assets (millions)	$216,900	$216,900	$213,700
Net income	458	(457)	722
Total capital	15,900	17,080	20,100
LDC loans*	10,100	6,300†	7,100†
LDC reserves	2,352	521	300
LDC loans/assets	4.6%	2.9%	3.3%
LDC loans/capital	63%	37%	35.3%
LDC reserves/LDC loans	23.2%	7%	4.2%

Based on data from the 1990, 1991, and 1992 Annual Reports.

*All cross border outstandings in refinancing countries.

†Includes debt/equity swaps.

Citicorp had extricated itself from some of its problem loan portfolio through write-downs and swaps. It was a larger bank in terms of assets, but not as profitable a bank as it had been in prior years. By moving to more extensive loans to consumers and corporations and on commercial real estate, it had substituted new troublesome areas for the old ones, judging from the continued volatility in earnings and the commentary in later annual reports.

In the meantime, having itself become a beleaguered, overextended debtor, Citicorp was selling off "nonstrategic" assets and chasing investors for preferred stock in order to shore up its capital. At one point it agreed with federal regulators to closer supervision, making the bank even more like "troubled" Third World debtors who could no longer be completely entrusted with managing their own financial affairs. Overall, the bank should have had no complaint about overregulation from the government, since at many times in the period the bank was insolvent and the U. S. banking regulators cooperated with the measures the bank took to extricate itself from trouble.

Stepping outside Citicorp's affairs for a moment, Brazil, Mexico, and Argentina, where Citicorp had extensive loans, all had as much or more external debt in 1992 as they had four years earlier.

EXTERNAL DEBT

	1988	1992
Brazil	115.7	119.7
Mexico	100.8	108.0
Argentina	58.7	67

Source: The Economist; EIU 1993, reports on the individual countries.

The debt trap was not necessarily over, but it had been redefined with new principals—more public involvement and less private bank involvement.

II. AS WE HAVE SOWN, SO SHALL WE REAP?

Does the United States as the leading debtor nation of the world have a unique future with respect to its proliferating debt, or will it experience what countless heavily indebted countries have experienced? We open this brief section with a series of three short articles from the *Wall Street Journal* on United States–Japan trade relationships, exchange rates, and investment policies. They were all written within a week of each other, and should be taken as a word, but by no means the last word, on these subjects.

TRADE SURPLUS OF JAPAN GREW 44% LAST MONTH

GAP WITH U.S. WIDENED 23%, GIVING AMERICANS MORE GRIST FOR BATTLE

*By John Bussey, Staff Reporter**

TOKYO-The U.S. got more grist for its trade battle with Tokyo as Japan announced that its world-wide merchandise trade surplus soared 44% in April from a year earlier to $10.25 billion.

That's the 28th consecutive monthly widening in the nation's surplus and the biggest jump ever for an April. Japan's surplus with the U.S. widened 23% to $4.03 billion in April, while its surplus with Asia rocketed 78% to $4.71 billion. Its surplus with the European Community narrowed 6.4% to $2.62 billion.

The April numbers are one of the Clinton administration's first readings on how the strengthening yen has affected the trade imbalance. Mr. Clinton has made a stronger yen a cornerstone of his trade policy, and comments by Mr. Clinton and members of his administration have sent the currency soaring against the dollar in the past several months.

White House Goal

The administration's idea is to make Japanese products more expensive for U.S. consumers in dollar terms, and thus cut Japanese exports. At the same time, U.S. products become cheaper for

*Source: Reprinted by permission of the *Wall Street Journal*; May 19, 1993 issue.

Japanese consumers in yen terms, theoretically giving a boost to U.S. exporters. It's a controversial policy at best—many trade experts believe a stronger yen is a mixed blessing—and the April numbers indicate the approach will take time to have an effect.

Indeed, a stronger yen actually widens the trade imbalance in the short run even if the amount of two-way trade remains the same. The reason: Trade is denominated in dollars, so it takes more dollars to buy the same amount of Japanese goods the so-called J-curve effect.

The value of Japanese exports to the U.S. jumped 14% in April when compared with the year-ago month. But about eight percentage points of that increase are attributable to the strengthened yen, said Peter Morgan, an economist with Merrill Lynch Japan Inc. But the volume of goods from Japan, which is in the midst of an economic slump, is also increasing, which is what worries Washington. "You're definitely seeing the trend toward pushing up the surplus," Mr. Morgan said.

Reason for Increase

Said Sozaburo Okamatsu, an official with the Ministry of International Trade and Industry: "I think the reason why the imbalance is increasing so rapidly is the slowdown in the Japanese economy."

In April, Japan's total exports were $30.68 billion, up 13% from a year ago. Total imports were $20.43 billion, up 1.7%.

The U.S. has been vigorously rattling the trade saber, and has told Japan it wants progress made in bilateral disputes in several sectors before the Group of Seven industrialized nations meets in Tokyo in July. Japan insists that its markets are open, that the U.S. is being unreasonable, that disputes should be resolved through the multilateral General Agreement on Tariffs and Trade, and that Japan may retaliate if the U.S. harangue persists.

Another notable trend in the April trade statistics is Japan's booming business with Asia, a jump that reflects the strength of economies throughout the region. China in particular has been absorbing increasing amounts of Japanese investment and goods. Japan's exports to China jumped 56% in April, led by products such as transportation equipment and passenger vehicles. In value terms, Chinese purchases of Japanese passenger vehicles rose 940% in the period.

YEN'S RISE ISN'T LIKELY TO DRIVE JAPANESE TO BUILD MORE PLANTS ABROAD THIS TIME

*By Masayoshi Kanabayash, Staff Reporter**

TOKYO – The last time the yen surged in value against the dollar, in the mid-1980s, Japan's manufacturers responded by building a huge base of factories overseas, where operating costs are lower.

Now the value of the yen is rocketing again—it's up almost 14% this year and traded at 107.15 yen to the dollar in late New York trading yesterday—which would seem to foretell another big shift of production abroad.

**Source:* Reprinted by permission of the *Wall Street Journal;* May 23, 1993 issue.

Don't count on it, at least in the near term, say government and industry offcials. And that means the latest currency shift could be more painful for Japan's businesses this time around. What's different today? Thanks to recessions around the world, Japan's blue-chip companies are already saddled with overcapacity and generally don't need more plants. What's more, earnings have been poor, and in many cases the money isn't there to build plants abroad.

The companies are "occupied with restructuring domestic operations," says an official at the Ministry of International Trade and Industry. "Now, there isn't such an explosive atmosphere" for overseas investment.

Clinton Drives Down Dollar

Since taking office in January, the Clinton administration has jawboned the dollar down against the yen to try to cut Japan's mammoth trade surplus. The dollar's latest free fall was triggered earlier this week by a Treasury Department official's remarks before Congress that currency traders interpreted as supporting a weaker dollar.

Those comments, like earlier Washington statements, infuriated Japanese officials. "It's a problem, when Japan is making all-out efforts to bring back its economy, that U.S. government officials splash cold water on the recovery," says Yuji Tanahashi, vice minister of MITI. Japan is worried that a stronger yen will make the nation's exports more expensive abroad, driving away customers.

Lack of Money to Invest

There's no question Japanese executives are tempted to shift more production abroad. A rate of 110 yen to the dollar "is the very limit for Japanese manufacturers to be able to keep domestic operations," said Takeshi Nagano, president of the Japan Federation of Employer Associations, this week.

But try finding the money to move production offshore. Many of Japan's top companies this week released horrendous earnings reports for the fiscal year ended March 31. Overall, corporate Japan has posted lower profits for the third consecutive year, an unprecedented streak. Profits are expected to fall again this year. Corporate capital spending also is down for the second year in a row, the first two-year drop since the oil shock in the mid-1970s.

Another reason companies won't invest so heavily in the coming months is that they overspent the last time, and already have plenty of unused factory space in foreign countries. Nippon Columbia Co., an audio equipment maker, recently said that by next year its overseas plants will make 60% of the company's goods, up from 25% now. But the company doesn't need to build any factories; the increase will be carried out at existing plants in Taiwan and Germany.

Similarly, Ricoh Co. will soon make 80% of its cameras overseas, up from 60% now, by increasing production at an existing plant in Taiwan.

For at least one Japanese exporter, the high yen has left only one choice, to go out of business. This week, Watanabe Seisakusho, a small tableware maker, went bankrupt, leaving about 438 million yen ($4 million) in unpaid debts. The 70-year-old company, which reaped 70% of its revenue from overseas sales, is the first such victim of the yen's recent appreciation, according to Teikoku Data Bank Ltd., a credit research institute.

JAPAN NO. 1 CREDITOR NATION*

Japan was the top creditor nation again last year, with the value of its overseas assets exceeding foreign liabilities by a record $513.6 billion. Foreign assets rose 1.4% to $2.04 trillion from 1991, as private investment and purchases of stocks and bonds edged up. Liabilities fell 6.3% to $1.52 trillion.

The Finance Ministry tally may intensify calls by Japan's trading partners for stronger efforts to pare its big trade surpluses. By selling more goods abroad than it buys, Japan has spare cash for overseas loans and investments.

Since 1985, when industrial nations coordinated monetary policies to boost the yen's value, Japan has been the world's largest creditor nation except in 1990, when it was bumped out by Germany. The move was part of efforts to cut Japan's trade surplus by making its goods more expensive abroad and foreign goods cheaper in Japan. But this also made it easier for Japanese to buy foreign assets and hasn't dented the surplus.

Comments

1. These stories remind us of several themes that are worth keeping in mind:
   a. Debt has comparable characteristics regardless of who the debtor is—an individual, a farmer, a corporation, or a government.
   b. Debt when it becomes unmanageable limits choices and flexibility—in this case the sovereignty of the United States and its ability to set economic policies.
   c. The economies of Japan and the United States are intimately connected. Japan will worry that an exchange rate of less than 110 yen to the dollar might imperil Japan's economy. At the same time, every asset and all wages in the United States have been reduced to the Japanese investor exchanging yen for dollars.
   d. Not all of the effects of trade imbalances, exchange rates, and investment policies are completely foreseeable. One wonders whether those who want a cheaper dollar have reckoned every single consequence.
2. The temptation to bash Japan or reopen World War II hostilities should be resisted, since the United States has had much more control of the post-World War II economic world than Japan. Debtors ought not to blame creditors for their own failure to set reasonable limits! In fact, some of the investment policies of Japan, including the purchase of U.S. debt, have financed U.S. prodigality.

**Source:* Reprinted by permission of the *Wall Street Journal;* May 26, 1993 issue.

IMF Austerity in the United States—A Possibility

Kendall Stiles opens his text on the IMF[36] with an ominous hypothetical situation: the United States finding itself so heavily indebted that it must agree to IMF austerity measures.

NEGOTIATING DEBT

Kendall Stiles

The date is November 10 of the year 2000. A new president of the United States has been elected on a promise of "no new taxes." With the federal budget deficit at $400 billion and the public debt at five trillion dollars, confidence in the U. S. economy is at an all time low abroad. Slowly at first, then with increasing velocity, dollars are being exchanged for Japanese yen and Deutsche marks on international markets. A panic erupts when the value of the dollar finally breaks the psychologically important 100 yen mark. Within minutes reports arrive at Washington that the dollar will be worth only 85 yen by the end of the day, with more dismal prospects for the rest of the week. The president-elect calls the chairmen of the four central banks in Europe and Japan as well as the Bank for International Settlements only to learn that they are all unwilling to coordinate an intervention to shore up the dollar's value. He is informed that his only hope is to immediately begin negotiations for a loan from the International Monetary Fund . . . Overnight the United States slips into foreign financial dependency.

The scenario, though unlikely, is not at all far-fetched. In November of 1988, George Bush's electoral victory was met with a 100 point drop in the Dow-Jones Industrial Average and a roughly ten percent drop in the dollar's value relative to the yen . . . It is entirely possible that in the next fifteen years the United States will go to the IMF to negotiate a conditional transfer of hard currency just as have Great Britain, Brazil, Mexico, Argentina and many other nations . . .

Comments and Questions

1. Stiles broaches an unpleasant subject: Will the United States be subject to the same hardships as every other problem debtor of the past few decades? Will there be a progressive loss of national control over what is produced, by whom, and for whom?

   If the United States has had one of the highest standards of living in the world, will the standard of living in the future be out of the control of the United States and in the hands of its creditors?

   We can reflect on the IMF austerity measures imposed elsewhere, and wonder how they would affect life in the United States. Would IMF–World Bank experts determine the sectors of the United States economy that offer the best prospects for "development?" The most promising "motors" of U.S. growth? Will it be corn, soy beans, and Northwest timber for export? Light industry in export processing zones?

[36]*Negotiating Debt: The IMF Lending Process* (Boulder: Westview, 1991). Copyright © 1991 by Kendall Stiles. Reprinted by permission of Westview Press.

Must the ownership and control of all valuable assets be open to foreign investment to alleviate debt service problems? Should the dollar be devaluated further to make foreign investment and exports attractive?

And what of government expenditures—on health care, pensions, education, physical infrastructure in roads, bridges, water, sewage, and so on? Must these be cut to facilitate debt service?

The foregoing questions, which have all been routinely asked about other countries and other economies, make Americans squirm, and they should. For years the financial and industrial multinationals headquartered in the United States have been the beneficiaries of IMF–World Bank austerity measures and structural adjustments. In the scenario sketched by Stiles, the worm has turned and the IMF, if it pursues a comparable course to the one it has taken in the past, becomes the agent of others, and the prospects for average citizens of the United States don't look so nice.

2. As previously noted, the United States owes its debt in its own currency. The impulse to print money and instantaneously "pay off its debt" could prove irresistible. In that event, hyperinflation, along the lines of countries that have been heavily indebted—Argentina, Brazil, Bolivia, and Peru—would occur. Further back in history, the devastating inflation in Germany in 1923 becomes a case in point. There, a basket holding stacks of worthless currency was worth more than the currency itself, and printing presses ran 24 hours a day, printing money.

FOREIGN DIRECT INVESTMENT

One solution when a country cannot meet its international obligations is foreign direct investment. In the short term, these investments offset shortfalls elsewhere in a country's balance of payments. For example, where there is an excess of imports over exports, foreign investment can make up the difference. However, in the longer term, when profits on foreign investments are repatriated, the deficiencies in the balance of payments can recur.

Foreign direct investments are troubling in terms of control of an economy since, by definition, foreign direct investment means that pieces of an economy have been sold off, and the buyer under existing rules of property and investment law can do what it chooses with the assets purchased.

Sometimes it is said that the nationality of owners makes no difference to the people who are directly affected by an enterprise—workers, customers, and the communities where the assets are located. In some senses this may be true, but in terms of control over what is produced, by what methods, for whom, and with what allocation of returns, foreign ownership may compound the already troublesome situation of too little local control over critical enterprises. No country wants to be a chess piece moved around on an international board by players of unknown sympathies. Ask any Brazilian who is not part of the multinational gravy train about foreign direct investment.

The excerpt that follows introduces a small corner of foreign direct investment in the United States. The mechanism for making such investments is easy to understand. In the example that follows, German investors simply exchange deutsche marks for dollars and invest the dollars in the Carolinas.

As noted, foreign direct investments of this type help offset trade imbalances in the short term. In the longer term they may create problems, ranging from repatriation of profits on U. S. assets acquired, to the overall control of direction of the economy when chunks of it have been transferred to foreign investors. In short, FDI, as it is termed, can raise problems of the type that been experienced everywhere in the world since World War II—but in reverse. This time it is the United States that could be losing control of its economic system.

UNLIKELY SITES

WHY GERMAN FIRMS CHOOSE THE CAROLINAS TO BUILD U.S. PLANTS

*By Michael J. McCarthy, Staff Reporter**

SUMMERVILLE, S.C. —When Corey Lutynski took a new job at the Baker Material Handling Corp. plant here, she found the German-owned forklift maker a bit short on Southern gentility.

Once, when her new German boss wanted his stapler filled, he threw it from his desk out into her office. "It took some getting used to," the executive secretary says.

Germans and Americans are trying to get used to each other all over the Carolinas. Baker is one of more than 200 German companies that have made the two states leading magnets for German industry. Together, North and South Carolina have attracted about $4 billion of the $42 billion German investment in the U.S.; that is second only to Texas, which attracts a huge share of overall foreign investment.

And with the German companies have come a lot of German managers. In fact, so many German speeders have been ticketed along one stretch of Interstate 85[sic] that links the Carolinas that state troopers have nicknamed it "the Autobahn." Says Alan Schafer, who runs South of the Border, a fireworks bazaar in Dillon, S.C., "the place is crawling with Germans."

The Recent Influx

Last summer, Adidas AG moved its U.S. headquarters to Spartanburg, S.C., from Warren, N.J. In October, Siemens AG's medical systems division opened a, $20 million training center in Cary, N.C., and Helima Helvetion International started up an auto-radiator tubing plant in Duncan, S.C. Bayerische Motoren Werke AG broke ground last fall in Greer, S.C. for its first auto plant not located in Germany and has raised its investment to more than $350 million.

Now, Mercedes-Benz AG is widely expected to build its first U.S. auto-assembly plant in North Carolina. Officials of the Daimler-Benz AG subsid-

**Source*: Reprinted by permission of the *Wall Street Journal;* May 4, 1993 issue.

iary recently indicated that the planned $300 million facility would probably be located near one of four U.S. heavy-truck factories operated by Freightliner Corp., another Daimler unit. Three of those plants are in the state.

Why the Carolinas?

On the face of it, the German connection seems unlikely. Germany, after all, is one of the world's most heavily industrialized countries; it is distinguished for precision-engineered automobiles, sophisticated machinery and electrical instruments. The Carolinas, too have a lot of industry, but much of it in less glamorous fields such as textiles and poultry processing. Outside the Research Triangle technical park, the Carolinas aren't at the leading edge of high technology.

Educational Disparity

In addition, Germany has one of the world's best-educated work forces, North Carolina and South Carolina rank as the 43rd and 46th states, respectively, in adult literacy in the U.S. Many German nationals living in the Carolinas shun the public schools and send their children to private institutions.

Except for Charlotte, N.C., the Carolinas aren't noted as a hot spot for U.S. corporate relocations. Even many American companies still "assume everybody talks slow, they're dumb – and do they even wear shoes?" says James Schriner, a vice president of PHH Fantus, a consultant that helped BMW pick a plant site.

But the Germans have gravitated toward the Carolinas precisely because the two states weren't trendy—and they have benefited by being big fish in a small pond. For example, South Carolina recently found a German investment important enough to split the bill with the recently recruited German company to fly some local people to Germany for training.

Low Labor Costs

The newcomers have turned some economic-development axioms on their ear. The Carolinas haven't become an international transportation hub; but the Germans have been able to keep other costs, particularly labor, so low that they could afford to pay more for shipping. Never mind that the Carolinas lack the concentration of research universities that exists in New England and California; the Germans consider the Carolinas' top-notch trade schools more valuable than Harvard or Stanford. And German managers have found the laid-back Southern workers more malleable than some of the aggressive unionized people up North.

"The workers are very loyal," says Willy Ruefenacht, Helima Helvetion's president. The tubing factory was supposed to be closed during Christmas week, but not one of the 60 employees griped when asked to clock in to help with a burgeoning workload.

"In New York," Mr. Ruefenacht says, "ask someone to come in on a Saturday and they'll say, 'You're crazy.' "

Of course, problems sometimes result from what the Germans consider a different work ethic. Manfred Baumann, the chief engineer for Baker Material Handling, recalls that his workers once left a critical component out of the final blueprints for a product; it turned out they had assumed there would be built-in opportunities for fixing mistakes and lapses. "I've learned I have to give them more detailed instructions than I have to give in Germany," he says.

And shortly after Baker opened its Summerville plant in the mid-1980s, its German managers suspected that they faced labor problems when many of the workers called in sick one day. The real problem, they soon learned: It was the opening day of hunting season.

The unlikely alliance began three decades ago, as the Carolinas struggled to turn their agrarian economy into an industrial one. Both states created ambitious technical schools to transform farmers into skilled production workers. And they sought out foreign multinationals to employ the graduates.

The first big German transplants provided chemicals and dyes as well as precision-engineered machinery to the region's textile industry. They included Bayer AG, which settled in Charleston, S.C., and BASF AG and Hoechst AG, both of which landed in Charlotte. Then, word-of-mouth brought in other German companies.

South Carolina's Hard Sell

South Carolina, especially, turned on the hard sell. In the late 1960s, Richard Tukey, then a backslapping development official, often traveled to Germany to call on industrial prospects. Back home, he poured on the Southern hospitality, kicking off Oktoberfests in Spartanburg, treating German executives to lunches with the governor and, at strategic locations, flying the West German flag.

Culture also helped draw German companies to Charleston. In 1966, George Struzyna, a Bayer engineer, picked the city for the company's new chemical plant partly because it was near its textile customers and had affordable real estate but also because it seemed to offer a cultured ambience that Germans would embrace. Back in Germany, his South Carolina proposal left company directors cold. So he invited them to Charleston, and they were charmed by its European air: cobblestone streets, wrought-iron balconies, the 18th-century Dock Street Theatre. Soon after their visit, ground was broken.

Because the Germans tended to look at the textile-rich Carolinas as a single region, North Carolina, too, benefited from South Carolina's efforts. Both states have marketed themselves as low-wage and low-cost. And South Carolina, in particular, doled out generous incentive packages. Last year, for instance, it offered BMW $130 million, including $71 million in tax breaks—one of the most lavish incentive plans ever offered to attract a foreign car plant. It bought the land for the plant site and agreed to get a runway extended at Greenville-Spartanburg airport to enable it to handle big cargo planes.

Of course, the Carolinas are quite different, as shown by the relative strengths of their economies. With robust tobacco exports, and money flowing into Charlotte, the growing banking and financial center, North Carolina weathered the recession particularly well. While employment dipped slightly in 1991, the Tar Heel State more than recovered lost ground. Employment jumped 3% last year, well above the U.S. average of 0.55%. And North Carolina's number of jobs in 1992 exceeded the pre-recession total, outpacing the U.S. as a whole, which still hadn't caught up.

South Carolina's recession was postponed somewhat by a surge in construction following 1989's Hurricane Hugo coastal disaster. Employment fell 2.7% in 1991, but bounced back 2.4% last year as the Palmetto State recovered. Economic vitality remains spotty. Foreign investment around Greenville and Spartanburg has kept the area thriving, but Charleston is bracing for a major naval base closing. Tourism, including an influx of overseas visitors to the state's golf courses and beaches, mitigated some of the recessionary impact.

For German companies wanting to invest in start-ups and long-term projects, cheap real estate makes the Carolinas particularly attractive. Unlike the British or Japanese, who are more prone to acquire American businesses or form joint ventures, Germans usually insist on starting operations from scratch.

Seizing a Bargain

In 1979, Korf & Fuchs Systems Inc. decided to open a furnace plant in Salisbury, N.C., where it found a big factory building and 3.5-acre site for $500,000. Employment has mushroomed from three people to about 80. "We bought more [real estate] than we needed, but we bought for future growth," says Karl Bleimann, a former president. "And the price was so damn good we couldn't resist."

In the Carolinas, Germans have also found a work force willing to tolerate management practices that Americans often find idiosyncratic, if not obnoxious. Like many German companies, the Robert Bosch GmbH plant in Charleston insists on an orderly workplace. Sweaters and jackets aren't draped over chairs; they are to be stowed in lockers. Employees are organized by assigned code names, making them sound like library call numbers. The top training manager is known as UO-ch/TRN, and that is how his memos are addressed, even though his name is James Winkler. Under him are UO-ch/TRNl, UO-ch/TRN2 and so forth. "I hated it at first," says Mr. Winkler, who reports to the plant manager, UO-ch/PM.

"People sometimes refer to it as 'alphabet soup,' " says MAS1, or marketing services' Margret Nordquist. But the employees have adapted. "You avoid having to write all those long names, and if the person [in a particular job] changes the correspondence will still go through."

Such adaptability has more than made up for the skill levels of many of the workers. In fact, it has enabled companies such as Bosch to mold employees the Bosch way. Bosch won't even consider an applicant for a production-line job who hasn't attended a state-funded, pre-employment training program, complete with a session on Bosch history. It requires laborers who wish to advance into some of the best factory jobs to attend a $2^{1}/_{2}$-year training program in Charleston that is modeled after Bosch's apprentice system in Germany.

The apprentice program involves hard work and starting pay half that of top-skilled employees. Apprentices take 1,000 hours of courses on subjects such as pneumatics and physics to prepare them to assemble Bosch's auto fuel injectors, which are measured in dimensions as small as 1/100th of a human hair. Although the workers eventually use high-tech machinery, they begin by spending some 60 hours learning to hand-file metal scraps to precise dimensions. "I got real tired of filing," says Stephanie Herndon, a 23-year-old apprentice graduate, in a deep Southern drawl. "I do believe they were trying to instill patience in us."

German ways don't always sit well with the half-a-million Americans who work for them, of course. One tricky issue is the German managers' habit of keeping their office doors closed. In chilly Germany, they do so to conserve heat, which is expensive. Moreover, closed doors, to Germans, are orderly.

But to Baker's American workers, who were used to affable, good-old-boy

Southern bosses, a closed door indicated an aloof, uncaring boss. "It drove people nuts," says Ms. Lutynski, the executive secretary. Morale has improved since Mitch Milovitch, an Atlantan, became president in 1991. He greets staffers at their desks, visits the factory floor and has coffee with production workers.

Even more important issues concern pay and working hours. At home in Germany, Germans have some of the world's highest wages and longest vacations. When transferred to U.S. divisions, they typically keep their six-plus-week vacations, annoying U.S. workers stuck with the skimpier American plan. "They're constantly gone, while the poor American stiff is here doing his work," complains Evelyn Albert, a former Bosch secretary.

An Aid to Unions

U.S. unions view such disparities as an organizing weapon. The United Auto Workers worries that BMW will pay its South Carolina workers less than the $17-an-hour the average U.S. auto worker makes. The union plans to make wages an issue to win support when the plant opens in 1995. The union has made inroads at German companies in the Carolinas; three years ago, it got representation rights at Mercedes's Freightliner plant in Mount Holly, N.C.

But in the Carolinas, most employees have wanted no part of unionization. They choose instead to vent their frustrations in less confrontational ways. Bored with some of the German apprenticeship system he had to teach, Mike Bryan, a trainer at Bosch, designed a project more relevant to himself and his friends, who grew up racing go-carts and restoring Corvettes. He devised a three-month project for the apprentices to build a scale-model replica of a 1904 Harley-Davidson.

And as for Ms. Herndon, she is now grateful for all those boring hours of filing metal. Her Bosch factory job pays $11.63 an hour, a lot better than a previous stint waiting tables at Howard Johnson's. "It's a good opportunity," she says.

Questions and Comments

1. There is no mention in the article of the relationship between the rise of foreign direct investment in the United States and trade deficits and the increasing debtor position of the United States. As the dollar falls in value with respect to other currencies in the world, including the German mark, all assets in the United States become cheaper.

   What has happened in other countries when currency has been devalued applies equally with respect to the U. S. dollar. As the article notes, some German companies found U. S. wage rates and land costs a bargain. (Compare a cheap Latin American vacation spot where the U. S. dollar goes far.)

2. In 1992, the level of foreign direct investment in the United States was actually far lower than it had been in prior years. From its high point in 1988 at $72.69 billion and $26 billion in 1991, it declined to $13.5 billion in 1992. Meanwhile, net capital flows from the United

States were higher, \$3.9 billion going out as compared to \$11.5 billion of net inflow in 1991.[37]

3. People in the United States have distinctively mixed sentiments about the foreign ownership of land and facilities. It would probably not be difficult to get popular approval of a flat prohibition on foreign companies' owning industrial sites or manufacturing facilities in the United States. (None has been proposed, because everyone in politics, regardless of party, knows the iron laws of international debt. They also know the ongoing investment practices of U.S.-based multinationals abroad.)

   At the same time that there is hostility to foreign investment, many states have established offices in foreign countries to attract investment, in order to provide jobs for their citizens. Moreover, they have often offered subsidies, as has South Carolina, financed out of local taxation, to make location in a state attractive.

   Because of this ambivalence about foreign presence in the United States, there have emerged no coherent law and policy regarding foreign direct investment. There are fears about foreign control of too much of U. S. business, or too much control of critical elements of U. S. business, but the fears are offset by expediency—getting jobs or bringing some economic activity into areas that have been chronically depressed.

4. We get little sense from the article of where the output from the factories is going, what the levels of profits are, and where the profits are going. We do, however, get some feel for the culture shock and resentments that accompany foreign direct investment. These might be comparable to those felt everywhere else in the world where multinational corporations have chosen to locate.

   Ought the residents of South Carolina to be grateful for the interest taken by German companies in their state?

5. How might the increasing presence of German companies in a particular state affect the political process either at the state level or at the national level? Might there be less and less difference between people elected to Congress from South Carolina and lobbyists for foreign governments, who are now required to register? This growing influence of other countries and their multinationals in state and federal legislatures has been considered in a journalistic account, *Buying Into America*.[38]

6. Make a study of the level of foreign direct investment in your state. To facilitate your work, you can consult the data compiled by the United States Department of Commerce. The data includes the level of foreign direct investment by country of origin, by industry, and by the state where investments have been made.

[37]*Wall Street Journal*, June 9,1993.

[38]M. Tolchin, op. cit.

Make an assessment, to the extent possible, of the impact of foreign direct investment in your state, and how it has affected such institutions as schooling and local government.

If there has been a state office established for the attraction of foreign investment, it would be worth study, as would the subsidy structure put in place by the state to sweeten the prospects of foreign investors' locating in the state.

As a class project, prepare a feature story of the type done by the writers for the *Wall Street Journal* on foreign investments in the Carolinas.

HYPERINFLATION USA

Harry Figgie, Jr. is the CEO of Figgie International, an international conglomerate. In a speech given in 1988, he asked a question comparable to the one asked by Stiles about the IMF: what if the U.S. dollar became worthless in a hurry? What would be the general effects of runaway inflation, and could his company operate under monetary conditions comparable to the ones that have occurred in heavily indebted Latin American countries?

SURVIVING HYPERINFLATION

Harry E. Figgie, Jr., Town Hall, Los Angeles, June 1988.[39]

. . . [M]y subject is not a pleasant one. I'm going to talk about hyperinflation, specifically about the lessons we learned in a study we recently conducted in South America.

I want to address three aspects of the subject of hyperinflation. The first, why I think hyperinflation is a timely concern. Secondly, I'll describe what our research team found in South America. Finally, I'll discuss what I think has to be done in relatively short order to keep this country from falling victim to hyperinflation.

I'm basically a businessman, and I don't consider myself an alarmist . . . [I]n the early 80's, I became concerned about our country's future and the possibility of hyperinflation because we projected an enormous future national debt.

In trying to learn more about it, we at Figgie International found that virtually nothing had been written on hyperinflation or how you operate a company under hyperinflationary conditions, so we sent a team to study hyperinflation in South America, viewing it as a laboratory for what we in the United States might expect.

I greatly hope that hyperinflation never comes to the United States, but I am concerned today because we have ... destroyed the flexibility of our great economic system. And I think that in the next decade we will either follow a path through disinflation and deflation to depression, or we will go into hyperinflation . . .

Now, why do I say we have destroyed our flexibility? Let me talk first about industry, and secondly about

[39]LV *Vital Speeches*, Nov. 1, 1988, pp. 47–51. Reprinted by permission.

government. Nonfinancial industry has a debt to equity ratio of .9 to 1, which is the highest ratio in history. We have $1.8 trillion in corporate debt, and an average of $9 billion in annual defaults. The earnings . . . coverage on interest used to be 26 times; it has fallen to 2.

As far as the government goes, we have lost our flexibility because of our huge deficits. The United States has created more debt in the last five years than in the entire prior history of our republic. We have doubled the debt from just over 1 trillion to almost 2.4 trillion, and that is peanuts compared to what lies in front of us . . .

[I]n 1982 the deficit was about $128 billion annually, up from about $40 billion just a few years before, and $5 billion in 1974 . . .

[T]he Grace Commission [1982] found that the debt will reach $13 trillion by the year 2000 . . . the annual deficit will be $2 trillion and the interest on the debt will be $1.6 trillion.

Now if you look at the period from 1986 to the year 2000 . . . and you graph the increase in debt, it really becomes shocking . . .

As a result, I think we face a 50 percent chance of hyperinflation in the 1990s.

I recognize there are economists who think we are going the other way, toward a depression. Either way, what has happened is that we have lost our flexibility and, in all likelihood, the president elected in 1988 will have to face a recession . . . and our next president is not going to be able to throw money at the problem because if he does, the deficit will immediately shoot through the roof and exacerbate a problem that is already very serious.

That's why I believe we will be at a crossroads in about six years.

Faced with this prospect, I decided about two years ago that our company better prepare for hyperinflation ... We decided that the French and German experiences in 1923 were just too old for our purposes . . .

Their assignment [for the three-person team] was to travel to Argentina, Brazil, and Bolivia and study inflation ... What we wanted from them was a handbook on how you operate in a hyperinflationary environment.

They made four trips . . . and talked to better than 80 leading bankers and industrialists and a considerable number of ordinary citizens . . . After one trip Dr. Swanson [said] that for years he had been teaching that deficits cause inflation, but now he had actually seen it first hand. When I asked how much notice you can expect before inflation turns into hyperinflation, he said there was a case where there was only three days' warning . . .

The worst news, however, was the widespread opinion . . . that the United States is on the same course their countries were on 20 to 30 years ago . . . They point out that the United States shares the same hyperinflation-causing features as their countries: large deficits, a rapidly expanding money supply, deterioration in our international balance of payments, calls for protectionism, eroded confidence in our national currency, and finally our currency's declining international exchange value.

They further pointed out that the United States has the lowest savings rate in the industrialized world, is the largest debtor nation, and has tripled its annual deficit in six years.

The South Americans see serious trouble ahead for us, and they can't believe we don't see it coming ourselves. They are absolutely amazed, for example, that our banks still offer 30-year fixed rate loans.

One Bolivian bank director . . .: "Your investments in productive assets are down, growth in non-productive sectors is up, and you purchase more than you produce. Sometimes I wonder how the United States holds together."

Although the team's principal objective was to study how to operate a business in hyperinflation, they also looked into its impact on the average citizen, and I will tell you that it is devastating. Pensions, bonds, savings and insurance policies become absolutely worthless. Paychecks have to be converted immediately into hard goods. Time is so essential that banks sometimes move their offices right onto the floors of the companies so workers can get cash immediately.

. . . Our team went into a supermarket in Argentina and watched someone pick up a loaf of bread. Between the time he picked it up and the time he checked it out, the price increased.

. . . There is a running joke that it is cheaper to take a cab than a bus because you have to pay the bus when you get on, and you don't have to pay the cab until you get out. By then the money is worth less . . .

Fifteen years ago when our company was making graders in Brazil, a team of doctors used to buy a new grader from us each year, park it in a garage, sell it the year following, and then buy another grader. They used that hard asset to protect . . . against . . . inflation.

As far as business operation, the impact of hyperinflation is also tremendous. There is no stability: prices skyrocket, supplies dry up, and wages continually rise. At Bolivia's inflationary peak, companies gave raises almost weekly. They paid wages every two or three days, and had no funds available for capital improvements . . .

[C]ompanies become extremely vulnerable to corruption and internally run employee black markets. The smaller companies put family members in key positions to stop black market drain. Short-cutting government regulations becomes all-pervasive, and everyone plays the black market.

Companies don't worry about business management; they worry about cash management . . .

Some manufacturers actually permit their manufacturing to halt and instead rely on speculation . . .

Companies never let their cash stay idle. Cash is invested overnight, renewed daily, and converted into one of two things: inventories or U. S. dollars. Dollar-denominated accounts become the common hedge, and minimal cash balances are kept in the local currency.

The companies generally maintain relationships with several banks, first because it maintains credit availability, but also because it protects them in case one of the banks goes bankrupt . . .

Bank funds become virtually unavailable because reserve requirements are so high . . . Most funds that are available go to the government.

When loans can be gotten, the interest is exorbitant. Rates in Brazil are currently about 18 percent monthly. During one of the researchers' visits to Brazil, interest rates moved up from 330 percent to 430 percent in one week.

I might point out that a number of people like inflation, because they can make so much money taking advantage of it . . . They keep their receivables to a minimum and drag their payables, and they end up with cash they can either arbitrage against the dollar, or lend. An Argentine accountant told our team that one of his clients earned over half its $220 million pretax profit by lending and currency speculation . . .

Companies in South America use local currency to accumulate debt. They accumulate cash in hard currencies, but they seldom touch hard currencies for debt.

They are very careful in extending credit to customers, and there are no long term, fixed price contracts. In Brazil, terms of sales for capital goods usually include a 50 percent down payment . . .

Companies have to change prices continually, and all prices are indexed to reflect inflation. They sell only high gross margin products because small margins can be wiped out overnight.

They also keep as many as four sets of books—one in old currency, one in new currency, one in units of production, and one in dollars . . .

I asked, . . . what are we going to arbitrage against [when the dollar is worthless]? I am still pushing for an answer, but obviously there are very few answers. The first few companies will arbitrage against the Swiss franc, the Dutch guilder, or the German mark, and the rest . . . will probably hedge against commodities.

It is easy to pass off the South American warnings by saying these countries are backward, but this wasn't always so. In the early part of the 20th century, Argentina was the fifth most productive nation in the world. It has since dropped down to 70th. In 1985, its inflation was 1000 percent. Now, in 1988, it is back down to 200 percent . . .

Brazil, which is the sixth most populous country in the world, has the eighth largest economy. Its 1985 inflation rate was 400 percent, and 1988 projections range up to 1000 percent.

Bolivia is the most potent example of all. Its deficit spending is incredible: in 1985, taxes covered only 15 percent of government expenditures, and inflation was running at 20,000 percent, with bursts up to 50,000 percent. There was one period where the equivalent of $5,000 in Bolivian money fell in only a few months to a value of just 50 cents. Bolivia's inflation is now back to double digits, but their economy is running well below capacity and unemployment is extremely high.

All of the countries we studied changed their currencies within the last two years, mostly by lopping off 3–6 zeros . . . The team took a picture of a man carrying a sack of money on his back to exchange at the bank, looking a little like Santa Claus. The bankers didn't worry about the denominations on the currency, they didn't even look at the money in the sack ... They just weighed the sack of money and gave him the new currency . . .

One thing we learned is that the governments find it virtually impossible to control hyperinflation once it gets started. We also have to face the prospect that we might lose our form of government if hyperinflation takes hold in this country . . .

All the governments tried to overcome inflation with wage and price controls . . . and all failed. In Brazil 50 percent of the people work for the government. The Brazilian government would put in wage and price controls and immediately raise government wages to avoid labor dissent . . .

I would like to stress some of the major findings from our study . . . First of all deficits cause hyperinflation. Sometimes you have less than three days' notice before hyperinflation takes off. And once hyperinflation starts to run its course, it's very difficult to reverse . . .

As I said earlier, our problem in the United States is that we've destroyed our flexibility. This is compounded by the fact that we don't believe it can happen here . . . I think hyperinflation could hit us sometime between 1994 and 1998 . . . [Figgie makes five recommendations: balance the federal budget; raise new taxes through gasoline and alcohol; privatize social security to make it less available to numbers juggling and more available as a source of investment capital; cut government waste, and promote more government–business cooper -ation as is common in countries like Japan. —Ed.]

In my judgment, 1992 will be too late to effect the changes needed. The President and Congress that come in in 1988 must act. And it is important that we don't adopt the attitude that hyperinflation cannot happen to America, because I can almost assure you that it *can* happen here . . .

Comments and Questions

1. During the Bush Administration, the annual deficits increased, and the national debt increased at a rate even faster than the one that had troubled Figgie. President Bush blamed the Congress, and the Congress blamed President Bush and the gridlock he was able to engineer through vetoes and large enough Congressional coalitions to sustain the vetoes.

   Partisan debate aside, nobody could contest the fact that deficits were larger, and that the national debt had been grown to around 4 trillion.
2. Compare the commentary of Figgie with the series of articles on U.S.–Japanese relations and the Skiles excerpt on the possibility of IMF austerity for the United States.
3. President Clinton's proposals for deficit *reduction* and tax increases can be evaluated against the list of recommendations made in the talk.

CONCLUSION

Tim Congdon in his book, *The Debt Threat*, warned about making prophecies about the future of economies. One has only to consider the grand transformation of the old East Block, the changes in "communist" China, and the current reopening of Vietnam to foreign investment to acknowledge the correctness of his warning. But he himself argues that extensive and growing debt inevitably creates trouble, even if the exact form of the trouble cannot be precisely predicted. Unmanageable debt transforms debtors and creditors. Some possibilities for thought have been offered here.

United States–Japanese relations present but one facet of contemporary debtor–creditor relations. Stiles writing on the IMF, poses another—the possibility of the United States under IMF austerity. Heavier foreign direct investment in the United States presents still another possibility. And Figgie wonders whether hyperinflation will be the outcome of long-standing carelessness about national debt of all types.

When Spanish speakers say "Ojo" and point to the eye, it's not a bad idea to do what they advise: "Be vigilant—eyes open—watch out!" As we have sown, so may we reap.

CHAPTER 12
Law and the Environment

The environmental movement in the United States can be dated from the appearance of *Silent Spring* by Rachel Carson in 1962. One reviewer insightfully predicted that her book would have the same effect as *The Jungle* written by Upton Sinclair around the turn of the century. Sinclair had so graphically described the rotten and diseased carcassses routinely processed by the meatpacking industry in Chicago that the public demanded the Pure Food and Drug Law of 1906. Carson's text had the same potential; if the environmental degradation she observed in and around agriculture were to continue, all living creatures would die. Something had to be done, but as Shakespeare cogently observed: "If wishes were horses, poor men would ride." Since 1962 many pieces of legislation have been passed, thousands of environmental regulations issued, and many cases have been processed. Whether their overall impact has been beneficial or not is the subject of ongoing debate from every political perspective.

The last 30 years have seen a difficult struggle to match increasing consciousness about the environment with what are seen by some to be the iron laws of industrial economy. Will it be spotted owls, or timber jobs in the Pacific Northwest? Steel or air? Bumper crops with fungicides, pesticides, and fertilizers, or marginal crops without them? Sometimes these so-called irreconcilable splits are false ones and are meant simply to short-circuit debate and rationalize what is expedient from a short-term perspective. But the debate can run deep, and it could well be that an industrial economy and a healthy environment are incompatible.

Agriculture in the United States has been transformed into an industrial process and an extractive enterprise like mining: petrochemically intensive methods, low labor intensity, larger and larger spreads, with a few key crops grown for market rather than home use, and maximizing yields even at the expense of long-term sustainability. Agriculture being very close to nature, it was understandable that Carson would begin her famous book with a fable about the predictable end point of modern farming.

A FABLE FOR TOMORROW[1]

There was once a town in the heart of America where all life seemed to live in harmony with its surroundings. The town lay in the midst of a checkerboard of prosperous farms, with fields of grain and hillsides of orchards where, in spring, white clouds of bloom drifted above the green fields. In autumn, oak and maple and birch set up a blaze of color that flamed and flickered across a backdrop of pines. The foxes barked in the hills and deer silently crossed the fields, half hidden in the mists of the fall mornings.

Along the roads, laurel, viburnum and alder, great ferns and wildflowers delighted the traveler's eye through much of the year. Even in winter the roadsides were places of beauty, where countless birds came to feed on the berries and on the seed heads of the dried weeds rising above the snow. The countryside was, in fact, famous for the abundance and variety of its bird life, and when the flood of migrants was pouring through in spring and fall people traveled from great distances to observe them. Others came to fish the streams, which flowed clear and cold out of the hills and contained shady pools where trout lay. So it had been from the days many years ago when the first settlers raised their houses, sank their wells and built their barns.

Then a strange blight crept over the area and everything began to change. Some evil spell had settled on the community: mysterious maladies swept the flocks of chickens; the cattle and sheep sickened and died. Everywhere was a shadow of death. The farmers spoke of much illness among their families. In the town the doctors had become more and more puzzled by new kinds of sickness appearing among their patients. There had been several sudden and unexplained deaths, not only among the adults but even among children, who would be strickened suddenly while at play and die within a few hours.

There was a strange stillness. The birds, for example—where there had they gone? Many people spoke of them, puzzled and disturbed. The feeding stations in the backyards were deserted. The few birds seen anywhere were moribund; they trembled violently and could not fly. It was a spring without voices. On the mornings that had once throbbed with the dawn chorus of robins, catbirds, doves, jays, wrens, and scores of other bird voices there was now no sound; only silence lay over the fields and woods and marsh.

On the farms the hens brooded, but no chicks hatched. The farmers complained that they were unable to raise any pigs—the litters were small and the young survived only a few days. The apple trees were coming into bloom, but no bees droned among the blossoms, so there was no pollination and there would be no fruit.

The roadsides once so attractive were now lined with browned and withered vegetation as though swept by fire. These too were silent, deserted of all living things. Even the streams were now lifeless. Anglers no longer visited them for all the fish had died.

In the gutters under the eaves and between the shingles of the roofs, a white granular powder still showed a few patches; some weeks before it had fallen like snow upon the roofs and the lawns, the fields and streams.

No witchcraft, no enemy action had silenced the rebirth of new life in this stricken world. The people had done it themselves.

[1]Rachel Carson, *Silent Spring* (1962).

Carson followed her fable with the question at the center of her book: What has *already* silenced the voices of spring in countless towns in America? Her answer, which is now part of every school child's understanding: irreversible adulteration of all environments by the indiscriminate use of chemicals, which have proliferated in types, poundage, and applications in agriculture. Their largely unknown properties are killing everything along with the unwanted pests and weeds. What looked like a short cut to abundance via single-crop agriculture is now acknowledged to be sure-fire destruction of whole ecosystems on which every living creature ultimately depends.

Carson's thesis aggregated the ecological knowledge that had been quietly building far from the petrochemical world. Those in biology could not help but see the effects of a variety of chemical agents on life. Perhaps they were involuntarily drawn toward the field of agribusiness by their investigations.

It might be surprising to learn that a book that has come to premise much contemporary education for even the tenderest of minds received a mixed reception. Supreme Court Justice William O. Douglas called *Silent Spring* "the most important chronicle of this century for the human race." But spokespeople from schools of agriculture and the variety of businesses that would be threatened by a sharply diminished public confidence in their products and services promptly counterattacked with the argument that the Carson thesis was unduly alarmist, argumentative, and unscientific.

Professor L. Baldwin, an entomologist at the University of Wisconsin, contended, "*Silent Spring*, is not a 'judicial review or a balancing of gains and losses' but rather the prosecuting attorney's impassioned plea for action against these new materials that have received such widespread acceptance."[2] *The Economist* also criticized the author more than the author's thesis:

> Miss Carson's book . . . is a tract: an angry, shrill tract against modern farm chemicals. It is propaganda written in white-hot anger with words tumbling and stumbling all over the page (rare are the passages where Miss Carson shows her normal elegant command of language). Propaganda is not expected to give both sides of an argument; others have told of the advantages of these chemicals, Miss Carson now lists their drawbacks . . .
> Is this cause for alarm? No one knows . . . here is a case where science does not know the answers and it is no use getting ... offended when people like Miss Carson start making snide remarks about it.[3]

The battle that ensued over *Silent Spring* is the same one that continues today, and along the same lines. Environmentalists are routinely challenged as being "argumentative," "emotional," and either unscientific or unwilling to consider scientific positions different from their own. (If "no one knows" exactly what harmful effects there are and when, then those presently in positions of economic–political power win, since the burden of proof on environmental questions rests upon those who wish to challenge the status quo.

[2]Quoted in *Book Review Digest* (New York: Wilson, 1962), p. 203.
[3]*The Economist 206*, (1963), p. 711.

The long–standing resistance to the virtually incontrovertible evidence that tobacco kills demonstrates the difference between knowledge systems and power systems.) In agriculture, when there is a failure to win the scientific argument, advocates of petrochemically intensive methods deftly shift the argument to the necessity for "trade-offs"; will it be bread or pure air and water? Many, inside and outside agribusiness, seem willing to trade short-term bread for long-term wheat.

Sometimes companies go even further, and come on as "champions" of the environment—a nubile college graduate prances across a wheat field in anticipation of taking a socially responsible job for a chemical company; healthfulness, chemicals, and an ethical career merge. An owl is pictured on the cover of a petroleum company magazine, suggesting that the company is just as mindful of environmental priorities as a "rabid" conservationist. Again, the companies need not win the war over public images—a tie will do.

Those persuaded by environmental concerns consider their position long-term realism; those antagonistic to such concerns call environmentalists unrealistic, pious, and purist. In the last three decades, the thesis of Rachel Carson has prevailed as a matter of truth and knowledge, but the chemical industry and agribusinesses have prevailed as a matter of environmental law and policy. As noted, knowledge is not power; power is—with, at most, occasional, minor adjustments, when the truth can no longer be totally denied. Moreover, power systems inspire supporting knowledge systems—legal, economic, and scientific—which can make life very hard for the songbird and its listeners.

BASELINE FOR THE STUDY OF INTERNATIONAL ENVIRONMENTAL ISSUES

As the United States experience in the legal regulation of environmental problems has gone, so will go the experience in regulating international environmental problems through the rule of law. This prediction can be stated even more severely: if a survey of the role of law in curbing environmental problems in the United States shows limited success, there is all the more reason to believe that the rule of law will be inconsequential in many other countries where multinationals do business. The latter position is based on the fact that there are many environmental laws in place in the United States, and there are at least some prospects for remedies and enforcement. Abroad, in many countries there are far fewer rules, and far less enforcement of what rules do exist. One must expect that the international experience in exerting consequential environmental controls will be more bleak than what has occurred domestically.

The distinct lack of enforceable environmental restrictions when firms go abroad has affected the debate over the free trade agreement with Mexico (NAFTA). Environmentalists in the United States wanted assurances that there would be an adequate environmental regulatory structure in place in Mexico. If not, companies locating in Mexico will be able to "externalize" all environmental costs, and make more profit than they could in the United States, where there is more effective environmental regulation. The arguments by environmentalists opposed to NAFTA do not require a wholesale endorsement of the environmental successes of the United States—which, as we shall see, could not be persuasively made. They need only argue that relative to Mexico's, the United States environmental record is a smashing success.

There is also the belief among those opposed to NAFTA that a weak environmental protection structure in Mexico would simultaneously weaken environmental enforcement in the United States, since every business operating in the United States would be able to raise the specter of moving to Mexico unless federal- and state-imposed environmental restrictions are made less intrusive upon them. The common business strategy of finding the least restrictive legal structure applies with special force in the environmental field. And as we learned from the deterioration of state control over corporations in Chapter 5, poorer law drives out better law, given the mobility of enterprises.

Two things can be learned from a brief survey of the United States' experience with environmental law and its enforcement: first, the array of *environmental problems* that have been the subjects for successive legislation, regulations, and contested cases; and second, the interplay of *science and law* and *economics and law* that has made effective environmental law and enforcement difficult. Once this domestic baseline has been articulated, the learning can be carried into the international sphere, where environmental law and enforcement is even more difficult.

THE U.S. EXPERIENCE

At common law, environmental questions were part of the law of nuisance; one property owner was alleged to have used property in a way antithetical to the uses of property of another. Cases fell under the Latin maxim, *sic utere tuo ut alienum non laedas* (use your own property in such a manner as not to injure that of another.[4]) The maxim was not all that helpful in resolving concrete conflicts. An aggrieved party had "a case" actionable in court for money to compensate for losses, or an *injunction* to prevent future nuisances.

This down-home approach on a case-by-case basis became inadequate to cope with the overall problems generated by a changing economy, and inadequate to protect *general* or *public* interest, which would at most be only incompletely articulated in a private lawsuit with limited scope and purposes.

[4]Blackstone, 1 *Commentaries* 306.

MADISON V. *DUCKTOWN SULPHUR, COPPER & IRON CO.*

83 S.W. 658, 13 TENN. 331 (1904)

Neil, J.

These three cases . . . embrace . . . the same facts and the same questions of law, and will be disposed of in a single opinion.

The bills are all based on the ground of nuisance, in that the two companies, in the operation of their plants at and near Ducktown, in Polk county, in the course of reducing copper ore, cause large volumes of smoke to issue from their roast piles, which smoke descends upon the surrounding lands, and injures trees and crops, and renders the homes of complainants less comfortable and their lands less profitable than before. The purpose of all the bills is to enjoin the further operation of these plants; the first bill having been filed against the first-named company, the last bill against the second company, and the intermediate bill against both companies . . .

Prior to 1870, one Rhat began the operation of a copper mine at Ducktown, and worked it for several years. Subsequently it was owned by the Union Consolidated Mining Company, Mr. Rhat's successor. These operations were continued until the year 1879, and were then suspended until 1891. During the latter year the Ducktown Sulphur, Copper & Iron Company commenced operating the properties . . ., and has continued to operate them ever since. The Pittsburgh & Tennessee Copper Company began operations at Ducktown about the year 1881, and continued until about 1899, when it sold out to the defendant Tennessee Copper Company. The latter began its operations in 1900, and commenced roasting ores in May, 1901. It has continued its works ever since.

Ducktown is in a basin of the mountains of Polk county, in this state, not far from the state line of the states of Georgia and North Carolina. This basin is six or eight miles wide. The complainants are the owners of small farms situated in the mountains around Ducktown.

The method used by the defendants in reducing their copper ores is to place the green ore, broken up, on layers of wood, making large open-air piles, called "roast piles," and these roast piles are ignited for the purpose of expelling from the ore certain foreign matters called "sulphurets." In burning, these roast piles emit large volumes of smoke. This smoke, rising in the air, is carried off by air currents around and over adjoining land.

The lands of the complainants in the first bill, Carter, W. M. Madison and Margaret A. Madison, Verner, and Ballew, lie from two to four miles from the works. The land of Farner, complainant in the last bill, lies six or eight miles away. The distance of McGhee's land is not shown. . . .

These lands are all thin mountain lands, of little agricultural value. Carter's land consists of 80 acres, assessed at $80; Verner's, 89 acres, at $110; Ballew's, 40 acres, at $66; Madison and wife, 43 acres, at $83; W. M. Madison, about 100 acres, at $180; Isaac Farner, 100 acres, at $180. Avery McGee has 75 acres. W. M. Madison has a tract across the Georgia line, and Mrs.

Madison also one of 100 acres there. The assessed value of these last three tracts does not appear. All of these lands, however, lie in the same general section of country, and we assume their value to average about the same in proportion to acreage.

All of the complainants have owned their several tracts since time anterior to the resumption of the copper industry at Ducktown in 1891. . . .

The general effect produced by the smoke upon the possessions and families of the complainants is as follows, viz.:

Their timber and crop interests have been badly injured, and they have been annoyed and discommoded by the smoke so that the complainants are prevented from using and enjoying their farms and homes as they did prior to the inauguration of these enterprises. The smoke makes it impossible for the owners of farms within the area of the smoke zone to subsist their families thereon with the degree of comfort they enjoyed before. They cannot raise and harvest their customary crops, and their timber is largely destroyed. . . .

There is no finding in either of the cases that the output of smoke by the Ducktown Sulphur, Copper & Iron Company has increased to any extent since 1891, when the business of mining and reducing copper ore was resumed at Ducktown. There is likewise no finding as to this matter in respect of the Tennessee Copper Company since it began roasting ores in May, 1901.

There is a finding that the Ducktown Sulphur, Copper & Iron Company acquired its plant in 1891, and that it has spent several hundred thousand dollars since that time in improving and enlarging the plant.

The Court of Chancery Appeals finds that the defendants are conducting and have been conducting their business in a lawful way, without any purpose or desire to injury any of the complainants; that they have been and are pursuing the only known method by which these plants can be operated and their business successfully carried on; that the open-air roast heap is the only method known to the business or to science by means of which copper ore of the character mined by the defendants can be reduced; that the defendants have made every effort to get rid of the smoke and noxious vapors, one of the defendants having spent $200,000 in experiments to this end, but without result.

It is to be inferred from the description of the locality that there is no place more remote to which the operations referred to could be transferred.

It is found, in substance, that, if the injunctive relief sought be granted, the defendants will be compelled to stop operations, and their property will become practically worthless, the immense business conducted by them will cease, and they will be compelled to withdraw from the state. It is a necessary deduction from the foregoing that a great and increasing industry in the state will be destroyed, and all of the valuable copper properties of the state become worthless.

The following facts were also found, viz.:

That the total tax aggregate of Polk County for the year 1903 was $2,585,931.43, of which total the assessments of the defendants amounted to $1,279,533. It is also found that prior to the operations of these companies there lived in the district where these works are located only 200 people, whereas there are now living in this district, almost wholly dependent upon these copper industries, about 12,000 people.

It is also found that one of the defendants, the Tennessee Copper Company, employs upon its pay roll 1,300 men, and that the average pay roll is about $40,000 per month, nearly all of which employees have been drawn from the population of Polk and neighboring counties.

It is further found that one of the defendants, the Tennessee Copper Company, consumes approximately 3,000 tons of coke, 2,800 tons of coal, and 1,000 cords of wood per month, and that it purchases and uses 2,110 car loads of coal, coke, wood, etc., per annum. In the year 1901 it purchased and used approximately 1,100 car loads of cord wood, cross-ties, lumber, and quartz. It was also found that 80 percent of these supplies were purchased from, and delivered by, the citizens of Polk county. The aggregate paid out for supplies is not stated in the findings of the Court of Chancery Appeals, and cannot be here stated accurately, but certainly the amount is very large; and it seems from the figures stated that one of the defendants alone, the Tennessee Copper Company, pays out annually in wages in Polk county nearly a half million of dollars. The Court of Chancery Appeals finds that the other company employs between 1,100 and 1,200 people, and from this it may be inferred that the company pays out in wages and for supplies annually nearly as much as the Tennessee Copper Company.

It is quite apparent that the two companies pay out annually vast sums of money, which are necessarily of great benefit to the people of the county, and that they are conducting and maintaining an industry upon which a laboring population of from ten to twelve thousand people are practically dependent; and it is found, in substance, by the Court of Chancery Appeals, that, if these industries be suppressed, these thousands of people will have to wander forth to other localities to find shelter and work. . . .

We shall now state the principles which, as we conceive, should control the merits of the controversy involved in the several cases before the court:

While there can be no doubt that the facts stated make out a case of nuisance, for which the complainants in actions at law would be entitled to recover damages, yet the remedy in equity is not a matter of course. Not only must the bill state a proper case, but the right must be clear and the injury must be clearly established, as in doubtful cases the party will be turned over to his legal remedy; and, if there is a reasonable doubt as to the cause of the injury, the benefit of the doubt will be given to the defendant, if his trade is a lawful one, and the injury is not the necessary and natural consequence of the act; and, if the injury can be adequately compensated at law by a judgment for damages, equity will not interfere . . .

And the equitable remedy by injunction must be applied for with reasonable promptness. . . .

In addition to the principles already announced, the following general propositions seem to be established ...: If the case made out by the pleadings and evidence show with sufficient clearness and certainty grounds for equitable relief it will not be denied because the persons proceeded against are engaged in a lawful business . . . or because the works complained of are located in a convenient place ...; nor will the existence of another nuisance of a similar character at the same place furnish a ground for denying relief if it appears that the defendant has . . . contributed to the injury complained of. . . . Nor is it a question of care and skill, but purely one of results.

But there is one other principle which is of controlling influence . . . This is that the granting of an injunction is not a matter of absolute right, but rests in the sound discretion of the court, to be determined on a consideration of all of the special circumstances of each case, and the situation and surroundings of the parties, with a view to effect the ends of justice.

A judgment for damages in this class of case is a matter of absolute right, where injury is shown. A decree for an injunction is a matter of sound legal discretion, to be granted or withheld as that discretion shall dictate, after a full and careful consideration of every element appertaining to the injury...

[W]hat is the proper exercise of discretion . . . ? Shall the complainants be granted . . . damages ..., or shall we go further, and grant their request to blot out two great mining and manufacturing enterprises, destroy half of the taxable values of a county, and drive more than 10,000 people from their homes? We think there can be no doubt as to what the true answer to this question should be.

In order to protect by injunction several small tracts of land, aggregating in the value less than $1,000, we are asked to destroy other property worth nearly $2,000,000, and wreck two great mining and manufacturing enterprises, that are engaged in work of very great importance, not only to their owners, but to the state, and to the whole country as well, to depopulate a large town, and deprive thousands of working people of their homes and livelihood, and scatter them broadcast. The result would be practically a confiscation of the property of the defendants for the benefit of the complainants—an appropriation without compensation. The defendants cannot reduce their ores in a manner different from that they are now employing, and there is no more remote place to which they can remove. The decree asked for would deprive them of all of their rights. We appreciate the argument based on the fact that the homes of the complainants who live on the small tracts of land referred to are not so comfortable and useful to their owners as they were before they were affected by the smoke complained of, and we are deeply sensible of the truth of the proposition that no man is entitled to any more rights than another on the ground that he has or owns more property than that other. But in a case of conflicting rights, where neither party can enjoy his own without in some measure restricting the liberty of the other in the use of property, the law must make the best arrangement it can between the contending parties, with a view to preserving to each one the largest measure of liberty possible under the circumstances. We see no escape from the conclusion in the present case that the only proper decree is to allow the complainants . . . damages, and that the injunction must be denied to them . . .

Questions and Comments

1. In this case we see a sample of an early judicial approach to pollution. One private party is pitted against another private party to secure particular remedies—in this case money, or an order closing the smelter. The case is oriented around property rights, and the devaluation of property *in the past and at the moment*; there is no separate "environmental" or futuristic perspective besides the one crudely raised within the rule structures of property law.

Once the court decides that the case is inapt for the issuance of an injunction, the maximum amount the company would have to pay to the plaintiffs is the fair market value of the farms, which by the court's reckoning was trifling. This "monetizing" of all costs in most legal disputes complicates resistance to environmental damage: what is the value of a trout caught from a stream running through a subsistence farm? The family garden plot? The smell of honeysuckle? The scenery?

Review some of the elements of the common law approach. With contemporary awareness, could you prepare an opinion in which an injunction would be granted?

Imagine yourself to be a judge in the original Ducktown case. What pressures would you feel upon yourself in rendering the decision?

2. This case occurred relatively soon after the post-Civil War transition from an agriculture–craft economy to an industrial economy. Could the court have made a better accommodation to these disparate values, or were the two economic organizing principles fundamentally incompatible?

   The court did make some compromise, ordering the company to pay the farmers money for their losses. Evaluate.
3. The court also seemed to use a form of cost–benefit analysis, taking into account the offending behavior, losses incurred by the farmers, losses on shutdown, and the overall contributions to society that the copper smelting was making. Evaluate.
4. In legal cases there is frequent discussion of the need for a court to "balance conflicting interests." Does this discussion of balancing simply mask the real reasons for decisions, or does it appear that there is real balancing going on? The reason that this question is asked is that once an issue is framed in terms of balancing, the choice of either alternative becomes almost automatically defensible.
5. In the *Ducktown* case, there is a distinct lack of scientific evidence about the environmental impacts of the air pollution (as one would expect in a case from this period). Was it the lack of science that made the farmers fail? What difference might contemporary understandings from environmental sciences have made on the outcome of the case?
6. Apparently, silly though it may appear from a modern perspective, the company was using "up to date" technology. What ought to be the decision where manifest environmental losses and "best available" manufacturing techniques occur in the same case? Should the burden be on the plaintiff to prove there is a better technique, or ought it to be enough for a plaintiff to show irreparable environmental damage?
7. Although it is not discussed in the case, it would seem that the company would have had the advantage in mobilizing legal and political support for its position. If so, the case would be reappraised, the material considered in Chapter 3 on power and powerlessness in coal mining or the cases studied in Chapter 9 on elite law practice.

OHIO V. WYANDOTTE CHEMICALS CORP. 401 U.S. 494 (1971)

Mr. Justice Harlan . . .

Ohio seeks to invoke this Court's original jurisdiction. . . . The action, for abatement of a nuisance, is brought on behalf of the State and its citizens, and names as defendants Wyandotte Chemicals Corp. (Wyandotte), Dow Chemical Co. (Dow America), and Dow Chemical Company of Canada, Ltd. (Dow Canada). Wyandotte is incorporated in Michigan and maintains its principal office and place of business there. Dow America is incorporated in Delaware, has its principal office and place of business in Michigan, and owns all the stock of Dow Canada. Dow Canada is incorporated, and does business, in Ontario. A majority of Dow Canada's directors are residents of the United States.

The complaint alleges that Dow Canada and Wyandotte have each dumped mercury into streams whose courses ultimately reach Lake Erie, thus contaminating and polluting that lake's waters, vegetation, fish, and wildlife, and that Dow America is jointly responsible for the acts of its foreign subsidiary. Assuming the State's ability to prove these assertions, Ohio seeks a decree: (1) declaring the introduction of mercury into Lake Erie's tributaries a public nuisance; (2) perpetually enjoining these defendants from introducing mercury into Lake Erie or its tributaries; (3) requiring defendants either to remove the mercury from Lake Erie or to pay the costs of its removal into a fund to be administered by Ohio and used only for that purpose; (4) directing defendants to pay Ohio monetary damages for the harm done to Lake Erie, its fish, wildlife, and vegetation, and the citizens and inhabitants of Ohio. . . .

That we have jurisdiction seems clear enough. Beyond doubt, the complaint on its face reveals the existence of a genuine "case or controversy" between one State and citizens of another, as well as a foreign subject. . . .

[M]uch would be sacrificed, and little gained, by our exercising original jurisdiction over issues bottomed on local law. This Court's paramount responsibilities to the national system lie almost without exception in the domain of federal law. As the impact on the social structure of federal common, statutory, and constitutional law has expanded, our attention has necessarily been drawn more and more to such matters. We have no claim to special competence in dealing with the numerous conflicts between States and nonresident individuals that raise no serious issues of federal law. . . .

Thus, we think it apparent that we must recognize "the need [for] the exercise of a sound discretion in order to protect this Court from an abuse of the opportunity to resort to its original jurisdiction in the enforcement by States of claims against citizens of other States." . . .

[W]e believe that the wiser course is to deny Ohio's motion for leave to file its complaint. . . .

In essence, the State has charged Dow Canada and Wyandotte with the commission of acts, albeit beyond Ohio's territorial boundaries, that have produced and, it is said, continue to produce disastrous effects within Ohio's own domain. . . .

History reveals that the course of this Court's prior efforts to settle disputes regarding interstate air and water pollution has been anything but smooth.

The difficulties that ordinarily beset such cases are severely compounded by the particular setting in which this controversy has reached us ... [A] number of official bodies are already actively involved in regulating the conduct complained of here. A Michigan circuit court has enjoined Wyandotte from operating its mercury cell process without judicial authorization. The company is, moreover, currently utilizing a recycling process specifically approved by the Michigan Water Resources Commission and remains subject to the continued scrutiny of that agency. Dow Canada reports monthly to the Ontario Water Resources Commission on its compliance with the commission's order prohibiting the company from passing any mercury into the environment.

Additionally, Ohio and Michigan are both participants in the Lake Erie Enforcement Conference, convened a year ago by the Secretary of the Interior pursuant to the Federal Water Pollution Control Act. . . . The Conference is studying all forms and sources of pollution, including mercury, infecting Lake Erie. The purpose of this Conference is to provide a basis for concerted remedial action by the States or, if progress in that regard is not rapidly made, for corrective proceedings initiated by the Federal Government. . . . And the International Joint Commission, . . . between the United States and Canada . . . issued . . . a comprehensive report, the culmination of a six-year study . . . concerning the contamination of Lake Erie. That document makes specific recommendations for joint programs to abate these environmental hazards and recommends that the IJC be given authority to supervise and coordinate this effort.

In view of all this, granting Ohio's motion for leave to file would, in effect, commit this Court's resources to the task of trying to settle a small piece of a much larger problem that many competent adjudicatory and conciliatory bodies are actively grappling with on a more practical basis.

The nature of the case Ohio brings here is equally disconcerting. It can fairly be said that what is in dispute is not so much the law as the facts. And the fact finding process we are asked to undertake is, to say the least, formidable. We already know . . . that Lake Erie suffers from several sources of pollution other than mercury; that the scientific conclusion that mercury is a serious water pollutant is a novel one; that whether and to what extent the existence of mercury in natural waters can safely or reasonably be tolerated is a question for which there is presently no firm answer: and that virtually no published research is available describing how one might extract mercury that is in fact contaminating water. Indeed, Ohio is raising factual questions that are essentially ones of first impression to the scientists. The notion that appellate judges, . . ., might appropriately undertake at this time to unravel these complexities is, to say the least, unrealistic. . . . Other factual complexities abound. For example, the Department of the Interior has stated that eight American companies are discharging, or have discharged, mercury into Lake Erie or its tributaries. We would, then, need to assess the business practices and relative culpability of each to frame appropriate relief as to the one now before us.

Thus, entertaining this complaint not only would fail to serve those responsibilities we are principally charged with, but could well pave the way for putting this Court into a quandary whereby we must opt either to pick and choose arbitrarily among similarly situated litigants or to devote truly enormous portions of our energies to such matters. . . .

What has been said here cannot, of course, be taken as denigrating in the slightest the public importance of the underlying problem Ohio would have us tackle. Reversing the increasing contamination of our environment is manifestly a matter of fundamental import and utmost urgency. What is dealt with above are only considerations respecting the appropriate role this Court can assume in efforts to eradicate such environmental blights. We mean only to suggest that our competence is necessarily limited. . . . Motion denied.

Mr. Justice Douglas, dissenting.

The complaint in this case presents basically a classic type of case congenial to our original jurisdiction. It is to abate a public nuisance. Such was the claim of Georgia against a Tennessee company which was discharging noxious gas across the border into Georgia [This case was subsequent to the Ducktown case excerpted above. The state of Georgia was able to get an injunction against the copper smelting factories. —Ed.], *Georgia* v. *Tennessee Copper Co.*, . . . The Court said:

"It is a fair and reasonable demand on the part of a sovereign that the air over its territory should not be polluted on a great scale by sulphurous acid gas, that the forests on its mountains, be they better or worse, and whatever domestic destruction they have suffered, should not be further destroyed or threatened by the act of persons beyond its control, that the crops and orchards on its hills should not be endangered from the same source." . . .

Dumping of sewage in an interstate stream, *Missouri* v. *Illinois*, . . . or towing garbage to sea only to have the tides carry it to a State's beaches, *New Jersey* v. *New York City*, . . . have presented analogous situations which the Court has entertained in suits invoking our original jurisdiction. The pollution of Lake Erie or its tributaries by the discharge of mercury or compounds thereof, if proved, certainly creates a public nuisance of a seriousness and magnitude which a State by our historic standards may prosecute . . .

The suit is not precluded by the Boundary Waters Treaty of 1909 . . . [It] does not evince a purpose on the part of the national governments of the United States and Canada to exclude their States and Provinces from seeking other remedies for water pollution. Indeed, Congress in later addressing itself to water pollution in the Federal Water Pollution Control Act, . . . said in Sec. 1(c):

"Nothing in this chapter shall be construed as impairing or in any manner affecting any right or jurisdiction of the States with respect to the waters (*including boundary waters*) of such States." [Emphasis added.]

This litigation, as it unfolds, will, of course, implicate much federal law. The case will deal with an important portion of the federal domain — the navigable streams and the navigable inland waters which are under the sovereignty of the Federal Government. It has been clear since *Pollard's Lessee* v. *Hagan*, . . . decided in 1845, that navigable waters were subject to federal control. . . .

Congress has enacted numerous laws reaching that domain. . . . the Rivers and Harbors Act of 1899, . . . which forbids discharge of "any refuse matter of any kind or description whatever other than that flowing from streets and sewers and passing therefrom in a liquid state" as including particles in suspension. . . .

In the 1930's fish and wildlife legislation was enacted granting the Secretary of the Interior various heads of jurisdiction over the effects on fish and wildlife of "domestic sewage, mine, petroleum, and industrial wastes, erosion silt, and other polluting substances." . . .

The Federal Water Pollution Control Act . . . gives broad powers to the Secretary to take action respecting water pollution on complaints of States, and other procedures to secure federal abatement of the pollution . . . The National Environmental Policy Act of 1969 . . . gives elaborate ecological directions to federal agencies and supplies procedures for their enforcement.

On December 23, 1970, the President issued an Executive Order which correlates the duties of the Corps of Engineers and the Administrator of the new Environmental Protection Agency under the foregoing statutes. . . .

Yet the federal scheme is not preemptive of state action. Section 1(b) of the Water Pollution Control Act declares that the policy of Congress is "to recognize, preserve, and protect the primary responsibilities and rights of the States in preventing and controlling water pollution." . . .

The new Environmental Quality Improvement Act of 1970, . . . while stating the general policy of Congress in protecting the environment, also states: "The primary responsibility for implementing this policy rests with State and local governments." . . .

There is much complaint that in spite of the arsenal of federal power little is being done. That, of course, is not our problem. But it is our concern that state action is not preempted by federal law. Under existing federal law, the States do indeed have primary responsibility for setting water quality standards; the federal agency only sets water quality standards for a State if the State defaults. . . .

There is not a word in federal law that bars state action. . . . Much is made of the burdens and perplexities of these original actions. Some are complex, notably those involving water rights. The drainage of Lake Michigan with the attendant lowering of water levels, affecting Canadian as well as United States interests, came to us in an original suit. . . .

The apportionment of the waters of the Colorado between Arizona and California was a massive undertaking entailing a searching analysis. . . .

The apportionment of the waters of the North Platte River among Colorado, Wyoming, and Nebraska came to us in an original action. . . .

But the practice has been to appoint a Special Master which we certainly would do in this case. We could also appoint—or authorize the Special Master to retain—a panel of scientific advisers. The problems in this case are simple compared with those in the water cases discussed above. It is now known that metallic mercury deposited in water is often transformed into a dangerous chemical. This lawsuit would determine primarily the extent, if any, to which the defendants are contributing to that contamination at the present time . . .

The problem, though clothed in chemical secrecies, can be exposed by the experts. It would indeed be one of the simplest problems yet posed in the category of cases under the head of our original jurisdiction.

The Department of Justice in a detailed brief tells us there are no barriers in federal law to our assumption of jurisdiction. I can think of no case of more transcending public importance than this one.

Questions and Comments

1. Evaluate the position of the majority of the court and the position taken by the dissenting justice. Where do environmental concerns fall on the majority's list of priorities for the Supreme Court's case agenda? On the dissenter's list?

   What are the implications of the Court's ruling here?

2. The Court rules that it could hear the case, but that it ought not to on the ground that it would be handling a small part of a larger problem best left to others. Evaluate.

   Both opinions note the many statutes, regulatory agencies, and interstate and international bodies that bear on the condition of Lake Erie. Does the case support the proposition that *the more* law and and regulation *potentially* applicable, the *less* law will *actually* be applied?

   If the foregoing proposition is true, how would it affect the strategy of businesses and their lawyers in environmental cases? In their political activism in the U. S. Congress and before the regulatory agencies?

3. If there is a division of responsibility between courts and political bodies— *state–state* (New York, Michigan, Pennsylvania, and Ohio all border on Lake Erie); *state–federal* (the Great Lakes fall within the maritime jurisdiction of the U.S. national law); and international (United States and Canada)—how would you envision that environmental protection would be subverted? Did subversion occur here?

4. The Court alludes to difficulties present in every environmental case that may be summarized in question form:

   Who did what, when?

   Was it harmful, Is it still harmful?

   What law governs?

   What remedies, if any?

   There are always questions of fact, scientific and otherwise. Where there are joint actors, as was the case with Lake Erie pollution, there may be a problem of causation or the assessment of responsibility among polluters, and allocation of damages or other remedial action among the implicated parties.

5. Besides the complications in active cases and controversies, there are other sources of chaos in environmental policy, law, and enforcement. To name three:

   a. Many statutes with sometimes overlapping purposes, administered by different governmental agencies—*several hundred* statutes of which the Environmental Protection Agency administers twelve major ones [5]

[5]Walter Rosenbaum, *Environmental Politics and Policy* (Washington: Congressional Quarterly Press, 1991), pp. 17, 18.

b. Multiple regulatory agencies with different budgets, personnel, enforcement (or nonenforcement) philosophies—the EPA, Labor Department (Occupational Safety and Health), Department of Agriculture and the Department of the Interior are the principal ones, joined by at least five other departments and many "Commissions"[6]

c. Divided and subdivided legislative responsibilities in the House and Senate of the Congress, as reflected in the number of committees and subcommittees that have environmental issues on their agendas; they number more than 100![7]

Ronald Reagan used to speak of the overregulation of business and asked when government was going to get off the backs of business. A better question would have been whether there can be effective regulation when there are so many participants at all levels of environmental law and enforcement. Has there been "deregulation" by virtue of the very condition that Reagan said he despised—proliferation of law and "enforcement" agencies?

Would enterprises want the environmental laws "cleaned up" and simplified, with swift, effective enforcement?

Measuring the Effectiveness of Environmental Enforcement in the United States

If one stands back from the Congress, the regulatory agencies, and the courts, just how clean is the U. S. environment? If it is not so clean, then at least three conclusions might be drawn: first, the environmental law has failed; second, the environment is bad, but it might have been a whole lot worse were there no environmental law and enforcement in place; or third, environmental law has been largely irrelevant to the practices of businesses. The third is different from the first in that it states that the two worlds have not intersected at all.

Even moderate commentators are not all that thrilled with the record of environmental protection since 1970. Rosenbaum talks about the 1980s as a virtually lost decade:

> . . . the Reagan years meant above all dangerous drift and in decision, almost a decade of lost opportunities and intensifying environmental ills.[8]

What concrete evidence did he give for this overview?

—Toxic waste sites. By 1986, the EPA had identified more than 27,000 abandoned hazardous waste sites, of which 1000 were especially da-

[6]Ibid., pp. 89–92.
[7]Ibid., pp. 82–86.
[8]Ibid., p. 5.

gerous. Six had been cleaned up.[9] New Jersey alone had more than 100 sites.[10]

—Surface water. "The nation did not eliminate all pollution discharges into its waters by 1985, nor did it make all, or even most, waterways "fishable and swimable" . . . [sic] the national permit system for pollution dischargers have prevented the further degradation of many surface waters, reduced pollution in others, and undoubtedly saved some high quality water from degradation. But the evidence of a long-term improvement in the overall quality of the nation's surface waters is elusive."[11]

—Drinking water. "Fragmentary evidence suggests that many of the nation's water systems, including some of the largest have been infiltrated by dangerous concentrations of chemical and biological contaminants, ... for which no standards exist and, consequently, no regulatory controls exist"[12]

—Airborne toxins. "More than 300 toxic chemicals are emitted into the air annually. The EPA is currently evaluating about 30 of these, but only 8 are currently regulated."[13]

—Urban air pollution. As the 1990s began, the only major urban area in the United States that met federal and state air-quality standards was Minneapolis. Despite more than two decades of effort, more than 77 million Americans were living in urban areas where serious, sometimes dangerous air-quality problems remained.[14]

—Agricultural Runoff. Agriculture (pesticides, fertilizers, fungicides, sediments, and animal wastes account for more than one third of water pollution from "nonpoint" sources. (Nonpoint sources are general sources rather than an identifiable source, such as a municipal dump, a factory, or a mine.)[15]

Businesses cannot be tagged with all of the responsibility for environmental problems. Businesses, governments, and individuals each contribute to growing environmental problems. For example, it is estimated that it will cost the U. S. government over $100 billion to clean up the radioactive waste from the U. S. government's nuclear weapons plants.[16] Individuals contribute their share through the use of automobiles and household garbage (1300 lb/capita/year; 3.5 lb/day).

But some aspects of the problem do fall heavily onto business. Many toxic wastes originate in the chemical industry.[17] And industry as a whole,

[9]Ibid., p. 213.
[10]Ibid., p. 218.
[11]Ibid., p. 199.
[12]Ibid., p. 207.
[13]Ibid., p. 193.
[14]Ibid., p. 189.
[15]Ibid., p. 201.
[16]Ibid., p. 7.
[17]Ibid., p. 45.

despite its continual lament of being bankrupted by environmentally mandated expenditures, spent under 2 percent of its capital outlays on pollution abatement in 1987.[18]

The foregoing is only an abbreviated inventory and fails to take into account the 1500 new chemicals introduced each year with properties that are not fully known. The review does not take into account the newer environmental threats—global warming or ozone layer depletion. Nor does it consider the "multimedia" effects of pollution, for example, air pollution acidifying rain, which then pollutes lakes or damages woodlands. Where regulatory agencies are discretely organized by the form of pollution—for example, air *or* water *or* soil—multimedia pollution can inject more regulatory ambiguity into an already confusing setting.

INTERNATIONAL ENVIRONMENTAL ISSUES

International environmental issues reach the American public sporadically and by dramatic case. Under the dogged surveillance of Greenpeace, a ship loaded with garbage sails around the world hoping to dump its cargo. A chemical plant in India "leaks" cyanide gas; 2000 are killed and hundreds of thousands are injured. A fire at a chemical company in Switzerland results in tons of toxic chemicals being dumped into the Rhine River, polluting water all the way to the North Sea. The top blows off a nuclear plant at Chernobyl, creating a radioactive wasteland. A television report documents the deforestation of the Amazon and the potential loss of the "lungs of the world." A major U. S. multinational is accused of bribing a dictator to sell a nuclear plant to be built on an earthquake-prone site. Poison is reported in Chilean grapes; they must be pulled from U. S. grocery stores. An oil slick threatens the north coast of Scotland. The Rio Grande River, which runs between Mexico and Texas, is reported to be an open sewer due to the wastes from industrial processing zones and overcrowded cities along the border.

We open this section with excerpts from one such news story, raise some questions about it, and then go on to sample other international environmental issues as remaining space permits.

[18]Ibid., p. 19.

GOING SOUTH

U.S. MINING FIRMS, UNWELCOME AT HOME, FLOCK TO LATIN AMERICA

*By Marj Charlier, Staff Reporter**

LA JOYA, Bolivia–In the thin air of the Altiplano, a barren plateau some 12,000 feet above sea level, shiny new mills, drill rigs and rumbling 85-ton trucks signify more U.S. jobs lost to foreign nations.

But there isn't much hue and cry back home. These jobs are in a mine—the Kori Kollo gold mine operated by Houston's Battle Mountain Gold Co.—and mining isn't welcome now in much of the U.S.

After nearly three centuries, the U.S. mining industry is looking to Latin America for its future operations. In 1992, the number of U.S. and Canadian mining companies exploring or operating in Latin America doubled from the year before. While exploration spending slipped 13% in the U.S. in the past two years, it more than doubled in Latin America.

Environmental Opposition

And as existing mines play out, the companies are leaving the U.S. with the blessing, if not open encouragement, of the Clinton administration and Congress, which are proposing even stiffer environmental regulations and new royalties on metals on public lands. Mining's critics contend that the U.S. won't lose much economically. The shrinking industry now employs only about 500,000 U.S. workers and, critics predict, will return after plucking the easy deposits elsewhere.

Battle Mountain's contrasting experiences in the U.S. and Bolivia illustrate why mining companies are leaving. In the state of Washington, the company and a partner have been battling for 18 months environmentalists who oppose their Crown Jewel gold mine. The necessary mining permits are still at least six months away. But here in Bolivia, Battle Mountain was welcomed as a source of jobs and tax revenue and even as a protector of the environment. The company received all needed permits the day it got the go-ahead from lenders.

"A U.S. mining company has to go international or it runs a very high risk of going out of business," says Kenneth Werneburg, Battle Mountain's president.

Better Prospects

In moving south, miners are also following their noses. In the U.S., most of the high-quality and cheap-to-mine ore has been extracted. But in South America, where dictatorships, leftist governments and constitutional provisions held down exploration for years, democratic reforms have now stabilized once-volatile political environments, and the mountainous terrain seems a bonanza awaiting modern exploration techniques.

"In the U.S., there are 10 geologists for every prospect," says Les Van Dyke, a Battle Mountain spokesman. "In Bolivia, there are 10 prospects for every geologist."

That may change soon. One recent morning, the Plaza Hotel cafeteria in La Paz was serving geologists from Amax Gold Inc., executives from a Salt Lake City mining-service firm and managers

*Reprinted by permission of the *Wall Street Journal*; June 18, 1993 issue.

from Battle Mountain's joint-venture company in Bolivia. Having breakfast there the next day were representatives of Tucson's Arimetco International Inc., San Francisco's Mineral Resources Development Inc. and Denver's Minproc Technology Inc.

And U.S. companies aren't merely looking around. Newmont Mining Corp., of Denver, will spend $18 million of its $30 million exploration budget next year overseas—much of it in Latin America. Cyprus Minerals Corp. has leased some Bolivian prospects for exploration and is considering joint-venture offers from state-owned companies in Chile and Peru. Phelps Dodge Corp. and American Resource Corp. recently constructed major gold mines in Latin America.

Green Movements

Certainly, it isn't all golden south of the border. Some opposition to foreign investment lingers on, especially in areas where mining unions have been strong. The state-owned Corporacion Minera de Bolivia (Comibol) has laid off tens of thousands of superfluous miners, and the Comibol union fears that foreign investment will cause further loss of members and clout.

In addition, an environmental movement is arising. A Chilean environmental agency forced Phelps Dodge to relocate a port for a new copper mine after complaints from a nearby scallop farm. And, aided by $67,000 appropriated by the U.S. Congress, a U.S. agency and some European countries proposed an environmental law for Bolivia last year that would have killed all mining projects in the country; a less-stringent law was passed.

Since 1988, however, eight job-hungry Latin American countries have rewritten their mining laws to encourage foreign investment. Peru eliminated price controls, lifted foreign-exchange restrictions and started privatizing state ventures. Mexico abolished mining royalties. Gonzalo Sanchez de Losada, chairman of Bolivia's biggest private mining company, was recently elected the country's president. And many miners, once strongly socialistic, have changed their minds about foreign investment and capitalism, thanks to such successes as Kori Kollo.

In the U.S., rural Western counties, already reeling from declines in the number of farms and ranches and cutbacks in the defense industry, will be the hardest hit by the flight of the mining companies. Their departure mirrors what happened earlier in the oil industry, where the U.S. has lost 500,000 jobs in the past decade. And as in the case of oil, the U.S. will have to import more metal, to the detriment of its already-lopsided balance of trade.

Miners haven't had much success countering their critics in Washington, where the sparsely populated states in which they operate have little political clout, especially with the environmental orientation of the Clinton administration. Jim Hill, a Newmont Mining spokesman, says "our biggest political risk is in the U.S.," even though the company's Peruvian mining project requires heavy security against the Shining Path guerrillas.

U.S. indifference to mining is just fine with Latin Americans. At a recent mining conference in Miami, Fausto Miranda Paz, a Mexican attorney, joked that his country, a major beneficiary of U.S. mining investment, should make campaign contributions to the legislators proposing high royalties in the U.S. "We are very grateful," he said. This summer, Peru, Bolivia and Argentina have sent or will send official mining delegations to Denver to court U.S. companies.

Problems in the U.S.

The industry's problems in the U.S. are evident in Olympia, Wash., where the permit process for the Crown Jewel mine owned by Battle Mountain and Crown Resources Corp. is dragging on and on. Environmentalists make no bones about what is happening. "We will certainly challenge it every step of the way," says Christopher Carrel, executive director of the Washington Wilderness Coalition.

The coalition of 22 environmental groups has assailed the project at three public hearings and subsequently submitted 600 pages of comments to which the companies, under the law, must respond. "It's not a lot of fun to hike around an open pit," Mr. Carrel says. Besides, he adds, the group isn't convinced the cyanide solutions used to process ore can be contained safely, and worries about water supplies.

The group proposed a 40-page bill that would have lengthened the state's permitting period to at least five years—a surefire project-killer, the companies say. When the bill didn't pass the legislature, the coalition sponsored newspaper ads and radio spots advocating declaration of a state of emergency, which would have triggered a moratorium on mining. The governor wouldn't do that, but the group is still pushing him to sign a moratorium until stiffer regulations are enacted.

Even without new legislation, the Crown Jewel mine must receive 56 different permits from 32 different agencies to proceed. Preparing the 1,000-page environmental-impact statement alone is occupying 250 people, 100 more than the mine itself would employ. It also is adding $5 million to Battle Mountain's initial development costs, which total $70 million.

Getting Started in Bolivia

All this frustration, along with falling reserves at its Fortitude, Nev., gold mine, hastened Battle Mountain's decision to look south for new prospects. In 1989, the company found Kori Kollo, which was a small mine here owned by Zeland Mines Ltd., of Panama, and had been mined off and on since the 1700s. With Battle Mountain funding, however, a gold deposit of 4.7 million ounces was defined, and Inti-Raymi SA—as the partnership between Zeland and Battle Mountain is known—promptly started negotiations with townspeople to buy the land around the deposit.

When Inti-Raymi officials rang the ancient church bells at the tiny village of Chuquina to call a town meeting, only two people showed up. The adobe huts had long since been abandoned; their owners had moved to hunt for jobs in the cities. In nearby La Joya, just 25 residents remained, barely scratching out a living by farming and small-stakes mining.

All that changed after Inti-Raymi agreed to relocate Chuquina, supplying materials and architects for new homes, a new school, a new church, a government building and a hospital. It also brought in water, sewers and electricity. In return for the community-owned land in La Joya, it brought in electricity, drilled water wells, remodeled the old La Joya church and built a new school and first-aid clinic.

Today, Chuquina's population is back to 500 and La Joy's 1,000, mostly because of work at the mine. All but two of the 550 jobs there are held by Bolivians.

They are an obliging work force. After all, pay at Kori Kollo averages about

$400 a month, compared with an average Bolivian factory worker's $100 a month. And mining jobs are scarce; in the past five years, Comibol employment has dwindled to 6,000 from 35,000. Not surprisingly, Inti-Raymi's recent negotiations with two unions were resolved in just two days.

Battle Mountain has also been pleased with its operations here. It was able to recruit some of the country's best mining engineers and geologists, who ensured a quick startup. Miners were easily trained, and construction crews were efficient. While the company has spent about $235 million, including development costs, for its 85% stake in the mine, low labor costs have kept cash operating costs low—about $180 an ounce, compared with a U.S. average of about $240 an ounce.

Inti-Raymi also completed the processing mill two months ahead of schedule, despite the difficult terrain—the Altiplano is ringed by 20,000-foot peaks—and the lack of paved highways—Bolivia, a country the size of France and Spain combined, has just 1,000 miles of them. Battle Mountain built a 45-mile power line and, to bring in supplies, a 250-mile gravel road from La Joya to Arica, on the Chilean coast. It built a town for its managers and an airstrip.

Battle Mountain and Zeland also are trying to avoid the ruthless, colonialist image that long plagued the industry in Latin America and led to the nationalization of mines in the 1950s and 1960s. The joint venture's Inti-Raymi Foundation has started $1.8 million in charitable projects, introducing better strains of grain and livestock, improving water systems and building 14 schools. Twenty women, many of whom used to pan for gold to support their families, now weave scarves at a cooperative set up by the foundation.

Sitting at a primitive loom, Nancy Quispe De Lopez, 32 years old, recalls once being unable to find a teaching job, but now she earns $100 a week, more than a teacher makes, weaving in a new brick building close to La Joya's maze of adobe homes. Combined with her husband's mining pay, her earnings enable the family to put fresh fruit on the table—a luxury on the barren plains.

Local residents also hail Battle Mountain's environmental policies. The company says it follows U.S. Environmental Protection Agency standards at Kori Kollo, as demanded by most international lending agencies and banks. It has constructed a closed system that recycles the chemicals and water used in the mining and milling. That is a change in South America, a continent overrun by lone-wolf prospectors who have poisoned streams with mercury and whose hydraulic jets have washed tons of mountain soil into rivers.

Even Philip Hocker, president of the Mineral Policy Center, a U.S. environmental group, concedes that the big U.S. and Canadian companies have generally followed good environmental practices abroad. "There is a faction within the industry that understands that they cannot go on operating badly," he says. However, he remains skeptical of smaller companies, especially those with bad environmental records in the U.S.

But for the foreseeable future, Bolivia's hunger for economic development and jobs will probably carry more weight than environmental concerns anyway. "The needs of this country are very different" than those in the U.S., says Mario Mercado, who runs Zeland. "Work, taxes, roads and schools—this is what the mining industry offers."

Questions and Comments

1. What is the difference between a news story and a political tract? Separate what is news in the foregoing story from what comes closer to politics. By politics is meant the direction the author–reporter would want the environmental law and regulations to take. For example, one political position seems to be that environmentalists have made it impossible for even the most conscientious and technically advanced mining companies to operate in the United States. Small wonder that they are heading for Bolivia, and so on.

   Once you are adept at separating fact from political argument, you will have gone a long way toward establishing a more solid basis for your own thinking on the subject of multinationals and their impacts both in the United States and abroad. Any text, including this book, must be read with that same care and enlightened skepticism.
2. To get a complete answer on capital flight to avoid stringent environmental restrictions, one would have to make an inventory of the regulations of the place from which the flight takes place, and an inventory of the regulatory scheme of the country where activities are scheduled for the future. In addition, to assess their long-term and short-term impacts, one would have to examine carefully all of the production methods that the fleeing companies have in mind for gold mining and ore processing (and waste products therefrom) in any new location.
3. The author of the article seems to have confidence in companies' voluntarily assuming environmental responsibilities rather than having them legally imposed upon them. Evaluate.
4. Just how dangerous is gold mining, and what might impel environmentalists to want to make a mining company cross every *t* and dot every *i* in the permit process? Has modern technology rendered mining and related activities utterly safe, as the Bolivians have apparently been led to believe, or is there still cause for concern?

   A few days in the library will reveal that gold mining and ore processing for gold has been and will continue to be a source of serious pollution.[19] The history of mining companies' cutting environmental corners is written all across the American west. Even Nevada, a state not known for intrusions into dubious desires, enacted law in 1987 to control water pollution from mining.[20] (Of the United States, Nevada is the largest gold producing state.)

[19]J. Jacus et al., "Law of Mine Waste: A Primer," 35 *Mineral Law Institute* (1990), pp. 9-2–9-62. J. Jacus, et al., "The Emerging Federal Law of Mine Waste," *Land and Water Law Review* (1991), 25-35, pp. 462-485.

[20]J. Draper, et al., "Environmental Laws and Regulations Governing Gold Mining in the West," *Mineral Law Institute* 36 (1990), pp. 5-1–5-58.

There are some common assumptions about gold mining that turn out to be untrue. For example, a pile of rock put aside as valueless-during some phase of mining may appear to be harmless to persons unschooled in chemistry. They might ask what difference can there be between rock in a pile and the same rock before it was taken from the earth? Or, if a pit is dug to extract ores, how can harm occur when the material left over after mining is put back into the hole?

The technical answer is that rock exposed to air and water generates sulfuric acid. Sulfuric acid dissolves heavy metals, which will be carried by water to underground water supplies and streams with highly toxic potential. The heavy metals associated with gold mining include arsenic, cadmium, copper, manganese, and zinc. So the pile of rock or waste material is not as neutral as the amateur to mining would be inclined to believe.[21]

Second, it might be assumed by the lay person that mining does not involve water. As it turns out, large amounts of water may be needed to process ore. Low-grade gold ore is often heaped in piles over which a cyanide solution is sprayed. The gold in trace amounts bonds with the cyanide in solution and drains to collecting pipes. The resulting gold-enriched solution is then put through a carbon process that picks up the gold from the cyanide. The cyanide solution, stripped of gold, will then be returned to the ore pile or heap for a repeat of the first step until the pile yields no more recoverable gold. (A spent heap can create pollution if not properly "neutralized".)[22]

There are huge debates about the ability to control the cyanide solutions flowing though the piles and forming in pools. The mining companies put barriers of various types under the piles of ore, which are to protect the underlying ground from penetration by the cyanide solution. The words "barriers of various types" are used advisedly, since there is substantial debate over what types of barriers are to be used and in what thicknesses. As one would expect, the companies argue that the environmentalists' standards are too stringent and may be unnecessary for the place where the ore processing is to take place. (For example, fewer precautions are said to be needed in arid places where there is less uncontrollable runoff. The companies also argue that less control is necessary in *remote* areas, where contamination of air and water have fewer harmful effects.)[23]

Waste of various types, with differing contributions to pollution, are generated from the extraction of ore, ore enrichment, and smelting, all of which have a variety of impacts on air and water quality.[24]

[21]Ibid., pp. 5-16—5-18.
[22]Ibid., pp. 5-5—5-18.
[23]Ibid., pp. 5-6, 5-11.
[24]Jacus, "Law of Mine Waste", pp. 9-4–9-28.

Students can read up on mining technology and its attendant risks just as environmentalists must do when they oppose the companies *or* regulatory agencies. After study they may come away chastened and arrive at the same conclusion reached by the Roman writer Agricola two thousand years ago:

> Further, when the ores are washed, the water which has been used poisons the brooks and streams and either destroys the fish or drives them away. Therefore, the inhabitants of these regions, on account of the devastation of their fields, their woods, groves, brooks, and rivers, find great difficulty in procuring their necessities of life... Thus it is clear to all that there is greater detriment from mining than the value of the metals which the mining produces.[25]

5. What connection might be drawn between Bolivia's being open to gold mining ventures and it perennial problems with international indebtedness and generating foreign exchange?

   The journalist contends that there has been substantial betterment of living and working conditions among Bolivians attributable to this new interest in Bolivian mineral development. Evaluate.

   It would also be worthwhile to check back on gold mining in Bolivia five years hence.

The following excerpt presents an overview of the relationship of multinationals to the environment in developing countries.

MULTINATIONAL CORPORATIONS, ENVIRONMENT, AND THE THIRD WORLD*

Charles Pearson, Ed.

The perceived relationship between environment and development has undergone a remarkable transformation. In the early 1970s these two concerns were seen as being largely incompatible, with societies forced to choose between them. Since then our understanding of the environmental–development nexus has broadened and deepened, with the result that today one finds in international circles a much "increased acceptance of the view that environmental considerations are an essential and integral part of sustainable national, and even global, economic development . . .

Consider first the ways in which the activities of multinational corporations . . . may have greater adverse impacts on natural systems and environmental management . . . as compared with local enterprises. The production processes of local enterprises tend to be less capital-intensive, with the result that locals may rely less on productive processes that are energy and synthetic intensive, and . . . pollution intensive. The technologies and products of local enterprises may also be more appropriate to local conditions with regard to diet, climate, and culture and thus less likely to cause adverse environmental consequences than alien technologies and products developed under different conditions. If the local enterprises are state owned, they may not need to pay dividends or worry about bankruptcy, may have preferential access to state financing, and

[25]Ibid., pp. 9-15.

*Durham, NC: Duke Univ. Press, 1987), pp. 4-12

may enjoy monopoly power, protected markets or hidden subsidies. It may thus be easier for them than for privately owned multinational corporations to incur environmental control expenses. And perhaps most importantly, local enterprises are likely to enjoy fewer options and less flexibility in resource allocation . . .

For other reasons MNC's may have fewer adverse impacts on natural systems and environmental quality or be in more compliance with governmental regulations than local firms. Multinationals operating in a host country may, for example, be under greater scrutiny and be more vulnerable to adverse publicity and punitive action. Local firms may enjoy greater influence with governmental regulators and may be granted preference with respect to the stringency and timing of environmental performance standards . . .

The multinational may also represent a channel for transfer of productive and environmentally sound technology and may be more in touch with environmental developments and innovations abroad . . . MNC's can play, and many believe should play, a demonstration and leadership role, and be an agent for change. The MNC's role is facilitated by the fact that the multinational corporate subsidiaries are typically larger firms than their local rivals and tend to be more profitable. They may be better able to absorb the costs of environmental controls. In addition, the technologies and equipment employed by transnational affiliates tend to be more modern, more recently constructed, better maintained, and more efficient in terms of waste control management. The affiliates typically also employ more professionally qualified managers on average than local enterprises do, and may also employ better skilled workers, given their generally higher wages. Finally, MNC affiliates, unlike their domestic rivals, tend to be more vulnerable to demands and pressures emanating from home and host countries with respect to social responsibility.

Multinational corporations operate in a heterogeneous world of environmental problems and policies—sovereign nations have been going about the business of environmental and health protection at different speeds, with different degrees of rigor, using different techniques. A great deal of environmental policy is in place in some of the highly industrialized countries. It is just beginning to emerge in others. In still others—particularly in the least developed—it will probably be some time in coming. As of 1986, a ballpark estimate would be that 95% of all environmental laws, environmental agency personnel and environmental spending around the world are concentrated in the Western industrial nations here.

But things have been changing. At the Stockolm Conference in 1972 only twenty-six countries had national agencies that dealt in some way with environmental issues. A survey ten years later showed that 144 countries had established such institutions (Mere creation of an institution, of course—especially if it is staffed by only a few people as is the case in numerous nations—implies little about the ability to implement effective environmental policy) . . . A recent survey of people involved in environmental protection issues in seventy-two developing nations showed that a large proportion (88 percent) believed that present environmental protection efforts in their nations were inadequate . . .

Despite this scattered evidence of progress it is important to recognize . . . that most developing countries face severe problems in planning and management of natural systems . . . Hufschmidt and his colleagues have identified ten critical management problems . . .

1. Inadequacies in monitoring and enforcement . . .
2. Extensive poverty that puts a premium on current income producing activities . . .
3. Scarcity of financial resources . . . to protect natural systems
4. The often perverse distributional effects of environmental quality plans . . . which may worsen existing inequitable distribution of income.
5. Difficulty in controlling the environmental effects of private-sector and public-sector development activities
6. Inadequacies in . . . expertise
7. Widespread market failures, which require extensive use of shadow prices . . .
8. Minimal participation . . . by the general public
9. Inadequacies in . . . data . . . trends and baselines
10. Wide diversity in cultural values which increases the difficulty of social evaluation of environmental quality effects.

The consequences of these shortcomings are serious. A recent cataloging includes rapid degradation of agricultural land via desertification; pesticide related deaths estimated at 10,000 per year in developing countries, with persons affected by acute pesticide poisoning estimated at 1.5 million to 2 million; rapid deforestation . . . accelerating habitat destruction . . . air pollution from major urban centers . .. widespread water contamination; and a staggering incidence of environmentally related disease—affecting over one billion people . . .

On top of this sobering set of constraints, a number of factors related to multinational corporations may further conspire to make purely national control systems either evadable, inefficient, incomplete, unenforceable, exploitable, or negotiable . . .

One factor to consider is the flexibility, mobility and leverage of multinationals. The global production, logistics and marketing systems of many pollution-intensive multinationals give them wide options . . . their autonomy concerning public policies has increased and conversely, their accountability . . . has decreased. This is especially the case for host countries, but increasingly also true for home countries. It is fair to assume that the typical MNC as a global profit maximizer tends to react to host government policies so as to minimize any impairment of expected profits . . .

A second limiting factor relates to communication and control gaps within multinational corporations. Their management systems vary from "closed" to "open" depending on the intensity of the parent's supervision of the subsidiaries and the density and communications links between them . . .

A third factor . . . is MNC secrecy . . . In many nations, governments lack the resources to monitor properly . . . exports, imports, product sales, investment and waste disposal activities. Such conditions explain the lack of solid information with regard to the export and import of hazardous products and the near absence of policy concerning the international movements of hazardous wastes . . .

The fourth complication is limits on transnational corporate accountability and responsibility. There does not yet exist a uniform or global concept of what a parent company's responsibilities for their subsidiaries should be . . . Questions of liability for accidents and environmental or occupational health damage becomes very ambiguous and troublesome when the enterprise is only partially owned by an MNC (when for example it is a joint venture), is owned by the transnational only indirectly (for example, a transnational affiliate of a transnational affiliate), or is a subcontractor (for example, a fly by night waste disposal company with one employee) . . . Other factors that diffuse or limit MNC responsibility for environmental damage include monetary ceilings or limits on liability (such as with oil tanker accidents), temporal limits on liability (. . . long abandoned waste landfills or long latency periods in the manifestations of occupational disease), institutional and legal barriers to cross border adjudication of disputes . . . and variations in the basic concept of liability from one nation to another . . . The consequence of these ambiguities, limits, and barriers is that many victims go uncompensated or inadequately compensated for losses . . .

A summary description of the current approach of most developing nations to environmental policy would include such words as embryonic, short term, narrow, fragmented, exclusionist, discontinuous, ad hoc, reactive, superficial, under-resourced, and negotiable . . .

Questions and Comments

1. Reread the excerpt from the *Wall Street Journal* on mining and compare it to this overview on the ability of underdeveloped countries to effectively control the environmental effects of multinationals. Make of list of questions that you wish the reporter had asked the company, or the environmentalists opposing the U. S. operations of the mining company. What background information do you wish the author had included in the article? Do some research on the subject of mining and rewrite the story in light of your findings.
2. Pearson opens his overview with a good question: will local firms or international firms be more likely to discharge their environmental responsibilities? Review the reasons he gives for either being the better candidate.

   It could also be that neither local nor multinational firms are inclined to meet environmental responsibilities, but for different reasons. The local firm may be using environmentally primitive methods, may not have the requisite capital for improvement, or may simply be desirous of avoiding costs; the international firm, given its options to choose among countries for certain activities, might choose a location with lax environmental enforcement to maximize worldwide profitability.
3. The debate on environmental impacts of multinationals cannot be answered as an abstract matter. Particular industries and companies within them must be understood in greater detail: their production processes and methods, how they dispose of unwanted waste from production, in what locations they are carried out, with what

impacts. Have an industry and companies within an industry been enthusiastic about environmental safety or resistant to it and, if so, for what reasons?

Mining, as discussed above, has been especially conducive to environmental degradation. The same would be true of the chemical industry, which generates substantial toxic waste even when production methods are highly sophisticated. However, when capital investments are high and immovable, companies might have less bargaining power once they have set up an operation. In an industrial processing zone, sewing clothes will have different environmental and workplace hazards from electronic assembly.

Similarly, in Third World agriculture, methods and environmental impacts may differ by the crop, who grows it, and in what quantities. Wendell Berry once recorded the consummate environmental sensitivity of Andean Indians, who from time out of memory have grown food on tiny plots in five climate zones, ranging from tropical lowlands to Andean highlands. These Indians are not slouches when it comes to concrete agricultural science. Multinationals engaging in monoculture on large plantations for export would present a shorter, different record. In many ways their methods are dazzling in sophistication, but in others are dazzling in crudity, and, from a peasant's perspective, profoundly wasteful.

These prerequisites for intelligent evaluation of environmental issues are what cause environmental activists to become detectives regarding company practices (and governmental practices, too, since the government often qualifies as a polluter), avid readers of scientific reports, and diligent students of the labyrinthine laws and regulations on the environment.

To get some feel for the heterogeneity about which Pearson speaks, it would be valuable to do a research project on the environmental aspects of a particular industry or company. What are the principal processes used, where do they take place, and with what environmental impacts? Perhaps in the area where you live there is a convenient topic for study—oil and gas production or refining, steelmaking, coal mining, timbering, electronic assembly, chemical manufacturing, cattle ranching, or grain production. It is probably safe to assume that the techniques you investigate in your area will be no worse than those used in a Third World country. They could be substantially better.

An alternative to the foregoing project would be to begin with an environmental disaster and trace it back to company or industry practices. Was the so-called accident predictable, given the practices in the industry where it happened? This is the technique employed by Noel Mostert in *Supership* (Chapter 3). Writing well before *Exxon Valdez*, he predicted environmental disasters in ocean transport of oil, based upon ship size, seaworthiness, navigation, and other aspects of the already dismal historical record of large oil tankers. He was asking whether an "accident" that is just waiting to happen can really be considered an accident.

4. One of the most potent discoveries about the old East Block industries, once they came open to outside inspection and inventory, was the fact that environmental degradation was so widespread in them. While this revelation was taken by western chauvinists as further proof of the deficiencies of state-run enterprises, the more important lesson should have been that ownership, public or private, may not be as important in assessing environmental risks as the techniques used in industry, mining, and agriculture, or in other more common governmental activities—supplying water, waste disposal systems and utilities.
5. In his closing commentary Pearson concludes that there are no effective compensation systems for victims of environmental and workplace hazards. Compare this dismal conclusion with the cases and materials in Chapter 9 on the strategies employed by multinationals and their lawyers in litigation.

   At the end of the excerpt there is a burst of adjectives on the prospects in developing countries for effective environmental control systems. Some of these might be kept in mind when the next environmental episode flashes across the television screen.

Bhopal

The release of cyanide gas into the air from a chemical manufacturing plant in Bhopal, India on December 3, 1984 was the worst industrial accident in history. The gas immediately killed 2000 people and more than 200,000 people were injured, some of whom later died. The death toll was complicated by the fact that some of the people who were killed were so poor that they had no official identity. Their kin simply prepared a funeral bier and cremated the bodies.

The case raised every conceivable question, large and small about industry, and industry in the Third World. After a short description of the event in the following excerpts* selected issues are considered.

Poison Gas Leak . . . Kills Hundreds, Injures 10,000

Wall Street Journal—December 4, 1984.

Poisonous gas leaking from a Union Carbide pesticide plant ... killed at least 410 people yesterday and injured more than 10,000 others ...

The spokesman [for Union Carbide] said the fumes caused fatalities and injuries to a number of people in the city of 630,000.

Company officials . . . were sketchy on the exact cause of the leak which occurred at one of three underground tanks and spread over a 25 square-mile radius . . .

Methyl isocyanate—described as flammable and highly toxic—attacks the mucous membranes, eyes, nose, and throat . . .

A company spokesperson said that scrubbers at the plant usually remove the lethal properties of methyl isocyanate, which is used to make the agricultural chemicals . . . Union Carbide sells . . . under the trade names Sevin and Temik . . .

Company spokesmen in Danbury [Connecticut] didn't know when the tanks were last inspected or what kind of inspections were required by Indian or U. S. regulations . . .

Union Carbide also makes the chemical at a plant in Charleston, West Virginia . . .

The company said . . . it has been safely manufacturing and handling methyl isocyanate for more than 25 years . . .

Union Carbide's managing director in India, Y. P. Gokhale [was quoted—Ed.] as saying the gas leaked for forty minutes before being stopped . . .

Union Carbide stock plunged $2.37 . . . in reaction to the news.

Wall Street Journal—December 5, 1984

Death Toll in India climbs to over 750 . . .

Union Carbide's president Warren M. Anderson . . . will fly to India to direct the investigation of the gas leak

The company confirmed more than 2,000 critical injuries. Doctors in India said that as many as 200,000 people were affected and 20,000 serious [ly] . . .

Union Carbide executives haven't yet spoken to their counterparts at the India plant which is 51% owned by Union Carbide and 49% owned by the Indian government. While the company on Monday denied that several managers at the plant were arrested . . . the company said yesterday three to five managers were believed to be under "house arrest."

Officials told the news conference that a fail-safe device may have failed to work when pressure built up inside the tank. Such fail-safe devices will be checked at the West Virginia and Woodbine, Georgia plants and at Union Carbide plants using methyl isocyanate in France and Brazil . . .

The company isn't sure exactly what happened but said all safety precautions had been taken and were believed adequate . . . There were indications, however, that some types of safety-related equipment used in the industry weren't in place at the India plant. A Carbide spokesperson said that the company's West Virginia plant uses a computerized early warning system to detect the buildup of temperatures and pressures in tanks that could permit the liquid chemical to turn into a gas. But the spokesperson said such a system had not been installed at the facility in India. He maintained, however, that the instrumentation used there was as effective as the computer-driven systems that have become standard safety features in the U.S. chemical industry in recent years . . .

Methyl isocyanate . . . expands rapidly under heat and pressure. To prevent explosions, storage tanks are fitted with escape valves to vent deadly gas. To neutralize the gas, the plant in India used a chemical scrubber system as well as a "flare tower" that should incinerate any gas that escapes the scrubber. The Union Carbide spokesperson said both the scrubber and the flare tower apparently failed to operate . . .

While the cause of the disaster is a major question, officials in India are also worried about possible long term effects of exposure . . . on the survivors. Mr. Browning [Union Carbide's director of health safety and environmental affairs] said that while the company believes there isn't likely to be a "major" effect, the company could not rule out the possibility because exposures on such a scale are "beyond our experience."

Under federal regulations . . . U. S. workers may not be exposed to more than .02 part of methyl isocyanate per million parts of air in an eight-hour day.

In the next weeks the *Journal* was filled with more details on Bhopal and related issues: death and injury counts; emergency efforts; a visit by the CEO that resulted in his temporarily being put under arrest; trying to get to the bottom of just what happened; sorting out the mixed commentaries of corporate spokespeople; determining whether chemical manufacturing in the United States presented comparable risks; finding who in the two Union Carbide companies—the U. S. parent or Union Carbide-India—were responsible for construction, operation, safety, and maintenance; U. S. personal injury lawyers in India signing up claimants against Union Carbide on a contingent fee basis; the impact of the accident on the solvency of the parent U. S. company; establishing how much insurance Union Carbide had and with what companies; reporting allegations by the company of sabotage; evaluating the adequacy of the Indian court system for the handling of hundreds of thousands of claims, as compared with the U. S. court system, and more.

For a fascinating story with unpredictable twists, students can read a sampling of the 100-odd items that appeared in the *Wall Street Journal* from December 4, 1984 through May 1985. To understand Bhopal and its aftermath is to understand the nature and limits of industrialization, the relationship between the First and the Third World, and the acceptance and denial of responsibility in worldwide company networks.

Taking the largest questions first, how do we gather information about disasters; are we likely to get the straight story? Is Bhopal an isolated instance or simply a dramatic manifestation of risks that are common in chemical manufacturing? To get some idea of what lies behind these questions, we turn briefly to a novel set in the United States. Don DeLillo in *White Noise* writes of an average family in an average town with average income and average tastes—take-out Chinese food and family television rituals that numb the imagination. The family is slowly awakened from its torpor by news that a toxic chemical has escaped from a ruptured rail car—a mini-Bhopal very close to home.

What the family encounters is a series of contrived misinformation, some of which they are suckers for, given their habit of getting their information exclusively from television and radio. The toxic news is broken in stages: first the toxicity is described as a "feathery plume,"[26] next "a black billowing cloud,"[27] then as an "airborne toxic event"[28] and finally: "Cloud of deadly chemicals, cloud of deadly chemicals."[29] A "feathery plume" sounds light and unthreatening; a "dark billowing cloud" is more frightening and must be sanitized by the abstract and scientific phrase "airborne toxic event." Then reality—"deadly chemicals"—clears the verbal air as it poisons the actual air. The family must evacuate.

While filling the family car with gas to get away, the father is exposed for a few minutes to the chemical—"Nyodene D," about which he knows noth-

[26]Don DeLillo, *White Noise*, (New York: Viking, 1984), p. 111.
[27]Ibid., p. 113.
[28]Ibid., p. 117.
[29]Ibid., p. 119.

ing. His conversation with a computer-technician-bureaucrat about his health risks yields the same noninformation as the early description of the escaping chemical as a feathery plume:

> Jack: Am I going to die?
> Technician: Not as such.
> Jack: What do you mean?
> Technician: Not in so many words . . . We'll know more in fifteen years. In the meantime we definitely have a situation.[30]

De Lillo later contends that the line between toxic events and abiding environmental conditions has been crossed, a fact that contributes to the need for experts in and out of government to obscure more about our true situation than they reveal. When the toxic "event" is officially over and the family returns home, do things get back to normal? Not quite:

> B: The dogs have sniffed out only a few traces of toxic material on the edge of town.
> H: That's what we're supposed to believe . . . If they released the true findings, there'd be billions of dollars in law suits. Not to mention demonstrations, panic, violence and social disorder . . .
> B: There's no reason to think the results aren't true as published . . .
> H: Industry would collapse if the true results of any of these investigations were released.
> B: What investigations?
> H: The ones going on all over the country.
> B: That's the point . . . Every day on the news there's another toxic spill. Cancerous solvents from storage tanks, arsenic from smokestacks, radioactive water from power plants. How serious can it be if it happens all the time? Isn't the definition of a serious event based on the fact that it's not an everyday occurrence?[31]

Bhopal, India was at once more than a feathery plume, but the story followed the same overall rhythm between harsh reality and half-truths, quarter-truths and outright lies. Euphemisms were presented alongside body counts; by odd circumstance the best portrayal of the gravity of the disaster was the stock price of Union Carbide which plummeted in the weeks after December 4. The company could not avoid acknowledging just how big the disaster was, but at the same time it gave assurances that the "accident" was not likely to occur elsewhere. Other plants of Union Carbide were "safe," and other prominent companies in the chemical industry came forth to defend the industry and assert their own impeccable safety procedures. In short, Bhopal was an unique event rather than what might happen anywhere at any time.

Jackson Browning, in charge of health, safety, and environmental affairs for Union Carbide USA was asked about the long-term effects of cyanide poisoning:

[30]Ibid., p. 140.
[31]Ibid., pp. 173,174.

> [W]hile the company believes there isn't likely to be a "major" effect, the company doesn't rule out that possibility because exposures on this scale are "beyond our experience."
>
> Browning was also asked about safety at Bhopal. According to the *Journal*:
>
> The company isn't certain exactly what happened, but said that all safety precautions had been taken and believed adequate. "What we can tell you is that everything that could have been installed . . . was installed," the company said. There were indications, however, that some types of safety related equipment used in the industry weren't in place in the India plant.[32]

In face of the fact that cyanide gas had been released over a 25-mile radius, the company was in a bit of a bind on safety claims. Second, it had to confront the Bhopal aftermath at the same time it had to assure that a plant making the identical chemical in West Virginia was safe. Calling the Bhopal plant completely safe would warn West Virginians that they better watch out. Calling the West Virginia plant more safe than the Bhopal plant exposed the company to the charge that it had exported a dangerous process to the Third World with substandard safety measures. (Congress had immediately called for an investigation of Union Carbide's safety procedures in West Virginia to see if they were adequate and different from those that had failed in Bhopal.) A Union Carbide strategy to pacify domestic worries would simultaneously arouse charges of racism and help sew up the Bhopal liability case against Union Carbide (including punitive damages). Perhaps it was this irreconcilable position which led the company to allege sabotage by disgruntled workers.

The chemical industry as a whole was caught in a comparable bind. It might have wanted to lend mutual support to Union Carbide, knowing that a disaster for Union Carbide was a disaster for every company in the industry. At the same time, other chemical companies wanted to put some distance between themselves and Union Carbide to render themselves more immune from the criticisms being leveled at Union Carbide. The standard press release of companies was that the industry as a whole was safe, and their own plants were even safer. In the end, the approach taken by Union Carbide and the industry was the same. Bhopal was an "event" rather than an extreme case arising from the day-to-day risks in chemical manufacturing. Every chemical plant—except Bhopal—was satisfactory.

Another aspect of this acceptance–rejection pattern that is closer to legal issues concerned the relationship between Union Carbide USA and Union Carbide-India. The public would have found it unbelievable that the Indians were "controlling" a plant in which the U. S. parent had a 51 percent stake. At the same time the parent corporation's impulse to put distance between itself and the subsidiary grew as the gravity of Bhopal disaster intensified. Moreover, the separation of the companies rather than their being joint fit an overall legal argument that the parent did not cause the disaster or otherwise do anything wrong. Possible connections between the com-

[32]*Wall Street Journal*, December 5, 1984.

panies included the plant's design, construction, operation, maintenance, and safety systems as well as decisions about the storage of toxic chemicals. The thread, such as it was, running through many of the company statements was that, of course, the parent company was responsible overall, but, of course, the parent company could not be responsible for everything that occurred in India. This was a variation on the war crimes defense, where generals who cannot deny their place in the hierarchy nevertheless claim that underlings cannot be kept under minute-by-minute control.

Before the case was fully "legalized," that is, company principals told by their lawyers to keep their mouths shut until told how and when to open them, the CEO of Union Carbide, Warren Anderson, was reported to have made statements that suggested the assumption of responsibility by the parent company for what had happened in India. From the *Journal*:

> —Mr. Anderson said he was confident that the victims of the disaster can be fairly and equitably compensated without any material adverse effect on the company's financial position.
> —Mr. Anderson said that he hoped the compensation issue could be resolved swiftly rather than in lengthy litigation.
> —Mr. Anderson said that he expected to spend the balance of [his] professional career helping Union Carbide recover from the disaster. "We have a stigma. We can't avoid it." he said. "We're going to spend a long time trying to make sure that the name of the company doesn't stand for the disaster in Bhopal."[33]

By the time the U. S. legal case involving Bhopal was decided in 1986, any language of responsibility had disappeared and the separation of parent company from subsidiary was in full evidence. The company submitted an affidavit saying that after design of the plant, everything from construction through operation and safety was in the hands of Indians (Union Carbide India Ltd), and out of the hands of U.S.-based principals:

> On the liability question Union Carbide asserts that the Bhopal plant was managed and operated entirely by Indian nationals, who were employed by UCIL.... the Bhopal plant is part of UCIL Agricultural Products Division which was a separate division of UCIL for at least 15 years, and that the plant had "limited contact" with UCIL Bombay headquarters, and almost no contact with the United States.[34]

The court had before it a preliminary question—*forum non conveniens*. Was India a more appropriate place to try the case than the United States? In ruling for Union Carbide the court ended what had been an intense legal battle over where the claimants would get a proper recovery. As noted after the disaster, some of the most prominent U.S. personal injury lawyers had gone to Bhopal and signed up thousands of clients on a contingent fee basis. It was this group that was fighting to keep the case in the United States fed-

[33]*Wall Street Journal*, December 11, 1991.
[34]*In re Union Carbide Corp. Gas Plant Disaster,* 634 F.Supp. 842, (1986) at 853.

eral courts. (Even with their contingent fees, they would probably have done far better for their clients than an early offer of settlement to the Bhopal victims—$100 in a death case, and $500 for an injury case.)

The claimants lost another critical fight when their cases were consolidated into one cause of action to be brought *by India* on their behalf, with distribution of proceeds to be done by a government agency. Claimants do usually have their own individual cases, but in 1985 India passed a law consolidating all of the individual cases into one claim.

When the case ended, Union Carbide had prevailed. The case was to be handled in India and not the United States, and the company had only one party with whom to negotiate the settlement. Like many a divorce case, the case came down to money. In 1991, the case was settled by the Indian government with Union Carbide for $470,000,000. (The estimated number of deaths was 3800 and the permanently disabled 20,000; there were thousands of other claims.) As of October 1991, "only a miniscule amount" of the civil settlement had been distributed by the government to the Bhopal victims.[35]

As concluded, the *Bhopal* case was far removed from the concrete suffering of hundreds of thousands of victims, and the issues surrounding chemical manufacture in the Third World.

Oil

A major source of ocean pollution is the unintended or deliberate discharge of oil from tankers or other ships. The words "oil spill" are usually applied, but the phrase trivializes just how much oil is lost when a ship founders, collides with another ship, explodes, or catches fire. The mind runs to a child spilling a glass of milk and not to 25,000,000 gallons going overboard, damaging marine life and habitats and washing up onto miles of shoreline. The word "spill" like the words "feathery plume" has its politics.

Exxon Valdez, when it lost 11,000,000 gallons of Alaska crude oil in a pristine bay, changed popular awareness in the United States of the impact of oil on the environment. If surveyed people might think that the *Exxon Valdez* created the worst oil pollution in history, but against the world list[36] of oil losses from ships and undersea wells, *Exxon Valdez* does not make the top ten.

[35]*Wall Street Journal*, October 4, 1991.
[36]*World Almanac* (New York: Pharos, 1993).

TOP TEN OIL LOSS LIST

	Date	Gallons*
Ixtoc oil well (Gulf of Mexico—blowout)	1979	176,000,000
Nowruz (Persian Gulf—blowout)	1983	176,000,000†
Atlantic Express (Off Trinidad—collision)	1979	88,000,000
Castillo de Bellver (off South Africa—fire)	1983	73,040,000
Amoco Cadiz (off France—grounding)	1978	65,562,000
Torrey Canyon (off England—grounding)	1967	34,986,000
Sea Star (Gulf of Oman—collision)	1972	33,810,000
Urquiola (La Caruna, Spain—grounding)	1976	29,000,000
Hawaiin Patriot (North Pacific—fire)	1977	29,100,000
Othello (Sweden—collision)	1970	23,520,000†
. . .		
. . .		
. . .		
Exxon Valdez (Alaska—grounding)	1989	11,000,000

*Tonnage was converted to gallons (7 barrels/ton; 42 gals/barrel).

†Estimated.

At least two more ship losses push *Exxon Valdez* further down the list (1992, *Aegean Sea* off Spain—24 million gallons; 1993, *Braer* off Shetland Islands—26 million gallons). There was a fire aboard a third ship, *Maersk Navigator*, carrying 260,000 tons near Indonesia with partial loss of cargo. Within a 24-hour period of *Valdez* there were three smaller spills in the coastal waters off Rhode Island, in the Delaware River, and on the Houston ship channel.

One more possibly unknown fact is that the big losses presented on the list are only a tiny fraction of the oil lost at sea in routine shipping activities. The cumulative effect of these "minor" losses dwarfs the effects of the more visible ones. It is safe to assume that as you are studying in this course there will be oil losses of either type. Be alert for what news there is of them.

The key tensions in the law and oil pollution involve two irreconcilable goals. Maritime powers, who have dominated the international conventions on oil pollution, desire to freely navigate in coastal waters and to limit their liability when their ships get into trouble. The coastal states, whose water quality and shore lines are likely to be damaged, want to exert more control over international shipping and to secure full compensation when pollution occurs. *Exxon Valdez*, since it was a ship owned and operated by a U. S.-based multinational and polluted the waters off Alaska, forced a choice by the U. S. Congress. Congress could either continue to subsidize ocean shipping by lenient petroleum pollution law and enforcement, or hold polluting companies fully accountable. For a long time companies had never been forced to internalize the costs of pollution, but there was intense public pressure after *Valdez* to change archaic rules and raise the level of damages collectable against a polluting company.

Perhaps out of the furor of the moment—in the American imagination Alaska stands as the last pristine frontier—Congress passed the Pollution Control Act of 1990. A central provision of the Act changed a nineteenth-century rule of maritime law that allowed polluting companies to limit their liability. Impossible as it may sound, given the extensive harm that follows from a major shipping disaster, liability under the 1851 law was limited to the value of the ship and the cargo (after the accident!). Under the 1990 statute the liability was raised to $1200 per gross ton, and where there was "gross negligence or willful misconduct," no limit on damages would apply.

Pollution on an impressive scale having become so common, Congress recognized other exigencies beyond cleanup and compensation. There was slow recognition of the point made as early as the mid-1970s: when more and more oil is transported in larger and larger tankers, there are *inherent* risks that go far beyond the usual maritime risks. Prevention and safety had to receive more attention. Included in the 1990 Act was everything from monitoring crews for alcohol to the requirement of double hulls for supertankers to give better protection upon grounding or collision. The latter provision applied to new construction, and wrote into law an oil industry standard already in place on forty supertankers.

Exxon Valdez was so highly publicized that it overshadows the usual oil pollution case that makes the news for only a few days. Exxon Corporation was facing a major loss of its U. S. customer base, and settling the case for a fraction of one year's profit must have appeared to the company to be a better alternative than stretching the case out for a decade. Moreover, the recoveries from lawsuits were payable over time and qualified, along with cleanup costs, as "ordinary and necessary business expenses" for tax purposes, making the case less painful for the company to settle.

The case was also free of the technicalities that accompany the usual international case. *Exxon Valdez* went aground in U. S. territorial waters. The claimants were U. S. citizens, states of the United States, or the U. S. Government. This was not a case where a U. S. multinational was operating abroad or on the high seas, where claimants were of another nationality, or where there was insufficient notoriety in the U. S. media to limit the impulse to drag the case out as long as possible.

By contrast, the *Amoco Cadiz* case[37] is far more representative of the legal thicket that can follow when a substantial ship founders and loses its cargo. In many ways the *Amoco* case replays some of the themes considered in Chapters 9 and 10: many litigants, all of whom are well funded with elite legal representation, countless preliminaries, and many substantive questions of law on liability and damages. One of the court opinions devoted exclusively to issue of damages ran more than 500 pages. (The case was in the U. S. federal court system from 1978 to 1992 and almost outlived the professional career of at least one judge; he was brought out of retirement to handle some of the last phases of the case.)

Following a brief summary of the event and the cast of parties involved, two issues have been selected from the many possibilities; first, corporate networking in shipping and how legal networks complicate the assessment of

[37]954 F. 2nd 1279, 1992.

liability and damages; and second, whether in light of some of the evidence and legal tactics found in the *Amoco* case, the public can safely rely on a voluntary assumption of good shipping practices by multinationals rather than placing reliance on regulatory control and legal sanctions.

The ship was built by a Spanish company, Astilleros Espanoles, a firm that goes back to the fleet of Columbus. Standard of Indiana (Amoco) was the buyer but operated through subsidiaries, Amoco International Oil Company, and Amoco Transport (Transport was a Liberian corporation that "owned" the ship). At the time it went aground the *Amoco Cadiz* was under charter to Royal Dutch Shell Ltd., and its subsidiary companies. (Shell's claim for the value of its oil was ultimately granted.)

The *Amoco Cadiz,* which had lost its anchor and steering, was under tow of the *Pacific*, a tug owned by a German company, Bugsier. The tug could not control the vessel, and it ran aground on the north coast of France, broke apart, and lost 220,000 tons of crude oil (approximately 65 million gallons, or six times *Valdez*). The plaintiffs against Amoco, the shipbuilder, and the towing company included France, a French department (province), French communes (towns), businesses that suffered losses, and environmental groups from France.

One significant dimension of the case was the corporate structure of Amoco for the international shipment of oil. The parent company, Standard of Indiana, had attempted to insulate itself from liability, and otherwise escape legal restrictions, by using subsidiary corporations and foreign flag registry for the operation and ownership of the vessel. After the accident the parent then tried to invoke the 1851 law referred to in the discussion of *Exxon Valdez,* which would have limited the liability of the Amoco companies to a paltry $700,000, the value of *Amoco Cadiz* after it had sunk (France later recovered $200,000,000).

The strategy backfired when Amoco needed it most. The court found a basis for holding the *whole* Amoco system liable for negligence. The court first deftly bypassed the parent company's legalism on limitation of liability by a legalism of its own; only the "owner" may invoke the limitation of liability and technically Amoco-Indiana did not own the tanker—Amoco Transport did. The second reason for holding the parent liable was not so legalistic. The court simply collapsed the "separate" legal entities into one corporation to find negligence:

> AIOC (Amoco International) — the party in charge of operation, maintenance and repair of the *Amoco Cadiz* and the selection of its crew—shared liability for the negligently designed, maintained and operated steering gear. Standard—the entity that exercised control over AIOC and Transport and that was initially responsible for the design, construction, and management of the *Amoco Cadiz* was liable for its own negligence as well as that of AIOC. . . . The structure of Standard was so highly integrated, each of the subdivisions was a mere instrumentality of the parent corporation . . .[38]

[38]Ibid., p. 1303

The French claimants got their justice after 12 years of the toughest litigation that one can imagine.

Perhaps the foregoing in itself discredits any claim that oil multinationals are anxious to settle claims arising from the carriage of oil by sea. But as one digs deeper into the case, there is even more troubling evidence that corporate good will and voluntarism will probably not safeguard ocean environments. The evidence showed that from the inception the hydraulic system that controlled the steering and rudder of the *Amoco Cadiz* was grossly deficient. This was noted on several inspections and every day the crew had to add hydraulic fluid to replace what had been lost by leakage. The builder of the ship had furnished critical replacement parts, which were left stored on deck while the crew continued to use the most primitive methods to keep the ship in service.

Why no repair? Money. The *Amoco Cadiz* was under contract and would lose $28,000 for every day it was in dry dock for repairs. This is a serious accusation. It says that because of a trifling loss of revenue the whole coast of Brittany was polluted. What evidence is there that Amoco bypassed rudimentary maintenance to maximize profits? From the court's opinion:

> The record [from the trial court—ed.] is replete with reference to the fact that it was Amoco's deliberate policy to defer drydocking and repairs in order to minimize the loss of charter hire that would have been incurred by taking the ship out of service . . .
> Zimmerman [AIOC] wrote his superiors that Amoco should turn down Astilleros's [the shipbuilder] offer of replacement parts, take a cash credit and defer repair until after the time charter expired . . .
> Amoco later decided that eight running days would be the limit [for recommended repairs]. Amoco is extremely concerned about the possibility that the vessel will be delayed from sailing as scheduled and agreed. The vessel is committed to a charter and any delays could result in a severe penalty to Amoco ...
> Amoco canceled the renewal of the bushings and packings because the job would have taken more than fourteen working days of two shifts per day ...
> The charter hire of $28,000 per day vessel multiplied by the estimated time in drydock of 30 days per vessel [there were two with the same hydraulic problem—ed.] is equal to $1,680,000 of incoming money that otherwise would not be realized . . .[39]

The court also documented the crude measures taken by the crew to cope with chronic *steering system* leakage problems:

> The manufacturer . . . recommended that the hydraulic fluid be kept free of contamination for proper operation of the hydraulic system ... Impurities in the oil cause wear on the internal parts of the main pumps, clogging of the filters, failure of seals, and scoring of the rams. Particulate matter in hydraulic systems acts like a grinding compound between points with close running tolerances . . .
> The hydraulic fluid in the steering system was not filtered or changed between

[39]Ibid., pp. 1299, 1300.

> September 1977 and March 1978, and no steps were ever taken to check for contaminants. The drums containing hydraulic fluid were stored on the open deck. They were not covered with tarpaulins. When the drums expanded and contracted because of temperature changes, the rainwater, dirt, soot, and sea spray that collected in the recessed drum heads was sucked in around the head of the drum.
>
> In addition, Amoco used improper procedures in refilling . . . [R]efilling was done in a rudimentary way. Crewmen would climb a ladder and pour a plastic bucket of hydraulic fluid into the tank without filtering. The bucket . . . was kept uncovered in the steering gear room which was dirty and moist . . .
>
> The bucket method of pouring fluid . . . produced agitation that would cause air bubbles . . . The steering system was never purged to remove entrapped air . . . The fluid's exposure to air . . . allowed foreign matter to enter the system. Water contamination decreases the lubricity of hydraulic fluid, which exacerbates the wear on closely moving parts . . .[40]

Only a small fraction of the issues raised over the twelve years of litigation have been considered here. The *Valdez* and *Amoco Cadiz* cases remind us of the complex relationships that arise when massive amounts of oil are shipped in tankers of dubious seaworthiness. Some of the complexity is by legal design and some is traceable to the fact that more and more oil is now shipped in supertankers, which give the best economic belt for the least buck. The risk of human error and from natural forces add more factors into the risk equation.

United States Mexican Pollution Problems

The environmental conditions in two geographical areas of Mexico have received most attention. The first is Mexico City, which remains the center of population and industry. Given the air and water problems that excessive concentration bring, it is doubtful if the city can continue to grow. For this reason Mexico, in opening the country for more foreign investment, has determined that Mexico City is not the best place for more manufacturing.

The second area is the maquiladora industrial processing zone that runs all along the 2000-mile border between Mexico and the United States. Under liberalized investment rules, maquila factories may be located elsewhere in Mexico under the same terms as those set up in the border cities. The environmental conditions at the border are taken as good evidence of what environmental conditions will be like after the North American Free Trade Agreement goes into effect.

There are, of course, pollution problems that are neither large-city nor maquiladora-based. For example, oil production, refining, related chemical manufacturing, distribution, and use in cars, trucks, and buses raise the same apprehensions in Mexico about air and water quality as they do in other places.

[40]Ibid., pp. 1297,1298.

The maquiladora experience is instructive on a number of counts: the types of pollution that are generated, the effects of pollution; and the regulatory structures that have been enacted *and enforced* by Mexico to counter pollution ("and enforced" is emphasized because the difference between law on the books and law in practice can be vast).

We turn first to journalistic accounts of environmental quality in one maquiladora zone, the very large one between El Paso, Texas and Juarez, Mexico.

POISONING THE BORDER

*Michael Satchell**

. . . Close to 2,000 plants employing about half a million people are now strung along the 2,000 miles of border from Matamoros in the East to Tijuana in the West. Here, the industrial dynamism of the First World and the poverty of the Third dovetail in what is widely viewed as a mutually beneficial arrangement. U.S. companies enjoy cheap labor and generous tax breaks from both nations; Mexican workers get steady jobs and the chance to improve their lives. The program last year pumped $3.5 billion in foreign exchange into the Mexican economy—second only to the $9 billion from oil exports. Says Alfred Rich, president of the Western Maquila Trade Association: "This is a program in which everyone benefits."

But that portrait is incomplete. The border region is paying a growing environmental price for allowing the Mexican-based firms to operate beyond the restraints of the U.S. Environmental Protection Agency and the Occupational Safety and Health Administration. Some companies admit they have moved south to avoid expensive U.S. environmental requirements. The result: They are creating more pollution there than they would in the United States. And while Mexico enacted tough new cleanup laws in 1988, scant resources have been made available to enforce them.

As the Bush administration presses forward with plans for a free-trade pact with Mexico, critics in Congress and organized labor cite present environmental and social conditions as a reason to block the treaty. They point to a report last June by the American Medical Association, which described the region as "a virtual cesspool and breeding ground for infectious disease." The AMA concluded: "Uncontrolled air and water pollution is rapidly deteriorating and seriously affecting the health and future economic vitality on both sides of the border." Treaty opponents argue that conditions will worsen if the border is fully opened. And these growing concerns about pollution have prompted several federal agencies to consider whether U.S. Trade Representative Carla Hills should order an environmental impact statement, which could delay the pact for years.

Advocates of a free-trade agreement argue that economic development, while inevitably creating some pollution, frequently spurs prospering nations to significantly improve their environmental enforcement and to enact more stringent workplace rules. In addition, President Carlos Salinas de Gortari is more determined than any predecessor to clean up

**U.S. News and World Report*, May 6, 1991. Copyright © 1991 by U.S. News and World Report; used by permission.

pollution, suggesting a brighter future for workers and the environment. But a *U.S. News* survey of current conditions reveals:

- Indiscriminate dumping or long-term storage of industrial garbage and hazardous wastes is trashing the landscape and poisoning the water and soil.
- A slumgullion of chemical-laced industrial waste water and raw sewage pumped into canals and rivers is causing widespread gastrointestinal illness, hepatitis and other long-term health problems—including a suspected increase in mortality from certain cancers.
- Massive discharges of toxic fumes have occurred in chemical plants and other factories. In the Matamoros–Reynosa region alone, seven major accidents since 1986 have sent more than 350 people to hospitals and forced thousands to flee their homes.
- *Maquiladora* employees—most of them women, who sometimes start work as young as 13 years old—are exposed to toxic substances and other workplace health hazards without being given safety instructions of basic protection like masks and gloves. There is also evidence of severe birth defects suffered by infants born to workers.

. . . The case of Yolanda Carrillo, who lives and works in the FINSA park, is typical. . . . Home is a wooden shack with a dirt floor, cardboard covering the window holes and wind whistling through cracks in the walls. A *colonia* canal flows nearby, its milky water badly polluted by industrial wastes. "Even the goats won't drink it," . . .

Interviews with dozens of employees in border communities turned up complaints of headaches, vision and respiratory problems and skin diseases caused by soldering fumes, solvents and other chemicals—particularly in the electronics-assembly industry. Some plants supply protective gloves, but few women wear them because they hamper dexterity and prevent the workers from maintaining the fast-paced production schedules. "They take advantage of us because women are more docile," says Reynosa worker Apolonia Resendiz, 39. "The men complain, so they don't get hired."

Catalina Denman, a professor at El Colegio de Sonora in Hermosillo, has studied health conditions among maquila women in Nogales since 1985. Among other problems, she finds that workers in the American-owned plants are three times as likely to give birth to infants of low weight as are other local women; half of these underweight babies are born prematurely. "We suspect toxics," Denman says. "We need to study just what the long-term effects are from being exposed to all these chemicals and fumes."

The Mallory children. Dr. Isabel de la O Alonso knows all too well. Over the past eight years, she has pieced together evidence strongly suggesting an environmental tragedy that has gone largely unnoticed. In 1982, while operating the Matamoros school for special education, she began seeing retarded children with unusual physical characteristics that fell outside well-documented conditions such as Down's syndrome. The children, with degrees of retardation ranging from mild to profound, had broad noses, bushy eyebrows, thin lips, webbed and deformed hands and feet and other distinctive birth defects. A clinical history of their families revealed a single common thread: Each of their mothers worked during her pregnancy at a now defunct electrical components maquila then called Mallory Capacitors.

Dr. de la O has located 25 living Mallory children, has documented another half dozen who died shortly after birth and suspects there are several others. The mothers all told her their jobs involved washing capacitors—small devices that hold electrical charges—in a chemical mixture they knew only as *electrolito*. As they worked with the liquid it would cover their hands and arms and splash onto their faces.

Now in charge of special education for the state of Tamaulipas, Dr. de la O suspects that the women were exposed to polychlorinated biphenyls, or PCBs, widely used in the electrical components industry before they were banned by the United States in 1979. Today, the Mallory children have passed the age of puberty, and the insidious genetic defects continue. Most of the girls have not begun menstruation, and many of the boys have undescended testicles.

In the absence of tort laws or strictly enforced EPA- and OSHA-style regulations, U.S. companies in Mexico are under little more than a moral obligation to protect either their workers or the environment. Some corporations—Union Carbide for example—are lauded by activists for treating workers and the environment well. Others can't claim the same honors. And maquila owners say attempts to operate their plants up to EPA standards are sometimes stymied by the slovenly practices of workers. "There's a lot of ignorance on the shop floor and old habits die hard," says David Flowers, head of Pulse Engineering in Tijuana.

SEDUE is the acronym for the Mexican federal agency charged with enforcing the nation's environmental laws. René Altamirano, its director of pollution prevention, vows: "The border will never become a pollution haven for the United States." But despite the best of intentions, Altamirano concedes, his agency is under severe handicaps. SEDUE has multiple responsibilities nationwide, including housing and parks, but its entire annual budget is just $10 million. While the United States will spend $24.40 per capita this year on environmental protection, Mexico can afford to spend only 48 cents—a major increase from the 8 cents it spent in 1989. Altamirano's financially strapped agency, for example, has only two inspectors in each of the six border states to investigate and ferret out environmental scofflaws.

This inadequate supervision invites problems. Under a binational agreement, maquilas are required to ship their hazardous wastes back to the United States for disposal and to notify the EPA. But transportation and EPA-approved disposal of a single 55-gallon drum of hazardous waste can cost anything from $150 to $1,000. As a result, most maquila wastes are stockpiled, buried, dumped, flushed, burned or "donated" to charities for "recycling"—an environmental charade permissible under a loophole in Mexican law. In 1989, reports the EPA's Kathleen Shimmin, the agency received just 12 notifications of hazardous-waste shipments being returned to the United States across the California and Arizona borders. Last year, the total rose to 85. "That's a small drop in the bucket," Shimmin says. "Besides jawboning, we have no legal means to force these companies to comply."

Those who monitor the maquila industry believe that big corporations, with their modern plants and their keen eye on public image, are more likely than small factories to voluntarily follow EPA and SEDUE standards. Yet controversy has even tainted some of America's giants. General Motors, for example, operates 34 border plants employing 41,500 people. Spokesman John Mueller says the auto maker has factories in 35 nations and "complies with local environmental standards and cultural norms." At the FINSA industrial park in Matamoros, some 1,200 workers at GM's $80 million RIMIR plant manufacture 6,000 automobile bumpers daily. RIMIR officials say their hazardous wastes are recycled locally or repatriated to the United States, and the plant appears to be a model of industrial efficiency and environmental rectitude. "We play by the EPA and SEDUE rules, we have to keep our nose clean and we are the environmental leader of the other maquilas," says Chuck Almquist, RIMIR's managing director.

Battle over numbers. Now, however, there is a dispute over the company's practices. Environmentalists claim their tests of discharges from the RIMIR plant showed much higher readings than GM's own tests. Last year, the Boston-based National Toxics Campaign Fund collected some 100 separate samples from discharge pipes at 22 U.S. plants in Mexico. Chemist Marco Kaltofen says NTCF's federally approved laboratory found that the RIMIR sample contained xylenes—common solvents that can cause lung, liver, kidney and brain damage—in a concentration of 2,800 parts per million (ppm). Kaltofen also says he measured discharges of ethyl benzene at 430 ppm, acetone at 56 ppm, methylene chloride at 41 ppm and toluene at 5.7 ppm. The EPA's cumulative permissible limit for all toxic organic chemicals discharged from industrial plants like RIMIR is 2.13 ppm, and some state standards are even lower. SEDUE's standards closely parallel the EPA's.

RIMIR officials say they are mystified by the high readings and are anxious to correct any deficiencies. Their routine tests conducted by an independent laboratory at roughly the same time as Kaltofen's last year showed xylene discharges of 0.56 ppm. Their tests for the other chemicals all showed readings of less than 1 ppm.

Pollution problems are evident elsewhere along the border. NTCF's tests at other plants found concentrations of hazardous materials in some samples that were too high to measure accurately. Water samples at 16 of the 22 sites, says the NTCF, violated Mexican and U.S. water-quality standards; some in Matamoros contained pH levels so severe they would cause acidic or caustic burns to skin.

Beyond the discharges, other practices by some U.S. firms also degrade the environment. Adjacent to the Reynosa industrial park that is home to several major corporations is a massive open dump that contains acre after acre of industrial detritus—plastic, metal, rubber, resins, paint sludge. Foul-smelling slime leaks from drums marked "Zenith Plant No. 12." Zenith Electronics Corp. spokesman John Taylor acknowledges that the company, which employs as many as 10,000 workers at its Reynosa facility, dumps its bathroom, kitchen, office and nonhazardous industrial trash here but says toxic wastes are returned to the United States. "This [site] is a SEDUE-licensed disposal facility and anything we do is in accordance with the law," Taylor says. "We are a good corporate citizen in Mexico." Both SEDUE and Reynosa municipal officials, however, say they have not authorized the area to be used as a dump.

The public-health threat from the kinds of solid wastes found at the Reynosa dump is generally confined to the local area. But polluted industrial effluent and untreated sewage from the exploding populations of the cities and *colonias* are migrating into the United States and creating serious water-borne health problems north of the border. In Tijuana, toxic effluent from the industrial park at Otay Mesa mixes with 12 million gallons of raw sewage discharged daily into the Tijuana River. The river then flows north before emptying into the Pacific Ocean at Imperial Beach, Calif., south of San Diego. Some 2.4 miles of shoreline are quarantined, and local officials estimate the closed beach and the area's befouled reputation cost more than $100 million a year in lost tourism and recreation opportunities.

California officials describe the New River, some 120 miles east of San Diego, as the filthiest waterway in the state—if not the entire United States. It flows north out of Mexicali, a booming maquila city, and into the Salton Sea, a large lake southeast of Palm Springs. Tests show the New River contains some 100 different industrial chemicals and 15 viruses capable of causing outbreaks of polio, dysentery, cholera, typhoid, meningitis and hepatitis.

Continuing east, the pattern is repeated. Up to 30 million gallons of untreated sewage flow out of Nogales each day and into Arizona's Santa Cruz River. An underground plume of carcinogenic solvents—including trichloroethylene—along with chromium, lead, manganese, cadmium, arsenic and mercury has badly polluted an aquifer that provides drinking water for thousands of *colonia* residents. The plume has migrated 10 miles beneath the border, forcing the closing of at least 12 wells on the U.S. side. In Texas, more than 100 million gallons of raw sewage laced with solvents, heavy metals and pesticides empty each day into the Rio Grande from Ciudad Juárez, Nuevo Laredo, Reynosa and other cities. Tissues of fish caught in the river show high levels of copper, selenium and mercury, and untreated human wastes turn the Rio Grande—literally—into the nation's biggest open sewer.

"This is a public-health disaster waiting to happen," says Dr. Reynaldo Godines, president of the Tri-County Medical Society in Laredo, Texas. The incidence of hepatitis between Brownsville and El Paso, he points out, is already six times the national average. In the El Paso *colonia* of San Elizario, 35 percent of children 8 years old and under are infected with hepatitis A, and 85 to 90 percent of adults contract the disease by the age of 35. At the University of Texas Health Science Center at Houston, epidemiological studies by Dr. Irina Cech reveal significantly elevated liver and gall bladder cancer mortality rates in the 33 counties along the Rio Grande that get their drinking water from the river. Dr. Cech suspects a combination of factors is responsible, including poor living conditions, high levels of fecal pollution in the water and toxic chemicals from the maquilas.

Heading south. One fear of free-trade opponents—industries fleeing south to avoid U.S. environmental laws and the skyrocketing costs of waste disposal—has already been validated. Between 40 and 50 furniture manufacturers, unable to meet Southern California's air quality standards, have relocated in Mexico. Joseph Haring, director of the Pasadena Research

Institute, monitors the trend and says furniture-industry employment in Southern California has shrunk from 85,000 workers in 1987 to 55,000 today. Over the next five years, he predicts, half of the region's 125,000 metal-finishing jobs will be lost to Mexico. "These industries can operate down there with fewer precautions and, in fact, create pollution," Haring says. "Almost to a man, that's what happens." Analysts say other industries that generate large amounts of toxic garbage—metal plating, chemicals, plastics, fiberglass and electronics—are also migrating south.

What are the prospects for change? Observers like Roberto Sánchez of El Colegio de la Frontera Norte believe the Mexican government, eager to foster industrialization, will never lean hard on the plants unless forced to by massive environmental tragedy. There is some possibility, though, that the Bush administration will promise a more serious and comprehensive crackdown on polluters. Trade Representative Hills will unveil a proposal this week, designed to win the backing of Democrats for her trade talks with Mexico, that is expected to seek stronger bilateral enforcement of pollution standards and suggest that U.S. assistance might be available for environmental programs in Mexico.

The Bush administration is also being pressured by critics like the Coalition for Justice in the Maquiladoras—an umbrella lobbying group—to find ways to improve wages and conditions for the Mexican workers. And American companies are coming under increasing fire from liberal lobbying groups. For industry and the Bush administration, the challenge from opponents is clear: Find ways to clean up the *maquiladora* mess, or the prospects for a free-trade agreement will get worse.

ACROSS THE RIO GRANDE: A TALE OF TWO TROUBLED CITIES

*Linda Robinson**

"This is one city, not two," says El Paso Mayor Bill Tilney, gazing out his 10th-floor window. "This is the future. We may be out of the Washington loop, but we're the front door of the change that's coming."

The future needs some attention. Across the Rio Grande, Ciudad Juárez has grown to some 1.2 million people. The number of *maquiladoras* has almost tripled since 1980, straining the region's resources. Juárez and El Paso share two aquifers, and Texas Water Commission official Hector Villa worries that the water table is dropping 10 feet a year. El Paso's hepatitis rate is five times the U.S. norm, due to ground-water contamination.

A plan worked out by Mexican President Carlos Salinas de Gortari and former President George Bush pledged $460 million in Mexican funds and $179 million in U.S. funds to clean up the border. Mexico's attorney general for the environment, Sergio Oñate, compares the task ahead with the Great Lakes cleanup. He has closed 46 polluting companies in six months. "We are spending what we can afford," Oñate says. "No one believes it's enough. The total solution requires billions, not millions."

But only one of the 1992 projects is underway—a sewage-treatment plant at Nuevo Laredo, which is now dumping 24 million gallons of raw sewage into the Rio

**U.S. News & World Report*, March 1, 1993.

Grande each day. Although 55 million gallons of sludge flow daily into an 18-mile canal beside the Rio Grande, plans for a sewage-treatment plant in Juárez are stalled. An illegal toxic-waste dump was discovered in Juárez last year, littered with 600 55-gallon drums all bearing U.S. marks. We haven't even begun tracking how far the chemical plumes have spread underground," says Villa.

A total of 163 anencephalytic or brainless babies—an alarmingly high number—have been born in Juárez in the past four years, and more than 90 more downriver in Matamoros and Brownsville, Texas. A U.S.-Mexican study has found no link to pollution or workplace hazards. But Olivia Robles, who suffers from skin lesions over most of her body, says the sores disappear whenever she takes leave from her job at Electro-Componentes, a General Electric assembly plant in Juárez. Because no link to the factory has been established in her case, either, Robles's sick pay is $2.26 a day—not enough to feed her two sons.

Other services are strained to the breaking point on both sides of the border. In Colonia Sparks, a desolate clump of concrete block on the edge of El Paso, newcomers dig their own cesspools. Gregorio Rojas bought a dilapidated trailer whose roof is held down by tires, and he is waiting for waterlines to be laid in June.

Squatters. Still, El Paso's *colonias* are middle class compared with those of Juárez. Rancho de Anapra, a Juárez *colonia*, lacks waterlines and paved roads, and most residents are squatters with no title to the land. They cannot qualify for government housing credits and instead scavenge cardboard and trash to build homes. Labor lawyer Gustavo de la Rosa scoffs at the housing credits, funded by employers: "To buy a low-income house, a minimum-wage earner would have to work 200 years."

El Pasoans like Tilney and Villa know that they can help themselves and their city by helping Juárez. They hope Bill Clinton will agree.

Questions and Comments

1. Stand back from the particulars of pollution. What is your *overall* assessment of the present problem and the likely future of the area? In what direction do solutions seem to lie? For example, would a solution be adequate that makes adjustments to the present system of location and industrialization, or is more fundamental change needed?
2. Turn now to the particulars—what has happened, who has caused what, who will clean up what?

   Who should pay for cleaning up prior pollution, and who should pay for future prevention? Possibilities include the companies, taken singly and collectively, residents of the affected areas, the local and national government in Mexico, parent companies based in the United States and other countries, and the government of the United States and other countries where the parent companies are based.
3. There are a number of types and sources of pollution: first, those that are part of the industrial process itself (workplace hazards such as those that would be covered by OSHA in the United States—fumes from soldering, toxic cleaning agents, cotton dust, and so on) and second, toxic and nontoxic wastes from the industrial process, air and

water impacts, and sanitation burdens. There is also the pollution generated by the work forces attracted to the zones and living with their families under the environmentally degraded conditions described.

This is a book about multinationals who are the principal operators of maquila factories. What is their responsibility for paying for the cleanup of prior pollution of the types mentioned? Of preventing future pollution?

4. One of the issues concerns direct effects and indirect effects. There can be little doubt about the case of particular factories generating particular pollution; under the current standards, they should pay for their prior pollution and control their own future pollution.

   But what about the pollution of the area *as a whole* by the industrial system *as a whole*? Should this be an expense borne by government, and, if so, what ought to be the government's sources of revenue to cover this "general" pollution?

   As to the pollution in the areas where workers and their families live (some of this has its source in the factories, and some comes from the householders themselves), is this pollution properly assessable to the companies who need a work force and have attracted people to the area? Or does the responsibility of companies stop closer to the factories and their known effluents, with residential pollution a problem to be addressed by government?

   To put the question another way, is El Paso–Juarez like a large "company town," where the collective duty of all companies should extend beyond the factory gates to housing, sanitation, education, and all other needs that a captive work force and their dependents require?

   If all of the costs associated with manufacturing in the maquiladora zone were to be assessed against the companies (internalized), would there be any advantage for a company to locate production there? (Review the discussion of internalizing–externalizing costs of enterprise found in Chapter 2.)

5. In the articles there is mention of contributions to be made by the Mexican and the United States governments for projects designed to abate pollution. There is also mention of the fact that companies are not expected to pay for these projects. Evaluate.

6. Are all costs reflected in the prices of products that we buy? Were all costs to be included in prices, would there be any such thing as a "cheap" Mexican-made television set?

   Who or what is subsidizing the production of so-called cheap consumer products?

Mexican Environmental Law and Practice

Visitors to Mexico who want to feel good about the environmental regulatory systems presently in place are advised to leave their eyes and noses at home. In the maquiladora areas they would see and smell the following:

> . . . large amounts of hazardous substances . . . spent solvents and thinners . . . either stored or discarded in back lots, on streets, or in town dumps ... in Nogales . . . companies . . . dumping toxic chemicals directly into municipal drains . . . in Tijuana, secret dumps and illegal recycling plants receive some of the toxic waste maquiladoras generate, while other waste is left outside to evaporate in factory yards.[41]

Official versions of reality can be distinctively more pleasant than the unofficial ones quoted above. In 1983 the United States and Mexico signed the La Paz agreement characterized by sympathetic commentators as "a framework for long-term cooperation between United States and Mexican environmental authorities in addressing environmental problems in the 'border area.' "[42] (A hard-nosed lawyer would characterize La Paz as an agreement by the two countries to try to agree, later—if they could—meaning that nothing had been agreed.)

The most critical dimension of the La Paz agreement was that each country would enforce its own laws within its boundaries, at its own discretion, and without coordination of enforcement between the two countries. (Since at the time Mexico had no comprehensive environmental policy, law, or enforcement structure, this reliance upon Mexico guaranteed that nothing was being changed by the agreement. At the time Mexico then had three environmental inspectors keeping track of 650 maquiladoras.) Multinationals, always inclined to penetrate beneath surfaces, knew that nothing noteworthy had been changed by the agreement.

In 1990, Presidents Bush and Salinas advanced a "border improvement plan," which was also long on rhetoric and short on concrete prospects. One skeptical commentator observed that "It took the agencies 200 pages to say what could have been said in one sentence: the United States and Mexico need to work harder . . ."[43] The so-called plan did have a purpose in the United States, but it had nothing to do with improving the environment in the border areas. President Bush wanted to put the best face on Mexican regulatory activism to improve the chances of getting Congressional approval of NAFTA.

Both the Bush administration and the Clinton administration expressed overall support for NAFTA, but their stances on the environmental aspects of the agreement were slightly different. The Bush administration, which negotiated the NAFTA agreement, cited the very recent developments in Mexican environmental enforcement (such as adding 100 more environmental inspectors) as proof positive that there would be zealous protection of the environment after NAFTA. Clinton, allegedly more responsive to the claims by environmentalists that the current Mexican "efforts" were only cosmetic, said

[41] S. Ables, "The Integrated Environmental Plan for the U.S.–Mexican Border, *Arizona Journal of International and Comparative Law* pp. 5, 487, 490, 491 (1992).

[42] V. Engfer, et al., "By-Products of Prosperity: Transborder Hazardous Waste Issues . . ." *San Diego Law Review* 28 (1991) pp. 819, 834.

[43] Ables, op. cit., p. 502.

that "side agreements" to the main NAFTA agreement would cure the deficiencies in the agreement regarding environmental regulation which threatened NAFTA ratification. At the time this text went to press, this side agreement was still being debated and a lower federal court had ruled that an *environmental impact statement* would have to be made before the NAFTA treaty could go forward.

The late 1980s did see a comprehensive law passed in Mexico styled along the environmental protection laws of the United States. This General Law of Ecological Equilibrium and Environmental Protection was to be administered by the Secretariat for Urban Development and Ecology.[44] It was to this agency that 100 inspectors were added as part of the new emphasis on the environment in 1991.

Before turning to the Mexican law as written and applied, one must consider the "mordida" or "bite" that has been exacted by any Mexican official with enforcement powers across all of Mexican history. The mordida is a bribe and therefore outside the parameters of polite conversation. Even in this writing, the author is reluctant to say that bribery of Mexican officials is rampant, lest it be mistaken for a general indictment of the trustworthiness of the Mexican people. First, the average Mexican will laugh in recognition–disgust at the mention of the words "la mordida," suggesting that *by Mexican standards* the mordida is (1) a fact of life and (2) repugnant. It should be remembered that many Mexicans have been on the wrong end of bribery transactions. Second, talking about bribes can preoccupy readers with character defects in Mexican officials, and understate the complicity of U.S.-based multinationals in these corrupt practices; for every prostitute there is a john, and if bribery did not result in a net advantage to polluting corporations the practice would probably atrophy in short order, given the extensive influence that foreign businesses have had in the law–government system of Mexico.

In one of the Bhopal stories, the *Wall Street Journal* reported:

> In Mexico, U.S. companies will tell you off the record that their biggest problem is Mexican pollution inspectors who arrive with their hands out and say, "This could take weeks; why not just settle it today?" . . . One had an inspector show up every day for a month, continuing to hold his hand out, never taking measurements.

Later in the same article:

> Many Latin American nations don't have well developed water disposal operations . . . Empty barrels lately have been turning up in Mexican slums, used by the poor as water barrels.[45]

The foregoing reports acknowledge that the practice of bribery is endemic in the dealings between Mexican officials and businesses. Like most other U.S. commentaries on the practice, the article fails to acknowledge the

[44]For a description of the main features of this law, see Enger, op.cit., pp. 825-833.
[45]*Wall Street Journal*, December 13, 1984.

encouragement by multinational corporations of bribery, and the willingness of multinationals to pay for advantages.

The following, more contemporary, comment both acknowledges the practice and consoles the reader with the fact that U. S. law forbids it:

> A maquiladora which attempts to pay a "mordida" violates the United States Foreign Corrupt Practices Act . . . The Act . . . prohibits the promise of money or other gifts to persuade a foreign official to use his influence in favor of a United States company.[46]

We see in the foregoing a blurring of the distinction between law on the books and law in practice.

The 1988 Mexican law on pollution seems to be adequate, as written. There are ample investigatory powers; many sources of pollution are covered; both past practices and future prevention are included, and legal and civil penalties may be assessed against violators.[47] There nevertheless remains enforcement, and one must wonder whether journalists visiting Mexico in the future will bring back the same tales of corruption and the dismal everyday life at the border.

The following article discusses a federal court challenge made by consumer and environmental groups in the United States to NAFTA. Whatever the eventual outcome of the case, it shows how the battle lines between proponents and opponents of the trade agreements will be drawn.

JOLT TO NAFTA: FEDERAL JUDGE'S RULING COULD BE DEATH BLOW TO FREE-TRADE ACCORD

*Bob Davis and Asra Q. Nomani**

WASHINGTON — With the North American Free Trade Agreement in such perilous political shape that any delay could be fatal, a federal judge here handed down a ruling that could become a death sentence for the pact.

Federal District Court Judge Charles Richey ruled that the Clinton administration must file an environmental-impact statement evaluating the effects of the trade accord—a process that could take months or even years to complete. With the trade pact with Mexico and Canada already floundering, "it would be the death of Nafta," says Julius Katz, the former U.S. trade official who negotiated the agreement. Indeed, the requirement is so onerous, Mr. Katz says "it would take the U.S. out of the business of negotiating trade agreements."

Appeal Expected

Treasury Secretary Lloyd Bentsen vows that the administration will appeal the ruling. "It violates the president's authority to carry on foreign relations for our country," he said in an interview. Though the administration will push for an expedited appeal, even that could take months. And during that time, Mr. Bentsen says, it is unclear whether the ruling "precludes us from working on side

[46]Ibid., (1991), p. 848.

[47]Ibid., pp. 825–843.

*Reprinted by permission of the *Wall Street Journal;* July 1, 1993 issue.

agreements" to the trade accord on environmental and labor issues that President Clinton has promised to negotiate.

The administration had been pushing to get Congress to ratify Nafta by the end of this year so that it could be put into effect on Jan. 1. The delays created by yesterday's court ruling disrupt that timetable.

And if a vote in Congress is pushed off into next year, Ross Perot and other Nafta foes will have more time to organize and weaken the resolve of wavering lawmakers. Hours before yesterday's court ruling, House Foreign Affairs Committee Chairman Lee Hamilton, an Indiana Democrat, warned: "Nafta will be a lost cause if the campaign for it does not begin soon and in earnest."

Leadership Doubts

The newest threat to Nafta, which comes just before President Clinton jets off to Tokyo for a summit of the leaders of the seven major industrial powers, further complicates his efforts to exercise world leadership. The administration had once hoped to make significant progress on world-trade talks and Japanese trade issues at the summit, but those hopes have faded with the fall of the Japanese government and renewed resistance from France. Now, with Nafta in doubt, "it weakens Clinton's hand" further, says Michael Aho, director of economic studies at the Council on Foreign Relations. "If we can't do Mexico, who can we do?"

In Mexico, the effects of a Nafta defeat could be profound. Mexican President Carlos Salinas de Gortari has made the prospect of free trade with the U. S. a cornerstone of his economic and political strategy, using it to cushion the blows of tough economic decisions. A delay or rejection in Nafta would both hurt him and complicate Mexico's process of presidential succession. Over the next few months, Mr. Salinas is expected to nominate his successor, which is tantamount to election because the ruling party has never lost a presidential race.

The Salinas government had hoped to have the treaty in hand before next summer's presidential elections as a sign that its policy of rapprochement with the U.S. had borne fruit. A delay would strengthen the hand of Mexican leftists, who have opposed the pact with Mexico's historic nemesis.

Retaining Investor Confidence

The immediate challenge is maintaining the confidence of foreign investors, who hold about one-fifth of Mexico's equities and half of its treasury bills. The government has relied upon the foreign investment, most of it very liquid, to fund a huge deficit in the current account. If capital inflows stop or if capital begins moving out of Mexico, the stability of the peso would be placed in jeopardy. A peso devaluation would wreck the president's economic-reform program and greatly diminish his popularity.

The news prompted a slide on the Mexican stock market yesterday, with the Bolsa de Valores's key IPC index falling nearly 2%.

Commerce Secretary Jaime Serra Pucha tried to minimize the effects of the court decision, saying the ruling "will not affect the parallel accords."

Similarly, the Canadian government, describing the case as "an internal U. S. procedure," says Ottawa "has no reason" to believe that the agreement won't be implemented as planned.

For the U.S., a defeat of Nafta could mean reduced growth in trade with

Mexico, which has become the U.S.'s third-biggest trading partner. In addition, any hope of expanding Nafta to include fast-growing nations in Latin America would evaporate. President Clinton had talked about negotiating a free-trade pact with Chile after Nafta was approved, while Argentina has been positioning itself to become a partner.

The Clinton administration vowed to fight hard to head off any consequences of Judge Richey's ruling, and sought to sound optimistic. "The fact is that it doesn't affect our commitment to negotiating both labor and environmental supplemental agreements. . . . It will not delay the legislative process," said Clinton trade representative Mickey Kantor at a White House briefing.

'Human Quality' Cited

In his Nafta ruling, Judge Richey said that U.S. law requires an environmental-impact statement for "federal actions significantly affecting the quality of the human environment"—and then cited a Bush administration study that said Nafta could worsen environmental problems already existing along the U.S.–Mexico border area. As a result, he said the Clinton administration was required to prepare a statement before it submitted the accord to Congress.

The breadth of such an environmental evaluation could be vast. Along with the border problems, Judge Richey cited concerns that Nafta's reduction of trade barriers could lower prices for farmers and ranchers, "thus creating pressure to intensify domestic production methods which will have a detrimental effect on the environment." To answer those concerns, the administration would have to review the environmental impact of Nafta on farms and ranches throughout the U.S.

In addition, Judge Richey raised the question of whether Nafta would create "pollution havens" in Mexico as U. S. companies moved their operations to Mexico to avoid more-stringent pollution requirements. The Clinton administration already had been grappling with the issue of whether the U.S. must prepare environmental-impact statements for actions that affect other countries. In March, President Clinton decided not to appeal a federal court decision requiring such an assessment before the U.S. built an incinerator in Antarctica.

In appealing Judge Richey's ruling, the administration is expected to argue that the alliance of environmental and consumer groups that brought the suit lacks the standing to sue the administration, and that the ruling represents an unconstitutional interference with the president's authority. That appeal will be heard by the U.S. Court of Appeals for the District of Columbia.

In theory, the appellate court could move the process quickly. On rare occasions, notes Arnold Reitze, a law professor at George Washington University, the court has acted on a case "literally within a matter of days."

'Not Enough'

But for that to happen, the administration probably would have to show a pending national emergency, which doesn't seem likely in this instance, Mr. Reitze says. "I don't know that this fact—that some politicians in other countries might get upset—is enough." Even the Clinton administration isn't betting on a quick review. A senior U.S. official said the administration doesn't expect its appeal to be heard until September at the earliest. And then, the official said, it could take "some weeks" for a decision.

Judge Richey, a 69-year-old Nixon appointee who once said in a speech that district courts must "say what the law is even if the law is unpopular," provided some political cover for the Clinton administration in his decision. "The court notes that this agreement was negotiated by President Bush . . . and this lawsuit should not be construed as a failure of the present administration."

The decision took the White House by surprise. By late afternoon, top White House officials hadn't yet been able to meet and discuss how to deal with the setback. Shortly before dinnertime, they held a press briefing with Mr. Kantor, who tried to assure the world that the treaty was still on track to ratification.

Other Problems Loom

The administration's best hope now, obviously, is that the courts agree to move quickly, then overturn the decision and let the process resume. But even in that case, the ruling could set off political forces that still pose big problems for Mr. Clinton, who has regularly voiced his support for the trade pact, even as his administration negotiates side agreements with Mexico and Canada to bolster the environmental and labor provisions.

For one thing, the ruling's warnings on the environmental impact of the trade deal are likely to give added ammunition to foes of the pact. Even before the ruling, the trade agreement was in trouble, especially in the House, where many of the 110 freshman lawmakers campaigned against it. Commerce Secretary Ron Brown calculates that a third of the House was "adamantly, vehemently, unequivocally opposed" to the agreement, one-third was "unequivocally" for it, and one-third was undecided. But a string of lawmakers have said that if the vote were held now, the agreement would go down to defeat.

Democratic Rep. Robert Matsui of California, leader of pro-Nafta lawmakers in the House, calls the ruling "a shocking development." He adds that "we can't have trade agreements subject to environmental laws like this." And Sen. Max Baucus of Montana, chairman of the Environmental and Public Works Committee, says the ruling means "Nafta is dead on arrival without strong environmental side agreements."

But some lawmakers, from both parties, argue that Nafta actually could benefit from a delay. Majority Leader Richard Gephardt, the most influential House member on trade matters and a Nafta skeptic, says the administration must focus on getting tough side agreements, "whether they're early or late." But for the most part, Nafta opponents were rejoicing. "I'm encouraged by this decision as it is clearly one more impediment to approval," says Sen. Howard Metzenbaum, an Ohio Democrat.

The ruling leaves in tatters the administration's strategy of dividing the environment opposition, by trying to win the Sierra Club's support for the pact. As one of three groups that brought the suit—the others were the Public Citizen advocacy group affiliated with Ralph Nader and the Friends of the Earth environmental organization—the Sierra Club seems to show that its allegiance to the anti-Nafta forces is greater than ever. "This is a defining moment for the future of trade agreements," crows Michael McCloskey, the Sierra Club's chairman. Indeed, one of the environmental groups that had said it would support Nafta, the National Audubon Society, praised the ruling.

Mr. Aho, the trade analyst for the Council on Foreign Relations, says the administration would have to rely on other environmental groups to lobby for the accord. But most of them are holding back until they see whether the administration can persuade Mexico and Canada to accept provisions that would allow the U.S. to impose sanctions if those nations don't enforce environmental and labor laws.

Both Mexico and Canada have rejected those proposals as infringements on their sovereignty—and are unlikely to make concessions so long as the U.S. can't offer assurances that it will approve the agreement anytime soon.

Robert Hormats, a vice chairman at Goldman, Sachs & Co. and a former U.S. trade negotiator, warns that if Judge Richey's ruling stands, it could be used as a precedent for pressing environmental concerns in other negotiations. "You could use an [environmental] challenge for arms-control agreements or world-trade talks."

—Matt Moffett and Dianne Solis in Mexico City and John Urquhart in Ottawa contributed to this article.

Comments and Questions

1. One of the problems in writing as book on multinationals is that the book may be out of date before it is printed. For example, this case was later overruled; NAFTA was approved in Congress and some of the issues outlined in the article were resolved, but some were not.

   There are issues raised by NAFTA that accompany all trade agreements. What does a country give up in terms of its sovereignty—including the ability to make its own laws—and the ability to control its own economic destiny, and what does it gain from the agreement? What groups come forward to support trade agreements, and what groups are most resistant to them? In this instance, the largest companies as well as the governments of Mexico and the United States were for the agreement, but labor and environmental groups did not want it. These alignments are worth following in a number of contexts.
2. Additional aspects of the article might be worth a second look.
   a. What message is conveyed by the phrase. "If we can't do Mexico, who can we do?" Would this phrase have different meanings to Mexican readers and to U. S. readers?
   b. According to the Mexican left, the United States has been Mexico's nemesis. What is a "nemesis?" Based on the U. S. presence in the maquiladora processing zones, can the validity of that charge be assessed?
   c. A very common argument made against environmentalists is that a complainant must be involved in a *case or controversy* and not simply be raising amorphous opposition to what the government wants to do.

      Should groups opposing trade agreements be able to raise their environmental concerns as done in this case, or should a court require more concrete showing of direct losses in order for a group to be allowed to sue?
   d. The case also involves a question of separation of powers among

the executive branch, the Congress, and the judiciary. Should NAFTA have been debated in the courts, or are treaties better subjects for the executive and legislative branches of the government.

e. Left-leaning theoreticians (see Chapter 3) predict that the various branches of the state will move in the same direction on matters affecting the economy rather than in opposition to one another. What about this case?

Costa Rica

The last reading in this chapter returns us to the questions raised by Rachel Carson, who found that modern agricultural practices would eventually undercut survival. In Costa Rica, substantial land has been devoted to bananas, which require heavy pesticides if they are to be exported free of spots and blemishes.

BANANA DEVELOPMENT IN COSTA RICA

*Christopher vanArsdale**

San Jose, Costa Rica—Costa Rica, named for its luxuriant Caribbean shoreline as seen by Christopher Columbus in 1502, has long been known for its rich natural endowment and unique biological diversity. Its 20,000 square miles (about the size of West Virginia) account for only .003 percent of the Earth's surface, yet are home to nearly 5 percent of the plant and animal species known to exist on the planet. Strong health and education programs, a stable democracy and the relatively large proportion of national territory set aside for parks and protected areas have bolstered Costa Rica's image as a nation concerned about the conservation of its natural resources and the just treatment of its citizens. In recent years, however, this image has begun to fray at the edges, largely as a consequence of a development model which encourages large-scale agricultural production for export in order to service foreign debt.

The banana industry, the country's second largest and an important source of foreign exchange, is currently undergoing a dramatic expansion. The government has proposed bringing nearly 21,000 hectares under banana cultivation with a target production goal of 90 million boxes of fruit for export annually. Spurred by tax breaks and incentives, banana companies are buying up new lands or re-occupying old plantations to the tune of 2,000 hectares per year, according to industry representatives. By some estimates, Costa Rica will overtake Ecuador this year as the number one exporter of bananas worldwide.

The costs of surging banana production are high, however. Expansion is hurting a withering natural resource base and local populations are defenseless against exposure to large doses of toxic agrochemicals. Costa Rican indices of pesticide contamination and deforestation are now among the highest in the world. According to conservation groups and the Catholic Church, the continued

*Christopher vanArsdale is executive director of the Costa Rican Audubon Society.
Multinational Monitor, January–February, 1991. Reprinted by permission.

unbridled expansion of the banana industry threatens to unravel the country's hard-won social and environmental achievements of the last four decades.

Poisoning the workers

Though consumers in the First World have become increasingly concerned with pesticide residues on fruits and vegetables, workers and their families in producer countries suffer the detrimental impact of exposure to agrochemicals more directly. The banana industry in Costa Rica is responsible for the largest proportion of total pesticide use in the country, accounting for 25 to 30 percent of all pesticide imports. On the plantations, pesticides account for 50 to 55 percent of the total cost of material inputs. One of the main reasons that Costa Rica has been capable of producing such a large volume of bananas for export is the heavy application of fungicides, herbicides, nematicides and other agrochemicals.

Workers, their families and local populations near banana plantations, however, are literally absorbing the real costs of this heavy pesticide use. Although accounting for only 5 percent of the nation's rural population, approximately one-third of all reported pesticide poisonings occur in the banana-growing regions. Field workers suffer 250–300 pesticide intoxications annually . . . [W]orkers continue to suffer the effects of acute pesticide intoxication, dermatitis, eye problems and chronic respiratory disorders caused by their exposure to chemicals on the plantations, and Costa Rica's nationalized health insurance company, the National Insurance Institute, is left to foot the medical bills of the poisoned workers.

[The author discusses the cases of Costa Rican workers vs. U.S. pesticide manufacturers. See Chapter 9.]

Poisoning the environment

The expansion of plantations and the heavy application of agrochemicals also take a devastating toll on neighboring eco-systems. For optimum production, plantations must have an array of drainage ditches, all of which eventually empty into the region's rivers and canals. A large percentage of the applied pesticides are washed into these waterways and carried ultimately to the sea, with toxic consequences both for aquatic life and for the local human populations which depend on the various intermediate bodies of water for sustenance. Moreover, at least 25 percent of the pesticides applied by aerial spraying never reach their target but are instead unintentionally applied directly into ponds and streams or on farmland surrounding the plantations.

All along the rivers and canals which run through dense jungle parallel to the shoreline from the city of Limon to the Nicaraguan border, the evidence of contamination from plantations is visible. Shreds of pesticide-saturated blue plastic, which comes from bags used to cover the bananas until harvest, dangle from tree branches near the canals' banks, clearly indicating the high-water mark. The bags, washed through the drainage ditches by heavy rains, also end up on beaches, clinging to coral or lodged in the stomachs of sea turtles.

Local inhabitants of the canal areas, who depend upon aquatic life for food, have become accustomed in recent years to finding large numbers of fish floating dead in the waterways, killed by pesticide poisoning. Last July, in perhaps the largest single fish-kill to date, as many as half a million fish were found belly-up in the canals. In public announcements, the Ministry of Agriculture and the Ministry of Health exonerated the nearby banana companies of all responsibility for the accident, claiming that the kill was probably perpetrated by local fishers. Local people and conservation groups are skeptical of the government's pronouncements, especially since, according to Carmen Roldan of the National University's Environmental Science Department, "public access to the official investigation was denied."

In another scene of environmental degradation, the once crystalline and vibrant array of coral reefs along Costa Rica's Caribbean shore is now nearly 90 percent dead as a result of pesticide runoff and sedimentation, mainly from banana plantations. In a 1987 study of Costa Rica's Caribbean coral, the International Marine Life Alliance states that of all activities "that have driven material, debris and wastes into the sea, none can equal the sheer annual tonnage of sediment that flows from the Atlantic-slope banana plantations." Erosion from the plantations along the Sixaola, Estrella and Matina rivers has sent volumes of pesticide-laden soil into the waterways which eventually finds its way to the shore and smothers the fragile reefs.

The impact of coral death goes far beyond its scenic value for beach-goers. Living coral is a primary determinant of productivity in shore fish and invertebrate populations, providing a sink for nutrients which form the base of a complex aquatic food chain. The coral colonies support populations of lobster, crab, snapper, bass, jack and a large variety of tropical ornamental fish, all of which represent economic resources for local communities. Thousands of people, especially descendants of Jamaican immigrants whose culture is closely tied to the sea, depend upon the continued productivity of the reefs. Local fishers say, however, that fishing for a living has become exceedingly difficult in the Caribbean coastal waters over the last 10 years. Marketable ornamental species, which are perhaps the most coral-specific of all fish in the area, are also declining in numbers. If present trends continue, the region's capacity to support ecologically sound development alternatives, such as harvesting ornamental fish, oysters and lobster, may be eliminated.

The expansion of banana plantations in the area and the visible environmental damage that results also clash with the economic interests of the tourism industry. Tourism, the third largest industry behind bananas, depends on the maintenance of Costa Rica's scenic beauty and its conservationist image abroad. The Caribbean is an extremely popular destination for sports fishing and tourism and accounts for a substantial percentage of the industry's total income. Few tourists, however, will be attracted by dead rivers and poisoned beaches. Modesto Watson, a tour boat operator in the region, comments, "I'm afraid we don't have too many years left before they kill this area off."

According to many agricultural scientists, the plantations could reduce their agrochemical use while maintaining reasonable levels of production. Integrated pest management, biological controls and other organic farming techniques offer ecologically responsible alternatives to complete dependence on chemical pesticides. Hernán Rodrígues, an expert in integrated pest management with the National University of Costa Rica, says, "the technology used on today's plantations is based on the idea imported from industrialized countries that yield increases can only come from massive use of chemical pesticides. This technological package is inappropriate for our reality." A switch to practices less dependent on agrochemicals, however, would probably require a lowering of cosmetic standards for fruit in consumer countries. None but the most perfect, unblemished bananas ever reach the supermarkets of Europe or the United States. Consumers in these countries may have to learn to accept slightly blemished or smaller bananas if pesticide contamination in producer countries is to be reduced. . . .

In the 1989 year-end Pastoral Letter of the bishopric of Limón province, church leaders issued a scathing condemnation of conditions created by the expansion of banana plantations and called on the government to re-evaluate its policy of expansion. The church leaders focused especially on the unstable and migratory nature of plantation work and its effect on families and communities: "The traditional structure of our families is suffering a grave alteration due to the instability and the economic uncertainty caused by the continual migration of family members. The consequences are becoming more and more evident: disintegration of families (incomplete families), deterioration in the education of children, conjugal infidelity and a lack of time and space for family dialogue and recreation."

Banana companies "maintain about 60 percent of their workers on a permanent basis, but keep the other 40 percent on temporary contracts which can be renewed every two and a half months," according to Carlos Acuna, former director of labor relations for the Del Monte subsidiary, Bandeco. This not only allows the companies to avoid making social security payments for nearly half their employees, but also assures that labor will remain quiescent. "Workers are afraid they will be placed on the computerized blacklist maintained by the companies and never again be able to find a job. Any worker known to have participated in union activities in the past will be denied work. I know because I managed that list when I worked for Bandeco," explains Acuna. . . .

Dr. Isabel Wing-Ching, sociologist at the University of Costa Rica . . . added that "today's bread is not for everyone." The wealth created in the production of bananas is concentrated in the hands of a few multinational companies. Though the banana industry provides needed jobs and some tax revenue for the state, the government has not scrutinized the long- and short-term costs and benefits of banana expansion. The already visible environmental and social damage caused by the activity portends more drastic consequences in the future. . . .

Comments and Questions

1. At times, people in the United States have become concerned about pesticide use in the Third World for the wrong reasons. One right reason would be the legal–ethical implications of selling agricultural chemicals in Third World countries that have been banned outright or are severely restricted in the United States. A second good reason would be concern for workforces and people living adjacent to plantations who will be poisoned by the applications of banned chemicals or

the misapplication of dangerous chemicals. (Recall the *Alfaro* case in Chapter 9 on the permanent disability of banana workers from DPCP, a pesticide banned for use in the United States.) A third good reason is the degradation of agricultural land and surrounding land and streams from chemicals and runoff of chemicals.

The wrong reason alluded to above is the fear among people in the United States that imported agricultural products will have toxic residues. The unstated inference to be drawn from the way this fear is expressed might be that it is one thing for *Third World people* and *their* land to be affected by toxicity, but it is another when the pesticides get into our own food. The not-so-cryptic racism implicit in becoming preoccupied with the purity of our own food parallels the assumption that workers in industrial processing zones are cheap lives.

Circle of Poison[48] documented the differential practices regarding chemicals and their use in the First and Third Worlds. The authors were talking about a circle, with poisoning at a number of places around the circle. In the legal sense the pesticide problem falls under extraterritoriality—whether the United States would choose to control practices beyond its borders or leave the problem to Third World countries to resolve. Concern about the quality of food in the United States forced the matter onto the Congressional agenda.

2. Multinationals enter the banana cycle at several critical places. They are involved in the production, which connects them to Third World countries and work forces there, and they are involved in the distribution of bananas in the United States and Europe. If the circle of bananas is also a circle of harm, how can the circle best be broken?
3. Costa Rica is a place of tourism as well as a place for bananas, coffee, and cattle. To the author of the article, reminding the Costa Ricans of the importance of tourism seems to be a good way to counter environmental degradation; what visitor to Costa Rica wants to swim or fish in polluted water?

   Think through the idea of tourism as a means of economic sustenance. Does tourism create problems while it resolves them?
4. "Banana plantations create jobs." Evaluate.
5. What is the role of the Costa Rican government in promoting banana production? The role of international lenders to whom Costa Rica owes its debt?
6. As between "development" and ecology, what has been the dominant orientation? What about the future tensions between banana production and environmental sensitivity?
6. Costa Rica, once largely rain and cloud forest, has been substantially deforested, with cleared land used primarily for cattle grazing. The

[48]David Weir, et al. (San Francisco: Institute for Food and Development Policy, 1981).

terrain is steeply graded, and environmentalists worry about long-term erosion problems.

7. The Amazon basin raises comparable problems of deforestation. The cycle there is deforestation, crop agriculture for a few years until tropical soils play out, and then a few years of cattle grazing until the land will no longer support grazing. Finally, the land is good for nothing—except mining. Deforestation finances clearing and clearing supports mineral rights which would otherwise belong to Brazil.

The relationship of multinationals to the deforestation of the Amazon is difficult to chart. The Amazon, like Alaska in the United States, is regarded by Brazil as a frontier and a social safety valve; there is clearly, therefore, a domestic impetus for Amazon development in those regions controlled by Brazil. Poor people, who may have been displaced by the internationalization of the Brazilian economy, may migrate to the Amazon to homestead. When they can no longer sustain themselves, they wind up in cities and abandon their land claims (as noted, these are important for mineral rights). The Brazilian government and the international lending agencies have both contributed to the stratification of economic returns from the Amazon, and supported practices which exacerbate environmental losses there. But clearly defined roles of actors, domestic and international, and firm causal connections beyond these rudiments are more difficult to establish. For an excellent survey of the Amazon, past practices, and likely futures, readers can consult *Development or Destruction: The Conversion of Tropical Forest to Pasture*[49].

CONCLUSION

In this chapter a sample of representative environmental questions have been considered. Mining, manufacturing, ocean shipping, industrial processing zones, and agribusiness suggest the range of the relationships between economic orders, now international, and the environment.

Environment is a broad term covering land, air, and water. Economic activity invariably creates some intrusion into the natural order, but Carson and others have argued that some forms of economic activity are far more intrusive and destructive than others. The word "sustainable" has been attached to words like "development," "agriculture," and "growth" to distinguish between the semi-miraculous record of industry and agribusiness, and alternative forms of economic activity that will be available for the foreseeable future.

Law as it affects the environment has within it the same tensions that obscure the distinction between useful economic practices and destructive ones. In general, the legal order has resolved these tensions in favor of economic activity rather than by imposing limits. The inescapable conclusion

[49]Theodore Downing, et al., eds. (Boulder: Westview, 1992).

from a survey of domestic law and environment issues must be that environmental sensitivities have not been matched by zealous enforcement. This is true despite the proliferation of environmental laws and the professional staff charged with their enforcement. Environmentalists are not ready to give up entirely on the rule of law, as their frustration during the Reagan-Bush years of probusiness inactivity attests, but they also know too much to be all-weather believers in the prospects for environmental wholesomeness through the rule of law.

When one moves to the international sphere, the environmental prospects become bleaker rather than brighter. Multinational mobility contributes to their bargaining power with other countries on the content of environmental law and the diligence of enforcement, even where the officials of those countries are well-intentioned. Where they are corrupt or coopted, the prospects are even worse.

The presence of unpayable international debt devalues the long-term and rationalizes the worst short-term expedients. Choices may be falsely put in terms of dying now or dying later, in which case the short-term expedient will be preferred. If the environmentalists are right, participants in ill-conceived ventures will die both now and later depending on their resiliency to harm.

"Average people," from the Amazonian Indian to the farmer and factory worker in the United States, do not know quite what to do about environmental questions. To the Indian, unprecedented practices must be just plain bewildering. By contrast, farmers in the United States no longer have a frame of reference to judge petrochemical methods; they may take them as an inexorable fact of life rather than a very recent and historically rare technique. Factory workers might fear that becoming uppity on the environment will only land them on the unemployment line. Perhaps what these groups share is a sense of powerlessness.

CHAPTER 13

Land and Land Use

In the next two chapters we stay close to land and labor. In the previous two chapters on debt and the environment we were close to these themes, but not close enough. Debt transforms economies, determining the types of land use and the kinds of industry a country will keep, and in the course of adjusting to debt, countries change the lives of people and communities. Hence debt was called the ultimate control system.

Chapter 12 on the environment brought us closer to the land, and we were reminded that nature can impose its own ultimatums: live and work within reasonable limits, or die a quick, or a slow, death. In work environments, fair and foul, people spend half their waking hours.

We are presented daily with contrasting examples of land and labor; a starving child in Somalia against a background of parched earth; a suburbanite in a fitness center trying to take off "those extra pounds." A peasant farmer stooped over with a mattock raised to strike forbidding ground; a modern farmer in a John Deere tractor, with air-conditioned cab and stereo, effortlessly plowing multiple rows in the U. S. midwest.

There is an auto worker at a plant closing, pointing to a sign that says "Will the last person to leave please turn off the lights?" Or a white collar worker, caught in the "downsizing" or "rightsizing" of a company, who has joined a support group to (1) ease the identity crisis; and (2) write a new resume. Alongside these redundant workers there is a conference of new-age business people convened by President Clinton to chart new paths for everyone in the United States.

The poverty of the Third World (now a misnomer, since there are fourth and fifth worlds that have fallen below the old third world levels) stands against the cornucopia of the U.S. shopping mall that is filled with goods sometimes made in the very places where the pictures of poverty and hunger were taken. Perplexed workers everywhere can be contrasted to international managers who are drawing new big pictures that they, and perhaps only they, will ever be able to see.

We are at once living in a world that is said to be coordinated on a world scale by the best minds, and yet simultaneously bordering on entropy (forces pulling toward chaos). Conflicting evidence should refute arrogant claims of organizational success, but the protagonists for an international commercial order (see, for example, George Ball's essay in Chapter 5) argue that there is still some mopping up to be done before all of the rough edges of international coordination can be smoothed. (Who or what is to be mopped up often remains unclear; it could be peasants standing in the way of "modern methods," workers turning off lights in abandoned factories, or mid-range executives adjusting to downsizing).

Corporate visionaries contend that notions of nationalism, sovereignty, and other parochialisms die slowly. If only people would put more trust in the multinational, everyone, everywhere, would be better off—if not at the moment, then certainly in the long run.

Antagonists to multinationals contend that in this new regime most people are living largely by their wits. Guineans (Chapter 11) know that cocoa is of interest to outsiders, but it does not feed Guineans; peasants caught in IMF–World Bank planning eventually find themselves in serious peril. Traven's farmer–basket maker (Chapter 1) knows his own corn, but does not know what income from baskets made on an industrial scale will yield to him and his family. Income can be a giant step away from food, even though those trained in supermarket psychology may not see it that way.

Redundant workers in the United States speculate on how long their unemployment, severance pay, and life savings will hold out. Unemployment provides no health plan, and they pray that they will not get sick. They could be "retrained," but they often ask a question they are not officially allowed to ask: for what job am I being trained, or is the training for the Great Employer in the sky? They could conclude that retraining is an extension of unemployment benefits, and nothing more. When workers are still on the job, they are encouraged to be loyal, but they cannot identify the object of their loyalty; experience tells them that the company could disappear overnight.

Are multinational corporations good users of land and reliable producers of industrial products? These last chapters attempt to arrive at answers—not because the questions are easy to manage and yield ready answers, but rather because it is necessary to assess the worth of multinationals given their worldwide preeminence. We must also link the dominant methods of agriculture and industry to law–government systems: where has systemic weight been thrown in the grand transformations of agriculture and industry that have occurred since World War II?

The land and labor themes are related. Peasants in a third world country who no longer farm migrate to cities, where they hope to find work in the "informal sector" (read: scratching out a living) or in newly created industrial processing zones. The movement of people from rural areas to cities (including the manufacturing centers of the United States since the turn of the century) has been the largest migration of people in all of human history. One of the claims of multinationals is that they are easing pain on both the rural and urban fronts: producing more food to feed more people, many of whom are no longer growing food for themselves; and employing otherwise jobless masses in the cities to which they have moved from the countryside.

Their opposites argue that large-scale agribusinesses have destroyed subsistence farming and in doing so have exacerbated population shifts to cities. The work that is provided by industrial multinationals there will not relieve their poverty, and will destroy work forces, rather than provide them with an alternative means to subsistence. These are the main lines of the debate, which will not be resolved to complete satisfaction in two chapters.

AGRICULTURE

Culture and agriculture cannot be separated, and it is not accidental that "agriculture" carries the word "culture" within it. The idea of farming being a "way of life" and not simply a means of subsistence should not be strange to Americans.[1] Even though "family farms" are becoming rarer by the year, the phrase still has overtones that move the emotions. These symbols find their way into television and films at the very time when small farming has all but disappeared; a benefit concert for bankrupted farmers blends art with reality, probably marking the virtual obsolescence of what the concert purports to help save.

Agribusiness has a different ring. As an agribusiness, growing crops becomes comparable to industry—bigger, faster, more, specialized, for sale, profit per units of cost, and so on—or comparable to mining—land as "resource" to be tapped until the soil plays out and there is nothing left to extract from the mine–farm.[2]

Given this psychology, agribusiness embraces no thought of farmers on the same land seven generations hence. Agribusiness makes land a means to an end and not an end in itself. In agribusiness, to ask what the land needs or wants would be a sentimental personification of nature, a useless distraction from crop management. Similarly, affection for the land will be dismissed, since it is impossible to get misty over what is equivalent to a production line or a mine shaft.

Subsistence farming, in which the vast majority of people have been engaged for most of human history, carries its own messages. Subsistence means basic, not to be trifled with, lest one die. However, "subsistence" in modern usage triggers a companion word "mere," as in the phrase *mere subsistence agriculture*. It is implied that the subsister could do a lot better, if sights were set higher; could make better use of time, energy, and the land itself. In this usage, subsistence does not look like a commendable achievement—life over death—but more like failure.

The subsister is an agricultural "underachiever." And from a larger perspective, subsistence farmers could be public enemies: what would happen if every farmer simply grew for use and sold only small surpluses in local markets far from the din of cities, and international trade? By this extension, subsistence becomes an anti-social act of selfishness.

Subsistence systems can also be written off as quaint, interesting, but irrelevantly anachronistic. The local market is the place where subsisters meet to sell and barter their surpluses. One such market can still be found at Zaachila in southern Mexico, where people don't even know that their market can best be classified as part of a "minireciprocity system."

[1]Wendell Berry, *The Unsettling of America: Culture & Agriculture* (San Francisco: Sierra Club, 1986), pp. 39–48.

[2]Ibid., pp. 7–9.

MORNING IN ZAACHILA[3]

John Bonsignore

Thursday is market day in Zaachila, the ancient capital of the Zapotec Indians of Oaxaca, Mexico. Before the bright morning sun has let the people forget the sharp mountain night, rough tables are set up in the market with everything from tomatoes and citrus fruits to local crafts. Children roam around underneath the tables, sharing the space with live turkeys and chickens, which will either be sold on the claw or brought back home for future reference. The trading is done by women, never more than 4 feet 10 inches tall, who chatter in high-pitched voices that would be shrill were it not for their muted volume.

The men are off at the livestock market, where each of them might stand all day in a dusty lot holding a lone animal on a rope, waiting for a customer. It is hard to tell who is captive of whom. If all else fails, the animal can, along with unsold turkeys or chickens, be brought back home.

Notions of efficiency cry out for a system of brokerage—one farmer holding multiple ropes, letting other farmers go free, and saving them from the tedium of waiting for a buyer who may never come. It doesn't happen; the Indians seem to know that to change the way it is done will change a way of life. And so, Time is not money in Zaachila; it is plain old time that can sometimes include long waits.

Transactions in both markets occur with less than lightning speed. To the Zapotec buyers and sellers, every article or animal is unique; something of the person who grew it, made it, or raised it resides in what is to be traded—to say nothing of the variations in the articles or animals themselves. Buyers are also unique: one, a *muy rico*, like an American who is just passing through; another, a local who will show up again on the following Thursday. The sale must take everybody and everything into account. Zapotecs can get "antsy," as the day wanes and they think about lugging untraded goods home, but they barely show it.

Two women squeak gently to one another as if they were two birds on the same branch of a tree. One has small dried fish in slightly different sizes that look pretty much alike to the untrained eye. The other has roughly one-inch-square pieces of kindling, all split from the same log. Like jewelers, the women do find differences in the fish and wood and the deal hovers over one of two fish separated from the rest, in exchange for between four or five pieces of wood. The wood lady proposes two pieces of wood for one-half a fish, motioning with her finger to show how the fish might be cut, but it is clear that the fish lady does not want to deal in fractions.

Seeing limits, she pushes the less favored of the two fish forward and gives up the smallest of the five sticks. The wood lady puts the punier stick back and removes a slightly larger stick, placing it next to her bundle without putting it away.

The fish lady in a this-should-do-it move takes the smaller stick out again, restores the larger stick, but changes the fish for the one that the wood lady had wanted in the first place. Both know that a deal has been completed; they pack up and say goodbye.

[3]This story is based on a visit to the market by the author in 1983, and on many trips to Oaxaca.

Questions and Comments

1. Is the wood–fish transaction simply "quaint," or is it "practical?" Are the people in the produce–crafts and livestock markets wasting their time?
2. Were a modern organization specialist to come to Zaachila, what changes would be recommended?
3. If Zaachila is obsolete, should it be preserved as a theme park? Would figurines of the wood lady, the fish lady, and the livestockman sell?
4. If Zaachila were replaced by a full-service grocery store, where would the wood lady, the fish lady, and the livestockmen fit in? What would the store sell?
5. In some poshy circles in the West some practices of peasants seem to be highly valued—breastfeeding, eating unprocessed foods from rustic crockery, having a home garden, wearing natural fibers, and so on. Does this mean that peasant life is being rediscovered after a long process of trial and error, or does it mean that peasant life is obsolete, and merely an art form among people who have a great deal of discretionary income?[4]
6. The observation on which the foregoing account was based took place in 1983. The women were old. Were they a monument to the past, or participants in a market with a future?

Small-scale agriculture has far fewer spokespeople than miracle farming. One stellar exception to this rule is Wendell Berry, who started his worklife on a small farm in Kentucky and returned there after working as a writer. He now writes-farms or farms-writes as the seasons of land, mind, and body allow.

EXCERPTS FROM *THE UNSETTLING OF AMERICA*[5]

In order to understand our own time and predicament and the work that is to be done, we would do well . . . to say that we are divided between exploitation and nurture. . . . The terms exploitation and nurture . . . describe a division not only between persons but also within persons. We are all to some extent the products of an exploitive society, and it would be foolish and self-defeating to pretend that we do not bear its stamp.

. . . I conceive a strip-miner to be a model exploiter, and as a model nurturer I take the old-fashioned idea or ideal of a farmer. The exploiter is a specialist, an expert; the nurturer is not. The standard of the nurturer is care. The exploiter's goal is money, profit; the nurturer's goal is health—his land's health, his own, his family's, his community's, his country's. Whereas the exploiter asks of a piece of land only how much and how quickly it can be made to produce, the nurturer asks a question that is much more complex and difficult:

[4]Susan George, "The SNOB Theory of Underdevelopment," in *Ill Fares the Land* (Washington, Institute for Policy Studies, 1984), pp. 89–93.

[5]Berry, op. cit., pp. 7–14. Copyright © 1977 by Wendell Berry. Reprinted with permission of Sierra Club Books.

What is its carrying capacity? (That is: How much can be taken from it without diminishing it? What can it produce *dependably* for an indefinite time?) The exploiter wishes to earn as much as possible by as little work as possible; the nurturer expects, certainly, to have a decent living from his work, but his characteristic wish is to work *as well* as possible. The competence of the exploiter is in organization; that of the nurturer is in order—a human order, that is, that accommodates itself both to other order and to mystery. The exploiter typically serves an institution or organization; the nurturer serves land, household, community, place. The exploiter thinks in terms of numbers, quantities, "hard facts"; the nurturer in terms of character, condition, quality, kind.

It seems likely that all the "movements" of recent years have been representing various claims that nurture has to make against exploitation. The women's movement, for example, when its energies are most accurately placed, is arguing the cause of nurture; other times it is arguing the right of women to be exploiters—which men have no *right* to be. The exploiter is clearly the prototype of the "masculine" man—the wheeler-dealer whose "practical" goals require the sacrifice of flesh, feeling, and principle. The nurturer, on the other hand, has always passed with ease across the boundaries of the so-called sexual roles. Of necessity and without apology, the preserver of seed, the planter, becomes midwife and nurse. Breeder is always metamorphosing into brooder and back again. Over and over again, spring after spring, the questing mind, idealist and visionary, must pass through the planting to become nurturer of the real. The farmer, sometimes known as husbandman, is by definition half mother; the only question is how good a mother he or she is. And the land itself is not mother or father only, but both. Depending on crop and season, it is at one time receiver of seed, bearer and nurturer of young; at another, raiser of seed-stalk, bearer and shedder of seed. And in response to these changes, the farmer crosses back and forth from one zone of spousehood to another, first as planter and then as gatherer. Farmer and land are thus involved in a sort of dance in which the partners are always at opposite sexual poles, and the lead keeps changing: the farmer, as seed-bearer, causes growth; the land, as seed-bearer, causes the harvest.

The exploitive always involves the abuse or the perversion of nurture and ultimately its destruction. Thus, we saw how far the exploitive revolution had penetrated the official character when our recent secretary of agriculture remarked that "Food is a weapon." [during the Nixion administration —Ed.] This was given a fearful symmetry indeed when, in discussing the possible use of nuclear weapons, a secretary of defense spoke of "palatable" levels of devastation. Consider the associations that have since ancient times clustered around the idea of food—associations of mutual care, generosity, neighborliness, festivity, communal joy, religious ceremony—and you will see that these two secretaries represent a cultural catastrophe. The concerns of farming and those of war, once thought to be diametrically opposed, have become identical. Here we have an example of men who have been made vicious . . . by their *values*. . . .

The concept of food-as-weapon is not surprisingly the doctrine of a Department of Agriculture that is being used as an instrument of foreign political and economic speculation. This militarizing of food is the greatest threat so far raised against the farmland and the farm communities of this country. If present attitudes continue, we may expect government policies that will encourage the destruction, by overuse, of farmland. This, of course, has already begun. To answer the official call for more production—evidently to be used to bait or bribe foreign countries—farmers are plowing their waterways and permanent pastures; lands that ought to remain in grass are being planted in row crops. Contour plowing, crop rotation, and other conservation measures seem to have gone out of favor or fashion in official circles and are practiced less and less on the farm. This exclusive emphasis on production will accelerate the mechanization and chemicalization of farming, increase the price of land, increase overhead and operating costs, and thereby further diminish the farm population. Thus the tendency, if not the intention, of Mr. Butz's confusion of farming and war, is to complete the deliverance of American agriculture into the hands of corporations.

The cost of this corporate totalitarianism in energy, land, and social disruption will be enormous. Husbandry will become an extractive industry; because maintenance will entirely give way to production, the fertility of the soil will become a limited, unrenewable resource like coal or oil. . . .

Meanwhile, the dust clouds rise again over Texas and Oklahoma. "Snirt" is falling in Kansas. Snow drifts in Iowa and the Dakotas are black with blown soil. The fields lose their humus and porosity, become less retentive of water, depend more on pesticides, herbicides, chemical fertilizers. Bigger tractors become necessary because the compacted soils are harder to work—and their greater weight further compacts the soil. More and bigger machines, more chemical and methodological shortcuts are needed because of the shortage of manpower on the farm—and the problems of overcrowding and unemployment increase in the cities. It is estimated that it now costs (by erosion) two bushels of Iowa topsoil to grow one bushel of corn. It is variously estimated that from five to twelve calories of fossil fuel energy are required to produce one calorie of hybrid corn energy. An official of the National Farmers Union says that "a farmer who earns \$10,000 to \$12,000 a year typically leaves an estate valued at about \$320,000"—which means that when that farm is financed again, either by a purchaser or by an heir (to pay the inheritance taxes), it simply cannot support its new owner and pay for itself. . . .

The first principle of the exploitive mind is to divide and conquer. And surely there has never been a people more ominously and painfully divided than we are—both against each other and within ourselves. Once the revolution of exploitation is under way, statesmanship and craftsmanship are gradually replaced by salesmanship. Its stock in trade in politics is to sell despotism and avarice as freedom and democracy. In business it sells sham and frustration as luxury and satifaction. The "constantly expanding market" first opened in the New World by the fur traders is still expanding—no longer so much by expansions of territory or population, but by the calculated outdating, outmoding, and degradation of goods and by the hysterical self-dissatisfaction of consumers that is indigenous to an exploitive economy.

This gluttonous enterprise of ugliness, waste, and fraud thrives in the disastrous breach it has helped to make between our bodies and our souls. As a people, we have lost sight of the profound communion—even the union—of the inner with the outer life. Confucius said: "If a man have not order within him/ He can not spread order about him. . . ." Surrounded as we are by evidence of the disorders of our souls and our world, we feel the strong truth in those words as well as the possibility of healing that is in them. We see the likelihood that our surroundings, from our clothes to our countryside, are the products of our inward life—our spirit, our vision—as much as they are products of nature and work. If this is true, then we cannot live as we do and be as we would like to be. There is nothing more absurd, to give an example that is only apparently trivial, than the millions who wish to live in luxury and idleness and yet be slender and good-looking. We have millions, too, whose livelihoods, amusements, and comforts are all destructive, who nevertheless wish to live in a healthy environment; they want to run their recreational engines in clean, fresh air. There is now, in fact, no "benefit" that is not associated with disaster. That is because power can be disposed morally or harmlessly only by thoroughly unified characters and communities.

What caused these divisions? There are no doubt many causes, complex both in themselves and in their interaction. But pertinent to all of them, I think, is our attitude toward work. The growth of the exploiters' revolution on this continent has been accompanied by the growth of the idea that work is beneath human dignity, particularly any form of hand work. We have made it our overiding ambition to escape work, and as a consequence have debased work until it is only fit to escape from. We have debased the products of work and have been, in turn, debased by them. . . .

But is work something that we have a right to escape? And can we escape it with impunity? We are probably the first entire people ever to think so. All the ancient wisdom that has come down to us counsels otherwise. It tells us that work is necessary to us, as much a part of our condition as mortality; that good work is our salvation and our joy; that shoddy or dishonest or self-serving work is our curse and our doom. We have tried to escape the sweat and sorrow promised in Genesis—only to find that, in order to do so, we must forswear love and excellence, health and joy.

Thus we can see growing out of our history a condition that is physically dangerous, morally repugnant, ugly. Contrary to the blandishments of the salesmen, it is not particularly comfortable or happy. It is not even affluent in any meaningful sense, because its abundance is dependent on sources that are being rapidly exhausted by its methods. To see these things is to come up against the question: Then what *is* desirable?

One possibility is just to tag along with the fantasists in government and industry who would have us believe that we can pursue our ideals of affluence, comfort, mobility, and leisure indefinitely. This curious faith is predicated on the notion that we will soon develop unlimited new sources of energy: domestic oil fields, shale oil, gasified coal, nuclear power, solar energy, and so on. This is fantastical because the basic cause of the energy crisis is not scarcity; it is moral ignorance and weakness of character. We don't know *how* to use energy, or what to use it *for*. And we cannot restrain ourselves. Our time is characterized as much by the abuse and waste of human energy as it is by the abuse and waste of fossil fuel energy. Nuclear power, if we are to believe its advocates, is presumably going to be well used by the same mentality that has egregiously devalued and misapplied man- and woman-power. If we had an unlimited supply of solar or wind power, we would use that destructively, too, for the same reasons.

Perhaps all of those sources of energy are going to be developed. Perhaps all of them can sooner or later be developed without threatening our survival. But not all of them together can guarantee our survival, and they cannot define what is desirable. We will not find those answers in Washington, D.C., or in the laboratories of oil companies. In order to find them, we will have to look closer to ourselves.

I believe that the answers are to be found in our history: in its until now subordinate tendency of settlement, of domestic permanence. This was the ambition of thousands of immigrants; it is formulated eloquently in some of the letters of Thomas Jefferson; it was the dream of the freed slaves; it was written into law in the Homestead Act of 1862. There are few of us whose families have not at some time been moved to see its vision and to attempt to enact its possibility. I am talking about the idea that as many as possible should share in the ownership of the land and thus be bound to it by economic interest, by the investment of love and work, by family loyalty, by memory and tradition. How much land this should be is a question, and the answer will vary with geography. The Homestead Act said 160 acres. The freedmen of the 1860s hoped for forty. We know that, particularly in other countries, families have lived decently on far fewer acres than that.

The old idea is still full of promise. It is potent with healing and with health. It has the power to turn each person away from the big-time promising and planning of the government, to confront in himself, in the immediacy of his own circumstances and whereabouts, the question of what methods and ways are best. It proposes an economy of necessities rather than an economy based upon anxiety, fantasy, luxury, and idle wishing. It proposes the independent, free-standing citizenry that Jefferson thought to be the surest safeguard of democratic liberty. And perhaps most important of all, it proposes an agriculture based upon intensive work, local energies, care, and long-living communities—that is, to state the matter from a consumer's point of view: a dependable, long-term food supply.

This is a possibility that is obviously imperiled—by antipathy in high places, by adverse public fashions and attitudes, by the deterioration of our present farm communities and traditions, by the flawed education and the inexperience of our young people. Yet it alone can promise us the continuity of attention and devotion without which the human life of the earth is impossible.

Questions and Comments

1. Berry classifies activity by its being either exploitative or nurturing. When we take this idea through a variety of contexts and questions, what do we learn?
   a. Do the women in the Zaachila marketplace look like nurturers or exploiters? How can one tell the two groups apart?
   b. We take a course in college and ask what we got out of it. Is that the right question? Do we think of education as a nurturing process, or is it an exploitative process?

   Are all of the institutions in which we participate of a single piece—that is, have the same cultural assumptions—or do they differ? Is school different from a farm, a church, a supermarket or a factory?

c. Reaching way back to the story of the Indian basket maker (Chapter 1), was he a nurturer or an exploiter? What of his counterpart, Winthrop of New York?
d. As one looks across the chapters of this text, does it appear that domestic and international enterprise has been premised on nurture or exploitation?
e. Is it possible to be a nurturer in a world premised on exploitation— dog-eat-dog, as it is sometimes put? Is the world of business by nature exploitative such that a person should not be surprised to find that characteristic predominating?
f. Would there be any international relationships at all if Berry's vision of community and local nurturing were to prevail?[6]

If international relationships were not ruled out altogether,what would relationships premised on nurture look like, and how close would such an image be to the configurations that contemporary international relationships have taken?

g. If each person has an equal opportunity to exploit others and everyone knows that exploitation is the rule of the day, is there any harm done?
h. Can nurturing be saved for home and private life, or must it be incorporated into the work day?
i. Adam Smith, in thinking of markets as exerting an invisible hand of control over the excesses of individuals, put less reliance on human character and virtue and more reliance on structures. A competitive market, in his judgment, curbed the excesses of those who might otherwise extort or exploit.

Are Smith's ideas of individual virtue and structure incompatible with Berry, or can the two explanations be made consistent with one another?

In thinking about what is best for us and the groups we frequent, is it better to place reliance on character or structure, or a blend of the two?[7]

Are the potential excesses of multinational corporations best controlled though character–virtue or controlled through structure such as legal regulation?

2. For an exploiter to be successful, it takes a patsy or an exploited party. What makes people susceptible to exploitation? (If it helps one can think back to Franz Kafka's parable,"The Refusal" in Chapter 1 and John Gaventa's discussion of powerlessness in Chapter 3.) Does Berry offer an escape route for people who do not accept being patsies?

[6]Wendell Berry considered this question in "Out of Your Car, Off Your Horse," *Atlantic Monthly*, February, 1991.

[7]For a discussion of this theme, see G. Orwell, "Charles Dickens" in *Collected Essays* (New York: Anchor, 1954), pp. 55–111.

3. What is it about physical labor that makes it offensive to many? "Labor-saving devices" seem intimately connected to the American dream. If given a choice between rototilling a garden or digging it by hand, would there be advantages to choosing to work by hand? Make a list of advantages and disadvantages of each method.

As might be inferred from the foregoing, Berry has not been enamored of modern farming techniques and agribusiness. In another chapter of the book from which the prior excerpt was taken, Berry critiques the central tenets of modern agribusiness:[8]

. . . [A] confirmed habit—even the theoretical context—of agricultural expertise, is suggested by an article in the October 1974 issue of the *American Farmer* (voice of the American Farm Bureau Federation). This article is about a "dream farm" of 2076 A.D.—a model constructed by a group of South Dakota State University agricultural engineering students. This farm of the future is described as follows:

"The farm of 9 square miles will use only about 1,800 acres, less than one-fourth of which is for production. The remainder will be a buffer or 'relaxed' zone for recreation, wildlife, and living under the 'blending with human values' aspect of the overall planning.

"Livestock will be housed (and products processed) in a 15-story, 150' x 200' building. It will also contain power facilities, administrative headquarter, veterinary facilities, repair shops, refrigeration and packaging units, storage, research labs, water and waste treatment facilities. At capacity, the high-rise building will house 2,500 feeder cattle, 600 cow-calf units, 500 dairy cattle, 2,500 sheep, 6,750 finishing hogs, space for 150 sows and litters, 1,000 turkeys, and 15,000 chickens.

"Crops will be grown year around under plastic covers that provide precise climate control in three circular fields each a mile in diameter. At any given time, regardless of weather, one field or crop will be in the planting stage, another in the growing state, and the third in the harvesting stage. Exceptionally high yields mean that only a fourth of the total 5,760-acre farm area would be needed for agricultural production.

"Only a half-inch of water will be needed for each crop. That's because evapotranspiration from growing plants would be recycled under massive, permanent plastic enclosures . . .

"Underground magnetic patterns, arranged to fit crop or machine, will attract specially-treated seed blasted from overhead tubes in the enclosures.

"If tillage is needed, it will be done by electromagnetic waves. Air-supported, remotely controlled machines will harvest entire plants because by 2076 A.D. the students believe multiple uses will be needed and found for most crops.

" 'Trickle' irrigation is to be electronically monitored to provide subsurface moisture automatically whenever needed.

"Recycling human, animal and crop wastes will be a key to the operation of the farm. Carbon dioxide from the respiration of live stock is to be piped into the circular enclosures for use by crops in

[8]Berry, op. cit., pp. 67–70.

exchange for the oxygen transpired by crops for use by livestock.

"Weed control is not anticipated as a problem because weeds would be eradicated under the field covers."

Soon after reading this article I wrote to Dr. Milo A. Hellickson, Associate Professor in Agricultural Engineering at South Dakota State University. My letter asked the following questions:

"1. Was any attention given to the possible social and economic effects of the projected innovations? Was it envisioned that this sort of farm would entirely replace the relatively small owner-operated farm? What would be its effect upon population patterns? Would it make food more or less expensive? What would be the energy requirements of such an operation, and what would be the sources of the required energy?

"2. What political consequences were anticipated? What, for instance, would be the impact...upon the doctrines of personal liberty and private property?

"3. What would be the effect upon the consumer? Would there be more or less choice of variety and quality?

"4. What would be the effect on the environment? For instance, roofing so large an acreage would present an uprecedented drainage problem. What did your students propose to do with the runoff? Would such a farm be built only in a desert area, or would it be feasible in an area of abundant rain fall?"

I received a prompt and very cordial reply from Dr. Hellickson, who responded to my questions as follows:

"Attention was given to the social and economic effect of the innovations. Essentially we feel that these developments would most likely fit individually into various farming operations and would not necessarily be all concentrated into one farmstead. As a matter of convenience in construction and so as not to alienate any particular phase of the agricultural industry, the model is constructed incorporating all the areas. Therefore, it would be equally possible in the future to maintain the smaller owner-operated farm and this then would cause little change in the distribution of the population. Specifically, we are thinking of energy captured from the sun, solar energy, as the sole energy source. I wouldn't even attempt to make a guess concerning expense, since this is such an area of dynamic change.

"Hopefully the above paragraph also answers question two. We are in no way advocating the elimination of the free enterprise system or the reduction of privately owned land.

"As per question three, I would see little change in the variety or quality of products available....If anything, quality might be improved through the reduction or elimination of disease and through better handling systems.

"Hopefully this system would improve the environment by eliminating air pollution from the livestock building and also eliminating erosion from the cropped area. Runoff from the roof areas is proposed to be used as the water source for the irrigation system and for livestock and humans. Naturally, adequate facilities must be included to handle unusually large rainfalls."

There is no quarreling with the professed aim of either of these farms-of-the-future, which is an abundance of food. And they have other aspects that are praiseworthy: the conversion of wastes into fertilizer and the reliance of the South Dakota model on solar energy. But we are still left with the question of what will be the costs, not just of construction and materials, which would be passed onto the consumers in the price of food, but costs of other kinds: social, cultural, political, nutritional, etc. And we still must ask if there may not be less costly ways to achieve the same ends.

The issue that is raised most directly by these farms-of-the-future is that of control. The ambition underlying these model farms is that of total control—a totally controlled agricultural environment. Nowhere is the essential totalitarianism and the essential weakness of the specialist mind more clearly displayed than in this ambition. Confronted with the living substance of farming—the complexly, even mysteriously interrelated lives on which it depends, from the microorganisms in the soil to the human consumers—the agriculture specialist can think only of subjecting it to total control, of turning it into a machine.

Questions and Comments

1. At one point the agricultural engineer referred to dynamism in agriculture as a reason why costs were hard to estimate with precision. How adaptable would his model farm be to dynamic conditions? Does the creation look static or dynamic?
2. How would the model farm be likely to look five years after it was unveiled?
3. What is the role of "labor saving" in the plan? In many older elementary school books there used to be charts demonstrating that it takes far fewer farmers to feed the nation using newer methods as compared to older ones. At the left end, representing earlier history, the charts usually had many little black silhouettes of farmers, and at the right end—modernity—far fewer silhouettes. See, boys and girls, how many people have been freed up by modern techniques!

   The numbers were rigged. Should people who drill for oil be included as farm labor when farms run on diesel or gas? People in the factories who make farm implements? Truck drivers, train crews, and merchant mariners who haul product? Food processors? Clerks at grocery stores? Bureaucrats in the Department of Agriculture? One must wonder, were there to have been a complete counting of "agricultural labor," whether the charts that amazed schoolchildren for so many years could possibly show such grand gains.

   Taking as an example the "model farm" imagined by the South Dakotans, what would be the labor necessary to create and operate the farm? To process and distribute its output?
4. Do agricultural engineers really think the way the model suggests, or is the 2076 farm just extracurricular speculation?
5. Berry developed the following list to evaluate when a new tool was worthy of adoption:[9]

[9]Wendell Berry, *What Are People For?* (Berkeley, CA: North Point Press, 1990), pp. 171, 172.

1) The new tool should be cheaper than the one it replaces.
2) It should be at least as small in scale as the one it replaces.
3) It should do work that is clearly and demonstrably better than the one it replaces.
4) It should use less energy than the one it replaces.
5) If possible, it should use some form of solar energy, such as that of the body.
6) It should be repairable by a person of ordinary intelligence, provided that he or she has the necessary tools.
7) It should be purchasable and repairable as near to home as possible.
8) It should come from a small, privately owned shop or store that will take it back for maintenance and repair.
9) It should not replace or disrupt anything good that already exists, and this includes family and community relationships.

Evaluate the list. Review the "farm of 2076," keeping his criteria in mind.

The U.S. Baseline

In prior chapters the point has been frequently made that an intense study of the United States experience can offer valuable leads for studying other places. This would seem to be especially true for agriculture, since the United States has been preeminent in producing vast agricultural surpluses. Taken as a self-evident success story, the U. S. system of agriculture–agribusiness might seem to be ready for export to other places "at earlier stages" of "development."

The words and phrases are in quotation marks because many scholars have refuted the idea of stages of development, and the belief that countries everywhere ought to be inching their way to the exact shape of United States agriculture, with variations by locale, climates, and crops, but no variation in technique.[10] Moreover, many scholars have learned the lessons that have been written on the bodies of Third World people—the preeminence in certain crops carries the price of alternatives forgone, and the now highly visible charges—ecological, cultural, social, and personal—that accompany one-dimensional agriculture.[11]

Three of the many possible themes preoccupy us here: (1) the way U.S. agriculture has changed from farming to agribusiness; (2) the place of the family farm in the transformation, and (3) the role of the U.S. law-government system in facilitating the main lines of contemporary agriculture.

[10]Peter Klaren et al., *Promise of Development* (Boulder, Col.: Westview, 1986), 3–31; A. Revel et al., *American Green Power* (Baltimore: Johns Hopkins, 1986).

[11]Frances Lappe, *World Hunger: Twelve Myths* (New York: Grove, 1986).

Highlights of U. S. Agricultural History

Farming has undergone profound transformations since the nineteenth century.[12] Whereas once a farmer would have been interested primarily in producing for use and selling or trading on the market whatever surpluses occurred, most modern farmers use little or nothing of what is produced. Almost everything goes to market for cash with which to pay all expenses, right down to the family groceries purchased at the nearest supermarket. The once common expression "At least on a farm you can always eat well" has no contemporary meaning, if it refers to home-grown food.

The farmer grows a single crop or perhaps two crops—for example, hogs and corn, or corn and soy beans—and sells them as commodities to others who will process them further into a wide variety of products. There is little organic method employed, such as manures generated by farm animals, and there is no crop rotation. Gone is the oats-clover-corn rotation that marked Corn Belt farming for many years. Rather, the farmer purchases all of the necessary inputs—seeds, fertilizers, pesticides, herbicides—and farms with equipment run on gasoline or diesel. The outputs of monoculture have been staggering, but by ironic twist, farmers have staggered along with their outputs; fewer and fewer remain, and those that remain are larger and larger, and more and more at the mercy of market forces across the globe.

Statistics reflect the decline in the numbers of farmers and larger land holdings for each farm. The number of farms has declined from a high point in 1930 of 6.5 million averaging 151 acres each to 2.1 million in 1987, averaging 462 acres. For farms with sales over $10,000, the average size was 782 acres that year. The top 5 percent of the farms had 50 percent of the sales in 1982. The disastrous 1980s took still more farmers out, reducing the number of farmers and concentrating farming even further. Now up to 50 percent of the farms are rural residences, so named because families that live on them must support themselves through nonfarm income. The farms in this group account for only 3.2 percent of all farm revenues.[13]

Agricultural labor and demographics reflect the changing structure of U. S. farming. During the 1930s the nation was still 50 percent rural. In 1920, 30 percent of people lived on farms but by 1987 the number had fallen to two percent (5 million people, including 1.05 million hired farm employees).[14] The mass migration of people from rural areas to cities and industrial employment matches the decline of farm populations and rural employment (on and off the farm). The 1980s intensified the long-term trend; a combination of interest rates, increasing input expenses, declining prices, unpayable loans, declining land values, and foreclosures applied an almost final blow to smaller farmers.

[12]D. Constance et al., "Agrarian Policies and Agricultural Systems in the United States" in A. Bonanno, ed. *Agrarian Policies and Agricultural Systems* (Boulder, Col.: Westview, 1990), pp. 9–75.

[13]Ibid., p. 18.

[14]Ibid., pp. 14, 17.

Surviving farmers, now called *commercial* farmers since the abandonment of production for home use and their focus on specialized crops for market, are caught between two sets of market forces beyond their control. On the input side, when they buy seed, tractors, chemicals, or whatever, they confront oligopolistic sellers whose prices are not the result of competition. On the output side, farmers are increasingly encountering oligopsony, the name for relatively few buyers who, like the suppliers of inputs, are not restrained by the forces of market competition.[15] Meanwhile, the farmers themselves are in full competition since even though farms are larger and larger, no single farmer can have any effect on supply and price; it is for this reason that the government for the last 50 years has had to enter the scene with price supports or supply reduction programs lest the farmers, regardless of size, disappear. The alternative of making other phases of the farm-to-market cycle more competitive was not chosen, as might be inferred from Chapter 6 on antitrust.

In addition, once farmers are integrated into markets that are now worldwide in scope, they have very few options. The farmer has land and its output as principal assets. As was noted in the earlier materials on debt, when income streams to farms are full, land values and the ability to borrow reflect this good fortune. When prices fall, land values fall, loans are called, farms are foreclosed, and there is one fewer unit of farm production.[16] (In most instances farm failures result in further concentration of land holding in larger units.)

One of the most interesting dimensions of the changing farm structure has to be the way that it closely parallels what has gone on in the rest of the world—decline of subsistence or mixed agriculture, increasing mechanical and petrochemical intensity, declining numbers of farmers and farm laborers, and more and more people migrating to the cities. A summary of the history of U. S. agriculture, which might be the summary for many other countries throughout the world, follows:

> With the rapid decapitalization of U. S. agriculture in the middle 1980s, the fate of the family farm in a world of large, specialized commercial farms, transnational input and processing oligopolies, and vertically integrated corporate farms is called further into question. A dual agriculture is emerging, consisting of a small percentage of large, integrated commercial and corporate farms which grow most of the food and a large percentage of smaller, marginal farms dependent on off-farm income which grow a small amount of food.[17]

[15]Ibid., pp. 52, 53.
[16]Ibid., pp. 46, 47.
[17]Ibid., p. 52.

FARMING AND THE U. S. LAW-GOVERNMENT SYSTEM

Domestic Law and Policy

From practically its inception the U.S. government has been involved with various agricultural policies and with interest groups in different degrees of political strength. At first, agriculture was part of national land management; subduing Indians, settling the frontier, and homesteading. Next there was the general promotion of agriculture and scientific methods in agriculture; transcontinental railroads, land grant colleges, agricultural experiment stations, and so on. There followed a mediation by government between farmers and their antagonists—railroads, business trusts, and banks.

With the growing difference among farmers—family farmers on the one hand and commercial farmers on the other—Congress had to choose whether farmers *in general* were worthy of abiding support, or if only *commercial farmers* should be subsidized. The commercial farmers prevailed, even though many of the subsidy programs affecting prices and the supply of agricultural products appear on the surface to be of equal application to both commercial farmers and family farmers. This preference is reflected in the strata of farmers who have received the most from U. S. support systems: the largest commercial farmers got the most; smaller farmers went bust on their own, without subsidies.

As agriculture became agribusiness, other power blocks entered the political economy of food. Farmers demanded an adequate relationship between costs and revenues; urban dwellers, voicing their positions through consumer advocacy groups, wanted cheap food. Later when it became apparent that petrochemically intensive agriculture was contributing to soil erosion, water pollution, and sometimes contaminating the food supply itself, the demands of environmentalists were voiced in Washington. When exports of agricultural products became important to eliminate surpluses, support friendly countries, and balance trade, the large commodity associations asserted themselves more forcefully in Washington (for example, the National Corn Growers Association or the American Soybean Association).[18]

So did the very large privately held companies in the world grain trade. For more than a century, five companies, all privately owned, have controlled virtually all of the world grain trade. (Since a merger of Matsui, a Japanese multinational, with Cook, a small United States-based company, there are now six principal companies.) Thus whether it is Canadian wheat or Australian wheat or United States wheat that is moving in trade, the same small group of grain merchants handle all significant trading and logistics between producers of the commodities and end users. In the case of soy beans, Cargill and Continental Grain control most of the beans grown in the United States. Once the crop is off the farm—in elevators, on barges, in processing plants, or on board ships as oil or meal—these major grain traders will be involved.[19]

[18]Ibid., pp. 19–37.

[19]Dan Morgan, *Merchants of Grain* (New York: Penguin, 1980). For additional discussion, see Chapter 4.

In summary, markets had changed from the strictly local to the national to the international. A political concern for farmers in general yielded to a concern for commercial farmers who had adapted to modern techniques. Commercial farmers then found themselves integrated into an international market of specialized commodities and big traders. Over time, farmers as a group lost political power and influence, except as it could be asserted though *commodity-based* associations; farmers for political purposes were soybean or cotton growers and not simply farmers. Demographics also hurt in Washington: rural areas experienced long-term population declines and lost political influence relative to cities and suburbs.

International Aspects

Debt, Trade, and Agriculture As noted, the multinational grain companies operate in all countries of the world and organize trade independent of the specific countries where large amounts of grain and related commodities are produced: Argentina, Canada, Australia, Brazil, or the United States. The case of Brazil and the introduction of soybeans there can be instructive. Prior to Brazilian production the United States was far and away the largest producer and exporter of soybeans.

After the late 1970s, Brazil had serious international debt problems. One of the ways out of debt is to move from crops grown for local use and sale to crops of interest on the international market where foreign exchange can be generated. The promotion of extensive soy estates in southern Brazil changed land and land use in Brazil, moving the country in the same direction that has already been outlined for United States agriculture; aggregation of land formerly in subsistence or mixed farming, larger and larger producers on larger tracts, with petrochemically and mechanically intensive methods.

The product of Brazil (bought by international grain merchants like Cargill) competes on the international market with soy grown in the United States (much of it also bought by Cargill and a handful of other companies). It can already be seen that the partial "solution" of Brazil's debt problem complicates U.S. agricultural law and policy, and U. S. export strategies. But the business prospects of the multinational grain companies may be improved by virtue of having multiple sources for soybeans.[20]

Other Latin American debtors figure in the international trade in agricultural commodities. Under the usual IMF conditions, indebted countries are expected to cut imports, using the returns from austerity to pay debt. This takes them out of the market as buyers of United States-grown agricultural commodities (and industrial products as well).

What arises from the foregoing is an irreconcilable conflict of policies within and between all of the countries involved. Brazil may pay more debt, but in doing so may be ruining the prospects of feeding its people, or balancing population in rural and urban areas. As it "solves" one problem, it gener-

[20]Ibid., pp. 288, 308, 326–328; Revel, op. cit., pp. 34, 139, 182; Lappe, op. cit., p. 124.

ates deep social unrest, especially as Brazilians realize that the returns from agricultural transformations in Brazil are highly stratified.

With respect to other heavily indebted countries, the United States wants international debts paid *and* a market for U. S. exports (in which agricultural exports figure heavily). It cannot have both, since countries cannot limit imports and buy U. S. agricultural products at the same time. United States agricultural law and policy designed to promote domestic stability in agriculture via international trade are more than offset by international debt policies which curtail U. S. exports and weaken U. S. farm prices.

This small illustration suggests that the integration of agriculture into a global economy will not necessarily produce clear-cut gains; there will be an identifiable stratification of the gains and losses when production and marketing are organized in this way. Some profit handsomely—operators of the large soy estates in Brazil, equipment and input suppliers, international grain merchants. But small farmers in Brazil may lose, as will some farmers in the United States. The U. S. government will be caught between fundamentally irreconcilable policies.

THE LESSONS OF PUBLIC LAW 480—FOOD FOR PEACE

United States Public Law 480—later named Food for Peace—has had a profound effect on farming, the distribution and sales of grain and other commodities; on ocean shipping; on foreign relations with other countries, friendly and otherwise; and on the food and nonfood policies of other countries. At times it has been pivotal in determining who eats and who goes hungry both in the United States and abroad. One can only wonder why such a monumentally important piece of legislation has been bypassed not only in professional legal education but also in legal education for nonprofessionals. The author does not know of a single legal textbook which includes any coverage of this law at all.

For the skeptical, only a few facts need be kept firmly in mind to establish the importance of Public Law 480. Over the first 20 years of its operation, 245 million tons of wheat, 177 million tons of wheat products, 43 million tons of feed grains and over 13 million tons of rice were shipped, along with other commodities.[21] The consequences, domestic and international, can be fully documented only by the scrupulous historian. Who got the proceeds and benefits, and where, would make for still other labyrinthine investigations.

Public Law 480 sits across many U. S. problems and interest groups. First, there have been chronic agricultural surpluses. Over almost a century, as farming became more and more oriented toward specialized crops for market, there has been too much of a number of commodities for markets to absorb.

[21]U.S. Congress, Senate Committee on Agriculture, *American Foreign Food Assistance: Public Law 480,* 94th Congress, Second Session, 1976 p. 34. Cited hereafter as Senate Committee on Agriculture, *Food Assistance,* 1976.

A second element in the farm and food sector is the United States government, which since the 1930s has been the buyer of last resort of agricultural surpluses to support agricultural prices. The government, through P.L. 480, uses the largest grain trading companies to dispose of some of the surpluses, and finances the movement of U. S. agricultural products internationally.

A third element is ocean shipping. American ship owners prefer foreign crews on board ships to hiring American merchant mariners at greater cost. American merchant seamen need work, but, as we learned, have been priced out by crews from other countries who sail on ships of foreign registry.

A fourth element is the State Department of the United States, which throughout the post-World War Two period has wanted to keep the world free of "unfriendly governments," and open to commercial penetration by businesses based in the United States and other industrial countries.

A fifth element is the foreign country that may need food regularly or from time to time, and that may be friendly or unfriendly to the United States. In many cases they have no "hard currency," the name given to money that traders will accept.[22]

A sixth element is people, mentioned last because they often come last in the calculus of food and its distribution. Existing simultaneously have been conditions that on the surface appear to be unthinkable: surpluses, satiation, and abundance for some; shortages, chronic hunger, and malnutrition for others. (A sad fact of domestic and international nutrition is that food moves toward money and not need; the need for food is not always matched by the money to buy it.)[23] With neither food nor money to buy it, people have little to lose by rebellion either against their own governments, or outsiders.

Enter Public Law 480, first passed in 1954, and amended numerous times. The law in some form or another addresses all of the foregoing, and in its totality establishes what can only be described as a major element of the political economy of food.

The plan under P.L. 480 was to move agricultural products out of the United States to countries we wanted to help—that is, who were our allies in cold or hot wars and who were willing to create trade relationships with the United States instead of closing themselves off as sources of raw materials or as markets for exported goods. For example, countries like Korea were seen as places for "offshore" production by United States-based multinational corporations, and to the extent that such countries needed food or had suffered dislocations from industrialization, P.L. 480 commodities such as rice could be made available.

What about money? The P.L. 480 program was funded by United States taxpayers. It is important to remember that actual money never left the country, although many commodities did. Under P.L. 480 the United States government can agree to either grant loans to a country for the purchase of

[22]Revel, op. cit., pp. 161–167.
[23]Morgan, op. cit., pp. 443–463.

food, or accept local currency to finance food purchases. This made shipment on credit or for internationally unacceptable money possible. (Those in the grain trade granted no credit and did not get "local currencies"; they were paid in full. The accumulation of loans, even when made at less than market rates of interest, promoted dependency on the United States, and contributed to longterm debt problems, considered earlier.)[24]

The grain traders made profits on storage, transportation and sales, with payment at all stages coming from the United States government.[25] (This says nothing about the profits made on the grain exchanges of the world, where the leading grain traders are always a presence, or gains on export subsidies which are paid to sellers of United States agricultural products when world prices are lower than domestic agricultural prices. Farmers have long complained that the "middle men" have been the chief beneficiaries of governmental programs like P.L. 480. They claim that none of the traders have gone out of business, but many farmers have.)

What about the owners of U. S.-flagged vessels, who might lose grain shipments to foreign-flagged vessels that operate more cheaply? A provision of P.L. 480 requires that 50 percent of the products shipped be carried in U. S. registry ships. United States registry simply means that U.S. crews will be hired to run the ships and not bargain crews from other countries. This subsidy is also paid by the U. S. government.[26]

What did the United States do with the local country currency it sometimes received for P.L. 480 food shipments? The following were the permitted purposes:

Promoting economic development

Developing new markets for American farm products

The payment of U. S. obligations abroad

International educational exchanges

Procurement of military supplies and military expenditures

Carrying out programs of U. S. government agencies

Purchases of goods and services

Purchases of strategic materials [27]

What P.L. 480 did in the early days of its operation, then, was create a minitreasury of foreign currencies from which many activities, some commendable and some not so commendable, could be carried out. Everything from funding population control (to help development) to financing the military of cooperative regimes and discouraging uncooperative ones, could be done with 480 money.[28]

[24]Senate Committee on Agriculture, *Food Assistance* 1976 (See note 21, above.) pp. v, vi; 1-3.

[25]Morgan, op. cit., pp. 146, 173, 176–178.

[26]Report, Government Accounting Office, Public Law 480, September 1985, pp. 13, 18, 23, 25.

[27]For a brief history of Public Law 480, as amended, see Senate Committee on Agriculture *Food Assistance,* 1976 (note 21, above) pp 5–15.

[28]Morgan, op. cit., pp. 301, 338, 339, 342, 376.

The leverage traceable to food aid led some people to wonder whether the United States had committed itself to help feed a hungry world, or whether food was just another device by which the United States could insinuate its way into the internal affairs of other countries, while dumping unwanted surpluses.[29]

The relationship between food aid and war was even more direct when one considers P.L. 480 and the fighting in Vietnam. Food shipments (in this case rice, which because of its being in chronic surplus in the United States, was covered under P.L. 480) were made in huge quantities to South Vietnam and Cambodia to support the war effort. In 1974 just before American troops pulled out, Cambodia and Vietnam got $400 million of the total of $425 million going to East Asia.[30] Two years later, Vietnam and Cambodia yielded to Korea, which became the sole recipient of P.L. 480 rice shipments to East Asia. The connection between P.L. 480 rice for Korea and the commercial penetration of Korea by U. S.-based multinationals should not be missed.[31] Nor can the substitution of U.S. grain for indigenous agriculture be overlooked; P.L. 480 both established international markets and undercut the potential for locally produced food supplies.[32]

The intention here has been to illustrate the close connection between U. S. agricultural policy and law and international relations of all types. It is difficult to reach the limits of the effects of P.L. 480, since food "aid" can take the student down so many paths of geopolitics.

AGRICULTURAL DIMENSIONS OF NAFTA

The environmental and labor aspects of NAFTA have received most attention, but what will be the effects of NAFTA on agriculture in the United States and Mexico? It depends on the commodities one is talking about, but in general Mexican agriculture will be drawn further into international trade in commodities and further away from small scale-farming. Very large agriculture in the United States will ship more commodities as the Mexican tariffs decline, including corn, oils, and beans which are staples in the Mexican diet.

For other facets of U. S. agriculture the picture is different. Winter vegetables will come in greater quantity from Mexico, as will citrus fruit. Opposition based on this prospect was heard frequently in Washington from Florida and California growers. Distributors of fruits and vegetables, like the distributors of grain spoken about earlier, will welcome enlarged sources of supply.

[29]Ibid., pp. 334–365.

[30]Senate Committe on *Food Assistance,* 1976 (note 21, above) p. 37.

[31]For the connection between P.L. 480 rice and Korean development, corruption in U.S. and Korean politics, and profits for companies specializing in the rice trade, see Morgan, op. cit., Chapter12.

[32]Revel, op. cit., pp. 166, 167.

[T]estimony on NAFTA reflected the transformation of U. S. agriculture. "Farm" groups have declined in importance relative to the myriad specialized crop associations who testify in Congress on the impact of NAFTA on their corner of the agricultural world. In addition to these heavies—the American Soybean Association, the National Cattlemen's Association, and so on—there are smaller groups, for example, the California Avocado Commission and the Florida Fresh Fruit and Vegetable Association. The latter association has overlapping membership with the national United Fresh Fruit and Vegetable Association. In that instance, the national association is for the treaty and the more local association was not, a division indicative of contemporary agriculture being broken into subsets and not of one voice on trade policy.[33]

The largest agricultural associations were for the treaty. Their testimony before a number of Congressional committees can be captured in a few paragraphs:

> Prospects for U. S. soy exports are bright . . . U. S. soybean growers and processors greatly value their present commercial relationship with Mexico. Mexico is already the fourth largest export market for U. S. soybeans, the fifth largest for U.S. soybean meal and the sixth largest for U. S. soybean oil.
>
> Both ASA (American Soybean Association) and NOPA (National Oilseed Processors Association) share enthusiasm for the NAFTA . . . Mexico currently imposes an import duty on soybeans and soybean oil . . . ASA and NOPA support reduction and elimination of Mexico's import duties on soybeans, soybean oil and soybean meal . . .[34]

Other associations divided along the line of the prospects of serious competition from Mexican product as in the case with citrus, winter fruits and vegetables, and sugar. Resistance to the treaty also came from other smaller pockets within U. S. agriculture.[35]

The family farmer, if such still exists on any serious scale, appeared to have only nominal input to the NAFTA debate. Nevertheless, the smaller farmer associations did appear before Congress, as the next excerpts of testimony on the treaty show. Whether these voices were heard, or carried any weight, is a distinctly different question.

[33]U. S. Congress, House Committee on Agriculture, Review of Issues Relating to . . . NAFTA, April, 1992.

[34]Ibid., p. 139.

[35]Ibid., for example, pp. 37–39; 29,30;234,235.

TESTIMONY OF DENISE O' BRIEN[36]

I am pleased to testify today as vice president of the National Family Farm Coalition and my experience as a diversified family farmer from Iowa raising chickens, organic fruit, and a 50-cow dairy herd.

The impact of both the current GATT and the NAFTA negotiations on farm survival remains high on the agenda of the family farmers in this country as well as in Canada, Mexico, Europe and Japan . . . It is not a farmer against farmer issue but a farmer versus agribusiness situation that is controlling our future as family farmers.

The NFFC represents a broad spectrum of family farm producers. Our 41 member organizations span 32 states and include producers of corn, soybeans, wheat, hogs and cattle in the Midwest and Northern Plains; poultry, peanuts and tobacco in the South; dairy in the Northeast, West, Southeast and Midwest; and fruits and vegetables in California and the South. The farmers of the NFFC contribute to the economic and social vitality of their communities both as agricultural producers and as community leaders. They share a commitment to the family farm system of agriculture, environmental stewardship, and vital rural communities.

I speak today as someone very concerned about the future of family farm agriculture in this country as well as in Mexico and Canada. What will happen to our rural communities when our jobs and farm loss escalate and put on an even faster track than it has been during the 1980s? A recent Iowa study of the structure of agriculture predicts that the 108,000 Iowa farmers in 1987 will shrink to 69,000 in 2007—a massive drop in only fifteen years.What are the real costs of this free trade agenda and does this Congress want to truly address sustainable rural development that includes economically and environmentally sustainable agriculture? . . .

[T]he over 480-page draft text . . . clearly states the ... priorities that are part of the NAFTA negotiations—increased concentration of land and production, continuing lower world commodity prices, lower food safety standards, and the elimination of a country's capacity to manage its own programs and manage its own supply. While this direction is no shock to us, it is a confirmation of our worst concerns . . .

[T]he negotiators have been heavily influenced by transnational corporations in determining the trade agendas. Why else would the Mexican proposals for special treatment provide incentives for agribusinesses while virtually ignoring the needs of their family farmers whose entire livelihood [is] threatened. Millions of Mexican basic grain farmers are threatened by the elimination of import restrictions on corn . . . Many of these farmers will be displaced, forced into urban centers, or the U.S. . . .

We remain concerned that these international agreements are attempting to establish the thwarted agenda of the Reagan–Bush agricultural policies in an arena that is far less accountable to the citizens of this country . . .

[36]Ibid., pp. 115–119.

STATEMENT OF DON ERET ON BEHALF OF THE FOOD FOR PEACE CAMPAIGN[37]

April 8, 1992

I am representing Food for Peace, an organization of producers and consumers. I am a farmer near Dorchester, Nebraska, producing grain sorghum, soybeans and wheat. From 1983 to 1987 I was a state senator in the Nebraska Legislature where I served on the agriculture committee.

Farmers from thirty states support the findings and farm policy proposals of Food for Peace. Our position is to oppose the proposed North American Free Trade Agreement (NAFTA) on the grounds that it would harm commodity producers in both the United States and Mexico. . . .

[F]ree trade, in general, since the Tokyo Round of the General Agreement on Tariffs and Trade in 1979, simply has not worked. The original theory of free trade was that of Comparative Advanatage: that a nation should produce what it is most efficient at producing, and that those nations that are not as efficient at producing that item should cease producing it, but should import, at a presumably lower cost, from the more efficient producer. . . .

The USDA's [U.S. Department of Agriculture] "Interim Report . . ." on NAFTA . . . leaves no doubt that the result . . . of the U. S.–Mexican free trade agreement will be to eliminate food production for domestic consumption in Mexico. The perspective of the report conforms to the policy perspective of a genocidal financial elite whose goal is reducing the world's population by two billion people. The targets of this policy are primarily the black and brown populations of the developing sector.

The USDA report says that the Mexican government has shifted away from a policy of national sovereignty over food production to a policy of dependence on food imports. The report describes it as a change from a policy of food "self-sufficiency," or "import substitution," to a policy of "food access," on the part of the Mexican government, under pressure of paying Mexico's enormous external debt. The report also states that recent gains in U. S. exports to Mexico would be in danger if Mexico returned to a policy of food self-sufficiency, thus admiting that the growth in the U.S.–Mexico export market has been at the expense of Mexico's domestic production to meet basic consumption needs. This means that Mexico will become totally dependent on imports, a state of affairs which will lead quickly to widespread starvation . . .

Under a free trade agreement such as the proposed NAFTA agreement, agriculture will follow the lead of the notorious maquiladoras assembly plants which manufacture inside Mexico for export. Through them, Mexico is becoming a runaway sweatshop for manufacturers in the U.S. As with the maquiladoras, Mexico will become a center of labor-intensive agriculture, producing for export food which should be feeding their own population. U.S. grain will be sent to Mexico to feed cattle in feedlots there, which will be slaughtered in Mexico and shipped out, destroying producers in the United States. Dairies and fruit and vegetable production will shift to Mexico from the United States to take advan-

[37]Ibid., pp. 123–135.

tage of cheap labor. Dairy products, fruits and vegetables will be exported back into the United States, again destroying producers.

Everywhere that free trade destroys producers, it also destroys markets. A market is no more than the purchasing power of producers. Meanwhile, Mexico's own producers of grain will be displaced as the more cheaply produced U.S. grain displaces them. Worldwide the weakening of nations' support for agriculture has caused a reduction in the volume and quality of food produced. When production drops, prices increase. This means starvation for a country like Mexico, whose domestic production is being eliminated through free trade and who must rely on increasingly costly imports.

Prior to 1980, Mexico was self-sufficient in wheat, beef, corn, and dairy. Today, since many restrictions on imports have been lifted, Mexico is . . . the largest importer of nonfat dry milk. Cheaper . . . imported milk from the United States destroyed the profitability of Mexico's domestic milk production. Then the Mexican government stopped supporting the dairies when their profitability fell. In the meantime, low . . . prices in the United States, coupled with the reduction in dairy herds, . . . has created shortages of dairy products. Nonfat dry milk, which was originally sold to Mexico at $450 per ton, is now $2,200 per ton.

On March 25, 74 Mexican agricultural organizations from 14 states came out against including grains in a NAFTA agreement, citing the potential for horrible damage to Mexico's economy and population. Leaders from 4 of the largest of these orgaizations gave a press conference at which they said that free trade in grain would spell ruin for more than 3 million farmers of Mexico's unirrigated land. Corn production in Mexico is less mechanized and cannot compete with corn imported from the United States. Mexican yields are 1.8 tons/hectare, compared to 7 tons for the U.S. The press release said that the main problem is the undercapitalization of Mexico's farms.

A free trade agreement between Mexico and the United States could not possibly increase agricultural markets for U.S. producers over the long term because the controlling feature of the Mexican economy is its enormous foreign debt load. . . .

The more the domestic economy is reoriented to producing for export to pay the debt at the expense of capital goods investment and infrastructure, the more internal consumption will decline. In fact, per capita consumption of meat, milk, corn, and beans, the staples of the Mexican diet, have declined 20–30% over the last decade. Estimates are that as many as 80% of the Mexican population are malnourished. Mexican production of meat and milk has declined 30% since 1980. Production of corn and beans has been similarly reduced.

Imports of corn, rice, wheat, dairy, beef, and beans have increased steadily as domestic production collapsed under the "liberalization" or free trade introduced by the Salinas government. But because price supports have been eliminated for all but corn and beans, and because unemployment has grown to close to 50% as producers were displaced, per capita consumption of food staples has fallen. Even so, the demands of debt service [are] forcing Mexico to export food. Export licenses which restrict exports of agricultural produce until domestic needs have been met have been dropped to allow food to be exported. . . .

Import tariffs of beef and slaughter cattle have been removed in Mexico, causing beef herds to decline from 37 million head over the past six years to 29 million head today. Nevertheless, Mexican exports of feeder cattle to the U.S. have doubled over the past decade. Mexico is so short of beef for its population that all import restrictions have been removed.

Five slaughterhouses have recently been established to process Mexican beef for export to the U.S. Historically this has been restricted for health regulations. Now the USDA inspects the meat on site and there are spot checks on the border. When the remaining protection on feedgrains are lifted in Mexico, feedlots will shift there from the United States.

Infrastructure investiment is not part of the NAFTA program. The lack of sanitation and health care in Mexico will soon lead to the spread of diseases, like cholera, which have been spreading into Mexico from Peru, into the United States. . . .

As Canadian Farmer's Union spokesman Wayne Easter said at the National Farmer's Organization convention in December 1990 about Mexico, "I've never seen such poverty and exploitation. Mexico used to be self-sufficient in corn and edible beans. Now, it isn't. International interests have seen to it that the best land is used for growing exportable grains and the poorest soils for growing domestic food. The result is hunger." . . .

Questions and Comments

1. Ms. O'Brien's testimony parallels the earlier commentary of Wendell Berry on the inverse relationship between size and good husbandry in agriculture. Evaluate.

   She also contends that the treaty will further the undesirable movement away from local control of agricultural law and policy. If the small farmer has lost in national legislation to large farm interests, the losses will be compounded in a treaty that displaces national and state law altogether. Evaluate.
2. Eret disputes the usual assumption that more "free trade" will even out differences across countries over time. Rather than being a force for long-term equilibrium and evening out the returns from agriculture, Eret argues that the new trade patterns will reinforce inequalities, and given the demographics of the affected populations can only be described as racist and genocidal. Evaluate.

AGRICULTURE IN THE THIRD WORLD

Law and Policy in Third World Countries

As a last dimension of this brief survey of agriculture some of the main lines of Third-World agricultural practices need to be summarized. From prior materials we may already have some feel for agriculture elsewhere—henequen in the Yucatan, bananas in Honduras and Costa Rica, cocoa in Equatorial Guinea, soybeans in Brazil, and dirt farming in Mexico.

There is a war, now in its late stages, being fought between international agribusinesses and indigenous farmers. The war is in the late stages because since World War II deep transformations in agriculture have already displaced many people and practices that were in place from time immemorial. The focus here is on the displacement of indigenous methods and their replacement by agribusiness methods, and the role of government in the transformation.

The Green Revolution

The Green Revolution, which is shorthand for the application of scientific methods to all aspects of agriculture, promised more for everybody, everywhere. The approach mirrored the approach taken by the South Dakotans in designing their model farm. Science plus determination would feed a growing world population, help countries using near-Stone Age methods, and earn a profit for those who cooperated with changes in the Third World countries and those who directed the changes from the first world—the U.S. and European-based multinational corporations.

This mixture of altruism and American knowhow, and of world peace and prosperity, can be found in the following Cold War account of what agricultural science could do for the world:

> The Rockefeller Brothers Fund report . . . made one fact plain. Growing pressure of population and the demand of all populations for an adequate standard of living will compel a wider base for any economic republic than can now be comprehended within the national borders of any existing State. This implies one of two things. Either the world will be divided into two zones, Communist and free, each attempting self-sufficiency, or a break will have to be found in the current impasse between the two. Such a break could be accomplished by conquest—but this means war, with destruction so great that either system, conquering or conquered, would have to begin over again. The alternative would be finding some avenue of cooperation . . .
>
> Common arrangements should be possible to supply underdeveloped areas with products, machinery, and techniques which they need, accompanied by a common understanding that they will share the benefits available to everyone concerned from the enhanced production thus engendered. Cooperation in such measures is theoretically entirely possible. American commercial power groups working with their government are quite as capable of accommodating to such arrangements as Soviet State production pyramids.[38]

Putting the cold war rhetoric aside, the policy position of the Report was that the United States would furnish technique and the Third World would let those techniques be employed, with the proceeds divided. There were to be no losers in development so envisioned. "American commercial power groups" in tandem with the U.S. government would solve problems (and not make life worse) for the teeming populations of the underdeveloped world.

[38]A. A. Berle, *Power Without Property* (New York: Harcourt, 1959), pp. 152, 153.

The Green Revolution was the agricultural dimension of this grand transfer of industrial technique. As it ran its course, Third World agriculture would be a mirror image of U. S. agriculture, with local variations within the overall parameters of the U. S. model of farming outlined above—large tracts, chemical intensity, mechanical displacement of human and animal labor, "best methods"—seeds, soils, weed and pest control, irrigation, harvesting and distribution.

The following excerpt shows the main reasons why high-tech agriculture failed, despite practically universal government support from all levels in all countries.

CULTURE AND AGRICULTURE[39]

The Green Revolution requires far more use of chemical pesticides. The richer vegetation is a haven for insects, and the frequent use of a single crop variety means that a disease can spread rapidly through a population. As noted above, the selection process is for a plant with immunity to local diseases, such as the Mexican wheat rust. This immunity makes a plant quite valuable, and farmers will adopt the new variety for its immunity as much as for its response to fertilizer. Invariably, however, a disease appears or evolves that can attack the new plant. Regions that once used a half dozen or more traditional varieties have converted to a single high-yielding variety, whether of wheat, rice, corn, cotton, or other commercial crop. As a result, whole river valleys have been decimated when a new rust or disease attacked a high-yielding type. The botanists, of course, are seeking different strains that will be imune to the disease, but in the meantime heavy doses of pesticide are used to protect the crops. . . . Such usage may become fairly standard practice; because farmers have already invested heavily in water and fertilizer, they cannot afford to lose crops should a novel pest come along just before harvest.

The value of the crops means that farmers and food processors now must take more serious and costly steps to protect their harvests from pests. In addition to the care of growing crops, attention must be given to storage, transportation, and marketing. All along the way the valuable product is subject to insects, bacteria, viruses, and fungi. The engineers fighting these threats face an enemy that numbers in the thousands. They have developed an astounding array of chemicals with which to wage war, but their knowledge and resources often are not as effective as the long, selective process that through trial-and-error protects the traditional varieties. Invariably, farmers see a season in which the modern varieties are decimated by pest while the old standbys may suffer but will persist in the face of a new disease or insect.

Animal pests are only half the problem. Heavy applications of water and fertilizer favor weeds as much as domesticated plants. They grow much more thickly, and new varieties of weeds appear that adapt to maximize use of the fertilizer nutrients. The weeds grow tall to get more sunlight to photosynthesize nutrients while the rice and wheat they compete with have been bred as dwarf varieties to prevent lodging. Even the rapid

[39]Ernest Schusky, *Culture and Agriculture* (New York: Bergin & Garvey, 1989), pp. 132–137.

growth of the high-yielding varieties does not help much in the competition for sunlight. Although the domesticates often have the edge in initial growth, their vertically arranged leafs and stems allow sunlight to reach the nutrient-rich soil. Thus the weeds are little hindered once they begin their race for the sun.

The principal response of Green Revolution farmers has been to apply more and more herbicides. This part of the pesticide package has become a major expense in some regions; in most places farmers probably err in the direction of applying too much rather than too little because of the value of their investment. Overall, the step is simply part of an investment spiral. More and more protection of investment must be given once farming begins with a large expenditure. As a result, Green Revolution farmers in developing countries are following the same course taken by farmers in the developed world. They are applying more energy, in the form of fossil calories, than they are getting in return, in the form of food calories.

Likewise, changes in the social and political life of rural communities undergoing the Green Revolution have been as extensive as in the West, but in the developing countries the social and economic changes can be measured yearly, whereas the parallel change in North America occurred over decades. Obviously, given the great differences in physical and political climate among northwest Mexico, India, the Philippines, and scores of other locales, it is difficult to generalize about the direction of these changes, yet some underlying themes are common almost everywhere.

For example, it is obvious that the demand for high energy use requires a substantial change from the original subsistence farming, for which the only major capital investment is in the form of land. Planners have often recognized that small farmers will be at a disadvantage in shifting to the new package of resources, but nowhere have plans evolved that give small subsistence farmers a competitive edge in raising the necessary capital to finance the modern technological complex that comprises the Green Revolution.

Norman K. Nicholson found that, in some places, developers have simply favored the large farmer who was already using capital-intensive methods, such as mechanization and perhaps some fertilizer and pesticides with traditonal varieties. Elsewhere, special extension services and credit funds have been made available only to poor rural farmers to give them some equity with farmers who were already small entrepreneurs. Still, no government invested nearly enough to insure that the poor could compete with others. Invariably, the Green Revolution stepped up inequality in the countryside, encouraging the growth of farm size though small holders sometimes extensively adopted the new practice.

Much of this process is simply inherent in the nature of the technology. Joan Mencher reports that the traditional varieties which were adapted to a region could best survive the idiosyncrasies of a region, be they prolonged droughts or swarms of insects. In contrast, the high-yielding varieties were custom engineered primarily to convert chemical nurtients into food calories. Any unusual challenge to them had to be met by human ingenuity that almost always relied on energy inputs—water that was delivered at exact times in precise amounts or heavily applied pesticides, aimed at diseases, insects, or weeds.

All these inputs derived from outside the farming community. Instead of relying upon the knowledge of past generations, outsiders who were often trained or dependent upon foreigners, supplied the knowledge for the new crops. The chemical fertilizer and the energy to run the irrigation system also came from the outside. All of these things had to be purchased, and even the money for them had to come from the outside. Credit usually arrived from some government bureaucracy, but much of it also came from the market. A future crop, or the land itself, was the usual collateral for such credit, whether public or private. In either case, the farmer lost much control over the production process.

In effect, what appeared to be a simple way of increasing production was in fact a radical transformation—from independent, subsistence peasant to commercial farmer. A. T. Mosher found that rapidly increasing cost of production required farmers to produce for a profit; they became dependent upon a market economy. Economies of scale meant they tended to specialize, and no longer grew all their own food. Rapid commercialization brought traditional peasants into complex relations with a national market in a matter of several years. Further, a national market such as that of India is no longer limited to a nation's boundaries. The price of wheat may be set by the government, but that decision will be influenced by the availability of American food aid. And that aid will depend upon factors such as demand by the U.S.S.R. and supply by Argentina or Australia.

All the unknowns of commercial agriculture totally transform the nature of the occupation. Subsistence farmers are in complete control of production and consumption decisions. The unknowns in their life are natural ones, the weather and pests. Traditional controls have evolved to protect those farmers from nature's vagaries, and tradition makes for conservatism. Jim Park . . . notes that commercial agriculture controls much of nature; drought and disease are treated with irrigation and chemicals. The market becomes even more of an unknown than nature. Its ups and downs demand more gambling. On occasion, farmers may make profits never before dreamed of, just as they may lose everything the next year.

Controls over the market are completely different from traditional ones over production. Predicting market trends becomes more important than predicting the weather. Getting credit to purchase fertilizer or increasing a share of water from a government-owned tubewell often requires political contacts that involve relations with sophisticated outsiders, persons ordinarily shunned by a traditional peasant. Thus, literate and better-educated farmers have a major advantage over the traditional peasant. The new conditions favor the entrepreneurs, who are willing to turn their backs on traditional and customary values.

Another way to perceive the likely changes is to recognize that commercial agriculture is a capitalist endeavor. Sources of capital are critical, and profitability is the primary goal. Economies of scale are recognized; mechanization is likely unless labor costs remain very low. All of these factors favor large farms, and, typically, farms have grown rapidly where the Green Revolution has established itself. Governments have recognized that such growth is probable; sometimes they have encouraged it. Mostly, though, policies have been established to limit the growth so rural populations would stay in the countryside.

Nonetheless, the processes of commercialization have regularly defeated the goals of policy.

The necessity to take advantage of economies of scale is largely in the area of purchases for production. A tractor and its related machinery are simply uneconomical for many small fields because they were borrowed outright from the West. Smaller, more appropriate power tools have been developed over the past decade, and this innovation has helped small farmers compete. Even so, large purchases of fertilizer, pesticides, and fuel will lower per-unit costs; likewise, delivery costs are lower for the farmer who has more to sell. Such transactions usually mean that the large cultivator will develop more urban contacts, become familiar with outside ways, and be more adaptable to modern influences by the seed sellers or extension agents teaching the latest methods of horticulture.

In regions where the Green Revolution has been judged highly successful, it has often been found that small farmers were quickly driven off the land to become day laborers for large landlords. Since land values rose quickly, urban investors sometimes bought up agricultural lands, and they created all the problems of absentee landownership. More often, however, the investors were local farmers who expanded or returnees to the land who reentered farming. That is, the commercial farmer was an owner-operator who invested in and improved upon the farm, but these families varied considerably in their composition and their strategies.

In a few places, the farmers adopting the new technology have come from all social strata. Success was a matter of survival. Shigeru Ishikawa has ...documented that generally the initial adopters simply did well enough that they could start buying out their more traditional neighbors. Government policy, encouraging adoption across the various strata, may have been important. Most of these cases for analysis are from India, although a similar process occurred in the Philippines. A more common pattern is for farmers of the upper strata to make the transition to commercialization. Only they can afford to make the initial investment, particularly where land must be newly irrigated or where the government does not subsidize fertilizer or fuel. With sudden large profits, land values may double or even triple, and the poor, indebted peasants can suddenly find wealth that was beyond their dreams. Of course, sale of land most often means a future life of hired labor, and then wages drop because of competition from other peasants who have sold their land. A variation on this latter pattern is for noncultivating landlords to return to their farms and directly oversee operations. Since more skills are involved, plus much higher profits, commercial agriculture generally has more prestige. Typically, the landowner may retain some of the former tenants as wage laborers, depending upon the degree of mechanization. Finally, cases are known where tenant farmers have been the major adopters of the Green Revolution. In these examples, however, the farmers were already engaged in commercial agriculture and experienced the shift as simply a change in productive techniques. Similar to this pattern is the case of landlords who have directed tenants in commercial agriculture. Such people are quite likely to take up quickly the techniques required by the new seeds.

Regardless of the type of adopter, the innovation in farming that increases dependency upon the outer world means that the old, local power base—often an hereditary monopoly—loses out to the individuals who can manipulate the ties between the local community and the state or external market. In nations where a government bureaucracy dominates, as in India, the contacts are in the offices of law and order, health, public works, and commerce, as well as in agriculture or economic development. Favorable contact with these agencies is facilitated by political party organization, so a "successful" farmer must usually have contacts with party officials both in and out of office, as well as a good working relation with a village level worker, who can assure delivery of seeds and fertilizer. In those nations where the market is less controlled by the government, it is just as critical to have good relations with a credit broker or bank, along with contacts who insure reliable transportation and access to nearby markets. And no developing country is so free of government direction that a good working relation with political party officials will not improve the producing and marketing processes. . . .

Questions and Comments

1. In Chapter 3 a theory of power and powerlessness was introduced. Review the theory and apply it to the Green Revolution and its outcomes. Is there any point when a peasant would be alerted to the onset of powerlessness?
2. In this chapter an outline of the changes in U. S. agriculture was included. Compare the U. S. experience with the experience in Third World countries.
3. As noted above, the original promise of improved agricultural technique was mutual gain for all participants. Compare the promise with the outcomes.
4. In some countries land reform is demanded which would return the control of land to the tillers of the land. What complications might accompany efforts to return to agriculture as it was done at an earlier time?
5. The relationship among land use, migration to cities and hunger is close. For extensive discussion of hunger as a problem of maldistribution of land and its proceeds and not one of excessive population, see Frances Lappé, *Food First*.[40]

In *Twelve Myths*, Lappé addressed the question of whether free trade in commodities had alleviated the hunger problem. She found that hunger had increased over the same period that more and more of the world agriculture had been integrated into the multinational agribusiness system. For example, in Mexico, India, Thailand, the Philippines and Zimbabwe, as agricultural output rose, hunger increased. There was more food and more hunger.[41]

[40](New York: Ballantine, 1979) and see Lappé, *World Hunger,* note 11.
[41]Lappe, op. cit. (*Twelve Myths*), pp. 49–51.

CONCLUDING CASE STUDY: AGRIBUSINESS IN THE PHILIPPINES

The operations of Castle and Cooke (Dole Pineapple, or Dolefil) on the island of Mindanao in the Philippine Islands[42] reveals the intimate connection between government and multinational agribusiness. Growing pineapples requires large amounts of land to accommodate a three-year, two-crop cycle, heavy mechanization and supporting facilities such as a cannery and warehousing, and access to a seaport for the export of canned and fresh product.

Complications to the aggregation of land occurred for two main reasons. First, the Philippine constitution prevented ownership by foreign businesses of land in excess of certain amounts (2500 acres). In keeping with a policy that smaller tracts would reward the tiller of the land with the product of the land, in pre-Dolefil days each family in the area had been given a home lot and about 30 acres. Second, the land that was desired for the plantation was in private hands already.

The government through its National Development Corporation, leased 8000 hectares (almost 20,000 acres) to Dolefil with rent based on production, with a minimum fee. (It was not clear from the case how the government corporation aggregated the land in the development corporation, but the Marcos regime was not above strong-arm methods.) The legal authority of the development corporation to lease land to foreign companies was also in doubt for the obvious reason that the corporation was doing indirectly what was legally prohibited. The remaining land (about 5000 acres) was leased by private individuals on long-term *fixed-rate terms,* with some premium for the quality of pineapples produced on the leased acreage. Fixed-rate rentals meant that as the Philippine peso lost value, the rental owed by Dolefil for the use of the land dropped.

As the land came under more and more production of pineapple, the locals lost control, and their returns were largely limited to wages from Castle and Cooke. Fresh pineapples went to Japan and canned pineapple was also exported. The case study is instructive on a number of themes besides the aggregation and control of land for an export crop and the displacement of subsistence farmers: cooptation of agricultural labor unions; the use of a dictator's cronies as "advisers" to the company (Juan Ponce Enrile, a close associate of the dictator, was "general counsel" for Dolefil); the environmental impacts of growing with petrochemical intensity more than 25,000 acres exclusively in pineapple; and the stratification of work forces, by pay, regularity of employment, and living conditions.

Complicity of government, from the national on down to local level, was needed for the pineapple venture to succeed. Average Filipinos derived little beyond wages which for seasonal workers were probably at or below subsistence. There were always plenty of workers available to the company, which could be taken as evidence that the company was regarded by the people as

[42]The full case report with commentaries can be found in L. Tavis, et al., *Multinational Managers and Third World Poverty* (South Bend: University of Notre Dame Press, 1982).

making a valuable contribution to the area. The abundance of workers could also attest to the foreclosure of alternative means of subsistence which the very presence of Castle and Cooke had dramatically altered. The officialdom in government and the unions no doubt skimmed some return from the multinational's presence; how much and to whom, would not be data that comes tumbling from public records for inclusion in academic case studies.

Returning to the original vision of mutual gains through peaceful international cooperation designed to serve all populations, the Dolefil venture was a cruel hoax. It could be blamed on the "wrong people" in charge in the Philippines—the corrupt Marcos regime. But probably the participants were "average," or just a cut worse than average, just as the principals of Dolefil were "average." For both, the land and the people of Mindanao were means to an end and not ends in themselves. But then, what is agribusiness, on either a national or international scale?

CHAPTER 14

Internationalization of Labor

To assess contemporary labor problems one must look at labor in general—how has it fared since World War II and the internationalization of the labor process. Immanuel Wallerstein, the political economist whose work was discussed in Chapter 4, argued that there are no longer any local or national economies. If so, the key question is where places of work or workers fit into the international scheme of things.

He contended that for the two decades after World War II, from which the United States emerged as the only industrial power, management and labor in the United States could get along reasonably well because there was plenty to go around, and any increased costs from higher wages and benefits could be passed on to others in the United States or abroad. This cozy relationship eventually broke down as the percentage of world industry controlled by the United States declined relative to Europe and Japan. From the late 1970s to today, management–labor relationships have become more contentious, and peaceful coexistence has been displaced by open antagonisms to labor, supported from the management side by worldwide options for production.[1] Although their techniques are less direct,[2] overall management tactics compare to the times when company goons battled trade unionists on the picket line to prevent the organization of work forces. The Caterpillar strike and Chapter 7 on Labor considered these developments.

Stephen Hymer, a political economist whose work was also considered earlier, made some startling prophecies in the early 1970s[3] that are worth keeping in mind as contemporary labor issues surface. Hymer saw the multinational as a marvel of organizational efficiency that would run into political trouble once those whose lives were affected by multinationals began to see that the benefits from the enterprises were highly stratified by country and privileged group.

He predicted that discontentment could occur in the home countries of multinationals, once capital flight and rival cheap labor eroded the economic

[1]Immanuel Wallerstein, *The Politics of the World–Economy,* (Cambridge: Cambridge University Press, 1984), pp. 71–75.

[2]See, for example, Kevin Delaney, *Strategic Bankruptcy* (Berkeley: University of California Press, 1992).

[3]S. Hymer, "The Multinational Corporation and Uneven Development", in Jagdish Bhagwati, ed., *Economics and the World Order* (New York: Macmillan, 1972), pp. 113–140.

security of domestic workers. In the host countries to which multinationals shifted production, rebellion could be precipitated by the failure of international companies to make an equitable allocation of returns to host country participants. According to Hymer, even if the multinationals were to be still viable as economic entities, their political viability could become more and more precarious—too many governments to pacify, more elites than available high places, and too little return trickling down to the vast majority.

THE MULTINATIONAL CORPORATION AND UNEVEN DEVELOPMENT[4]

Stephen Hymer

1. The multinational corporation, because of its great power to plan economic activity, represents an important step forward over previous methods of organizing international exchange. It demonstrates the social nature of production on a global scale, and as it eliminates the anarchy of international markets and brings about a more extensive and productive international division of labor, it releases great sources of latent energy.

2. But the multinational corporation is still a private institution with a partial outlook and represents only an imperfect solution to the problem of international cooperation. It creates hierarchy rather than equality, and it spreads its benefits unequally. As it crosses international boundaries, it pulls and tears at the social and political fabric and erodes the cohesiveness of national states.

3. Whether one likes this or not, it is probably a tendency that cannot be stopped. Through its propensity to nestle everywhere, settle everywhere, and establish connections everywhere, the multinational corporation destroys the possibility of national seclusion and self-sufficiency and creates a universal interdependence.

4. This applies to the United States as well as to other countries. Continued growth of U.S. direct foreign investment at its present rate of 10 percent per year implies an increased cleavage between international and national interests, i.e., more dependence upon the world economy, greater difficulty in controlling large corporations, and greater involvement in maintaining law and order to protect international private property.

5. However, in proportion to its success, the multinational corporation leads other groups, particularly labor and government to mobilize their power; it creates counterforces in the form of conflicts within major centers, between major centers, and between the major centers and the hinterland.

6. The present crisis may well be more profound than most of us imagine, and the West may find it impossible to restructure the international economy on a workable basis. One could easily argue that the age of the Multinational Corporation is at its end rather than at its beginning. The present hearings may be the epitaph of the American attempt to sustain the old international economy, and not the herald of a new era of international cooperation.

[4]U.S. Congress, Joint Economic Committee, Subcommittee on Foreign Economic Policy, Ninety-first Congress, Second Session, 1972, pp. 906–910.

THE COMING CRISIS OF THE MULTINATIONAL CORPORATION

Since the beginning of the Industrial Revolution, there has been a tendency for the representative firm to increase in size from the *workshop* to the *factory* to the *national corporation* to the *multidivisional corporation* and now to the *multinational corporation.*

Until recently, most multinational corporations have been from the United States. Now European corporations, as a by-product of increased size, and as a reaction to the American invasion of Europe, are also shifting attention from national to global production and beginning to "see the world as their oyster." If present trends continue, multinationalization is likely to increase greatly in the next decade as giants from both sides of the Atlantic (though still mainly from the U.S.) strive to penetrate each other's markets' and to establish bases in underdeveloped countries, where there are few indigenous concentrations of capital sufficiently large to operate on a world scale. This rivalry may be intense at first but will probably abate through time and turn into collusion as firms approach some kind of oligopolistic equilibrium. A new structure of international industrial organization and a new international division of labor will have been born.

So profound a change in economic structure will require correspondingly radical changes in the legal, political, and ideological framework. At present "practice is ahead of theory and policy," . . . Multinational corporations, through their everyday business practice, are creating a new world environment, but policy makers (and theoreticians) are lagging behind.

In other words, the situation is a dynamic one, moving dialectically. Right now, we seem to be in the midst of a major revolution in international relationships as modern science establishes the technological basis for a major advance in the conquest of the material world and the beginnings of truly cosmopolitan production. Multinational corporations are in the vanguard of this revolution, because of their great financial and administrative strength and their close contact with the new technology. Governments (outside the military) are far behind, because of their narrower horizons and perspectives, as are labor organizations and most non-business institutions and associations. Therefore, in the first round, multinational corporations are likely to have a certain degree of success in organizing markets, decision-making, and the spread of information in their own interest. However, their very success will create important tensions and conflicts which will lead to reactions by other groups.

Thus, whether foreign investment can continue to grow at 10 percent per year, as it has for the past twenty years, with drastic implications such an expansion has for world order, is an open question. Economic factors, in the sense of an expanding world market, are favorable. Political factors are a different matter. Since economic power cannot long be out of phase with political power, multinational corporations must mobilize political power, or they will not be able to create the new world economic order we hear so much about.

Uneven Development

Suppose giant multinational corporations (say 300 from the U. S. and 200 from Europe and Japan) succeed in establishing themselves as the dominant form of international enterprise and come to control a significant share of industry (especially modern industry) in each country. The world economy will resemble more and more the United States economy, where each of the large corporations tends to spread over the entire continent and to penetrate almost every nook and cranny. What would be the effect of a world industrial organization, decentralization and centralization? ... To what extent would it perpetuate the present system of uneven development, i.e., the tendency of the system to produce poverty as well as wealth, underdevelopment as well as development?

The growth of firms involves a double movement: differentiation and organization, decentralizational and centralization. On the one hand, the multinational corporation because of its power to command capital and technology and its ability to rationalize their use on a global scale, will probably spread production more evenly over the world's surface than now is the case. At the same time, it will tend to centralize strategic decisions in regional coordinating centers and in corporate headquarters. Horizontal expansion of corporations through the world will be accompanied by a vertical differentiation of levels of command (symbolized by the corporate skyscraper) and a stratification of employees from operatives to executives, with wide differences in authority, status, remuneration, horizons, mobility, mental demands, and development.

The spatial or geographic implication of the corporate structure lies in the close correspondence between the centralization of control within the corporation and centralization of control within the international economy. A system of North Atlantic Multinational Corporations would tend to produce a hierarchal division of labor between geographical regions corresonding to the vertical division of labor within the firm. It would tend to centralize high-level decision-making occupations in a few key cities in the advanced countries, surrounded by a number of regional subcapitals, and confine the rest of the world to lower levels of activity and income, i.e., to the status of towns and villages in a new Imperial System. Income, status, authority, and consumption patterns would radiate out from these centers along a declining curve, and the existing pattern of inequality and dependency would be perpetuated. The pattern would be complex, just as the structure of the corporation is complex, but the basic relationship between different countries would be one of superior and subordinate, head office and branch plant.

One would expect to find the highest offices of the multinational corporations concentrated in the world's major cities—New York, London, Paris, Hamburg, Tokyo. These along with Moscow and perhaps Peking, will be the major centers of high-level strategic planning. Lesser cities throughout the world will deal with the day-to-day operations of specific local problems. These in turn will be arranged in a hierarchal fashion: the larger and more important ones will contain regional corporate headquarters, while the smaller ones will be confined to lower-level activities. Since business is usually the core to the city, geographical specialization will come to reflect the hierarchy of corporate decision-making, and the occupational distribution of labor in a city or region will depend upon its function in the international economic system. The best and most highly paid administrators, doctors, lawyers, scientists, educators, government officials, actors, servants, and hairdressers will tend to concentrate in or near the major centers.

The new economy will be characterized by a division of labor based on nationality. Even within the United States, ethnic homogeneity increases as one goes up the corporate hierarchy; the lower levels contain a wide variety of nationalities, the higher levels become successively more pure. A similar phenomenon will probably develop on a world scale as firms try to balance the need for adaptation to local customs and circumstances with a centralized strategic point of view.

Day-to-day management in each country will be left to the nationals of that country who, being intimately familiar with local conditions and practices, are able to deal with local problems and local government. These nationals remain rooted in one spot, while above them is a layer of people who move around from country to country, as bees among flowers, transmitting information from one subsidiary to another and from the lower levels to the general office at the apex of the corporate structure. In the nature of things, these people (reticulators) for the most part will be citizens of the country of the parent corporation (and will be drawn from a small culturally homogeneous group within the advanced world), since they will need to have the confidence of their superiors and be able to move easily in the higher management circles. Latin Americans, Asians, and Africans will at best be able to aspire to a management position in intermediate coordinating centers at the continental level. Very few will be able to get much higher than this, for the closer one gets to the top, the more important is "a common cultural heritage."

The multinational corporate system thus does not seem to offer the world national independence or equality. Instead it would keep many countries as branch plant countries, not only with reference to their economic functions but throughout the whole gamut of social, political, and cultural roles. The subsidiaries of multinational corporations tend to be among the largest companies in the country of their operations; and their top executives play an influential role in the political, social, and cultural life of the host country.

Yet these people, whatever their title, occupy at best a medium position in the corporate structure and are restricted in authority and horizons to a lower level of decision making. The governments with whom they deal tend to take on the same middle management outlook, since this is the only range of information and ideas to which they are exposed. In this sense, one can hardly expect such a country to bring forth the creative imagination needed to apply science and technology to the problems of degrading poverty.

CORPORATIONS AND NATIONS

"For a worldwide enterprise, national boundaries are drawn in fading ink," wrote *Business Week...* as a headline with reference to George Ball's now famous argument that corporations are modern institutions and nation states are old-fashioned institutions rooted in archaic concepts. What does this mean in particular for the United States, the most powerful national state of all?

In the first place, one should note that the conflict is not really between corporations and nation states, but between groups of people within corporations and nation states struggling over who decides what and who gets what, i.e., between big multinational corporations over the share of the world market, between big business which is internationally mobile and small business and labor which are not; between the middle class of different countries over managerial positions, between high wage labor in one country and low wage labor in another; and between excluded groups and elites within each country over the direction development is to take.

The importance of these conflicts depends upon the scale of foreign investment. The rapid growth of U.S. foreign investment over the last twenty years has already revealed certain cleavages between the interests of international investors and the rest of the domestic economy over taxation, balance of payments, extraterritoriality, and foreign aid. For example, multinational corporations have pressed for relief from taxation on foreign income and from regulation by antitrust and other laws. They would like the United States to adjust its balance of payments by deflating the economy or controlling imports rather than controlling foreign investment. At the same time, they would like freedom to produce where costs are lowest, unhampered by tariffs and trade. On these issues they conflict with other domestic taxpayers who wish equal taxation for foreign income; firms who cannot meet the challenge of foreign competition through investment but must rely on exports or on the domestic market; and certain classes of labor threatened by foreign competition.

These types of problems will grow as foreign investment continues to grow. Three major types of complications are likely to emerge.

First, the United States will become increasingly interdependent with the world economy. The multinational corporation is a medium by which laws, politics, foreign policy, and culture of one country intrude into one another. Already United States antitrust laws and balance of payments controls quickly feed into other countries via multinational corporations and then quickly react back on the United States Government. More of this can be expected in the future, as the multinational corporation acts as a viaduct for transmitting pressure from one country to another, thus reducing the sovereignty of all nations and requiring the building of supranational institutions to coordinate policy and reduce conflicts. To many, this is its most positive feature.

Second, the ability to control large corporations will be reduced. Multinational corporations because of their worldwide horizons and scope of operations have a certain flexibility for reducing the control of any one country over them. This applies to monetary policy, fiscal policy, and a host of others, and is perhaps best illustrated by tax questions. In an environment of free capital movements and free trade, a government's ability to tax multinational corporations is limited by the ability of those corporations to manipulate transfer prices and to move their productive facilities from country to country. Countries become like cities competing for branch plants.

Third, because the multinational corporation is associated with world stratification and inequality in property, power, and income, it creates a goal in those lower down the hierarchy to try to change it. This tendency is dampened to the extent that the system provides continuous improvement and opportunity for everybody. The multinational corporation, because of its dynamic qualities, has a certain stabilizing effect in this regard. But the available evidence indicates that it can provide some degree of participation for at most one-third of the world's population. The remaining two-thirds, who get only one-third of income, gain little. And, along with the many dissatisfied of the upper third, present a continuous challenge. The United States, because of its special position, pays the largest part of the cost of maintaining the system in face of these challenges. The costs have been rising rapidly and may easily come to exceed any benefits the nation as a whole is alleged to gain from them (as opposed to the substantial gains accruing to the limited sector directly involved in foreign investment). At any rate, this is what happened to the British Empire.

Comments and Questions

1. There might be a tendency to think of multinationals as so strong that their power would never be open to challenge. This thought has received more support since Hymer wrote; more nooks and crannies of the world have been integrated into the world economy. Multinationals are seen as an inevitable fact of economic life.

   What are the sources of instability that multinationals face? If we were to make a sample reading of the *Wall Street Journal* for a single week, could we find evidence of multinationals coping with instability?
2. In examining particular multinationals, can one find status and return on a hierarchical scale according to nationality, race, and gender? One place to look for answers is in the reports of companies to the S.E.C., which are carried on microfiche in some libraries.

   Could multinationals improve their long-run chances for survival by sharing more of the status and returns that the organization generates, or is there not enough to go around to make that a feasible means toward political stability?

   If hearts cannot be peaceably won over, what is the role of force in maintaining a multinational's security?
3. What do you see to be the most severe limit on mobilizing labor power as a counterweight to multinational power in either home or host countries?
4. What are the limits of home and host country governments, even when operating in good faith and for the public welfare, in countering multinational power? Can these limits be overcome?
5. Two law–government strategies are commonly advanced for coping with abuses of multinational power: first, world government, which would match worldwide political–regulatory power with worldwide economic systems; second, the reinforcement of national and local law–government systems to control the multinational.

   Which do you find more practical?

   Which of these two alternatives might a multinational prefer, if it had to choose?
6. Hymer predicts that multinationals based in different countries will not eat each other alive through competition. Rather, he anticipates oligopolistic arrangements where the multinationals would cooperate along the lines that domestic oligopolies and international cartels have done. To assess this prophecy one could follow international

mergers, joint ventures, or other forms of cooperation; and the international rivalries between multinationals in the same lines of business. Cooperation between Siemens of Germany and IBM of the United States is a sample of the first; the battle between GM and Volkswagen over trade secrets and industrial espionage is a sample of the second.

7. How do Hymer's prophecies look 20 years after he made them?

The purpose of bringing Wallerstein and Hymer back for renewed attention is to provide a background against which to measure contemporary conflicts. At no time in recent history has labor, whether organized into unions or not, been so aroused as it has been over NAFTA and the prospects of intensified capital flight to Mexico. Speaking to this fear was the largest single appeal of Ross Perot; Americans are very afraid that they no longer figure into the multinational equation of world production. Whether Ross Perot—or any other leader—would do anything about labor problems presents an entirely different question. But the responses to some of his appeals may have been one rumbling of the increased political activism that Hymer predicted.

The following excerpt contains a vision of the U. S. labor future that should be of special interest for two reasons: first, it was written by Robert Reich, the present U. S. Secretary for Labor; second, the commentary was prepared by Reich when he was at Harvard to assist his students in their career planning.

THE FUTURE OF WORK

Robert Reich[5]

It' s easy to predict what jobs you shouldn't prepare for. Thanks to the miracles of fluoride, America, in the future, will need fewer dentists. Nor is there much of a future in farming. The federal government probably won't provide longterm employment unless you aspire to work in the Pentagon or the Veterans Administration (the only two departments accounting for new federal jobs in the last decade). And think twice before plunging into higher education. The real wages of university professors have been declining for some time, the hours are bad, and all you get are complaints.

Moreover, as the American economy merges with the rest of the world's, anyone doing relatively unskilled work that could be done more cheaply elsewhere is unlikely to prosper for long. Imports and exports now constitute 26 percent of our gross national product (up from 9 percent in 1950), and barring a new round of protectionism, the portion will move steadily upward. Meanwhile, 10,000 people are added to the world's population every hour, most of whom, eventually, will happily work for a small fraction of today's average American wage.

[5]*Harper's,* April 1989, pp. 26–30. Copyright © 1992 by Harper's Magazine. Reprinted by special permission.

This is good news for most of you, because it means that you'll be able to buy all sorts of things far more cheaply than you could if they were made here (provided, of course, that what your generation does instead produces even more value). The resulting benefits from trade will help offset the drain on your income resulting from paying the interest on the nation's foreign debt and financing the retirement of aging baby boomers like me. The bad news, at least for some of you, is that most of America's traditional, routinized manufacturing jobs will disappear. So will routinized service jobs that can be done from remote locations, like keypunching of data transmitted by satellite. Instead, you will be engaged in one of two broad categories of work: either complex services, some of which will be sold to the rest of the world to pay for whatever Americans want to buy from the rest of the world, or person to person services, which foreigners can't provide for us because (apart from new immigrants and illegal aliens) they aren't here to provide them.

Complex services involve the manipulation of data and abstract symbols. Included in this category are insurance, engineering, law, finance, computer programming, and advertising. Such activities now account for almost 25 percent of our GNP, up from 13 percent in 1950. They already have surpassed manufacturing (down to about 20 percent of GNP). Even in the manufacturing sector, executive, managerial, and engineering positions are increasing at a rate almost three times that of total manufacturing employment. Most of these jobs, too, involve manipulating symbols. Such endeavors will constitute America's major contribution to the rest of the world in the decades ahead. You and your classmates will be exporting engineering designs, financial services, advertising and communications advice, statistical analysis, musical scores and film scripts, and other creative and problem solving products. How many of you undertake these sorts of jobs, and how well you do at them, will determine what goods and services America can summon from the rest of the world in return, and thus—to some extent—your generation's standard of living.

You say you plan to become an investment banker? A lawyer? I grant you that these vocations have been among the fastest growing and most lucrative during the past decade. The securities industry in particular has burgeoned. Between 1977 and 1987, securities industry employment nearly doubled, rising 10 percent a year, compared with the average yearly job growth of 1.9 percent in the rest of the economy. The crash of October 1987 temporarily stemmed the growth, but by mid-1988 happy days were here again. Nor have securities workers had particular difficulty making ends meet. Their average income grew 21 percent over the decade, compared with a 1 percent rise in the income of everyone else. (But be careful with these numbers; relatively few securities workers enjoyed such majestic compensation. The high average is partly due to the audacity of people such as Henry Kravis and George Roberts, each of whom takes home a tidy $70 million per year.)

Work involving securities and corporate law has been claiming one quarter of all new private sector jobs in New York City and more than a third of all the new office space in that industrious town. Other major cities are not too far behind. A simple extrapolation of the present trend suggests that by 2020 one out of every three American college graduates will be an investment banker or a lawyer. Of course, this is unlikely. Long before that milestone could be achieved, the nation's economy will have dried up like a raisin, as financiers and lawyers squeeze out every ounce of creative, productive juice. Thus my advice: Even if you could bear spending your life in such meaningless but lucrative work, at least consider the fate of the nation before deciding to do so.

Person to person services will claim everyone else. Many of these jobs will not require much skill, as is true of their forerunners today. Among the fastest growing in recent years: custodians and security guards, restaurant and retail workers, daycare providers. Secretaries and clerical workers will be as numerous as now, but they'll spend more of their time behind and around electronic machines (imported from Asia) and have fancier titles, such as "paratechnical assistant" and "executive paralegal operations manager."

Teachers will be needed (we'll be losing more than a third of our entire corps of elementary- and high-school teachers through attrition over the next seven years), but don't expect their real pay to rise very much. Years of public breast beating about the quality of American education notwithstanding, the average teacher today earns $28,000—only 3.4 percent more, in constant dollars, than he or she earned fifteen years ago.

Count on many jobs catering to Americans at play—hotel workers, recreation directors, television and film technicians, aerobics instructors (or whatever their twenty-first-century equivalents will call themselves). But note that Americans will have less leisure time to enjoy these pursuits. The average American's free time has been shrinking for more than fifteen years, as women move into the work force (and so spend more of their free time doing household chores) and as all wage earner are forced to work harder just to maintain their standard of living. Expect the trend to continue.

The most interesting and important person-to-person jobs will be in what is now unpretentiously dubbed "sales." Decades from now most salespeople won't be just filling orders. Salespeople will be helping customers define their needs, then working with design and production engineers to customize products and services in order to address those needs. This is because standardized (you can have it in any color as long as it's black) products will be long gone. Flexible manufacturing and the new information technologies will allow a more tailored fit—whether it's a car, machine tool, insurance policy, or even a college education. Those of you who will be dealing directly with customers will thus play a pivotal role in the innovation process, and your wages and prestige will rise accordingly.

But the largest number of personal service jobs will involve health care, which already consumes about 12 percent of our GNP, and that portion is rising. Because every new medical technology with the potential to extend life is infinitely valuable to those whose lives might be extended—even for a few months or weeks—society is paying huge sums to stave off death. By the second decade of the next century, when my generation of baby boomers will have begun to decay, the bill will be much higher. Millions of corroding bodies will need doctors, nurses, nursing home operators, hospital administrators, technicians who operate and maintain all the fancy machines that will measure and temporarily halt the deterioration, hospice directors, home care specialists, directors of outpatient clinics, and euthanasia specialists, among many others.

Most of these jobs won't pay very much because they don't require much skill. Right now the fastest growing job categories in the health sector are nurse's aides, orderlies, and attendants, which compose about 40 percent of the health-care work force. The majority are women; a large percentage are minorities. But even doctors' real earnings show signs of slipping. As malpractice insurance rates skyrocket, many doctors go on salary in investor-owned hospitals, and their duties are gradually taken over by physician "extenders" such as nurse-practitioners and midwives.

What' s the best preparation for one of these careers?

Advice here is simple: You won't be embarking on a career, at least as we currently define the term, because few of the activities I've mentioned will proceed along well defined paths to progressively higher levels of responsibility. As the economy evolves toward services tailored to meet the particular needs of clients and customers, hands-on experience will count far more than formal rank. As technologies and markets rapidly evolve, moreover, the best preparation will be through cumulative learning on the job rather than formal training completed years before.

This means that academic degrees and professional credentials will count for less; on-the-job training, for more. American students have it backwards. The courses to which you now gravitate—finance, law, accounting, management, and other practical arts—may be helpful to understand how a particular job is *now* done (or, more accurately, how your instructors did it years ago when they held such jobs or studied the people who hold them), but irrelevant to how such a job *will* be done. The intellectual equipment needed for the job of the future is an ability to define problems, quickly assimilate relevant data, conceptualize and reorganize the information, make deductive and inductive leaps with it, ask hard questions about it, discuss findings with colleagues, work collaboratively to find solutions, and then convince others. And *these* sorts of skills can't be learned in career-training courses. To the extent they are found in universities at all, they're more likely to be found in subjects such as history, literature, philosophy, and anthropology—in which students can witness how others have grappled for centuries with the challenge of living good and productive lives. Tolstoy and Thucydides are far more relevant to the management jobs of the future than are Hersey and Blanchard (*Management of Organizational Behavior*, Prentice Hall, 1988).

Questions for discussion

1. Your first question is the best one: where do I fit in if Reich is correct? What will my four—or more—decades of work be like? Will I have a say about it?
2. Reich contends that workers of the future will be required to continually adapt to new workplace demands and not simply work their way up into known hierarchies of power, status, and economic return. What are the implications of this prophecy?

Compare the foregoing to the prophecy about the importance of hands-on experience. Wouldn't more of that kind of experience come with time? Would such a differential create differences in status, and returns? In power?

Reich also says that hands-on experience will count more than formal rank and formal education. What implications follow from this?

Compare the need for hands-on experience with the need for conceptual thinking. Can there be hands-on experience with conceptual thinking, or at that point has the hand metaphor run amok?

3. If no trustworthy prophecies can be made about the future, what is an expert? If Reich were to say to his students, "The future is anybody's guess," what effects would that have?
4. At one point Reich makes the point that too many pencil pushers in service jobs would make the economy dry up like a raisin. Compare this prospect with his recommended habits of mind—conceptualization, seeing complex situations, asking tough questions, and talking answers through. Do these sound like production, or services that would operate like fruit dryers? Who will feed these new-age managers, if farmers become increasingly obsolete?
5. Reich's vision seems to come down to a prediction that the heads will be in the "developed world" and the hands will be in the "underdeveloped world." What would happen if those countries whose role it is to furnish "cheap goods" and food to the conceptualizer–servicers, refuse to do so? (For example, if "cultural products" like films and television reruns no longer hold their charm?) Is this where the military and the CIA come in?

The author of this text distributed the following story to his students in 1984. It can be compared to the foregoing essay by Robert Reich.

SERVICE ECONOMY

John J. Bonsignore

I

Never get pinned in a corner at a family gathering. Whenever possible stay near the center of the room, or near a doorway. Charles knew this, having just seen "The Graduate" on his VCR, but before he could position himself properly, he found himself wedged between the trash compactor and the refrigerator in the kitchen. A doorway was in plain sight, but he knew he would never reach it. Besides, his Uncle Nunzio deserved at least a word. Just six months had gone by since he had given Charles twenty-five dollars for his high school graduation. Hi, Uncle Nunzio, Charles waved to his uncle coming toward him.

As soon as his uncle had seen Charles alone, his face had brightened. In mid-sentence he had stopped, brushed aside the people he was with, and made straight for Charles. "Chollie, my favorite nephew, howahyah?" he asked, throwing his arms around him in a bear hug. The bottom button on Nunzio's shirt almost gave out, holding back a huge Thanksgiving dinner and decades of pasta. "Gosh, it's good ta see yah. Offta college. What are ya gonna take up?

Charles would have said prelaw if he had had a chance—he had already learned that law sounded practical and shifted the burden of conversation from himself. Relatives usually said, "That's good. Nice to have a lawyer in the family. Someone you can trust."

Nunzio hadn't waited for an answer. After a quick sweep of his tongue to clear his teeth, he blurted, "Communications. Everything's electronics." He opened his arms and raised his hands to follow the trend. To add precision, he began pointing his finger just below Charles' chin. "I tellya, what I would do if I was you is computers. It's growing."

Nunzio might know. At his auto repair place, he looked longingly for cars from the early 1970s—"Cars you can fix. Not like the new ones . . . You can't tune 'em. They drive ya nuts."

Charles nodded appreciatively at his uncle's advice, eyeing the doorway, but not impolite enough to make for it yet. Instead he covered himself, "Yeah, I plan to take a few courses in computers."

The television in the other room interrupted them: *"GETTING AN IDEA OF WHERE IT NEEDS TO BE IS AS IMPORTANT AS THE IDEA ITSELF!"* Nunzio appreciated the boost: "See, what'd I just say? Get in on it. You won't be sorry."

Now Nunzio himself wanted out. He heard that desserts and coffee were ready.

II

Years passed. Charles had graduated from college with a degree which, if not as crisp as one in computer science, was at least enough to land a position as a securities account manager trainee. One corner of Nunzio's advice had stuck. He had escaped the family grease pit, could work sitting down, in an expensive suit, with a custom haircut, and shiny shoes. His salary compounded like the balances in his customers' accounts. Within a short time he had broken all of the family records for income in a single year.

Occasionally his old friends from high school would poke at him: "Chollie, you got a bullshit job. You don't do nothin. You don't make nothin." Charles never got angry at these prisoners of the industrial culture. The world had blipped on by them and they deserved compassion.

III

One day Charles noticed a small hole in his right shoe. After an old injury, he put more weight on his right leg, making his right shoe wear out first. I'll take care of it during lunch, he thought, getting back to his computer terminal. On a small side street near the high-rise office building where he worked anything from clothes to hardware could be bought. At noon, he made his way toward the familiar sign of Monarch Shoes, a large copper replica of an English riding boot. It had been there so long it had turned green.

He had been there before and a polite clerk, dressed just about like Charles right down to a well-preserved pair of Monarch's finest, welcomed him warmly, "Good to see you again, Mr. Argento."

Charles returned the politeness. "Thanks. Good to see you. I don't need much of your time. I'm happy with the style I have on. 10D."

"I won't be a minute," the clerk said, and he was true to his word. Forty-five seconds later he returned from the back room with a piece of white paper carefully folded. "Will you take them this way or will I put them in an envelope? That will be $89.50, tax included."

Charles reached for the paper and opened it:

> Charles Argento
>
> One pair of shoes
>
> 10D
>
> "The same style he has on"

"What is this? This is ridiculous," Charles laughed, hoping the clerk would join in. He then shifted his weight from his right leg to his left leg. (It is not known whether he did this to save wear on the shoe that already had a hole in it.)

The clerk felt a need to speak: "Six months ago we moved to a new concept here at Monarch. Ninety-five percent of business today is communications—moving information from place to place, accurately, cheaply, and, above all, quickly. Have you ever received faster service here than you got today? . . . Only a few have complained."

Charles was now a little beside himself, and the clerk sensed the need for a fall-back position. "In emergencies, like the one you seem to be having, there is a Maintenance Program—for people hooked on old-time shoes. In addition to the computer printout, you can get a color Polaroid of the shoes you are wearing. Or you can pick out any others from our 500-page catalog. Some people get six color prints at a time. Hey, I understand. Nobody wants to go barefoot, especially in winter!"

Charles quickly left the store, stepping adroitly over a small puddle on the sidewalk. He would take the afternoon off, spend it quietly at home—if his Volkswagen in the parking garage would start.

In real life, Charles probably would have bought a pair of shoes assembled in an industrial processing zone located in the Third World. He may not have paid less for them than he would have had they been made in the United States. The story of Sadisah of Indonesia sewing shoes for Nike (Chapter 8) typifies the current pattern. When companies go abroad they commonly employ female labor, and low labor costs are not passed on to consumers.

THIRD WORLD WOMEN AND WORK: SADISAH OF INDONESIA REVISITED

Sadisah of Jakarta, Indonesia is not alone. Her position typifies the position of women in all parts of the Third World, and many feminist scholars have convincingly found that Third World women have many counterparts in the First World, where women are similarly trapped by gender, class, and race in destructive roles[6]; the women of Saco, Maine, the last site of U. S. production of Nike footwear, may have more in common with Indonesian assembly line workers than meets the slovenly eye.

Mindful of the analogy that makes the Third World woman, not totally unique, the overall position of the Third World woman can be further described. The following commentary presents a general picture and is therefore subject to the criticism of being "painted with too broad a brush" or

[6]John Bonsignore, et al., *Before the Law* (Boston: Houghton Mifflin, 1993), Chapter 9.

failing to take into account "differences in the position of women depending upon time, place, and circumstances." To borrow a point from law, the burden of proof should have shifted by now. It is up to those who wish to carve out exceptions to the general status and place of women in industry to come forward with countervailing evidence to that piling up on their abysmal condition.

The Third World woman is exploited regardless of the setting in which she works, that is, as a factory worker, as a home worker, in the "informal sector" (this includes sidewalk minirestaurants and tiny stands for selling), or as an agricultural worker.

She is often simultaneously at the bottom of the local hierarchy and at the bottom of the international hierarchy,[7] making her the principal victim of local and international exploitation. Sometimes she tries to stay in the country, where many peasants have been left landless, as more and more land is removed from subsistence food production and allocated to the production of cash crops for export; male and female peasants share this rural transformation just as they do much of urban squalor. Her husband, or man, may leave her with the children in the country as he flees outright to the city, or leaves in hopes of finding new possibilities for the family left in the country.

Aihwa Ong in her book on Malaysian women records the multiple facets of gender hierarchy in the workplace (a Japan-based multinational) and in the culture at large.[8] The Malays, like many Third world people, have become landless and for want of rural opportunities have migrated to the cities. The industrial processing zone has found a large labor pool of workers who have literally no experience with industrial practices and the discipline required of them. Ideal factory workers were young, fresh, "single" women, meaning that workers aged 16 to 24 had preference over "older workers" (aged 25 to 28).

Microscope work required the very young, who did not last long:

> Cash rewards were paid for particularly stressful tasks, such as the use of microscopes in electronics factories ... [F]resh recruits were routinely used so that by the time their eyesight had deteriorated in a couple of years, they would be replaced by new operators. A few might continue at the same tasks, wearing prescription glasses, or be transferred to other tasks; others resigned because their physical capacity for the work had been literally used up...out of the original batch of 300 microscope workers recruited in 1975, only 30 were still thus employed after four years.[9]

[7]See generally, Jeanne Bisilliat, et al., *Women in the Third World* (London: Associated University Press, 1987); Lynne Brydon, et al., *Women in the Third World* (New Brunswick: Rutgers University Press, 1989), 161-178; and H. Standing, "Employment" in Lisa Ostergaard, *Gender and Development* (London: Rutledge, 1992), pp. 57–75.

[8]A. Ong, *Spirits of Resistance and Capitalist Discipline* (Albany, New York: SUNY Press, 1987).

[9]Ibid., p. 166.

All of the common stereotypes of women and their tractability found their way into Malaysian investment brochures or managerial comments on the inevitability of the prevailing hierarchical division of labor based on age, gender, and ethnicity.

> *Promotional Brochure:*
> Her hands are small and she works fast with extreme care. Who therefore could be better qualified by *nature and inheritance* to contribute the efficiency of a bench assembly production line than the oriental girl? (Ong's own emphasis)
> *A Japanese manager:*
> [F]emales [are] better to concentrate [on] routine work [which may be] compared to knitting . . . young girls [are] preferable to do the job than older persons, that is because of eyesight.
> *Malay manager:*
> [W]e feel that females are more dexterous and more patient than males.
> *Chinese engineer:*
> You cannot expect a man to do very fine work for eight hours . . . Our work is designed for females . . . If we employ males, within one or two months they'd run away . . . Girls [sic] under thirty are easier to train and easier to adapt to the job function.[10]

Not quite. As Ong demonstrates, there was resistance of the women to being enslaved at every turn, but they were separated from their home areas, their families, and familiar life cycles, and often made the best of a very undesirable round of work and boarding house living. In the end the victims were blamed for a condition that was not of their own making, and were called *minal letrik*—hot stuff. Not a compliment in a Muslim country, the phrase says the women were naturally wild and, by extrapolation, that they deserved social ostracism and whatever treatment they got in the factories.

Ong is an anthropologist who records more than just the cultural and psychic impacts of industrialization. She analyzes the ethnic and gender patterns in the organizational structure of a Japanese electronics factory. The factory she studied in detail happened to be owned by a Japanese company, but was representative of all factories in the processing zone:

Transistor Assembly

Production manager (J)	J = Japanese
4 Supervisors (3C;1I)	C = Chinese
9 Foremen (5C, 2M, 1I) includes 1 female	I = Indian
7 Technicians (4C; 2M; 1I)	M = Malay

All in the hierarchy, except one, are male, and most are non-Malay. As one descends in the hierarchy, the work force is more female and more Malay:

[10]Ibid., pp. 152, 153.

Typical Work Team

Foreman (C)
3 Changehands (all female)
6 Line leaders (all female)
89 Operators (all female; 81M, 5I, 3C)[11]

The highest rank on the shop floor was changehand, of which there were 25 positions among 800 operators. Women earned M$3.50 (U.S. $1.50) to, M$4.00 (U.S. $1.80) per day (as compared to unskilled males, who earned from M$3.75 (U.S. $1.80) to M$4.80 (U.S. $ 2.15) per day (Ong's study ran from 1979 to 1981). The work week was six eight-hour days, and some Sunday overtime, with intense supervision and piece rates. Though the wages look low to Americans, the Malay women faced displacement from automation and were forced to accept frequent "speed ups" and multiple machine tending.[12]

The plight of the women of the Philippines is another example. When a Filipina comes to Manila, usually as an unattached female (sometimes leaving her children with relatives in the country), she will share a room with other unattached women, perhaps in the Tondo, one of the largest slums in the world.[13] She has two choices. Either she can become part of the "tourist trade," a euphemism for sex tours or other forms of prostitution in the red light district in Ermita. (She shares the sex trade with teenage boys billed as "the finest male models in the world," or with children to cater to pedophiles). Or she can go to the "zones" as an assembly worker in electronics, textiles, toys, or other labor-intensive light industry. (Some women live in dormitories at the factory with rent deducted from their pay.)

Whichever choice she makes, she will be burned out by her mid- to late twenties by long hours, low pay, substandard housing, poor nutrition, and perhaps disease, traceable either to industrial overwork or high-risk sexual labor, or both. By this time she will have long since been "washed up" as a potential mate even though she is still "young" by First World standards, and she will yield the field of pristine romance to the younger women who are in the identical position that she was in a few years before. If she is "lucky" she will catch a 60+ expatriate American, Australian, or European reject with money and declining vigor, who will keep her as a mistress or wife. In the culture the mistress-concubine-wife role is tolerated even when it involves what are in an outsider's eyes absurd age disparities, as just another way to earn one's living in a forbidding place. Moreover, if the woman "strikes it rich" in this way, she will be expected to cut her extended family in on the good fortune and share her, and where possible his, resources with them.[14] (Remember, they are also probably destitute.)

[11]Ibid., p. 170.

[12]Ibid., pp. 155–170.

[13]The Philippine migration and boarding house living are documented in Loraine Gray's film, "Global Assembly Line" (Educational Television and Films, 1986).

[14]Author's interview in the Philippines, January and February, 1990.

Ann Warner's profile of the *maquila* workers of Mexico sounds very much like the ones already drawn for Malaysia and the Philippines:

> Multinationals have primarily employed young women aged 16-24. In the early stages of *maquiladora* development they constituted up to 90% of the Mexican export processing labor force in border communities. Women were predominately hired for assembly work. Electronics *maquiladoras* teach workers a series of repetitive . . . work tasks. Managers have repeatedly indicated that they prefer to hire women for these tasks because they have greater dexterity and visual acuity and are more patient than men.[15]

Like the Malaysian women, the women of *maquila* are rarely above the lowest places in the company hierarchy. Technical and managerial positions, which carry higher pay, are reserved for men. A *U.S. News and World Report* story tells about work and living in the maquiladora zone:

> *Maquiladora* employees—most of them women who sometimes start work as young as 13 years old—are exposed to toxic substances and other workplace health hazards without being given safety instructions or basic protection like masks or gloves. There is also evidence of severe birth defects suffered by infants born to workers.
>
> The *maquiladoras* . . . have sustained explosive growth of 15 to 20% over the past five years. As a result, tens of thousands of workers are now packed in shantytown *colonies*, living in hovels built from cinder blocks, tin sheets, scrap lumber, plastic and cardboard without electricity, sewers, or potable water.
>
> Some of these conditions might be endurable if the prospect of upward economic mobility weren't so distant...Wages start at 82,000 pesos ($27) for a 49 hour week. The average weekly salary is about $47 in a border economy where food and other necessities are as expensive as in the United States.
>
> *The industry response:*
>
> *V.P. Electronics:* "We're in a foreign country and it's a big mistake to impose U.S. values."
>
> *Trade Association Chief:* "Are these people better off with me or without me? The small wages gives them the ability to enjoy a decent lifestyle. They may not be living in the lap of luxury, but they aren't starving."[16]

To generalize further, the Third world woman inherits her unenviable position from the colonial era, when she was on the bottom of both externally imposed and internally imposed power–status hierarchies. The problem may go even deeper than the last few centuries. The novelist Albert Camus puts the following words into the mouth of his false prophet:

> [O]ne can't get along without dominating or being served. Every man needs slaves as he needs fresh air. Commanding is breathing—. . . . And even the most destitute manage to breathe.

[15]A. Warner, "The Sociological Impact of the Maquiladoras," in Khosrow Fatemi, ed., *The Maquiladora Industry*, (New York: Praeger, 1990), pp. 187, 188.

[16]*U.S. News and World Report*, May 6, 1991, p. 46. See also Chapter 12 for more details.

> The lowest man in the social scale still has his wife or his child. If he's unmarried, a dog. The essential thing, after all, is being able to get angry with someone who has no right to answer back . . . Power . . . settles everything.[17]

The responsibility for this indefensible structure is local and international; local in that men have been accomplices rather than antagonists to the outside forces that shape all of the important facets of local economies and their accompanying law–government regimes[18]; locals will often try to make themselves part of the opportunity structure offered by the multinational, even though if they thought about it, the deal they strike threatens a generation of workers in its long term effects.

Outsiders, such as the principals of a multinational enterprise, stay at least one step away from the blood, delegating the violence to subsidiaries, along with production schedules and factory inputs. Their crime ranks higher in heinousness, since it cannot be partially justified by situational necessity.

This is the story. There are ways to prettify the picture by talking about new and independent roles for women, or their improved bargaining power in their family, or with their mates, as they become wage earners. There is talk of learning "new skills," and finding "new relationships with other women" that can lead to profound political changes.

Where the unenviable position of women as workers is more squarely acknowledged, it is sometimes dismissed as a transient condition analogous to industrial women of the First World who were eventually more empowered than they were as "housewives." All of the foregoing may be true, but for the critical present these palliatives are patently out of keeping with the more persistent realities of a Third World woman's life. She often must perform all roles: preparing food, tending children, working at home and "at work," and face being turned into an utterly exhausted and dispirited person, if she survives at all.

Question for Research

It is often said in the case studies of particular countries that it is impossible to generalize on the economic-cultural conditions of women, and how they respond to their situation. Others, including the author, say that there are general conditions traceable to the forms of international production being advanced everywhere. Make a study of a country and the place of women in it. The references in the footnotes might be a place to start, but there are now abundant studies done on many countries. After research, compare notes to see whether the experience of women is of a single piece or unique and dependent on the place where they live.

[17]Albert Camus, *The Fall*, trans. Justin O'Brien (London: Hamish Hamilton,1957), pp. 34, 35.

[18]Cheryl Payer, *The Debt Trap* (New York: Monthly Review Press, 1974), pp. 43, 44.

SOUTH OF THE BORDER—MEXICAN VIEWS ON NAFTA

The most commonly heard views from Mexico on NAFTA came from the Mexican government.[19] As one would expect, having studied Mexican investment policy and the maquiladora policy, the Mexican central government views NAFTA as a logical step to promote foreign investment and export-led growth. These policies have been formulated in consultation with the IMF and World Bank to improve the ability of Mexico to service debt.

Most Americans, when hearing resistance to NAFTA in the United States, have assumed that all Mexicans are unqualifiedly in favor of the treaty. On closer study they will learn that many Mexicans have a list of fears as long or longer than many people in the United States.[20] They don't trust their government, and they fear the expansion of U.S. economic power in Mexico.

Their government is a dictatorship run by a single political party, the PRI, which has been in power since 1929. In recent elections there have been well documented cases of vote fraud, which renders the party's claim to legitimate authority specious.[21]

The party has maintained its position by an elaborate system of patronage and interest-group favoritism. Unfortunately, patronage and party influence go all the way back to prerevolutionary days and the dictatorship of Porfirio Diaz. B. Traven in his novel-treatise *Government* describes point-blank the pre-1911 practices:

> The government was represented in the eastern district by Don Casimiro . . . Like every other jefe politico, Don Casimiro thought first of his own interests. He served his country not for his country's good, but in order to profit at its expense. He worked better on those terms and, above all, he lived better. If a man can earn no more as a servant of the state than he can by running a snack bar, there is no reason whatever why he should aspire to devote his energies to his country's service.
>
> After he had taken care of himself he thought of his family. Then came his intimate friends. These friends had helped him obtain his post and now he had to humor them so they would let him keep it...
>
> Every member of his family to its remotest branches . . . all were taken care of. They were given jobs as tax collectors, postmasters, chiefs of police, justices of the peace as long as he could hold his . . .
>
> The manner of administering the public welfare began at the top with the president, Don Porfirio, was carried on in the same fashion by his secretaries; it was taken up in turn by his generals, copied exactly by the governors of the various states, and handed to the mayors of the smallest towns and villages...
>
> Since little if any ability was visible at the top, even less was looked for at the bottom. People were grateful to be allowed to live at all. And if a man was murdered because he had gotten heated over some administrative roguery or fla-

[19]See, for example, J. Puche, "The North American Free Trade Agreement," *Vital Speeches*, LIX, April 15, 1993, pp. 395–398.

[20]Sidney Weintraub, *A Marriage of Convenience* (New York: Oxford, 1990) pp. 27–66.

[21]Ibid., pp. 42–49.

grant example of bribery and corruption, his neighbors and friends were only thankful that they had escaped. The victim was buried and forgotten, and all he had by way of epitaph was, "What did he want to burn his fingers for?"[22]

That was pre-1911-revolution—what about today?. Writers in 1983 summarized the current status of corruption: "Aspirants out of political office now peacefully await their turn at corruption as well as power."[23] Sidney Weintraub describes practices differing only in intensity and scale from the ones described by Traven:

> Any analysis of corruption in Mexico must deal not only with overt bribery, excessive enrichment by public officials, and the spoils for members of the PRI, but also with the discretionary use of import licenses and import exemptions . . .[24]

Later he adds:

> The PRI controls the spoils. It can make or break political careers and distribute jobs to the faithful. The very existence of much of Mexican industry is due to the PRI, and so industrialists look to the government, and therefore to the PRI, for import privileges, tax concessions, and procurement . . .[25]

The Mexicans thus have good reasons not to trust their government. The government has, for more years than Mexicans want to think about, been an opportunity structure for some at the expense of many.

Mexicans have also seen the distribution of returns in Mexico. Whether from industry or government, Weintraub finds the returns stratified:

> The big winners for the past fifty years have been the business community, professionals (such as lawyers and engineers), organized labor, large scale farmers and the bureaucracy. These groups dominate the political structure and have the largest incomes. Those who have benefitted less include unorganized labor, small farmers, especially those cultivating crops in rain-fed areas, and persons flooding into the cities because of the lack of opportunity in rural areas. Intellectuals have mostly been in the more privileged group.[26]

Lest this writer be accused of quoting Weintraub for some purposes and then sidestepping his conclusion, Weintraub favors the "opening up" of the Mexican economy and the Mexican political system through free trade. Why the dismal record that he recounts will not repeat itself, or even be intensified after new trade relationships, is not altogether clear. But then, his book on Mexican–United States relationships is entitled *A Marriage of Convenience* and does not purport to record a relationship founded on oceanic love.[27]

[22]B. Traven, *Government* (London: Atleson & Busby, 1980), pp. 1,2.

[23]Daniel Levy, quoted in S. Weintraub, op. cit., p. 52.

[24]Ibid., p. 33.

[25]Ibid., p. 39.

[26]Ibid., p. 27.

[27]In an article after the NAFTA debate opened, Weintraub characterized NAFTA as an episode in the relationship between the two countries and not an endpoint. S. Weintraub, "The economy on the Eve of Free Trade," *Current History,* February 1993, pp. 67–72.

Distrust of their own government does not mean that dissatisfied Mexicans will welcome increased U. S. presence with open arms. Most Mexicans distrust the United States as much or more than their local antiheroes. Four hundred years of Mexican history tell why thinking Mexicans would be testy at the prospect of opening of Mexico to more foreign direct investment under NAFTA. Since the Conquest in 1519, there has been a constant struggle over Mexican wealth, which, to put it mildly, the Mexicans have not always won.

Spain ruled Mexico until after 1821, when independence finally prevailed, but independence did not end the sometimes abrasive relationship with outsiders. The United States fought the Mexican War in 1846 and eventually took control of what are now the states of California, New Mexico, and Arizona. Texas had already been annexed. The map of 1820 Mexico in Figure 14-1 shows just how big a territorial bite the United States took from the old Mexican empire. Spain, Great Britain, and France were also extensively involved with Mexico throughout the nineteenth century. After floating loans that went unpaid, they invaded the country in 1862.[28]

The 1911 Mexican Revolution was an attempt at overthrow of both domestic and foreign controls. The revolution still lives in the Mexican memory and casts its long shadow across the current free trade debate. Porfirio Diaz, discussed above, who ruled from 1876 until his overthrow in 1911, financed his regime through a combination of international and domestic alliances, both of which exploited Mexico's rural and urban poor.[29] Foreign investors were given concessions, while Diaz consolidated domestic control through political patronage and the protection of rural estates and nascent industry.

Why this digression into the history of Mexico? The first reason—a not especially good one—is that everyone needs background to understand the tensions over NAFTA. This is of course true. But a better reason exists. A study of history tells us the right question to ask. With the new trade treaty, are the two countries beginning a new round of dominance–subservience with highly stratified returns, or has some new scheme been invented, with mutual benefits up and down the line for all participants?

Following are two voices from Mexico.

[28]Howard Cline, *Mexico: Revolution to Evolution 1940–1960* (New York: Oxford, 1963), pp. 7–29.

[29]Traven, op. cit., pp. 44, 71, 128, 133. For a highly readable account of pre-Revolutionary Mexico, see Traven's "jungle series" of six novels (*Government* is the first).

FIGURE 14-1

Source: Howard Cline, *Mexico: Revolution to Evolution* 1940–1960 (New York: Oxford, 1963), p. 16.

MEXICAN DEVELOPMENT CONCERNS

Dr. Gustavo del Castillo Vera[30]

. . . I . . . have always been an academic specializing in U.S.–Mexico trade policy making.

Those of us who have studied and experienced events in Mexico since the middle of the 70's have been concerned about the future of the country; this concern has been magnified since the economic crisis of 1982 which left Mexico with an intolerable debt burden, high rates of inflation, galloping unemployment, and the general worsening of the lives of most Mexicans. Between 1981 and 1987, the minimum wage in Mexico City fell by 50 percent; between 1981 and 1985 the number of workers receiving salaries below the minimum wage grew from 13 to 40 percent. The worsening of economic conditions has also severely affected the dietary intake and health of middle and working class populations.

By the early 1980's it was clear that Mexico needed to implement drastic changes in order to overcome a bankrupt

[30]U.S. Congress, House Committee on Banking, Subcommittee on International Development, 102nd Congress, First Session, April 1991, pp. 119–128.

economy and regain the confidence of a disillusioned people. A development plan was enacted in the early 1980's, the culmination of which now rests on securing a North American Free Trade Agreement.

Mexico's Development Model

The changes that continue to be envisioned by Mexican policy makers involve the redesign of Mexican economic thinking. The old model of import substitution and endogenous capital accumulation as the primary source of capital must be abandoned, and a new model of economic development must be formulated where growth is the result of the dynamic incorporation of Mexican production into regional and global markets. The search for free trade at a continental level through a tripartite free trade agreement . . . is a critical part of this model . . .

Over the past decade, the model has aimed at restructuring foreign economic policy through: (1) Adjusting foreign debt payments to the capacity of the country to pay. (2) Creating conditions to convince international lenders to make further capital available to Mexico which would serve the developmental process and to stabilize the currency. (3) Securing stable trading conditions for Mexican products which would guarantee already established market shares and provide favorable conditions for new Mexican products.

Internally the model aimed to drastically reduce the role of the state which had commanded a virtual monopoly of economic development policies through the control of investments in infrastructure, employment, prices and credit. The control had led to runaway public sector spending, converting the state into the greatest source of internal debt. The new model places the private sector as a primary actor in defining economic development . . . through free markets . . .

Overcoming Short-Term Costs and Securing Long-Term Benefits

A free trade area is not necessarily a guarantee that the costs of economic integration will be distributed equally within the countries involved or among the populations within these countries. In fact, the most recent empirical studies indicate that the costs . . . will not be shared equally . . . and that elements of success will differ between the short term and the long term.

The data indicates that in the short run (up until 1995), the U.S. stands to gain much more than Mexico from a free trade agreement . . . The University of Maryland study predicts a short-term loss of some 200,000 jobs in the Mexican agricultural sector due to U.S. agricultural exports, and substantial job losses in the Mexican machinery exporting sector . . . [T]he primary question here is whether . . . other employment opportunities will be created . . .

The generation of employment in Mexico is contingent upon direct foreign investment. . . . Furthermore . . . the nature of the investment is also important. If development strategies of firms favor capital intensiveness, then the question of Mexican employment will still linger . . .

One other related dimension . . . is its effects on Mexican income distribution . . . Since Mexico now counts as the second worse Latin American country in terms of the distribution of income, one has to ask how this trend could be reversed . . . Initial data demonstrates that since Mexico joined GATT and opened its economy, 80 percent of Mexican exports have come from the operations of ten companies, only two of which are Mexican. There is little doubt that increases in capital accumulation follow established patterns of concentration. Therefore, one should be concerned that income distribution patterns not follow the same trend as the concentration in export industries.

A related question is what effect this concentration of economic activity in a few enterprises will have on the price structure within Mexico. Cartels can manipulate internal prices, thereby raising the cost of imports and obviating [sic] the assumed benefits of lower consumer prices.

Finally if foreign firms do receive national treatment, the problems of unemployment, price distortion and capital accumulation might be exacerbated through the takeover of existing national firms. Under these conditions, open markets and liberalized investment rules would have negative effects in Mexico which cannot be ignored. This is true not only because of their negative economic effects, but also because of the political reaction in Mexico at the sight of disappearing Mexican industries, and of the transference of profits to centers outside the country.

In spite of the many issues which concern individual nations, a more general development issue has to be addressed; should economic issues be addressed solely under a national perspective, or should continental concerns be resolved on a common basis? This question is of special relevance today as we see the rise of transnational production blocks such as the European Economic Community and the Pacific Basin and the overwhelming presence of Japanese interests there. In more general terms, the question that has to be answered is whether North America will be in a position to face increasing competition from other regional blocks as well as the growth of regional protectionism . . . If the answer . . . is yes, steps must be taken to insure the national interest of each of these countries is defined in terms of the long-run collective economic security of the entire region and not through the expression of parochial interests . . .

Forging a North American Free Trade Agreement is a critical next step . . .

Questions and Comments

1. In light of Castillo's summary of the recent economic history of Mexico, is NAFTA Mexico's first choice or a last resort?
2. There is a question as to how Mexico's very young and growing labor force will fit into newer trade relations. If development is labor-intensive then youth and numbers will be valued, but to the extent that it is capital-intensive, labor will be less valued. The type of international investments will also determine the strata of Mexican society which will benefit most from liberalized trade. The more capital-intensive, the more highly stratified will be the returns.
3. Castillo warns of the problem of economic concentration after freer trade is initiated. This fear harkens back to the material on antitrust in Chapter 6, and the failure in the United States to limit concentration, or the control of markets and prices by oligopolistic firms.

His point also has nationalistic overtones, since the concentration of enterprise could be non-Mexican, placing Mexican welfare beyond Mexican control.

4. Castillo Vera's concerns border on the question of national sovereignty and the ability of nationally based political systems to exert consequent control over the directions of enterprise and the costs and benefits attendant to them.

   His answer seems to be that there should be full harmonization across the three countries joined by the treaty, leading one to assume that there would be less differences over time across the territories now demarcated by national boundaries. This would raise the standard of living in Mexico to the levels in the United States and Canada.

Do multinational corporations thrive on harmonization and evening out of differences among the different countries where production and distribution take place, or do they thrive on differences? If the latter, what are the prospects of Mexico and Mexican citizens becoming equal partners in joint prosperity?

TESTIMONY OF ADOLFO ZINSER ON NAFTA[31]

... I am a professor and Senior Researcher at the Center for Studies of the United States ...

The free trade negotiations between our three countries represent an historical opportunity to transform our intense economic relationship into a genuine association of mutual prosperity, cooperation and social development. However, we can easily misuse this opportunity. Short-term political objectives and misguided illusions could persuade us that a quick and narrow agreement of limited scope is sufficient to promote growth and productivity in Mexico, to create jobs, and to raise automatically the income levels of many Mexicans without significantly damaging the welfare of Americans and Canadians ... On the basis of such expectations many Americans have already been persuaded that ... a narrow free trade deal is desirable because it will cause a drastic reduction in migratory flows of Mexican workers to the United States. To expect that a restricted free trade agreement will automatically put into motion the kind of economic process necessary to overcome Mexico's ancient development gaps is, I think, a serious miscalculation ...

The economic and social integration of Mexico and the United States has been underway for more than six decades and it is precisely that experience which we must examine to determine the kind of economic pact we need ... What we think are the most dynamic and successful areas of our economic integration are often equally the cause of serious disruptions. This is, for instance, the case of the maquiladora investments in the border region. Today, more than twenty-five years after the maquiladora program started, the single most important contri-

[31]U.S. Congress, House Committee on Foreign Affairs, Subcommittee on International Economic Policy, The North American Free Trade Agreement, 102nd Congress, First Session, March 1991, pp. 40–49.

bution . . . is the half million jobs they give to Mexican workers. Although no significant backward linkages have been established (less than 3% of maquiladora inputs come from Mexican suppliers) employment is clearly an achievement. However, even if it is true that the salaries in the maquiladoras are perceptibly higher than average salaries in the rest of Mexican industry, the income levels of the maquiladora workers have not risen significantly in this period, certainly not at the same rate as labor productivity has increased. Border integration is today an overwhelming reality; however, such integration has not automatically induced a harmonization of norms regarding the protection of the environment, occupational safety and other working conditions. On the contrary the two most characteristic features of the Mexican border environment—cheap labor and poor environmental controls—are seen as incentives for foreign investors . . .

Free trade must above all be an instrument of prosperity. Without the social development dimension . . ., this initiative will at best serve only to promote growth restricted to the northern regions of Mexico, where the economic integration with the United States is really taking place. This will happen at the expense of regional development and economic equity in most of the country. Instead of boosting Mexico's overall economic and social development, the agreement will help to concentrate income in few hands and in few places, it will jeopardize the environment, it will restrict economic opportunities, it will intensify social resentments and polarize demands; ultimately it will promote the consolidation of the authoritarian antidemocratic system of government suffered by Mexico . . .

Mexico is not a democracy and not even the best and most comprehensive Free Trade Agreement can modify that. Only Mexicans can change the authoritarian regime. However . . . a fair and equitable trade pact . . . can help Mexicans to struggle for their economic rights and civil liberties.

The discussion of the FTA has . . . already caused some democratic outcomes; labor unions, environmental groups, human rights organizations, concerned scholars, and independent social critics of our three countries have spontaneously inaugurated a direct and frank civic dialogue that has no precedent in our relationship . . .

Mexicans do not live in a political environment where people can openly express views and opinions that challenge official creeds. Mexican authorities have tried to prevent an open debate about free trade. The government exercises almost a monolithic control of all political messages transmitted through the mass media, particularly television. Nothing about the FTA goes on the air that is not strictly consistent with the views of the authorities. The limited freedom enjoyed by the written press is constantly suffocated by a combination of mechanisms including corruption [and] outright intimidation of critics and by unrestricted use of public funds for official propaganda. Despite these restrictions and often in defiance of government controls, many sectors of Mexican society have . . . spoken out, manifesting their deep concerns about . . . what Mexicans should expect to gain and lose from the agreement. The Mexican government has responded to these concerns, resorting to character assassinations, calling its most vocal critics traitors . . . assuring the public that in the FTA there are only winners, no losers . . .

The majority of Mexicans are not in principle opposed to the FTA. In fact, never before has Mexican society been better inclined to negotiate a broad economic agreement . . . However, concerned Mexican citizens are opposed to the authoritarian methods by which the government wants to resolve this issue. There is in Mexico a growing fear that in the process of these negotiations some fundamental social concerns will be ignored, that Mexican authorities, urged by their own short-term political necessities, will make costly concessions and make a bad deal when a mutually beneficial agreement is deemed possible.

These suspicions refer mainly to three fundamental questions. First and foremost is the fear that oil resources will be traded in the agreement for commercial concessions or investment commitments. Oil has a central role in Mexico's modern struggle for independence; it is not only a symbol of sovereignty, it is widely recognized as a collective patrimony, a resource Mexicans should use responsibly to develop and should preserve for future generations. No other national asset has this prominence. Although many Mexicans recognize that our national oil industry has not been administered prudently or efficiently, I am convinced that Mexican society is not and will never be prepared to give up this responsibility, transferring the administration of the oil industry partially or totally to private and foreign interests . . . [N]ot even the most energetic commitments of the authorities . . . [have] dissipated public suspicions. On the one hand the war in the gulf has been perceived in most sectors . . . as a reminder of the strategic importance the U.S. government attaches to oil . . . On the other hand many Mexicans think that given the eagerness and readiness of the government to sign an FTA, oil can still be included as a last-minute hidden or disguised clause . . .

The second area of public suspicion relates to the fear that the FTA will only benefit a few industrial, commercial and financial monopolies who control most of Mexico's assets and wealth. The experience of the past few years proves that economic liberalization and privatization . . . [are] not necessarily conducive to decentralization of political and economic power. Free trade might phase out from the economic scene small and medium size industries, leaving the industrial and commercial base of the country in the hands of big sharks and foreign investors. In any event most Mexicans are aware of the fact that market-oriented economic policies are not adopted in Mexico at the expense of government's power to arbitrarily impose its might on economic actors. Wage controls that have cost a 60% reduction in real income since 1982 are a vivid example of how the government combines economic freedom with political imposition. As long as the investment promotion policies . . . are based on low wages, and while independent and democratic unions continue to be suppressed, Mexican workers know that salaries will not increase when jobs are created nor when productivity rises. A social charter and an effective dispute settlement mechanism . . . will reassure Mexican workers that the purpose of the continental economic pact is really to close the gap between the rich and poor.

The third major concern expressed by the Mexican public is the future of subsistence agriculture. This is not a sector like any other; it will require outright protection and significant support for an indefinite period of time . . . exposing it to indiscriminate international competition would simply be disastrous for ten million people . . .

Questions

1. Zinser does not seem to be content with the current state of the Mexican economy, or its law–government system. While he acknowledges that most Mexicans are for the trade agreement, he observes they are forlorn about the future well-being of the average Mexican. What are they concerned about? Against the background of your study of multinationals in many places, do these concerns seem well founded or fanciful?

   If you were an adviser for various Mexican groups *outside* the circle of business–government power, what would you recommend?
2. Zinser wonders whether NAFTA will reinforce authoritarian rule and stratification of power and wealth in Mexico. Evaluate.
3. Sometimes in the United States press the opening of trade is called "reform" and equated with enhanced freedom. Will increased trade inevitably lead to greater political freedom, or must political freedom precede trade agreements?
4. Should the end point of U.S.–Canada–Mexico relationships parallel those now being worked out in Europe—elimination of borders, free movement of people, common currency, and so on? Common citizenship and a *continental* legislature with representation based on one person one vote?

   If the United States cannot envision such end points, what would this say about the good faith of U.S. motivations regarding NAFTA?

   If no deep interconnections are anticipated, is it likely that there will be a long-term evening out of wages, working conditions, or the improvement of environmental conditions in Mexico?
5. Zinser endorses the abiding importance of subsistence agriculture. If the United States can export the staples of the Mexican diet—corn and beans—then why should there be such concern over the preservation of subsistence farming?

NORTH OF THE BORDER

One of the ways both the Bush and Clinton administrations have tried to console workers in the United States on free trade agreements such as NAFTA is that the treaties will extend the practices common in enterprise processing zones, without eliminating the best jobs in the United States. If the international production system were put in terms of the human body, the *head* will stay in the First World while the *hands* will be in the Third.[32] (The hands in many industries will be female hands, although the breakdown of contemporary international employment by gender does not receive enough discussion.) The exported jobs have been written off by experts as "low end jobs" or "simple assembly."

[32]Richard Barnet, *The Lean Years*, (New York: Simon & Schuster, 1980), pp. 267–294.

The continuation of this hierarchy of world labor runs throughout the NAFTA debate as conducted by elite U. S. spokespeople. Few people in the labor movement believe that the treaty will mean more and better employment in the United States, or that existing companies will be in the same production configuration five years hence, and one third of the people on the streets of the United States agree.

The primary focus of the contemporary debate on the future of U.S. labor has been the NAFTA debate, although the movement of production abroad has been going on for a long time, and will probably continue, if current law and policy continue. Following are four excerpts: the first shows the existence of consequential automobile production in Mexico. This excerpt corrects the common misconception in the United States that when NAFTA is implemented production *will* move. Production *has already moved*, in part because of the liberalization of Mexico's trade and investment laws (see Chapter 11) and the reduction of U.S. tariffs to 3–6 percent on imports. The battle over NAFTA concerned whether the movement to Mexico would be expanded even further than existing laws already facilitate.

A major auto industry has been growing in Mexico, as the next reading shows.

WE DO WHAT THE MEXICANS DO[33]

Jerry Flint

While the auto business flags in the U.S., it is booming in Mexico. Domestic sales there have doubled in the last three years, and so has the number of cars produced for export, mostly to the U.S. And guess what? Honda and Toyota aren't the winners. They don't sell in Mexico. The winners are Ford, General Motors and Chrysler, plus Volkswagen and Nissan. A new Ford Taurus costs around $25,000 in Mexico, about 50% more than in the U.S. Yet Mexicans will buy 650,000 new cars and trucks this year, against 550,000 last year. But there are still only 66 cars for every 1,000 people in Mexico, versus 500 cars for every 1,000 people in the U.S. Closing that gap to, say 120 cars per 1,000 people would bring the Mexican car market to 1 million sales.

Thanks to protection against outsiders, the companies that have invested in Mexico are making good money even on their relatively low volumes.

But Mexico offers more than a good market. It is an increasingly favorable place to build cars and parts. With its hardworking people and low wages, Mexico is becoming a key piece in Detroit's entire effort to become profitable again.

Of the nearly 1 million vehicles currently being produced in Mexico, close to 400,000 finished cars are for export, mostly to the U.S. and Canada. These include Mercury Tracers, Dodge Shadow convertibles, Buick Centurys, Volkswagen Golfs, plus millions of radios, engines and other parts. Total value: $7 billion shipped to the U.S. last year.

[33]J. Flint, "We Do What the Mexicans Do," *Forbes*, September 2, 1991, pp. 72–80.

The volume is likely to grow, particularly with the free-trade rules being drawn up now.

Volkswagen is creating an export-oriented production base in Puebla, two hours outside Mexico City, in the shadow of the smoking Popocatépetl volcano. This year VW will send 400,000 engines and 200,000 axle sets back to Germany; from the fall of 1992 every VW Golf and Jetta sold in the U.S. and Canada will come from Puebla. "For the first time in our life, we're in sight of real economies of scale, and for our suppliers, too," says Martin Josephi, chairman of VW de Mexico.

Ford is spending $700 million to upgrade—and build new small engines at—its Chihuahua engine plant, which exported 270,000 engines last year. Nissan has proposed spending $1 billion on parts-producing plants and a new assembly plant in Mexico. Mercedes plans to assemble cars in Mexico and, if that works well, maybe export them to the U.S. Why? Because those Japanese luxury cars are killing Mercedes on price.

That Mercedes is interested in Mexico says something about the country's manufacturing quality. Last year a Massachusetts Institute of Technology study group called Ford's plant in Hermosillo better than the best plants in Japan. (The plant makes Ford Escort station wagons and Mercury Tracers for export only.) GM's chairman, Robert Stempel, says his engine plant in Mexico is his best worldwide, and his car plant at Ramos Arizpe is getting one discrepancy per car—"pretty top drawer for anybody."

"They [the foreign companies] are all over us on quality," says an executive from Grupo Summa, a major Mexican auto parts producer. "If we don't get Q1, we won't get the business. No Pentastar, we lose Chrysler. But that's all to the good." This businessman expects to triple his $100-million-a-year business in three to five years.

Mexico's basic attraction is, of course, its huge reserves of low-cost labor. In the U.S. wages and benefits run past $30 an hour for automakers. In Spain the figure is $16 an hour. In Mexico it's $1.55 an hour on the border and around $5.50 in Mexico City. That's for American companies. Mexican-owned partsmakers may not be nearly as generous. In the Mexico City area, for instance, the minimum wage is $4 a day.

Okay, wages are low, but how's the productivity?

At Chrysler's plant at Toluca, 4,000 production workers turn out 30 automobiles an hour. In a typical U.S. plant, 2,400 workers would roll 60 a hour. So the U.S. plant is three and a half times more productive. But U.S. workers are at least ten times more expensive than their Mexican counterparts; net, the advantage swings to Mexico—and will continue to do so as new investment lifts Mexican productivity.

Not surprisingly, the United Auto Workers union is resisting the proposed U.S./Mexico free-trade agreement. But Martin Josephi, head of VW in Mexico, points out,"If the American companies don't . . . shift to Mexico and get lower costs, they'll close the plants and lose the jobs anyway."

In one sense the Mexican plants may be saving some U.S. jobs. GM Chairman Stempel points to GM's Deltronicos *maquiladora*—foreign parts, Mexican assembly—plant in Matamoros, where 4,000 workers assemble 3 million car radios a year. This is no sweatshop operation. The plant is clean, air-conditioned and filled with electronic equipment, even a laser etcher. Its workers, mostly women in their early 20s, are better dressed at work than are people on the streets of Matamoros.

The plant's radios are shipped to the U.S. for installation in American-made GM cars and trucks. In a curious way, this low-wage plants helps preserve the jobs at GM's electronics complex in Kokomo, Ind., where 10,000 people work. "The high-tech in Kokomo is balanced with the manual work offshore," Stempel says. By investing in Mexico, he says, "we saved jobs rather than migrating jobs."

Rimir, another GM *maquiladora* at Matamoros, makes plastic bumper facias (fronts) and trim. A sister plant, in Anderson, Ind., makes similar parts. Rimir's low costs average down GM's total facia bill. "If I wasn't here our sister plant in Anderson wouldn't be here. We'd be out of the facia business," says Chuck Almquist, the plant manager. But Almquist makes another point. "Look, if we were just asking for cheap labor, we'd have all the plants in Haiti. GM likes to build where we sell. This is a $100 million investment. We're not talking about 15 sewing machines."

In the longer run wages will rise in Mexican automobile plants, but that will not end Mexico's advantage: There is still plenty of room to offset the cost increases with more investment in equipment. While a few Mexican auto plants, like Ford's Hermosillo plant, are state-of-the-art, most are years, decades, generations behind in technology. Cars are painted by hand with spray guns. Bumps and dings are filed down and polished with handheld files and metal finishing discs. You hear the pounding of hammers on metal; there are greasy pits with men working beneath cars. Fits are measured on old-fashioned jigs. Henry Ford—the original Henry Ford—would have felt at home in the Nissan plant at Cuernavaca.

It helps that Mexican labor is highly motivated. Roberto Gutierrez, the swarthy manager of Chrysler's Toluca plant, manages 4,000 production workers. He tells Forbes: "I said we don't do what the Japanese or anybody else does. We do what Mexicans do. People say we don't like to work too much. You like siesta. You don't want to be active. 'Okay,' I tell my people, 'continue that way. But do the job right, the first time.'

"We are very proud to say that [our quality] is better than the U.S.," Gutierrez continues. "People always ask me how many robots I use to build car. I say I have 4,000 robots."

"A man loses this $1.50-an-hour job, he goes to 25 cents an hour, or maybe nothing," says Chrysler de Mexico's president, Carlos Lobo. "He cannot afford to lose the best job he will ever have." Mexican unions, unlike their U.S. counterparts, let the companies run the factories.

The carmakers are anxiously awaiting the final drafting of the U.S./Mexico trade pact. While presenting them with opportunities, the agreement has its pitfalls for them, too. A special auto side pact is under negotiation now.

It's too early to know what the agreement will provide. But it is clear that the five automakers in Mexico, having invested billions in Mexican industry at the demand of the Mexican government, want protection.

They don't want to see Toyotas and Hondas taking their profitable volume away with cars exported south from new nonunion plants in Kentucky and Ohio. Nor do they want to see "screwdriver plants" in Mexico, with Mexican workers putting Japanese vehicles together from Japanese parts and shipping them north duty free, as Mexican cars.

In a larger sense, both countries have a lot to gain from the continued development of the Mexican industry. The U.S. wants a prosperous, stable Mexico, and the automobile industry is a magnificent engine for raising unskilled workers into the middle class. It creates not only better-paying jobs but also a class of skilled workers and managers, and demand for roads, services, gas stations, drive-ins, repairs.

Perhaps most important, it creates mobility and enables people to look about for the best job, the best price, the best place to live. Yes, growth of the Mexican industry will cost U.S. autoworkers jobs, but these jobs may be doomed anyway. As David Hendrickson, manager of GM's Deltronics plant in Matamoros, put it: "I'd rather see a job go to Mexico than to Taiwan."

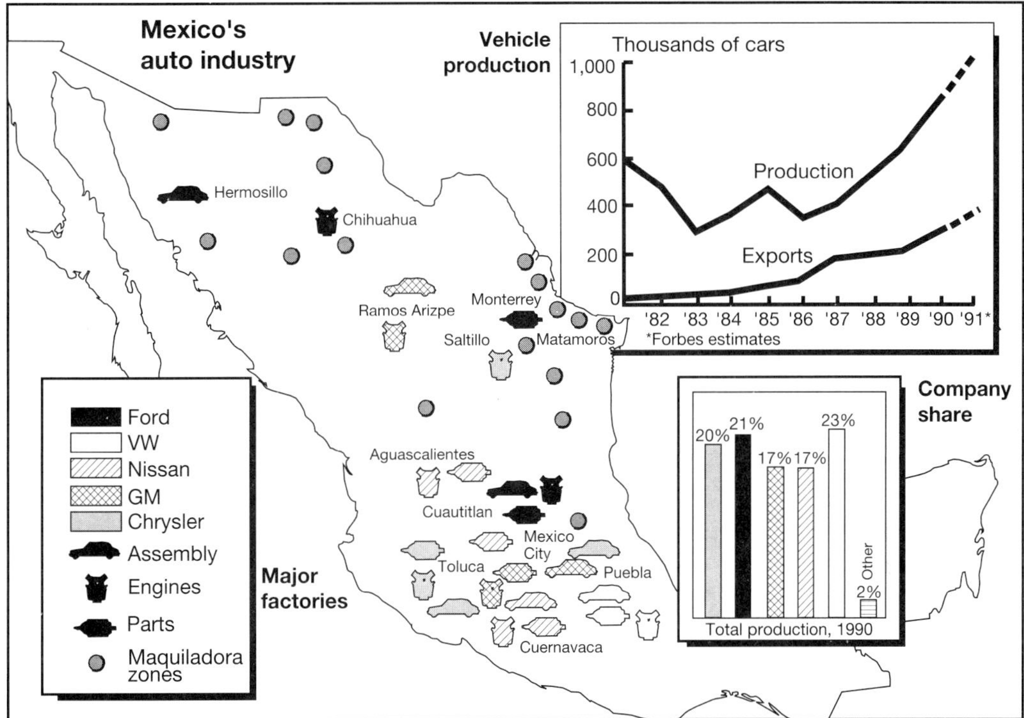

FIGURE 14-2 Five companies share Mexico's car/truck growth. Old plants ring Mexico City, while new factories and maquiladora parts plants are sited in the north and along the border.

Comments and Questions

Based on the current practices in automobile manufacturing, is it safe to say that, after NAFTA, the production of inputs to cars will remain in the United States, even if more assembly is done in Mexico?

This question concerns the likelihood of forward and backward integration of phases of production. Is the next logical step from assembly to the production of inputs for assembly? Or if the production is of inputs, is it predictable that the assembly of the inputs into other products will likely be next?

Forward and backward integration becomes important because both the Bush and Clinton administrations have derived the employment impacts of NAFTA from current levels of exports to Mexico. Implicit in this projection is that historical patterns of phases of production will continue.[34] How safe is it to assume that there will be no structural changes after NAFTA is ratified?

The foregoing material on automobile production in Mexico should also remind us that the liberalization of Mexican trade and investment law has already brought a great deal of investment to Mexico.

As one peruses the many Congressional hearings conducted on the impacts of NAFTA, one must be struck by the overall enthusiasm of the largest U. S. businesses and their associations for the treaty.[35] This enthusiasm found its way into the many *Wall Street Journal* stories that conveyed the idea that NAFTA would confer an unalloyed blessing on the United States.[36]

The largest manufacturers, all multinationals, were enthusiastic about NAFTA for obvious reasons. If they want to continue to produce in the United States they can and will, and if they want to relocate production in Mexico they can and will; the treaty adds to their location choices and puts nothing at risk. As noted in Chapter 7 on labor, international options, especially when they are so close geographically, dramatically strengthen the collective bargaining position of employers in the United States.

Smaller manufacturers, sometimes tied to the United States as their sole place of business, and sometimes linked as suppliers to multinationals engaged in U. S. production, find the NAFTA treaty to be reducing options rather than enlarging them. In one hearing devoted to the impact of NAFTA on small business, their testimony was given.

[34]See, for example, White House press release, "North American Free Trade Agreement–Fact Sheet," 1, 2; Office of the Trade Representative, "U. S. Jobs and Adjustment," August 1992; and Lloyd Bentsen, "United States Economy" *Vital Speeches*, LIX, July 15, 1993, pp. 578–580.

[35]For a partial list, see, U. S. Congress, House Committee on Public Works, Subcommittee on Economic Development, Fast Track Authority, 102nd Congress, First Session, May 1991, pp. 79–84.

[36]*Wall Street Journal*, August 13, 1992.

TESTIMONY OF M. L. CATES[37]

. . . My name is Mac Cates, Jr. I am Chief Executive Officer of Arkwright Mills in Spartanburg, South Carolina.

My company is 94 years old. You might be interested in the reason why I qualify as a small business. Over the last 20 years I have closed two out of three plants due to imports and have gone from providing 1000 jobs to employing 300 people. The first plant I closed was the lowest-cost, most efficient plant in its market area. In fact I won a case before the old Tariff Commission [for] adjustment assistance for my workers and my company. So I know first hand what a unilateral free trade policy can do to a company and to an industry . . .

My company now employs 300 people in one plant with annual sales of approximately $25 million. We sell our fabric to U. S. producers of work gloves and other types of apparel, and I am very concerned about the impact of a North American Free Trade Agreement on my company and my industry.

Since 1986, imports of cotton gloves have gone from 15 million dozen to 20 million dozen . . . Over 57 percent of all woven work gloves are now imported. The fabric we make is directly competitive with the fabric in these imported gloves.

A free trade agreement with Mexico could cause even more trouble . . . Specifically I am thinking that work glove producers in Mexico will either: (1) purchase fabric from Far Eastern suppliers rather than from U. S. and Mexican suppliers; or (2) become pass-through or transshipment operations where they would relabel products actually manufactured in the Far East . . .

In addition to my duties at Arkwright Mills, I am also First Vice President of the American Textile Manufacturers Institute (ATMI), a trade association whose members. . . account for 75 percent of the fiber consumed by the domestic textile mill products industry.

ATMI has just completed a study . . . of the Uruguay Round [international talks designed to reduce quotas and tariffs —Ed.] Within ten years, the combination of eliminating quotas and cutting tariffs will seriously cripple if not fatally injure what is today America's largest manufacturing sector.

By way of background, U. S. imports of textile and apparel products during 1990 amounted to more than 12 billion square meters . . ., triple the amount imported in 1980. This trebling . . . has forced the closing of hundreds of producing facilities and the loss of 400,000 jobs since 1980 . . .

Mexico has been a contributor to this injury. Mexico was this country's sixth largest foreign supplier of textiles and apparel during 1990, having more than trebled its textile and apparel exports to the U.S. between 1980 and 1990 . . .

The Multifiber Arrangement (MFA) which has been the framework...since 1974 is likely to be phased out as part of the... Uruguay Round . . . The Uruguay Round phase-out...will devastate the U. S. textile and clothing industry as we know it today. [The phase-out] will dis-

[37]U.S. Congress, House Committee on Small Business, United States–Mexico Free Trade Agreement, 102 Congress, First Session, May 1991, pp. 52–54.

place two-thirds of U. S. textile and clothing production and take away the jobs of 1.4 million U. S. textile and apparel workers. U. S. cotton, wool and man-made fiber producers will be especially damaged . . .

In other words, with a Mexico Free Trade Agreement we will struggle to compete.

But with a Uruguay Round Agreement, we will struggle to survive.

I am leaving today for a meeting of my Board of Directors. We are down to one plant, built in 1968, and that has been modernized four times. Do I ask my Board to continue to modernize? What do I tell my workers about the future of their jobs?

TESTIMONY OF JOHN HIGBIE . . .[38]

AES is a supplier of wiring harnesses to the automotive industry. At peak levels, AES employs 200 people, has sales of $8 million a year, and 65% of our business ships to a supplier of the General Motors Corp. based in Kokomo, Indiana. This supplier operates two maquiladora facilities in Mexico, and 50 percent of our product ships to these factories in Mexico. The remainder of our product supplies the truck and bus industry in the United States and Canada, the U. S. Navy, as well as two Japanese transplant automotive radio manufacturers.

AES is known as a contract manufacturer. AES manufactures product to blueprint. Our expertise is in our assembly skills and product knowledge. We sell no product on the consumer market. Our bank considers us a strong company and we consider ourselves a conservative company . . .

The story of AES, I suppose, would have to be one of adapting to the comings and goings of the large industrial concerns of the Midwest in the 1970's and 1980's. There are two major events which have influenced our actions in the last decade.

The first event was an upward wage spiral in the late 1970's. By nature, our product requires labor-intensive hand assembly. By 1986, it became apparent that AES was pricing itself out of its hand assembly operations at our Avon location. Company and union-negotiated labor costs were averaging nearly $7 an hour in relation to our competitor's minimum wage levels.

In order to maintain our... sales, AES opened a second facility in Kirklin, Indiana, 30 miles north of Indianapolis, at 25 cents above minimum wage. An IUE (International Union of Electrical Workers —Ed.) local was organized in mid-1988, to which half of the Kirklin employees now belong. The opening of our Kirklin factory allowed us, and still allows us, to ship product at prices acceptable to our Midwestern customers.

By 1988, Kirklin was shipping product to Kokomo, Indiana and to the maquiladora facilities located across the Texas border from Brownsville and McAllan. The employees at our original Avon, Indiana location were retrained for high-technology work such as mil-spec soldering for the Navy, and building higher-priced cable assemblies for the truck and bus industry.

. . . Our customer's Reynosa, Mexico facility decided to fill excess capacity by producing internally one particular product line that had been assembled at Kirklin. This business equaled $1 million a year in sales and 14 full-time employees . . .

[38]Ibid., pp. 49, 50.

However, our customer has since backfilled the Kirklin facility with additional business, in order to maintain competitive pricing for the harness business remaining in Indiana . . . It is fortunate for AES and its employees that our customer had additional product to award that was deliverable within Indiana. Whether that business remains in Indiana and, therefore, whether our business remains in Indiana, is a source of friction between our customer and the UAW, AES will remain adaptable to our larger business needs in order to maintain satisfactory business levels and also by obtaining new lines of business.

The second event was, and continues to be, a requirement of the transportation industry, brought on by foreign competition, for continuous improvement of our product . . . and closer contact between customer and supplier . . .

By mid-1988, our customer's Matamoras, Mexico facility expressed a desire to be supplied from a location closer than Kirklin, Indiana in order to allow their personnel in Mexico to assist AES in maintaining higher quality and process control.

Again we were faced with a decision of losing 50 percent of our business or moving south. Accordingly, AES decided to open a facility in Harlington, Texas, 20 miles from the border.

Why did we not move to Mexico at that time? Being from the Midwest, and not familiar with the Hispanic culture, I felt that learning the customs and legal requirements for doing business in Mexico too great a burden, considering the short time allotted to begin production . . .

Before some questions are raised for discussion, consider the following excerpt from a labor union leader.

TESTIMONY OF WILLIAM H. BYWATER[39]

. . . I am William H. Bywater, President of the . . . IUE . . . I appreciate this opportunity to submit this statement on . . . a free trade agreement . . . with Mexico. It is our view that this agreement would be devastating for millions of American workers . . .

The IUE represents production and maintenance workers in a wide spectrum of industries, including electrical-electronics, transportation, fabricated metal, power-generation equipment, furniture and automotive parts. At one time, our union had 360,000 members. Today we have 165,000. This dramatic decline . . . has been due, in large part, to our members having been displaced, as their employers have cut back or completely closed their U.S. operations in favor of offshore lower-wage labor markets. While millions of American homes now contain color televisions, compact disc players, major appliances and other electronic goods with American brand names, the majority of these products are no longer made in this country. *The United States has already lost entire industries—radio and black and white television manufacturing are but two examples—and many others are sure to follow if exploitation of cheap foreign labor continues to be a cornerstone of U.S. trade policy.*

Cheap labor, however, is precisely the foundation of the proposed agreement with Mexico. "Free trade". . . means that all workers are put into competition with the most impoverished workers of the world. It does not mean decent wages and full employment.

[39]Ibid., pp. 87–92.

Indeed, for the FTA proponents, Mexico's most outstanding attraction is the poverty of its citizens and their corresponding willingness to work for subsistence wages. The skill and productivity of American workers becomes irrelevant in this context. Under no circumstances can U. S. workers compete with Mexican workers who earn, on average, 59 cents per hour. A free trade pact between countries of such unequal economic status is, in fact, unprecedented.

IUE members know first-hand from our experience with the Mexican maquiladora program what happens when companies go abroad for cheap labor. The "maquiladoras" are assembly plants that have been established in Mexico by foreign corporations. Ninety-percent of them are U. S. owned. Maquila workers are paid the abysmal wage of 60 to 70 cents an hour.

. . . During the past decade many of our employers, including Bendix, Chrysler, General Electric, General Motors, Litton Industries, North American Philips, RCA, Sylvania, United Technologies, Westinghouse, and Zenith have abandoned assembly operations in this country and relocated them . . . across the Rio Grande . . .

Our experience with the maquiladora program offers a preview of what American workers may expect from a free trade agreement . . . The proposed pact would vastly expand the territory from which the companies could recruit low-wage workers. It would increase opportunities for multinational corporations to circumvent U. S. laws intended to protect workers and the environment.

It is a widespread practice of American-based companies to make components here, ship them to their maquila plants . . . for assembly, and then return the finished product to this country for sale. Currently about 95% of the components used in the maquilas are produced in the U.S. . . . [T]he proposed pact would allow Mexico to produce *more* of the *component parts* . . . Such a shift would mean the exportation of even more jobs from this country.

Five years ago U.S. firms had invested nearly $2 billion in the maquilas and we lost nearly 300,000 manufacturing jobs. Since 1986, many American-based companies have expanded their existing operations in Mexico . . . There are now some 2000 maquilas along the border employing nearly a half million workers . . .

Such investment abroad has not been without domestic repercussions. The number of workers officially counted as unemployed is now 8.6 million. When the millions of others who have been forced to accept part-time employment are counted, along with those who are too discouraged to continue their search for work, the number of American suffering from partial or total income loss is a staggering 15.8 million . . .

Our members are enraged that the Bush Administration is forging ahead to negotiate a FTA . . . against this backdrop of recession, job loss, and increasing demands that U. S. workers take wage and benefit cuts . . .

The following are but a few examples of the disastrous impact that our economic relationship with Mexico has already had on IUE members:

1. *IUE . . . Jefferson City, Tennessee:* In 1978 with 2000 production workers . . . IUE members made electronic components for televisions and video games, and television cabinets for Magnavox, Philco and Sylvania.

   In 1982, the Company (North American Philips) shifted production . . . and laid off 950 . . . Eight hundred jobs were relocated to Mexico . . . With wages at only $5.40 an hour NAP was hard pressed to argue that its labor costs were making it unprofitable. Indeed the company did not even try to seek wage concessions from the local union because it realized that even at minimum wage, the Tennessee workers could not possibly compete with Mexican workers . . . [at] 65 cents an hour—$5.20 a day . . .

2. *IUE . . . Evansville, Indiana*: . . . 850 Zenith workers . . . Today we no longer represent any Zenith workers there. Both plants have been closed. The work was moved to Mexico . . .
3. *IUE . . . Louisville, Kentucky*: Roper range is now being built in Mexico.
4. *IUE . . . Warwick, Rhode Island*: In 1987, 550 wiring assembly jobs at this GE plant were lost to Mexico . . .
5. *IUE . . . Warren, Ohio:* In 1973, IUE represented some 13,000 production workers . . . By 1986 GM's Packard Division had seven plants along the Mexican border, with more than 15,000 workers . . . only 8,200 jobs remain in Warren.
6. *IUE . . . Brooklyn, New York: . . .* 600 jobs . . . Matamoras, Mexico . . .
7. *IUE . . . Pittsfield, Massachusetts:* Fifteen years ago GE employed 15,000 . . . Today, only 1000 hourly jobs remain . . .
8. *IUE . . . Memphis, Tennessee:* In 1989 . . . 400 workers . . . GE announced that . . . jobs would be moved to Mexico.
9. *IUE . . . Troy, Illinois*: Since 1982 employment at Basler Electric has declined . . . relocated to Reynosa and Matamoras, Mexico.
10. *IUE . . . Kirkland, Indiana: . . .* Many IUE members work for small companies which rely on larger corporations for their business . . . Delco Products, a General Motors subsidiary, subcontracts to AES . . . IUE members at this plant . . . make $5.00 an hour. The business there has been threatened and the jobs of members lost because Delco turned to another supplier across the border . . .

Our union could furnish this committee with many other examples of IUE members who have lost their jobs . . . There are, in addition, thousands . . . [who] have been forced to accept inferior wage and benefit agreements because their employers have threatened to move their jobs to Mexico . . .

Questions

1. Based on the testimony of the three witnesses, what is happening here? What is your prediction as to future events? What is the relationship among what is happening, what will likely happen, and the law?
2. Are the unions (IUE or UAW) causing the problems for AES, or its principal customer, or are the unions simply responding to rapidly changing industrial conditions?

   Average wages in northern Mexico are now a little more than $1 per hour with minimum fringe benefits. What should American workers and their unions do in face of these figures?

3. The strategy of AES is adaptation to the decisions of customers. Is the handwriting on the wall for him and other small manufacturers as U.S.-based producers?

   If it is unlikely that AES can stay in business in the United States, what does this say about the confidence of both the Bush and Clinton administrations that current levels of exports from the United States will be unaffected by the treaty?
4. The association of textile manufacturers eventually came out in support of the NAFTA agreement.[40] What might this mean for the future of textile-related employment in the United States?
5. In the list of places in the United States that have lost factories, many are low-wage areas. What does this say about future employment prospects in those areas, and other areas of the United States that are not presently low-wage areas?

CONCLUSION

In quieter moments many Americans might admit to being afraid. Fear is of two types: the irrational fear of a child that darkness inevitably means danger; and the rational fear of real trouble against which precaution should be taken whenever possible. Americans could be afraid that in the future the American horn of plenty will yield only a fraction of what it once yielded; many middle-aged Americans believe that what could be routinely expected for their generation might not be available to their children—access to advanced education without lifetime debt, a home of one's own, reasonable job security, health care at affordable cost, and dignified retirement. Of course, for the American poor, the horn of plenty never yielded more than crumbs, and they see their abiding ill fortune being shared by more and more people.

Fear is never more than a thought away from reflections on the economy, economic futures, and our place (if any) in them. To the extent that the economy of the United States and virtually every other place has become more and more affected by multinational corporations, the relationship of fear to the multinational corporation must be examined as carefully as possible. Will we, like the child who outgrows his fear of the dark, be able to dismiss our fears over this new pattern of business organization, or will our worst fears about multinationals be substantiated?

At least two schools of thought prevail on personal futures as they are touched by multinationals. The first is that if the organization of world finance, production, and distribution is allowed to run its course, there will be greater material return for everyone, everywhere. Whatever domestic diffi-

[40]U. S. Congress, House Committee on Ways and Means, Subcommittee on Trade, The North American Free Trade Agreement, 102nd Congress, Second Session, September 1992, pp. 278–281.

culties that may arise—for example, concentration of control over critical enterprise decisions like plant closings and relocations; wage and benefit reductions; the deterioration of working conditions; and toxic "spills" or environmental hazards—will be short run and will be ironed out as economic activity is perfected on a world scale, over time, by worldwide organizations. The free market, with modest regulation by government, if unchallenged by popular resistances will *in the end* yield more for more people in more places than economic systems of earlier vintage, such as those organized along strictly local or national lines.

The second school of thought is that multinationals constitute a giant wrong turn in history. While there are extensive returns when enterprise is organized on a world scale, the returns are highly stratified; a few people benefit handsomely while the majority suffer far more than they would have under older forms of economic organization. According to this view, multinationals constitute a new form of colonialism with returns from the margins, the less developed countries, aggregated at the center in the developed countries.

They contend further that even in the developed countries there is not an across-the-board sharing of the fruits of world enterprise. On the contrary, the burdens of international enterprise are carried *both* by the people in the home country where the multinationals are headquartered *and* by the people in the host countries where the multinationals carry on many of their business activities. For example, given the power of multinationals, the workers in both Mexico and Michigan may be long-run losers; The success of multinationals does not necessarily trickle down to lower-level participants. Mexican workers, who may appear to be gainers under NAFTA, may next be pitted against workers elsewhere in Latin America, making the prospects of Mexican wages rising to the levels in the United States and Canada dismal.

If the first school of thought about multinationals proves to be correct, then our troubles are over, our fears unfounded. We would simply train ourselves up for roles in multinational enterprise—learning several foreign languages, mastering the complexities of international trade, becoming adept at negotiating in multiple currencies, understanding worldwide transportation logistics, and so on. Even though training regimes might be more complex than the usual business curriculum, at least the goal would be *adaptation* to multinational business rather than *resistance* to its spread, or trying to invent whole alternatives.

If the second appraisal about the role and reach of multinationals proves to be correct, then the educational task becomes far more imposing. Instead of learning to adapt, a one-step assignment, a person could be faced with a threefold assignment: first, the anatomy of the multinational corporations and its consequences; second, a determination of what is wrong with multinationals and whether what is wrong is fixable, and in what way; and third, if they cannot be fixed, that is, if they are inherently and irretrievably flawed, what might be some promising alternatives?

If the investigation of multinationals takes us beyond simple adaptation, we might be inclined to delegate the responsibility for monitoring multinational activity to government, to legal experts, or to a political messiah like Ross Perot. Identifying the public interest, safeguarding the public from abuses, and protecting people from the excesses of private decisions have been among the traditional justifications for government and legal systems. Perhaps we need to study multinationals and their regulation only to the point where we can feel secure that government and the legal system will effectively regulate multinationals.

But what if further study discloses that government and the legal system have never imposed serious restrictions on undesirable multinational activity? And what if study also discloses that the government and the legal system have *actively fostered* the multinationalization of enterprise at the expense of other organizational possibilities? If the net effects of multinational enterprise are beneficial, we need not worry. But if the net effects prove detrimental to billions of people, then what?

Conclusion

After Thomas Malthus predicted that population would outstrip the productivity of land, and that death, war, pestilence, and famines would be the only limits on population growth, economists were said to be dismal scientists. All through the writing of this text the author believed he too was involved in a dismal science. The idea that multinationals were a gigantic wrong turn in human history, taken either consciously or unconsciously, kept intruding into every theme, whether it was size and alienation; labor and living; debt and chronic dependency; land, crops, and hunger; responsiveness of government; law and justice; or environmental degradation.

Like bleary-eyed gamblers well beyond what could be passed off as a bad streak of luck, people everywhere were looking tired, broke, and running out of material and spiritual collateral to continue. When troubles in the world economy are explained as a "population problem," people might feel added guilt for taking up life space, or making the most trifling material demands—taking food out of the mouths of the rich, so to speak. I assumed the role of spokesperson for average people, doing an autopsy on the dead body of worldwide economy.

The impulse of any person with a joy for living who is caught in such a persistent nightmare is to find bright spots, offsetting forces, or countervailing influences to the ones currently in the foreground. Friends and family reinforced this tendency, punctuating discussions of "the book" with moderate statements: "Well, wouldn't people be worse off without multinationals?" or "Aren't there some good multinationals who are helping?" The author felt at times like an invalid getting vague encouragements from loved ones, lest a debilitating illness take irreversible hold. In some cases, friends and family were trying to save me from embarrassment, or worse: "Will they publish the book, if you write it this way?" (With family, everything is satisfactory once the book comes out.)

The impulse for moderation could not be accommodated, despite the temptation to follow the advice of loved ones. As often as the words "practical," "balance," "growth," "development" were dredged up for renewed consideration, they were crowded out by painful facts and ordinary morality. Euphemisms lost out to their opposites—"foolish," "imbalance," "dwarfism," and "destruction." The desire for equilibrium was there, and the preference for optimism dies slowly, but what is a person to do?

I eventually came to an answer that made me more willing to stand in sparser company, unconsoled. The multinational phenomenon presents extremes rather than a debatable middle ground. A student in one of my multinational seminars was asked by his father, who works for a multinational, about my overall position: "Is he *for* or *against*?" In the father's mind there was no middle ground. Either I was presenting an apology for multinationals or drawing a broad indictment of their practices. The father did not ask about topics or other details. He wanted the political bottom line. His cutting through to the conclusion attests to the lack of middle ground in the field.

Upon learning that my politics were different from his own, the father might have pressed forward: "Has he got any alternatives?" My student probably would have had to answer no. The student might have added, "He's looking for some, but seems old-fashioned—maybe he was born in the wrong century."

If the field is one of extremes, then one cannot expect the usual pros and cons that accompany a more tranquil area of study. But who or what created the extremes that force grand choices rather than the usual fine tuning of particulars and the suspension of judgment? The best answer is that the multinational form of enterprise drives out rival forms of economic activity, and once it is in preeminent place, there is nothing left to fine tune. This may be what makes people cling to local control wherever it can be preserved; people are far less mobile than multinationals.

Trends become stubborn as alternatives are more definitively forgone. When this happens—and we are reminded every day that we are in a global economy in which everything local is secondary—a range of choices disappears, and one is left, like Traven's basket weaver, with a simple yes or no. I approve, or I disapprove.

A person either has work or doesn't, and to the extent that multinationals are a prime source of employment, one either likes the labor conditions that multinational enterprises and their surrogates offer, or one rebels. There may be no alternative job around the corner, because there are no corners; every person is a point on a hierarchically drawn straight line. And when agriculture becomes oriented toward market rather than use, husbandry disappears and world-scale management and marketing appear; one either embraces the change or feels queasy about it.

With regard to the environment, the Amazon basin is either cleared or continues as a rain forest; trees cannot be simultaneously cut and continue to grow. Similarly, debt is either manageable and put to good use, or it strangles, as any householder knows who has been buried by credit card purchases. People in government either pursue a general purpose for the vast majority of the citizenry, or speak for special interests, use public office as a private opportunity structure, and abandon the quest for legitimacy.

Moderation thus loses to a forced choice among extremes. The richness of alternative choices and variety gone, one cannot postulate them back with lawyerlike assumptions that "There are two sides to every story," "Nothing is an either/or proposition," or "Life is complex." Corporate publicists and their legal advocates do tell many stories, often leaving their opponents speechless, since language, images, and meaning have themselves become the objects of corporate takeover like coal, VCRs, or ships. But their stories upon closer study often turn out to be incredible (from the latin *in credere*—not to be believed), and their use of language perverse. The largest businesses, often with government complicity, have been the teachers of cynicism and extremism.

Unconscious awareness of this characteristic may be what sent people running for their lives on hearing that everyone everywhere will gain from NAFTA. Popular cynicism can be traced to the lies told by private (and governmental) spokespeople; and weekly viewing of "60 Minutes" recharges the cynicism, just as hope begins to creep back into the heart.

Upon study, the dynamics of multinationals proved not complex *in results*, despite the proliferation of economic, political, and legal networks that are complex. When they are evaluated by results, multinationals present a mindless simplicity reinforced by power. If multinational enterprises are the final form of economic organization, complexity and richness of experience, thought, and action will have been displaced.

Richard Barnet and Ronald Muller in their early book, *Global Reach*, said it as well as it can be said, and their prophecy applies as poignantly to contemporary conditions in the "First World" as in the "Third World," which was the principal focus of their study:

> The confrontation between the multinational corporation and its enemies promises to influence the shape of human society in the last third of the century more than any other political drama of our time. To survive and to grow, certainly to fulfill its promise to create a rational, integrated world economy, the global corporation must forge a new global consensus on the most fundamental questions of political life: What kind of social and economic development meets the needs of twentieth-century man? What is a just social order? What is "freedom," "justice," or "need" in a world in which 4 billion inhabitants are struggling for food, water, and air? What does "efficiency" or "growth" or "rationality" mean in such a world?
>
> And in the end they must answer ... the same question that has confronted every new elite aspiring to political leadership and social management: by what right do[es] a self-selected group of druggists, biscuit makers, and computer designers become the architects of the new world? To establish their political legitimacy, the aspiring World Managers must be able to demonstrate that the maximization of global profits is compatible with human survival.
>
> . . .
>
> [W]e try to assess what their current operations and future plans mean in the daily lives of ourselves and our children—not only in the United States but in the rest of the world. Does the rise of the World Managers offer a new golden age or a new form of imperial domination? Is the global corporation mankind's best hope for producing and distributing the riches of the earth, as the World Managers contend—or, as their critics argue, is their vaunted rational integrated world economy a recipe for a new stage in authoritarian politics, an international class war of huge proportions, and ultimately, ecological suicide?*

They wrote their primer on multinationals in 1974, twenty years ago. Their ideas are not "old" but simply appeared before general consciousness could encompass their import. They said the hour was late for the necessary reconciliation between people and system. Is it any earlier now?

*Richard Barnet et al, *Global Reach* (New York: Simon & Schuster, 1974), pp. 24, 25.

INDEX